Solid Shape

Solid Shape

Jan J. Koenderink

The MIT Press
Cambridge, Massachusetts
London, England

Third printing, 1993

This book was printed and bound in the United States of America

Library of Congress Cataloging-in-Publication Data

Koenderink, Jan J.
　　　Solid shape/ Jan J. Koenderink.
　　　　　　p.　　cm.
　　　Includes bibliographical references.
　　　ISBN 0-262-11139-X
　　　1. Geometry, Differential--Data processing. 2. Computer-aided design. I. Title.
QA641.K74　1990　　　　　　　　　　　　　　　89-29193
516'. 06 ---dc20　　　　　　　　　　　　　　　CIP

Contents

Series Foreword

Artificial intelligence is the study of intelligence using the ideas and methods of computation. Unfortunately, a definition of intelligence seems impossible at the moment because intelligence appears to be an amalgam of so many information-processing and information-representation abilities.

Of course psychology, philosophy, linguistics, and related disciplines offer various perspectives and methodologies for studying intelligence. For the most part, however, the theories proposed in these fields are too incomplete and too vaguely stated to be realized in computational terms. Something more is needed, even though valuable ideas, relationships, and constraints can be gleaned from traditional studies of what are, after all, impressive existence proofs that intelligence is in fact possible.

Artificial intelligence offers a new perspective and a new methodology. Its central goal is to make computers intelligent, both to make them more useful and to understand the principles that make intelligence possible. That intelligent computers will be extremely useful is obvious. The more profound point is that artificial intelligence aims to understand intelligence using the ideas and methods of computation, thus offering a radically new and different basis for theory formation. Most of the people doing work in artificial intelligence believe that these theories will apply to any intelligent processor, whether biological or solid state.

There are side effects that deserve attention, too. Any program that will successfully model even a small part of intelligence will be inherently massive and complex. Consequently, artificial intelligence continually confronts the limits of computer-science technology. The problems encountered have been hard enough and interesting enough to seduce artificial intelligence people into working on them with enthusiasm. It is natural, then, that there has been a steady flow of ideas from artificial intelligence to computer science, and the flow shows no sign of abating.

The purpose of The MIT Press Series in Artificial Intelligence is to provide people in many areas, both professionals and students, with timely, detailed information about what is happening on the frontiers in research centers all over the world.

J. Michael Brady
Daniel G. Bobrow
Randall Davis

*Nothing is more important than to see the sources of invention
which are, in my opinion,
more interesting than the inventions themselves.*
—GOTTFRIED WILHELM LEIBNITZ (1646–1716)

Preface

About a dozen years ago I happened to come across that wonderful book written by Hilbert and Cohn-Vossen entitled *Anschauliche Geometrie* (translated into English as *Geometry and the Imagination*). When I read the footnote on Felix Klein's conjecture, which contains a postage stamp size picture of the Belvedere Apollo with the parabolic curves drawn on its surface, I became hooked on differential geometry. Since then I have read everything on the subject—ancient or modern—that I could lay my hands on. I also started to apply the concepts and methods of differential geometry to my own discipline which happens to be visual perception (both experimental psychophysics and theoretical work on the neuroscientific and eco-optical foundations of that subject).

By sheer coincidence Thomas Banchoff happened to review one of the papers my wife and I wrote upon the subject. This triggered off a new phase as Banchoff presented some of his movies to us during a visit to our laboratory (*Banchoff-Strauss-Productions*, if I remember well): it was a revelation to see what computer graphics could do to foster intuitive insight into the most abstruse mathematical tangles. My wife and I started on a project to develop the discipline of "computational differential geometry." This really paid off: soon we could demonstrate to our mathematical colleagues that many of the concepts of which they possessed a mere formal grasp could be handled and manipulated in such a way that the intuition gained a firm hold on them.

I am not a mathematician and am apt to regard the subject of differential geometry of the submanifolds of three-dimensional space such as appear as models of the surfaces of solid objects ("Solid Shapes") as essentially *a branch of mathematical physics*. Although I used to be rather out of tune with the times in this regard, it would appear that the times are changing now: in such fields as *robotics*, *machine vision*, and others the subject has acquired many practical applications. I may soon be out of tune with the times again, because the subject is being turned into an engineering field now, rather than mathematical physics. Anyway, there is a wide demand for texts on extrinsic differential geometry of three-dimensional space at present, stressing intuitive understanding and heuristics rather than mathematical rigor and elegance for its own sake. This book is a first attempt to fill the gap.

I wrote a rough outline within two weeks during a summer school in the Italian Apennines, then finished the first complete draft during a four-month stay at Oxford University: I am grateful to University College which appointed me as the first Douglas Holder Fellow, to the Royal Society and General Electric Company which helped sustain me, and to the department of Engineering, especially Professor Mike Brady, who provided a stimulating environment and an office overlooking University Park.

Peter Giblin read the first draft and I am highly indebted to him for his numerous and most useful remarks.

Of course I am also indebted to Knuth for his TeX program: this made it possible for me to design the book much as I liked at the mere cost of some initial frustration and a lot of time.

MIT Press, especially in the person of Terry Ehling, has been most understanding and helpful.

My family and my students had to bear the brunt of the endeavor. I thank them all for their patience and understanding. Without the help of my wife with the logistics I would have been lost.

Needless to say I am solely to blame for the numerous faults the careful reader is certain to encounter.

Notes to the reader

There are a few things you have to note if you want to use this book
in the most effective manner:

- Use the figures! At a great many places the text will appear opaque
  and uninformative if you don't spend as much time with the figures
  as with the words. The converse is also true. (Use the text!)
  You may have to read a paragraph twice and you may have to
  look at a figure twice. You don't necessarily understand a text
  by reading the letters and you don't necessarily grasp a figure by
  glancing at it. Both reading text and reading figures are only
  possible through the active intellectual participation of the reader.
  Careless reading or casting a mere glance here and there is a mere
  waste of time, especially in the case of this book. You won't even
  have the satisfaction of having duly nodded at every little step of
  a long proof (like reading letters this may make you feel good but
  it doesn't necessarily convey much sense): there are none of such
  here.

- Look out for *Intermezzi*, which can be recognized through the "♠"-
  sign. They are breaks in the main flow of the text. You had better
  skip them, except when you have read the main text at least once
  already, or when you find the book easy going (but then you may
  be wasting your time). Think of them as of "footnotes" that were
  too long-winded to be contained in the lower margin of the page.

- Skip all the footnotes too (at least on first reading). I can assure
  you that you won't miss anything important.

- Use the *glossary* to get some enlightenment in the case of strange
  concepts not properly introduced earlier or to refresh your memory
  when a nonstandard expression recurs. I use quite a few expressions in this book that you won't find elsewhere. Many of them
  are introduced in a lighthearted (and extremely concise) manner
  in the glossary.

- Don't expect many useful hints on obscure literature (even if very
  pertinent) scattered throughout the text: there are essentially no

such references worked into the main text. Sorry! In an appendix
I have gathered some indications on how to carry on. Get your
references from these sources. Since this is not a research report,
nor a formal textbook, I'm not ashamed of myself. If you think
I'm doing other authors an injustice, let me state once and for all
that I owe all that is in this book to others.

- There is no particular reason why you should waste your time on
  the citations. I merely threw them in because I am freaky that
  way as well as for reasons of layout. However, you may be in need
  of light distraction at intervals.

- When I say of something that it is "simple" or "obvious" in some
  way or other, you should wake up. These are technical terms that
  should trigger the introspection. You're supposed to nod and read
  on if you agree, to stop pondering or backtracking if not. Don't
  feel bad if the "obvious" isn't obvious to you. The terms merely
  indicate that you should be able to figure it out for yourself; they
  don't imply that you should be able to do it on the fly.

- Maybe you are intent on reading this book because you want to
  become an expert in differential geometry, or maybe because you
  already are one: in both cases you will find it a waste of time. The
  aims of the text are outlined in the first chapter.

I hope you'll read the book for fun and profit!

*The eye, which is called the window of the soul, is the chief means
whereby the understanding may most fully and abundantly
appreciate the infinite works of nature.*
—LEONARDO DA VINCI (1452–1519)

I PROLOGUE

1 Introduction

> See, I answer him that asketh, "What did God before
> He made heaven and earth?" I answer not as one is
> said to have done merrily (eluding the pressure of the
> question), "He was preparing hell (saith he) for pryers
> into mysteries." It is one thing to answer enquiries,
> another to make sport of enquirers.
> —ST. AUGUSTINE (A.D. 400), *Confessions*

1.1 About this book

At the present time, there is increasing activity in applications dealing with three-dimensional shape. Among the more obvious reasons
are the technological breakthroughs that make it possible to generate
non-trivial shapes (Computer-Aided-Manufacture[1]) and to handle shape
models conveniently (Computer-Aided-Design[2]). Moreover, there is cur-
rently much interest in sophisticated methods to describe the structure
of mechanical and optical operations that involve shape in the robotics
of manipulation and in computer vision. The community interested in
these matters barely overlaps with the community that traditionally developed the methods to handle these problems originally, namely mathematicians with an interest in geometries of different kinds. Not only
are the aims and foci of interest rather divergent, but quite naturally
familiarity with the available tools also differs enormously.

To summarize the difference, or maybe to caricaturize it a bit: the
mathematician usually doesn't use computers to do differential geometry, whereas the robotics engineer is unlikely to know much about vector
bundles[3] or the history of the subject. One result of this mismatch is
that the mathematician—if he is interested in such things at all—can
amuse himself perusing the recent literature by noting how the engineer
invents the wheel every other day. At the other side, the engineer is
likely to be disgusted by the mathematical literature which is—from his
particular vantage point—in no way fit for any use in the real world.

There appears to be a real need for texts that lead the non-
mathematician to an appreciation of the wealth of material that waits

---

[1]Perhaps more familiar as "CAM."

[2]Usually known as "CAD."

[3]Don't let technical terms worry you one bit! If I use them before introducing
them formally, you may substitute "abstruse technicality" and read on. If you are
the curious type, you will already have discovered the index and the glossary.

to be used and has been amassed by mathematicians over decades or
even centuries. The engineering community has yet to absorb Gauss's
thoughts on the subject. The engineer seeks an educated intuition for
the powerful tool kits that he—as a non-mathematician—might pick up
right away. With "non-mathematician" I don't refer to people without
mathematical training at all, but rather to those for whom mathematics
is not a profession but a *tool*, that is to say, the engineer or the natural
scientist. Such people usually have the training to pick up the technical
facility needed to do symbolic manipulation fast enough. Yet they often
find that such a facility is not sufficient to let them solve *real problems.*

What is lacking is an intuitive picture or "gut feeling" for what is
really going on. I mean the ability to guess at an answer and be more
often right than wrong. What is needed is a body of heuristics that
fails to be conveyed by the mathematical texts.[4] This is essential in the
natural sciences. Tools will only be used at all if a "feel" for them has
been developed. It seems curiously immaterial whether they are actually
understood in the mathematician's sense. The history of science abounds
with examples. As a result practical people would rather solve problems
their own way, which amounts to saying that they'd rather invent the
wheel anew if that enables them to use it. And rightly so, for although
this is a shame in principle, it also makes solid pragmatic sense.

Typical problems arise in different ways at the start and at the finish
of a project. At the *start* there is the ignorance of existing material;
thus you have to start from scratch, whereas you could "stand on the
shoulders of giants." At the *finish* there is the inability to round off
a project successfully because of an unfamiliarity with the tools of the
trade. Both problems can be met with through suitable education. Then
you are left with the problems in the *middle*, namely those connected
with the development of the project. It seems that these are hardly
being taught at all: the ability to use intuitive, heuristic tools to shape
the problem, if necessary to *redefine it.* This often spoils much of the
fun after an initial euphoria due to the necessity of learning to handle
a few new tools. Although you may be able to prove theorems given
as "problems" or do sums that have been formulated carefully by the
teacher or author, you discover to your chagrin that you are in no position to produce something off track by yourself. The theory "doesn't

---

[4] "Heuristics" or the *Ars Inveniendi* denotes the study of the methods and rules
that lead one to invention and discovery. Heuristic reasoning is based on induc-
tion, analogy, and metaphor, not necessarily of a purely discursive, but often of an
aesthetic kind (such as visual or kinesthetic, "gut feelings," *etc.*) Descartes and Leibnitz planned (but never published!) treatises on the *Ars Inveniendi* of the moderns
Bolzano especially may be mentioned.

get you anywhere." In this text I try to concentrate on this most elusive part and—I hope—to do something about it.

In this book I attempt to show the way to the great body of useful existing knowledge on the mathematics of the three-dimensional shape of natural objects. I try to stress the conceptual, heuristic side of the matter and to evoke the kind of mental pictures that are such a great help in intuitive thinking. I basically refrain from presenting formal tools or proofs. There is a wealth of literature on that, which can be used once you understand what is going on. The ability to find what you need in this literature is obviously also of decisive importance. I try to give hints on this problem.

I have not included any material without a clear motivation to do so; either it is necessary for discussions in later chapters or I know of an application, mostly in the theory of visual perception of shape. (This derives from my personal hang-ups; it doesn't mean that you couldn't find exciting applications in your own area! Applications are waiting for you all over the place.)

1.2 The necessary background

You are supposed to possess the kind of mathematical maturity that may normally be expected from the engineer or physicist. This will enable you to convert much of the geometrical picture into algebraic or algorithmic form right away. If not, then the text should have given you the intuitive keys to get what you need from the mathematically slanted textbooks.

I take it for granted that you will only have a marginal interest in such subjects as proofs of existence, singular cases ("freaks") or geometrical objects that you are unlikely to meet with in nature such as self-intersecting or non-orientable surfaces. Such things take up little space in this book. This is really a bit dangerous and will rightly be scorned by the mathematician.

"Partial proofs" are dangerous in principle and tend to be judged as in rather bad taste by the mathematically inclined. For the engineer and to a lesser degree the physicist they are often sufficient or even necessary, however. Partial proofs are useful to memorize if they throw some light on a theorem—at least if that theorem happens to be correct. Complete proofs that yield no real insight on the other hand can be forgotten once you have convinced yourself of the truth of that theorem. You may even skip such proofs completely if you don't mind accepting an expert's

authority. They have no further use. The "truth" of the physicist or
the engineer is of a different, more pragmatic, kind from that of the
mathematician. In this book I will often cross the borderline of what is
generally considered mathematical good taste. I hope that at least the
natural scientist will not object. On the other hand you can expect a
"bird's-eye view" of wider scope than you will find in more formal texts
of similar length.

It is also expected that you have at least some rudimentary ability
to picture geometrical objects in your head. There definitely do exist
people with an almost purely formalistic thinking process for whom this
text is consequently not the book to read. You may test yourself by scanning through the following books that in my view anyone interested in
geometry as a heuristic tool should have read: Aleksandrov, Hilbert and
Cohn-Vossen, Coxeter, Berger.[5] If you don't feel the urge to buy your
own copy of Hilbert and Cohn-Vossen's book, then you should probably
stop reading right here. These texts also give a good background for
the present book and are highly recommended. The value of the faculty
of "visualization" of geometrical objects can hardly be overrated and
should be exercised and developed continuously.[6] The reader should
not rest before each subject developed in this text stands out vigorously
clear in his "mind's eye." "Doodling" while reading will help and at the
same time helps develop your ability to express geometrical relations
summarily through simple sketches.[7]

I have collected some notes on the art of sketching differential geometric entities and on "reading" them—which is also something of an
acquired art—at the end of the book.

[5] Authors mentioned within the body of the text without the hint of a reference
can usually be traced in the bibliography at the close of the book. If not, then I'm
just being nice to somebody. You can be sure that you don't miss a thing because
I'm withholding a reference! Don't you worry.

[6] Everybody remembers from high school geometry how a proof that looked very
hard suddenly became a mere formal exercise after somebody made a small drawing,
or pointed out a certain sub- or superstructure in a figure that solved the problem
"visually."

[7] According to Polya the method of starting the examination of a problem of
construction by drawing a sketch on which, supposedly, the condition is satisfied,
goes back to the Greek geometers, and is hinted at by the short and somewhat
enigmatic phrase of Pappus: "*Assume what is required to be done as already done.*"

1.3 Where the emphasis is

> *I concluded that I might take as a general rule the principle that*
> all things which we very clearly and obviously conceive are true:
> *only observing, however, that there is some difficulty*
> *in rightly determining the objects which we distinctly conceive.*
> —RENÉ DESCARTES (1596–1650), *Discourse on Method*

I had to make a few decisions with regard to the form in which the subject matter is presented. They are the following:

Wherever possible I use descriptive geometry rather than analysis. In many cases this will mean that *pictures* are used together with some lines of text that attempt to bring you into a state in which you try to convince yourself that some statement is true, or —even better—is obvious, by using the picture to shape your thoughts. You should not confuse this handwaving with mathematical proof. This should be self-evident.

Both reading and sketching figures is something of an acquired art. I think especially of sketching as a kind of "experimental approach" to the study of geometry. Pictures are by their very nature *concrete* and form a welcome antidote to the formal apparatus. They alone allow the mind to get a firm hold on the subject matter. For formal proofs you can always take recourse to the literature. Here you meet with a curious dichotomy that splits the scientific community into two opposite camps.

Assumption: *For the mathematician, figures and solid object models are merely illustrations of the formalism, nice but superfluous. For the readers of this book, however, I take it that the latter are the real essence and in fact the matter itself whereas the formalism is merely about them.*

Wherever possible, I use discrete *models*, usually so-called "finite elements" models. For instance, I will model a space curve as a chain of rigid rods joined by universal joints. This greatly aids the intuition of the typical natural scientist; moreover, it shows a possible route to computer implementation.

As a matter of principle I use generic—that means essentially "garden variety"—examples and avoid degenerate cases in which nontypical geometrical relations confuse the issue. The literature typically picks degenerate cases to illustrate things because they can be selected so as to yield exactly solvable problems. This may be all right for classroom use to illustrate the point in question, but at the same time it usually misrepresents other relations. It destroys the intuitive "setting." This tends to blur your intuitive feel by no small amount. Thus the teacher may actually do his pupils a disservice with "simple" examples. (Since this happened to me several times I assume it to be a universal evil. I notice the phenomenon with my students too.)

For example, I have met many people who were of the honest opinion that the boundary of visible and occluded patches on an object is a planar curve, or that the visual rays are orthogonal to this curve. They probably have pictures of spheres in their head for which these assertions happen to be true. In many texts on the subject of "artificial vision" the sphere is indeed used as the paradigmatic case to explain the "occlusion boundary." These assertions are in fact false for almost any other surface. Just think of a cube. Already Leonardo knew better, and maybe the ancient Greeks already did. I haven't researched the history of the matter. Such observations could be amplified *ad libitem*.

Never use a nongeneric example to memorize some geometrical relation because this will thwart future attempts to visualize relations. Examples like that—although simple—are really no help at all, but rather hindrances to the intuition that cannot fail to clog up your mind's eye.

Another disadvantage of selected simple cases is that the pupil obtains a completely false idea about the range of problems that can be solved analytically. The moment he attacks a *real* problem he is in serious trouble because the classroom methods don't work. This commonly leads to much frustration because the pupil tends to underestimate the singular nature of the typical classroom problem and tends to blame his own inability to handle the tools. It is the cause of much unnecessary suffering.

Wherever possible I use representations that most easily lend themselves to computer implementation. It is in fact possible to do sophisticated "computational differential geometry" on a simple micro. This makes it possible to "experiment" with geometrical objects, and if the graphics are at all reasonable, it is an enormous help in developing the intuition. I heartily recommend such experimentation. At many places in the book I have inserted sections that give explicit—be it rather succinct—instructions on how to build simple differential geometry programs using a dialect of "pidgin PASCAL or MODULA-2." Although this is hardly any trouble for anyone with a modicum of computer literacy, I have witnessed professional mathematicians being raised to euphoric states when they were given access to such a package. In short, you are most strongly urged to build yourself a differential geometry package and thus bring many "abstract theorems" to "life."

1.4 What not to expect

The subject of "shape" is too enormously varied to treat even superficially in a text like this. I had to be very selective. Some of the more interesting subjects that were left out—taken in random order—are:

- statistically defined shapes, such as textures or foams;

- regular and quasiregular tesselations of space and surface patches, so called patterns;

- arborizations of all kinds;

- thoroughly crumpled surfaces such as the by now well-known and even popular "fractals";

- subjects of integral geometry, which are of considerable importance in integral geometrical methods of morphometry;

- the venerable subject of regular polyhedra ...

and so on. Thus the title of the book is rather presumptuous. In view of the complexity of the natural world you can only be awestruck. But of course every small piece of nature that you pick out for closer attention is entertaining for its own sake. *Today's small piece is basically about arbitrary smooth lumps of three-dimensional space such as could be occupied by your typical potato or favorite torso, say.*

EPIRHEMA

Müsset in Naturbetrachten
immer eins wie alles achten;
Nichts ist drinnen, nichts ist draußen,
denn was innen, das ist außen.
So ergreifet ohne Säumnis
heilig öffentlich Geheimnis
—JOHANN WOLFGANG VON GOETHE (1749–1832)

2 Shape and Space

Ubi materia, ibi geometria.
—JOHANNES KEPLER (1619)

... la géometrie est une magie qui réussit ....
—RENÉ THOM *(quite recently)*

2.1   An operational view of space

When I speak of "shape," I mean a structure of a simultaneous presence
as defined by certain operational methods that may differ from case to
case. For instance, you may try to clarify to yourself what you really
mean by such conventional notions as the shape of a dog, a stellar con-
stellation, an atomic nucleus, a cloud ... Could you implement them in
some artificial intelligence? Would a single datastructure suffice in all
these cases?

Certain abstract relations between measurements are repeatedly valid,
regardless the specific shape you deal with. Examples of such relations
include incidence, inclusion, overlap, juxtaposition, and so forth. This
kind of invariant backbone of simultaneous presence is *physical space*.
You usually describe the relations of physical space in terms of mathematical entities called *geometries*.

Geometries are abstract descriptions of structured sets. The applied
scientist usually interprets the elements of such a set as "blobs" of
"space" that could be occupied by some object. The additional structure
is defined in abstract terms. Such relations might be inclusion, overlap,
incidence, juxtaposition, betweenness ... The terms are borrowed from
people's intuitive notions of certain relations in physical space, mostly
dealing with rigid objects. The mathematical relations should not be
confused with those. They are defined through *axioms* that tell you the
rules of the game, but they have no other significance.

For instance, in the "projective plane" the notions of "line" and
"point" are interchangeable. Thus it doesn't make sense to conceive of
"lines" as "very thin taut wires" and of "points" as of "extremely tiny
fly specks." The moment you do this you have to discard the notion of
"duality" of point and line.

These geometries are objects of great beauty but are not necessarily
useful in a physical context. In the case of the world on a human scale
you don't care much about problems involving infinities or infinitesimals,

whereas you certainly care whether something is line-like or point-like. Yet you have to assume some standpoint with respect to geometry since geometrical theories are obviously going to be your tools in shape description.

Geometries will be *models* like any physical theory and only relevant within your range of application as constrained by tolerances of your measuring apparatus and the size of your laboratory. Thus I will assume a strictly utilitarian viewpoint and regard mathematics as nothing but rigorous abstractions from ordinary experience.

Such different approaches to the subject of geometry have a long history, although the philosophical positions only became explicit in recent times. Leibnitz's position is an early example of a thoughtfully formulated epistemological view of space. The dichotomy signaled here is beautifully brought out in a comparison of two important papers from the second half of the previous century, namely the famous (1854) paper by Riemann "On the *hypotheses* that form the basis of geometry" and a lesser-known paper by Helmholtz published only a little while later "On the *facts* that form the basis of geometry." The very titles of the papers summarize the diametrically opposite epistemological positions of these nineteenth-century giants of science.

Historically, Helmholtz's contribution has been debunked about as much as Riemann's has been praised. His mathematics was a bit clumsy because he did not possess the apparatus of Lie groups. This hardly diminishes the magnitude of his achievement, however. I am convinced that justice will still be victorious in the long run. Different as they may be, both papers were seminal, each in their own way.

What you need are both *operationalizations*, which are methods of physical measurement, and *conceptualizations*, which are mathematical models, of such important notions as size, order, displacement, and so on, augmented with a set of *correspondence rules*. I will not make a big deal of this in the present text, although this subject is relatively poorly developed and certainly merits a good deal of attention. I will merely review a few possibilities and notions to set the scene in this introductory chapter, and then I will delve right away into more technical matters without caring too much about careful definitions. This is not the right way to proceed either in mathematics or in physics, but it is a quick way to grab an intuitive feel of a subject, which is after all the goal of this book. Of course I will consider only theorems that can be interpreted rather directly in experiential terms.

2.2 Basic entities and methods

> *The description of right lines and circles,*
> *upon which geometry is founded, belongs to mechanics.*
> *Geometry does not teach us to draw these lines,*
> *but requires them to be drawn.*
> —SIR ISAAC NEWTON, *from the preface to*
> *the 1687 edition of the Principia*

A "place" is a part of the simultaneous presence that you can trace back because it has some distinctive characteristic. This may be called a "tag" or "mark." "The city well" is a place. A "position" is a rule for pointing at a place, like putting a mark somewhere or spotting a thing between other similar things, at the hand of a description that tells you how to move with respect to certain fiducial places. The familiar description of where the treasure is in a pirate story is a prototypical position: "From a rock shaped like a man's skull, take thirteen paces south, seven east, and dig to twice the depth of a man's height."[1]

Because you don't specify what kind of thing exists at a given position in order to give the rule to arrive at it, the notion of position is a kind of abstraction of that place. A position is devoid of physical properties except for some numbers called *coordinates.* You obtain the numbers through some recipe like "from here take so many steps in the direction of ..." and so forth. I also call positions "points," not so much because they are that "which has no extension" but rather because the idea of extension doesn't make any operational sense in this case.

The basic entity is the "blob-like region." These are portions of space that can appear as actual "apertures" or "windows" in physical measurements. Blobs have an extension, one that is given either by the lower limit on the resolution of your apparatus—then they could be called "atomic blobs"—or by your *choice.* For instance, if you want to measure the density of biomass in a treetop, you have to choose a window of maybe a cubic foot. Ten times less and you sample either a single leaf or a blob of air. Ten times more and you have almost reduced the tree to an operational point.[2] Such decisions have to be made all the time

---

[1] Many examples. For instance in Poe's "The Gold-Bug" the mysterious MS has (when properly decoded): "A good glass in the bishop's hostel in the devil's seat—twenty-one degrees and thirteen minutes—northeast and by north—main branch seventh limb east side—shoot from the left eye of the death's-head—a beeline from the tree through the shot fifty feet out."

[2] For instance, a single pixel from a satellite image may encompass a wood.

in the experimental sciences. In "image processing" and similar fields the blobs are commonly known as "pixels" or "voxels." Their physical significance is that of a weighing function for measuring some intensive parameter, and in terms of information theory they represent a single datum, a so-called "degree of freedom," or "point."

Mark well: *Even large blobs are technically "points" when you have chosen not to investigate their inner structure or their "shape".*

Sets of blobs, most often overlapping sets of blobs, are "regions," or volumes. These are the basic building blocks of physical space. Note that they are *volumometric* entities. "Surfaces" and "curves" are always *derived entities*, volumes are the primary ones.

This makes it possible to handle many tricky problems in a simple way. For instance, I define *area* in terms of the number of atomic blobs needed to just cover the boundary of a region, such as for instance the number of cobbles needed to cover a city square; and *length* in terms of the number of atomic blobs you have to string together to cover a stretch such as the number of beads that a string will accommodate.

By way of an example, the curve shown in figure 1 has a length of seventeen resolution units between its endpoints.[3] That this kind of definition is *necessary* is clear from the fact that it is mathematically possible to cram a surface of infinite area onto a small region, just by putting in lots of tiny creases—so small that you couldn't hope to detect them. Area and length only make sense if you specify the resolution of your physical method.

The types of operations people use to define shape are extremely various. In most cases of interest you consider the shape as a *constraint* on certain physical possibilities, for example, the possibility of passing through a sieve or fitting a template. A region may put constraints of certain types on operations that go on in its ambient space. For instance, an opaque object limits the possibility of seeing things from all over space. From any viewpoint the opaque object has the ability to *obscure* other objects. Objects can be said to induce a "geometrical field" around them, a field that can be probed operationally. The structure of the field is the *shape* of the object. Notice that "shape" is not only a property of the object but equally of the method you actually use to probe it.

---

[3]You find a figure by its number. Any figure appears at a place in the text *at* or *beyond* the place at which it is first referred to. Thus you should usually be able to find a figure on the page you are reading (if you are in luck) or the next page or page thereafter, but *never* one or more pages back. Except, of course, when the figure has already been referred to earlier in the text.

Fact: *"Shape" is only operationally defined. Thus things do not "have a shape" the way Santa Claus has a red suit.*

Things have a shape for *you*, the person in whose perception the things exist.[4] Shape depends on the perception— that is, the mode of interaction and the expectation (your "theories" or "models").

In general the emphasis will be on the "things" rather than on the "space they are in." "Space" only figures as the possibility of displacement and simultaneous presence or order. This mere potentiality is what used to be called the *"plenum."* When you try to measure space, you convert it to a thing. For instance, I will consider rigid frameworks on which you can attach other rigid things and then use the relation to the frame to specify their "position" (fig. 2). When you employ regular crate structures as frame, the relations become "Cartesian coordinates."

The figure illustrates $\mathbf{R}^3$, that is, the "Cartesian product" of three copies of the real axis (denoted $\mathbf{R}$ or $\mathbf{R}^1$). A Cartesian point is an ordered triple of real numbers like (x, y, z) and you can find it by moving distances x, y and z into the direction of the three orthogonal X, Y, and Z axes from an arbitrary fiducial point (labeled "origin" for the occasion) in the time honored manner described by Descartes.

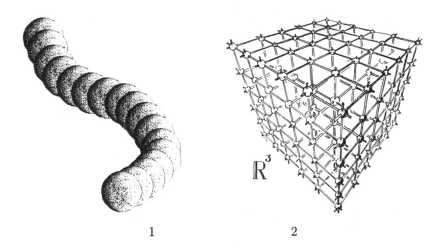

$\mathbb{R}^3$

1   2

---

[4]As bishop Berkeley said, *"Esse est percipi,"* but of course, Parmenides had already said: *"What is ... is identical with the thought of what recognizes it."*

2.3   How to define constraint

There exist a great many nonequivalent ways to define "curves," "surfaces," and so forth mathematically. A few are of interest to the study of shape in a more general sense and I will briefly review them here.

A notion that I will use often, is that of a *level set*. Suppose you have measured the density of some physical property with a certain tolerance or blob size. Then I define an "object" as the region where the density exceeds some given "fiducial value." The fiducial value is essentially *arbitrary*, that is, it is up to you to specify it. Nothing is required from the mathematical viewpoint. However, the physical nature of your problem typically constrains the range of reasonable values very much. Clearly, "what the object is" is a matter of *physics*. You decide on the corner of the natural world you are going to study. Once you have decided on this, you can draw upon mathematics as a tool.

The "level set" for the fiducial density is that portion of space where the empirically determined density *equals* the fiducial value. Clearly the level set bounds the object, whereas the object is a region that depends both on the resolution of the measurement of the density and on the fiducial value. The shape of the level set is not "sharp," but a bit fuzzy. To appreciate this fact, consider that you may define a *boundary* or *transition layer* as the region where the measured density is within some tolerance of the fiducial value. This is real life, not mathematics, remember?

In order to grasp what I mean to say here, it is probably best to consider a simple example.

A useful example of a level set to keep in mind is a *cloud*. A continental cumulus cloud is a portion of the earth's atmosphere where the density of condensed water, measured at a level of resolution of about one meter, exceeds some conventional fiducial value. A ballpark value is in the neighborhood of 0.2 grams per meter cubed.

Figure 3 shows a set at two different levels of resolution with the transition layer indicated in grey tone.

The level sets are mathematically as nice as can be; they are generically everywhere smooth and without self-intersections. This method to define a shape is both mathematically attractive because it avoids many of the problems associated with the alternative definitions and makes solid operational sense. An example would be the shape of the dry land region of the earth as depicted on geographical maps. Their coast line is the level set of all portions of the solid earth that are above sea level (fig. 4).

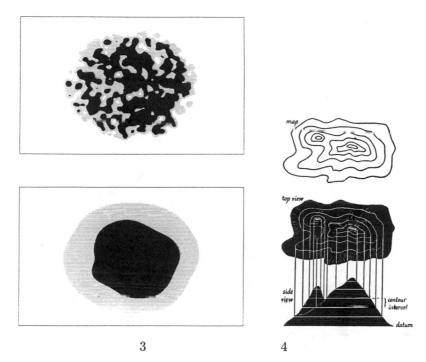

3   4

Another way to define constraint is to consider invariances under transformations or symmetry operations. This actually makes almost tangible operational sense too, because you often *generate* objects in such a way. For instance, a *plane* can be defined as a surface that remains invariant against translations that are linear combinations of two arbitrary fiducial translations; a *sphere* can be defined as the surface that is transformed into itself by arbitrary rotations about axes that are concurrent, and so forth.

In all these cases the identity that should occur after the symmetry operation has been performed has to be assessed in terms of a certain *tolerance* (operationalization) of course. Otherwise a material sphere could not exist at all.

Still another way is to consider *mappings of simple objects*. For instance, you define a *curve* as a map from the unit interval of the reals ("time") into space. This also makes lots of sense because it often enables you to describe complicated things in terms of simpler ones. It makes some operational sense insofar as you may identify a map with a rule to establish a position.

A geographical atlas provides an example: "City such-and-such is at F 7." Much like the usual chess notation. But "F 7" is on the flat map as well as on the spherical earth. The convenience of such methods is great and I will often use maps or parametrizations. Their operational significance is a bit less direct than that of the previous methods, though. Moreover, the *definition* of surfaces in terms of maps is a rather problematic matter, full of subtle problems arising from the desire to avoid such singularities as self-intersections, or worse.

In this book I use maps only as convenient labeling systems for surfaces that are defined not by way of the map but as the level surfaces of densities measured with a finite level of resolution.

There actually do exist a few methods to define *surfaces* or curves operationally *without taking recourse to volumometric methods.*

For instance, surfaces have physical relevance when they appear as apertures involved in measuring the flux of some *current*. This makes it possible to define a surface as something that maps currents on fluxes. This interesting possibility has rich mathematical consequences in the theory of "variforms." The definition is very attractive indeed, because it is entirely based on *integrals*, or *measurable quantities*. It should especially appeal to the physicist, and I am amazed that I have not yet come across an application in theoretical physics. Because you deal with fluxes, this method cannot "see" such fine singular structures as "hairs" on the surface, just because these catch no flux. Thus you automatically skip many of the problems that typically cause trouble in the usual mathematical definitions of surfaces.

Nice as the method may be though, I won't consider it further in this book.

2.4   Constraint defined operationally

Just as the introduction of the irrational numbers ... is a convenient myth [which] simplifies the laws of arithmetic ... so physical objects are postulated entities which round out and simplify our account of the flux of existence ... The conceptional scheme of physical objects is [likewise] a convenient myth, simpler than the literal truth and yet containing that literal truth as a scattered part.
—WILLARD VAN ORMAN QUINE (1960)

The ways to interact with shape and to generate shape are so various that I can hardly review all of them. New methods are being devised every day. A cursory overview will have to suffice. I include it because it is important to grasp the fact that there exists an infinite variety of operations that might be relevant in some practical context. Geometry will somehow have to abstract the essences from this. The very *value* of the geometrical approach is that it permits you to abstract from the infinite variety of real-life physical operationalizations. It prepares you for the methods that might be invented tomorrow.

Many interesting ways to generate shapes exploit invariances under symmetry transformations. For example, the most precise way to produce a spherical mirror even in our technologically advanced age is to *rub two slabs of glass against each other.* These only fit in all positions if they are both spherical and have the same curvature. Any deviation from a true spherical shape is soon abraded away. If you take three pieces and rub them pair-wise, you generate planar surfaces, for only if all three are planar will they fit in all positions and all combinations. Similarly turning on a lathe or throwing on a wheel generate "surfaces of revolution"; any perturbation is cut away in no time. This is one reason why invariances under symmetry operations might interest you.

There are many other ways of generating shapes that use different principles, of course. Some use *physical laws* to obtain defined shapes, for instance crystalization, freezing of liquids that have formed horizontal surfaces under gravity, blowing bubbles, bending flexible rods, and putting strings under tension. Others use existing objects to form other objects (molding, casting, stamping, drilling ...), while still others form by *combining* (gluing, nailing, screwing ...). Theories that treat shapes due to physical laws abound. Theories for agglomerated shapes have only recently attracted interest. This is the case because of the increased interest in CAD-CAM applications.

Ways to measure or define shape are extremely various indeed. A great many kinds of interaction essentially yield different kinds of shape information. For a given piece of metal you may treat the moments of inertia, the electrostatic capacity, the aerodynamic resistance, the scattering cross section for different radiations, and so forth, as essentially so many *shape measures.* This usually entails the rewriting of the physical formula in terms of some dimensionless "geometrical factor," of course.

"Geometrical factors" occur quite commonly in physics and they are synonymous with "shape," although physics textbooks rarely stress this fact. Any one of these could be of decisive importance in some application. Shape is not just what you measure with calipers, it comprises a much wider class of notions.

Mark well: *Different meanings of "shape" are not necessarily closely related.*

It is useful not to mix up the meaning of the word shape in the "shape of a dog" and the "shape of an atomic nucleus." You might get confused. Many people are. In high school they taught me to think of electrons as little blue spheres. Protons and neutrons where somewhat larger spheres, colored red and white, respectively. Although I know this is bogus, I can't stop my inner vision from presenting me with this image when I think of elementary particles. Of course these entities *have neither shape nor color* in our everyday visual sense: the interaction of electromagnetic radiation from the electromagnetic spectrum with an apple is quite different from that with a single electron in the apple. Only entities larger than a few wavelengths of such radiation (roughly 5000 Å) possess a "visual shape" in any reasonable sense.

Shape is by necessity *operationally defined* and the method is as much part of the definition as the object is.

Of course you don't necessarily want a shape measure of the *numerical* type. In many cases you just want a *taxonomy*, for instance. You may roughly consider the following disciplines:

morphology: The descriptive method, in other words a taxonomy or the use of "nominal scales." Examples are "ovoid" or "egg-shaped," "pretzel-shaped," "vermiform" or "worm-like," "galliform." (That means something like "helmet-shaped." This type of shape is treated in much detail later in the book. I call it "bell shaped" there.) In this text I will often name certain equivalence classes and thus mark shapes on a nominal scale. Examples are "convex," "concave," "synclastic," "anticlastic," "gutter-point," and many more. Such equivalence classes are usually based on such things as the signs of certain geometrical invariant measures, like the principal curvatures of a surface patch.

There is no reason to consider such "merely qualitative" measures as in any way *inferior*; in fact, they are perhaps the most important shape descriptors in use. It would be considered great progress if you could build a machine that glances at an object and ventures a classification in this sense.

morphography: The method of the physical models such as blueprints, computer sculpted surfaces (so called "scale models"), and so forth. I illustrate an early—fifteenth-century—example (fig. 5). Nowadays a morphographical description will typically be a CAM-object, or maybe the depiction of a CAD object on a CRT screen.

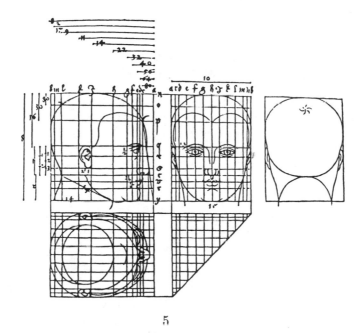

5

Notice that a "morphographical description" is really not a *description* at all, but in essence merely a *copy*. As such it is as yet "uninterpreted": it contains less explicit information than the morphological description, but of course more implicit information.

morphometry: Methods to specify certain features of the shape numerically, for instance the largest diameter in inches. A well-known example is the discipline of "craniometry." In this science of "skull measuring" one specifies various parameters such as height, depth and width, facial angle, volume of the brain cage, and so forth. In this text the values of various curvatures as a function of arclengths play such a role.

Notice that any morphometric description needs a "scaffold" (such as a blueprint) to attach the numbers to. No mere list of numbers as such can be a shape description.

morphonomy: Methods that aim at a complete description of the shape in numerical form, such that one could reproduce the shape from the description alone. Note that this could hardly take the form of a "telephone book," because ultimately the numerical data have to be interpreted in terms of some conventional or communicated "format" or recipe, basically an algorithm that allows you to construct a (scale) model on the basis of the description.

You need a datastructure that is fit for the kind of use you plan to make of the description, augmented with numerical data.

In most cases you need all methods simultaneously. This could be done through a blueprint with measures printed on it, for instance. (A combination of a morphographic and a morphonomic description.) Figure 5 shows an example of many centuries ago. It is an anthropomorphic study of Albrecht Dürer. This is really obvious material that has been around for ages. I won't pretend to tell you anything novel.

In order to illustrate the broad spectrum of shape measures, I consider just a few mechanical and a few optical measures in this chapter. Remember that the possibilities are virtually unlimited.

If you open your eyes so much as to decrease your height by one-fourteenth and spread and raise your arms so that your middle fingers are on a level with the top of your head, you must know that the navel will be in the centre of a circle of which the outspread limbs touch the circumference;
and the space between the legs will form an equilateral triangle.
—LEONARDO DA VINCI (1452–1519)

2.5   Mechanical operationalizations

I am coming more and more to the conviction that the necessity of our geometry cannot be demonstrated, at least neither by, nor for, the human intellect ... geometry should be ranked, not with arithmetic, which is purely aprioristic, but with mechanics.
—KARL FRIEDRICH GAUSS (1817)

Even the purely mechanical measures are extremely various in nature. You can use interaction with rigid objects, or with flexible strips and wires, but just as well with fluids ... Just consider the following operations (they by no means *exhaust* the possibilities):

fitting The paradigmatic example is the use of a template. You can handle almost arbitrary shapes as long as there is no "undercut." Examples include the time honored straightedge and the square. You also use piecewise rigid templates connected with hinges and joints, such as the many different types of dividers.

Different implements are used for "outer" and "inner" measures (fig. 6). Special implements have been developed for specific shapes, for instance spherical surfaces, such as the spherometer for optical lenses, or skulls, as you can see in books on "craniometry."

Problems arising in many contexts arc due to kinematical constraints. An example is the use of a straightedge to test the planarity of a billiard table. In that case *two points of contact completely determine the situation kinematically.* You simply cannot expect a contact along the length of the straightedge in *any* case. You can only hope to be able to decrease the deviations to an unnoticeable extent for a given method of measurement. One typically puts a piece of cigarette paper between the straightedge and the table surface and tries to blow it away in order to test the quality of the contact.

The typical spherometer (fig. 7) is a good example of sound "kinematical design." Three points determine the position of the instrument with respect to the surface, then you find the point of contact for a fourth rod that can be moved orthogonally to the plane defined by the three points of contact. The contact of the fourth point can be enforced through a spring or can be judged mechanically by noting the nature of the "wobbling." Another

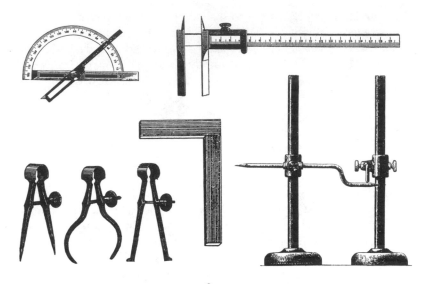

6

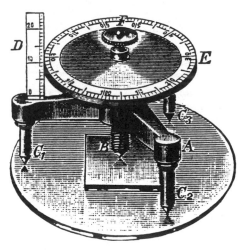

7

method is to notice the position of the fourth rod in relation to its reflected image (fig. 7).

Such things are bread and butter for the engineer, of course, although they have only fairly recently fired the imagination of the mathematicians.

grading Grading through sieves is a method that is only marginally different from the use of templates. However, you usually don't expect the object to "fit" the apertures of the sieve very well. This is indeed the key difference. As long as the object gets through or is held back, everything is just fine. The worry is that your objects could get stuck in the holes of your sieve.

Exceptions occur for some recognition processes, such as locks and keys. For the typical case of grading through sieves, precision is obtained by using a *set* of sieves to "bracket" the description.

"Negative sieves" are commonly used to gauge the size of holes or the separation of components (such as the gap of a spark plug). If you are able to pass a certain thickness of blade between two parts, you know that their separation must exceed this thickness.

application of strips The application of flexible strips, either with the broadside or "edge on," yields shape information. These are ways to define "geodesics" and "asymptotic curves" (fig. 8). The terms are explained later.

application of strings Taut strings define geodesics, the shape of the parallelograms of the fishnet yields information about the "Gaussian curvature."

It is a generally recognized fact among vaudeville directors that the shape of female legs is brought out to best advantage by the shapes of the mazes in a tightly fitting, wide-mazed stocking. Notice that you can only pull strings taut when they pass over convexities. They "lift off" when they pass over concavities.

slicing You can slice simply by taking off a chip or by taking actual sections. For the case of a chip the shape of the "wound" gives curvature information; it is known as "Dupin's indicatrix" and I will discuss it in detail in a later chapter.

When you section a surface in different orientations, you effectively reduce the study of three-dimensional shape to that of the study of families of planar curves. Precisely herein lies the attractiveness

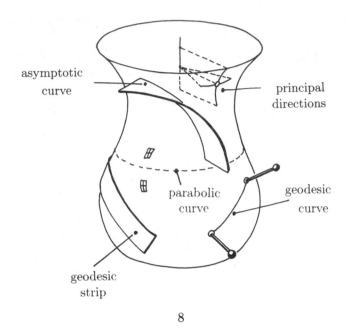

asymptotic
curve

principal
directions

parabolic
curve

geodesic
curve

geodesic
strip

8

of the method: it is a way to simplify the complicated. This is one
of the classical methods in the study of curved surfaces, dating
back to the eighteenth century. It is associated with the names of
Meusnier and Euler.

peeling If you peel an apple and spread out the peel on the flat table,
you can reconstruct a lot of the curvature of the apple, namely
the "intrinsic curvature." Peeling is a special case of the unfolding
method discussed below.

"dressing up" The shape of the pieces of cloth used to sew a man's
suit reveal a lot about his shape. Similarly, the regular polyhedra
are quite often characterized by way of their unfoldings in the
plane. This method can be quite powerful; for instance, convex
polyhedra are completely described by their faces.

For nonconvex objects, or for surface patches that are not closed,
the method is less powerful. And even in the case of convex polyhedra you really need this prior knowledge because it may well
be possible to paste up a nonconvex polyhedron from the same
fold-out.

pointing Basically this method implies that you take coordinates with

respect to a rigid fixed frame. This is the method of choice that
sculptors use to define shape for copying in marble. The sculptor
starts with a roughly rectangular block and first of all drills a lot of
holes in the direction of the cartesian axes to such a depth that the
hole just touches the desired shape. The more holes you drill, the
better you can define the final shape. Then the process of rough
"blocking out" and subsequent more precise chisel work—taking
off little chips at a time—is carried out. This is hard and relatively
stupid work and is best left to apprentices. Only in the very latest
stage, the sandpapering, does the sculptor (the master himself!)
dare to remove the pits due to the drill holes. It is then said that
"the master brings the surface to life." On many finished statues
you can still detect the pits quite easily, so maybe the hand of the
master never entered here.

pouring You may pour liquids on the shape. "Hollows" can *contain*
liquids; they drip off from other parts. Dipping an object in a
liquid is an ancient way to find level sets of the height function, a
primitive "ranging device." This messy method has a long literary
history. It is described in renaissance technical treatises on art.[5]
Despite the writings, the actual use can be debated though.

et cetera You may amuse yourself by thinking of countless other examples.

2.6 Optical operationalizations

Possible optical interactions are again extremely diverse in their nature.
Some of the interactions depend merely on the rectalinear propagation,
that is on *perspective*. Others are of a photometrical nature. Still others
depend on the wave character of the radiation. The possibilities are
extremely diverse, as you will appreciate when you scan an armful of
optics journals. (Try recent years of the *Journal of the Optical Society
of America*, or *Applied Optics*.)
  Consider the following:

- The shape of the cast shadow for different positions of the point
  source. This is often called the "silhouette." It is a very ancient
  method to study solid shape. It is related to the art of drawing

---

[5]For example, Vasari's technical appendix to his *Lives of the Artists*, and Cellini's
autobiography (*Vita* ...), which contains numerous pieces of good technical advice.

which reputedly was invented by an ancient Greek woman who traced the outline of her lover's shadow on the wall. For several obvious reasons this touching scene has attracted many painters throughout history.

For a convex object you can *reconstruct* the object from its silhouettes. When the object has deep "potholes," this is obviously not possible. You have a better chance if you study the cast shadows of X-rays though.

- The edge of the body shadow in the case of an object that is being irradiated with a point source (fig. 9). This edge is intuitively a curve on the object where a cone of light rays with its apex at the source touches the object.

9

Draftsmen traditionally equate the shadow edge with some mysterious entity known as "the edge between the major planes of the model." They use the term even if the model is a nude that tends to resemble a human body rather more closely than a polyhedron! I will clarify this in a later chapter.

- The isophotes of the illumination of the surface. You could study this for the case of a point source, or for a large diffuse radiator. The latter type of illumination actually yields the better results.

The light-dark distribution, or "chiaroscuro," basically reveals the orientation of surface patches with respect to the dominant light direction.

That chiaroscuro yields very powerful shape cues is evident from the use of shading by graphical artists. It is easy to paint a chiaroscuro depiction of a plaster relief that is visually indistinguishable from the real thing, even at a surprisingly short viewing distance.

In modern "machine vision" this has led to the method of "photometric stereo." It is easily the worst method ever implemented for shape measurement. I'm sure there is room for improvement though,

- The outline of the object as seen from different viewpoints. Intuitively at least, an object is completely determined if you have recorded its outline from all directions, at least when the object doesn't contain deep undercuts.

In a way this is similar to the recording of cast shadows: here "visual rays" take over the function of "light rays." The mathematics is absolutely identical, only the physics is different.

- The specularities in case of a reflecting object. Figure 8 indicates how to spot "parabolic curves"—the term is explained later. Again, a specularity reveals the orientation of surface patches, this time with respect to both the direction of the source and of the line of sight.

- The caustics of the light rays in space for a reflecting object. For instance, you can easily distinguish convex and concave mirrors on account of their image-forming properties. Sometimes you observe interesting light patterns on the bows of ships that would reveal the shape of the water surface if you knew how to interpret them.

We are not used to making sense of caustics in ordinary vision. In physics, where one often depends on scattering experiments for the knowledge of an object's shape, caustics are often very important though.

- The vignetting effect of one part of the object with respect to another. For instance, the fact that eye holes always come out as dark patches in photographs of people of caucasian complexion, even in diffuse light fields, reveals their nature as concavities.

This effect is very important as a visual cue, and artists very often use it. You can make "a hole" in a piece of marble with a piece of coal just as effectively as you can with a drill. We know that the

famous baroque sculptor Bernini drew the pupils of the eyes on
marble busts, to do the (merely mechanical) job of the hollowing
out afterward.

- The interreflections ("reflexes") on a white object. Again, these
  basically reveal concavities, or at least deviations from convexity.

  A hemispherical boss and a hemispherical dimple on a plane look
  similar in many ways. In fact, they are often visually confused (in
  case these people also misjudge the position of the source). Only
  the interreflexes, the cast shadows and the vignetting show the
  difference in an objective manner.

- The differential scattering cross section as a function of wavelength. This is our main source of information concerning the
  shape of aerosol particles that drift about at high altitudes in the
  earth's atmosphere.

  I doubt whether you ever use this cue in vision.

- The "optic flow," that is, the deformations of the images that
  a moving camera obtains from the object. Figure 10 shows the
  distorted shapes of what were originally the squares of a Cartesian
  mesh that have been carried along with the optic flow for a spell.
  This most vividly illustrates the deformation of local detail induced
  by the flow. Note that you don't see the actual object but *only its
  deformations* here. In modern "machine vision" this is known as
  the "shape from motion problem."

  There can be little doubt that this is a very powerful shape cue in
  daily life.

- Again, you may want to think of still other examples yourself.

All such methods reveal different aspects of the "shape" of the body,
some being relevant in some situation, and some in others. Many of the
methods mentioned in this section have recently gained popularity in
the engineering community. The field of "machine vision" is indeed ma-
turing rapidly. Some methods have already been developed to the point
where they have become true quantitative methods of measurement. It
is to be expected that these methods will grow much more sophisticated
in the foreseeable future. Differential geometrical methods such as are
explained in this book will certainly play a key role in the development
of these methods.

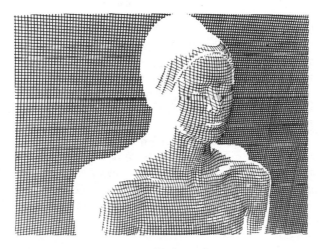

10

It will be clear that the aim cannot be to study such diverse methods in detail. Instead, the description of shape should be so general that it is easily adapted to any particular method. This is the true geometrical approach. Yet all theorems will again have to be interpretable in experiential terms, usually via either one of the mechanical or one of the optical operationalizations. The mathematically inclined textbooks always—and rightly so—stop short of this final step. Here you reach the domain of physics where no mathematician dares enter.

It will be clear that there can be no such a thing as a "mathematical theory of shape." The very notion of shape belongs to the natural sciences. Nevertheless I will play down the physical methods and concepts as much as possible in this book. On the surface the treatment will look "mathematical." Don't let this fool you.

Und belehr ich mich nicht? wenn ich des lieblichen Busens
Formen spähe, die Hand leite die Hüften hinab.
Dann versteh ich erst recht den Marmor, ich denck und vergleiche,
Sehe mit fühlendem Aug, fühle mit sehender Hand.
—JOHANN WOLFGANG VON GOETHE, *Römische Eligien (1788)*

2.7   Shape tolerances

*. . . , in the channels of rivers, the bends in foliage, the angles in salts,
crystals and other bodies, in the tips of the claws that appear to the
naked eye to be very sharp in the case of certain animals; if a
microscope were used to examine them, in no case would the point
appear to be quite abrupt, or the angle altogether sharp, but in every
case somewhat rounded, & so possessing a definite curvature &
apparently approximating to continuity. Nevertheless in all these cases
there is nowhere true continuity according to my Theory; for all bodies
of this kind are composed of points that are indivisible & separated
from one another; & these cannot form a continuous surface; . . .*
—ROGERIO JOSEPHO BOSCOVICH, S.J., *Theoria Philosophiæ Naturalis*
(1763)

In the previous section I tacitly assumed that "the object" was some
coherent blob. In many practical cases this may actually be far from the
truth. Dispersed systems abound, either systems consisting out of many
distinct components, such as the droplets of a cloud, or those that are
characterized by extreme articulations, such as arborizations. Think of
a tree or a soot particle.[6]

There exist several feasible methods of approach. One method is to
look for the "overall shape" first. This can be done via the blob approach
if you take a sampling aperture that is, so large that the shape—that is
the level set—apparently *coheres* again.

Such a method works well for the cloud and is in fact implicit in the
common notion of what a cloud is. If the aperture is large enough, it is
intuitively evident that any sample within the region of the cloud will
contain many droplets, irrespective of the precise position. The method
cannot "see" the spaces between the individual droplets, in that case.
Then you describe the microstructure as a *texture*. Thus you prepare
only a *statistical* description. An example would be the distribution
of droplet size in the cloud. If you merely "shuffle" the droplets—as
the natural aerodynamics does all the time in nature—the "cloud" as a
superstructure remains largely unaffected.

Important observation: *On a microscale the cloud is a completely
different object every other second, but on a macroscale it is an
enduring entity.*

---

[6]Soot particles owe many of their peculiar and often disagreeable properties, such
as their remarkable floatability in the air (very much like snow flakes) and their
stickiness, to their fractal-like structure.

It is even possible to describe the shape at several or even many levels of resolution *simultaneously*. This is often a very practical and desirable method, since the more "overall" representatives can be used to "organize" the wilder high resolution ones. Figure 11 shows *the same object* at several levels of resolution. What is a dispersed cloud at one resolution looks like a coherent blob at another. Many *different* shapes at a high level of resolution can lead to essentially *identical* shapes at a low level of resolution. Viewed from a low level of resolution the high level detail is either completely irrelevant, or treated as "texture," that is, merely in an overall statistical manner.

You need a way to put two clouds with "the same shape" but in general a different texture—such as clouds in which you have "reshuffled" the droplets—into a single *equivalence class*. What you need is a *shape metric*.

You can obtain a useful metric in the following way:

1. First I define the "ε-neighborhood" of a point as the spherical region of radius ε centered on that point.

2. Then define the "spherical ε-neighborhood" of an *arbitrary region* as the union of all ε-neighborhoods of the points belonging to that region. You may think of the ε-neighborhood as a slightly "thickened" shape.

3. With these preliminaries understood, you can proceed to define the "distance" between two shapes: the distance between two shapes is the smallest value of ε for which it is the case that each shape is contained within the ε-neighborhood of the other, perhaps after some arbitrary displacement.

4. As a result you are all set to define the equivalence class of a given shape for a given resolution: shapes within a distance given by the resolution are considered equivalent.

Figure 12 illustrates the case of a line segment and a point pair. In the lower part of the figure you see the ε-neighborhoods for a value of ε that is sufficiently large to ensure that the line-piece easily fits in the dilated point pair, and *vice versa*. At this value of ε the two shapes are indistinguishable. This means that their mutual distance is less than ε.

The notion of an "ε-neighborhood" allows me to make the previous definition of *surface area* more precise. You just take the difference of the volumes of the two times ε-neighborhood and the ε-neighborhood and divide it by ε cubed. The result is a pure number that specifies the

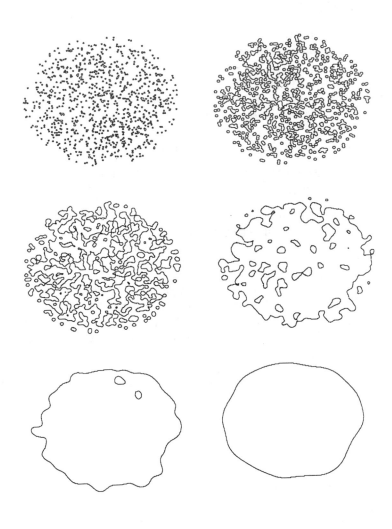

number of "cobbles" of atomic size needed to "pave" the surface. Of course this "area" depends on ε, but what do you want? No "limit for ε to zero" would make sense for a real object. There is no way to avoid this, because it isn't clear at all that there exists anything like a "true area" in the first place.

You would be well advised to stick to the operational definition as there is no way to avoid the resolution dependency. In specifying the surface area of a person's skin, do you want to count the area subtended by the inside of the pores? For some applications yes, for others no. This is by no means a *mathematical* problem. It is a decision you make on purely pragmatic and operational grounds. "Surface area" is a physical parameter for which you have several mathematical models. This type of definition has been pioneered by Minkowski.

Fact: *The notion of "surface area" is devoid of any meaning unless you specify the resolution at which it is to be assessed. The same goes* ipso facto *for the notion of "arc length".*

Any statement concerning the shape of an object makes sense only if it holds equally well for all members of the equivalence class of the object. The equivalence class is defined by your method. Because of the finite tolerance you always deal with equivalence classes and never with any singular "mathematically defined" object. You can't "mathematically define" anything with the physical methods at your disposal. Although this is obvious in a physical sense, it gives rise to many problems of a mathematical nature. For instance, many important shape characteristics are defined in terms of *derivatives*. Clearly the mathematical concept of a derivative is of no use here. In an equivalence class they could have essentially *arbitrary* values for the various members of that class.

Although it is possible to solve such problems in a neat way, this is quite involved and takes great care. Intuitively what you should do is something like the following. You substitute *averages* over blobs of a diameter equal to the resolution for point properties, and you substitute *differences* over a distance of the order of the resolution for the derivatives. This is essentially what the neat methods do in a mathematically acceptable way. Figure 13 shows the sampling window for the value at a point $\mathcal{P}$ and the sampling windows used to arrive at the derivative at the point $\mathcal{Q}$. The estimate of the derivative is the difference of the samples obtained from the offset spheres divided by the separation of their centers. The method works tolerably well only if the separation and the diameters are in some reasonable proportion. This is indeed intuitively

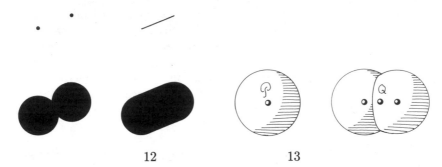

12   13

evident. It is elaborated upon in the next subsection, but you may skip
it on first reading.

We have learned that to examine how scored and pitted
smooth skin looks under the microscope
does not help us to conceive the satin flesh as leather, ...
—ADRIAN STOKES, *Reflections on the Nude (1967)*

2.7.1 Blurred derivatives

♠ INTERMEZZO—A TECHNICALITY.

Remark: *I use the "spade-suit sign" (♠) to mark those sections which contain material that you would be well advised to skip on a first reading. They usually constitute a break in the main line of argument, so it may indeed be best to skip them if you read through in one go. Sometimes these sections go somewhat deeper into technicalities, sometimes they offer you a handle on possible applications. Most often, however, they are true* intermezzi, *inserted for the sake of distraction.*

The present intermezzo gives a short background on "physically acceptable" definitions of derivatives.

The notion of a physical *sampling window* is worth some closer attention. Suppose you measure an intensive parameter via its averages over spherical volumes, a so-called "hard" window. Then it is well known that you will have to reckon with *spurious resolution*. By this people indicate that the sampled density may show structure "that shouldn't be there."

You can easily demonstrate this effect with an unfocused slide projector. Just pull the focus back and forth and study the fine detail. You will notice that light-dark contrast may actually reverse! This happens because this blurring method convolves the image with a neighborhood operator that is almost a uniform circular disc. The equivalent frequency transfer function has positive and negative lobes: hence the contrast reversal. This effect is very objectionable, because the image may in places become unrecognizable. Portrait photographers have a keen sense for this effect: with the best (very sharp) lenses the ears will look like a mess if you focus on the eyes. They prefer "soft focus lenses," for which the spurious resolution is much less.

The only way to avoid spurious resolution is to use a "soft," smooth window. (The portrait photographer's "soft focus objective.") In fact, it has been shown mathematically that the only correct sampling method, which is the one that completely avoids spurious resolution in a sense to be made precise later, is the *Gaussian window*. This window has the weighing function

$$G(\vec{x}, \vec{x}') = \frac{e^{-\frac{\|\vec{x}-\vec{x}'\|^2}{4t}}}{(4\pi t)^{\frac{3}{2}}}.$$

Suppose your density at some very high resolution is $D(\vec{x})$; then your sampled density will be the convolution $D(\vec{x}, t) = D \otimes G$.

Mathematically this is equivalent to a "diffusion process" if you interpret the resolution parameter as the "time." But don't get confused: there is absolutely nothing temporal going on here! The parameter t is a measure of the spatial resolution; it doesn't represent time. There is no diffusion process in the usual physical sense.

A *blurred derivative* is defined as a garden variety derivative of the blurred density. However, it turns out that you may compute it directly from the *unblurred* density via a convolution with a derivative of the window. That this is the case follows from the trivial relation (for simplicity I write the one-dimensional formula)

$$\frac{\partial(D \otimes G)}{\partial x} = D \otimes \left(\frac{\partial G}{\partial x}\right).$$

Thus the kernel $\frac{\partial G}{\partial x}$ describes a "neighborhood-operator" that permits you to compute the blurred *derivative* by way of a weighted *integration*. Very convenient indeed.

You obtain arbitrary mixed partial derivatives in the same way. The blurred differentiators are very robust operators because they are defined through an *integration* process that can be applied to any, even a noise-polluted, situation. The result depends critically on the resolution, of course (fig. 14). The

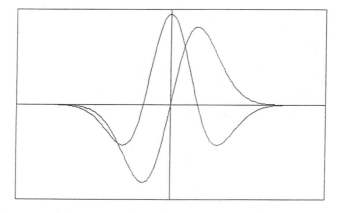

14

figure shows the weighing functions of the first- and second-order blurred differentiators for the one-dimensional case, whereas figure 15 shows the mixed partial derivatives $\frac{\partial}{\partial x}$, $\frac{\partial^2}{\partial x^2}$ and $\frac{\partial^3}{\partial x\, dy^2}$ for the two-dimensional case.

Although this whole construction is fairly trivial in a way, it opens up a field of useful applications. Moreover, it is possible to interpret the process in ways that are helpful to the intuitive notion of what goes on in the "infinitesimal domain." Notice how you can "blow up the infinitesimal domain" and operate with *finite neighborhood operators* if you use blurred derivatives. This can be interpreted as a *physically realizable model* of the differential calculus. You can use this method as a "microscope" that opens up the infinitesimal domain for

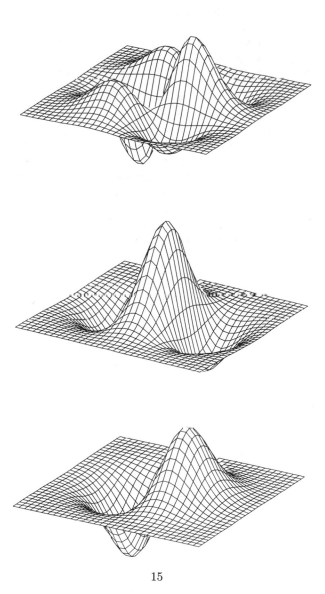

15

you! The method solves at least a few of the well-taken objections of bishop Berkeley against "infinitesimals." It is also connected with the (very) modern method of "hyperreal numbers."

The blurred derivatives are also eminently *practical* tools. In many cases it suffices to take a mathematical result and blandly substitute neighborhood operators for the mixed partial derivatives in order to arrive at a viable engineering implementation of that result. It is the preferred way to translate results of the differential calculus to the physical domain.

The human visual system may also be wise to this trick, because many of the cortical receptive fields have sensitivity profiles that closely resemble the derivatives of Gaussian kernels.

In physics this kind of thing (the substitution of finite neighborhood operators for differentiation) is going on all the time, without people so much as mentioning—or perhaps even noticing—it. It is worth your while to try to detect this procedure and generally be aware of it. But come to think of it, the limit for whatever size to zero has never made any physical sense.

Salviati: ... when you want to show me that a material sphere
does not touch a material plane in one point,
you make use of a sphere that is not a sphere,
and of a plane that is not a plane.
—GALILEI GALILEO *Dialogues (1629)*

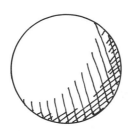 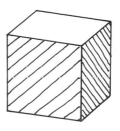

16

2.8   Shape models and their use

In a way *any* shape description is a "model." Indeed, the only way you can approach reality is by way of modeling it. However, in this section I will consider substitutes for shapes that have additional structure that is regarded as irrelevant but is nevertheless retained because it helps you to understand the shape better. This may sound mysterious, so let me give an example right away.

Take *polyhedral models*. As models for smooth shapes, the vertices, faces, and edges of a polyhedral model must be considered irrelevant. However, the value of a polyhedral model as a heuristic tool is exactly that it has these features. Figure 16 shows a sphere and a polyhedral model of that sphere. In other settings the sphere might be used as a model of the polyhedron. The relation "being a model of" being completely conventional.

Models are used as heuristic tools to sharpen your intuition. Usually they are of a finite, combinatorial type and easily lend themselves to computer implementation. They usually also lend themselves to simple mechanical implementation—for instance, polyhedral models from pasted paper or wire models. In some cases of an engineering nature they may be of interest for practical implementation, too.

It is important to know what the *essential* elements of a model are supposed to be if you are really going to use it. Consider the simple example of a polyhedral model. The essential elements could be either the *vertices* or the *faces*. That this really makes a lot of difference becomes evident when you build computer models and are confronted with the problem of numerical tolerances. A small "play" in either the position of the vertices or the position and orientation of the facets leads to completely different *qualitative* behavior.

If the *faces* are given, you will typically obtain vertices at which three edges meet in a stable fashion; when the *vertices* are given, this number may vary. If the vertices are given, the faces will only be stable if they are of triangular shape; if the faces are given, they may be more complicated planar polygons, but you cannot depend on the fact that the number of vertices will be well defined (fig. 17).

In any case you should strictly observe the distinction between the *model* and the *approximation*. This difference lies in your aims. It is not at all intrinsically due to the mathematical structure. A *model* captures some features of the object that it is supposed to model, but it isn't meant to be used as an approximation at all. It usually simplifies matters conceptually when you leave out the unessentials. You use models to help answer questions of a qualitative or a general nature. The *approximation* on the other hand is specific and quantitative but it need not be "simple" in any obvious way. An approximation is good if you can use it instead of a given object for a specific type of interaction.

What you need to know about models in order to use them intelligently is:

- Their *structure*. Supposedly that is an easy matter, for unless you are a masochist you pick only models that lend themselves to elegant descriptions.

- What to consider as important *properties*, that is, how to interpret these in terms of your real problem.

- What to *disregard*.

The latter two points are to be considered a vital part of the model. That this is not as a gratuitous remark as it may well appear at a cursory glance is evident from the observation that you will often encounter scientific discussions in which an apparent disregard of the third entry of the list is the effective cause of the polemics. This is one of those sad facts of life that makes a scientist's hair turn gray at an early age.

A few models will find repeated application in this text. They are discussed below. More detail will follow when I will actually use them.

2.9 Models for curves

Two models are in general use, the *linked rod model* and the *folding model*.

The linked rod model consists of any number of rigid rods, usually of a fixed length, that have been linked by universal joints (fig. 18). The

Perturb

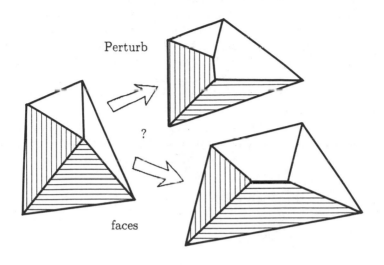

faces

Perturb

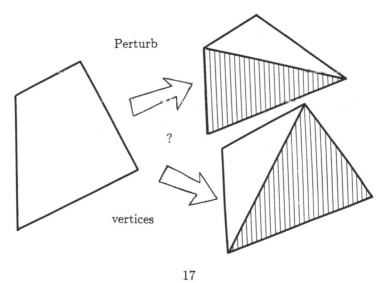

vertices

17

model makes most sense if subsequent rods are almost—but not quite—
collinear. Every curve can be used to generate such a model in the
following way: I pick a first point on the curve and then each time find a
subsequent point by traversing the curve in the positive direction until
the chord between the two points has reached a certain fiducial length.
The chords then are replaced by the rods. Notice that you could have
obtained this configuration by flexing an originally straight rod model
at the joints. Thus it is intuitively obvious that you can bend *any* space
curve into *any* other.

A planar curve may similarly be represented by a bicycle chain. Instead of universal joints you use hinges with a single degree of freedom
(fig. 19).

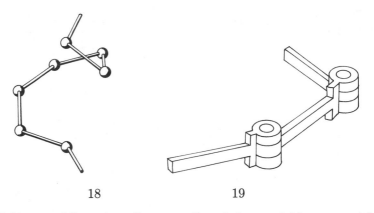

18   19

The *folding model* consists of any number of planar, rigid sectors with
very acute angles that have been joined by hinges along the edges in
such a way that each subsequent sector sticks out by a fixed amount.
These free pieces of edge together describe the curve, as the rods did in
the linked rod model. You can deform the curve by flexing the hinges;
for instance, you can flatten it out or make it into a space curve.

Notice that this model has less freedom than the rod model because
the sector angles must remain fixed during the bending. The rod model
with universal joints has two degrees of freedom per joint, whereas the
folding model has only a single one. The chain model also has but a
single degree of freedom but clearly of a completely different nature.

In the chain model you are free to change the "curvature," whereas
the curve has to remain planar. In the folding model the curvature
has been fixed once and for all, but by flexing the model you may still
change its appearance. You may turn the structure from a planar into

a general space curve by changing the curve's "torsion." In the linked rod model you have full control over both the curvature and the torsion. It is intuitively evident that the linked rod model is as free as can be, in other words that curvature and torsion somehow specify the shape of the structure completely. These notions are discussed in detail in a later chapter.

A folding model may be obtained from a curve by first finding its linked rod model and then defining the plane of the sectors through the planes spanned by subsequent rods (fig. 20).

The folding model clearly represents more structure than the linked rod model. The latter gives merely the "first derivative," that is the change of position in tangential direction, whereas the former also gives the "second derivative," which is the change of the sector planes, that is, the dihedral angles. The linked rod model may be endowed with additional interesting structure though. For instance, you may attach *normal planes* in the middle of each rod. This is not feasible with a mechanical model but no worry in case of a computer model. Then a lot of additional structure appears, such as the lines into which successive normal planes intersect, the series of points into which successive triples of normal planes intersect, and in fact several other entities of rather immediate geometrical interest.

2.10 Models for surfaces

For surfaces I will employ several different models, namely *polyhedra*, *triangulated patches*, and *nets*. Nets are linked rod models.

Polyhedra can be used as models, since they have the advantage that all the curvature is in the edges and the vertices. For instance, the cube can often be used as a convenient model of a sphere. Notice that this is the same as figure 16, but now the other way around.

The catch is that polyhedra are difficult combinatorial objects. This is mainly so because it is so hard to label the elements, namely the faces, vertices, and edges, in a consistent logical manner, although this certainly can be done in *some* cases. That is the reason why I will use polyhedra for only the simplest purposes.

Regular triangulated patches (fig. 21) have almost all the advantages of polyhedra, but can also be easily labeled. They are my preferred models for patches of curved surfaces. I usually take a regular triangular tessellation and fit it to the surface. This can be done in many possible ways; you really have an awful lot of freedom in this respect. In many

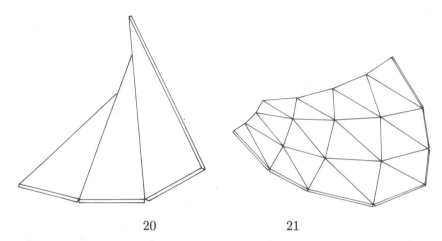

20   21

cases you may exploit this freedom to find *special* triangulations that
are convenient for certain tasks.

For instance, you may pair triangles to quadrilaterals and try to find
triangulations in which the quadrilaterals are planar. This is known as
a triangulation based on a "conjugated net." Alternatively you may
require that the "coordinate" edges of quadrilaterals (mark well: not
the "diagonals") that meet at a vertex are in a plane. This is known as
a triangulation based on an asymptotic net. Many alternative choices
are possible and may in fact be advantageous in a given context. I will
discuss such constructions in a later chapter. Sometimes you will be
able to find triangulations with the desired properties, sometimes this
will prove to be impossible.

Such different models have quite different properties, as you can imagine. As said before, many other methods are possible and are equally
interesting and useful. You always have to tailor the model according
to the specific application.

Sometimes you may be able to *bend* such a model by flexing it at
the hinges, but usually it proves to "give" only a little bit or even to
be completely rigid. This is a quite different situation from what you
experience with the linked rod model for space curves. The linked rod
model somehow has more freedom.

A special case of a triangulation is that of a *strip*. To make a strip
you hinge triangles together such that the patch is only one triangle

"deep" but possibly many triangles "long." Such a strip can be a model for a "peel" or a strip of paper that you bend into complicated spatial configurations. Its aptness depends very much on a judicious choice of the "hinges" (fig. 22).

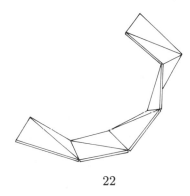

22

Clearly every strip is bendable, although it is equally obvious that you may not expect to be able to bend just any given strip into another one. This is at least intuitively obvious because of the following heuristic argument: first bend the strips that are to be compared in such a way that both are planar. (Just "iron them out.") If they aren't congruent as planar figures, you can entertain no hope of changing this with a bending that doesn't tear the material. In this respect the strips hold an intermediate position between space curves and surfaces.

Strips are so simple that you often won't bother to construct triangulation at all, at least not for purposes of intuitive doodling. Instead, imagine thin paper strips as models. Better still, take out your scissors and cut yourself a few.

A surface patch can often very conveniently be modeled by a sheaf of such strips, at least in the neighborhood of a point. You think of the point as a "puncture" and proceed to "mend" it by the application of many strips of adhesive tape in a criss cross manner. The curvature and twist of the strips depend on the direction of application and do reveal a good deal about the way the surface patch curves in space.

Nets are basically what you end up with when you keep only the edges of the quadrilaterals in a triangulation and interpret them in some mechanical way. Some nets are of special interest as simple models, for instance those where all edges are of equal length, the so-called "Cheby-

shev nets."[7] They are similar to tightly fitting sexy tights that reveal
shape through the variation in the angles of the quadrilaterals. When
you replace the taut wires of a net by rigid rods and the vertices by
universal joints, you obtain a linked rod model of a surface, the two-
dimensional equivalent of the linked rod curve model.

2.11   Volumometric models

A very special model that I will use now and then is not primarily
surface-like, but is actually *volume based*. It consists of a conglomerate
of elementary volume elements. If you consider all of space filled up
with a regular pile of "sugar cubes," that is, unit cubes in a regular
array, then you may map any blob on a pile of sugar cubes such that a
given cube is a member of the model if it has a point in common with
the blob. Alternatively you may require it to have more than half the
volume of the cube in common. It doesn't matter very much which. I
will refer to such models loosely as "piles of sugar cubes" (fig. 23). Sugar

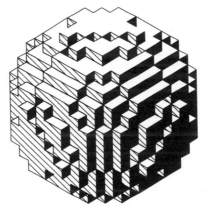

23

cubes work very well for simple doodling at the coffee table. For more
serious experimentation, however, children's "lego-blocks" are much to
be preferred. You can actually attach blocks to each other and thus
produce "undercuts" without contracting a major disaster.

---

[7]Variant spellings of the name are Čebyšev or Tschebyscheff. The latter spelling
occurs predominantly in German papers, the former one may have been used by
Čebyšev himself, but I didn't check this.

Note that any blob can be arbitrarily well approximated by such models in terms of the positions of points, although the surface area of the model can hardly be expected to converge to that of the blob. This model does not represent anything remotely *like a surface* in any useful way. It can be extremely convenient in various types of integral geometry though. For instance, it is rather easy to find the *volume* of a blob if you consider such a model. Basically this just amounts to a count of the cubes. Contrast this with the problem of how to find the volume of a closed hinged triangle model of a surface. Moreover, many empirically determined objects are actually *given* in this format.

Further on in the book, you will meet other models that model specific features of blobs. They may even be further removed from the real thing. For instance, you may think of a *wire model*—say from pipe cleaners—of a man. In this example you model a blob with a branched curve. Yet many aspects of the shape of a human being are being well represented by such a model. Everybody immediately perceives it as a "model man." Again you should not confuse "models" with "approximations." Indeed, the pipe cleaner model isn't a very good approximation at all; you would immediately notice it if somebody entered your office looking like that, or would you?

We obtain the idea of bodies through the senses; and the senses cannot in any way judge on a matter of accurate continuity; for very small intervals do not fall within the scope of the senses. Indeed we quite take it for granted that the continuity, which our senses meet with in a large number of bodies, does not really exist. In metals, marble, glass & crystals there appears to our senses to exist continuity, of such sort that we do not perceive in them any little empty spaces, or pores; but in this respect the senses have manifestly been deceived. This is clear, both from their different specific gravities, which certainly arises from the differences in the numbers of the empty spaces; & also from the fact that several substances will insinuate themselves through their substance. For instance, oil will diffuse itself through the former, & light will pass quite freely through the latter; & this indeed indicates, especially in the case of the latter, an immense number of pores; & these are concealed from our senses.
—ROGERIO JOSEPHO BOSCOVICH, S.J., *Theoria Philosopiæ Naturalis*
(1763)

II SPACE

3 Euclidean Space

Quoiqu'il soit vrai qu'en concevant le corps, on conçoit quelque chose de plus que l'espace, il ne s'en suit point qu'il y a deux étendues, celles de l'espace et celles du corps; car c'est comme lorsqu'en concevant plusieurs choses à la fois, on conçoit quelque chose de plus que le nombre savois res numeratas, et cependant il n'y a pas deux multitudes, l'une abstraite, savoir celle du nombre, l'autre concrète, savoir celle de choses nombrées. On peut dire que de même qu'il ne faut point s'imaginer deux étendues, l'une abstraite de l'espace, l'autre concrète du corps; le concept n'étant tel que par l'abstrait.
—LEIBNITZ (1646–1716), *Nouveaux essais sur l'entendement humain, II 4*

3.1 Geometries

In this book I deal only with your trusty "everyday" *Euclidean space*. This is a space without any *a priori* singled-out origin, fitted with the full machinery for the measurement of distances, areas, volumes and angles. That is to say, you can freely carry yardsticks, carpenter's squares, and so forth around and hold them up to the objects of interest for purposes of "measurement."[1]

Although Euclidean space offers a very nice environment indeed, it will be worth your while to be acutely aware of the "genealogy" of geometrical properties and not to despise a look at more "primitive" geometries. I mean roughly that it is often rewarding to think of Euclidean geometry as being the final evolutionary result of a series of geometries with steadily increasing structure, defined through groups of operations that conserve shape, throughout the series. The power of this view was forcefully argued by Felix Klein in his famous Erlangen program. It is one of those important modern viewpoints that the Greeks somehow managed to miss completely.

The more primitive geometries that will figure in this book are mainly *topology*, in which basically only neighborhood relations are recognized, and *affine* geometry, in which one abstains from carrying yardsticks and protractors around with the mad abandon one takes for granted in Euclidean spaces. *Projective* geometry, which primarily deals with the incidence relations of the "flats" of space—all space, planes, lines and

---

[1] "Measurement" means comparison, usually noting the incidence of certain landmarks of the object with certain fiducial marks on your yardstick.

points—will hardly figure explicitly, despite its fundamental importance.

Basically, geometry is about *structures* or *relations* defined on sets. A set has no geometrical structure whatsoever except that of "simultaneous presence," which yields the potentiality of acquiring geometrical structure. A set is merely a bag of "objects." The only relation between the objects is that they are members of the same set. For instance, you may take "blobs of space" for the objects, say the portions of space contained in spherical shells.

It is easy to set up an abstract, algebraic *model* for this in terms of four-tuples of real numbers to make this model respectable. The subsection 3.1.1 explains this idea in somewhat further detail.

Let there be a *lower limit on the diameter* of the blobs. Then the smallest blobs may as well be called *points*. They are members of the set of blobs.

One basic relation between blobs that generates geometrical structure in the model is that of *overlap*. This would be expressed as an algebraic inequality in the "respectable model." Another is that of *inclusion*. It is remarkable that the relation of inclusion can actually be expressed in terms of *overlap*.[2] Thus

blob $\mathcal{A}$ is included in blob $\mathcal{B}$ if and only if for *any* blob $\mathcal{C}$ that overlaps with $\mathcal{A}$ it is also true that $\mathcal{C}$ overlaps with $\mathcal{B}$.

A blob that includes a point is called a neighborhood of that point; the set of all neighborhoods of a point is called the "neighborhood system" of that point. This is a very important notion because it defines a *topology* on the set of blobs. A set, when given a topology, is the simplest kind of geometry that I will consider here. Many important relations in Euclidean space can actually be traced to this basic ancestor. They are called *topological properties*.

In this book I will never use intricate facts or methods from point set topology directly. Although it remains true that point set topology lies at the basis of every operation in the study of differential geometry, you don't need deep results at this introductory level. This is mainly the case because I don't *prove* any statements but merely try to make them understandable or even intuitively "obvious." Because I discuss shapes only at coarse levels of resolution, most mathematical monstrosities such as curves filling areas, or curves without direction, don't occur anyway. Don't let this fool you into believing that a basic knowledge of topology

---

[2] At least for convex blobs, such as spheres.

is not necessary if you want to "turn the crank" yourself. You *have* to study it if you want to be able to use the machinery of differential geometry in a reasonably "safe" and intelligent fashion.

I will merely use such notions as "dimension," "boundary," "connectivity," and I will do so in a rather naive manner, counting on your prior exposition to these matters. "Combinatorial" or "algebraic" topology is quite another subject which I will consider later.

A very useful and basic notion is that of the *convex hull* of a set of blobs. It is a volume—that is, a subset of all blobs—such that a point is contained in that volume if and only if *any* sphere that contains the set of blobs also contains that point. This definition is very much in the spirit of Huntington's model of Euclidean geometry. It is by no means the conventional way to introduce convexity. I will point out more conventional definitions later.

It should be intuitively evident that if you take the convex hull of a convex hull then this does not present you with anything new.

The convex hull of sets of disjunct points is known as the *join* of those points. People often use special terms for joins; for instance, the join of a pair of distinct points is a "line piece" (fig. 24); of three points (distinct and "in general position"), a "triangle"; of four points (same reservations), a "tetrahedron."

You can actually define the *dimension* of space through the joins:

> If there exist joins of $(n + 1)$ points that contain blobs that are *not* contained in *any* of the joins of the n-tuples of points obtained by deleting one of the original $(n + 1)$-tuple, then the dimension of the space must be at *least* n.

You understand this intuitively if you visualize how in three-dimensional space a tetrahedron contains interior points—not contained in any of its faces—whereas a cube can be dissected into tetrahedra without any loss.

If you extend a join, as when you elongate a line piece to both sides (easily defined in terms of convex hulls), you obtain the "flats" of the space: points, lines, planes, and space itself. The joins are in a natural hierarchical relation, a *lattice* in the technical sense. Thus the triangle covers the edges, the edges cover the vertices, and the vertices cover the null set for any given join of a triplet of points as shown (fig. 25).

The flats and their mutual relations are of extreme importance in geometry. They are in a hierarchical relation with respect to each other; thus points lie on lines, lines lie in planes, planes lie in space. The flats satisfy certain "incidence relations," thus planes may have a line

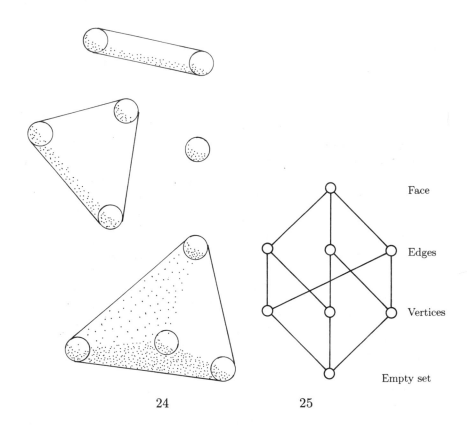

Face

Edges

Vertices

Empty set

24   25

in common, lines in a plane may have a point in common, and so forth.
Moreover, two points usually define a *line*, two intersecting lines or a
point and a line usually define a *plane*, two planes or a point and a
plane usually define *space*. The discipline of *projective geometry* aug-
ments the flats with some "ideal elements" in order that such relations
hold universally, and is essentially the study of these relations. Many
important properties of Euclidean space are actually inherited from this
geometry; people call them *projective properties*.

One important view of geometry is to consider *groups of transformations* and to study such properties as remain invariant under actions of
the group. This view originated with Felix Klein. For instance, arbitrary smooth deformations leave invariant what are called "topological
properties." Hence the term "rubber geometry." Central projection of
one plane on another leaves the projective relations in the plane invariant; hence the term "projective" geometry. A very important group of
transformations is that of the *affine* transformations, which are arbitrary
anisotropic dilations and parallel translations of space. An affine space
is like a linear vector space lacking an origin. A great many properties
of Euclidean space that are discussed in this book are actually inherited
from *affine geometry*.[3]

Euclidean properties are invariant under *isometries*, which are the
rotations and *translations*.[4] I leave out the *reflections* in this book.
Two figures are *congruent* if they can be superimposed by an isometry.
If they can be superimposed only if an additional reflection is used, I
call them "enantiotropic" rather than congruent.

Rulers and protractors may be moved to places of interest and can
be used to *measure distances and angles*. Helmholtz has shown that
the hypothesis of *free mobility of rigid bodies*, which captures more or
less the common physical notion of space, constrains the possible space
forms to spherical geometry, Euclidean geometry and hyperbolic (or
Lobachevskian) geometry. Several simple assumptions then suffice to
constrain the possibilities further such that only Euclidean geometry
remains. For instance, the assumption that similar triangles of arbitrary

---

[3]Here, as at many other places in this book, I really don't have the space to fill you
in on all details. In this case you are assumed to be at least superficially familiar with
the notion of "affine geometry." If you have such problems, it may be wise to consult
introductory level texts. In this case I recommend Berger (for the mathematically
inclined) or Misner, Thorne and Wheeler (strongly appeals to the physicist).

[4]I say this although I am well aware of the fact that Euclidean geometry can
be based on the reflections alone! Successive reflections in parallel planes define
the translations, in mutually slanted planes the rotations. My reason is that in the
pragmatic view left and right gloves are different, whereas the operationalization of
the multiple mirror tricks presupposes the translations and rotations!

sizes exist suffices to bring this about. Euclidean geometry is in a way just affine geometry augmented with a metric or machinery to measure distances and angles.

I will predominantly deal with *curved surface patches*, and also with the curves lying on them and the *shapes* they enclose. Shapes are defined in an operational manner. You may think of a physical quantity, a *density*, that has been measured all over space. Then the shape is a portion of space where the density exceeds some fiducial value. The surface is the *boundary* of this portion as defined through the topology of neighborhood systems. Thus I have also to deal with the structure of real functions on Euclidean space. These are called "scalar fields" from here on. The density is a physical quantity; it has been measured with finite spatial resolution. You could say that the method of measurement doesn't "see" the molecular structure at all. Then the level sets will be nice and smooth.

Remark: *This is the reason why it makes sense to study "smooth surfaces" even if there may or may not be anything smooth in nature.*

It is a very hard task to study things that are curved in space, but here is a simple trick to get a handle on it:

Advice: *Use myopic vision.*

Remember that people used to believe the earth was flat, whereas it is really—always in the right approximation—spherical. This happened because of the short-sightedness of our forefathers. If you sufficiently restrict your field of view any curvature vanishes and you are left with a study of the flats of space. This is why you should be so much interested in the flats in the first place. *Locally* any curve is not different from a line segment, any surface not different from a plane. *Globally* you perceive that the "line" changes orientation from place to place and the "plane" rotates and turns. This is where "connections," or *differentiation* comes in. The basic strategy is to study the "microscopic" situation first, and then "patch the microscopic views together." The turns and twists necessary for the patching then reveal the curvature itself in a neat and operationally clear manner. Trivial as this may sound, there is really no concept in differential geometry that is more powerful or doesn't depend on this notion. The ability to see the earth as flat is the cornerstone of the study of shape; myopia may be a necessary condition for the geometer.

3.1.1 Huntington's disc geometry

♠ INTERMEZZO—BLOBBY POINTS: A CURIOSITY.

An elegant construction of Euclidean geometry on the basis of overlap relations of circular discs has been proposed by Huntington more than half a century ago. In this geometry "points" are "one-inch-spheres" and Huntington suggests that his geometry can be realized with physical blobs of chalk on the blackboard. (This is bogus, but I won't explain why.) The importance of the idea is that the model provides a neat example of the construction of a geometry on the basis of the single simple relation of *overlap*. The whole construction is extremely elegant, and Huntington's paper is most entertaining.

An element is a triplet of real numbers, say (x, y, R), with x and y arbitrary, R positive. A relation of "overlap" holds between two triplets whenever for (a, b, c) and (p, q, r) it is the case that

$$(a - p)^2 + (b - q)^2 < (c + r)^2$$

that is—in the geometrical interpretation—when the circular discs with centers at (a, b) and (p, q), radii c and r have points in common. The whole theory can be founded on this *algebraic* model, which—for some people at least—has the virtue of making the model "respectable."

Huntington arrives at the construction of "lines," "triangles," and so on by fully logical reasoning and combinatorial processes and proceeds to show that his model is actually isomorphic with Euclidean geometry. The exercise is largely of academic interest, of course. Yet it remains true that you can base geometries on the overlap or inclusion relations of convex blobs, which is a valuable insight and will delight the experimental physicist.

Es ist schwer, die genauen Grenzen des Begriffes "kleinste Form" zu ziehen—der Punkt kann wachsen, zur Fläche werden und unbemerkt die ganze Grundfläche bedecken—wo währe dann die Grenze zwischen Punkt und Fläche?
—WASSILY KANDINSKI, *Punkt und Linie zu Fläche (1926)*

3.2   Convex sets

A *convex* set may alternatively be defined as a region that completely
contains the line segments joining any pair of its points. This is more like
the conventional definition. The *convex hull* of an arbitrary set is the
smallest set that is convex and does contain the given set. If a set equals
its convex hull, it is obviously "convex." I have earlier defined the convex
hull by way of the relation of inclusion of spherical blobs. Intuitively the
present definition is equivalent to the one previously given.

A convex set is called "strictly convex" if the join of each pair of its
points lies completely in its interior with the possible exception of its
end points. A strictly convex set will be called "ovoid" in this book.
The ovoids are among the very simplest shapes I can possibly imagine.
On a sufficiently low level of resolution *any* shape appears as an ovoid.
Conversely, and intuitively perhaps more appealing, you may consider
the ovoid as a kind of "primordial egg" that can develop any shape on
"deblurring."[5] This is why ovoids are of such a central importance in
the study of shape.

Alternative definitions of the convex hull are often useful. For instance, you may call a set convex if it is the intersection of possibly
infinitely many *half-spaces*. (A half-space is the portion of space on
one side of a plane.) This definition closely mimics a common method
to *produce* such objects in the machine shop. The boundaries of half-
spaces are candidates for tangent planes of the convex hull, the so called
support planes.

Ovoids seem to hold an extraordinary fascination for members of the
human race. Witness their frequent appearance in religions, philoso-
phies, and such prescientific endeavors as alchemy. Just consider the
"world egg" or the "philosophical egg," well known from the quaint illustrations taken from Renaissance hermeneutic and alchemic literature.

A plane that contains a point of a convex set and is situated such that
the set lies completely on one side of that plane is called a *support plane*.[6]
For ovoids the support planes have only a single point in common with
the set. Non-convex sets may also have support planes. The points being
touched by support planes are known as *exposed points*.[7] The ovoids are

---

[5] This will be elaborated upon in a later chapter.

[6] For an obvious reason: if you put the ovoid on a table, such that the point
$\mathcal{P}$ touches the table, then the tabletop clearly supports the ovoid physically and is
also the tangent plane at $\mathcal{P}$. This disregards the statics of the situation, however.
Geometers don't worry about centers of inertia!

[7] Again, for almost obvious reasons. You can see the point from a halfspace: this
is the highest degree of exposure any point on a smooth surface can have. "Smooth"

"completely exposed" in this sense. Notice that the mathematical notion of "being exposed" has a very vivid visual meaning.

If a shape is not convex, then there will be support planes that have *more* than a single point in common with the shape. Typically you expect *bitangent and tritangent planes*. Good physical horse sense reveals that if you place an object on the table—or any flat surface—there are generically three possibilities (fig. 26):

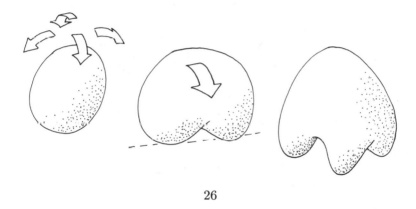

26

1. the object touches the table on a single point and can roll in all directions without slipping or turning;

2. the object touches the table on two points and can only roll in a single direction;

3. the object touches the table on three points and cannot be rolled without lifting one of the three points, and then it can roll in exactly one of three possible directions, that is, with only a single degree of freedom.

A contact with *more* than three points is not stable. It is intuitively obvious to practical people that even an infinitesimal deformation makes a four legged table wobble.[8] Such objects as "ideal tables"—or even worse shapes—do not exist in real life, so there seems to be little reason to develop any mathematics that would admit such animals.

---

is necessary here: you can see the apex of a pyramid from *more* than a halfspace!

[8] Equally obvious is the fact that a tripod will never wobble—unless it deforms.

In case 3 the surface of the tabletop is a *tritangent plane* of the object (fig. 27).   Visually, the tritangent planes whose vertices are exposed

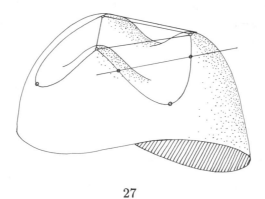

27

must be part of the convex hull. In case 2 the rolling involves a rotation about the line that connects the points of contact. These lines are called limiting "bitangents." Some thought will reveal that there also can exist bitangents that are not in such intimate contact with the convex hull. These will be considered later in this book. The limiting bitangents are the intersections of successive *bitangent support planes*. Continuous one-parameter families of bitangent support planes envelope a surface on which the limiting bitangents lie. This surface is curved, but it can be spread out flat in the plane. The exercise described above gives a mechanical demonstration of this. Therefore it is called "developable." The limiting bitangents are the "generators" of these developables. The bitangent developables are part of the convex hull if their contact points are exposed.

The tritangent planar parts of the convex hull are triangularly shaped. Again, there may also exist nonexposed tritangent planes. I will consider them later.

At each side of the triangle a piece of bitangent developable is attached. The length of the segment between the (bitangent) points of contact is variable along the developable. It may *reduce to zero* in which case the developable ends in a double point of contact. But of course this *need* not happen. The developable could also be closed or attached to a triangle at both sides.[9]

------

[9]But no two triangles can hold an edge in common for the simple reason that any

Thus the local structure of the convex hull of a generic smooth shape can assume the following forms (fig. 28):

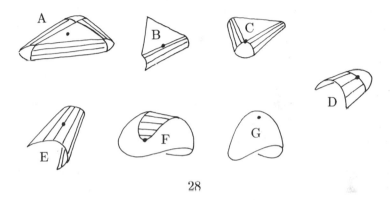

28

- a tritangent plane. A triangular, flat piece (fig. 28, point $\mathcal{A}$)

- a point on the "seam" between a tritangent plane and a bitangent developable (fig. 28, point $\mathcal{B}$)

- a vertex of the tritangent triangle (fig. 28, point $\mathcal{C}$)

- a point of bitangency (fig. 28, point $\mathcal{D}$)

- a point on a bitangent generator (fig. 28, point $\mathcal{E}$)

- the end point of a bitangent developable (fig. 28, point $\mathcal{F}$)

- a generic exposed point, that is a point that has a single point in common with its support plane (fig. 28, point $\mathcal{G}$).

It is easy enough to make local models of the convex hull. The surface of the convex hull has either a point, a line piece, or a piece of a plane in common with the support plane. Thus you can easily form yourself a *complete picture* of the *local* shape of *arbitrarily* complicated convex hulls.

This is a general phenomenon, worth sticking to your mind:

point on a smooth object has a unique tangent plane.

Remark: *It is often possible to obtain a complete taxonomy of local shapes even if the global complexities may well elude you.*

It is yet another case where going myopic pays off.

Convex sets have many interesting and useful properties. For instance, you may derive many nice inequalities that relate diameter, area and volume of convex sets. Of practical importance is the fact that convex sets have remarkably simple properties with regard to their contact with lines and planes. Either mechanically or optically this is of obvious importance. General surfaces are much more complicated. In many practical cases you may take advantage of that and approximate an object by its convex hull, for instance, in object avoidance problems of navigation, the so-called "better safe than sorry" strategy. People *have* actually flown small aircraft through the opening in the Arc de Triomphe in Paris, but in general the safer strategy would be to treat this hole very much as a part of the space that is occupied by this obstacle, that is, to reckon with the convex hull. This would be different for the pedestrian, of course. Evidently these are in no way *mathematical* problems.

In many manufacturing processes the convex hull is in fact a preliminary stage, for hollows are usually scooped out or drilled at the latest stages, after an initial roughing out.

Very useful also is the fact that the projection of convex hulls equals the convex hull of the projection of a set. This has many important implications in computer graphics and image processing.

In many ways the ovoids are the simplest compact smooth objects. The term "primordial egg" is indeed directly applicable to solid shape. *Any shape* can be regarded as a special evolution starting from an ovoid. This makes the ovoids worthy of special study. I will discuss their properties again and again in this text.

3.3 Coordinate systems

1.1 Definition Euclidean 3-space $\mathbf{E}^3$ *is the set of all ordered triples of real numbers. Such a triple* $\mathbf{p} = (p_1, p_2, p_3)$ *is called a* point *of* $\mathbf{E}^3$.
—O'NEILL, *Elementary Differential Geometry (1966)*

Intuitive, heuristic thinking in geometry really depends on imagery and hardly ever on combinatorial or analytic techniques. Counting beyond three is a rare capability in vision and has to be subsumed under the heading of combinatorics. Almost by definition you don't use coordinates in geometrical reasoning.

Figures of a sufficiently sloppy type are the main tool. They stand for large equivalence classes of geometrical situations rather than for special cases. This is a most interesting fact: although pictures are by their very nature *specific*, they are used to indicate the general case! Of course pictures should not be confused with proofs. Our vision is very powerful, but only gets things right "most of the time": mistakes are frequent enough.

This process of intuitive geometrical reasoning is greatly assisted by the rather modern insistence on *coordinate-free* descriptions of *geometrical objects*.

The generic example, of course, is the notion of a *vector*. You don't think of a vector as an ordered set of numbers although you often represent them as such in your computer.[10] Rather, you think of a vector as a geometrical entity that exists in its own right.

Typically, you have a picture in your mind of an arrow with tip and tail at specific positions in space. This is the view of a vector as a *bilocal* entity, say an "ordered pair of points" (fig. 29). Such arrows are often referred to as "free vectors" because their tails can be anywhere. If you combine vectors, for instance by "vector addition" via the parallelogram construction, you always combine vectors with their tails at the same point. People then speak of "bound vectors."

Although I often draw sloppy pictures it is understood that the tips of all vectors with their tails at a certain point ($\mathcal{P}$, say) are *not in the space proper*, but instead exist in their own "tangent space" that is "attached" to the point $\mathcal{P}$. You visualize space with a tangent space attached to each of its points, aptly called the "tangent bundle" of the space. The tangent space is just a local, that is a linearized, picture of the space itself.

For a smooth surface the tangent space at a point is the *tangent plane* at that point. The notion of tangent space merely generalizes the notion of tangent plane.

If you want to do differential geometry you must become intimately familiar with such notions as tangent bundles. In Euclidean spaces the tangent spaces are isomorphic to the base space, which has no need of linearization, and you can forget about what are then mathematical hair splitting exercises. For curved surfaces the tangent spaces, or "tangent planes," are not identical to parts of the surface, and the notion becomes crucial. But even so the notion of the tangent bundle also crispens your

---

[10]I'm being optimistic here: I frequently meet people who *do* think of vectors as ordered sets of numbers. Let's hope this regrettable fact is part of a passing phase of history.

visualization of Euclidean space.

Whenever you have the opportunity to do numerical calculations, that is when you exercise "computational geometry," you are almost *forced* to use coordinates, or at least some *numbers*, no matter what you choose to call them. I assume that you are well acquainted with this monumental construct of Descartes. In shape studies things are more complicated than in college geometry, though. You usually attach a *different* coordinate system, or coordinate "frame," to every point of the space. This makes a lot of sense because you want to pick the coordinate frames that are best fitted to the job in all cases.

An example may be instrumental to drive this point down. The inhabitants of the earth can hardly be dissuaded from taking the vertical as one of the axes of their coordinate frames, which means that the frames are different in New York, Sydney or Amsterdam (fig. 30). Even if you

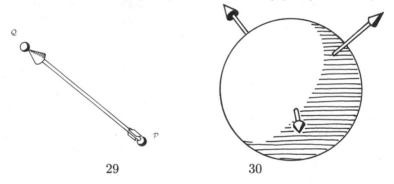

29   30

view the globe from the distant perspective of "the Eye of Eternity" you can hardly do otherwise, lest you give unequal treatment to different loci, which would certainly be self-contradictory in this case. The problems connected with this are treated later on. For the moment I note that *locally*, in any given frame of reference, things will always be very simple, in fact just the old-fashioned Cartesian way. Typically, you don't worry very much about spherical coordinates when going about your daily business, unless you happen to be an airplane pilot or a navigator at sea. Once again, myopia helps you see.

The whole machinery of "linear algebra" can be put into use to do calculations in local frames. These are really big guns. It will be reviewed in a summary fashion later on in this chapter.

Problems arise mainly when you want to compare geometrical entities that live in *different* frames. You have to find a "connection" for your "frame field" in some way or another. The most convenient way to do this was formulated by Élie Cartan in his method of "moving frames," the *"repère mobile."*[11]

Cartan's methods are so powerful that, apart from yielding a convenient environment for numerical work, the moving frames yield all the classical stuff on differential geometry as simple corollaries of a few basic and elegant relations. The main problem is to appreciate what you get instead of discarding the results carelessly as "obvious" and "trivial" because they were obtained at so little cost. Cartan's methods carry a rather immediate intuitive content.

I consider Cartan's method in a later section after a review of the basic multi-linear vector algebra. Although this is very elementary material, I cannot boot you up from scratch. It is absolutely necessary that you have been exposed to the usual linear algebra course in order to be in the right position to appreciate these sections. All engineers, physicists and mathematicians went through these exercises, of course.

I review most of what is needed, but that is only because I want to encourage you to adopt certain *pictorial attitudes* that will enable you to use the tools of multilinear algebra in an intelligent way, and to acquaint you with the really minimal formalism used in this text, *but not at all with the objective of teaching you technique.* You are supposed to possess this power already.

The usual courses are devised in such a manner that the full generality of the subject is brought out to the best advantage, an objective that is not without a certain *grandeur*, but has the unfortunate consequence that a conscious effort is made to prevent the student from developing a feel for the obvious application in a very special case, namely that of three-dimensional spatial structure. Some painful experiences in trying to explain even very simple applications led me to include the present chapter on these very elementary matters in this book.

Of course, this emphasis on three-dimensional space does indeed make that the present review lacks the full generality of a more formal approach. This will not be a problem if you are an applications-oriented person. If you are going to apply the ideas in quite different contexts, you will need to consult other texts in order to erase the specialized definitions from this book.

Some subjects of great power that do certainly have a true geometrical appeal will not be treated here, mainly because I have made an

---

[11]Élie Cartan (1869-1951) may be the single most influential person in modern differential geometry. He is perhaps best known for his invention of the "exterior derivative" in 1901. Most of his work in differential geometry he did after the age of fifty. He should be one of your heroes!

attempt to keep the introductory parts concise in order to move to real "shape" applications as fast as possible. One example is the theory of Lie derivatives, Lie algebras, and groups. I feel a bit bad about that; on the other hand I think I managed reasonably well without these tools.

All the problems of geometry can easily be reduced to such terms that thereafter we need to know only the length of certain straight lines in order to construct them.
—RENÉ DESCARTES, *Discourse on Geometry (1637)*

3.4 The myopic view

*I regard it as an inelegance, or imperfection, in quaternions, or rather
in the state to which it has been hitherto unfolded, whenever it
becomes or seems to become necessary to have recourse to x, y, z, etc.*
—HAMILTON, *as contained in a letter from Tait to Cayley.*

3.4.1 Linear Vector Spaces

Linear vector spaces are the bread and butter of geometrical analysis in
the infinitesimal domain. The reason for this is simple enough: smooth
things are well approximated by linear entities *in the small*. A function
can be approximated with a linear map, its "differential." A curve can
be approximated with a straight line, its "tangent" or "velocity" if the
curve is an orbit. Finally, a surface can be approximated with a plane,
the "tangent plane." You then enjoy the benefits of linearity, such as
easy cascading or inversion of maps and so forth. Thus people don't use
linear algebra because it makes calculations easy, although this is often
suggested as the major reason. The real point to be grasped is that
all of the calculus is nothing but a form of exploitation of local linear
approximations. Without linear algebra there is really preciously little
of interest in nonlinear analysis left.

The very expression MULTILINEAR ALGEBRA may sound forbidding
but in fact this discipline is as intuitively appealing—because simple—
as it is practically useful. In order to make the subject manageable
you should strictly distinguish between the machinery of algebraic ma-
nipulations, either in terms of coordinates or in terms of higher order
"datastructures" such as vectors and so forth, and that of the description in terms of easily grasped and imagined *geometrical objects*. The
first part is usually taught and is extremely useful, even necessary, in
any practical project. The second part is not so often taught, or rather
suppressed at all cost, but is essential if you want to understand the
"why" instead of just "knowing how" and to think out new things yourself. This part uses simple pictures to assist and fire the imagination.
They tend to be essential to the understanding and heuristic reasoning
but are usually suppressed in introductory courses.

Many people seem to understand that linear algebra is a discipline
that stands on its own and has little or no connections with analysis,
probably because these fields are usually taught in separate courses.
Nothing is farther from the truth though. I repeat that all differential
geometry is for a large part nothing but linear, or rather multilinear,

algebra. You can't study shape without a solid background in linear algebra.

In this book I merely present the intuitive content. Anyone who needs to master the machinery can find plenty of textbooks to guide him. In a later section I give some hints on how to implement these structures as actual computer programs.

3.4.2   The simplest entities

I already referred to vectors as "bilocal" entities, namely arrows with tip and tail (fig. 29). This is often a very useful view, a vector as an ordered pair of points. After all, one main use of vectors in this book will be as models of oriented line segments.

A vector is *an ordered pair of (infinitesimally close) points.*

Mathematicians have developed many other views, however, in their attempts to make vectors "respectable." Several of these alternative views are actually very helpful in intuitive reasoning. Any additional viewpoint enriches your concept of an object and makes it more widely useful because of a greater possibility of association. As a general rule you shouldn't go for a single view if you can help it but rather try to be as eclectic as possible.

One very useful view of vectors is to regard them as the *velocities of orbits* (fig. 31). Orbits are maps from the reals ("time," say) into space

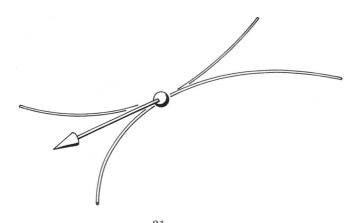

31

and thus have a rather simple structure. You can use them to define vectors. A "tangent" vector is an equivalence class of orbits, namely those orbits with the same velocity at the origin. This is a bit nicer than the "bilocal" concept for the following reason. Consider a curved surface and a point on it. The tangent space at the point is just the tangent plane. Pictorially speaking it contains all "tangent vectors" (fig. 32). Thus the tips of the vectors are *in the tangent plane and not*

 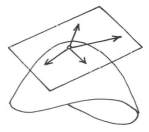

32

on the surface. This is a problem for the bilocal concept. You solve this tricky problem if you consider tangent vectors as velocities of orbits on the surface, that is, as equivalence classes of orbits.

A vector is *an equivalence class of orbits.*

The curves are neatly on the surface at all times. You can define the equivalence classes without leaving the surface at all. Of course, you draw the velocity as leaving the surface. But then you don't intend the tip to represent a point of the surface. Thus this especially elegant construction of vectors as equivalence classes of curves has a very geometrical flavor and makes it possible to define vectors in a way that is completely *intrinsic* to the surface. As a result it is very easy to derive the transformation laws of vectors for changes of maps on the surface.

Still another view of vectors is to think of them as *derivations*. The idea is simple and already implicit in the bilocal concept. If f is a function from points to the reals (for instance the "temperature") then the value of f at the tip of a vector $\vec{v}$ minus the value at the tail (I write $\vec{v}[f]$ or—especially in later sections—also $\nabla_{\vec{v}}f$) is a measure of the change in f; in fact, if divided by the separation it is an approximation to the directional derivative of f in the direction of $\vec{v}$. You think of $\vec{v}[f]$ as the vector $\vec{v}$ "taking a bite" of the field f: "The difference in temperature between tip and tail of the arrow."

A vector is *a directional derivative operator.*

The type of bite defines the vector in an operational sense. You can make this precise if you take the difference for a vector that is a zillion times shorter than $\vec{v}$ and rescale the difference by the same factor.

It is also implicit in the view of the vector as an orbit, for when you traverse the orbit you may monitor the change of some scalar variable such as the temperature. The rate of change of the temperature with time is just the directional derivative again. Figure 33 attempts to illustrate the process. The moving point on the curve takes a thermometer with it and measures the instantaneous—that is local—rate of change. Here vectors appear as *rates* (or, perhaps more accurate although rather more cumbersome, "rate-taking operators").

Mathematicians reverse this correspondence: they define vectors as directional derivatives. Although this may appear odd at first glance, it is really easily justified on logical grounds because all the different viewpoints can be reconciled, as they lead to isomorphic structures.

Remark: *To the abstract eye these views are identical. To the practical eye one view may be more apt than another, depending on the problem at hand.*

I use the bilocal concept, the velocity concept, and the idea of the vector as derivative as completely interchangeable and often switch from one view to the other right in the middle of an argument. You should try to do the same and to "fuse" all these approaches in your own mind. The derivative idea is so useful, however, that I often let it show through in my *notation*. Thus I think of $\frac{\partial}{\partial x}$ (or in abbreviated notation $\vec{\partial}_x$) as a *vector*, namely "the derivative in the x-direction." In my *pictures* I mainly use the velocity idea of "vectors as arrows" or the bilocal idea of a "vector as an ordered pair of points."

The vector operations are linear in the two obvious senses (a and b denote constants; f and g scalar fields; $\vec{v}$ and $\vec{w}$ vectors)

$$(a\,\vec{v} + b\,\vec{w})\,[f] = a\,\vec{v}\,[f] + b\,\vec{w}\,[f]$$
$$\vec{v}\,[a\,f + b\,g] = a\,\vec{v}\,[f] + b\,\vec{v}\,[g],$$

moreover, they satisfy the Leibnitz rule for the differentiation of the product of two functions, namely

$$\vec{v}\,[fg] = \vec{v}\,[f]\,g + f\,\vec{v}\,[g].$$

You may check for yourself that the vector operations satisfy the well-known axioms that define a linear vector space. The basic operations on vectors are, I assume, sufficiently well known to you. Essentially, only two of them exist. They are, first, the multiplication of a vector by a scalar, which is a scaling operation; thus "$\alpha \vec{v}$ is an arrow of α-times the length of $\vec{v}$." Then, second, you have the addition of two vectors via the construction of the "parallelogram of forces." Figure 34 illustrates

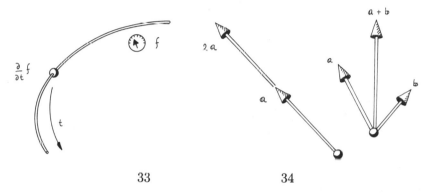

33   34

the multiplication by a factor of two and the summation of two vectors. These operations are basic and should be visualized quite without effort and very vividly.

A *frame* is a set of three orthonormal vectors (fig. 35). Any vector can be expressed uniquely as a linear combination of the frame vectors. This is Descartes's basic idea that enables the use of coordinates. A *basis* is *any set* of three noncoplanar or "independent" vectors. In most applications you would typically pick an "orthonormal basis," three mutually perpendicular unit vectors, that is, a *frame*. The frame vectors are often denoted

$$\{\vec{e}_x, \vec{e}_y, \vec{e}_z\},$$

or

$$\{\frac{\partial}{\partial x}, \frac{\partial}{\partial y}, \frac{\partial}{\partial z}\},$$

or

$$\{\vec{\partial}_x, \vec{\partial}_y, \vec{\partial}_z\}.$$

They are all one and the same. Thus $\vec{e}_x$ denotes the unit vector in the x-direction and $\vec{\partial}_x$ the directional derivative in that same direction.

A vector $\vec{v}$ then has the representation

$$\vec{v} = v^x\,\vec{e}_x + v^y\,\vec{e}_y + v^z\,\vec{e}_z.$$

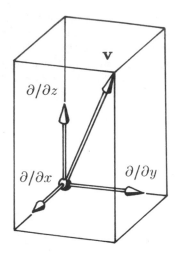

$$\mathbf{v} = v^x \partial/\partial x + v^y \partial/\partial y + v^z \partial/\partial z$$

35

Remark: *The numbers $v^{x,y,z}$ are known as the "components" of the vector. They depend on the frame vectors, of course, and do not possess an existence of their own as geometrical objects. Only the vector $\vec{v}$ as an integral entity has a geometrical significance.*

Figure 35 shows the decomposition of a vector in terms of its projections on the frame vectors in the classical Descartian manner.

The notation in terms of derivatives at once shows you how to calculate the directional derivative:

$$\vec{v}[f] = v^x \frac{\partial f}{\partial x} + v^y \frac{\partial f}{\partial y} + v^z \frac{\partial f}{\partial z}.$$

The funny notation with upper and lower indices looks a bit baroque at first sight, but it is really extremely convenient. The full advantage only becomes clear in fairly advanced analysis, though.

For the moment I just note a minor convenience, namely that in many expressions, a *summation* will always be over identical upper and lower indices. By convention, lazy people suppress the summation sign. This is known as the "Einstein summation convention." Thus the expression $v^i \vec{e}_i$ is commonly used to imply the summation over $i = x, y, z$. You then have the expression

$$\vec{v} = v^i \, \vec{e}_i,$$

which is certainly very convenient and elegant. It saves some writing, which is no big deal except when you use a word processor in which special symbols are a pain. It also has that slick professional look that people value so much.

In this book I will play down the importance of coordinate representations though, nice as they may appear from the point of view of the typography. You will no doubt appreciate this move if you just flip the pages of some text based on the index notation. A famous example is Schouten's well-known book on the "Ricci calculus" which is often quoted as the culmination of the typesetter's achievement (fig. 36). Some of the formulas that appear in this figure also figure in this book, but I hope that you will not be able to detect this at a glance.

A well-known entity from physics is the "gradient" or "differential" of a function—the temperature, say. This is not a directional derivative at all, but rather an entity that can be combined with any vector to yield a *number*, namely the difference in temperature between tail and tip of that vector. The differential "knows" this number for all vectors. This is a very useful concept.

The gradient is so useful that you can't do without it. In order to capture this notion I introduce the so called "covectors." The covectors are also often known as "forms," or also "one-forms." [12] Don't ask me how anyone came to think of the funny expression in the first place. [13] I'm afraid one is stuck with it.

The covectors are introduced as *linear maps on vectors*. Thus a covector $\tilde{\varphi}$ (say) can be combined with a vector $\vec{v}$ to yield a *number* $\tilde{\varphi}\langle \vec{v} \rangle$. If you want to sound like a professional you should announce that you "contract the vector on the covector." This process is linear in both $\vec{v}$ and $\tilde{\varphi}$. That means that you have

$$\tilde{\varphi}\langle f\,\vec{v} + g\,\vec{w}\rangle \;=\; f\,\tilde{\varphi}\langle\vec{v}\rangle + g\,\tilde{\varphi}\langle\vec{w}\rangle$$
$$(f\,\tilde{\varphi} + g\,\tilde{\psi})\langle\vec{v}\rangle \;=\; f\,\tilde{\varphi}\langle\vec{v}\rangle + g\,\tilde{\psi}\langle\vec{v}\rangle.$$

The "differential" of a function f is a form df such that $df\langle\vec{v}\rangle$ is the difference in the value of f between tip and tail of $\vec{v}$, in other words

$$df\langle\vec{v}\rangle = \vec{v}[f].$$

The differential is linear and satisfies the Leibnitz rule for the differen-

---

[12] Strictly speaking it would be better to reserve the term "one-form" for a covector *field* and to use only "covector" for the duals of the tangent vectors. However, in practice people often use the term interchangeably. I will conform to this malpractice.

[13] I'll venture a guess later on though.

§ 16. Die Gleichungen von Gauß und Codazzi für X_m in A_n[1]).

Aus (196a) folgt durch Differentiation und Alternation nach $\omega\,\mu$ unter Berücksichtigung der Symmetrie von $B_{\omega\,u}^{\beta\,\alpha}\,\Gamma_\beta\,B_\alpha^\delta = H_{\omega\,u}^{\cdot\cdot\,\delta}$ in $\omega\,\mu$:

$$
(210)\quad
\begin{cases}
B_{\omega\,u\,\gamma}^{\beta\,\alpha\,\nu}\,\Gamma_{[\beta}\,\Gamma_{\alpha]}\,v^\gamma = \Gamma'_{[\omega}\,\Gamma'_{\mu]}\,v^\nu - B_{[\omega\,\mu]\gamma}^{\beta\,\alpha\,\nu}\,\Gamma_\beta\,v^\delta\,B_\alpha^\varepsilon\,\underset{u}{\sum}\,(\Gamma_\varepsilon\,t_\delta)\,n^\gamma \\[2mm]
\qquad = \Gamma'_{[\omega}\,\Gamma'_{\mu]}\,v^\nu - v^\delta\,B_{[\omega\,\mu]\gamma}^{\beta\,\alpha\,\nu}\,\underset{u}{\sum}\,(\Gamma_\alpha\,t_\delta)\,\Gamma_\beta\,n^\gamma .
\end{cases}
$$

also, infolge von (II, 116), (201) und (203):

$$
(211)\qquad B_{\omega\,\mu\,\gamma\,\lambda}^{\beta\,\alpha\,\nu\,\delta}\,R_{\beta\,\alpha\,\delta}^{\cdot\cdot\cdot\,\gamma} = R'_{\omega\,\mu\,\lambda}^{\cdot\cdot\cdot\,\nu} + 2\,B_{[\omega\,\mu]\gamma\,\lambda}^{\beta\,\alpha\,\nu\,\delta}\,\underset{u}{\sum}\,(\nabla_\alpha\,t_\delta)\,\Gamma_\beta\,n^{\cdot\cdot}
$$

oder:

$$
(212)\qquad \boxed{\,B_{\omega\,\mu\,\gamma\,\lambda}^{\beta\,\alpha\,\nu\,\delta}\,R_{\beta\,\alpha\,\delta}^{\cdot\cdot\cdot\,\gamma} = R'_{\omega\,\mu\,\lambda}^{\cdot\cdot\cdot\,\nu} + 2\,H_{\lambda\,[\mu}^{\cdot\cdot\,\nu\,\gamma}\,L_{\omega]\cdot\,\gamma}^{\cdot\,\nu}.\,}
$$

Dies ist die Verallgemeinerung der *Gauß*schen Gleichung für X_m in A_n.

Setzt man:

$$
(213)\qquad
\begin{cases}
\overset{u}{h}_{\mu\lambda} = B_{\mu\lambda}^{\alpha\beta}\,\Gamma_\alpha\,\overset{u}{t}_\beta \\[2mm]
\overset{u}{l}_\mu^{\cdot\,\nu} = B_{\mu\beta}^{\alpha\,\nu}\,\Gamma_\alpha\,\underset{u}{n^\beta},
\end{cases}
$$

so sind die Integrabilitätsbedingungen der ersten Gleichung:

$$
(214)\quad
\begin{cases}
\Gamma_{[\omega}\,\overset{u}{h}_{u]\lambda} = B_{[\omega\,u]\lambda}^{\cdot\cdot\,\delta\,\varepsilon}\,\Gamma_\gamma\,B_{\delta\,\varepsilon}^{\alpha\,\beta}\,\Gamma_\alpha\,\overset{u}{t}_\beta = B_{[\omega\,\mu]\lambda}^{\gamma\,\alpha\,\varepsilon}\,\Gamma_\gamma\,B_\varepsilon^\beta\,\Gamma_\alpha\,\overset{u}{t}_\beta \\[2mm]
\qquad = B_{[\omega\,\mu]\lambda}^{\gamma\,\alpha\,\beta}\,\Gamma_\gamma\,\Gamma_\alpha\,\overset{u}{t}_\beta - B_{[\omega\,\mu]\lambda}^{\gamma\,\alpha\,\varepsilon}\,(\Gamma_\gamma\,B_\varepsilon^\beta)\,\Gamma_\alpha\,\overset{u}{t}_\beta \\[2mm]
\qquad = \tfrac12\,B_{\omega\,\mu\,\lambda}^{\beta\,\alpha\,\delta}\,R_{\beta\,\alpha\,\delta}^{\cdot\cdot\cdot\,\gamma}\,\overset{u}{t}_\gamma + B_{[\omega\,\mu]}^{\gamma\,\alpha}\,H_{\gamma\,\lambda}^{\cdot\cdot\,\beta}\,\nabla_\alpha\,\overset{u}{t}_\beta \\[2mm]
\qquad = \tfrac12\,B_{\omega\,\mu\,\lambda}^{\beta\,\alpha\,\delta}\,R_{\beta\,\alpha\,\delta}^{\cdot\cdot\cdot\,\gamma}\,\overset{u}{t}_\gamma - B_{[\omega\,\mu]}^{\gamma\,\alpha}\,\underset{v}{\sum}\,\overset{v}{h}_{\gamma\lambda}\,n^\beta\,\nabla_\alpha\,\overset{u}{t}_\beta
\end{cases}
$$

oder:

$$
(215)\qquad \boxed{\,2\,\Gamma'_{[\omega}\,\overset{u}{h}_{\mu]\lambda} = B_{\omega\,\mu\,\lambda}^{\beta\,\alpha\,\delta}\,R_{\beta\,\alpha\,\delta}^{\cdot\cdot\cdot\,\gamma}\,\overset{u}{t}_\gamma + 2\,\underset{v}{\sum}\,\overset{u\,v}{v}_{[\omega}\,\overset{v}{h}_{\mu]\lambda}\,,\,}
$$

wo:

$$
(216)\qquad \overset{u\,v}{v}_\lambda = B_\lambda^\alpha\,(\nabla_\alpha\,\overset{u}{t}_\beta)\,\underset{v}{n^\beta} = -\,B_\lambda^\alpha\,(\nabla_\alpha\,\underset{v}{n^\beta})\,\overset{u}{t}_\beta\,,\qquad\qquad u \neq v\,.
$$

Die Integrabilitätsbedingungen der zweiten Gleichung lauten:

$$
(217)\qquad \boxed{\,2\,\nabla'_{[\omega}\,\overset{u}{l}_{\mu]}^{\cdot\,\nu} = -\,B_{\omega\,\mu\,\gamma}^{\beta\,\alpha\,\nu}\,R_{\beta\,\alpha\,\delta}^{\cdot\cdot\cdot\,\gamma}\,\underset{u}{n^\delta} - 2\,\underset{v}{\sum}\,\overset{v\,u}{v}_{[\omega}\,\overset{v}{l}_{\mu]}^{\cdot\,\nu}.\,}
$$

Die p^2 Vektoren $\overset{u\,v}{v}$ liegen in der X_m und genügen den Gleichungen:

$$
(218)\quad
\begin{cases}
\nabla'_{[\omega}\,\overset{u\,v}{v}_{\lambda]} = \nabla'_{[\omega}\,B_{\lambda]}^\alpha\,\big(\nabla_\alpha\,\overset{u}{t}_\gamma\big)\,\underset{v}{n^\gamma} = B_{[\omega\,\lambda]}^{\beta\,\alpha}\,\nabla_\beta\,\big(\nabla_\alpha\,\overset{u}{t}_\gamma\big)\,\underset{v}{n^\gamma} \\[2mm]
\quad = \tfrac12\,B_{\omega\,\lambda}^{\beta\,\alpha}\,R_{\beta\,\alpha\,\gamma}^{\cdot\cdot\cdot\,\delta}\,\overset{u}{t}_\delta\,\underset{v}{n^\gamma} + B_{[\omega\,\lambda]}^{\beta\,\alpha}\,\big(\nabla_\alpha\,\overset{u}{t}_\gamma\big)\,\nabla_\beta\,\underset{v}{n^\gamma}
\end{cases}
$$

---

[1]) *Weyl* gibt 1922, 12 eine andere Behandlung der Krümmungstheorie einer X_m in A_n, bei der vorausgesetzt ist, daß die X_m eingespannt ist.

tiation of products:

$$
\begin{aligned}
d(f+g) &= df + dg \\
d\,fg &= g\,df + f\,dg.
\end{aligned}
$$

Remark: *A covector can be regarded as a "machine with a slot" that accepts vectors. If you insert a vector into the empty slot the machine will pop out a number in response.*

The reverse is also quite reasonable: to regard vectors as slot machines that accept covectors to present you with a number in response. There exists a nice symmetry (or as professionals say, "duality") between covectors and vectors. Very elegant!

The covectors are no whit less important than the vectors and you need a *picture* of them to be able to use them in geometrical reasoning. The simplest picture is this:

Covectors are *stacks of parallel planes* endowed with a well-defined progression and spacing. The "phase" of the planes is irrelevant and should be disregarded.

The contraction of a covector on a vector yields *the number of planes pierced by the vector*, from tail to tip, with positive sign if the direction of the vector is in the progression of the covector, negative otherwise.

Figure 37 depicts an example. The vector $\vec{v}$ contracts to *four* on the one-form $\tilde{\varphi}$ because it *pierces four levels* of the one-form between its tail $\mathcal{P}$ and tip $\mathcal{Q}$.

Because the "phase" is irrelevant you can always visualize the situation in such a way that one plane of the form contains the tail of the vector. The tip will then probably end up "between planes," but of course you can interpolate as many planes as you wish. In practical doodling you may just guestimate the interpolated value, of course.

When you think of a description of the (scalar) temperature field in terms of isothermic surfaces, then the differential of the temperature (a one-form) is a local approximation of these surfaces in terms of a stack of parallel planes.

Figure 38 shows the curves of equal distance to the eye for a human body.[14] If you contract a small bilocal vector on these parallel curves you obtain the depth difference for that displacement. Again, *locally*, the equal height curves look like parallel curves. The contraction of

---

[14]This is a 2D, not a 3D example!

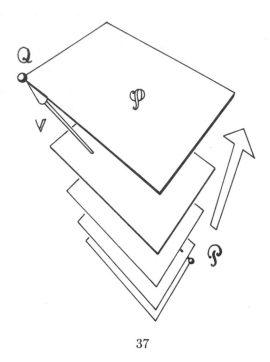

37

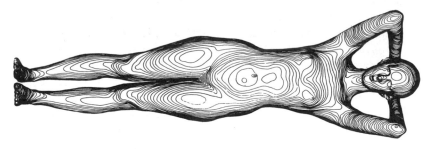

38

a displacement vector on these one forms yields the height difference traversed.

The covectors are conceptually every bit as simple and important as the vectors are, the two geometrical objects stand on equal footing. The thing to remember is that:

Fact: *Vectors are rates, covectors are gradients.*

The difference is obvious from the point of view of the physicist, although physicists and engineers usually neglect this obvious difference when they exercise vector analysis because they were raised in the old-fashioned metrical setting in which the difference becomes easily smothered in the formalism.

Pictorially, of course, vectors remain oriented line segments or ordered point pairs, and one-forms are stacks of parallel planes, defined through their spacing and order of progression. Just remember that their "phase" is immaterial.

You easily find a *basis* for the forms. In the usual Cartesian frame the coordinate values $\{x, y, z\}$ are scalar fields. Their *differentials* $\{dx, dy, dz\}$ are one-forms that can be used as elementary forms. The form dx is pictorially represented through a stack of planes at unit separation and all parallel to the y-z plane, such that the unit frame vector $\vec{\partial}_x$ exactly "fits" between two successive planes. A similar picture applies to the other basis one-forms. Any one-form $\tilde{\varphi}$ can be written as a linear combination of the dx, dy, dz (39):

$$\tilde{\varphi} = \varphi_x \, dx + \varphi_y \, dy + \varphi_z \, dz.$$

The contraction of $\tilde{\varphi}$ on $\vec{v}$ is simply $\varphi_i v^i$. Mind the summation con-

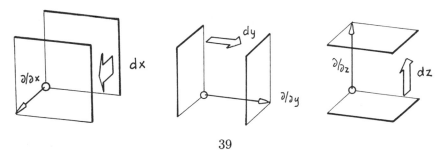

39

vention! Note the convenience of the upper and lower indices here. The differential of a function $f(x, y, z)$ is similarly

$$df = \frac{\partial f}{\partial x}\, dx + \frac{\partial f}{\partial y}\, dy + \frac{\partial f}{\partial z}\, dz.$$

The contraction of a basis form on a basis vector yields either one or zero. For instance, you have

$$dx \left\langle \frac{\partial}{\partial x} \right\rangle = 1$$

and

$$dx \left\langle \frac{\partial}{\partial y} \right\rangle = 0,$$

and so on. In general you have

$$dx^i \langle \vec{\partial}_{x^j} \rangle = \delta_{ij},$$

where the δ_{ij} are the Kronecker symbols, defined as zero when $i \neq j$ and unity otherwise. The bases are known as each other's "duals."

Such relations are intuitively so *trivial*—just try to conjure up the picture before your mind's eye—that there is really no need to memorize them. At least there shouldn't be if all is well. You should be perfectly in the clear about them and be capable of immediately visualizing such simple relations before your mind's eye.

Important milestone: *If you are even slightly hesitant, then stop reading right now and think it over again.*

You are familiar with the pictorial addition of vectors by way of the "parallelogram of forces" from the introductory mechanics courses. A quite similar construction applies to the one-forms. If you number the planes of the one-forms you may associate the sum of these numbers with the intersections of the "planes." These intersections are lines in 3D and points in 2D, but you may join them up to make "planes" again. You can visualize this if you think of the one-forms as *continuous progressions* of "planes" for a moment. These "planes" are those of the sum one-form. You may assign the "phase" in an arbitrary manner. A similar construction applies to subtraction. Since the addition of one-forms is no whit less important than the addition of vectors, you should be equally familiar with both constructions.[15]

---

[15] If you are a physicist it may help you to conceive of one-forms as *plane waves* such as the familiar scalar waves $\psi(x, y, z) = \exp i(k^x\, x + k^y\, y + k^z\, z)$ for a spell. The planes of the one-form are the isophasal surfaces $k^x\, x + k^y\, y + k^z\, z = 2\pi n$. Addition of forms then results from the addition of wave vectors.

3.4.3 The gauge figure

The concepts of vector, covector, contraction, dual bases, and so forth make perfect sense in *affine* geometry too. You have no need for the free movements of yardsticks and protractors. However, Euclidean space has additional structure, and it is about time I use it, for this will provide you with additional power.

In Euclidean space you have a simple mechanism to switch back and forth between forms and vectors, something unthinkable in affine geometry. It is called "the metric" when used as a geometric object, or "the metric tensor" in coordinate language, the "gauge figure" if you want to stress the pictorial, geometric content, and—finally—the "sharp operator" if you want to stress its operational character. Although *superficially* it may seem that you meet a lot of novel entities here, they really all boil down to the same notion. In fact heuristically they are but different manifestations of the same entity.

Although more general gauge-figures such as "Riemann metrics" or even "Finsler metrics" are often very useful, I will only employ a very simple one, namely the *unit sphere*. In Euclidean space this is the locus of all points at unit distance from some fiducial point which is the origin of the tangent space this entity lives in. Every mensuration is based on this important figure. In more general spaces the procedure is very similar, although more complicated structures than spheres take over the role of the sphere. For instance, in Riemannian geometry one uses a different *quadric* at every point of the base space.

Consider how to use it to associate a unique form with every vector— except for the null vector, of course (this is known as "metrical dualization").

From the tip of the vector I construct a cone mantle that is tangent to the sphere. (If the vector is shorter than unity you merely scale it up and then rescale the resulting form; this is reasonable because everything is linear anyway. This is not necessary, though, for with a little geometrical juggling you can do the job directly just as well.[16]) The cone mantle touches the sphere along a small circle and thus defines a unique *plane*, known as the *polar plane* for the tip of the vector. This

---

[16]You proceed as follows: consider the tip of your vector as the incidence of three (the number depends on the dimension of your space) arbitrary *planes*. Every plane can be assigned a unique point as follows: the plane meets the sphere in a lesser circle. There is a unique cone mantle with generators tangent to the sphere. The apex of the cone is the unique point determined by the plane. Thus you obtain *three points*. These determine a *plane*, which is the first plane of the form dual to your vector within the sphere. Got it? If not try it!

plane is taken as a plane of the form, the separation of the planes being
taken as the distance of that plane to the origin. Figure 40 illustrates

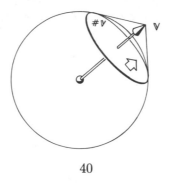

40

the construction. If you are familiar with analytical geometry you will
recognize the construction as merely the inversion in a sphere. Note that
likewise a covector—that is a plane—defines a point—that is a vector—
just by inverting the inversion. Thus the gauge-figure lets you associate
vectors with covectors and *vice versa* in a unique, purely geometrical
way.

Now for the next step: to use the gauge figure for the measurement of
the length of a vector. This is how you do it: if l denotes the length or
"modulus" of the vector, then the spacing of the planes of the form is
l^{-1}, as you may remember from elementary geometry. Thus *the vector
contracted on its own associated form* yields l^2, which you recognize as
the squared length of the vector. Notice that I have used the gauge-figure
to find the squared length of a vector in a purely *geometrical* manner,
that is, by construction and counting.

Given the ability to find lengths you can find many other interesting entities, such as the "scalar product," also called "dot product," or
"inner product" of two vectors $\vec{a}$ and $\vec{b}$.

I define:

$$\vec{a} \cdot \vec{b} = \frac{1}{4}(\|\vec{a} + \vec{b}\|^2 - \|\vec{a} - \vec{b}\|^2).$$

This is a remarkable formula for the scalar product that merely employs
squared lengths. The process is known as "polarization."

You easily convince yourself—by making a scribble if necessary—that
the scalar product equals the contraction of the associated form of $\vec{a}$ on $\vec{b}$,
or equally the contraction of the associated form of $\vec{b}$ on $\vec{a}$. People express
this by saying that the scalar product is *symmetric*. By construction it

is also linear in both factors ("bilinear," as people say).

The same thing can be done pictorially. You construct the dual of one vector—it doesn't matter which one—and contract the other on it. This is in fact the more geometrical method. It is pictorially evident that the scalar product of a vector with itself is positive definite. The locus of all vectors of modulus one is called the "gauge figure" and is, of course, just the sphere I started out with.

In many courses people introduce the scalar product directly as a bilinear symmetric operator and derive the metric from there. The present exposition seems geometrically more intuitively satisfying and transparent. If so desired, you can do it all by picture and algebra needn't come in at all. Algebra is not necessary, just convenient. I will introduce a suitable notation in a moment.

In official language the gauge-figure is represented by the metric tensor $\mathbf{G}$, a "machine" that converts vectors to forms; thus $\mathbf{G}\vec{a}$ is the form associated with the vector $\vec{a}$. Then the inner product $\vec{a} \cdot \vec{b}$ equals both $\mathbf{G}\vec{a}\langle\vec{b}\rangle$ and $\mathbf{G}\vec{b}\langle\vec{a}\rangle$. The metric tensor has a dual representation that lets you pull the trick the other way around, to convert a form to its corresponding vector. The coefficients of the dual are those of the inverse of $\mathbf{G}$ in the usual matrix notation. The matrix coefficients of the metric tensor are just the numbers $\mathbf{G}\vec{e_i}\langle\vec{e_j}\rangle$, of course. In component notation you have the almost obvious relations (mind the summation convention!):

$$(\mathbf{G}\vec{a})_i = G_{ij}a^j,$$

which is the one-form dual to $\vec{a}$, and

$$\mathbf{G}\vec{a}\langle\vec{b}\rangle = G_{ij}a^i b^j,$$

which is the "inner product" or "scalar product" of $\vec{a}$ and $\vec{b}$. For the duals you have similarly:

$$(\mathbf{G}\tilde{\omega})^i = G^{ij}\omega_j,$$

which is the vector dual to $\tilde{\omega}$. You can construct countless examples yourself. Note that the notion of the metric tensor and its "dual" really boil down to the same geometrical picture: *there is only one gauge figure.* The metric tensor belongs properly to the domain of symbolic manipulation, that is, to algebra. Please notice that its components (namely the numbers G_{ij}) have no intrinsic significance whatsoever. Only the integral "geometrical object" has any significance.

Since the tensor language usually is associated with impressive festoons of rococo indices, a more geometrical—because operational—

notion is that of the "sharp operator," which takes vectors to one-forms:

$$\sharp \vec{v} = \tilde{\nu}.$$

You should pronounce this, "nu is sharp vee." This is equivalent to the action of the metric tensor, of course. It focuses the attention on the *operational significance* instead of the *coordinate representation*, though. This is the preferred notation if you do *geometry* rather than *algebra*. Using the sharp operator, you can write the definition of the scalar product in the equivalent form:

$$\vec{a} \cdot \vec{b} = \sharp \vec{a} \langle \vec{b} \rangle = \sharp \vec{b} \langle \vec{a} \rangle,$$

which has a rather direct visual interpretation and useful intuitive content. If you read this notation you should automatically see the corresponding picture before your mind's eye.

I will use the sharp operator indiscriminately as a "type converter" in the sense of computer science that transforms *any* multivector into its corresponding multiform and *vice versa*.

The canonical coordinate system makes life very easy indeed. The basis vectors and basis forms are pair-wise associated, that is $\sharp \vec{\partial}_x = dx$, for example.

The coefficients G_{ij} are just the Kronecker symbols δ_{ij}, that is, unity if i equals j and zero otherwise. Thus a vector has *the same coordinates* as its associated form. This is convenient, *but also confusing*. You might tend to forget the distinction between forms and vectors. This would be regrettable because this equality doesn't hold in many other spaces that might interest you. Failure to make the distinction will hurt you more than the minor convenience is worth: believe me!

Notice that the squared length of a vector is

$$\sharp \vec{a} \langle \vec{a} \rangle = a^i G_{ij} a^j = (a^x)^2 + (a^y)^2 + (a^z)^2,$$

which is nothing but the venerable *Theorem of Pythagoras*. It has some impressive frills added to it, and consequently looks more professional, but basically this is just how the ancients did it.

Vectors and covectors are each others "duals" and you have an isomorphism between vectors and forms. The gauge-figure, or metric tensor, enables you to switch between the two in both directions. To "take the dual," as people say.

The space of forms is called the *covector space* and I generally consider either the tangent or the *cotangent bundle* according to convenience. Again, don't take these concepts as mere formal constructs, as the mathematician should. The tangent and cotangent spaces should be thought of as *local, that is linearized, pictures* of the spaces you are interested in. The vectors are rates, the dual covectors are gradients in these local linearized spaces.

Try to be able to visualize these spaces easily and as vividly as possible.

3.4.4   Multivectors and multiforms

You are not at all done with linear algebra yet, for you still lack many important concepts. For instance, you can't represent such elementary entities as areas or volumes. The road to these notions is *multivectors*.

A *bivector* is a geometric object that can best be pictured as an oriented planar patch of well-defined area but undefined shape. This probably sounds so vague that the imagination might well run into problems, but you will grow accustomed to it soon enough. People usually draw the orientation by means of a loop with an arrow on it. This can be understood as a sense in which the boundary of the bivector can be circumnavigated. Even though a thing without a shape may not have a clear boundary you can always—arbitrarily—assign one. Alternatively you can understand it as the definition of a surface normal defined via the motion of a right hand screw that is being turned according to the arrow on the loop that helps you distinguish one side of the surface from the other. Even better still you may get used to this notation as the natural, and hopefully even pictorially obvious, way to "orient a surface patch." Figure 41 shows an example.

The very name "bivector" suggests a relation of oriented areas with *an ordered pair of vectors*. This relation is known in beginner's classes as the "exterior product," "vector product," or also "cross product" of two vectors. Professionals understand the exterior product of two vectors $\vec{a}$ and $\vec{b}$ not as another vector, but as the *bivector* $\vec{a} \wedge \vec{b}$, which is a new geometrical object.

Don't panic if irresponsible people have taught you that the vector product is a *vector*. For the moment you may interpret this as the "normal vector" of the oriented area element. You have been unfortunate enough to have been taught the clumsy way, but you will soon enough get over it. Intuitively you think of the area formed by the parallelogram spanned by $\vec{a}$ and $\vec{b}$ endowed with a natural screw sense. Just turn $\vec{a}$ to $\vec{b}$ along the shortest route. Figure 42 shows an example.

If you turn your favorite cork screw in this direction it will travel in the direction of the surface normal. But *please hold on to your cork screw* because if someone swapped it for another one, this could lead you into utter confusion. The point is that there exist two types of cork

screws in this world, the so-called left- and right-handed ones. These
yield opposite normal directions.

A basis for bivectors is represented by the exterior products of the
basis vectors, namely $\vec{e}_y \wedge \vec{e}_z$, $\vec{e}_z \wedge \vec{e}_x$, and $\vec{e}_x \wedge \vec{e}_y$ (fig. 43). Any bivector

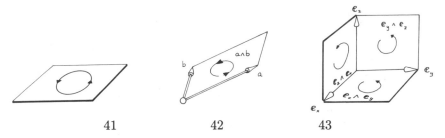

41   42   43

can be written as a linear combination of them. Intuitively they are the
oriented unit squares in the yz, zx and xy planes.

Please make it very clear to yourself that, for instance, the bivectors

$$\vec{e}_y \wedge \vec{e}_z, \quad \frac{\vec{e}_y}{2} \wedge 2\vec{e}_z \quad , \text{ and } \quad \frac{\vec{e}_y - \vec{e}_z}{\sqrt{2}} \wedge \frac{\vec{e}_y + \vec{e}_z}{\sqrt{2}},$$

denote the *same geometrical object*, although they certainly *look different*
as you will notice when you make sketches according to our standard
recipe. *Forget about the shape.*

The exterior product is linear in both factors, but—in contradistinction with the scalar product—is *antisymmetric*. Consequently, swapping
the vectors that make up the product reverses the orientation or sign of
the bivector.

The mutual relation between two vectors $\vec{a}$, $\vec{b}$ is only brought out fully
by the scalar and the exterior product together. From a knowledge of
both products you can compute their common plane, the angle between
the vectors and the product of their lengths. In a true geometrical
calculus, such as has been pioneered by Grassmann and by Cayley, the
scalar and exterior products would be *combined* into a single "vector
product" of which the scalar product would be the symmetrical and
the vector product the antisymmetrical part. I will not pursue such
an elegant and extremely powerful discipline of "multivector algebra"
further though. If I made you curious, you may want to take a look at
Hestenes's paper.

In physics you often use oriented area elements to find the *flux of some current*, such as the magnetic flux captured by a wire loop. Intuitively you count the "field lines" that cross the area element. That means the area bivector, of course. You can construct a suitable geometric object to do just that, the two-form. Abstractly a *two-form* is a bilinear antisymmetric map of pairs of vectors on the reals—that is, a "slot machine" with two slots that accept vectors, or a single slot that accepts a bivector, and pops out a number.

Intuitively, a two-form is a system of "tubes" endowed with an orientation. The contraction of the two-form on a bivector is the number of tubes, "field lines," or "flux tubes," that cross the bivector. You may construct two-forms from one-forms using the wedge product: $\tilde{\varphi} \wedge \tilde{\psi}$. The wedge product merely uses the planes of the one-forms as the walls of the tubes of a two-form. The orientation of the tubes follows from the orientation of the one-forms that enter in the wedge product. Figure 44 shows the intuitive picture of a two-form. You should imagine such "tubes" running all over space, filling it like a giant bundle of spaghetti. The picture is very close to the intuitive pictures of the magnetic field in physics.

The wedge product $\tilde{\mu} = \tilde{\varphi} \wedge \tilde{\psi}$ contracted on the bivector $\vec{b} = \vec{u} \wedge \vec{v}$ is nothing but the value of the pseudodeterminant:

$$\det \begin{vmatrix} \tilde{\varphi}\langle \vec{u} \rangle & \tilde{\varphi}\langle \vec{v} \rangle \\ \tilde{\psi}\langle \vec{u} \rangle & \tilde{\psi}\langle \vec{v} \rangle \end{vmatrix} = (\tilde{\varphi} \wedge \tilde{\psi})\langle \vec{u} \wedge \vec{v} \rangle = \tilde{\mu}\langle \vec{b} \rangle,$$

an expression that readily generalizes to higher order wedge products such as $\tilde{\varphi} \wedge \tilde{\psi} \wedge \tilde{\xi}$. The determinant form makes the completely antisymmetric nature of the wedge product explicit.

Figure 45 shows the contraction as you can picture it in your mind. Because the orientation of the bivector and the two-form agree, the result is positive, and because the area of the bivector accommodates four cross sections of tubes of the two-form, the amount is *four*. Thus the contraction yields the value *plus four* in this case.

The basis two-forms are $dy \wedge dz$, $dz \wedge dx$ and $dx \wedge dy$. The wedge product is bilinear and antisymmetric. Thus you have $dx \wedge dy = -dy \wedge dx$, as well as $dx \wedge dx = 0$ and so forth. The intuitive picture of tubes is indeed very useful, and with a little practice you should readily visualize two-forms in your mind. Think of $dy \wedge dz$ as a bundle of tubes of unit cross section running in the x-direction. Say the tubes with "walls" defined by letting the y and z coordinates assume integer values.

Oriented volumes are defined in a manner completely analogous to the oriented areas. People define the "triple product" of three vectors

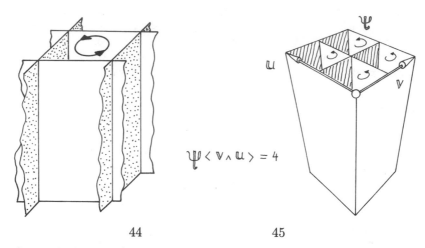

$$\psi \langle \vee \wedge u \rangle = 4$$

44   45

$\vec{a}$, $\vec{b}$ and $\vec{c}$ as $\vec{t} = \vec{a} \wedge \vec{b} \wedge \vec{c}$, where $\vec{t}$ is a new geometric object, a *trivector*. The triple product is trilinear and completely antisymmetric (the sign of $\vec{t}$ flips when you swap any two terms). I think of trivectors as oriented blobs of space with well-defined volume but undefined shape. Often I use a vision of a "soap box" or "crate" defined by the three vectors $\vec{a}$, $\vec{b}$, $\vec{c}$ which is OK as long as you don't put any significance on the shape.

Figure 46 shows the triple product of three vectors yielding a "crate." Figure 47 shows a more austere picture in which the vectors are gone and you are left with an oriented volume of undefined shape. The crate picture is a useful—though arbitrary—representation because it allows you to indicate the orientations induced on the faces.

Since the actual shape is immaterial, the only geometrical relevant entities are the *ratios of volumes* (or *areas*, in the case of bivectors). Any trivector in Euclidean three-space must be a multiple of the—unique— unit trivector $\vec{e}_x \wedge \vec{e}_y \wedge \vec{e}_z$, the scale factor being the determinant of coefficients of the three vectors. Pictorially, you think of the unit trivector as the oriented unit cube. Because *all* trivectors are merely multiples of a single unit trivector, they have a certain "scalar flavor," and are often called "pseudoscalars." However, if you change the orientation of your frame, the pseudoscalars flip their signs, whereas real scalars are, of course, not affected.

Oriented volumes are contracted on *three-forms* to obtain a number. This is equivalent to the physical use of *densities*. Thus charge density times an oriented volume yields a significant entity, the charge in the volume. People conceive of charge density as a swarm of flyspecks and count flyspecks in the volume. If you are a physicist you may prefer to think of "electrons" for the sake of concreteness. A three-form is best pictured as a cellular space structure, and the contraction on a trivector is merely the number of cells within the volume of the trivector.

Thus pictorially speaking a three-form is a giant space-filling honeycomb or—equivalently—an enormous warehouse of neatly stacked sugar cubes. You may construct three-forms through the wedge product from triples of one-forms (such as $\tilde{\psi} \wedge \tilde{\varphi} \wedge \tilde{\xi}$); all three-forms can be constructed in that way.

Figure 48 shows a single cell, but you should imagine them to be

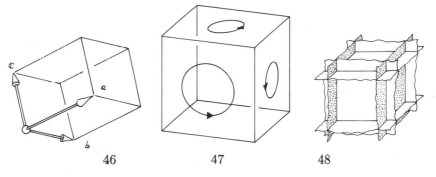

46   47   48

packed together in a giant honeycomb so as to fill all of space. The three-forms denote densities, and this is indeed the most intuitively sensible picture. Let each cell of the three-form contain a single particle; then the three-form represents the particle density. Contract it on a trivector and you get the number of particles inside the crate of the trivector.

There is only a single basis trivector, namely $\vec{e}_x \wedge \vec{e}_y \wedge \vec{e}_z$ or $\vec{\partial}_x \wedge \vec{\partial}_y \wedge \vec{\partial}_z$, and a single basis three-form, namely $dx \wedge dy \wedge dz$. The cells of $dx \wedge dy \wedge dz$ are a stack of unit cubes that completely fills space—at least if you don't insist on the importance of the cubical shapes of the cells. Clearly you have the "impressive" identity

$$dx \wedge dy \wedge dz \, \langle \vec{\partial}_x \wedge \vec{\partial}_y \wedge \vec{\partial}_z \rangle =$$

$$\det \begin{vmatrix} dx\langle \vec{\partial}_x \rangle & dx\langle \vec{\partial}_y \rangle & dx\langle \vec{\partial}_z \rangle \\ dy\langle \vec{\partial}_x \rangle & dy\langle \vec{\partial}_y \rangle & dy\langle \vec{\partial}_z \rangle \\ dz\langle \vec{\partial}_x \rangle & dz\langle \vec{\partial}_y \rangle & dz\langle \vec{\partial}_z \rangle \end{vmatrix},$$

which equals

$$\det \begin{vmatrix} 1 & 0 & 0 \\ 0 & 1 & 0 \\ 0 & 0 & 1 \end{vmatrix},$$

which again equals unity. You may pronounce these formulas in plain words: "A single cell of $dx \wedge dy \wedge dz$ fits into the soap-box $\vec{\partial}_x \wedge \vec{\partial}_y \wedge \vec{\partial}_z$" or "the volume of the unit cube is unity." The latter phrase especially does full justice to the geometrical content of the formulas.

Note that such formulas appear as mere *trivialities* when you observe them as simple geometrical relationships before your mind's eye, no matter how formidable the coordinate notations may look. Many people seem to be born geometers if they just use their eyes and don't think too much.

3.4.5   Euclidean three-space

The dimension of the space of bivectors equals that of the space of vectors: three. This is a peculiarity of dimension three. For instance, it doesn't work for dimension two. The vector space has dimension two but there is only a single independent bivector in the plane; thus the bivector space has dimension one. Historically, this has been the cause of much confusion. For instance the "vector product" $\vec{a} \times \vec{b}$ is known as an "axial vector" but is really the bivector $\vec{a} \wedge \vec{b}$ in disguise. People often switch back and forth between scalars (say λ) and trivectors (λ times $\vec{\partial}_x \wedge \vec{\partial}_y \wedge \vec{\partial}_z$) or vectors and bivectors. Sometimes this is reflected in the terminology; for instance, "capacities" and "densities" are trivectors and three-forms even if both are conventionally treated as if they were scalars. But more often the true status of physical entities is left very much in the dark.

People formalize this procedure through the star-operator on forms. This can easily be done for arbitrary dimension (n, say), where the star operator is defined in such a manner that it maps k-forms on ($n - k$)-forms. Moreover, the star operator is designed to be a linear machine:

$$*(\lambda \tilde{\varphi} + \mu \tilde{\psi}) = \lambda(*\tilde{\varphi}) + \mu(*\tilde{\psi})$$

and is most conveniently defined *recursively* as follows:

First you define the action of the star operator on *scalars*. The only reasonable definition for the result of $*1$ that I can think of is the unit three-form of positive orientation, so I take this as the axiom:

$$*1 = dx^1 \wedge dx^2 \wedge \ldots \wedge dx^n.$$

Then you may set up a recursion by means of an application of the sharp operator and the contraction. You could reason as follows:

Let $\tilde{\alpha}$ be a one-form. Then $\sharp\tilde{\alpha}$ is a vector. If you contract any form on a vector you lower its degree by one. Thus if $\tilde{\beta}$ is a k-form, and if the star operator is to perform as advertised $*\tilde{\beta}$ should be a $(n-k)$-form and $*\tilde{\beta}\langle\sharp\tilde{\alpha}\rangle$ should be a $(n-k-1)$-form. Notice that $\tilde{\beta}\wedge\tilde{\alpha}$ is a $(k+1)$-form, thus $*(\tilde{\beta}\wedge\tilde{\alpha})$ should also be a $(n-k-1)$-form.

Although this sounds complicated it does not ask for much more expertise than being able to count up to three.

Now you are in a position to start define a recursion by requiring that the star operator is such that it automatically respects the identity

$$*(\tilde{\beta}\wedge\tilde{\alpha}) = (*\tilde{\beta})\langle\sharp\tilde{\alpha}\rangle$$

for any one-form $\tilde{\alpha}$. In practice this means that you do it for the basis one-forms, of course. I could have introduced this axiom without more ado, but you might have been puzzled. Since this definition concerns only geometrical objects, the star operator is also guaranteed to possess true geometrical significance.

In order to see how this works out in practice I will explicitly write down the starred basis forms in two and three dimensions. You should really do the exercise yourself at least once, building things up from the recursion relation. In two-dimensional Euclidean space with the standard Cartesian coordinates you obtain:

$$
\begin{aligned}
*1 &= dx \wedge dy \\
*dx &= dy \\
*dy &= -dx \\
*dx \wedge dy &= 1
\end{aligned}
$$

and in three-dimensional space you get

$$
\begin{aligned}
*1 &= dx \wedge dy \wedge dz \\
*dx &= dy \wedge dz \\
*dy &= dz \wedge dx \\
*dz &= dx \wedge dy \\
*dy \wedge dz &= dx \\
*dz \wedge dx &= dy \\
*dx \wedge dy &= dz \\
*dx \wedge dy \wedge dz &= 1
\end{aligned}
$$

These simple examples will indeed be sufficient if you care only about operations in 2- and 3D. If you manage to memorize them, you can safely forget the abstract definition!

For three-dimensional space the double application of the star operator always returns you to the original form, thus you have the formal
relation $*^2 = 1$. This fact is not completely general, though, but depends on the dimension of the space, as you may figure out for yourself.
Thus, in the case of the plane the $*^2$ operator flips the sign for the basis
one-forms but preserves it for scalars and two-forms.

An easy way to keep track of the sign is to note the order of appearance of the factors dx^i in expressions like the above. All factors must
necessarily appear just once. If you read them from left to right (hopping
from the left to the right side of the equality in the process) you obtain
a permutation of the indices $(i = 1, \ldots, n)$. The sign of the starred form
is the sign of the permutation.

Thus the expression $*dy = -dx$ yields the permutation $\{21\}$ which is
indeed *odd*, whereas the expression $*(dy \wedge dz) = dx$ yields the permutation $\{231\}$ which is *even*.

Because you can easily switch between forms and vectors through
the sharp operator you can use the star operator to convert k-vectors
to $(n - k)$-vectors, too. For example, the area element of a surface
is properly a *bivector*, but is often replaced by a *vector* known as the
"surface normal" in the usual integrations performed in such physical
disciplines as electrostatics or hydrodynamics.

This kind of thing happens at the drop of a hat in mathematical
physics and theoretical engineering. It may lead to much confusion if
you are relatively inexperienced in these matters.

It will help you get a feeling for them if you spend some effort trying
to convert some physics that you are thoroughly familiar with into neat
geometrical form, letting rates be vectors and gradients be covectors
and so forth. If you haven't been exposed to this kind of thing before
you should not hesitate to take up this challenge. Electromagnetics is an
excellent touchstone. If you get stuck you may want to consult the rather
nice text by Flanders which appeals to mathematicians and physicists or
the wonderful giant pocket book by Misner, Thorne and Wheeler which
strongly appeals to the physicist.

3.4.6 The exterior derivative

In general you will not be satisfied with operations in the tangent space
of a single point. You want to be able to roam about space in order to
describe shape and so forth. Thus I consider not only single vectors but
vector *fields*, and not just single one-forms but one-form *fields*.

A vector field is a "cross-section" of the tangent bundle. Remember
that "tangent space" is the space containing all tangent vectors *at a*

point. The tangent bundle contains all tangent spaces, hence all tangent vectors for all points of the manifold. "Cross-section" means that at any point of the "base space" you pick just one vector from the attached tangent space in a smooth manner. Hence the term "cross-section." People usually refer to the tangent space as "the fiber over the point" in base space of the tangent bundle and the vector field as "cutting through the fibers"; a very useful intuitive picture (fig. 49).

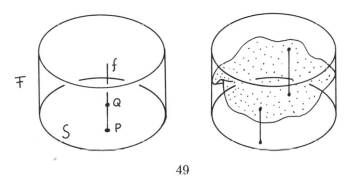

49

The vector bundle $\mathcal{F}$ is made up of a "base space" $\mathcal{S}$ and a "fiber space" f. Locally, but not necessarily globally, the fiber bundle is the Cartesian product $\mathcal{S} \times f$.[17] If the fiber bundle is a Cartesian product *globally* it is called "trivial." In the figure Q is a point in the "fiber over $\mathcal{P}$." The point $\mathcal{P}$ is a point of the base space. One says that $\mathcal{P}$ is the "natural projection" of Q.

The figure also illustrates the concept of a "cross section." It is a smooth way to associate an element of the fiber over arbitrary points of the base space with those points. As the figure illustrates, the term "cross section of the fiber bundle" captures the intuitive notion very aptly.

On the whole the language of modern differential geometry is agreeably descriptive and visual. In the cross section you move from one fiber to the next, that is, you hop from one local tangent space to the next. Although the local tangent spaces are linearized, their relations must reflect the nonlinear structure of the space, very much reflected in the fact that the verticals are different on different places on our globe.

Here—finally!—things start to become mildly interesting.

---

[17]I skip more general constructions here. I sketch the structure of a somewhat specialized notion of a "fiber bundle." The more general notions are not important in the context of this book.

An example of a cross-section of the cotangent bundle is

$$\tilde{\alpha} = a_x(x,y,z)\,dx + a_y(x,y,z)\,dy + a_z(x,y,z)\,dz.$$

Notice that the coordinates of $\tilde{\alpha}$—always in the tangent space over the point (x,y,z)—depend on the location in space. That's why $\tilde{\alpha}$ is called a covector-*field*. You have built an oriented stack of parallel planes in every tangent space, picked in a smooth, that is differentiable, way. A covector field is also called a "differential one-form," probably because it looks like something that might well appear under an integral sign. Indeed, here must lie the origin of that peculiar alias for a covector: "form."

One thing you can always do to any changing entity is, of course, to differentiate it, in order to see how it varies in the neighborhood of a point. This is standard technique. For every new object you meet it makes sense to worry about a sensible definition of its derivative.

For the multi covector fields this is done by way of "exterior differentiation." It is basically a rather simple process.

As an example you may consider the exterior derivative of the two-form $\tilde{\beta} = b_x\,dy \wedge dz + \dots$. You have:

$$d\tilde{\beta} = d(b_x\,dy \wedge dz) + \dots =$$

$$\left(\tfrac{\partial b_x}{\partial x}\,dx + \dots\right) \wedge dy \wedge dz + \dots = \tfrac{\partial b_x}{\partial x}\,dx \wedge dy \wedge dz + \dots$$

much as you would expect. You merely replace the coefficients with their differentials (one-forms) and factor out the resulting three-forms, dropping terms such as $dy \wedge (dy \wedge dz)$ which are perceived to vanish identically to the geometrically trained eye. They represent crates that have been "squashed completely flat." When necessary you rearrange factors; for instance, $dy \wedge (dz \wedge dx)$ equals $dx \wedge dy \wedge dz$, and so forth. The key point is to exploit the antisymmetry.

In order to understand what I mean by "squashed flat" or "squashed coordinate system" you may consider another simple example. Let the coordinates (u,v) be obtained from the Cartesian coordinates (x,y) by means of a member of a one-parameter family of affine transformations. The parameter is ψ. The family is defined through the equations

$$\begin{aligned} u &= & x &+ & \tanh\psi\,y \\ v &= & \tanh\psi\,x &+ & y. \end{aligned}$$

The new coordinates (u,v) are "sheared" with respect to (x,y). When you take ψ equal to zero you obtain nice Cartesian coordinates again (in fact $u = x$, $v = y$), but for large values of ψ the situation changes dramatically. Notice that du and dv are two unit one-forms and that the product two-form $du \wedge dv$ equals $(\text{sech}\psi)^2 \, dx \wedge dy$. When you let ψ approach infinity you observe that the cells of $du \wedge dv$ become flatter and flatter, whereas its modulus approaches zero. In the limit for very high values of ψ you have $u = v(= x + y)$! Then the one-forms du and dv *coincide*. They have become unfit as sides for a reasonable parallelogram and do no longer specify a two-form together.

Pictorially the cells become squashed to a line segment such that the product form vanishes. It is intuitively evident that (u, v) cannot be used as coordinates whenever this is the case, because the u and v coordinate directions are no longer transversal. This is an important example that you should fully understand. You can make precise drawings of the (u, v)-coordinate system for various values of the parameter ψ, because the example is *that* simple.

Fact: *The vanishing of the product of two one-forms means that they are unfit for the use as coordinate grids.*

The *exterior derivative* satisfies all the nice relations reminiscent of "Leibnitz's rule" from elementary differential calculus. Thus you have ($\tilde{\psi}$, $\tilde{\varphi}$ one-forms, f and g functions)

$$d(fg) = df\, g + f\, dg$$

$$d(f\tilde{\varphi}) = df \wedge \tilde{\varphi} + f\, d\tilde{\varphi}$$

$$d(\tilde{\varphi} \wedge \tilde{\psi}) = d\tilde{\varphi} \wedge \tilde{\psi} - \tilde{\varphi} \wedge d\tilde{\psi} = \det \begin{vmatrix} d\tilde{\varphi} & \tilde{\varphi} \\ d\tilde{\psi} & \tilde{\psi} \end{vmatrix}.$$

In the same manner you can differentiate forms of other orders, for instance, scalars. You obtain the "differential," which is a one-form for a scalar, a two-form for a covector-field, *etc.*

In the case that you differentiate a three-form-field the result is *always zero* because the terms will be of the type $dx \wedge dy \wedge dz \wedge dx$, which geometrically must vanish because they represent squashed crates. (In this case because the factor $dx \wedge dx$ occurs.)

A basic result of recurring applicability is that repeated exterior differentiation always yields zero:[18]

$$d^2 = 0,$$

a famous relation due to Poincaré. Store it into your mind in a gilded frame, for this relation is by far your most powerful tool in differential geometry!

Formally this relation merely restates the fact that terms like $dx \wedge dx$ must vanish because of the antisymmetry of the wedge product.

It is basically little more than the classical *equality of mixed partial derivatives*, but it packages things in a particularly neat way and is much more concise than the classical coordinate expressions. Thus the exterior derivative of a differential (say of the temperature) vanishes. In the parlance of classical vector calculus, one says "the *curl* of a gradient is identically zero." However, there exist one-forms—obviously not differentials of scalars—that *do not annihilate* when you differentiate them but yield a non-zero *two-form* instead. An example is $\frac{1}{2}(x\,dy - y\,dx)$, the differential of which is readily seen to equal the unit two-form.

People intuitively think of such "nonexact" one-forms as stacks of planes with extraneous half-planes inserted. An example would be the form $\tilde{\varphi} = x\,dy$. You have $d\tilde{\varphi} = dx \wedge dy$, which is a unit two-form. This should represent a unit density of "dangling planes." That this is indeed the case is pictorially evident. The spacing of the planes of $\tilde{\varphi}$ is x^{-1} (x planes per unit y increment) and thus varies in the direction parallel to the planes themselves. If you consider a rectangle with vertices (x, y), $(x+a, y)$, $(x+a, y+b)$, $(x, y+b)$, then this rectangle is represented with a bivector $\vec{A} = a.b.\vec{e}_x \wedge \vec{e}_y$. Notice that $x.b$ planes pierce the side (x, y), $(x, y+b)$, whereas a different number, namely $(x+a).b$ planes pierce the opposite side $(x+a, y)$, $(x+a, y+b)$. Thus $a.b$ planes have "dangling ends" within the rectangle, that is just one per unit area. This figures nicely with the formula $d\tilde{\varphi} = dx \wedge dy$ for $d\tilde{\varphi}\langle \vec{A} \rangle = a.b$ is the number of dangling ends within the rectangle. You geometrically attribute one extraneous plane of $\tilde{\varphi}$ sprouting from each cell of $d\tilde{\varphi}$.

Thus the contraction on a fixed vector depends on *where* the vector pierces the form. Figure 50 depicts such a "nonexact" one-form. *Nonexact forms always have such loose ends dangling around the place.*

---

[18]Try it in 2D for the scalar field $f(x, y)$: you obtain the two-form $f_{xx}\,dx \wedge dx + (f_{yx} - f_{xy})\,dx \wedge dy + f_{yy}\,dy \wedge dy$. Here the terms containing $dx \wedge dx$ and $dy \wedge dy$ vanish identically because they represent "squashed crates." The remaining two-form also vanishes identically, this time because of the *equality of mixed partial derivatives*. This is classical differential calculus!

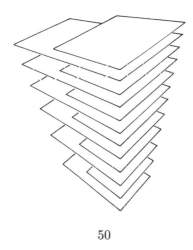

50

The boundaries of the loose ends are curves for one-forms, points for two-forms. This is the pictorial interpretation of nonexactness.

Here you have a *geometrical* handle on the significance of Poincaré's relation. You now see what the exterior derivative of a multi covector field means. Poincaré's relation states that the exterior derivative of a field can have no dangling ends. This can be restated in geometrical terms for the different orders.

Thus Poincaré's relation has the following simple intuitive content for the case of one-forms:

Remark: *The planes of a differential of a scalar field are level sets, hence necessarily closed; thus there can be no "dangling ends." This is the significance of Poincaré's relation for the case of one-forms.*

The density of the dangling ends is of course described by way of *some form*, a two-form for one-forms and a three-form for two-forms. These forms are just the nonvanishing differentials. Thus the differential of a two-form is a three-form and the cells of this three-form are the "sources" of the extraneous tubes of the two-form. Notice that this is exactly the physical picture of the electric field where the field lines are either closed or end on charges, that is, originate from the cells of the "charge three-form." If you are a physicist you should indeed already have a keen gut feeling for the meaning of the exterior derivative and of Poincaré's relation: these describe the relation between the "sources" and the "field."

The reverse of differentiation is *integration*. This is a very easy process, although mathematically not without its tricky traits. It can be simply understood intuitively. Notice that *contraction* is really an integration in the infinitesimal domain. The formal expression for the contraction already looks like the kind of thing that appears after the integral sign in the standard calculus classes.

The integral over a region (one-, two- or three-dimensional, as the case may be) of a form (one-, two- or three-form) is easily found by *approximating the region with multivectors* (vectors, bivectors, or trivectors, as the case may be). Just contract the form on these multivectors and sum the results; the process is always the same, although the corresponding pictures may look markedly different.

Thus a line integral of a one-form over a curve is found through the following procedure. You approximate the curve with a chain of vectors, that is with a polygonal arc. Then you pierce the vectors with the surfaces of the one-form one at a time and count the piercings, adding up the results of all vectors (fig. 51).

51

From this construction it is pictorially immediately obvious that *the line integral of the differential of a scalar field over a closed curve vanishes*. This happens because every surface that is pierced in one direction will eventually be pierced in the other direction. Similarly, the integral of the product of two one-forms over a closed surface must vanish because any tube that enters the volume bounded by the closed surface must eventually also leave it. On the other hand, a one-form with extraneous half-planes will not necessarily yield a zero result because in one direction you may pierce more planes than on the way back. That's essentially all there is to it (fig. 52).

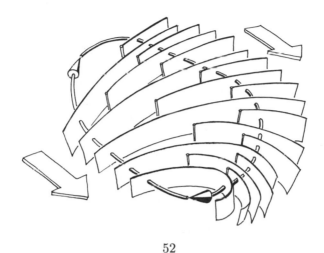

52

The classical result of Stokes gives the relation between the exterior derivative of a form and its integral over a closed surface. Let $\mathcal{A}$ denote a region and $\partial\mathcal{A}$ its boundary. Pictorially, you must have $\partial^2\mathcal{A} = 0$. For example, let $\mathcal{A}$ be a circular disc. Then $\partial\mathcal{A}$ is a circle. Because a circle is a *closed* curve, its boundary is *empty* and you have formally $\partial^2\mathcal{A} = 0$. It is indeed pictorially evident that this is a general (tautological) fact. As people are wont to say,

Fact: *"the boundary of a boundary is zero."* Or: $\partial^2 = 0$.

Thus you have $\partial^2 = 0$ as the formal analog of $d^2 = 0$. A while back I gave an intuitive interpretation of Poincaré's relation for the case of a covector field. You will appreciate that this also appealed to the intuitive notion that the boundary of a boundary must be empty.

The boundary inherits its orientation from the volume in the natural fashion. Thus you obtain the deservedly famous relation that the flux through the boundary of a region (think of the flux of the electrostatic field lines) equals the total amount of source material contained inside that region, or—formally—

$$\int_{\partial\mathcal{A}} \tilde{\varphi} = \int_{\mathcal{A}} d\tilde{\varphi}.$$

This is your trusty *Green's theorem*, but jazzed up to full generality. It is another of those theorems to be put into a gilded frame, but of course

practical people in physics and engineering knew this all along. It is one
of the major tools in classical electromagnetics, for instance.

From this relation you see immediately that

$$\int_{\partial \mathcal{A}} d\tilde{\varphi}$$

vanishes identically because $d^2 = 0$ or $\partial^2 = 0$, according to your taste.[19]
This relation formally captures the "conservation principles" of theories
of physical phenomena such as electromagnetics. Notice how such relations seem absolutely natural in the pictorial domain, although their
analytic justification is by no means a trivial job.

Most of the results discussed in this section have well-known counterparts in classical vector analysis. In the geometrical notation the
relations become much more intuitively clear, however.

In the classical vector analysis you have such well-known operations
as taking the "*curl*" or "*div*" of a vector, or the "Laplacean" of a scalar
field. These operations have close connections to the exterior derivative. The problem with the classical analysis is that entities which are
specified through three "components" are not distinguished (they could
be vectors, bivectors, covectors, or two-forms). You can patch up such
defects through a shrewd use of the sharp and star operators. By just
noticing what happens to the "components," you see that

$$d(a_x \, dx + \ldots) = (\frac{\partial a_z}{\partial y} - \frac{\partial a_y}{\partial z}) \, dy \wedge dz + \ldots$$

must be the classical "*curl*," whereas

$$d(a_x \, dy \wedge dz + \ldots) = (\frac{\partial a_x}{\partial x} + \frac{\partial a_y}{\partial y} + \frac{\partial a_z}{\partial z}) dx \wedge dy \wedge dz$$

must be the "*div*." Moreover, the Laplacean appears in the expression

$$d * d(\varphi) = (\frac{\partial^2 \varphi}{\partial x^2} + \frac{\partial^2 \varphi}{\partial y^2} + \frac{\partial^2 \varphi}{\partial z^2}) dx \wedge dy \wedge dz.$$

Thus the Laplacean operator as applied to a scalar field is seen to correspond to the $*d * d$ operator, and so forth.

---

[19] In physics the stress used to be on the "sources" of fields and on the law of
conservation of source material. In the modern view the fields are central and the
sources mere singularities of the field. Then it is attractive to regard the *tautological
fact* that "the boundary of a boundary is zero" as fundamental: physics without
machinery, essentially based on nothing at all! Strange as it may sound to the
layman, the ambition of he physicist must be to reduce all theory to a card house
built upon tautological truths! Then the fact that physics is a *natural science* is only
evident from the "correspondence rules," that is, the interpretation of the formalism.

3.4.6.1 Calculus in the plane

♠ SUPPLEMENTARY MATERIAL; USEFUL BUT DULL

Though it might appear that this is a rather special case it may well be the most commonly encountered one in applications. The reason is that you will no doubt do most of the calculus in the parameter spaces of your parametrized surface patches, and that usually means the Cartesian plane.

In the Euclidean plane you use a natural frame field through the parallel displacement of the two orthonormal vectors $\vec{I}$, $\vec{J}$ at the origin to the point of application. I denote the coordinate functions by x, y.

In this section I spell out a few of the more commonly used relations.

A one-form is

$$\tilde{\varphi} = f_x \, dx + f_y \, dy,$$

with $f_x = \tilde{\varphi}\langle \vec{I} \rangle$, $f_y = \tilde{\varphi}\langle \vec{J} \rangle$;

A two-form is

$$\tilde{\nu} = g \, dx \wedge dy,$$

with $g = \tilde{\nu}\langle \vec{I} \wedge \vec{J} \rangle$.

Let $\tilde{\psi}$ be another one-form with coefficients $h_{x,y}$ then the wedge product is

$$\tilde{\varphi} \wedge \tilde{\psi} = (f_x \, h_y - f_y \, h_x) \, dx \wedge dy = \det \begin{vmatrix} f_x & f_y \\ h_x & h_y \end{vmatrix} dx \wedge dy,$$

a result that should be well familiar from elementary calculus classes.

It is obviously the case that

$$\tilde{\varphi} \wedge \tilde{\psi} = -\tilde{\psi} \wedge \tilde{\varphi}$$

and consequently

$$\tilde{\varphi} \wedge \tilde{\varphi} = 0.$$

The differential of a function f is the one-form

$$df = \frac{\partial f}{\partial x} \, dx + \frac{\partial f}{\partial y} \, dy$$

and of a one-form $\tilde{\varphi}$ is

$$d\tilde{\varphi} = \det \begin{vmatrix} \frac{\partial}{\partial x} & \frac{\partial}{\partial y} \\ f_x & f_y \end{vmatrix} dx \wedge dy,$$

a relation that you will recognize as the *"curl"* operator in the plane.

You can easily check some simple rules, reminiscent of Leibnitz's rule and the concatenation rule from elementary differential calculus:

$$d(fg) \qquad = \qquad df\,g + f\,dg$$

$$d(f\tilde{\varphi}) \qquad = \qquad df \wedge \tilde{\varphi} + f d\tilde{\varphi}$$

$$d(g(f)) \qquad = \qquad g'(f)\,df$$

$$df \wedge dg \,\langle\, \vec{v} \wedge \vec{w} \,\rangle \quad = \vec{v}\,[\,f\,]\,\vec{w}\,[\,g\,] - \vec{v}\,[\,g\,]\,\vec{w}\,[\,f\,]$$

$$= \qquad \det \left| \begin{array}{cc} \vec{v}\,[\,f\,] & \vec{v}\,[\,g\,] \\ \vec{w}\,[\,f\,] & \vec{w}\,[\,g\,] \end{array} \right| .$$

People call a form *closed* if $d\tilde{\varphi} = 0$, *exact* if a form $\tilde{\xi}$ exists such that $\tilde{\varphi} = d\tilde{\xi}$. If a form is exact then it is also closed because $d^2 = 0$.

3.4.7 Important transformations

A few basic geometrical transformations occur over and over again, namely the Euclidean isometries and projections. You ought to be thoroughly familiar with them. They are easily described in terms of multivectors which then assume an *operational* rather than their usual *extensional* significance.

Projections are almost trivial, but highly important transformations. They are *idempotent operators*, by which term one understands that if you iterate a projection, there is no further change after the first application. In this book I will merely need the notions of projections on lines and planes.

Projection on a line is best described by using a unit vector $\vec{l}$ to define the line. Then any vector $\vec{a}$ maps on a multiple of $\vec{l}$. You have that

$$\Pi\,\vec{a} = \sharp\vec{l}\,\langle\,\vec{a}\,\rangle\,\vec{l}.$$

The "remainder" lies in the plane perpendicular to $\vec{l}$, thus it is obviously two-dimensional. People say that the "codimension" of the projection is two or that the "orthogonal complement" is the plane perpendicular to $\vec{l}$.

Projection on a plane can be described in a similar way. You define the plane through the unit normal $\vec{n}$. Then $\vec{a}$ maps on

$$\Pi\,\vec{a} = \vec{a} - \sharp\vec{n}\,\langle\,\vec{a}\,\rangle\,\vec{n}.$$

The codimension is one.

In "canonical coordinates" you just *ignore* one (in the case of projection on a plane) or two (for a projection on a line) coordinates. Then projection is trivially the restriction to a sub-flat of the base space. This is what you typically do if you project in a computer program. You transform into a representation in which the projection is trivial (people say: in "canonical representation") and disregard the superfluous coordinates.

This also works for more general projections, such as the "central projection" in which you map a vector $\vec{a}$ on its normalized direction $\|\vec{a}\|^{-1}\vec{a}$. In this case the canonical coordinates vary from vector to vector, however. The natural setting here is the spherical frame field, which will be extensively treated by way of an example later.

Of the Euclidean isometries I will only need translations and rotations.

Translations leave all tangent spaces unaltered, as they merely shift the origin.

Rotations also rotate the tangent spaces. Rotations leave sets of parallel planes invariant and can thus be thought to occur *in oriented planes*. The conventional description refers to the direction perpendicular to the planes, however. There is one fixed line, the axis of rotation, and the rotation is said to be "about the axis." This is peculiar to three dimensional space. For instance, in four dimensions the rotations would be "about planes" but they are also "in planes." The very idea of an "axis" thus loses most of its intuitive content. In two dimensions the rotation is about a point but—again—in the plane.

A general isometry, that is, a translation plus a rotation, thus affects the tangent spaces only through the rotational part.

The rules for concatenating rotations in three-dimensional space are very complicated and intuition is often confused by the fact that rotations don't commute.

The easiest way to handle the problem is to appreciate that rotations are like oriented planes and thus can be described by bivectors $\vec{R}$ (say). For a given vector $\vec{a}$ (say) you compute its dual $\sharp\vec{a}$ and contract the resulting covector on the rotation bivector. The result is a vector $\vec{v} = \sharp\vec{a}\langle\vec{R}\rangle$ that specifies the instantaneous velocity due to the rotation.[20]

---

[20] Here you could object that I haven't told you explicitly how to contract a *bivector* on a *one-form*. I think you can find out through some doodling how to do this. The geometrical idea is to draw the bivector in such a way that it is represented by a rectangle, one of whose sides is along a plane of the two-form. Formally it is easiest

Multiples of the vector $\sharp * \sharp \vec{R} = \vec{r}$ are invariant (check it!), thus $\vec{r}$ points in the direction of the "axis of rotation."

For a finite rotation you have to compute the *exponential* of a *bivector*. (You will discover this if you attempt to build a transformation from an infinite concatenation of infinitesimal steps. You obtain an infinite series that can be interpreted as the formal Taylor expansion of the "exponential" of the infinitesimal component.) I will not enter into these—very practical—matters further though. Such an idea leads directly to spinor or quaternion algebra, which are by far the most convenient tools to handle rotations in practice.

I manage to do without these tools in the present text, however. The reader will find useful references at the end of the book.

3.4.8   Symmetric forms

You very often have to deal with symmetric bilinear functions on vectors. The metric tensor is the standard example of such a function via its representation by the inner product. Thus $\vec{a} \cdot \vec{b}$ is symmetric and bilinear whereas the bivector $\vec{a} \wedge \vec{b}$ is antisymmetric and bilinear. This explains the common occurrence and general usefulness of these symmetric forms: *they are generalized metrics*.

One very useful and often most natural way to deal with such situations is to define a map of vectors on one-forms such that the one-form $\mathbf{S}(\vec{a})$ contracted on $\vec{b}$ equals the one-form $\mathbf{S}(\vec{b})$ contracted on $\vec{a}$. In geometrical terms this is nothing but a gauge-figure, a quadric that lets you map vectors on one-forms in a natural and unique way. The gauge-figure is usually the entity with the most direct intuitive content and you should always try to visualize it.   Figure 53 illustrates the construction for a special case. The gauge figure is used to convert the vector $\vec{a}$ into its dual covector $\sharp \vec{a}$. Then the second vector $\vec{b}$ is contracted on $\sharp \vec{a}$ so as to yield the value $\mathbf{S}(\vec{a}, \vec{b}) = 0.5$, because $\vec{b}$ pierces about half a level of $\sharp \vec{a}$.

In coordinates, the symmetric form is a tensor with components S_{ij} (with $S_{ij} = S_{ji}$) that can be contracted on two vectors $\vec{a}$, $\vec{b}$ to yield the number $S_{ij}a^i b^j$. Remember the Einstein summation convention; you have to sum over i and j. Although this is a useful representation, it carries no intuitive content and I will avoid it.

Useful heuristic: *It is preferable to consider the tensor as a "slot-*

---

to define the operation in terms of the basic multiforms and vectors. Then you have $dx\langle \vec{\partial}_y \wedge \vec{\partial}_z \rangle = 0$, $dx\langle \vec{\partial}_z \wedge \vec{\partial}_x \rangle = -\vec{\partial}_z$, $dx\langle \vec{\partial}_x \wedge \vec{\partial}_y \rangle = \vec{\partial}_y$ and so forth (by cyclic permutation).

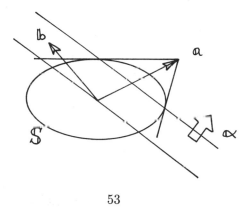

53

machine" with two slots. You drop the vectors $\vec{a}$ and $\vec{b}$ into the
slots and out pops a number that doesn't depend on the sequence.

This, of course, is exactly how the tensor appears in a computer program if you use a "hidden type."

If you fill only a single slot the "partly filled machine" is like a one-form that can be contracted on a vector to yield a number. Thus you may equally well regard **S** as *a map from vectors to one-forms.* Symbolically you have:

$$\mathbf{S}(\vec{a}, \vec{b}) = \mathbf{S}(\vec{a}, \bullet)\langle \vec{b} \rangle = \mathbf{S}(\bullet, \vec{b})\langle \vec{a} \rangle = \mathbf{S}\vec{a} \cdot \vec{b} = \vec{a} \cdot \mathbf{S}\vec{b},$$

where the dot ("•") conventionally indicates a missing argument or "empty slot." The operator **S** is also called "self-adjoint" for reasons that I will not explain here.

If you pick three mutually orthonormal vectors $\vec{g}_{1,2,3}$ with duals $\tilde{\chi}^{1,2,3}$ and three scalars $\lambda_{1,2,3}$ you can construct a unique symmetrical operator as follows:

$$\mathbf{S}(\vec{a}, \bullet) = \sum_i \lambda_i \, \tilde{\chi}^i \, \langle \, \vec{a} \, \rangle \, \tilde{\chi}^i.$$

This is called a "symmetrical tensor product." The symmetry is obvious from the construction. Notice that $\sharp\mathbf{S}(\vec{g}_i, \bullet)$ equals $\vec{g}_i$ again, but multiplied by λ_i. The three vectors are the "eigenvectors" of the operator and the three scalars the "eigenvalues." In the frame $\{\vec{g}_i\}$ the operator merely scales the components of an arbitrary vector by different factors; thus geometrically this represents an anisotropic dilation.

The metric tensor itself can be constructed in this manner from any orthonormal frame. Thus you can write symbolically:

$$\mathbf{G}(\bullet, \bullet) = (dx \, \langle \, \bullet \, \rangle \, dx + dy \, \langle \, \bullet \, \rangle \, dy + dz \, \langle \, \bullet \, \rangle \, dz) \, \langle \, \bullet \, \rangle,$$

an expression that looks deceptively like the Pythagorean theorem, and indeed, in the earlier literature this expression occurs as the famous "line element" or the so called "dee-es-square":

$$ds^2 = dx^2 + dy^2 + dz^2,$$

where physicists think of the terms as "infinitesimal displacements." If you think of it as a symbolic expression of the gauge-figure, everything is OK, for the geometrical expression for **G** given above can also interpreted as the gauge-figure, of course.

The gauge-figure idea also has its merits, as it will usually be possible to find simple, intuitively appealing meanings for the figure. This is how the nineteenth-century physicist managed to get a feel for the formidable coordinate expressions in mechanics, electromagnetics, and so forth. For

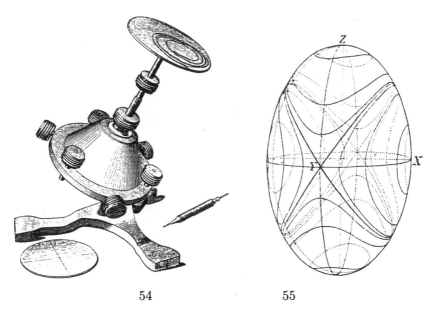

54   55

instance, the inertia-momentum ellipsoid used in the theory of the gyroscope (fig. 54) is just another gauge-figure that enables you to grasp the six components as a *single* geometrical object. Figure 55 shows this "Poinsot ellipsoid."

3.4.9   Computer Implementation

In computer implementations you have little choice but to use coordinates somewhere in your code, for the stupid machine just pushes bits around and doesn't really handle geometrical objects as such. "Virtual machines" can be defined that make this actually happen, in some abstract but intuitively very real sense, however. Higher languages like PASCAL or MODULA-2 let you keep some of the flavor of the essentially geometrical content of linear algebra by making it possible to *hide* the gory details. In MODULA-2 you can use opaque types and really hide the representation. In Pascal you have to be satisfied with a little less and hope to keep the adventurous user in check by means of comments. The user should under no circumstance make use of the specific implementation details of geometric objects as datastructures, but always use them through the handles you provide. If you yourself are the sole user this will save you from growing grey hairs at an early age.

In the **DEFINITION MODULE** you may refer to **TYPE**'s Vector or OneForm and handle them without caring about the actual data structures.

Coordinates are ordered sets—triples in your case—of reals, and in the **IMPLEMENTATION MODULE** the **TYPE**'s will either be declared as

> **CONST** DIM = 3;
> **TYPE** INDEX − [1 .. dim];
> **TYPE** VECTOR = **ARRAY** INDEX **OF REAL**;

or as a

> **TYPE** VECTOR = **RECORD** x,y,z : **REAL END;**

The latter method is nice because you can declare bivectors as

> **TYPE** BIVECTOR = **RECORD** yz,zx,xy : **REAL END;**

whereas the

> **TYPE** BIVECTOR = **ARRAY** INDEX **OF REAL**;

wouldn't show the difference. This is not a problem, though, because the user shouldn't see the implementation. It is nice to have an explicit definition of the index range. A drawback is that you sometimes would like to switch between vector and bivector representations in order to accommodate classical vector analysis. However, in my opinion it is better to have to deal with explicit type conversions which you export from the **DEFINITION MODULE** in order to preclude all-too-common mistakes. Similarly, it pays to distinguish between one-forms (say a

TYPE ONEFORM = **RECORD** DX,DY,DZ : **REAL END**;

definition) and vectors; sometimes it is even necessary to introduce the metric tensor explicitly. The metric tensor has 6 independent components. You either store them in a record and pick the same field for G_{ij}, G_{ji} or write a

FUNCTION G(I, J : INDEX) : **REAL**;

In the true geometrical spirit you again *hide* the representation and use **G** merely to convert vectors to one-forms and *vice versa*. The metric then appears in its guise as the sharp operator. This is by far the most natural representation. The metric tensor appears as a type converter between vectors and forms. You then don't export any components explicitly, although the user can always compute them via the available procedures—for instance, $G_{ij} = \mathbf{G}\vec{e}_i \langle \vec{e}_j \rangle$—but the choice of basis is up to the user.

It is a simple enough matter to write a basic library that handles the details. You have to implement vector addition, scalar multiplication, inner and exterior product, triple product, wedge product, contraction, taking the dual, and all that. Although this is a tedious job, it is worth the effort because it allows you to write your routines using the geometrical objects and operations without worrying about coordinates. You will not encounter any problems of a numerical nature: all you need is weighted sums. The creative part is in the definition of the data types, the "packaging" that has to allow you to use the defined entities as geometrical objects without the least worry about numerical trivia.

A coordinate transformation—I should really be saying a change of frame—usually means a lot of computing, and I try to avoid it whenever possible. In many cases you just postpone the transformations to the very end and then concatenate them all. It only pays to transform right away if you prepare a data file that is going to be used repeatedly: then the data must be in as convenient a frame as possible. Usually you can postpone the actual explicit definition of the frame to the very end, and then you are automatically doing the right thing. But such techniques are well known from computer graphics and are strictly irrelevant to the present issue.

Integration is not difficult in principle and it is a numerically stable process because in the end it boils down to counting. *The complication is in the representation of the domain.* This is especially hard if the domain is some curved surface. You will encounter suitable methods to cope with such problems later on. At the moment, they are probably too much for you to handle; if not, then you could stop reading now and use your time in a more productive manner.

Differentiation of scalars is quite another problem. The local geometry is simple enough, but the process is inherently sensitive to noise. In principle you just use differences, in practice you have to be very careful and do a bit of smoothing on the side. For instance, in order to compute a gradient you fit a smooth function through a cluster of data-points and use the fit to estimate the partial derivatives of the coordinates of the form. The algebra that follows is simple again. The differentiation of *vector and covector fields* will be considered in more detail at a later stage. It is complicated by the fact that the frame will usually vary from point to point and you will somehow have to differentiate it too. I will tell you how later on. Don't try your hand at such things before you have read further.

3.4.9.1 The Graphics

> *Animation is not just a series of funny drawings*
> *strung together in movement.*
> *At its most creative it is a truly beautiful art form*
> *and, by its very nature, it is magical.*
> —TONY WHITE, *The Animator's Workbook (1986)*

In this book I only consider the geometrical and differential geometrical problems. I will not give any hints on the *output* side of computational differential geometry. This will necessarily greatly depend on the application. For this book I built a package with a graphics output on CRT and plotter. The methods used are conventional and can be found in the literature on computer graphics. The reader who wants a package to "play" in order to sharpen his intuition in shape analysis will need the usual "pipeline" of routines for clipping and projection. I use parallel, perspective, and sometimes stereographic projection. The latter type is not often found in conventional packages but is a great asset for spherical images because one easily shows much more than a hemisphere at once. This is much better than a photographic "fisheye-lens." It also gives a conformal image; thus there are none of the deformations of details that are so irritating in linear perspective.

Another necessary feature is some way to suppress "hidden lines" or "hidden surfaces" in order to improve on the clarity of the presentation. I have found it absolutely necessary to be able to get pictures *without* the hidden elements elimination too. In most cases it helps a lot to see a wireframe image being written on the CRT screen from back to front or to let it rotate. The "kinetic depth effect" gives you vivid 3D and thus disambiguates the degeneracies due to the projection. In such cases the hidden element elimination can be completely skipped. It is more likely to be a hindrance than a help. For static images the hidden lines elimination often helps avoid confusion, although it inevitably also deletes a lot of useful information. If the aim is understanding rather than nice pictures, I recommend some form of "haloing." When lines cross in the projection, the nearest line gets a "halo" that obliterates a short stretch of the line farther away from the vantage point. This very clearly establishes the depth order in such a way that the eye isn't confused, yet much of the structure at the back of the figure may still "shine through." Such routines can be faster than hidden line elimination and they often don't suppress as much useful detail.

Animation is by far the most powerful and—you are in luck for once— also the easiest method around. It only works well on a moderately fast computer with quite a bit of RAM, however. On my (cheap) Atari ST this is my preferred method. Even though I only animate via about a dozen frames (cyclically) the result is very good. More frames would mean an impossible amount of computation, anyway. On my PC clone I have come to prefer either straight wire frame representations or haloed line routines. I save the hidden lines routine for "showing off," usually on a pen plotter (sigh!). If you are an employee of LUCASFILM, then naturally these remarks don't apply to you.

Drawing is putting a line round an idea.
—HENRI MATISSE (1869–1954)

3.5   Frame fields

3.5.1   The covariant derivative

The notion of a vector as a *derivative*, that is the definition of $\vec{v}[f]$ as the limit for vanishing t of the scaled difference

$$\lim_{t \to 0} \frac{f(\mathcal{P} + \vec{v}t) - f(\mathcal{P})}{t},$$

can equally well be applied to *vector fields*. Let $\vec{W}$ be a vector field, that is, a rule that assigns a vector to every point of space such that the projections of $\vec{W}$ on the Euclidean frame vectors are smooth, that is, differentiable, functions of position. Then you may consider the limit for vanishing t of the difference (fig. 56):

$$\lim_{t \to 0} \frac{\vec{W}(\mathcal{P} + \vec{v}t) - \vec{W}(\mathcal{P})}{t}.$$

This limit defines yet another vector field, which I will denote as $\nabla_{\vec{v}}\vec{W}$, the so called "covariant derivative of $\vec{W}$ by $\vec{v}$."[21] Note the intuitive geometrical meaning of this definition (that means, as always, make a sketch):

Heuristic: *The covariant derivative of the vector field $\vec{W}$ by the vector $\vec{v}$ at the point $\mathcal{P}$ is the initial rate of change in $\vec{W}(\mathcal{P})$ as the point $\mathcal{P}$ moves in the $\vec{v}$-direction.*

The covariant derivative is *linear in both* $\vec{v}$ *and* $\vec{W}$ in the following sense:

$$\nabla_{a\vec{v}+b\vec{w}} \vec{U} = a\nabla_{\vec{v}} \vec{U} + b\nabla_{\vec{w}} \vec{U},$$

here a, b denote scalars, $\vec{v}$, $\vec{w}$ vectors, whereas $\vec{U}$ denotes a vector *field*; and

$$\nabla_{\vec{v}} (a\vec{R} + b\vec{S}) = a\nabla_{\vec{v}} \vec{R} + b\nabla_{\vec{v}} \vec{S},$$

where $\vec{R}$, $\vec{S}$ denote vector fields. In addition you have the following rule that is reminiscent of Leibnitz's rule:

$$\nabla_{\vec{v}} (f\vec{R}) = \vec{v}[f] \vec{R} + f \nabla_{\vec{v}} \vec{R}.$$

---

[21] The funny symbol "$\vec{\nabla}$" is pronounced "nabla." The name derives from the shape of an Assyrian harp. Thus, when James Clerk Maxwell wrote his Tyndallic Ode (to the honor of Professor Tait), he alluded to Tait as "The Chief Musician upon Nabla."

  Of course, the vector $\vec{v}$ could as well be a value of another vector field $\vec{V}$; thus you can speak of the covariant derivative of one vector field by another. This is a noncommutative operation, by which I mean that the "bracket" or "commutator"

$$[\vec{V}, \vec{W}] = \nabla_{\vec{V}}\vec{W} - \nabla_{\vec{W}}\vec{V}$$

doesn't vanish in general (fig. 57). The bracket is by construction anti-

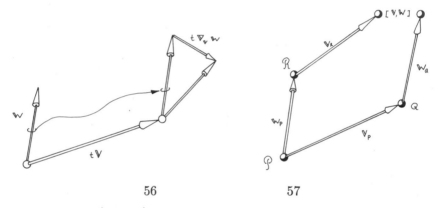

56   57

symmetric in $\vec{V}$ and $\vec{W}$, and although it would seem to be of the second order at first sight, it is actually yet another *vectorfield*.[22] This may need thinking over! It has important geometrical applications because it can be shown to vanish for a *coordinate basis*, that is, for a basis with basis vectors taken as the duals of the exterior derivatives of three arbitrary "coordinate functions," fondly known as a "holonomic basis."

  Perhaps an example will help you to understand what is going on here. Consider the coordinate functions $r(x,y) = \sqrt{x^2 + y^2}$, and $\varphi(x,y) = \text{arctg}\frac{y}{x}$. These can be taken as "polar coordinates in the plane." Their bracket $[\vec{\partial}_r, \vec{\partial}_\varphi]$ vanishes. On the other hand, for the *frame vectors* $\vec{\partial}_r$, $\frac{1}{r}\vec{\partial}_\varphi$ the bracket doesn't vanish but rather equals

$$(\frac{\partial}{\partial r})(\frac{1}{r}\frac{\partial}{\partial \varphi}) - (\frac{1}{r}\frac{\partial}{\partial \varphi})(\frac{\partial}{\partial r}) = -\frac{1}{r^2}\frac{\partial}{\partial \varphi} = -\frac{1}{r}(\frac{1}{r}\frac{\partial}{\partial \varphi}),$$

---

[22]Since a vector is a derivative operator you might well infer that the operation of two vectors in sequence is equivalent to a second order derivative, and hence that the bracket would be a second-order differential operator! Not so.

or—written in the usual notation—

$$[\vec{f}_r, \vec{f}_\varphi] = -\frac{1}{r}\vec{f}_\varphi.$$

Notice how *mirabile dictu*—the second order terms have canceled! This is seen to be a consequence of the equality of mixed partial derivatives. Thus the commutator is indeed of the first order. Geometrically it is also clear that the commutator must be just another vector field. You can even guess at its form: the reason is that the bracket is just the *error term* that is needed to close "quadrilaterals" formed from the points

$$\mathcal{P},$$
$$\mathcal{P} + t\vec{V}(\mathcal{P}),$$
$$\mathcal{P} + t\vec{V}(\mathcal{P}) + t\vec{W}(\mathcal{P} + t\vec{V}(\mathcal{P})),$$
$$\mathcal{P} + t\vec{W}(\mathcal{P}),$$
$$\mathcal{P} + t\vec{W}(\mathcal{P}) + t\vec{V}(\mathcal{P} + t\vec{W}(\mathcal{P})).$$

For a coordinate basis the quadrilaterals close trivially, as the figure shows, but for the frames they don't necessarily do so.

It is an easy and very instructive exercise to prepare a sketch for the case of the polar coordinate frame (fig. 58). It is a simple matter to derive the commutator from high school geometry from such a sketch. You should certainly do this if the definition isn't completely transparent to you already. As indicated in the figure, the width of the gap is proportional to the area of the quadrangle and to the bracket of the frame vectors that was calculated above.

You will have noticed that the commutator is arrived at by a somewhat sneaky limiting process. Just remember that:

Fact: *The bracket is the closer of quadrilaterals.*

Another way to express the same fact is to say that the bracket measures the fitness of two vector fields to define a curvilinear coordinate system.

The "Leibnitz rule" ensures that the connection only "sees" first order structure, thus that it behaves as a "derivation" should. The so-called "classical connection" is just

$$\nabla_{\vec{\partial}_{x^i}} \vec{\partial}_{x^j} = \sum_{k=1...3} \Gamma^k_{i\,j} \vec{\partial}_{x^k},$$

where the coefficients $\Gamma^k_{i\,j}$ are the familiar "Christoffel symbols," to be

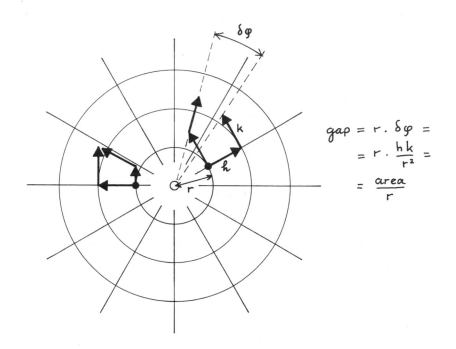

$$gap = r \cdot \delta\varphi =$$
$$= r \cdot \frac{hk}{r^2} =$$
$$= \frac{area}{r}$$

discussed in detail later in this text.[23] They are by no means the components of some tensor, as the impressive frills might well suggest to you.

The more elegant and modern method is to define the connection through a few well-picked axioms and then to show it exists, is unique, and has all the nice properties. This modern method is so *neat* that it is generally expected to bring tears to your eyes. This is possible not because modern man is so much smarter than previous generations, but merely because he now knows the answer from the very beginning. (You *have* to be cheating when you suddenly draw the right axioms out of a hat!) Earlier authors had to earn their money the hard way. Classically one started off with the Christoffel symbols and took it from there, building the house from the roof down. This introduced certain auxiliary problems that I am quite happy to skip here. The earlier literature is certainly no fun at times.

The Christoffel symbols can be useful, and so they certainly are, but they carry little intuitive content. Later on in this chapter I will introduce a better, more pictorial way to get a handle on what goes on. Take heart.

> *Only the motions of bodies relative to one another*
> *have an objective meaning.*
> —HERMANN WEYL *Space, Time, Matter (1921)*

---

[23]At least to the physicist, these should be familiar from the usual classical mechanics drilling.

3.5.2   The attitude transformation

Amongst the various branches of science studied in our
academies and places of public education there are
few of greater importance than the Use of the Globes.
—THOMAS KEITH, *A new treatise on the use of the globes ... designed*
for the instruction of youth (1869)

A frame field can be regarded as a cross-section of *six-dimensional*
"frame-space." In order to construct the frame space you attach the
space of all orthonormal frames, which is a three dimensional manifold,
to every point of space. I assume that the frames of a frame field change
continuously from one place to the other. As always there is nothing like
an example; thus I introduce the *spherical frame field* here, an example
that will be of use later on too.

I will illustrate this special frame field in much greater detail than is
usual even in introductory texts in order to let you get some intuitive
grasp of what's going on behind the scenes of the formalism, even at the
risk of boring you stiff. I wouldn't do this to you if I didn't think it was
good for you. From my own experience I know that new concepts are
most easily assimilated through specific examples.

A "frame" is given by a point $\mathcal{P}$ of frame space and a rotation A, such
that if you rotate the basis by A and then translate it to $\mathcal{P}$ you obtain
the local coordinate system. The rotation A determines the "attitude"
of the frame, and I will refer to it as the "attitude transformation." If
the attitude transformation is the *identity* you obtain the simplest frame
field in which all frames are merely shifted replicas of each other (fig. 59).
This is the "standard frame field" that you typically use as the "default"
option.

At this point I will attempt to clarify things through an extensive
example, worked out in all its gory detail—so be prepared! You should
not skip the example, however. I will use it to introduce some very
important concepts.

A spherical frame field can be picked in such a way that one vector
of the frame (call it $\vec{f}_\varrho$) always points away from the origin. I will pick
another unit vector ($\vec{f}_\varphi$) that is parallel to the x-y plane and orthogonal
to $\vec{f}_\varrho$. You will see in a moment which of the two directions to choose.
Then the third frame vector ($\vec{f}_\vartheta$) is completely determined because you
have $\vec{f}_\vartheta = -\vec{f}_\varrho \times \vec{f}_\varphi$ (fig. 60). I have chosen these vectors in the direction
of the gradients of the spherical coordinates $(\varrho, \varphi, \vartheta)$; the distance to the

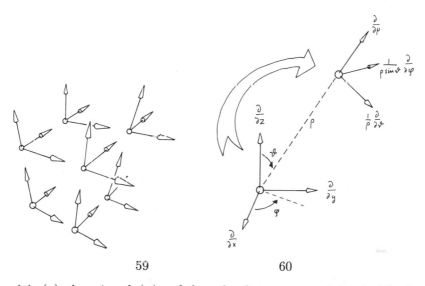

59   60

origin (ϱ), the azimuth (φ) and the polar distance, or co-latitude (ϑ). On the unit sphere ($\varrho = 1$) these coordinates become the usual geographic ones, thus φ denotes the longitude, whereas ϑ denotes ninety degrees minus the latitude which is often known as the "co-latitude." Thus $\vec{f_\varrho}$ points in the vertical direction for each inhabitant of this globe, $\vec{f_\varphi}$ points eastwards, and $\vec{f_\vartheta}$ points towards the south.

Although this type of frame field is obviously of great convenience to any inhabitant of the unit sphere, that is, the surface $\varrho = 1$, it easily confuses the outsider with a "global view" because the local frames are *different* for inhabitants of different places on the globe. The frame of the $\vec{f}$'s may be obtained by first rotating the basic frame (the vectors $\vec{e}$, say) about the vertical over an angle φ, then about $\vec{f_\varphi}$ over an angle ϑ. This specifies the attitude transformation. You can write it symbolically as the application of an attitude matrix A on the frames $\mathbf{f} = (\vec{f_\varrho}, \vec{f_\vartheta}, \vec{f_\varphi})$, $\mathbf{e} = (\vec{e_x}, \vec{e_y}, \vec{e_z})$:

$$\mathbf{f} = A\mathbf{e},$$

not a very exciting, but nevertheless, a very important equation.

In terms of the usual Cartesian coordinates, the spherical coordinate functions are the following. Figure 61 gives an impression of the ϑ, φ

dependence on direction.

$$\begin{aligned}
\varrho(x,y,z) &= \sqrt{x^2+y^2+z^2} \\
\vartheta(x,y,z) &= \arctan\frac{\sqrt{x^2+y^2}}{z} \\
\varphi(x,y,z) &= \arctan\frac{y}{x}.
\end{aligned}$$

Conversely you have

$$\begin{aligned}
x(\varrho,\vartheta,\varphi) &= \cos\varphi\sin\vartheta \\
y(\varrho,\vartheta,\varphi) &= \sin\varphi\sin\vartheta \\
z(\varrho,\vartheta,\varphi) &= \cos\vartheta.
\end{aligned}$$

Using conventional differential calculus you may find the one-forms of the spherical coordinate basis. The differentiation is a rather dull mechanical exercise, but I will get at the geometrical meaning of it soon enough. The coordinate one-forms are as follows (figs. 62 to 64):

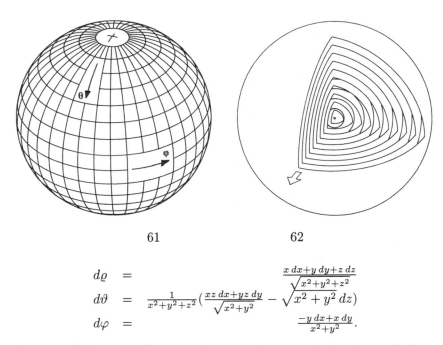

61   62

$$\begin{aligned}
d\varrho &= \frac{x\,dx+y\,dy+z\,dz}{\sqrt{x^2+y^2+z^2}} \\
d\vartheta &= \frac{1}{x^2+y^2+z^2}\left(\frac{xz\,dx+yz\,dy}{\sqrt{x^2+y^2}} - \sqrt{x^2+y^2}\,dz\right) \\
d\varphi &= \frac{-y\,dx+x\,dy}{x^2+y^2}.
\end{aligned}$$

As you will be painfully aware by now, the example is not exactly fun. I am by no means done yet, however.

Consider the geometrical meaning of these one-forms:

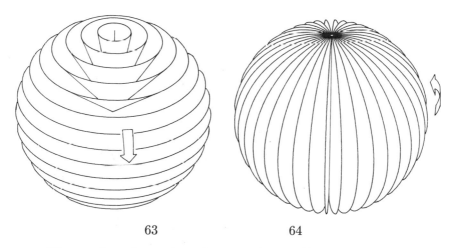

63   64

- The one-form $d\varrho$ consists of concentric, equidistant spherical shells.

- The surfaces of $d\vartheta$ are concentric cones.

- The surfaces of $d\varphi$ are a sheaf of concurrent planes, sharing the z-axis.

For $d\varrho$ the origin is a bad place, whereas for the other one-forms the z-axis is singular.

The basis one-forms can be used to construct a basis for two-forms ($d\vartheta \wedge d\varphi$, $d\varphi \wedge d\varrho$, and $d\varrho \wedge d\vartheta$) (figs. 65 to 67). Here you have a first nontrivial example of one-form level surfaces and two-form tube bundles. The two-form $d\vartheta \wedge d\varphi$ describes a geometry that is reminiscent of the electrostatic field of a monopole. The tubes replace the classical "lines of force" of the elementary physics courses, they radiate outwards from the origin in all directions. The strength of the field is not isotropic, however. You will see how to amend this situation in a moment. The tubes of $d\varphi \wedge d\varrho$ are horseshoe-shaped, with the ends of the horseshoe on the z-axis. The tubes of $d\varrho \wedge d\vartheta$ are closed rings that encircle the z-axis. For the two-forms the z-axis is a bad place, because the forms collapse there. It is not the space itself that is so bad, it is only the coordinate system that is to blame.

The three-form $d\varrho \wedge d\vartheta \wedge d\varphi$ (fig. 68) parcels space into roughly rectangular boxes. Again, the z-axis is not the place to be.

Of course the covectors really reside in the local tangent spaces. Figures 69 to 71 give an impression of the one-form fields, and figure 72 of

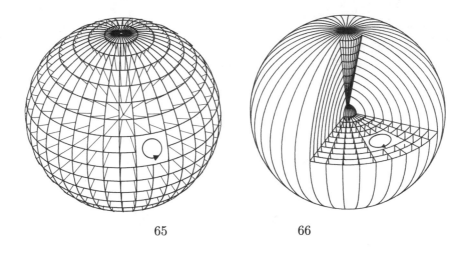

65   66

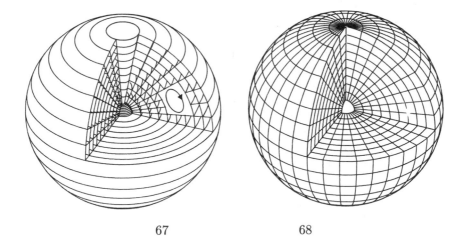

67   68

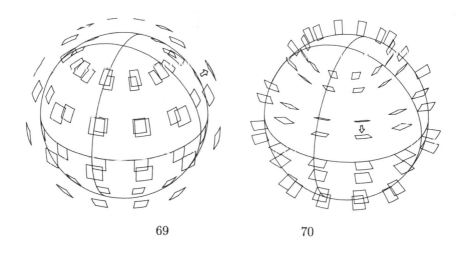

69   70

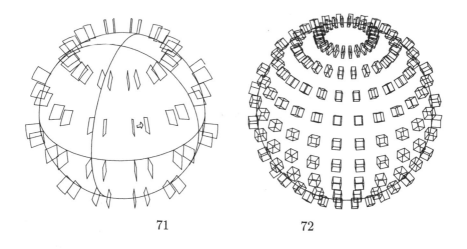

71   72

the basis three-form field. This kind of picture is about the best you
can do when you want to picture "a section of the cotangent bundle" in
your head.

When you take the duals you obtain the basis vectors of the coordinate
basis. They are $\vec{\partial}_\varrho$, $\vec{\partial}_\vartheta$ and $\vec{\partial}_\varphi$ and have the same coefficients as the one-
forms. The coordinate basis is obviously not orthonormal, although
you can easily confirm that it is orthogonal. (Yes, for once I picked
an overly symmetric example.) Figures 73 to 75 yield an impression of

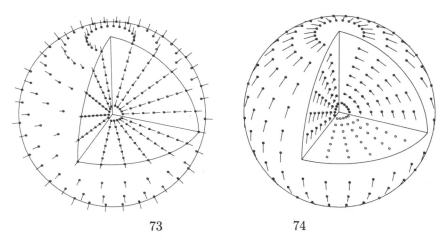

| 73 | 74 |

what the coordinate basis vector fields look like. The vectors $\vec{\partial}_\varrho$ radiate
outwards from the origin in all directions. They are in fact unit vectors.
The vectors $\vec{\partial}_\vartheta$ grow in size as you move out from the origin. They
are tangent to spheres concentric with the origin and point stubbornly
south. The vectors $\vec{\partial}_\varphi$ are also tangent to spheres concentric with the
origin, but they always point eastwards. They dwindle in size toward the
poles and toward the origin. Note that the basis vectors always contract
to unity or zero on the basis one-forms, as should be. Figures 73 to 75
probably come close to the intuitive picture the practical physicist has
from a vector field.

Notice that the coordinate basis is not a *frame*, for although mutually
orthogonal, the basis vectors are not unit vectors. Only after *normalization* of the coordinate basis do you obtain the *standard spherical frame*

field:

$$\vec{f_\varrho} = \frac{x\vec{\partial}_x + y\vec{\partial}_y + z\vec{\partial}_z}{\sqrt{x^2 + y^2 + z^2}}$$
$$= \cos\varphi \sin\vartheta \, \vec{\partial}_x + \sin\varphi \sin\vartheta \, \vec{\partial}_y + \cos\vartheta \, \vec{\partial}_z$$

$$\vec{f_\vartheta} = \frac{1}{\sqrt{x^2 + y^2 + z^2}} \left(\frac{xz\vec{\partial}_x + yz\vec{\partial}_y}{\sqrt{x^2 + y^2}} - \sqrt{x^2 + y^2}\vec{\partial}_z \right)$$
$$= \cos\varphi \cos\vartheta \, \vec{\partial}_x + \sin\varphi \cos\vartheta \, \vec{\partial}_y - \sin\vartheta \, \vec{\partial}_z$$

$$\vec{f_\varphi} = \frac{x\vec{\partial}_y - y\vec{\partial}_x}{\sqrt{x^2 + y^2}}$$
$$= -\sin\varphi \, \vec{\partial}_x + \cos\varphi \, \vec{\partial}_y.$$

This "anholonomic basis" is in practice often the most intuitively clear choice. It is certainly very practical, although you may be biased a bit since you use it daily to get about on our globe.

The unit trivector now has the same volume everywhere; thus the structure of the field is easily appreciated (fig. 76). Because you have to

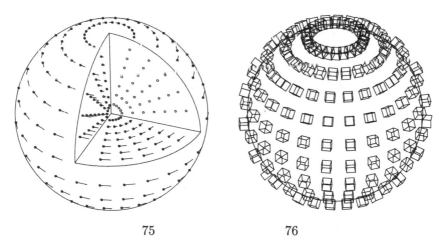

75   76

abstract from the precise shape of the crates, you will appreciate that this field is not different from $\vec{\partial}_x \wedge \vec{\partial}_y \wedge \vec{\partial}_z$, although it certainly *looks* different. You should adjust your mental spectacles such that this false impression vanishes.

The duals of the frame vectors are simply:

$$\begin{aligned}
\tilde{\sigma}^{\varrho} &= & d\varrho \\
\tilde{\sigma}^{\vartheta} &= & \varrho d\vartheta \\
\tilde{\sigma}^{\varphi} &= & \varrho \sin\vartheta d\varphi.
\end{aligned}$$

These expressions are well known from elementary calculus classes as the "infinitesimal displacements" for the spherical coordinate system. In fact this old-fashioned hat trick is the quickest way to get at the frame covectors in the first place. I could have skipped most of the math if I had behaved as a hard-nosed physicist right from the start.

As I argued earlier, the brackets for the coordinate basis must all vanish, whereas they don't necessarily do so for the frame vector fields. You may want to check for yourself that the only nonvanishing brackets are

$$\begin{aligned}
[\vec{f}_{\varrho}, \vec{f}_{\vartheta}] &= & -\tfrac{1}{\varrho}\vec{f}_{\vartheta} \\
[\vec{f}_{\varrho}, \vec{f}_{\varphi}] &= & -\tfrac{1}{\varrho}\vec{f}_{\varphi} \\
[\vec{f}_{\vartheta}, \vec{f}_{\varphi}] &= & -\tfrac{\cot\vartheta}{\varrho}\vec{f}_{\varphi}.
\end{aligned}$$

People say that the coordinate basis is *holonomic*, whereas the frame field is *anholonomic*.

From the expressions of the frame vectors you see that they are obtained from the standard Cartesian frame field through a rotation, as should indeed be the case. In fact, the rotation is just what I earlier called the attitude transformation. You can immediately read off the coefficients of the matrix that describes the attitude transformation from the expressions of the frame vectors. The explicit expression of the attitude matrix is (sorry about this!):

$$A(x,y,z) = \begin{pmatrix} \frac{x}{\sqrt{x^2+y^2+z^2}} & \frac{xz}{\sqrt{(x^2+y^2)(x^2+y^2+z^2)}} & \frac{-y}{\sqrt{x^2+y^2}} \\ \frac{y}{\sqrt{x^2+y^2+z^2}} & \frac{yz}{\sqrt{(x^2+y^2)(x^2+y^2+z^2)}} & \frac{x}{\sqrt{x^2+y^2}} \\ \frac{z}{\sqrt{x^2+y^2+z^2}} & \frac{-\sqrt{x^2+y^2}}{\sqrt{x^2+y^2+z^2}} & 0 \end{pmatrix},$$

or, when expressed in terms of the angles:

$$A = \begin{pmatrix} \sin\vartheta \cos\varphi & \cos\vartheta \cos\varphi & -\sin\varphi \\ \sin\vartheta \sin\varphi & \cos\vartheta \sin\varphi & \cos\varphi \\ \cos\vartheta & -\sin\vartheta & 0 \end{pmatrix}.$$

The matrix A depends on the position of the frame, of course. Figures 77 to 79 give an impression of the spherical frame field. The action of the

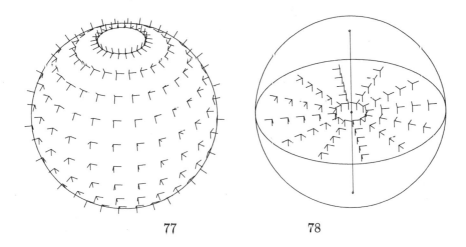

77   78

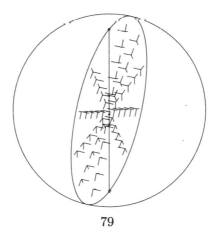

79

attitude transformation is to rotate the frame from place to place.

When you change the position, the matrix A changes: when you move from $\mathcal{P}$ to $\mathcal{P} + d\mathcal{P}$, the matrix changes from A to $A + dA$. The change of the frame vectors is thus $d\mathbf{f} = dA\mathbf{e}$ as expressed in the basic system $\mathbf{e}$.

The extremely useful insight of Élie Cartan was that

Flash of Genius: *it is most rewarding to express this change in terms of the local frame itself.*

You have obviously $\mathbf{e} = A^{-1}\mathbf{f}$, thus the change of the frame expressed in terms of the frame itself is $d\mathbf{f} = dA.A^{-1}\mathbf{f} = C\mathbf{f}$. I will call C the "Cartan transformation" or Cartan matrix. Because of the special form of the matrix A, the matrix of $C = dA.A^{-1}$ is skew-symmetric. You may want to prove this!

You may think of the Cartan matrix as representing *the "infinitesimal rotation" of the frame when you shift the point of application* a bit. Considered in this way, the skew-symmetry is almost self-evident. The three independent coefficients of the matrix can be interpreted as the coefficients of a vector of infinitesimal rotation if you like.

These relations are basic. Thus you could do worse than to commit the following relations to memory:

$$\begin{aligned} d\mathbf{f} &= C\mathbf{f} \\ C &= dA.A^{-1} \\ C + {}^tC &= 0. \end{aligned}$$

They are basic for all the differential geometry you're ever likely to do!

For the spherical frame field you calculate—sigh!—that

$$C = dA.A^{-1} = \begin{pmatrix} 0 & d\vartheta & \sin\vartheta\, d\varphi \\ -d\vartheta & 0 & \cos\vartheta\, d\varphi \\ -\sin\vartheta\, d\varphi & -\cos\vartheta\, d\varphi & 0 \end{pmatrix},$$

which is indeed a skew-symmetric matrix of one-forms. Like the attitude matrix, the Cartan matrix has a structure that you can actually *understand*, in the sense that you can easily figure out the coefficients through some doodling in the margin. It's worth your while to do this. For instance, take the frame vector in the radial direction. What happens to it when you move out from the origin? Clearly nothing; thus $d\varrho$ shouldn't appear in the Cartan matrix. What happens when you do a step $\Delta\vartheta$ "to the south"? Clearly the radial frame vector also turns to the south: this explains the coefficient C_{12}. What happens when you do a step $\Delta\varphi$ "to the east"? The radial frame vector also turns to the east, but the amount of turn depends on the latitude: clearly it vanishes at the poles. The coefficient C_{13} accounts for this quantitatively. In such a manner you can make sure that you obtain a solid gut feeling for all the coefficients, and eventually for the Cartan transformation itself.

I will denote the independent components of the Cartan matrix by $\tilde{\omega}^{ij}$. Clearly $\tilde{\omega}^{ij} = -\tilde{\omega}^{ji}$, and so forth.

Those one-forms are called the *connection forms* of the frame field. Their geometrical meaning becomes apparent when you rewrite them in terms of covariant derivatives:

$$\tilde{\omega}^{ij}\langle \vec{v} \rangle = \nabla_{\vec{v}}\,\vec{f_i} \cdot \vec{f_j} = \tilde{\sigma}^j\langle \nabla_{\vec{v}}\,\vec{f_i}\rangle.$$

Thus,

NEVER FORGET: $\tilde{\omega}^{ij}\langle \vec{v}\rangle$ *is the initial rate of turn of the frame vector $\vec{f_i}$ toward the frame vector $\vec{f_j}$ when the point of application moves in the direction of the frame vector $\vec{v}$.*

For example, the contracted form $\tilde{\omega}^{\varrho\varphi}\langle \vec{f_\vartheta}\rangle$ yields the initial rate of turn of the vertical toward the east when you move toward the south. This amount obviously vanishes for the example.

The connection one-forms are basic for the description of the twisting and turning of the frame, and it is of paramount importance that you know what they are about and that you intuitively see the effect of the connection forms before your mind's eye.

It is perhaps best to try to remember (or "feel") the effect of the components $\tilde{\omega}^{ij}\langle \vec{f_k}\rangle$. Remember that $\tilde{\omega}^{ij}$ is antisymmetric in i, j; thus $i \neq j$ or else the component vanishes. Moreover, swapping i and j merely reverses the sign. Thus you only have to memorize three components. Then you had best distinguish between the case that k equals i or j or that i, j and k are all different. Figure 80 illustrates the basics: all the combinations have been "drawn," although only the turn $\tilde{\omega}^{23}\langle\vec{f_2}\rangle$ has been implicitly indicated with symbols. Figure 81 illustrates this latter turn more graphically. It is a kind of "climb" in the $\vec{f_2}$-direction.

When i, j and k are all different, then the component $\tilde{\omega}^{ij}\langle \vec{f_k}\rangle$ describes a *spin* of the frame about the direction of movement when you move in the $\vec{f_k}$ direction. It helps the imagination to think of the movements of some vehicle, for instance a simplified toy aircraft. The case that k equals i or j describes a *left or right turn* or else a *nose dive or a climb*.

In the classical literature these components of the movement of the frame are known as the "Christoffel symbols." You have encountered

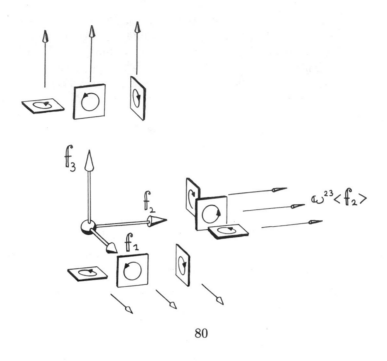

80

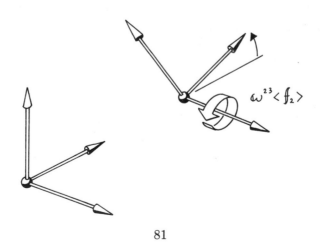

81

these before as algebraic entities, but now you may appreciate their full geometric significance. They capture the turning and twisting of the frame for any possible movement through space in the most vivid manner. It is essential that you get a solid intuitive (pictorial) grasp of these animals.

The Christoffel symbols quietly sit at a point, ready to do their thing when you need them. They don't really belong to the tangent space at that point, however. They are "local" rather than "punctal" entities. Once you have gotten hold of them, you can easily calculate the covariant derivatives of arbitrary vector or covector fields. In fact you have:

$$\nabla_{\vec{v}} \vec{W} = \sum_j \left(\vec{v}\,[W^j] + \sum_i W^i \tilde{\omega}^{ij} \langle \vec{v} \rangle \right) \vec{f}_j.$$

In this formula the W^i denote the coefficients of W in terms of the frame, that is $\vec{W} = W^i \vec{f}_i$. The connection coefficients appear as a "correction" on the mere differentiation of the components. The correction is—of course—necessary because of the turning and twisting of the frame from place to place. The correction only vanishes in the case of the default (uniform, Cartesian) frame field.

A typical correction term is $W^i \tilde{\omega}^{ij} \langle \vec{v} \rangle \vec{f}_j$. Consider what this contribution represents:

It is the contribution due to the turning of the the i-th frame vector into the direction of the j-th frame vector when you move from the tail to the tip of the vector $\vec{v}$. This contribution is merely the component of the vector $\vec{W}$ in the direction of the i-th frame vector multiplied by its rate of turn.

If you remember this geometrical picture you should be able to reproduce the formalism without really having to memorize "where all the indices go." I myself have never managed to memorize the index formulas, but I always somehow manage to mix things up. You may be better at this task. But if you're not there is no need to despair, because once you get the picture you should always be able to construct the right expressions from scratch.

The equivalent expression for the covectors is

$$d\tilde{\varphi} = \sum_j \left(d\varphi_j + \sum_i \varphi_i \tilde{\omega}^{ij} \right) \wedge \tilde{\sigma}^j.$$

In this expression the φ_i are coefficients of a one-form $\tilde{\varphi}$ in terms of the frame, such as for instance $\tilde{\varphi} = \varphi_i \tilde{\sigma}^i$. Again the connection forms appear in correction terms. A typical correction term is $\varphi_i \tilde{\omega}^{ij} \wedge \tilde{\sigma}^j$. This term involves the rate of turn of the i-th to the j-th frame vector for a progression in an unspecified direction.

In order to bring out the fundamental significance of the connection forms I will write symbolically

$$\mathbf{f} = (\vec{f}_\varrho, \vec{f}_\vartheta, \vec{f}_\varphi)$$

and then you have:

$$\nabla \mathbf{f} = \begin{pmatrix} 0 & \tilde{\omega}^{\varrho\vartheta} & \tilde{\omega}^{\varrho\varphi} \\ -\tilde{\omega}^{\varrho\vartheta} & 0 & \tilde{\omega}^{\vartheta\varphi} \\ -\tilde{\omega}^{\varrho\varphi} & -\tilde{\omega}^{\vartheta\varphi} & 0 \end{pmatrix} \mathbf{f},$$

or, even more concisely, and what is certainly easy enough to commit to memory:

$$\nabla \mathbf{f} = C\mathbf{f}.$$

People refer to the equations (i roams from 1 to 3)

$$\nabla_{\vec{v}} \vec{f}_i = \sum_j \tilde{\omega}^{ij} \langle \vec{v} \rangle \vec{f}_j,$$

or just $\nabla \mathbf{f} = C\mathbf{f}$ as *the connection equations of the frame field*. They are of basic importance if you move over the surface of our globe, for instance as a jet pilot, and want to keep track of your heading. I'm not trying to tire you with some mathematical hair-splitting exercise here: this is indeed very practical stuff, used on a daily basis by practical, hard-working people.

Any one-form may be expressed in terms of the duals of the frame vectors. You may symbolically write

$$\underline{\tilde{\sigma}} = (\tilde{\sigma}^\varrho, \tilde{\sigma}^\vartheta, \tilde{\sigma}^\varphi).$$

For the simple case of the differentials of the coordinates $d\mathcal{P} = (dx, dy, dz)$ you may then write a simple symbolic expression. People speak of $d\mathcal{P}$ as the "differential of a point," which has the merit that it certainly sounds good even if it doesn't mean very much. You have:

$$d\mathcal{P} = \underline{\tilde{\sigma}} \langle \mathbf{f} \rangle.$$

So far so good! I have now arrived at a complete description of the frame field, expressed by the (Cartan) "connection equations." These are the following:

First, you have the expression

$$dP = \underset{\sim}{\tilde{\sigma}} \langle \mathbf{f} \rangle,$$

which describes the "differential of a point" in terms of the frame;

Second, there is the relation

$$\nabla \mathbf{f} = C\mathbf{f},$$

which describes the change of attitude of the frame expressed in terms of the "moving frame" itself;

Third, you have the condition for the Cartan matrix

$$C + {}^{t}C = 0,$$

which describes the skew-symmetry of $dA.A^{-1}$, or, in more geometrical language, the Cartan matrix is an infinitesimal rotation.

These equations are so *basic* but (happy to say!) also so geometrically graspable that you should have no problem committing them to memory.

These equations are a marvelous tool in both practical applications and in intuitive exploration. Their geometrical content is evident, and it is worth your time to ponder these relations until you have fully absorbed them into your mental system. They should be so thoroughly familiar that they appear to you as self-evident truths. It is fair to say that there exists virtually *nothing* of any interest that you could do in differential geometry that does not involve these basic relations somehow.

I am happy to say this also concludes the somewhat longwinded example of the spherical framefield. Many of the notions that were introduced on the side have a very general range of applicability though. They are absolutely essential tools in the study of shape.

3.5.2.1 Good old "Infinitesimal Displacements"

♠ Intermezzo—Supplementary material.
Caution: This material may be shocking to decent people.

In the old-fashioned way taught in introductory physics classes you compute the length of an "infinitesimal displacement":

$$\begin{aligned}
dl^2 &= \\
&\|((\varrho + d\varrho)\sin(\vartheta + d\vartheta)\cos(\varphi + d\varphi)\vec{e}_x + \ldots) \\
&-(\varrho\sin\vartheta\cos\varphi\vec{e}_x + \ldots)\|^2 = \\
&d\varrho^2 + (\varrho d\vartheta)^2 + (\varrho\sin\vartheta d\varphi)^2.
\end{aligned}$$

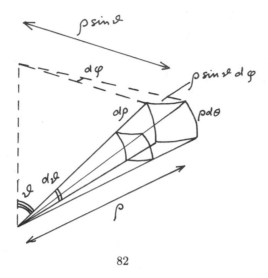

82

It is even more convenient to get this directly from the geometrical interpretation of a sloppy "back of the envelope" drawing showing "infinitesimals" (fig. 82).

From the expression for the squared length of the infinitesimal displacement, you most conveniently obtain the one-forms $\tilde{\sigma}$, which are the duals of the frame vectors:

$$
\begin{aligned}
\tilde{\sigma}^\varrho &= & d\varrho \\
\tilde{\sigma}^\vartheta &= & \varrho d\vartheta \\
\tilde{\sigma}^\varphi &= & \varrho\sin\vartheta d\varphi.
\end{aligned}
$$

This simple trick accomplishes what was done over the previous fifteen or so pages.

This perhaps gives some intuitive content to the interpretation of $\underline{\tilde{\sigma}}$ as the "differential" of a point" $d\mathcal{P}$. Indeed, it is the only sense I can make of it.

Thus, in retrospect, we have been taught some useful insights as young physics students. You can stop becoming red in the face and just pretend you don't understand why other people do *not* immediately guess at the correct form of $\underline{\tilde{\sigma}}$ and instead perform all those silly calculations! It is by far the quickest way to arrive at the expressions you need in the first place. Just don't tell your mathematical friends.

3.5.3   The integrability conditions

You have already seen that forms vanish when you apply the exterior derivative more than once ($d^2 = 0$). This expresses a fundamental property of space that may also be expressed in terms of the equality of mixed partial derivatives. Applied to the structure equations you have the conditions $d^2\mathcal{P} = 0$ and $d^2\mathbf{f} = 0$.

The first condition is sometimes plastically expressed as, "the second differential of a point vanishes."[24]. Geometrically it is nothing but the dual of the connection equations.

The second condition essentially expresses the fact that infinitesimal rotations commute in Euclidean space. (It expresses the fact that *Euclidean space is flat.*)

By algebraic manipulation you find that the conditions are equivalent to:

$$d\underline{\tilde{\sigma}} = C\underline{\tilde{\sigma}} \quad,$$

or—in more conventional notation

$$d\tilde{\sigma}^i = \sum_j \tilde{\omega}^{ij} \wedge \tilde{\sigma}^j$$

and

$$dC = C^2,$$

which—in the more conventional notation—can also be written

$$d\tilde{\omega}^{ij} = \sum_k \tilde{\omega}^{ik} \wedge \tilde{\omega}^{kj}.$$

These equations are often referred to as "the first and second structural equations."

You may find it instructive to check these structural equations for the spherical frame field.

Most of your applications of differential geometry will involve the use of the structural equations; thus it makes sense to memorize them. This shouldn't be much of a problem if you remember the abbreviated notation.

In a way, Cartan's "method of moving frames" is so powerful that these equations express all that is known about differential geometry. Of course, this will remain a rather vacuous remark until you get used to the techniques that are employed to get the information out. All further explorations in this book will be applications of these equations, attempting to extract as much geometry as possible by exploiting them and to provide you with some gut feeling.

---

[24]You can remove the magic by looking at an example: for the spherical coordinate system you have $d\mathcal{P} = \vec{e}_\varrho \, d\varrho + \vec{e}_\vartheta \, \varrho \, d\vartheta + \vec{e}_\varphi \, \varrho \sin \vartheta \, d\varphi$. Compute $d(d\mathcal{P})$ in the usual way and collect terms. You will be able to interpret the algebraic fact that the coefficients of $d\varrho \wedge d\vartheta$, *etc.* vanish identically in an obvious geometrical fashion

Important milestone: *If you got this far and understand it all on the*
gut level, then nothing will prevent you from going all the way! The
remainder of the book is largely an application of what you picked
up so far. You will repeatedly have to use these tools. If you are
hesitant, your best bet is to backtrack now.

3.5.4   Computer Implementation

Cartan's method of moving frames is admirably suited to computer implementation. You easily fit the frame fields to the problem at hand, and
a knowledge of the frame field lets you readily compute the geometry.

In some applications you may have an explicit algorithm for the frame
field, that is a **PROCEDURE** that takes a position and pops out the
attitude matrix **ATTITUDE**(P:VECTOR). Even better, you make
a **PROCEDURE** of the attitude transformation itself: you feed it a
position and it spews out the frame.

If you have an analytic expression for the attitude transformation, you
calculate the forms and Cartan matrix beforehand and write suitable
PROCEDUREs for them; otherwise you use differences to arrive at
these entities.

If you have explicit *data*, such as a set of points on a surface, you have
to fit a frame field to the data. For instance you could estimate local
tangent planes and take the frame vector $\vec{f}_3$ to be orthogonal to them,
and so forth. This is the most common case you are likely to meet with.
I will give specific details on how to handle this kind of problem later
on. In order to deal with it intelligently you have to know how to fit the
frames more snugly to the shape at hand.

The forms of virtue are erect, the forms of pleasure undulate:
Minerva's drapery descends in long uninterrupted lines; a thousand
amorous curves embrace the limbs of Flora.
—HENRI FUSELI (1741–1825), *Aphorisms on Art (item 194)*

4 Curved Submanifolds

The artist may admire in the outlines of this body the perceptual flowing of one form into another, and the undulating lines which rise and roll like waves, and become swallowed up in one another. He will find that no copyist can be sure of correctness, since the undulating movement which he thinks he is following turns imperceptibly away and leads both the hand and the eye away by taking another direction.
—JOHANN JOACHIM WINCKELMANN (1717–1768), *on the Belvedere Torso*

4.1 General considerations

In this book I only discuss the shape of "blobs," or portions of Euclidean space which are operationally defined in a physical way.[1]

One important aspect of "shape" is the curvature of the boundaries of the blobs, or of curves running over these boundaries. You will appreciate that several curves have interesting properties for practical purposes; for the moment the boundary of an attached shadow due to a point source of light may serve as an example. This is the reason why curved submanifolds, that is, curves and surfaces in Euclidean space, are of interest in the first place.

This viewpoint is totally different from that of the mathematician and thoroughly restricts the domain of interest. For instance, the main interest of mathematicians in the study of curved manifolds tends to be the *intrinsic geometry* of the manifold, that is, what can be known of the manifold if you do geodesy strictly *within* the surface. This is a subject that will hardly attract you, your main motivation probably coming from an interest in the *extrinsic geometry*—namely how you may interact with blobs from the outside.

Similarly, I am not too concerned about the *definition* of the very notion of "curved submanifold"; you are not going to meet Möbius bands or cross-caps anyway, since they don't occur as boundaries of blobs.

Likewise you have few problems with intricate structures of an arbitrarily small scale. Since you use operationally defined blobs, the resolution is finite and the problems lurking in the infinitesimal domain are blurred away.

---

[1]**blob**, *n.* [Prov.Eng., from Scot. *bleb*, *bleib*, *blab*, a bubble] (**1**) a drop or lump of something viscid or thick; a bubble; a blister.
In this book a "blob" always means a region $\{\vec{x} \mid f(\vec{x}) > a\}$ defined with respect to some physically determined density or scalar field f and some fiducial level a.

Similar observations apply to the very large dimensions. "Infinities" simply don't apply to the physically relevant situations. In short, you may assume a thoroughly Procrustean attitude:

1st convenience: *Real-life tolerances make everything smooth.*

2nd convenience: *All shapes will fit into my laboratory.*

Thus all surfaces are *locally flat*, all curves locally *straight*. Sometimes you tolerate exceptions, for instance when you use "models" to approximate blobs such as polyhedra or cones. Then you have to deal with *edges* and *vertices* that are—by choice—*not* locally flat, although the surfaces that they model *are*. I then use continuity arguments to deal with these singularities. For instance, I consider an edge as the limiting case of a "rounded-off edge" with locally very high curvature.

Mainly because of my stress on *extrinsic* properties and a certain neglect of "interesting special cases"—most of them mathematical monsters that you won't meet in practice—this text has a decidedly different flavor as compared to the usual treatments. I use the generic viewpoint throughout, being only interested in what really might exist. This means that most of the "nice" (classroom variety) examples will be of little interest.

For instance, I am only interested in those properties of the sphere that it holds in common with a large class of ovoids. If the sphere happens to illustrate a general property well, I don't hesitate to use it as an example: thus the sphere lies on one side of each of its support planes as any old ovoid does. But otherwise I will not use it. Thus the centro-surface of the sphere is of no interest here because it is thoroughly degenerate and would "explode" on the slightest change of shape. The triaxial ellipsoid would make a much better example in this respect, at least as long as you don't consider its affine properties, and so on.

4.2   Codimension

A *normal vector* is a vector that is orthogonal to the tangent space at a point of a curved manifold. As such it is the ultimate "extrinsic" geometrical object. Normal to the tangent space is as extrinsic as you will ever be able to get. The dimension of normal vector space is three (that is, the dimension of space) minus the dimension of tangent space.

Thus a *surface* has a one-dimensional normal space, or "codimension one," whereas a *curve* has codimension two.[2] Intuitively this means that a curve has a greater "freedom" than a surface, and is less constrained through the nature of the space it lives in.

Figure 83 depicts the sphere with a tangent space and a frame of which

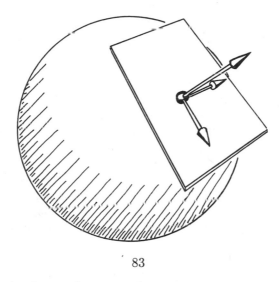

83

one frame vector is a surface normal.

Surfaces are *boundaries of volumes*; thus the two possible directions that a normal vector may have are *not equivalent*. People speak of the "inner normal" if the normal vector points into the "material" of the blob like the arrows in General Custer's hat, and of an "outer normal" if it sticks out like the spines of a porcupine. Thus the normal in figure 83 is an *outer normal* for the ball.

Surfaces that are boundaries of volumes are *orientable*. This means that you may pick smooth, nowhere vanishing normal vector fields that are purely of either the inner or the outer type. It doesn't matter in the least which convention you use for the surface orientation as long as you don't mix things up. In drawings I usually prefer the porcupine variety, simply because it looks better, whereas I have found that in most applications you can minimize the number of minus signs in your formulas if you stick to the General Custer's hat convention.

Note the difference with *curves* in this respect:

---

[2]Notice that the notion of the "codimension" of a submanifold is actually more important than its dimension here.

Note: *there is no conceivable way to assign "inner" or "outer" normals to a space curve.*

This is important because it means that you can't assign a unique sign to the curvature of space curves, whereas you can do so for surfaces. For them the curvature is either "with" or "against" the normal direction.

For some reason or other this tends to confuse people no end. You will see later that the curvature doesn't vanish anywhere for a generic space curve, and that you may as well consider it to be positive everywhere. Yet ordinary people continue to speak of "inflexion points" of space curves over and over again as though it made sense.[3]

The confusion probably arises because of everyone's familiarity with *planar curves*. Planar curves have codimension one, just like surfaces in three-space have, and thus possess well-defined inner and outer normal directions. Then the sign of the curvature makes sense, and so do inflexions. This is why the concept of codimension is essential. If space curves are *on a surface*, then the codimension *with respect to the surface* is again *one* and there is a sense in which you may speak of the sign of the curve's curvature. But then you mean something else with curvature, namely *geodesic curvature*, an *intrinsic* concept to be discussed in detail later.

4.3   Curvature, extrinsic and intrinsic

For a space curve, *all* the curvature is *extrinsic*. There is simply no way to define curvature through local geodesy. Of course, you could find out that a curve is closed by traveling around it, but that is a *global* matter.

Surfaces are different in this respect because there exist aspects of the curvature that are *intrinsic* and aspects that are *extrinsic*. You can appreciate the difference when you consider a polyhedral model. Clearly the faces of a polyhedron are *flat*, both intrinsically and extrinsically. Intuitively any curvature must reside in the *edges* and *vertices*.

Consider an edge. At both sides of the edge you may consider the unit outward normals. What is the normal at the edge itself? If you consider the edge as the limiting case of a piece of a cylinder mantle that smoothly blends the faces, you come to appreciate that the edge carries a continuous family of normals at each of its points. This family smoothly interpolates between the normals on the faces. Thus the normal turns over the *dihedral angle* of the faces when you cross an edge (fig. 84).

---

[3]Mathematicians know better, of course.

This amounts to saying that there is an *extrinsic curvature* associated with an edge for which the dihedral angle is a measure.

There is no *intrinsic* curvature associated with an edge. You can understand this in the following way: if you consider the faces as "hinged" at the edges, then you may use the hinges to spread out the two faces that meet at the edge such that the dihedral angle vanishes. This doesn't

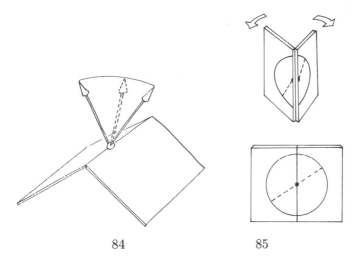

84   85

change the intrinsic geometry in any way; thus the edge (fig. 85) is intrinsically *flat*. The proverbial intelligent ant crawling on the surface would never notice the presence of the edge.

The vertices do have an *intrinsic* curvature, though. In general you cannot use the hinges to spread the faces that meet at a vertex in order to flatten it. The vertex can only be flattened if you *cut* the surface, for instance along an edge. Then the flattened surface will show a gap or an overlap.

This excess or deficit can also be detected intrinsically—for instance, by measuring the ratio of the circumference to the radius for a circle on the surface that has the vertex as center. The result will obviously be 2π minus the gap or plus the overlap.

For a vertex on a cube you find $\frac{3\pi}{2}$, for there is a gap of the amount $\frac{\pi}{2}$.

The interesting fact is that *you can detect the gap without any extrinsic operations*. You can define normals for a vertex as you did for the edge. They fill a solid cone that interpolates (fig. 86) between the normals

on the faces. The solid angle subtended by the cone equals the gap
("spherical deficit").

For the cube the cone fills one octant of a sphere, for instance, thus
the spherical deficit is $\frac{\pi}{2}$ again.

Consequently, there is an intrinsic curvature associated with a vertex
for which the spherical deficit (fig. 87) is a measure. The intelligent ant

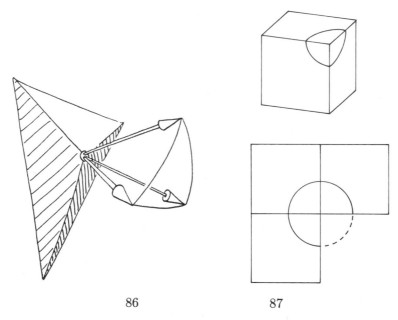

86   87

crawling over the surface could certainly find out about the presence of
the vertex: it would appear as a point singularity of locally concentrated
curvature.

Essentially the same situation holds for a smooth surface. There exist
two distinct and important notions of curvature: one *intrinsic*, the other
one *extrinsic*. They are known as the "Gaussian curvature" and the
"mean curvature," respectively. The Gaussian curvature is a measure
of the spherical spread of the surface normals. The mean curvature is
something very much like the average of dihedral angles. I will show
later how to define them precisely on a smooth surface. The average
is supposed to be calculated over all directions. I will get to precise
definitions later. Both the concept of the Gaussian and that of the
mean curvature will prove to be extremely important in the study of
shape.

4.4   The method of "Moving Frames"

The "method of moving frames" was already implicit in Frenet's treatment of the theory of curves. It was adapted to *surfaces* by Darboux (about 1880). Finally it was developed by Cartan to its full generality and power.

In order to apply Élie Cartan's powerful *method of moving frames* you have to fit a frame field to the curved submanifolds. For instance, *in the case of a curve* it makes obvious sense to let one vector of the frame be the unit tangent of the curve, whereas *in the case of a surface* it would make a lot of sense to let two-frame vectors define the tangent plane.

Then the turning and twisting of the frame acquires a direct geometrical content because it indicates how the submanifolds curve their way through space. You can often do better still by exploiting the local differential geometry.

In the case of a curve two "infinitesimally near" tangents in general define a plane, called the "osculating plane," and you may let two of our frame vectors define that plane. Then you have fitted a unique frame to the curve known as the "trieder of Frenet" and because the frame field is completely determined by the curve, *all* of the structure equations and integrability conditions must acquire a well-defined and intuitively obvious *geometrical content*.

Likewise, *in the case of a surface* you usually can fit the frame even tighter to the surface. Generically there exist two directions of extremal normal curvature on each point of a surface known as the "principal directions." Together with the unit normal they define a unique "principal frame" that is extremely convenient in practice.

By way of an example, you may think of a cone mantle. It makes obvious sense to let one of the two frame vectors that together span the tangent plane point along the local generator. Then you have fitted a principal frame to the cone mantle.

The methods discussed above only define the frame field on a piece of the submanifold *itself*, not on the surrounding space. However, this can easily be remedied. There always exists a region of space around the submanifold in which the different normal rays never meet. This is known as a "tubular neighborhood" of the surface or curve.[4] In a tubular neighborhood you can extend the frame field fitted to the manifold by translating it parallel to itself along the normal rays. All frames moved out over a distance ε are fitted frame fields for another submanifold

---

[4]The term "tubular neighborhood" is pictorially very apt for the case of curves.

known as the "parallel surface at distance ε." Parallel surfaces obviously have the same normals at corresponding points and parallel frames by construction (fig. 88).

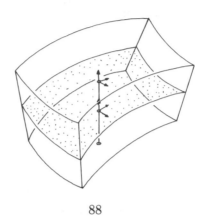

88

In most cases you don't need this extension of the fitted frame fields to tubular neighborhoods, however—namely when you restrict the discussion to the manifold itself. But the extended frame fields come in handy at times, especially if you are not quite sure where the surface is exactly located. Remember that the level sets have a certain layer of tolerance built into them.

When you have fitted a frame field the first thing to do is to find the attitude matrix and the Cartan matrix. Then you need the basic one-forms on the surface, the duals of the frame vectors. After that you are all set to start doing differential geometry.

The procedure is at least conceptually fairly simple. Take a sphere as an example. Then you have to consider the case of the *spherical coordinates*, again. Apparently, they are very suited to deal with spherical surfaces: the frame field is neatly adapted to them because $\vec{f}_\rho$ is the outward surface normal. The vectors $\vec{f}_\vartheta$, $\vec{f}_\varphi$ together span the tangent plane. If you only consider *tangent vectors*, they form a frame field for the surface.[5] They can be combined to form the unit bivector $\vec{f}_\vartheta \wedge \vec{f}_\varphi$, which is the bivector $\vec{\partial}_\vartheta \wedge \vec{\partial}_\varphi$ multiplied with the scalar field $1/\sin\vartheta$. Figures 89 and 90 show both $\vec{\partial}_\vartheta \wedge \vec{\partial}_\varphi$ and $\vec{f}_\vartheta \wedge \vec{f}_\varphi$. The duals of the

---

[5]This is an important point: at many places in the text, I will *restrict frame fields to the surface itself*. Sometimes you want the full 3-vector frames, sometimes just their restriction to the tangent spaces of the surface. Always try to make clear to

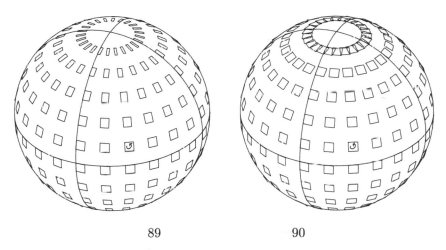

89   90

tangent vectors are $\tilde{\sigma}^\vartheta$ and $\tilde{\sigma}^\varphi$ (figs. 91 and 92). The form $\tilde{\sigma}^\rho$ doesn't exist if you consider only *geometrical objects in the tangent space.* The covectors can be combined to form the unit two-form $\tilde{\sigma}^\vartheta \wedge \tilde{\sigma}^\varphi$, which is the form $d\vartheta \wedge d\varphi$ multiplied by the scalar field $\sin\vartheta$. The unit two-form forms a mesh on the surface that allows you to find the areas of regions on the surface by counting the number of meshes they cover (fig. 93). Forms like the one-form $\tilde{\sigma}^\varphi$ have level lines that "don't mesh." Thus the forms associated with the frame vectors can only be properly drawn in the tangent planes (fig. 94 to 96). The gauge figure that allows you to dualize the vectors and covectors is, of course, just a unit circle in the tangent plane (fig. 97).

The connection forms gain a very special significance if you consider them in terms of the surface. The form $\tilde{\omega}^{\vartheta\varphi}$ describes a rotation of the tangent vectors about the normal in the tangent plane. *It leaves the tangent plane as a whole undisturbed.* Intuitively it seems therefore to have little to do with extrinsic shape.

The forms $\tilde{\omega}^{\rho\vartheta}$, $\tilde{\omega}^{\varphi\rho}$ describe the change of the normal as you move over the surface. This is extrinsic shape *pur sang.* For the sphere this is extremely simple, for it is evident that if you travel a distance t in any direction along a great circle, the normal turns over tR^{-1} (R denotes the radius of the sphere) about the orthogonal direction. The only movement of the frame is a "nose dive." This is peculiar for the sphere though,

---

yourself what is meant in specific cases.

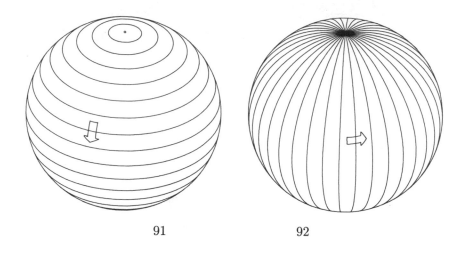

91   92

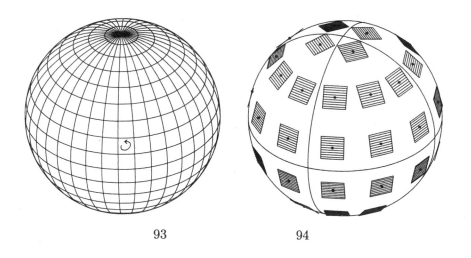

93   94

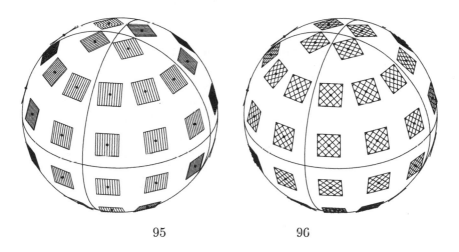

95 96

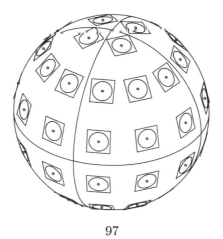

97

because for most surfaces there will also be some *twist*, that is to say, the frame will also spin about the direction of movement.

It will be apparent after this discussion that you will have to divide the connection and structural equations into two distinct groups, those that concern $\tilde{\omega}^{\vartheta\varphi}$ and those that concern the other connection forms.

These equations have been around for a long time in different forms under different names. They tend to look rather mysterious in the classical notations. In fact I have often wondered how people came to think of certain relations in the first place without a clear geometrical, that is visual, interpretation. In the modern notation, however, using the notion of Cartan's moving frames, you easily develop a solid gut feeling for their meaning.

If you label the coordinate directions 1,2 (in the tangent plane) and 3 (the normal direction), then the Cartan equations become:

First

$$d\tilde{\sigma}^1 = \tilde{\omega}^{12} \wedge \tilde{\sigma}^2$$
$$d\tilde{\sigma}^2 = \tilde{\omega}^{21} \wedge \tilde{\sigma}^1,$$

the so-called Gauss Connection Equations, or "First Structural Equations"

Second

$$\tilde{\omega}^{31} \wedge \tilde{\sigma}^1 + \tilde{\omega}^{32} \wedge \tilde{\sigma}^2 = 0,$$

known as the Symmetry Equation, or Weingarten's Equation

Third

$$d\tilde{\omega}^{12} = \tilde{\omega}^{13} \wedge \tilde{\omega}^{32},$$

The Gauss's Equation—another structural equation

And finally

$$d\tilde{\omega}^{13} = \tilde{\omega}^{12} \wedge \tilde{\omega}^{23}$$
$$d\tilde{\omega}^{23} = \tilde{\omega}^{21} \wedge \tilde{\omega}^{13},$$

the so-called Codazzi Equations, which are also structural equations.

In these forms the basic Cartan relations appear in surface theory.

For a *principal frame field* the equations simplify considerably because then you have, for instance, $\tilde{\omega}^{13} = \kappa_1 \tilde{\sigma}^1$ and so forth.[6] The symmetry equation is trivially satisfied. All equations assume a rather direct geometrical significance. I will consider this case in more detail in a later chapter. This case is important, because the principle frame field will be your prime choice in applications. Moreover, for this frame the equations assume such a simple and symmetrical form that they easily stick in your memory.

These equations contain about all of surface theory. They are usually rewritten using the "Gaussian curvature" K and the "mean curvature" H. These entities have simple and important geometrical meanings once you catch on, and will be considered in detail later on.

For the moment you may just accept the definition

$$K \tilde{\sigma}^1 \wedge \tilde{\sigma}^2 = \tilde{\omega}^{13} \wedge \tilde{\omega}^{23}$$

for the Gaussian curvature. Note that this concisely expresses the fact that K *measures the spherical spread of the normals for a unit area patch.*

The definition for the mean curvature is:

$$2H \tilde{\sigma}^1 \wedge \tilde{\sigma}^2 = \tilde{\omega}^{13} \wedge \tilde{\sigma}^2 + \tilde{\sigma}^1 \wedge \tilde{\omega}^{23}.$$

In this case the right-hand side can be interpreted in terms of *dihedral angles*. If you contract on the unit bivector you find that H equals the average of the "nose dives" in the two coordinate directions. For instance, the two-form $\tilde{\omega}^{13} \wedge \tilde{\sigma}^2$ contracted on $\vec{f_1} \wedge \vec{f_2}$ equals $\tilde{\omega}^{13}\langle \vec{f_1} \rangle$, which is the rate of turn of the normal in the $\vec{f_1}$ direction for a unit progression into that same direction. Because the coordinate directions $(1, 2)$ are essentially *arbitrary*—except for orthogonality—you find that H equals the *nose dive averaged over all directions*. This explains the term "mean curvature." The nose dive is also the dihedral angle, per unit spacing of the faces, for an edge in the orthogonal direction. Hence H also equals the "average dihedral angle" in a precise sense.

Gauss's equation can be written in the equivalent form

$$d\tilde{\omega}^{12} = -K \tilde{\sigma}^1 \wedge \tilde{\sigma}^2.$$

This is the famous *"theorema egregium"* (or "princely theorem"), which is one of the triumphs of nineteenth-century mathematics. What is so special about it is that *the index 3 doesn't appear.*

---

[6]These very important frame fields are discussed in considerable detail in chapter 6.

This amounts to saying that the intelligent ant exploring the surface from the purely intrinsic point of view could actually *measure K* through local geodesic exercises. You will appreciate that K appears to measure something that has to do with the turning of the frame about the normal, that is, with something that is amenable to some *intrinsic* definition. Again, a detailed discussion follows later.

4.5   Calculus on the manifold

In practice you will almost always use a *parametric description* of a surface S (say), that is, you use a *map* from a piece of the plane $\mathbf{R}^2$ (usually a rectangle or the unit square) with Cartesian coordinates (u, v) say to the surface, for instance, $M : \mathbf{R}^2 \mapsto S$. Thus you have an algorithm that allows you to find $\vec{x}(u, v)$, that is, a typical point of the surface, for all points of your map. The chart serves to *label* points of the surface. This is explicit in the computer implementation where the $[u, v]$ are merely indices or pointers.

Moreover, you also do much of the calculus on the surface in terms of your map. For instance a real function of the surface $f(\vec{x})$ can be "pulled back" to the chart and I use $f(\vec{x}(u, v))$ as a convenient *coordinate expression* of the function.

You have the simple relation

$$\vec{x}_u[f] = \frac{\partial}{\partial u} f(\vec{x}(u, v))$$

(and similar for v). Thus you have reduced the directional derivative to partial derivatives of coordinate expressions.

Note that any tangential vector field can be expressed as a linear combination of the "partial velocities" $\vec{x}_u$, $\vec{x}_v$, since these two vectors span the tangent planes. For *arbitrary* but nontangential vector fields on the surface, I use the normal as a third independent vector. They clearly form a *coordinate basis*. In general they will neither be normalized nor orthogonal. In practical applications you will usually replace them with an orthonormal *frame*.

The vectors $\vec{x}_u$ and $\vec{x}_v$ are the images of the natural Cartesian frame field of the map under the *Jacobian* of the coordinate function with respect to u, v. This linear map M_* maps the Cartesian frame vectors $\vec{e}_1$, $\vec{e}_2$ on the coordinate basis $\vec{x}_u$, $\vec{x}_v$. If $\vec{a}(t)$ is a curve in the parameter plane, then $M_*(\vec{a}(0))$ is the initial velocity of the corresponding curve on the surface. Linearity implies that $M_*(a\,\vec{v} + b\,\vec{w}) = a\,M_*\vec{v} + b\,M_*\vec{w}$.

For *forms* you can define a very useful operation: you can always "move" them between surfaces. For instance, if you have a map

$$G : \mathcal{A} \mapsto \mathcal{B},$$

that maps surface $\mathcal{A}$ to surface $\mathcal{B}$, and $\tilde{\varphi}$ is a form on $\mathcal{B}$, then the "pull back" $G^* \tilde{\varphi}$ of $\tilde{\varphi}$ is a form on $\mathcal{A}$ such that

$$G^* \tilde{\varphi} \langle \vec{w} \rangle = \tilde{\varphi} \langle G_* \vec{w} \rangle$$

(there is a similar expression for two-forms). Here G_* is the *Jacobian* of G that allows you to map tangent vectors of $\mathcal{A}$ to tangent vectors of $\mathcal{B}$. It is a linear transformation of one tangent space to another, the best linear approximation of G. It is often called the "push-forward."

Note that G_* "pushes forward," that is if $\vec{v}$ is on $\mathcal{A}$ then $G_* \vec{v}$ is on $\mathcal{B}$. In contradistinction, G^* "pulls back," thus $\tilde{\varphi}$ is on $\mathcal{B}$ whereas $G^* \tilde{\varphi}$ is on $\mathcal{A}$. The push-forward pushes vectors from one manifold to the next. For instance, $(\vec{\partial}_u, \vec{\partial}_v)$ are pushed to $\vec{x}_u$, $\vec{x}_v$. In general, *vectors cannot be pulled back. In most cases* you *pull back forms from the surface to the coordinate patch*. Then you can do the calculus in the Euclidean plane instead of on the surface. Thus the pull-back is extremely important in almost *any* application.

The pull-back behaves as nicely as you could possibly wish:

$$
\begin{aligned}
(G^* \tilde{\varphi}) \langle \vec{v} \rangle &= \tilde{\varphi} \langle G_* \vec{v} \rangle \\
G^* \tilde{\eta} \langle \vec{v}, \vec{w} \rangle &= \tilde{\eta} \langle G_* \vec{v}, G_* \vec{w} \rangle \\
G^* (\tilde{\varphi} + \tilde{\psi}) &= G^* \tilde{\varphi} + G^* \tilde{\psi} \\
G^* (\tilde{\varphi} \wedge \tilde{\psi}) &= G^* \tilde{\varphi} \wedge G^* \tilde{\psi} \\
G^* (d\tilde{\varphi}) &= d(G^* \tilde{\varphi}).
\end{aligned}
$$

Thus in the special case of the coordinate chart, the duals of $\vec{x}_u$ and $\vec{x}_v$ pull back to the forms du and dv through the action of M^*.

In general you can't expect to be able to pull back tangent *vectors*; the spaces might even have different dimensions. If the mapping is a nice diffeomorphism, you *can* pull back vectors and push forward forms, however. This is often useful in practice because you so often deal with coordinate transformations, which are supposed to be nice automorphisms. The map of your parametric description is a prime example: M_* pushes vectors from the Euclidean plane on the manifold, whereas M^* pulls back forms from the manifold to the Euclidean plane. But you can equally well pull back vectors or push forward forms. Of course, you should always be wary: there are dangers lurking in every corner.

These relations are intuitively rather obvious if you think of tangent vectors as bilocal entities and of forms as families of parallel curves and checkerboard patterns. Then $G^*\tilde{\varphi}\langle \vec{w} \rangle = \tilde{\varphi}\langle G_*\vec{w} \rangle$ merely expresses the fact that a vector pierces the same number of levels in the chart and in its image (fig. 98), which is visually almost obvious when you think of the image as just a warped, deformed, rubber-sheet version of the chart. Then the number of piercings will be trivially independent of

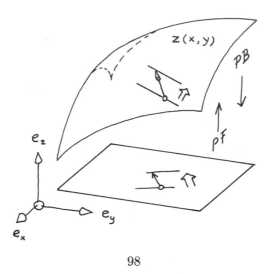

98

the warping. Technically the relations involve tricky relations between partial derivatives, however, and things are not so obvious. The fearless use of the pull-back gives you a lot of power indeed.

You use the pull-back in practice to compute *integrals*. Geometrically integrals are trivial. You *count* piercings for line integrals and cells for area integrals. However, to do the thing analytically or—more likely— numerically, you need a suitable representation. You have:

$$\int_{curve} \tilde{\varphi} = \int_{curve\ on\ chart} G^*\tilde{\varphi} \approx \sum_i G^*\tilde{\varphi}\langle \vec{w_i} \rangle,$$

where you approximate the curve with a chain of increment vectors $\vec{w_i}$ on the chart.

Similarly, for an "area integral"you have (approximately):

$$\int_{region} \tilde{\psi} = \int_{region\ on\ chart} G^*\tilde{\psi} \approx \sum_{i,j} G^*\tilde{\psi}\langle \vec{v}_i \wedge \vec{w}_j \rangle,$$

where you approximate the region with a set of "tiles" given through the increment bivectors $\vec{v}_i \wedge \vec{w}_j$ on the chart.

These approximations are very convenient if you want to program integrations of forms over curved submanifolds on your computer. The main problem is in the representation of the domain. When you pull back the multicovector field to your Euclidean parameter patch, this problem becomes at once trivial. Then numerical integration becomes a reasonable proposition. This is most important in computational differential geometry.

4.6 Transversality

When curved submanifolds *meet* you need some notion on how intimate the contact is. This leads to the *theory of contact* treated in the next paragraph. You also need some notion of how "likely" the contact is.

What is meant by that is clear when you think of a line and a plane in Euclidean 3-space. Clearly it would be highly unlikely for a line to lie in the plane or to be parallel to the plane if you drew them "at random." I am not going to discuss here what "drawn at random" could actually mean in this context. You can either try to form a clear image in your mind, or even better you could consult a standard reference on differential topology.[7] The notion should have some intuitive appeal though.

A typical line picked at random will surely have exactly one point in common with the plane. If that is the case I say that the line and the plane meet transversely. This is the notion of *genericity* or *infinitesimal stability*. If I change the position or the direction of the line—or maybe both at the same time—ever so slightly, I will destroy the incidence or the parallelity, but I can't destroy the transverse crossing as easily as that.

Whether two submanifolds meet transversely can be decided if you consider the *codimension of their tangent spaces*. The dimension of the intersection equals the difference of 3, the dimension of space, and the

---

[7]You may also want to take a look at texts dealing with "integral geometry," especially if you are an applications-oriented person.

sum of the two codimensions. The intersection is void if the difference comes out negative. Thus in the transverse cases you have the following table:

codim M	codim N	dim M∩N	significance
3	3	*	Two points don't coincide
3	2	*	A point isn't on a line
3	1	*	A point isn't on a plane
2	2	*	Two lines cross
2	1	0	A line intersects a plane
1	1	1	Two planes intersect

An asterisk means that the intersection is void. Notice how these relations are pictorially evident when you conjure up an image corresponding to the "significance" entries from the table before your mind's eye.

Figure 99 depicts the interesting cases. Figure 100 depicts a few

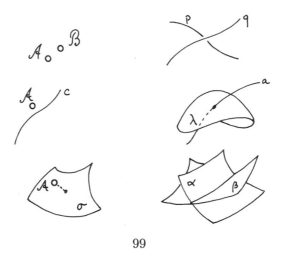

99

nontransversal cases.

I have left out the trivial cases. My main application will be to curves and surfaces. You see that two curves will never meet; when they do, in whatever manner, the crossing is not transverse. Thus, the only interesting transverse cases are those of two surfaces intersecting in a curve and of a curve crossing a surface. Again, these relations are completely obvious in the pictorial interpretation.

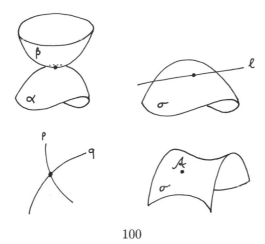

100

4.6.1 Computer Implementation

♠ INTERMEZZO—REAL WORLD WORRIES.

Since you almost always calculate with limited precision, you cannot expect to conserve nontransversal geometrical relations in numerical processes. If a point lies *on* a line, then it will in general lie *outside* the line after a transformation of coordinates. Thus the concept of transversality is a very practical one indeed. If you want to represent nontransversal situations, there are only two ways out:

- Use an excessively high precision. This is only a partial remedy, of course. It is expensive to boot. Because it is the simplest way out, it is also the most popular method.

- Treat the nontransversal configuration as an integral geometric object and devise suitable datastructures to represent it. This is obviously the desirable solution. It does the job exactly, even if you use a low accuracy.

For example, if you have to represent two concurrent lines in space you have to represent them by way of their common point and their directions. Other methods, such as representing the lines through two non-coincident points on each, will result in skew lines after a transformation.

Such problems are extremely common. They have to be attacked on an individual basis. The methods used are, in fact, those of the old-fashioned "kinematical design" known to most engineers.

Experienced people always pick the representations that automatically avoid these problems, so life is easy for them. If you ask them how to do it, they put on a big show of seeming puzzled by the question, since the bad

choices just appear so utterly contrived to them that they could only have
been thought off by diseased minds. This is not much of a help, and we less
experienced people had better spend some time making sure the approach
decided on is reasonable. If you proceed without caring, you are asking for
trouble.

4.7   Order of contact

I will have recurrent use for notions of the *degree of contact* of two
submanifolds. One application is in fitting a local model to a shape.
You want the contact to be as tight as possible. The other application is
in the type of interaction of probes with the shape. For instance, a light
ray may graze a surface in many different ways, the degree of contact
varying enormously from case to case.

People say that two planar curves have *no contact* if they have no point
in common, contact of the order zero if they have a common intersection,
and of the order one if their tangent directions also coincide. It is said
that two curves have contact of the order p if all their derivatives with
respect to arc length up to the pth order coincide, whereas the $(p+1)$-th
order is different. The order thus amounts to the order of the common
initial part of a Taylor series.

The order of contact also equals the maximum number of transversal
crossings that you obtain from a small perturbation minus one, as is
intuitively clear in view of the principal theorem of algebra. This is
the *pictorial interpretation* of contact, and in practice it often replaces
a formal calculation. When a curve grazes a surface it is immediately
obvious to the intuition that you may at most obtain a pair of transversal
crossings from almost any perturbation. Thus the contact is of the
first order. The perturbation used to study the multiplicity is generally
known as an "unfolding."

Similarly it is said for the case of two surfaces, that the order of contact
is p if all mixed partial derivatives up to the pth order for some mutual
parametrization $(\vec{x}(u,v), \vec{x}'(u,v))$ coincide, whereas this is not the case
for the $(p+1)$-th order. Thus first-order contact means $\vec{x}_u = \vec{x}'_u$,
$\vec{x}_v = \vec{x}'_v$ and at least one of the equalities $\vec{x}_{uu} = \vec{x}'_{uu}$, $\vec{x}_{vv} = \vec{x}'_{vv}$,
$\vec{x}_{uv} = \vec{x}'_{uv}$ is not true; that is to say, the tangent planes coincide but
the osculating quadrics differ.

A *curve* has contact of at least order p with a *surface* if there exists
a curve in the surface which has pth order contact with the curve. One
defines the contact of space curves in the same way as the contact of

planar curves mentioned earlier.

The case of contact of a straight line with a surface will be discussed in detail later on because of its great importance in practical optics.

Suppose the contact is at least of the first order. Order zero is trivial anyway. Then you pick a local frame such that the $\vec{e}_3$ is along the surface normal and $\vec{e}_1$ along the tangent to the line. The surface can be given as $(x, y, f(x, y))$ and the line as $(x, 0, 0)$. Then pth order contact means just that $\frac{\partial^s f}{\partial x^s} = 0$ for $s \leq p$ whereas $\frac{\partial^{p+1} f}{\partial x^{p+1}} \neq 0$.

Some general observations may be of use here. If you consider a surface and a line, contact of the order zero is certainly generic because the line pierces the object and intersects it transversely. Thus:

- for any point of space there exists a cone of lines with a finite solid angle that contains lines that pierce the object. The dimension of this space of piercing lines is *four*, because you can parametrize it by the points on the surface, which accounts for two degrees of freedom, and by a spatial direction, accounting for another two degrees of freedom.

- A line that *grazes* the surface generically has contact of the first order. From each point of space I have a cone mantle of such rays. The dimension of the space of grazing lines is *three*.

- If the surface contains saddle-shaped patches, then there exist regions of space such that each point in that region admits a finite number—typically just two—of lines that touch the object with second-order contact. The dimension of the space of such lines is *two*.

- There may exist surfaces in space consisting of lines that have third-order contact. The dimension of the space of such lines is only *one*. From this you may infer that these special lines describe a ruled surface that is somehow intimately connected with the surface. I will discuss this "biflecnodal scroll" in a later chapter.

- Then—finally—there exist a finite number of lines that sport fourth-order contact. The dimension of that space is *zero*, which is the minimum possible because it only represents a finite number of straight lines. You have to stay on the singular line in order not to lose the fourth order of contact. Notice that a small perturbation must yield as many as *five* almost coincident points where the line sticks through the surface. Few naive people can visualize such a complicated situation without a bit of coaching. I will discuss this case into more detail in a later chapter.

These relations are absolutely fundamental in the study of the optical interaction with surfaces. The lower orders of contact are fairly obvious in the pictorial interpretation, and you should try some "experiments" by making sketches until you fully grasp their meaning. The higher orders of contact are treated in a later chapter.[8]

4.8   The topologically distinct surfaces

I will use a few notions concerning the global topology, namely the connectivity, of surfaces. The situation is basically simple because I don't tolerate surfaces with self-intersections. Moreover, all surfaces will be smooth and of (very) finite size. After all, surfaces are boundaries of blobs, so how could they possibly self-intersect or otherwise misbehave?[9] Then the connectivity is completely defined by the *genus* of the surface (Riemann's "Geschlecht"), that is, *the number of through holes* in the blob (fig. 101). Thus the sphere has genus zero because it has no holes, the torus has genus one since it sports a single through hole, the pretzel has genus two because of its two holes, and so forth.

Apart from the genus I will use another characteristic number, the *Euler number* (or Euler "characteristic") of the surface, which is simply related to the genus as

$$\chi = 2(1 - g)$$

(where χ denotes the Euler number and g the genus).

The Euler number pops up in many, often unexpected, ways in differential geometry of surfaces that bound volumes. As an example you may consider the triangulations of surfaces, a subject of direct practical importance. You can triangulate any surface, that is, cover it with triangular patches such that any two oriented triangles may have either nothing, or one vertex, or an edge in common. The common edges have to be of opposite orientation. At any vertex you should be able to make a round trip through adjacent triangles. If you count the number of

---

[8]It depends on the power of your imagination what "high" and "low" actually mean here.

[9]In fact, ill-behaved blobs are not impossible. If you don't like what you've got, you should change the resolution and the threshold just a little. The odds are highly in favor on your ending up with a well-behaved blob, regardless of how you do it. I find this a comforting thought.

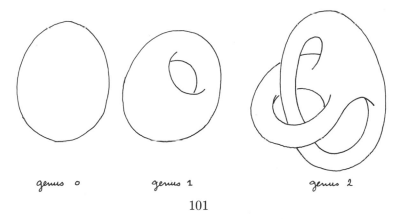

genus 0   genus 1   genus 2

101

faces (F), vertices (V), and edges (E), then it can be shown that

$$F - E + V = \chi.$$

If you don't believe it, the cure is first of all to spend some time drawing examples and counting. After that you may want to look at Aleksandrov's book, for instance.

I presume that you are very much interested in the problem of the triangulation of surfaces, because triangulations are the most practical means to represent arbitrary surfaces numerically.

Triangulations can be made in any odd way, but some methods are definitely more convenient than others. In practice you would like to have some control over the shape of the faces, because very elongated faces are bad from a numerical point of view. Moreover, you would like the number of faces that meet at a vertex to be limited. If it is very large the angles will necessarily be very acute and the triangles will be elongated again. Even better, you would appreciate a certain regularity such that it is easy to *index* the elements of the triangulation.

One of the neatest triangulations that I am aware of is obtained in a parametrization such that a regular triangular tiling on your chart maps on the triangulation. Then all vertices are such that exactly *six faces meet* there. It is obvious to the physical intuition that geodesy based on equilateral triangles is the optimum in terms of robustness with respect to the ever-present observational tolerances. For a patch that is the image of, for instance, the square, such a nice triangulation is always

possible. For a global surface, however, it will in general be impossible
to do this.

In order to investigate the problems, first note that I can always *refine*
a given triangulation such that I only introduce vertices of the 6-type.
Thus you need only investigate coarse triangulations (fig. 102) to find

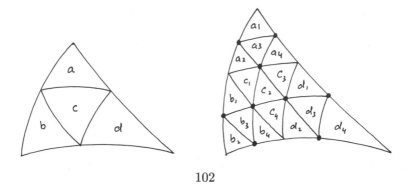

102

out about the problems. A simple way to refine a triangulation is to
subdivide every triangle into four new ones through the artifice of bisection of all edges and joining up the new points within the triangles. This
leads to elegant recursive refinement procedures that are very suitable
for computer implementation.[10]

It may help to consider a few examples. You can easily find a coarse
triangulation of the torus that is regular. Two faces suffice, suitably
sewn together (figs. 103 and 104). If you sew two triangles together, you
obtain a quadrangle. Sewing a pair of opposite sides of the quadrangle
together yields a cylindrical tube that is open on both ends. If you bend
the tube into a ring, you may also sew the other pair of sides together
and you are left with a torus. Easy, isn't it?

For the sphere you can't do that. You need a few vertices with less
than six faces meeting there. This can be done in *many* ways. For
instance, a regular octahedron is a topological sphere and contains eight
triangles that meet in six vertices in such a way that four faces meet at
each vertex (figs. 105 and 106).

For surfaces of genus two and more I can use a general scheme in
which I add a suitable amount of vertices at which *more* than six faces
meet. The simplest way to achieve this is by "plumbing."

---

[10]At least I find them suitable because they are so easy to program and thus save
me time. I know some people don't like recursion.

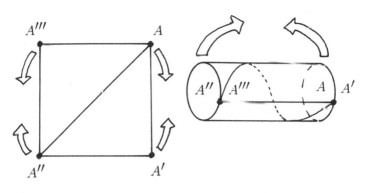

103

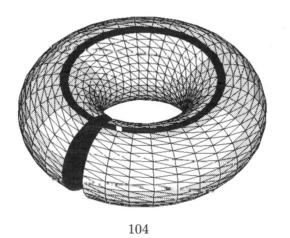

104

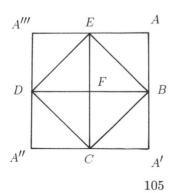

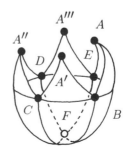

105

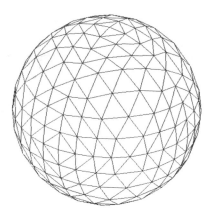

106

You have already seen how two triangles can be sewn together to form
a "tube" that is an open cylindrical surface. On each end there are two
vertices at which three faces meet and that have room for more. Pieces
of tube are one of the main raw materials in the art of plumbing. The
only other part you need is the T-piece, in order to make *junctions* in
your artwork.

From pieces of tube and T-pieces you can assemble arbitrarily complicated surfaces by soldering them together. You only use it for surfaces
of genus exceeding unity, of course. For a surface with genus g you will
need a number of T-pieces equal to $2(g - 1) = -\chi$.

Figure 107 shows how to assemble a T-piece by way of the "cute
pants" method. Each T-piece introduces three vertices at which eight
faces meet. Thus you will introduce $|3\chi|$ eight-vertices for a surface of
Euler number χ. (Remember that $\chi < 0$ in the cases of interest.)

When you refine the triangulations, the ratio of non-six vertices to the
six-vertices decreases and you can make the ratio as low as you want.
Then *almost all* of the vertices will be of the six-type. Moreover, you can
always cut up the surface in such a way that the bad vertices are located
on the corners of your patches. Then all patches are of the nice type
and the problems occur only when you try to sew the patches together.
Thus the use of merely 6-vertices is really not a restriction at all.

It is most convenient to use a standard method for your triangulations
in order to ease the task of labeling the components of the triangulation
and to keep track of the patches. This chore is usually the most involved
part of practical algorithms, thus it really pays to spend some effort on

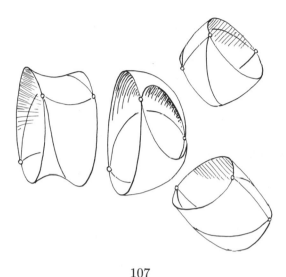

107

a general formalization. Of course, many methods other than the one I proposed here will work as well in practice. The point is to use a *method*—any method!—instead of reinventing the wheel for each next case you have to handle.

4.9 Singularities of vector fields

A scalar field on a surface is called *regular* at a point if its gradient doesn't vanish there. If the gradient *does* vanish the point is called "critical" and the value of the field is called a "critical value." Generically the critical points are finitely many, are nondegenerated, and are isolated, whereas their critical values are distinct. In this context "nondegenerate" means that the second-order terms in a Taylor expansion describe the structure sufficiently well whenever the gradient happens to vanish. If the field is indeed Morse, then it can be shown that a small perturbation cannot change the qualitative (topological) structure of the field, that is, cannot create or destruct critical points. (Of course, a large enough perturbation may well change the structure.)

For instance, if you make a radar map of a surface, you are interested in "the distance squared function," the squared distance from a "vantage point" to any point on the surface. I prefer distance *squared* in order to avoid some mathematical difficulties. It makes no difference to the argument. Then the distance squared field will be generic, or "Morse," as people call it, for almost every position of the vantage point.[11] If it is not Morse then an infinitesimal displacement of the vantage point will restore the nice situation. The "bad" vantage points lie on certain singular surfaces that I will discuss in detail later. There exist only very few such bad vantage points. If you pick an arbitrary point, the odds are infinitely against your having got one. If you happen to be unlucky for once, you can rest assured that there will be nice vantage points arbitrarily close.

Such conditions are also true for the other scalar functions that have a special interest, such as the "slant-function," that is the cosine of the angle between the surface normal and the direction of view from a vantage point. This field is of fundamental importance in many applications of an optical nature.

Tangent-vector fields are also of interest because the all important *frame vector fields* form an example. The bad news is that you cannot in general expect to be able to define a smooth tangent-vector field over all of the surface. There have to be "bad" points where the tangent field vanishes and its direction becomes undefined. Generically these are isolated singularities of simple types, which isn't so bad. What it means in practice is that you can't cover a surface with a single parametrization. Thus, you have no option but to use an "atlas" of charts.

For example you need at least two charts to cover the unit sphere completely (fig. 108) The map covers more than a hemisphere; thus two of such patches amply "clothe" the sphere. This coordinate mesh is just a "stereographical backprojection" of a Cartesian mesh on a tangent plane at the north pole. It can actually cover *all* of the sphere except for one point, namely the south pole. Unfortunately it turns out that the sphere owns one point more than the plane. This problem is a serious one in practical applications, and I will suggest how to handle it later on.

As in the case of triangulations, the singularities of vector fields can be classified in various ways and you can show that only certain combinations can occur on surfaces of a given genus. The basic property of a singularity that counts here is its *index*. The index equals the number of turns the vector field makes if you traverse a small circle encircling the singularity. If the senses are unequal, the index is negative. The "pole" of a planar polar coordinate system is the prime example of a singularity

---

[11] Here that means: the critical points are isolated and nondegenerate (thus extrema and the simplest type of saddles), whereas all critical values are distinct.

of index +1.

Poincaré has shown that the sum of the indices of all singular points equals the Euler characteristic. You may want to try this for the sphere. Pick a vector field pointing either south or east everywhere but at the poles. The poles are a problem, so there you let the modulus of the vectors go smoothly to zero. Both choices lead to singularities of index unity at the poles. (Check it by drawing!) This indeed neatly figures with the Euler number two.

Because only the surfaces of the topological type of the torus have a vanishing Euler characteristic they are singled out through the property that they can admit singularity free tangent vector fields. It is indeed simple enough to construct such fields on the torus. Just rotate the torus about its axis of rotational symmetry, and consider the velocity field on the surface created by this movement, for instance.

Thus the sum of the indices equals *two* for a sphere. From this you may conclude immediately that there exist no smooth vector fields on the sphere that vanish nowhere. As the saying goes: "You can't comb the hair on a sphere." As noted earlier, the field of all vectors pointing south on the globe has two singularities of index one, namely the poles. It is easy to find vector fields with only *one singularity* on the sphere: take all small circles that have a common tangent at a given point, namely the singularity, and consider the field defined by all their tangent vectors. It is not hard to figure out that the index of this singularity is +2, as it should be. It is a kind of "dipole"-like singularity; thus the index +2 makes some vague sense from a physical point of view. This is the type of singularity that will arise at the south pole in the example depicted in figure 108.

I illustrate one possible form of singularity for the sake of concreteness (fig. 109). As you see, singularities can be rather involved. You may encounter any number and sequence of "nodal," "elliptic," and "hyperbolic" sectors. In figure 109, you have a simple example of a "dipole-like" singular point in a tangent vector field. However, in practice you will meet only a few simple types in the vector fields on surfaces that are of interest here. In several cases I will point out the generic possibilities for the entities of most interest, without going into an extensive discussion though. The methods of differential topology that most directly apply to these problems are of an algebraic rather than of a geometric nature and fit rather badly into the present text.

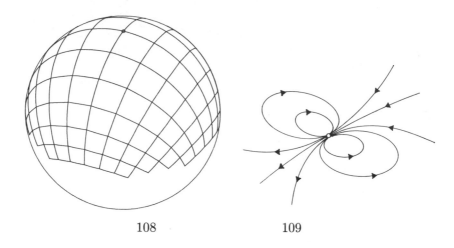

108   109

When you think of a body-norm in terms of component units, you will
emphasize units you are especially interested in. The way you shape
each of them will show how you feel about them. Analogy comes in
again here. You will find you may draw a chest like a box, a belly like
a bag, legs like pillars or a skull like a dome. This is actually one of the
great resources of art—metaphor, linking parts of the body with other
elements of experience.
—PHILIP RAWSON, The Art of drawing (1983)

III SMOOTH ENTITIES

5 Curves

... *because* [straight lines] *don't occur in nature and only exist in the mind of man. Whenever man employs them, the elements are destructed.*
—EUGÈNE DELACROIX (1798–1863), *cited by Kurt Badt*

... *the serpentine line, by its waving and winding at the same time in different ways, leads the eye in a pleasing manner along the continuity of its variety, if I may be allowed the expression; and which by its twisting so many different ways, may be said to inclose (tho' but a single line) varied contents.*
—WILLIAM HOGARTH, *The Analysis of Beauty (1753)*

5.1 Why study curves?

In this book I deal little with space curves as such, since they never occur as *objects* in their own right anyway. Curves are only of interest in the following respects:

- As *curves on surfaces* such as the shadow boundary, the intersection between two interpenetrating surfaces, and so forth. These are space curves from the *extrinsic* point of view, but their practically important codimension is usually to be assessed relative to the tangent space of the surface, and thus is only *one*. In such cases I regard the curve preferentially as a "carrier" of a surface strip. The theory of such strips will be dealt with in the next chapter.

- As *models* for regions like the "stick man." These are true space curves, although of a somewhat generalized kind because you may expect arborizations.

- As descriptions of certain physical phenomena which are used to interact with shapes–for instance, "light rays."

In this chapter I provide a short, but at least pictorially and heuristically, fairly complete review of space curves. Technically the review is sufficiently complete to point you in the right direction, but you will need to consult standard texts in order to be able to start any serious work.

5.2   Curves as orbits

Mathematicians usually prefer to describe a curve as a map from an interval of the real numbers into space, although alternatives are available and sometimes very useful. This makes good physical sense too if you think of curve as an *orbit*. An orbit maps the reals—say "clock time"—to space, that is, "momentary position." Since you are not really interested in the *dynamics of the orbital motion*, if you want to study the shape of the curve *per se* you may as well conveniently constrain the problem to orbits that are traversed with unit speed throughout. In that case the time elapsed since the movement passed some fiducial point equals the "arclength" along the orbit from that point. Mathematicians call this a "parametrization according to arclength." This makes life somewhat easier, since some of the irrelevant dynamics drop out, although it isn't strictly necessary, of course.

The *velocity* of the orbit is a unit vector, and it is usually known as the *tangent*. Because the tangent is a unit vector, the *acceleration* must be some vector *perpendicular* to the velocity. The *direction* of the acceleration is known as "the (curve) normal," whereas the *amount* of the acceleration is known as "the curvature." It is the centripetal acceleration that equals the square of the velocity divided by the radius of curvature, remember? Note that the *normal plane*, that is, the plane orthogonal to the tangent, is an *oriented plane*. The orientation is induced by the tangent direction and the orientation of space.

You can use the tangent and the normal to define a natural frame field on the curve. You take the three vectors $\vec{T}$, $\vec{N}$ and $\vec{B} = \vec{T} \times \vec{N}$, which are the *tangent*, the *normal* and the *binormal*. In figure 110, $\vec{T}$ is the tangent to the curve, $\vec{N}$ is orthogonal to $\vec{T}$ and lies in the plane defined by the infinitesimally close triple of points $\mathcal{P}$, $\mathcal{P}'$, and $\mathcal{P}''$. This frame is known as the *Frenet frame*. In the folding model (fig. 111) and linked-rod model (fig. 110) you can easily find the frame.

In the folding model the tangent is the part of the sectors that is actually on the edge and not on a hinge. The normal lies in the plane of the sector and is perpendicular to the tangent. The binormal is the normal of the plane of the sector.

In the rod model the rods themselves form the tangents. Two successive rods define a plane known as the "osculating plane." The sector planes in the folding model also indicate the osculating plane. The osculating plane is rather special; for instance, it is the only plane through the tangent direction that is *pierced* by a general space curve.

The normals of these osculating planes are the binormals. The normal

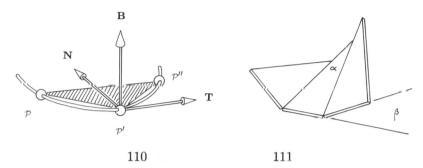

110   111

is the vector perpendicular to the rods in the osculating plane. You may
accept the convention that the osculating plane of a universal joint of
the rod model is the plane defined by the two rods that are joined there.
The *dihedral angle* β at a junction is the angle between the osculating
plane and the osculating plane of the succeeding junction. The "turn"
at a joint is the angle α between the rods. Then a little exercise in high-
school-type stereometry yields the relation between the frame $(\vec{T}, \vec{N}, \vec{B})$
at a vertex and the frame $(\vec{T}', \vec{N}', \vec{B}')$ at the succeeding vertex (figs. 112
and 111). You find:

$$
\begin{aligned}
\triangle\vec{T} &= & \cos\alpha\,\vec{T} & & +\sin\alpha\,\vec{N} \\
\triangle\vec{N} &= & -\sin\alpha\cos\beta\,\vec{T} & +\cos\alpha\cos\beta\,\vec{N} & +\sin\beta\,\vec{B} \\
\triangle\vec{B} &= & \sin\alpha\sin\beta\,\vec{T} & -\cos\alpha\sin\beta\,\vec{N} & +\cos\beta\,\vec{B}.
\end{aligned}
$$

The angles are supposed to be small for a good approximation to a
smooth curve; thus it makes sense to compute a first-order approximation to these equations. You obtain

$$
\begin{pmatrix} \vec{T}' \\ \vec{N}' \\ \vec{B}' \end{pmatrix} = \begin{pmatrix} 1 & \alpha & 0 \\ -\alpha & 1 & \beta \\ 0 & -\beta & 1 \end{pmatrix} \begin{pmatrix} \vec{T} \\ \vec{N} \\ \vec{B} \end{pmatrix}.
$$

You will recognize this expression as the *identity transformation*, corresponding to the translation of the frame along the rod, augmented with
an *infinitesimal rotation* of the frame as a whole. This part, of course,
is nothing but the Cartan matrix of the frame field along the curve. If
you approximate the same curve with shorter rods, the turn and the
dihedral angle will decrease in proportion. For the smooth curve, only
the limiting values of the ratios αL^{-1} and βL^{-1} (where L denotes the

rod length) are significant. These connection coefficients are known as the *curvature* and the *torsion*, respectively.

Thus what happens when you hop from one point to the next in the models is this: the frame rotates about the binormal by an amount equal to the sector angle, or—equivalently—the angle between the rods, and simultaneously rotates about the tangent by an amount equal to the dihedral angle between the sector planes. In the continuous case you have, in a "physical" notation,

$$\vec{T}' = \vec{D} \times \vec{T}$$
$$\vec{N}' = \vec{D} \times \vec{N} \quad \text{with} \quad \vec{D} = \tau \vec{T} + \kappa \vec{B},$$
$$\vec{B}' = \vec{D} \times \vec{B}$$

where κ and τ are the rates of change of the angles and the primed quantities now signify derivatives with respect to the arclength. The vector $\vec{D}$ is the instantaneous rotation vector of the frame and is known as the *Darboux vector*. Figure 113 shows a Frenet frame field that has

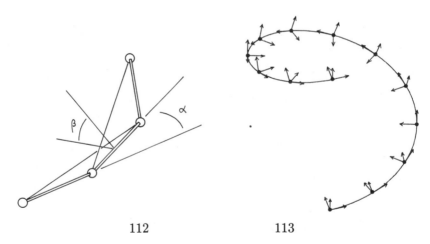

112   113

been fitted numerically to a general space curve. In a more conventional notation you may write:

$$\begin{pmatrix} \vec{T}' \\ \vec{N}' \\ \vec{B}' \end{pmatrix} = \begin{pmatrix} 0 & \kappa & 0 \\ -\kappa & 0 & \tau \\ 0 & -\tau & 0 \end{pmatrix} \begin{pmatrix} \vec{T} \\ \vec{N} \\ \vec{B} \end{pmatrix},$$

a set of equations that is commonly known by the names of Serret and Frenet. The matrix, again, is nothing but the Cartan matrix C of the

frame field; thus the skew symmetry should come as no surprise to you.
In fact, you could immediately have guessed such a relation on the basis
of the material discussed in the previous chapters and have asked right
away what the geometrical meaning of the matrix elements might be
in this special case. As it happens, C_{12} is the curvature and C_{23} the
torsion, whereas C_{13} vanishes, a fact that could hardly have been guessed
offhand. It is the result of the judicious choice of frame field. This is
a phenomenon that sometimes happens when you are fortunate in the
choice of your frame fields. Of course, it would be nice if you were
fortunate in your choices as often as possible. This is something of an
acquired art, although a pictorial insight into the geometry may often
guide you into the right direction. In any case, your degree of success
will be reflected in the simplicity of the resulting Cartan matrix.

Here, then, is a general rule for recognizing (and sometimes construct-
ing) "good" frame fields:[1]

Useful heuristic: *As many of the connection coefficients as possible
should either vanish or be constant.*

This is typical for the Cartan method of moving frames:

Observation: *the creative part lies in the choice of the moving frame;
all the rest is just a mechanical exercise,*

a going through the motions once again; you obtain the important
results almost for free. If you make sure that you pick a frame that is
fully determined by the geometry and has no arbitrary features, then
it must be true that the coefficients of the Cartan matrix do have an
immediate, coordinate-free significance.

Basically, the Serret-Frenet equations contain all there is to know
about space curves, and I could as well stop the discussion at this point.
However, it aids the intuition a good deal if you face some of the consequences explicitly so as to be able to acquire a pictorial knowledge
base.

The Darboux vector, together with the translation defined by a rod in
the rod model, defines an *instantaneous screw*. Intuitively the axis of the
screw is the common perpendicular of two successive normals (figs. 114
and 115). Figure 115 shows the normal rays for a circular helix; they
describe a "screw surface," or helicoid. In this case the axis of the screw

---

[1]Since the connection components have no immediate geometrical meaning (they
don't transform as tensors), their vanishing—strictly speaking—doesn't mean anything! This rule is a mere heuristic device. However, you will find it very useful in
practice.

is the same for all points of the curve. This is a serious degeneracy, of course, but it is a case that is especially easy to visualize and commit to memory. The ruled surface described by the normals of a general space curve is a "scroll," that is, a surface that cannot be developed into the plane.

The cotangent of the angle between the Darboux vector and the tangent vector is $\chi = |\frac{\tau}{\kappa}|$, and is known as the *conical curvature*. The conical curvature specifies the amount of turn of the binormal per unit turn of the tangent. The right circular cone with the Darboux vector as axis that osculates the tangent plane at the tangent direction has the same conical curvature as the curve and also as that of the "director cone," that is, the cone subtended by the tangent vectors considered as bound vectors at the origin. This "director cone" is nothing but the *spherical image* of the curve. The "conical curvature" is the curvature of this spherical image considered as a spherical curve. These notions will be explained fully in this chapter.

The formulas for the derivatives of the frame vectors are known as the Frenet-Serret (1847 and 1851, respectively) equations. As noted, they are nothing but *the Cartan connection equations*.

The parameter κ measures the deviation from collinearity for subsequent tangents; thus it measures the *curvature* in a pictorially rather obvious manner. Three successive joints of the rod model determine a *circle*. This is known as the "osculating circle." The radius of this circle

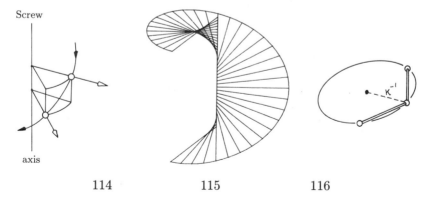

Screw
axis

114   115   116

(fig. 116) is just the reciprocal of κ. Thus the *pictorial interpretation* of the curvature is indeed evident.

The parameter τ measures the deviation from flatness of two subsequent sectors, "the dihedral angle of successive osculating planes"; it is known as the *torsion*. For instance, the shortest distance between tangent rays at points that are an infinitesimal distance apart is $\frac{1}{12}\kappa\tau$ times the distance cubed. Clearly the torsion can also be interpreted in rather direct, pictorial terms. In the classical literature the term "second curvature" is often used for the "torsion." One then speaks of "curves of double curvature" (as opposed to planar curves).

The planes orthogonal to the normals are known as the *rectifying planes*. They envelop a developable surface, known as the *rectifying developable* because of the remarkable property that the curve happens to become a straight line when you actually develop this surface in the plane. The generators of the rectifying developable (fig. 117) are parallel to the Darboux vector.

Indeed, the fact that the Darboux vector is the infinitesimal rotation vector of the frame means that the generators of the rectifying developable are the "hinges" of that surface, so it *has* to be developable. That the curve becomes *straight* when you push the rectifying developable flat seems little less than miraculous now, but it will appear intuitively obvious to you later, when you learn about "geodesic strips."

Figure 117 shows the rectifying developable for a circular helix. It is a fairly trivial affair, as you probably had anticipated already. It is nevertheless useful because so visually evident and easy to remember. The example is a nice one because I can use it to illustrate that this surface is quite distinct from the ruled surface generated by the binormals (fig. 118). I noticed that the distinction is neglected sometimes. The ruled surface of the binormals is a "scroll," that is, not even a developable surface.

By now you have been introduced to the essentials of the classical theory of curves. It is about time I introduce some simple examples to show some of the power of the machinery at your disposal.

A simple but instructive example is the *circular helix* (fig. 119), which in a way is the simplest space curve. The circular helices are curves with constant curvature and torsion. They are about the simplest nontrivial space curves. They can be shown to cling to the surface of some right circular cylinder much like a vine to a stem, in such a way that their "climb rate" is constant. They subtend a fixed angle with the generators of the cylinder. If you can't find a vine in your office, a coiled telephone cord will do if you wish to study the helices empirically.

You will probably guess offhand that the cylinder must have a close relation to the geometrical invariants of the curves, and right you are. Because the tangents to the helix subtend a fixed angle with the generators, it must be the case that the *spherical image* of the tangent is also

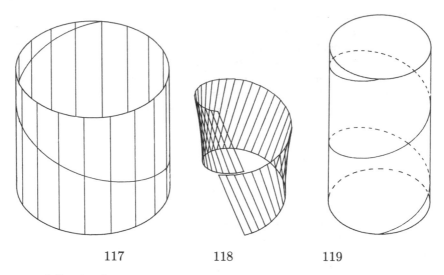

117   118   119

especially simple.

The spherical image of a vector field is merely the manifold subtended
by the directions of the vectors. You may imagine all tangent vectors
being transported in such a way that their tails are at the origin: then
their tips describe the spherical image of the tangent vector field along
the curve. This yields a vivid insight into the twisting and turning of
the frame along the curve.

In the case of the helices all tangents clearly must be confined to
a right circular cone with semi top angle equal to the angle between
the tangents and the generators of the cylinder. Thus the spherical
image is a small circle of the unit sphere. Note that it is a *closed curve*,
in contradistinction to the helix itself. The geodesic curvature of this
spherical image—geodesic curvature is explained in detail later—equals
the *conical curvature*. This explains the origin of that term. Notice
that the conical curvature vanishes only if the "climb rate" of the helix
vanishes and the helix degenerates into a circle. This indicates that the
conical curvature somehow measures the nonplanarity of the helix.

The axis of the cone of tangents has the same direction as the axis
of the cylinder and is just the Darboux vector of the curve. This is a
constant vector for the case of the helices. The normals of the helices
are the radii of the cylinder. They are the radii of the circles that you
obtain when you cut the cylinder with a plane normal to the axis. Note
that the common perpendicular of any two normals is nothing but the
cylinder axis, that is, the Darboux vector. Thus the *normal spherical*

image is a great circle. It is traversed once when the curve completes a full turn around the cylinder.

The curve makes a detour when it encircles the cylindrical surface because the length of a turn must equal the circumference of the cylinder divided by the sine of the angle between the tangents and the generators. Therefore the normal spherical image cannot be traversed at unit speed. The speed is $\lambda = \sqrt{\kappa^2 + \tau^2}$, the so-called *total curvature*. From this you obtain the value $2\pi\lambda^{-1}$ for the length of a complete turn around the cylinder. The distance traveled in the axis direction is $2\pi\tau\lambda^{-2}$. What is of interest in this little calculation is that the sign of this "pitch" is determined solely by the sign of the torsion. Thus the sign of the torsion decides between left-handed and right-handed helices, or the "helicity." In the case of the circular helices the *rectifying developable* is simply the cylinder that they lie on.

In summary, you may observe the following angular turns for the frame vectors per unit progression along the tangent. Please remember that these turns are the coefficients of the connection.

- The tangent turns over κ about the binormal, which amounts to a *turn* of the frame.

- The binormal turns over τ about the tangent, which amounts to a *twist* of the frame.

- The normal turns over the "total curvature." The total curvature (sometimes called "third curvature") amounts to the square root of the sum of squares of κ and τ about the Darboux vector. This amounts to a *combined twist and turn* of the frame.

For planar curves there is *no torsion*, of course. The curve remains stubbornly in the fixed osculating plane. This means that the Darboux vector is just κ times the binormal, and the binormal becomes a *constant vector*. You may as well forget about the binormal then. The frame rotates in the plane of the curve with angular rate κ.

If you *know a priori* that the curve will be planar, you can use the chain model. There is no further need to construct the normal from subsequent tangents; you just turn the tangent over $\frac{\pi}{2}$ to obtain it. *You can even define the normal if there is no curvature at all*, that is, when two subsequent tangents do not span a plane. This is unheard of in the case of space curves. The sign of the curvature now has an *absolute* significance. Again, this is *not* true for space curves. In the linked-rod model you can only define the osculating plane if two rods

are not collinear. Moreover, an absolute sign for the curvature makes no
sense, because unlike the constrained situation with the bicycle chain, I
can now rotate about the rods, so that turning to the "left" or to the
"right" becomes indistinguishable.

It is possible to show that for the generic space curve the curvature
nowhere vanishes. For the rod model this just signifies that the rods will
in general not be collinear, which will hardly surprise you. If two successive rods were collinear, an infinitesimal perturbation would certainly
cure that. If it ever happened you could also simply collate the rods into
a single one. I shall always consider the curvature to be positive. This is
a convenient choice since the decision about the sign is entirely arbitrary
anyway. The sign of the torsion is well defined; the curve can either be
like a left or like a right screw. The generic curve may have *isolated
torsion zeros*,[2] but in general the rate of change of the torsion does not
vanish at the torsion zeros.

You may obtain an impression of a torsion zero if you draw a left-
and a right-handed helix approaching each other from both sides of the
same cylinder. Clearly you will have to introduce a torsion zero somewhere if you are going to join up the two curves smoothly somewhere in
the middle. Such changes of helicity are often introduced in telephone
extension cords to prevent them from curling up into an ugly knot. You
may also notice them in the tendrils of certain weeds of the vine variety,
perhaps for a similar reason?

Typically, *a space curve pierces its own osculating plane*—that is,, it
moves from one side over to the other. In the case of a torsion zero, however, the curve does not pierce its osculating plane but merely *touches*
it. Thus the osculating plane at a torsion zero has a rather intimate
contact with the curve; the curve is locally rather "planar." For this
reason the torsion zeros are often called the "planar points" of the space
curve.

The influences of curvature and torsion on the shape of the curve are
clearly brought out in a power expansion with respect to arclength from
a fiducial point $\vec{x}_0$ of the curve in terms of the Frenet frame:

$$\vec{x}(s) = \vec{x}_0 + s\vec{T}_0 + \kappa_0 \frac{s^2}{2} \vec{N}_0 + \kappa_0 \tau_0 \frac{s^3}{6} \vec{B}_0.$$

This approximation ("Frenet approximation") is carried to the lowest
order in s per frame direction.

---

[2] Also called *planar points*, for reasons that will become apparent later on.

Take care: *This is not a general third-order power series in the arc-length.*

Nevertheless this is for once—a nice formula, so even I am able to remember it.

The zeroth order is simply the fiducial point itself; the first order is a straight line along the tangent direction; the second order, a parabolic arc in the osculating plane; the third order term describes the deviation from the osculating plane. If the torsion vanishes, you need the next order, depending on the rate of change of the torsion.

You may also consider the projections on the $\vec{N}\vec{T}$-plane, that is, the osculating plane; the $\vec{N}\vec{B}$-plane, that is, the normal plane; and the $\vec{B}\vec{T}$-plane, that is, the "rectifying plane." The projection on the osculating plane is just a parabolic arc; on the rectifying plane you see an *inflexion*; and the projection on the normal plane shows a *cusped curve* (fig. 120). This is easily verified (fig. 121) with the linked-rod or the folding model.

Figures 122 to 124 display the special case of the cylindrical helix. It is instructive because you can easily familiarize yourself with the phenomena for this case if you get hold of a common piece of coil spring. A telephone cord will also do rather well, especially if you pull it out a bit. The general case is quite similar.

Local models for these projections are sometimes convenient. In any case they provide you with an insight in the apparent shape of the curve as seen from different directions. By noticing how the curve passes from one octant of space to another and how it contacts the osculating, normal, and rectifying planes you obtain a vivid insight into the local behavior of the typical space curve. In their simplest form the projections are:

$$
\begin{aligned}
y &= Ax^2 \quad \text{with} \quad A = \tfrac{\kappa}{2} \quad &\text{a parabola} \\
z^2 &= By^3 \quad \text{with} \quad B = \tfrac{2\tau^2}{9\kappa} \quad &\text{a cusp} \\
z &= Cx^3 \quad \text{with} \quad C = \tfrac{\kappa\tau}{6} \quad &\text{a cubic}
\end{aligned}
$$

You may of course pursue the development to higher orders if you are so disposed, although the results are not particularly enlightening. The Serret-Frenet equations can be repeatedly applied to make this dumb exercise bearable. Such exercises are of little practical value, apart from their use in the drilling of students.

A few easy corollaries are of more than passing interest. These concern, for instance, the measurement of the torsion and the curvature from the change of the Cartesian coordinates in the Frenet frame. You

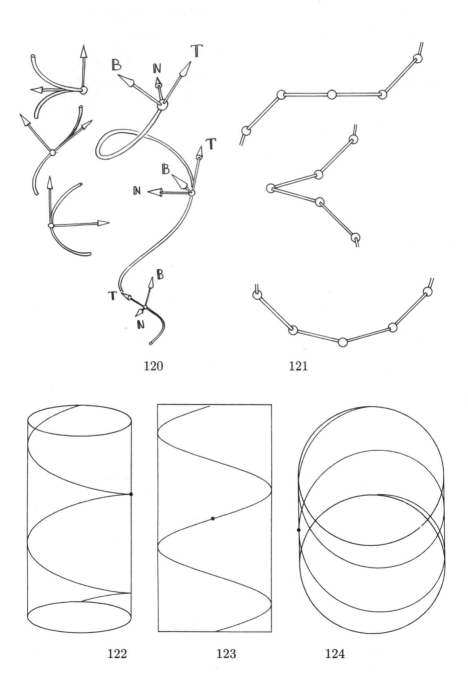

120   121

122   123   124

find for the curvature

$$\kappa = \lim_{s \to 0} \frac{2y}{x^2} \ .$$

This formula, due to Newton, clearly indicates how κ measures the deviations from a straight line. In the x-y-plane the curvature equals twice the deviation from the tangential direction divided by the square of the progression along that direction.

Similarly, you obtain for the torsion,

$$\tau = \lim_{s \to 0} \frac{3z}{xy} \ ,$$

a formula that clearly indicates how τ measures the deviations from planarity. The torsion equals thrice the deviation from the osculating plane divided by the area of the rectangle defined in the osculating plane by the progressions in the tangential and the normal direction.

For the length of a chord you obtain

$$\sqrt{x^2 + y^2 + z^2} = s\left(1 - \kappa^2 \frac{s^2}{24} + \ldots\right).$$

Thus the chords can be used to estimate arclength if they are short with respect to the radius of curvature: if the chord is less than half the radius of curvature, the deviation from the true arclength does not exceed about one percent.

Finally the length d of the common perpendicular of two tangents is

$$d = \frac{\kappa\tau}{12} s^3,$$

as has already been noted.

The expressions for the curvature and the torsion can be very useful at times in numerical work and as rule-of-thumb estimators.

The "FUNDAMENTAL THEOREM OF CURVES" is the treasured culmination of all curve theory and expresses the important fact that two smooth but otherwise arbitrary functions $\kappa(s)$, $\tau(s)$ with $\kappa(s) > 0$, $\frac{\partial \tau}{\partial s} \neq 0$ if $\tau(s) = 0$ define a curve $\vec{X}(s)$ of which $\kappa(s)$ and $\tau(s)$ are the curvature and torsion, and that this curve is uniquely determined except for an arbitrary Euclidean movement, that is, a "congruence." Thus, curvature and torsion tell you everything there is to know about the *shape* of the curve and absolutely nothing about its position and orientation.

Fact: *Through the specification of the curvature and the torsion you have effectively distilled the pure shape of the curve.*

All Euclidean shape properties must be functions of the curvature and the torsion alone. This is sometimes expressed: the "natural order of differentiation" is three in the case of space curves.

There is no additional shape information to be discovered in the higher order derivatives, which is a very comforting thought, isn't it? You might object that *the curvature and torsion are functions* and thus implicitly contain all derivatives. However, this objection is not quite to the point, since it is not at all required that these functions possess higher order derivatives in the first place. They need only be continuous. In numerical work you define a curve intrinsically through tabular values of the curvature and torsion, without worrying about differentiability for a moment. This will never put you into trouble.

Notice the decisive importance of the codimension in the case of curves living in spaces of different dimensions.

- The curvature vanishes. The torsion is irrelevant then: this is the degenerate case of the straight line. The tangent is a constant vector and the normal and binormal are not defined. This is your generic curve in one-dimensional space.

- The case of nonvanishing curvature but vanishing torsion: this is the degenerate case of the planar curves. The binormal is a constant vector. This is the generic curve in two-dimensional space.

- The case of nonvanishing curvature and torsion. The torsion may vanish at isolated points, but at such a point the rate of change of the torsion doesn't vanish. These are the general space curves. this, of course, is the generic curve in three-dimensional space.

Finally I list a few special cases that are of occasional interest in applications:

- The torsion vanishes; the curvature is constant: a circle.

- Both the curvature and the torsion are constant and different from zero: a circular helix.

- Curvature and torsion are in a constant ratio: a cylindrical helix, that is, a curve that clings to a general cylinder.

- The unpronouncable condition $\kappa^{-2} + (\frac{1}{\tau} \frac{\partial \kappa^{-1}}{\partial s})^2 = r^2$; with $\frac{\partial \kappa}{\partial s} \neq 0$: complicated though this condition may appear to you, it expresses the simple fact that the curve clings to a sphere of radius r. Such curves are very important in applications because spheres are so often used to study directional changes—of anything—through "spherical images."

Two curves that differ merely in the sign of the torsion are each other's *mirror images* and are called *enantiotropic*.

Scaling κ and τ by the same factor amounts to a scaling the whole curve proportionally.

5.2.1 Arbitrary speed curves

♠ INTERMEZZO—GOOD EXERCISE.

Let $\vec{x}(t)$ be a curve that is *not referred to arclength*; t is the "time," say. Then you have for the first temporal derivative of position

$$\frac{\partial \vec{x}}{\partial t} = \vec{v} = \frac{\partial s}{\partial t} \frac{\partial \vec{x}}{\partial s} = v\, \vec{T},$$

which is merely the velocity (v the speed, $\vec{T}$ the direction of movement). Similarly, the second temporal derivative of position is

$$\frac{\partial^2 \vec{x}}{\partial t^2} = \vec{a} = A\, \vec{T} + \kappa v^2\, \vec{N},$$

which is the acceleration. It is composed of two terms, namely the linear acceleration (A) which affects only the speed but not the direction, and the centripetal acceleration ($v^2 \kappa$), which has the effect of curving the orbit and thus defines the orbital plane. Finally the third temporal derivative of position is

$$\frac{\partial^3 \vec{x}}{\partial t^3} = \vec{b} = (\frac{\partial A}{\partial t} - \kappa^2 v^3)\, \vec{T} + (3A\kappa v + v^2 \frac{\partial \kappa}{\partial t})\, \vec{N} + \kappa \tau v^3\, \vec{B},$$

which is seen to be composed of three terms. There are corrections to the linear and the centripetal acceleration, and then there appears a third term which has the effect of deflecting the particle out of the orbital plane. This term contains the torsion. It also contains the curvature, a fact that should come as no surprise because vanishing curvature would imply an undeterminate osculating plane against which no torsion could be measured. In other words the torsion only exists relative to the curvature. These expressions are easily checked if you are the type who doesn't quit when things get a bit messy. The task is somewhat alleviated by the fact that you can make continual use of the Serret-Frenet equations to simplify the expressions. Conventionally $\vec{v}$ denotes the velocity vector, and $\vec{a}$ the acceleration.

From these expressions you immediately obtain the expressions for the curvature and the torsion in terms of the temporal derivatives:

$$\kappa = v^{-3}\|\vec{v} \wedge \vec{a}\|$$
$$\tau = \|\vec{v} \wedge \vec{a}\|^{-2} \|\vec{v} \wedge \vec{a} \wedge \vec{b}\| \; ;$$

thus the curvature is proportional with the modulus of the bivector constructed from the velocity and the acceleration, whereas the torsion is proportional with the size of the crate constructed from this bivector and the third temporal derivative of the orbit. For a unit speed curve the curvature is the magnitude of the second derivative, whereas the product of the torsion and the curvature equals the component of the third derivative orthogonal to the orbital plane.

The speed v, acceleration A and the derivative of the magnitude of the acceleration $\partial A/\partial t$ are *purely dynamical variables* that depend on the way the orbit is actually traversed.

If the speed is constant, the Serret-Frenet equations become simply:

$$\frac{\partial}{\partial t} \begin{pmatrix} \vec{T} \\ \vec{N} \\ \vec{B} \end{pmatrix} = \begin{pmatrix} 0 & \kappa v & 0 \\ -\kappa v & 0 & \tau v \\ 0 & -\tau v & 0 \end{pmatrix} \begin{pmatrix} \vec{T} \\ \vec{N} \\ \vec{B} \end{pmatrix},$$

as you could have guessed without any computation at all.

5.2.2   Spherical curves

♠ Intermezzo—A curiosity.

Curves that are constrained to cling to a unit sphere seem very special, but in fact they are very common and important in applications. This is the case because you are bound to make a lot of use of so-called "spherical images" when you have to deal with anything curved. The later chapters will yield plenty of examples.

If a curve is *a priori* known to be spherical, it makes no sense at all to stick to the Frenet frame. Instead you had better take the "Saban frame," which is defined as follows:

- The first frame vector is the outward normal of the sphere.

- The second frame vector is the curve's tangent.

- The third frame vector is completely determined by the first two.

It is pictorially evident that the Saban frame is intimately connected with the Frenet frame through a simple rotation about the tangent. Thus, it is an easy exercise to find the derivative of the Saban frame from the general Serret-Frenet equations. You may want to try to do the sums yourself. The result is:

$$\frac{\partial}{\partial s} \begin{pmatrix} \vec{S}_1 \\ \vec{S}_2 \\ a\vec{S}_3 \end{pmatrix} = \begin{pmatrix} 0 & 1 & 0 \\ -1 & 0 & \sigma \\ 0 & -\sigma & 0 \end{pmatrix} \begin{pmatrix} \vec{S}_1 \\ \vec{S}_2 \\ \vec{S}_3 \end{pmatrix}$$

The "spherical curvature" σ is just $\pm\sqrt{\kappa^2 - 1}$. Thus it vanishes for the great circles of the sphere. The great circles appear here as the analogues of the straight lines of the plane. You will meet the spherical curvature in later chapters as the "geodesic curvature" of curves on the sphere. The great circles are "geodesics." The name "geodesic" derives from the basic property of great circles to divide the sphere into equal parts.

Conversely, the curvature and the torsion of the spherical curves considered as general space curves are simply:

$$\kappa = \sqrt{1 + \sigma^2}$$
$$\tau = \frac{\frac{\partial \sigma}{\partial s}}{1 + \sigma^2}$$

Thus *torsion zeros are geodesic vertices.* Spherical curves of constant curvature are indeed planar, for they are just the small and great circles of the sphere.

Notice that *the spherical curvature has a well-defined sign.* This is possible, of course, because—as a spherical curve—it has a codimension of one, very much like the planar curves. Indeed, you could easily establish a 1–1 correspondence between planar curves and spherical curves by the artifice of perspective, or central projection. Then straight lines correspond to great circles. There are some loopholes in this, but I will leave it up to you.[3]

5.3   The edge of regression

The tangents on a circle cover the plane outside the circle *twice* but leave the inside area of the circle uncovered. In order to obtain a picture of the manifold of tangents you could take two copies of the plane with the circle punched out and "sew" them together along the circle. Each copy carries half a tangent.

If you cut both planes along one normal, you can deform the two planes into space structures without bending the tangents themselves. The planes then separate and hang together (figs. 125 to 127) only via the curve. You had to cut the structure along a normal plane in order to do this, and at the cut you see a sharp *cuspidal edge.* The figure shows the tangent developable of a circular helix.

It is most instructive to carry out this construction in a literal sense. After all you need only paper, scissors and a device to staple bits of paper together. If you are reading this book at your desk, you are probably all set, so what are you waiting for? There is no better way to make sure

---

[3]You can only map a hemisphere without its perimeter on the plane in this manner.

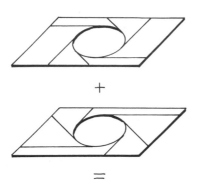

+

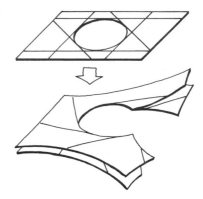

=

125

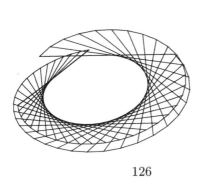

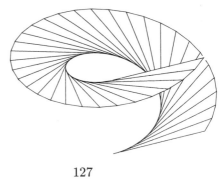

126   127

that these fundamental facts will enter your system; besides it is fun. If you are too lazy to try this, you may very well miss the point.

The sharp edge that you have produced is commonly known as the "edge of regression of the tangent developable." The surface is named "developable" because you can spread out everything flat again if you want. In many applications you need only one sheet, in which case you just curtail the tangent rays at the points where they contact the curve. Figure 127 also shows a single sheet of the tangent developable of the circular helix. The desire to disregard half of the surface arises, for instance, when the curve lies on a surface and only half of the tangent ray sticks out of the material bounded by that surface.

In the folding model you have the perfect model of (half of the) tangent developable. The notion of "developability" is indeed very strikingly implemented in this model: it is intuitively clear how you can use the hinges between the sectors to spread out the model in the plane.

Each space curve is the edge of regression on its own tangent developable. The tangents are called the "generators" of the developable. From the folding model you see that they are the lines along which subsequent osculating planes meet, that is, the hinges. I will indeed often call the tangent lines the "hinges" in this book

You may also regard the tangent developable as the *envelope of tangent planes*. Indeed, in the folding model the sectors *define* the tangent planes. If you conceive of the complete sector planes, you see that these form a congruence of planes that are tangent at the developable along the tangent lines. (A plane shares a "sector" with the developable, and a "sector" is a pair of—infinitesimally close tangent lines.)

The tangent developable cuts the osculating planes in planar curves with a curvature that equals four thirds times κ, a fact that you may not have guessed right away. This insight comes from Beltrami. You may want to prove it to your own satisfaction.

An easy to remember "local model" of the edge is $\mathcal{P}(x,y) = x\vec{e}_x + y^2\vec{e}_y + y^3\vec{e}_z$ (figs. 128 to 131).

Note that a tangent line runs on one sheet of the tangent developable and at the point where it touches the curve crosses over to the other sheet.

Figure 132 shows what the tangent developable looks like in the case of a torsion zero.[4] It has a "pinch point"-like singularity which is known

---

[4]You may find it amusing to build a model (kindergarten tools suffice). Take two sheets of note paper and cut out circular discs. Staple the sheets together along the circumferences of the holes. Cut the sheets in order to make them amenable to a twist. You obtain the typical forms of the edge of regression by twisting the thing

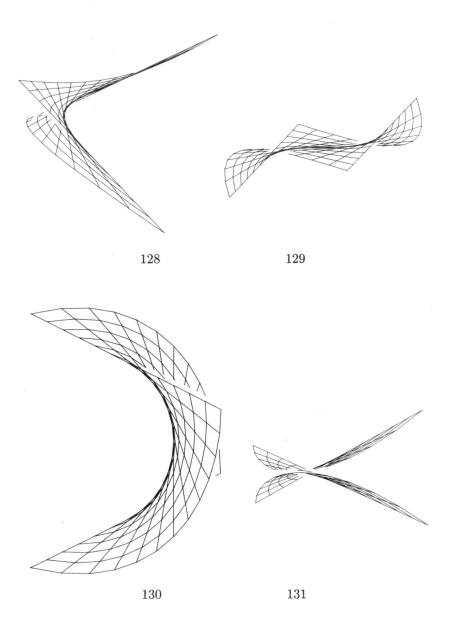

128   129

130   131

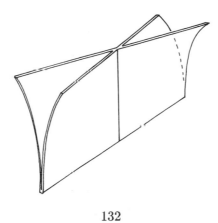

132

as "Whitney's umbrella" to differential topologists. If you happen to view the curve from the immediate neighborhood of a tangent at such a torsion zero you may see some complicated projections. There exist many fleeting impressions that arise when the vantage point is at exactly the right point. I will skip them; the "stable" views that don't change qualitatively when you move the vantage point are more interesting.

Figure 133 shows these "stable" possibilities. You can have a great

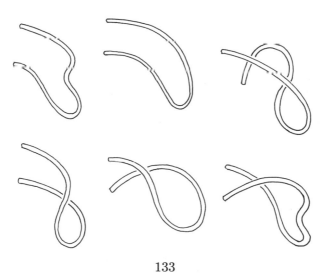

133

time if you borrow some copper wire from the lab and bend yourself

into spatial configurations (tearing is strictly forbidden!). Enjoy yourself.

some hairpins to view from various directions. It is almost necessary
to have done this at least once if you want to develop your intuitive
faculties. So why don't you do it and graduate to the "in" set?

5.4   The polar developable

Consider the linked-rod model with the normal planes attached. Two
consecutive normal planes meet in a line (fig. 134), which is known as
the *polar line*.

The polar line meets the osculating plane in a point that is the center
of the osculating circle, that is, the circle that has the highest order of
contact with the curve at that point.

Three consecutive normal planes (fig. 135) typically have *a point in*

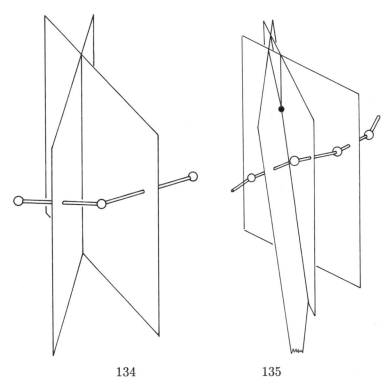

134   135

common. This means that consecutive polar lines are *not skew* but intersect in a point. This point is the center of the *osculating sphere*, introduced by Fuss (1820, *"De sphaeribus oscularibus."* The language alone should tell you that this is really very classical material). This is the sphere (fig. 136) that has the highest order of contact with the curve at that point. Its center is located at the point

$$\vec{x} + \frac{1}{\kappa}\,\vec{N} + \frac{1}{\tau}\frac{\partial \kappa^{-1}}{\partial s}\,\vec{B}$$

and the sphere has contact of the order > 2 with the curve.

Clearly the osculating circle is a small circle on the osculating sphere. Its center is located at the point

$$\vec{x} + \frac{1}{\kappa}\,\vec{N}$$

and the circle has contact of the order two with the curve.

Note that the centers of the osculating circle and osculating sphere *coincide* when the curvature is stationary.

At a torsion zero the osculating sphere degenerates into a plane. The center of the sphere then moves off to infinity. That's one reason why people call such points the "planar points" of the space curve.

For a planar curve the osculating circles are, of course, sufficient, and it makes little sense to look for the osculating spheres. Note that the osculating circles separate parts of the curve with smaller curvature from those with larger curvature. It is not a difficult exercise to show that successive osculating circles on arcs with constant sign of the curvature are *nested*. Thus you meet with the curious fact that all the osculating circles are nested, yet they envelop the curve. This fact was first noted by Kneser.

The polar lines are the generators of yet another developable surface, known as the *polar developable*. It *must* be developable because consecutive generators intersect. If you put *hinges* at the polar lines you can "develop" the surface into the plane. *It is the envelope of normal planes.* The polar lines must be the generators of the polar developable, and they are tangents of the edge of regression of this surface, called the *focal curve*, which is seen to be nothing but the locus of the centers of the osculating spheres. The focal curve is sometimes called the "evolute" of the curve, for good reasons that I won't explain here. The tangent to the focal curve is parallel to the binormal of the curve. The arclength between two points on the focal curve equals the difference of the radii of curvature of the corresponding points on the curve. At least if κ is monotonic on the interval.

The focal curve is nowhere linear and nowhere planar for the generic space curve. It is smooth almost everywhere. At isolated points it may have *cusps* though. At those points the polar developable has a "swallowtail" singularity (fig. 137). Such points correspond to "vertices"

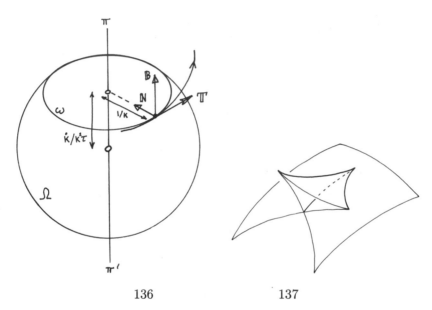

136   137

of the space curve. They appear to be the most natural generalization of the *vertices* of a planar curve. Note that they do not quite correspond to critical points of the "spherical radius of curvature." Contrary to what you might have expected, the curvature κ does not assume an extremum at such a vertex, nor does the radius of the osculating sphere assume an extremum there. Vertices are often conspicuous features of planar curves. Extrema of curvature are known as "hinges" in the jargon applying to geological strata, for instance. For space curves they may appear as "kinks." At a torsion zero the focal curve must have an asymptote because the osculating sphere degenerates into a plane there.

For closed planar curves there is a lot of theory on the number of vertices that you may encounter. For instance, you have at least four vertices on an ovaloid (the famous "Vierscheitelsatz"). However, the simplest "bumpy circle" is $x^2 + y^2 + \varepsilon(x^3 - 3xy^2) = 1$, which clearly possesses *six* vertices.[5] This looks somewhat like an egg with blunt and sharp ends. We owe this insight to Portuous. For space curves things are much more complicated because of the importance of the torsion, or—equivalently—because of the higher codimension. It would appear that there are still discoveries to be made for this case.

5.5   Curves in central projection

When you use computer graphics to study curves, you will usually observe them in central projection on a CRT screen. Thus, it is of some importance to have at least a rudimentary understanding of the shape of the projection as it is related to the shape of the curve and the geometry of the situation.

Let $\vec{r}$ denote the visual direction, Π the plane orthogonal to $\vec{r}$, and ϱ the distance. This means that if the vantage point is at $\mathcal{V}$, then the point on the curve is at $\mathcal{V} + \varrho\vec{r}$. Then I define the orientation of the curve with respect to the vantage point through two angles:

- α denotes the angle between the osculating plane of the curve and the plane Π. The angle α is called the "slant."

- β denotes the angle between the curve's tangent and Π. The angle β is called the "slant of the tangent."

Notice that α constrains the possible values that β may assume.

The *apparent curvature* of the projection is defined as the curvature of the central projection of the curve on a plane parallel to Π and at unit distance ($\varrho = 1$) from the vantage point.

When you do the sums (sigh!) end up with the relation

$$\kappa_{apparent} = \varrho\kappa\frac{\cos\alpha}{\cos^3\beta}.$$

From this formula you may draw several useful conclusions:

- The apparent curvature scales linearly with the distance. This is merely a trivial scaling effect expressing the basic fact of life that things look smaller when you view them from a greater distance.

- The apparent curvature is proportional to κ, as was to be expected from the very start.

---

[5]For a circle, the second order is fixed once and for all; thus the lowest-order perturbation is the cubic terms. One could say it's all a matter of definition.

- The proportionality to the cosine of the slant has an important
  effect. When the vantage point is in the osculating plane of the
  curve, the apparent curvature vanishes completely. This is understandable enough, think of a planar curve. Then you would obtain
  a straight line as projection.

- The proportionality with the reciprocal cubed cosine of the slant
  of the tangent also has dramatic consequences. If you look into
  the tangent direction ($\beta = \frac{\pi}{2}$) the apparent curvature becomes
  infinite. In order to treat this case, you have to be a bit careful
  because both α and β approach $\frac{\pi}{2}$. The projection shows a *cusp*,
  then. Note that this will happen if the vantage point is on the
  tangent developable, which is a *nontransversal* condition. Thus
  you will never encounter this case for random positions of the
  vantage point, but if the vantage point traverses some *orbit*, you
  will see cusps at discrete moments of time.

5.6 Computer Implementation

If you are provided with a sequence of points that are samples of some
curve, it is easiest to treat them as a linked-rod model. You simply interpret the chords as tangents. Then you find the planes of subsequent
tangents. If two tangents are collinear, you concatenate them and treat
them as a single rod. Thus you find the normals and osculating planes.
You then compute the binormals via the vector product. In most cases
the curve will not be in equal rod-length representation. Thus you compute the rod lengths, the angles between subsequent tangents and the
angles between subsequent binormals. The latter are the dihedral angles of the osculating planes. You then end up with a complete intrinsic
description of the curve, irrespective of its position and orientation in
space. The angular turns divided by the rod length yield convenient
estimates of the curvature and torsion.

If you have to *generate a curve from scratch*, it is best to use the
intrinsic description $(\kappa(s), \tau(s))$ and generate a linked-rod model via the
Frenet-Serret equations. As a bonus you automatically obtain the frame
field, which is a great help in geometrical algorithms. Specifically, you
immediately have the tangent developable, and it is easy enough to find
the polar lines and thus the polar developable and the focal curve. The
center of the osculating circle is at $\vec{x} + \frac{1}{\kappa}\vec{N}$ and of the osculating sphere

at

$$\vec{x} + \frac{1}{\kappa}\,\vec{N} + \frac{1}{\tau}\frac{\partial \kappa^{-1}}{\partial s}\,\vec{B}.$$

It is usually most convenient to progress at equal arclength intervals, but if you wish to be economical, you may move further if the curvature is low, setting a lower limit on the excursion from the straight line $\vec{x} + s\,\vec{T}$. Again, this usually isn't worth the effort because it complicates your program, and you end up trading your time against a machine's. Which is the more important? You only live once.

A simple algorithm is obtained if you specify $\kappa(s)$, $\tau(s)$ by way of functions and specify starting conditions by way of a starting position $\mathcal{P}$ and a starting frame $(\vec{T}_0, \vec{N}_0, \vec{B}_0)$. Moreover, you must specify the "rod length" $\triangle s$. Then you may compute the values of the arclength s, the position $\mathcal{P}(s)$ and the frame iteratively:

ALGORITHM FOR CURVE GENERATION:

---

constant $\triangle s = $ *something small*;
variable: $\tilde{T}_i$, $\tilde{N}_i$, $\tilde{B}_i$, $\tilde{T}_{i+1}$, $\tilde{N}_{i+1}$, $\tilde{B}_{i+1}$: unit vector;
variable: $\mathcal{P}_i$, $\mathcal{P}_{i+1}$: PositionVector;
variable: s_i, s_{i+1}: real;
function $\check{}(s\colon$ real): real;
function $\emptyset(s\colon$ real): real;
begin DoCurve
    Set $\mathcal{P}_i$ and $\tilde{T}_i$, $\tilde{N}_i$, $\tilde{B}_i$ *to initial values*;
    repeat *ad infinitum*
        $s_{i+1} = s_i + \triangle s$;
        $\tilde{T}_{i+1} = \tilde{T}_i + \check{}(s_i)\triangle s\,\tilde{N}_i$;
        $\tilde{N}_{i+1} = \tilde{N}_i + (-\check{}(s_i)\,\tilde{T}_i + \emptyset(s_i)\,\tilde{B}_i)\,\triangle s$;
        $\tilde{B}_{i+1} = \tilde{B}_i - \emptyset(s_i)\triangle s\,\tilde{N}_i$;
        $\mathcal{P}_{i+1} = \mathcal{P}_i + \triangle s\,\tilde{T}_i$;
        Use the new point of the curve, i.e., for graphics;
    end repeat *ad infinitum*
end DoCurve

A useful refinement is to renormalize the frame vectors every few steps
or so, just to make sure they don't drift off from being unit length.
That's all there is to it. All the rest is merely graphics or whatever your
application might be. Have some fun!

In every kind of practical activity and experience of nature we
constantly encounter curves ... of widely different forms. The path of a
planet in space, of a ship at sea, or of a projectile in the air, the track
of a chisel on metal, or a wheel on the road, of a pen on the tape of a
recording device, the shape of a cam-shaft governing the valves of a
motor, the contours of an artistic design, the form of a dangling rope,
the shape of a spiral spring coiled for some specific purpose, such
examples are endless.
—A.D. ALEKSANDROV, Curves and Surfaces (1956)

6 Local Patches

1. The surface is a limitation of the body.
2. That which is not part of any body is a thing of nought.
3. A thing of nought is that which fills no space.
The limitation of one body is that which begins another.
—LEONARDO DA VINCI (1452–1519)

6.1 Strips

6.1.1 The notion of a strip

In the folding model you have a model of a *curve* that happens to be a *surface* at the same time. Indeed it is possible to study surfaces by way of studying *strips* that are defined by curves on the surface, like the peel you usually discard when you peel an apple. In many practical cases you may be interested in strips for their own sake. An example would be when you intend to study the surface of an object in the neighborhood of a shadow boundary, a curve of equidistance from some vantage point, or a similar problem. Thus the subject is not merely of an academic interest. Moreover, it serves very well for a didactically attractive entry into the field of surface geometry in general. It is one easy way to obtain a "feel" for what surfaces can be up to, curvaturewise.

For a curve on a surface you wouldn't want to use the Frenet frame because it is so obviously ill-fitted to the surface. You can do much better than just letting the curve's tangent be a tangent vector to the surface. An obvious improvement would be that you take the first vector of the frame in the direction of the curve's tangent, then take the *surface normal* as the third-frame vector and construct the second vector so as to form a right-handed trieder. For the folding model you get the Frenet frame in this way, but usually you will obtain quite a different frame, one that is related to the Frenet frame by a rotation about the tangent.

This type of frame is known as the *Darboux frame*. The frame vectors are $\vec{T}$, $\vec{V}$ and $\vec{S}$ where $\vec{T}$ denotes the tangent and $\vec{S}$ the surface normal. Thus the strip lies in the $\vec{T}$–$\vec{V}$ plane.

It is visually evident that the surface elements only join up smoothly to a surface strip if the tangent of the carrier curve is orthogonal to the surface normals. Thus a necessary constraint for a strip *to be a strip at all* is $\vec{T} \cdot \vec{S} = 0$, and I will assume that this is the case (fig. 138). Otherwise you would get some funny constructions. To see what I mean, you may consider the extreme case $\vec{T} = \vec{S}$, which would correspond to a pile of coins or a deck of playing cards. *Where is the surface in such a case?*

In order to study strips in terms of the Darboux frame, but nevertheless be able to exploit the knowledge you acquired about the behavior of space curves in the Frenet frame, you have to hunt for an angle φ (say) that will depend on the particular point on the strip where you happen to be such that

$$\left(\begin{array}{c} \vec{V} \\ \vec{S} \end{array} \right) = \left(\begin{array}{cc} \cos\varphi & -\sin\varphi \\ \sin\varphi & \cos\varphi \end{array} \right) \left(\begin{array}{c} \vec{N} \\ \vec{B} \end{array} \right),$$

that is to say, the pair $\vec{V}$, $\vec{S}$ is just the curve's normal ($\vec{N}$) and binormal ($\vec{B}$) rotated as a pair about the tangent over an angle φ.

Figure 139 shows a very simple example where the strip is a latitude

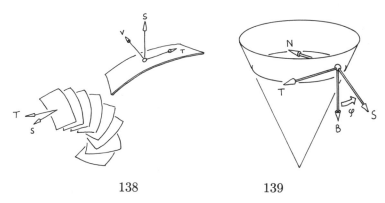

138   139

circle of a right circular cone. Then the angle φ is just the semi top angle of the cone. The angle φ in general depends on arclength. Figures 140 to 143 show a few possibilities. The "carrier" curve has constant curvature and zero torsion for clarity. The angle φ has the value 0 and 90 degrees for the first two pictures, 45 degrees for the third, and makes a steady turn of 180 degrees in total for the fourth example.

Apparently you can make some pretty weird ribbons this way. Of course, an additional torsion as well as torsion and curvature *trends* complicate things still further. The point I want to make here is that *ribbons are by no means trivial geometrical constructs*, although they are, of course, far simpler than full-fledged surfaces.

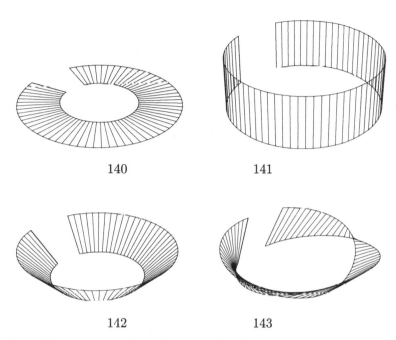

140   141

142   143

6.1.2   The geometrical invariants

It is a fairly light exercise to express the Frenet-Serret equations in terms of the triad $(\vec{T}, \vec{V}, \vec{S})$ instead of $(\vec{T}, \vec{N}, \vec{B})$. I denote the elements of the Cartan matrix as follows. I make use of the skew symmetry to reduce the number of independent coefficients right away to a mere triple.

$$\begin{pmatrix} \vec{T}' \\ \vec{V}' \\ \vec{S}' \end{pmatrix} = \begin{pmatrix} 0 & g & k \\ -g & 0 & t \\ -k & -t & 0 \end{pmatrix} \begin{pmatrix} \vec{T} \\ \vec{V} \\ \vec{S} \end{pmatrix}.$$

By comparison with the Frenet-Serret equations, you immediately find the relations:

$$\begin{aligned} g &= \kappa \cos \varphi \\ k &= \kappa \sin \varphi \\ t &= \tau - \tfrac{\partial \varphi}{\partial s}. \end{aligned}$$

As expected, the geometrical implications are pictorially evident. The invariant k is the component of the acceleration along the surface normal; it is called the *normal curvature*. It equals the curvature of the intersection of the strip with the $\vec{T}$-$\vec{S}$ plane. This is a so-called "normal section." Flexing a ribbon in a way that affects only k intuitively does not involve any stretch of its material. For instance, you may impose a normal curvature on any paper strip at your disposal. Try it at your desk. Paper, scissors, and your fingers are all you need. What are you waiting for?

The geometric invariant g is the component of the acceleration in the tangent plane. It is known as the *geodesic curvature*. You can't flex a paper strip such that you change the geodesic curvature without tearing it. If you want a paper strip with a different geodesic curvature, you have no option but to cut a new one from a fresh piece of paper.

The invariant t equals the torsion of the curve minus the rate of rotation of the Darboux trihedron about the tangent relative to the Frenet trihedron. Intuitively this measures the amount by which you will have to "twist" the folding model in order to make it fit the strip. The invariant t is known as the *geodesic torsion*, but I will often refer to it as the "twist." You can twist a paper strip as much as you like without tearing it, as some experimentation will reveal.

6.1.3   Curvature strips

In order to grasp these ideas in a more intimate way, you may want to consider a few special strips. Suppose the invariant t vanishes. Such an untwisted strip is illustrated here (fig. 144). Such a strip is technically known as a "curvature strip." It is special in the sense that the change of the surface normal is along the tangent. Thus you obtain a curvature strip if you bend a not-necessarily-straight paper strip such that the bending takes place perpendicular to the curve's direction.

Any strip on a sphere is a curvature strip; this shows you how special the sphere is. The sphere is completely determined through this property.

A folding model of a curvature strip consists of hinged quadrilaterals such that the hinges are bisectors of the "rods" (fig. 145).

The curvature strips are completely characterized through the property that the normals are generators of a developable surface. This is in fact a method to spot curvature strips on surfaces. The normal rays must be the tangents of some curve, namely the edge of regression of the developable. This "focal curve" is the locus of points where successive normal rays meet. Notice that the "focal curve" is often called "caustic curve" or "curve of centers," sometimes "evolute." All these terms can be used interchangeably.

Figure 146 shows the typical case. Notice that successive normals are *skew*. Figure 147 displays the special case of the curvature strip.

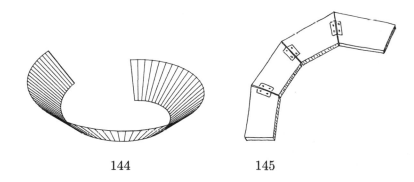

144   145

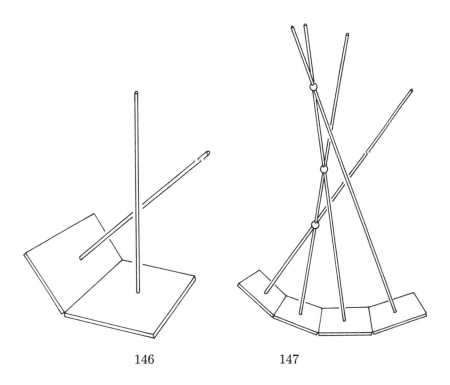

146   147

6.1.4 Geodesic strips

If the invariant g vanishes, the strip has no curvature in the plane of the strip. Such a "geodesic strip" is illustrated here (fig. 148). Such strips are *straight* when spread out in the plane. On the sphere you may take a strip along a meridian, for instance a sector $\alpha < \varphi < \alpha + \Delta\,\alpha;\ 0 < \vartheta < \pi$ (fig. 149).

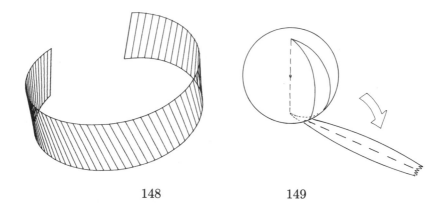

148   149

The straightening-out property suggests the way to build a folding model. Take a triangulation of a straight planar strip and use the hinges to make a space structure. Such strips are called "geodesic strips." If you paste a length of adhesive tape on a surface, it assumes the shape of such a geodesic strip.

The geodesic strips have a relation to *the shortest route problem.* Clearly a straight line is the shortest distance between the endpoints of the strip when it is spread out flat. But the distance *along the surface* doesn't change by bending the strip; thus the center line of the strip must be a shortest distance along the surface. You can also realize geodesic arcs mechanically by stretching wires tautly over the surface and using the curve of contact as the carrier curve for a geodesic strip to be cut out of the surface.

The "geodesic curvature" is the curvature of the plane curve that you obtain when you project the carrier curve of the strip, by parallel projection in the direction of the surface normal, on the tangent plane of the strip.

6.1.5   Asymptotic strips

If the invariant k vanishes, the strip has no normal curvature. It is *twisted*, and may possess a geodesic curvature. There exist no such strips on the sphere. An example of a purely twisted strip would be a ribbon about the edge of regression of a space curve where the "hinges" are the tangents of the curve. This is obviously not the kind of recipe that you could pass on to the machine shop!

Here is a more practical way to obtain a model of this type of strip: take any geodesic strip and stick pins in the sectors, perpendicular to the strip. Bend it any way you want. The pins then define the kind of strip you are after; it is called an *asymptotic strip*. But please notice that the pins cannot represent the hinges of the strip in this case.

You can't make a more direct model because the hinges have to be in the same direction as the strip's curve. That this trick works is clear from the fact that a rotation of a geodesic strip over $\frac{\pi}{2}$ along the tangent $(\varphi \rightarrow \varphi + \frac{\pi}{2})$ converts a geodesic strip into an asymptotic strip, and vice versa (fig. 150).

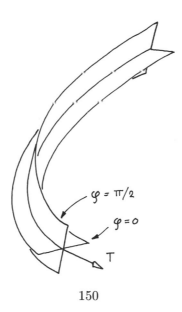

150

You may also cut a long straight, narrow strip from flexible but inextensible material such as paper and apply it to a surface. If you apply it with the broad side on the surface, you find a geodesic strip; if you apply it *edge-on*, that is, orthogonal to the tangent planes of the surface, you obtain an asymptotic curve on the surface. This has been illustrated in the chapter "Shape & Space" and may have looked mysterious at that place. Thus, you will never be able to apply a straight strip edge on to a sphere, a fact that will hardly come as a big surprise to you.

A folding model can approximate an asymptotic strip if you take a triangulation with very elongated triangles.

The asymptotic strips are completely characterized through the property that the osculating planes of the carrier curve coincide with the tangent planes of the surface.

6.1.6   Levi-Civita parallel transport

The strips are such nice models because you can so conveniently *deform* them, for instance so as to fold them out in the plane. This is intuitively obvious from the folding models. I will often make use of this property. For instance, you can easily measure the geodesic curvature in this way.

The geodesic curvature is just the curvature of the planar curve you derive by the process of ironing out. (Thus "geodesic curvature" is *not* the curvature of any geodesic. Beware!) When you peel an apple, you usually obtain a spiral with vortices of opposite sense at both ends and an inflection in the middle when you flatten the peel. Thus you obtain a curve with a marked geodesic curvature gradient. This is something to try right away if you can't visualize it very well. There is nothing like the hands on approach to burn relations of the natural world into your brain.

Another important concept that is easily demonstrated on peels is that of "Levi-Civita parallel transport."[1] The problem here is how to transport a tangent vector from one tangent space to the next. The catch that makes this task interesting and highly nontrivial is that this is an ambiguous process that *depends on the route.*

If you have defined a route on a surface, you can cut a strip along it and spread it out in the plane.[2] Then you transport vectors by Euclidean translation in the plane: no sweat! When you again apply the ribbon to the surface taking the vector with it, you have "Levi-Civita-transported" it. Basically that is all there is to it.

Figure 151 shows this for a latitude circle of the sphere. A closed

---

[1]Dates from 1917. Don't miss the fact that "Levi-Civita" stands for a single person!

[2]Of course, you may also roll the object over a flat table top. This alternative method works out in precisely the same way.

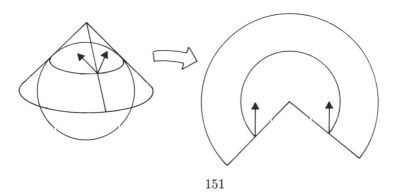

151

circuit usually can't be spread out without tearing, so you ruthlessly cut it open and—formally—identify the endpoints. A little experimenting will convince you that transport of a vector around a closed loop will in general rotate it, that is to say, after the circumnavigation of the loop the tangent plane has suffered a rotation about the normal.

This curious possibility is especially evident in the case of *closed geodesic loops*. Since a geodesic strip irons out to a straight planar strip, the tangents along a geodesic strip are Levi-Civita transported copies of each other. When you follow a geodesic, you may experience a situation in which you apparently circumnavigate a loop and return to a point you already visited. But you may be facing in another direction! Of course this means that the geodesic intersects itself.

Levi-Civita parallel transport can also be explained in an apparently slightly different, though actually equivalent way. Any geometrical entity at a point of the surface can be written as the unique sum of a tangential and a normal component. The sum of the tangential and normal components is a geometric object in $\mathbf{E}^3$, thus a fairly trivial affair. When you simply *discard the normal components*, you obtain operations and objects that belong to the tangent spaces of the surface.

In this view Levi-Civita parallel transport is simply the Euclidean parallel transport (how trivial can you get!) *projected upon the surface*. It is pictorially evident that this explanation is equivalent to the definition I gave earlier. When you write down the formal expressions, these explanations are indeed *identical*: it is only the *interpretation* that sounds (and looks) slightly different.

A very simple example is offered by the geodesics on a right circular cone. Since you can so easily develop a cone into the plane, this case is especially enlightening. It helps to make a sketch. Geodesics can indeed return to the same point on the cone mantle, and when they do so you find yourself facing in a new direction. It is easy to derive the angular difference through elementary geometrical considerations. It depends only on the semi-top angle of the cone. In fact the turn of the tangent equals the solid angle subtended by the normals at the apex.

This is a simple instance of a general phenomenon, originally noticed by Gauss, that will be discussed in some detail later. It is perhaps vaguely reasonable at this point if you still remember the fact from a previous chapter that the *theorema egregium* involves the form $d\tilde{\omega}^{12}$. This form must relate to this turn, and is again related to the Gaussian curvature, that is, the spread of normals. These mysterious relations will be cleared up at a later stage. They are important and interesting because they reveal relations between the intrinsic and the extrinsic geometry of a surface.

The tangent vectors of geodesic strips must be Levi-Civita transported versions of each other; so much is pictorially evident. Geodesics are "autoparallels." The geodesic can be defined as a route obtained by driving over the surface in your car without turning the steering wheel. (This is the intuitive content of the technical expression "autoparallel.") Notice that they are *not* the curves you obtain by *setting a heading and sticking to it*, for on the globe you would travel over a *loxodrome* then, a curve that takes you to the pole in spirals. Loxodromes can only be defined with respect to a coordinate system on the surface, such as a compass direction on our earth. The geodesics are completely independent of such an arbitrary choice.

A geodesic route between two points on the globe differs quite markedly from a loxodrome (figs. 152 and 153). Apparently the heading changes from point to point along the geodesic, whereas the loxodrome has constant heading but surely takes a detour between any two points. Points near opposite poles yield extreme examples.

Note that Levi-Civita parallel transport necessarily *rotates the tangent plane as a whole*; thus the mutual angular relationships of tangent vectors are conserved.

6.1.7   Focal properties

The curvature strips are of special interest. The hinges of the folding model are at right angles to the curve; moreover, they are generators of a developable surface. This should be pictorially evident given the fact that a curvature strip is by construction nothing but a strip from a tangent surface of some curve, cut in such a way that the strip tangent is everywhere perpendicular to the generators.

The *edge of regression* of the developable of the hinges is of evident

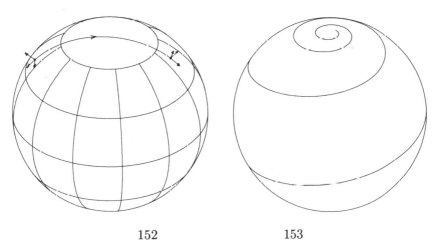

152   153

geometric importance, although it lies somewhere in space outside the actual strip. It is the *locus of centers of geodesic curvature* of the strip, as will be clear from the construction (fig. 154). The geodesic vertices and inflexions have geometric meaning and define special points on the strip.

For degenerated surfaces with special symmetry, as they often occur in human artifacts, you often can point out the curvature strips right away. For instance, in surfaces of revolution they are the meridians and latitude circles. In this case the developables of the strips are circular cones and general cylinders (fig. 155).[3]

For a general strip the hinges are not necessarily perpendicular to the strip curve. Their direction is given by the intersection of consecutive ribbon planes ($\vec{T}$-$\vec{V}$ planes), which is again given by the direction of $\vec{S} \times \vec{S}' = t\vec{T} - k\vec{V}$. You will recognize the similarity to the Darboux vector for curves. This is because the mechanical function of the hinges is to act as an axis of rotation (fig. 156). Only when the torsion vanishes, as for a curvature strip, do you have orthogonalty. *The directions of the hinges are called the "conjugates" of the tangent directions.*

From construction, the conjugated directions are the generators of a developable surface. Its edge of regression consists of the apices of the *osculating cones* that touch the surface along the ribbon.

---

[3]It is geometrically evident that all hinges along a meridional strip are parallel (hence "general cylinder"), whereas for a latitude strip the hinges must meet on a point of the axis of rotational symmetry (hence "right circular cones").

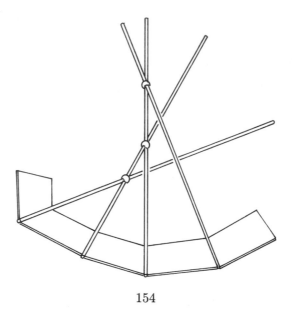

154

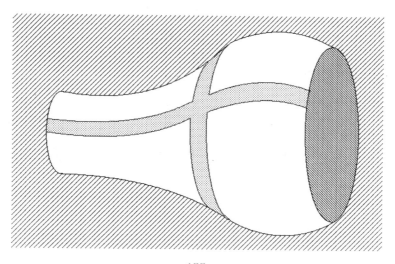

155

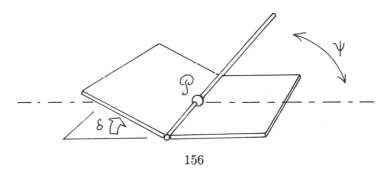

156

Here is an easy way to generate strips for which this developable is a true general cone: take a point source of light and consider all light rays that graze the surface of the object. They generate a general cone mantle that touches the object along a strip that is the terminator of the body shadow (fig. 157). All grazing rays are conjugate to the terminator.

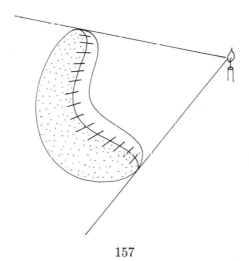

157

Next time you visit some suitable statue illuminated by the sun you may want to study these relations in detail!

Note that the rays need not be *perpendicular* to the terminator; in some cases they may even be tangential to it, such as when the normal curvature vanishes. This happens at points where the ribbon is asymptotic.

If you consider the *normals* along a strip, it is evident that in general they will be *mutually skewed*. Consider a normal $\vec{S}(s)$ and the "next one," that is, $\vec{S}(s + \triangle s) = \vec{S}(s) - k\vec{T}(s)\triangle s - t\vec{V}(s)\triangle s$. These two vectors are coplanar when the crate $\vec{S} \wedge \frac{\partial \vec{S}}{\partial s} \wedge \vec{T}$ vanishes, that is, when $t = 0$.

Any twist makes subsequent normals skew, as is immediately evident when considered pictorially. Thus the curvature strips are the only strips for which the normals are generators of a developable surface. The edge of regression of this surface is a locus of *centers of normal curvature*, where nearby normal rays intersect. It is an extremely important locus of great practical utility. Its operational interest, for instance, is evident from the fact that a point on a strip has to be a critical point of the distance squared function if the vantage point is a center of normal curvature.

6.1.8   Computer Implementation of strips

♠ INTERMEZZO—HOW TO HACK A STRIP SHOW.

Strips are particularly simple objects to represent in a computer. You can define them either by the normal and geodesic curvature with the geodesic torsion, or via a curve with an added twist. This twist is the relation between the Darboux and the Frenet frame. In the latter case the generation is almost completely identical to that of a space curve. If you have already made a program to generate curves via the Serret-Frenet equations, you can make it do double duty and generate strips to boot. It will be worth your while to do this and to play around with strips for a spell. It certainly helps to get a feel for these "almost" surfaces. This will greatly aid your understanding of "full fledged" surfaces.

A simple algorithm runs as follows. You have to specify functions κ, τ, φ of arclength and some initial conditions. The initial conditions are the position and starting Frenet frame. Then you compute the Frenet frame iteratively, just as you would do it for the space curves. From the Frenet frame you obtain the Darboux frame through a rotation over $\varphi(s)$. The ribbon can be drawn if you specify its width. Alternatively you may want to compute the "hinges" as the conjugate directions of the tangents. You compute the hinges at points halfway between the points you find through the iterative procedure. The hinges can be found via the vector product of successive normals from the Darboux frames.

6.2   Local surface patches

6.2.1   The moving frame

I still have to show how to fit a moving frame to a surface patch as tightly as possible in order to bring out the relevant geometry with a minimum of inessential overhead.

At the moment it is at least clear that one of the frame vectors should be the surface normal and that the other two would automatically span the tangent plane (fig. 158). This is illustrated in figure 159, which

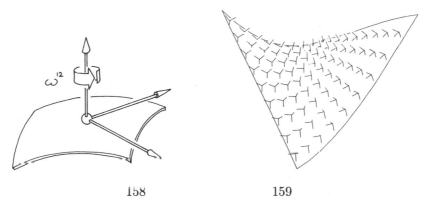

158   159

shows a typical frame field as I numerically fitted it to a patch. This type of structure is the foundation for most computational differential geometry.

This leaves you with only a single degree of freedom, namely a rotation of the frame about the normal to improve the fit. Several useful choices are possible, but it will take me a while before I can explain the rationale. Some additional insights are needed first.

Let the frame vectors be denoted $\vec{f}_{1,2,3}$, with $\vec{f}_3$ the normal. Then you first find the duals of $\vec{f}_{1,2}$, denoted $\tilde{\sigma}^1$, $\tilde{\sigma}^2$. The dual of $\vec{f}_3$ is trivial and I won't consider it now. Then you have to deal with the *connection form of the intrinsic geometry*, that is to say, $\tilde{\omega}^{12}$, which describes the turn of $\vec{f}_{1,2}$ about the normal when you move over the surface, and the forms describing the external geometry $\tilde{\omega}^{13}$, $\tilde{\omega}^{23}$, which describe how the normal turns about $\vec{f}_{1,2}$ when you roam about the surface. The latter two forms might well be call "extrinsic curvature forms." The former I will call the "spin form" because it describes the spin of the tangential coordinates about the normal. Sometimes I will call it the "intrinsic curvature form" because it really determines the intrinsic curvature of the surface, as you will see later on.

6.2.2   The second fundamental form

Before I proceed, I have to introduce an operator that defines the local *shape* in a convenient manner. Intuitively, *shape* is how the normal—or equivalently, the tangent plane—turns as you move in arbitrary directions over the surface. The shape clearly depends only on the extrinsic curvature forms. What you would really like to have at your disposal is some machinery that catches this intuitive notion closely.

The "second fundamental form" is the operator that catches the local shape. It has a great many faces, most of them useful in one way or another. An elementary definition regards II merely as the *Hessian of the height function* along the normal direction. However, I prefer to introduce II as an operator which reveals how the tangent planes change in the neighborhood of any point on the surface. This is what I mean:

Let $\mathcal{P}$ be a fiducial point on your surface. Let $\mathcal{Q}$ be another point in its vicinity. Let p and q denote the tangent planes at $\mathcal{P}$, $\mathcal{Q}$. Then q can (at least pictorially!) be interpreted as a covector in the covector space of $\mathcal{P}$ in the following way: Let $\vec{v}_{\mathcal{P}}$ be any tangent vector at $\mathcal{P}$. Then $\mathcal{P} + \vec{v}_{\mathcal{P}}$ is a point in the tangent plane p. The distance of this point to the tangent plane q at $\mathcal{Q}$ is d, say. Clearly d depends linearly on $\vec{v}_{\mathcal{P}}$, thus there must be a covector $\tilde{\delta}_{\mathcal{P}}$ such that $\tilde{\delta}_{\mathcal{P}}\langle \vec{v}_{\mathcal{P}} \rangle$ equals d. This covector represents q, that is, the tangent plane at $\mathcal{Q}$ in the tangent space at $\mathcal{P}$. Thus the tangent planes in the vicinity of $\mathcal{P}$ can be brought into correspondence with covectors in the tangent space at $\mathcal{P}$.

This notion neatly meshes with the intuition that the tangent planes are somehow like *first derivatives of the shape*, that is to say, linear functions that approximate the surface. Using this heuristic, the *shape* should be the *second derivative*, that is to say the "curvature," which should be a linear map of linear maps, that is, *a symmetric bilinear map*. Symmetry is to be expected because the relations between neighboring points on the surface should be reciprocal. Later on I will develop this heuristic somewhat further.

You have seen how any one-form in the tangent space may be considered to represent another *plane* that is *inclined with respect to that tangent plane* if you interpret the geometry extrinsically (fig. 160).

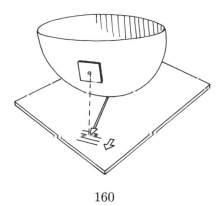

160

You can come to an understanding of this important idea as follows. Let $\tilde{\varphi}$ be a one-form: then $\tilde{\varphi}\langle\vec{t}\rangle$ for some tangent vector $\vec{t}$ is a number that can be interpreted as the normal deviation of a certain plane with respect to the tangent plane at the point $\vec{t}$. It is not hard to figure out how this plane is positioned in space. Just notice that the vectors $\alpha\vec{s}$ for which $\tilde{\varphi}\langle\vec{s}\rangle = 0$ are on the line of intersection of the plane defined by $\tilde{\varphi}$ and the tangent plane. Thus the inclination of the plane of $\tilde{\varphi}$ is merely the arctangent of $\tilde{\varphi}\langle\vec{p}\rangle$, where $\vec{p}$ is a unit vector orthogonal to $\vec{s}$.

As said before, *shape* intuitively means exactly that you have to reckon with different tangent planes for different points. Thus if you are at a point $\mathcal{P}$, then you need the tangent planes at nearby points $\mathcal{P}'$, or—equivalently—you have to specify a certain one-form for those points. This leads to the insight that

Important heuristic: *shape can be understood as a map that assigns one-forms to tangent vectors.*

Locally, everything will be linear; thus it makes good sense to look around and see if you can scare up some linear operator that will do the job for you. There is such an animal and it is called "II." Among its better-known names are "Second Fundamental Form"—hence "II"—or sometimes also "Shape Operator" or "Weingarten Map," for reasons that will become clear later on.

The operator $II(\vec{t})$ assigns a one-form to tangent vectors $\vec{t}$, such that this one-form defines the tangent plane for a point of the surface that is approximated by the tip of $\vec{t}$. Contracted upon another vector $\vec{s}$, you obtain a number $II(\vec{t})\langle\vec{s}\rangle$ that is the deviation at $\vec{s}$ of the tangent plane at $\vec{t}$ from the fiducial tangent plane. It is intuitively evident that II is a bilinear operator on the vectors $\vec{t}$ and $\vec{s}$ and that it is *symmetric*; thus $II(\vec{t})\langle\vec{s}\rangle = II(\vec{s})\langle\vec{t}\rangle$. This latter fact is pictorially evident because the geometrical relations between the tangent planes are *mutual*. I often write $II(\vec{t}, \vec{s})$ for either $II(\vec{t})\langle\vec{s}\rangle$ or $II(\vec{s})\langle\vec{t}\rangle$. (Thus I will write II sometimes with a *single*, sometimes with a *double* argument! Don't get confused!) This operator is classically known as "the second fundamental form" of the surface. The vector $\sharp II(\vec{t})$, which is nothing but the change of the surface normal, as a function of $\vec{t}$ is sometimes called the "Weingarten map."

If you guessed that there must be a "First Fundamental Form," you were right. This operator "I" or "First Fundamental Form" is nothing but *the gauge figure*. In the classical literature it is often called the "line element," or "dee-es-squared," because it defines the local metric. The operator I can accept two tangent vectors in its slots and pops out their scalar product in response. Thus you have simply $I = d\vec{x} \cdot d\vec{x}$. The first fundamental form is useful because it can often be used to find arc lengths, areas, and angles in terms of the surface parametrization. The classical textbooks tend to take it from I, all the rest builds on this *fundamental* form. I consider this to be a rather extreme view caused by an undue concentration on issues of intrinsic geometry.

The second fundamental form is a truly wonderful tool in shape analysis because—by construction—it *defines the totality of tangent planes in a neighborhood of any point.* If you fix the direction of $\vec{t}$, then $II(\alpha\vec{t})$ describes a stretch of a strip in the direction $\vec{t}$, namely a curve $\alpha\vec{t} + \frac{1}{2}\alpha^2 II(\vec{t}, \vec{t})\vec{f_3}$ with "hinges" $\vec{h}$ defined through the condition $II(\vec{h}, \vec{t}) = 0$. Thus II somehow packages all strips belonging to normal sections at a certain point of the surface into a single entity.

By comparison with the Cartan matrix, you obtain the explicit form of the second fundamental form:

$$II(\vec{t}) = \tilde{\omega}^{13}\langle\vec{t}\rangle\,\tilde{\sigma}^1 + \tilde{\omega}^{23}\langle\vec{t}\rangle\,\tilde{\sigma}^2.$$

From this expression it appears that the connection forms $\tilde{\omega}^{13,23}$ determine II, as could indeed have been expected from the start since these define the turn of the normal about $\vec{f}_{1,2}$. In retrospect the whole construct of the shape operator appears geometrically rather trivial. The operator $II(\vec{t})$ turns out to be simply the rate of turn of the surface normal toward the first-frame vector times the first-frame one-form plus an identical term for the second-frame direction.

Thus $II(\vec{t}, \vec{s})$ is the scalar product of the change of the surface normal from tail to tip of $\vec{t}$ with the tangent vector $\vec{s}$.[4] This is one of the classical definitions of the second fundamental form: "$II = d\vec{N} \cdot d\vec{x}$." You see that

---

[4]Or vice versa!

a study of the *change* of local shape over the surface must involve the exterior derivatives $d\tilde{\omega}^{13}$, $d\tilde{\omega}^{23}$. In fact you could say that the tangent plane is a "first derivative," the second fundamental form the "second derivative," and that the forms $d\tilde{\omega}^{13,23}$ are the "third derivatives" of the surface.

That the second fundamental form is like a second derivative is also evident from the fact that the value of $II(\vec{x'}, \vec{x'})$ for a curve $\vec{x}(t)$ on the surface is exactly the *normal component of the acceleration*, that is, the tendency of a particle traversing the orbit to leave the surface. This acceleration is velocity squared divided by the radius of curvature of the orbit, as you will remember from way back. Thus II measures the curvature of orbits on the surface, clearly a second-order property.

The third derivatives are at once obtained from the general Cartan equations. They are

$$d\tilde{\omega}^{13} = \tilde{\omega}^{12} \wedge \tilde{\omega}^{23}$$
$$d\tilde{\omega}^{23} = \tilde{\omega}^{21} \wedge \tilde{\omega}^{13},$$

a pair of equations that is generally associated with the names of Codazzi-Mainardi I will discuss them in a more convenient form later on.

People often write the shape operator $II(\bullet, \bullet)$ as a *matrix* with coefficients $II(\vec{f_i}, \vec{f_j})$. Thus the matrix is:

$$\begin{pmatrix} \tilde{\omega}^{13}\langle \vec{f_1} \rangle & \tilde{\omega}^{23}\langle \vec{f_1} \rangle \\ \tilde{\omega}^{13}\langle \vec{f_2} \rangle & \tilde{\omega}^{23}\langle \vec{f_2} \rangle \end{pmatrix}.$$

Please remember what these coefficients signify:

- $\tilde{\omega}^{13}\langle \vec{f_1} \rangle$ is the turn of the normal about $\vec{f_2}$ for movement along $\vec{f_1}$.

- $\tilde{\omega}^{23}\langle \vec{f_1} \rangle$ is the turn of the normal about $\vec{f_1}$ for movement along $\vec{f_1}$.

- $\tilde{\omega}^{13}\langle \vec{f_2} \rangle$ is the turn of the normal about $\vec{f_2}$ for movement along $\vec{f_2}$.

- $\tilde{\omega}^{23}\langle \vec{f_2} \rangle$ is the turn of the normal about $\vec{f_1}$ for movement along $\vec{f_2}$.

The diagonal elements clearly describe "nosedives" (turnings) of the frame, whereas the off-diagonal terms describe the twist. The determinant and the trace of this matrix are of special importance because they are *algebraic invariants*. They don't change when you rotate the frame about the normal. They are denoted K (the determinant of the matrix) and H (one half the trace of the matrix). Conventionally, K is known as the *Gaussian curvature*, H as the *mean curvature*. These terms will be discussed more fully later in this chapter. They can conveniently be expressed in terms of $\tilde{\omega}^{ij}$, $\tilde{\sigma}^i$. You have

$$\tilde{\omega}^{13} \wedge \tilde{\omega}^{23} = K\,\tilde{\sigma}^1 \wedge \tilde{\sigma}^2$$

and

$$\frac{1}{2}(\tilde{\omega}^{13} \wedge \tilde{\sigma}^2 + \tilde{\sigma}^1 \wedge \tilde{\omega}^{23}) = H\,\tilde{\sigma}^1 \wedge \tilde{\sigma}^2.$$

The sign of K roughly determines the qualitative shape of a surface as gauged by the eye. You can easily distinguish positive and negative Gaussian curvatures at a glance. Consider some examples:

The *sphere* is a surface with constant *positive* Gaussian curvature. You know a sphere when you see one! By way of contrast I depict here a surface with constant *negative* Gaussian curvature (fig. 161). It is known as the "pseudosphere," so called because in some old-fashioned sense, which really doesn't matter here, it is like a "sphere with imaginary radius." The Gaussian curvature leaves quite a bit of leeway to the extrinsic shape though. For example, I show two surfaces that are both of constant positive Gaussian curvature, just like the sphere (fig. 162). As you will appreciate they can certainly look (or *be*) quite different

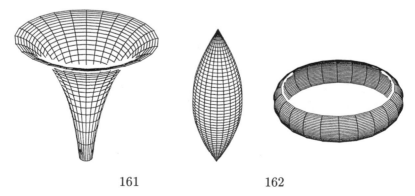

161   162

from spheres.

6.2.3 Geometrical invariants

Both the formulas defining K and H have a rather direct geometrical meaning. Consider the first one. The two-form $\tilde{\sigma}^1 \wedge \tilde{\sigma}^2$ is just the *element of area on the surface*. The two-form $\tilde{\omega}^{13} \wedge \tilde{\omega}^{23}$ is the solid angle spanned by the normals on this element of area. Thus the Gaussian curvature K is the ratio between the solid angle subtended by the normals on a small patch divided by the area (fig. 163). Figure 164 shows cases in which the

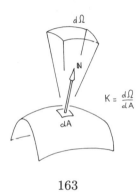

163

sign of K is positive, negative—the orientation of the spherical image reverses—and zero—the solid angle vanishes.

This relation is often somewhat differently expressed. People say that they map the surface on the unit sphere; that is—formally—they write[5]:

$$G\left(\vec{x}\left(u,v\right)\right) = \vec{f}_3(u,v).$$

This map $G : \mathcal{S} \mapsto \mathbf{S}^2$ from the surface patch $\mathcal{S}$ to the unit sphere $\mathbf{S}^2$ is generally known as "the Gauss-map" and the unit sphere is baptized "the Gaussian sphere" for this occasion. The number K is just the *area magnification of the Gauss map* and is known as the "Gaussian curvature."

Useful heuristic: *K measures the total spread of normal directions per unit surface area.*

The second equation also has a nice geometrical interpretation. Notice that a term such as $\tilde{\omega}^{13} \wedge \tilde{\sigma}^2$, when contracted on the unit bivector, is just $\tilde{\omega}^{13}\langle \vec{f}_1 \rangle$. This again is nothing but the rate of turn of the normal

---

[5]Don't confuse this mapping G with the metric tensor!

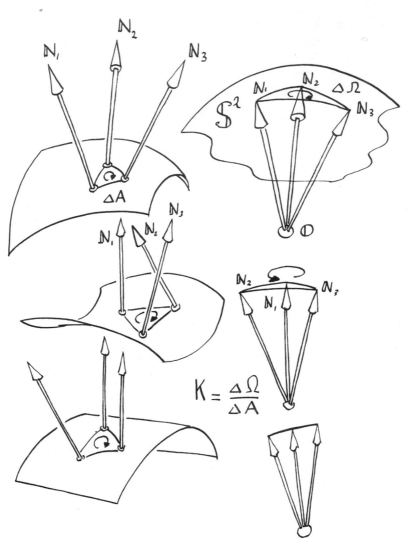

$$K = \frac{\Delta \Omega}{\Delta A}$$

in the first coordinate direction if you progress into that direction—in other words, a "nose dive" of the frame. Geometrically this nose dive is the result of the normal curvature in the first coordinate direction.

If you remember that the first coordinate direction is essentially arbitrary except for the obvious constraint that it has to be in the tangent plane, it follows that the mean curvature equals the average normal curvature taken over all tangent directions. This accounts for the term "mean curvature." I will postpone the full discussion of the mean curvature until I have discussed how to fit the frame still tighter to the surface.

Useful heuristic: *H measures the turn of the normal direction for a unit step along the surface averaged over all directions.*

Notice how the *algebraic invariants* of *II*—its trace and determinant—induce significant *geometric invariants*.

The general Cartan frame equations yield another interpretation of the Gaussian curvature K via the condition $d\tilde{\omega}^{12} = -K\,\tilde{\sigma}^1 \wedge \tilde{\sigma}^2$. This equation is conventionally known as the "Gauss equation." This formula has important consequences because it was used by Gauss, albeit in a quite different guise, to show that K can be defined through geodesy on the surface itself, and thus has intrinsic significance. This is the famous "*Theorema Egregium*," or "Princely Theorem." Gauss must have been rather pleased with himself, and rightly so! The interpretation is as follows:

The spin form $\tilde{\omega}^{12}$ describes a rotation that leaves the tangent plane as a whole undisturbed and is an *intrinsic* geometrical entity. This becomes clear when you consider alternative frames, rotated about the normal direction over an angle φ that depends on position. Then $d\tilde{\omega}^{12}$ changes merely by the one-form $d\varphi$. A Levi-Civita parallel transport of the tangent plane over a closed curve rotates the tangent plane over an angle that equals the area integral of the Gaussian curvature over the area bounded by the loop. This was called by Gauss the "*curvatura integra*"; the integral of $K\,\tilde{\sigma}^1 \wedge \tilde{\sigma}^2$, which might be translated as "total curvature." That this amount is independent of the choice of the frame is clear from the fact that the exterior derivative $d\tilde{\omega}^{12}$ for different frames differs by $d\varphi$, that is, an exact one-form whose integral over a closed loop must vanish identically.

The rotation of the tangent plane or "holonomy angle" can obviously be detected with *intrinsic* measurements. This is the Gaussian curvature in a completely different guise: the total curvature somehow packages the intrinsic properties of a patch in such a way that if you circumnavigate the boundary of the patch you can tell from the total curvature by what amount your trusty compass body will be off! No matter how mysterious this may appear, you should make a mental note of it:

Useful heuristic: *The total curvature of an area measures the net turn of the tangent plane about the normal for a full circumnavigation of that area.*

You end up with two totally different interpretations of the Gaussian curvature. On the one hand there is the extrinsic interpretation of K as the spread of surface normals per unit surface area. On the other hand there is the intrinsic interpretation of K as a density whose integral over an area yields the holonomy angle for a circumnavigation of that area.

One side of the Janus face reveals how the surface is embedded in three-space; the other side can be seen by the intelligent ant that only knows the surface. Small wonder that Gauss got excited about this! If you really want to understand surfaces in three-space, the miracle should somehow be transformed into a basic fact of life—a truth you hold to be self-evident ... Such can only happen through familiarity: playing around with surfaces in the real, in the abstract, and in the computer.

6.2.4 The nature of the spin form

The facts concerning "holonomy" can be described in various equivalent forms that may carry slightly different intuitive connotations, and thus are all valuable in various ways. One especially useful method is in terms of a "path lifting rule" on "fiber bundles." What this impressive blurb is supposed to mean is explained in this section. It is somewhat advanced material, presented in unduly popular form. Don't panic if you miss the point and skip this section. No harm has been done.

A "fiber bundle" is an entity that is constructed very much like the tangent bundle.[6] In fact the tangent bundle is the standard example of a fiber bundle and probably stood model for the concept. Consider the case in which you let the fibers be the unit vectors in the tangent plane, that is, the space of all directions on the surface. Locally this fiber bundle is the Cartesian product of the surface with this space of directions. It is known as the "unit sphere bundle." A *section* of this bundle is a field of directions on the surface.

Consider a direction $\vec{d}$ at a point $\mathcal{P}$ of the surface and a path on the surface that starts at $\mathcal{P}$. You may traverse the path and carry $\vec{d}$ along

---

[6]Here I'm taking some license. The notion of a "fiber bundle" is really more general than I am using it here. But the general, abstract definition would only cause confusion and it isn't really necessary in the context of this book.

with you, taking care to keep it parallel to itself (a "gyroscopic compass body," say). Then you obtain a path in the fiber bundle. Professionals say that you have "lifted" the path on the surface into the bundle. The spin form can be integrated over the surface path, and according to the princely theorem it will yield the fate of the direction $\vec{d}$.

You may think of the spin form as of a family of planar elements in the bundle, such that for each fiber the planes are parallel, although they may change from fiber to fiber.[7] When you follow the path on the surface, the planar elements give you the *slope* in the fiber bundle and enable you to lift the path. When you *circumnavigate a closed path* and return at $\mathcal{P}$, you will in general end up at another point of the same fiber over $\mathcal{P}$ because the lifted path does not necessarily close. This difference is the holonomy angle.

Clearly the holonomy angle will vanish whenever the planar elements mesh and are actually tangent planes of some *surface* in the fiber bundle. This should be at least pictorially evident, for when you circumnavigate a loop over an arbitrary landscape you are certain to end up at the same height. When the Gaussian curvature is different from zero, this does not happen in the fiber bundle. The closed loop lifts to a helix-like curve. The planar elements of the spin form don't mesh in that case. A measure of this mismatch is the exterior derivative, and by now you will appreciate how the derivative of the spin form must be closely related to the intrinsic curvature. This is the geometrical content of Gauss's "*Theorema Egregium.*"

Consider the simple example of a sphere of radius R. Suppose you circumnavigate the boundary of an octant subtended by the north pole and two points on the equator. You may run a cart over the globe without turning the steering wheel, for instance, except for two sharp right-angle turns. You pick a standard direction fixed to the cart, except that you counterrotate it by 90 degrees at the right-angled turns to ensure that it always "points in the same direction." Then you end up with a net turn of the fiducial angle that amounts to 90 degrees, which is the holonomy angle. But the integral of the Gaussian curvature equals one over R squared times the area of the octant, which is also 90 degrees. In this simple case you may even make a pretty drawing of the fiber bundle and discover for yourself what the nature of the "path lifting rule" is. All the necessary analysis has been done in the section on spherical frame fields, so this task should cause no hardship.

---

[7]It won't hurt to make a sketch.

6.2.5   The Riemann curvature tensor

If you carry a tangent vector $\vec{d}$ with you on a journey that circumnavigates an infinitesimal loop naturally defined via a surface bivector $\vec{A}$, you will find it changed by a certain amount $\triangle\vec{d}$ on returning to your point of departure. The change $\triangle\vec{d}$ must depend linearly on both $\vec{A}$ and $\vec{d}$, thus there must be some *linear slot machine* somewhere which has slots in which to insert $\vec{d}$ and $\vec{A}$ and which will pop out $\triangle\vec{d}$ after some turns of the crank. Call it $\mathbf{R}$, in honor of Riemann. You will guess that it will have a tensor notation like $\mathbf{R}^{l}{}_{ijk}$ in order to be able to contract on the inputs with a vector result.[8] This is usually called "the Riemann curvature tensor" of the manifold.

In the present case of surface patches the surprising fact is that the Gaussian curvature K seems to take care of everything in a most convenient and complete manner, although it obviously lacks the impressive festoons of indices and almost tends to look like a harmless scalar.

The explanation of this remarkable state of affairs is that the application of Riemann geometry to surfaces in three-dimensional space is a highly degenerated one. You may understand this if you consider the fact that *any bivector* on the surface must be a scaled version of the *same* unit bivector whereas the tangent space *as a whole* suffers a rotation. Thus it can hardly matter very much which *particular* vector and bivector you insert in the slot machine. The Gaussian curvature may be considered a suitable contraction of the full Riemann curvature tensor, and it happens to contain all the relevant information. Thus, it doesn't make much sense to invoke the full machinery of tensor technology in this case.

The point to keep in mind is:

Good to keep in mind: *The Gaussian curvature, harmless as it may seem at first sight, is really nothing but Riemann's formidable slot machine in disguise and will present you with a vector on contraction on an area bivector and a fiducial tangent direction.*

This is one important way to intuitively understand what the Gaussian curvature is up to.

6.2.6   The principal frame field

The symmetry of the second fundamental form suggests a way to tie the frame even tighter to the surface. Find the *eigenvectors* of II and use

---

[8]Thus $\mathbf{R}(\tilde{\sigma}^{l}, \vec{A}, \vec{d})$ is the component of the change of $\vec{d}$ along the l-th coordinate direction after circumnavigating an oriented area represented by the bivector $\vec{A}$.

these as your tangential frame vectors $\vec{f}_{1,2}$. This must be done at all points of the patch, and you must make sure that everything is smoothly joined. This leads to problems at times; they will be dealt with later on. The eigenvalues are $\kappa_{1,2}$ (say) and you obtain the simplification $\tilde{\omega}^{23}\langle \vec{f}_1 \rangle = \tilde{\omega}^{13}\langle \vec{f}_2 \rangle = 0$ as a bonus (thus no twists, only nosedives!); moreover, you obtain the marvelously simple and extraordinarily useful equations:

$$\tilde{\omega}^{13}\langle \vec{f}_1 \rangle = \kappa_1$$

and

$$\tilde{\omega}^{23}\langle \vec{f}_2 \rangle = \kappa_2.$$

We have to be thankful to Olinde Rodriguez (1816) for these truly wonderful formulas. They simply indicate that if you progress a distance $\triangle s$ in the first principal direction, the frame will rotate by an amount κ_1 times $\triangle s$ about the second. This is very similar to what you encounter on the sphere for *any direction*.

This representation allows you to describe the extrinsic curvature in the most concise and elegant way that is available to mankind.

The Codazzi equations become

$$\vec{f}_1[\kappa_2] = (\kappa_1 - \kappa_2)\tilde{\omega}^{12}\langle \vec{f}_2 \rangle$$
$$\vec{f}_2[\kappa_1] = (\kappa_1 - \kappa_2)\tilde{\omega}^{12}\langle \vec{f}_1 \rangle$$

They specify the change of the eigenvalues in one principal direction when you move in the orthogonal direction. These changes both vanish at an umbilical point, or even everywhere in the case of spheres.

A frame field like this will be called a "principal frame field." It is by far the most convenient representation of surface patches for practical applications.

For the principal frame field, the second fundamental form has the simple and pictorially significant representation[9]

$$II(\bullet, \odot) = (\kappa_1\tilde{\sigma}^1\langle\bullet\rangle\tilde{\sigma}^1 + \kappa_2\tilde{\sigma}^2\langle\bullet\rangle\tilde{\sigma}^2)\langle \odot \rangle.$$

This explicitly reveals the gauge figure associated with II, which is an object of great intuitive utility and which I will exploit fully later. This gauge figure even has a name: it is conventionally known as "Dupin's indicatrix."[10]

---

[9]Because you can easily show that $\tilde{\omega}^{13} = \kappa_1\tilde{\sigma}^1$ and $\tilde{\omega}^{23} = \kappa_2\tilde{\sigma}^2$, two equations that are nice in their own right.

[10]Dupin's indicatrix will be treated in detail later on.

It is pictorially evident that the curvature of any curve on a convex
or concave patch must exceed the value of the smallest principal curvature. Thus the fact that curves live *on a patch severely constrains them.*
Examples abound. Thus the geodesic torsion of any curve on a sur-
face equals $\frac{\kappa_1 - \kappa_2}{2} \sin 2\varphi$, where φ denotes the angle between the curve's
tangent and the first principal direction. It vanishes for the principal
directions and cannot exceed $\frac{\kappa_1 - \kappa_2}{2}$. The geodesic torsion reaches its extremal values for strips along the bisectrices of the principal directions
(fig. 165).

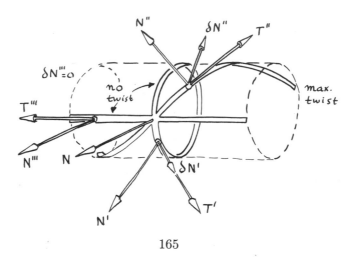

165

6.2.6.1   Classical Language

♠ Intermezzo—The skeleton in the cupboard.

In the usual literature you will often encounter the structural equations
under their conventional names, so you should be conversant with the custom.
A typical classification is:

A parametrization $\vec{x}(u,v)$, normal $\vec{n}$, coefficients of the "metric tensor"
(that is, the first fundamental form) E, F, G, coefficients of "second funda-
mental form" L, M and N ($L = \vec{x}_{uu} \cdot \vec{n}$, $M = \vec{x}_{uv} \cdot \vec{n}$, $N = \vec{x}_{vv} \cdot \vec{n}$):

Derivatives of $\vec{n}$ with respect to u, v:

"Weingarten's equations" (Weingarten, 1861), if u and v are along the principal directions also called the "Rodriguez formulas" (Rodriguez, 1816).

Derivatives of $\vec{x}_u$, $\vec{x}_v$ with respect to u, v:

"Gauss's equations" (Gauss, 1827). These equations contain the coefficients of the classical connection, the "Christoffel symbols" (Christoffel, 1869; but already known by Gauss—the *Disquisitiones*—much earlier). These equations, together with the Weingarten equations, are formally similar to the Frenet-Serret equations from the theory of curves and are often packaged together as the "Gauss-Weingarten-equations" of surface theory.

The "equations of compatibility," namely,

1. Gauss's "Theorema egregium":

The "princely theorem" from Gauss *Disquisitiones*, easily the most important contribution to mathematics from the early nineteenth century, which expresses the Gaussian curvature in terms of intrinsic geometry of the surface.

In the classical notation you have the following formula. I include it purely as a curiosity; don't ever try to memorize anything like this!

$$K\,(EG - F^2)^2 = (F_{uv} - \tfrac{1}{2}(E_{vv} + G_{uu}))(EG - F^2) +$$

$$\det \begin{vmatrix} 0 & F_v - \frac{G_u}{2} & \frac{G_v}{2} \\ \frac{E_u}{2} & E & F \\ F_u - \frac{E_v}{2} & F & G \end{vmatrix} -$$

$$\det \begin{vmatrix} 0 & \frac{E_v}{2} & \frac{G_u}{2} \\ \frac{E_v}{2} & E & F \\ \frac{G_u}{2} & F & G \end{vmatrix}.$$

I have never developed a taste for expressions like this, but some people I know get turned on by this impressive monument.

2. The "Codazzi-Mainardi-equations":

The equations of the form

$$L_v - M_u = L\Gamma_{12}^1 + M(\Gamma_{12}^2 - \Gamma_{11}^1) - N\Gamma_{11}^2$$
$$M_v - N_u = L\Gamma_{22}^1 + M(\Gamma_{22}^2 - \Gamma_{12}^1) - N\Gamma_{12}^2,$$

due to Mainardi (1856) and Codazzi (1860).

There are several reasons why you must be able to use the classical notation. One reason is that the earlier literature contains a great deal that is extremely relevant today and is not available at all in the modern notation. Another reason is that many modern authors in applied areas continue to use the classical notation. In the final chapter I recommend some texts that you can use to pick up the classical notation without unnecessary suffering.

I am of the opinion that tutors who in this enlightened era continue to pro-
mote the use of the E, F, G, L, M, N and so forth ought to be shot at dawn.
The only tolerable exception is the use of the classical language for certain
especially fortunate choices of the frame field such as, for instance, the principal frame field. However, even in these cases the modern notation is every
bit as transparent, and I can only classify these practices as manifestations of
advanced scientific arteriosclerosis. Don't say I didn't warn you.

6.2.6.2   How to fit a principal frame field

♠ Intermezzo—Practical matters.

In practice you are usually presented with a surface only at a finite number
of sample points. You certainly have the coordinates there, be it only to a
certain tolerance, and you may or may not have the normals, or tangent planes,
explicitly given. If the latter are not specified, you have to get them somehow,
usually by fitting some surface through the points. For instance, you may
fit planes through local groups of points. This typically leads to severe noise
problems. Later I will assume that the samples are *samples of tangent planes*
("surface facets"). This leads to much better numerical behavior.

If the surface is given algorithmically, you can usually let it yield both
positions and normals because normals are obtained from the positions by
differentiation, which is always possible. In the latter case, this would preferably be done analytically. Of course, nowadays one uses an algebraic package
such as REDUCE to reduce the suffering this entails.

In order to specify the shape, you need the curvature. The easiest way to
get at that is to pick a point and to consider the deviations of neighboring
points from its tangent plane. The deviations can be approximated with the
best fitting quadric. It pays to take advantage of the fact that you know
neighboring normals, too, although such a refinement is rarely necessary. In
local coordinates you have $x^3 = \frac{1}{2}(a_{11}x^1x^1 + 2a_{12}x^1x^2 + a_{22}x^2x^2)$ where x^3 is
the deviation orthogonal to the tangent plane and (x^1, x^2) the projections of
the neighboring points on the tangent plane. You have to diagonalize this form
and to fit a frame with $\vec{f_3}$ in the normal direction and $\vec{f}_{1,2}$ in the directions of
the eigenvalues.

It isn't at all difficult, although it is certainly a lot of work—just the kind
of job that computers were made for in the first place. You can probably
hack the thing together from standard library routines. If you use positions
and normal deviations at the N neighbors of a given vertex of a triangulation,
you obtain $3N$ conditions (that is, 18 conditions for the typical six-vertex). If
you fit a second-order approximation to the vertex, you have three unknowns
(a_{11}, a_{12}, and a_{13}). Your best bet is to find a SVD-routine (Singular Value
Decomposition, present in many linear algebra packages) to solve the resulting
linear least-squares problem in a robust manner.

The next problem is to *orient the frame globally*. This is the hard part; it may not even be globally possible. For suitably limited patches it is always possible, though. For a principal frame field your patch shouldn't enclose an umbilic. You are faced with two problems: first, to divide the principal directions into two distinct families; and second, to have principal frame vectors of the same family point in similar directions at nearby points. The first problem can always be solved; the second task is usually impossible, except for limited regions. The orienting can be done recursively with a kind of "painting algorithm" where you start with an arbitrary point and orient all others—neighborwise—with respect to it. Compared with the rather heavy number crunching involved in the first part, I'm always pleased to notice that this can be a surprisingly fast process.

The result is a *principal frame field*. Of course you need much more to go on, but at least this is a solid start. You have computed the second fundamental form, that is, the principal directions and curvatures, at the same time. They follow trivially from the eigenvalues of the quadric. Thus you are now in possession of H and K, too.

The fact that a global orientation of the frame is hardly ever possible never fails to bug me even after a lot of experience in computational differential geometry. It is a real curse because you need an atlas of charts with all the problems of correspondence that this carries with it. I have solved the problem by special means from case to case, but this is certainly not the way it ought to be done. Some effort to build the structure to handle the atlas as such in a thoroughly convenient manner would not be ill-spent. Such a package should include the usual operations you want to perform on atlases: just take the first chapter of almost any modern book on the differential geometry of surfaces and implement the "atlas" concept.[11]

In regions where the principal frame field is not orientable, you can at least *sort* by setting $\kappa_1 \geq \kappa_2$ and making sure that, for instance, $\vec{f}_1 \cdot \vec{a} > 0$, where $\vec{a}$ is some fiducial direction.[12] Such a procedure at least limits the bad places to curves. You can push these curves about by running the painting algorithm for limited regions. Thus you can do differential geometry in well-ordered pieces at least. Afterward you will have to sew the pieces together somehow.

6.2.7 The metric on the surface

The metric on the surface is simply the metric in the tangent plane induced by the unit circle as gauge figure. This makes the tangent planes equal to Euclidean planes. However, you often want to do metrical calculations on your *charts*. You obviously can't use a circle as gauge figure there. You need the image under the inverse Jacobian of the gauge figure on the tangent plane. Just "pull back" the gauge figure and you've

---

[11]Please send me a copy if you perform this good deed.

[12]In fact you can do better, because the distinction between the two families of principal directions can always be made.

got it. This then becomes an ellipse on the chart, an ellipse that may
vary from place to place.

You may also look at it from another point of view. The metric is a
machine that lets you associate a one-form with a vector. You can pull
back these one-forms and thus define a metric for the chart that is an
"image" of the metric in the tangent plane. Classically this is done via
the "first fundamental form." The classical coordinate expression is:

$$I((u,v),(u',v')) = E\,uu' + F\,(uv' + u'v) + G\,vv'.$$

This expression defines the scalar product for vectors $u\vec{e}_1 + v\vec{e}_2$, $u'\vec{e}_1 +$
$v'\vec{e}_2$ on the chart that corresponds with the Euclidean scalar product
in the tangent plane. The equation $Eu^2 + 2Fuv + Gv^2 = 1$ defines the
gauge figure and can be used for the usual geometrical constructions.
The E, F, G are the components of the metric in its guise as the metric
tensor. Classically one often writes "ds^2" for $I(\vec{x},\vec{x})$ because this expression looks very much like the Pythagorean theorem; thus ds is "the
arclength." Formulas very similar to the classical "dee-es-squared" are
obtained if you define "I" as a symmetrical tensor product, especially
when expressed in terms of principal coordinates. For instance, you
may write (remember that x^3 is measured along the normal direction
and doesn't come into play)

$$I(\bullet,\bullet) = dx^1\langle\ \rangle dx^1 + dx^2\langle\ \rangle dx^2,$$

which certainly looks a lot like the trusty "dee-es-squared." The pull
back on the (u,v) parameter patch is what people usually are prepared
to call "the first fundamental form."

For a Monge patch you get a nice geometrical picture.[13] The gauge
figures in the tangent plane can be "projected" on the chart, which is an
intuitive way to do the pull-back. The resulting ellipses can be used as
a gauge figure to do all—Euclidean—calculations in terms of the chart
(fig. 166). For a general chart you can't expect such a simple picture, of
course, but the idea is the same.

6.2.8   The osculating quadric

6.2.8.1   The second-order structure

The second fundamental form defines the local quadratic approximation.
For any tangent vector $\vec{t}$, the number $\frac{1}{2}II(\vec{t},\vec{t})$ defines the deviation in

---

[13]Basically a parametrization like $z = f(x,y)$ for Cartesian coordinates (x,y,z),
that is, a description by way of a "height function." More on Monge patches later.

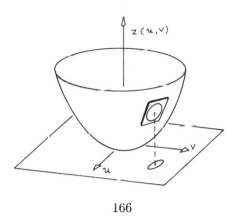

166

the normal direction from the tangent plane at position $\vec{t}$. I use the notation

$$x^3 = \frac{1}{2}II(x^1\,\vec{f_1} + x^2\,\vec{f_2}, x^1\,\vec{f_1} + x^2\,\vec{f_2})$$

for the osculating paraboloid. This expression ties II to the classical expression "$d^2\vec{x}.\vec{N}$," which is often used to introduce the second fundamental form.[14]

In case you wonder where the factor one-half suddenly springs from, you may want to consider the—completely analogous—one-dimensional case. For the parabola $x^2 = \frac{1}{2}\kappa(x^1)^2$ (please note that x^2 is the normal direction, now!) you obtain the "second principal form" $ii = \kappa dx^1\langle\ \rangle dx^1$. For a vector $\vec{a} = a\vec{\partial}_\tau^1$ you obtain $ii(\vec{a}) = \kappa a dx^1$, which indeed yields the slopes of the tangents: $ii(\vec{a}, \vec{e_1})$ equals κa which again equals $\frac{\partial x^2}{\partial x^1}$ at $x^1 = a$. Thus ii really does do everything for the *curve* that II does for *surfaces*. You can also see that the "osculating paraboloid" is $\frac{1}{2}ii(\vec{a}, \vec{a})$, which equals $\frac{\kappa}{2}\|\vec{a}\|^2$. This example is so simple that you can easily make precise drawings of everything that goes on. Go ahead. It helps.

In a principal frame field all this boils down to the convenient expression:

$$x^3 = \frac{1}{2}\kappa_1\,x^1 x^1 + \frac{1}{2}\kappa_2\,x^2 x^2.$$

In these coordinates the tangent plane at (x^1, x^2) is $dx^3 = \kappa_1 x^1 \tilde{\sigma}^1 + \kappa_2 x^2 \tilde{\sigma}^2$ and you have $x^3 = \frac{1}{2}dx^3\langle\vec{t}\rangle = \frac{1}{2}II(\vec{t}, \vec{t})$, which merely demonstrates the point of departure.

---

[14]The notation "$d^2\vec{x}$" is used for the Hessian in a normal frame. I won't go into details here (there are certain problems since the Hessian isn't a geometric object). If you are attracted to expressions like "$II = d^2\vec{x} \cdot \vec{N}$," you may—for instance—consult Lipschutz.

The eigenvalue, or principal curvature representation is usually the intuitively most obvious one. The principal directions tend to coincide with visually obvious symmetries. Objects of revolution yield pictorially evident examples. Figure 167 shows this vividly for the case of a "catenoid."

167

From this representation you immediately get Euler's famous formula (1760),

$$\kappa(\vartheta) = \kappa_1 \cos^2\vartheta + \kappa_2 \sin^2\vartheta = H + \frac{\kappa_1 - \kappa_2}{2} \cos 2\vartheta \quad .$$

This specifies the normal curvature of curves making an angle ϑ with the first principal direction. Thus it is an easy matter to obtain the normal curvature for whatever section you require.

The one-form dx^3 in effect merely defines the slope and orientation of the tangent plane at (x^1, x^2) with respect to the tangent plane at $(0,0)$ as is intuitively obvious, since dx^3 is just the gradient of the "height." This is how I introduced the second fundamental form in the first place: as a linear map of tangent vectors to covectors—which again are nothing but linear maps of tangent vectors to the real numbers, a "linear map of linear maps."

6.2.8.2 The indicatrix

I can indicate a simple geometrical construction that you can apply to arrive at the covectors that represent the tangent planes in the immediate neighborhood of a point: draw the locus of points $\vec{t}$ for which $\frac{1}{2}II(\vec{t},\vec{t})$

equals plus or minus one on the tangent plane. This figure is known as "Dupin's indicatrix" (Dupin, 1813). It is the gauge figure associated with II and thus represents II in a purely geometrical manner.

I like to conceive of the indicatrix as the circumference of the "wound" inflicted on the shape by a cut with a planar blade, carried parallel to the tangent plane. This interpretation enables me to visualize the shape of Dupin's indicatrix very easily and vividly. Perhaps the same works for you.

Among other things, Dupin's indicatrix indicates the one-forms dx^3. Remember that (pictorially) these are the tangent planes in the vicinity of your fiducial point. To get them, just use the indicatrix as you would the gauge figure of any metric; that is to say, the first equi-line of the one-form is the polar line of the vector or the first level line of the dual covector. In fact this is exactly the way I constructed the second fundamental form in the first place; there is nothing new here.

You can conveniently study Dupin's indicatrix on topographical maps of hilly landscapes featuring equi-height contour lines. The summits of the hills and the deepest points of kettle valleys reveal elliptical indicatrices, whereas the passes reveal hyperbolical structures. Indeed, the paradigm of the indicatrix as a height contour is worth keeping in mind.

The indicatrix of Dupin is really of great practical and intuitive value, except at so-called "planar points," which are points where the rank of the local Hessian is zero. Such points cannot be expected on your generic surface patch, however.

The indicatrix of Dupin is completely equivalent to the second fundamental form. It is to be preferred if you think geometrically and for sketching, whereas II is used for formal calculations. The indicatrix makes the *shape operator* a very tangible object and particularly easy to visualize. "Shape operator" is a term I use for the geometrical object involved. In its formal guise it is "II," in pictorial language, the indicatrix.[15]

Heuristic: *Dupin's indicatrix is the geometrical embodiment of the shape operator.*

---

[15] Here you have your first example of a significant symmetric bilinear operator that is not a metric. The indicatrix of Dupin is its "gauge figure." You use the indicatrix as you would use the gauge figure of the metric. Thus $II(\vec{a}, \vec{b})$ is like an inner product, $II(\vec{a}, \vec{a})$ like a squared length. Two directions $\vec{a}$, $\vec{b}$ for which $II(\vec{a}, \vec{b})$ vanishes are "orthogonal" in the sense of the second fundamental form; a vector $\vec{c}$ for which $II(\vec{c}, \vec{c})$ vanishes has "length zero" (but need not be the zero-vector!), *etc.* Such relations will be seen to have an intimate relation to extrinsic shape properties.

Once you have constructed the one-form dx^3, you can use the indicatrix to compute arbitrary combinations $II(\vec{t}, \vec{s})$. Notice that $II(\vec{t}, \vec{s})$ is computed in exactly the same manner as you would compute the scalar product through the gauge figure: you construct the one-form for one vector and then contract the other on it. Thus the indicatrix is a nice way to see *more geometrico* and thus intuitively what the second fundamental form is up to. This enables you to find *conjugated directions*, which are the directions $\vec{a}$, $\vec{b}$ such that $II(\vec{a}, \vec{b})$ vanishes, or *asymptotic directions*, which are the directions $\vec{a}$ such that $II(\vec{a}, \vec{a})$ vanishes. And so forth.

6.2.8.3   Conjugated directions

For a *sphere* the direction conjugated to any given one is the direction orthogonal to it. Then the indicatrix is a circle, and every pair of orthogonal diameters is a "conjugated pair." If you subject the circle with two orthogonal diameters to an arbitrary affinity, you obtain an elliptical indicatrix with two diameters that are—in general—no longer orthogonal, but they are still called "conjugated." You see that in this way "conjugation" generalizes the concept of "orthogonality" in the affine sense.

If $\vec{a}$ and $\vec{b}$ are tangent vectors with tail at the center of, tip on the indicatrix, then these vectors represent conjugated directions if it is the case that $\vec{a}$ is along the tangent to the indicatrix at $\vec{b}$ and *vice versa*. Notice that this entails orthogonality of the vectors in the case that the indicatrix is a circle, but that this definition uses only affine properties (fig. 168).

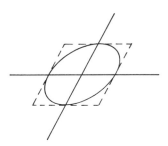

168

Conjugation is a very basic relation with numerous practical applications. Consider an example: if a light beam shines in the direction of $\vec{a}$, then the edge of the attached shadow will be along $\vec{b}$ and *vice versa*.

This example suggests that conjugation generalizes the relation between adjacent facets of a polyhedron and their common edge for the case of smooth surfaces. This is a notion with great heuristic power. For points $\mathcal{A}$ and $\mathcal{A} + \lambda \vec{a}$ on the surface you have that their tangent planes intersect along a line in the direction of $\vec{b}$, where $\vec{a}$ and $\vec{b}$ are conjugated directions on the surface. More about this later on.

Thus:

Useful heuristic: *The edge of two facets at $\mathcal{P}$ and $\mathcal{Q}$ is conjugated to the direction $\mathcal{PQ}$. (And vice versa!)*

6.2.8.4   The first and second fundamental forms in triangulations

♠ INTERMEZZO--CARRY IT TO THE COMPUTER.

Suppose you use a triangulation as a model of the patch. The vertices are at the gridpoints $(u, v) = (i, j)$ with $(i, j = 0 \ldots N - 1)$ of the chart. Let $l_{(i,j)(i',j')}$ be the length of the directed edge from (i, j) to (i', j') on the surface, and let φ_{ij} denote the sector angle between $l_{(i,j)(i+1,j)}$ and $l_{(i,j)(i,j+1)}$. Then the coefficients of the first fundamental form are simply ($I(u, v) = E \, du^2 + 2F \, du \, dv + G \, dv^2$):

$$
\begin{aligned}
E &= l_{(i,j)(i+1,j)}^{\,2} \\
F &= l_{(i,j)(i+1,j)} l_{(i,j)(i,j+1)} \cos \varphi_{ij} \\
G &= l_{(i,j)(i,j+1)}^{\,2}
\end{aligned}
$$

Thus the first fundamental form describes the size and shape of the triangles. This is just the definition of the metric through triangulation as it is conventionally practiced in the art of geodesy.

The second fundamental form depends also on the *dihedral angles between the facets*. It describes how the triangulation curves in space. It is easy enough to derive equations for the coefficients, but they are rather complicated and I won't need them any further, so I won't consider them here in detail.[16]. It is much more useful to derive solutions for the case that the discrete, polyhedral structure is in fact due to the discrete sampling of some unknown smooth surface.

The case of a triangulation based on the two families of curves of principal curvature is instructive though. In that case the dihedral angles at the

---

[16]The interested reader may consult Sauer's "Difference Geometry," but watch out for the typos! You can derive these expressions by substitution of the parameter values (i, j) in the second fundamental form and equating it to the deviation of that vertex from the fiducial facet for which you want to find the L, M and N. This height depends (among other things) on the dihedral angles. If you do it algebraically, you obtain Sauer's formulas. This is a lot of very boring work. It is easy to do the thing numerically, of course. Thus you can find II for any triangulation without much ado. Sauer's formulas are of no obvious use in practice.

"diagonal" edges vanish; thus the parameter line meshes are planar. Then the dihedral angles at the other edges equal the principal curvatures times the edge lengths. You will find this a simple application of Rodriguez's formula. In this case you immediately see geometrically how the dihedral angles determine the second fundamental form.

In the general case described above you proceed as follows: if you have the positions $\vec{x}_{ij}$ and normals $\vec{n}_{ij}$ for a number of data points indexed with (i,j), such that the immediate neighborhood of a point is $(i + / - 1, j + / - 1)$, you can find the differential geometric descriptors in the following way:

First you may observe that the osculating quadrics contain only three unknowns since the tangent planes are already given. Thus, a least squares fit for even a small neighborhood immediately leads to a solution. You are faced with a nice (because linear!) overcomplete set of equations. In most cases you will need the osculating cubic too, which amounts to an additional four unknowns. Again a comparatively small neighborhood leads to a simple solution via a least squares fit. For a typical vertex with six neighbors you obtain eighteen equations, *i.e.*, sufficient to fit even higher-order approximations. This is how I did the computational differential geometry for this book.

If you have only the positions, not the tangent planes, *you are in trouble!* In principle you can follow the same route after you have estimated the tangent planes somehow. Alternatively you may attempt to fit a general quadric at a point through a small region, which involves the simultaneous estimate of nine unknowns. But straightforward as this procedure may seem, this tends to be a rather noise sensitive process in my experience. When you sample a physical surface you must always prefer methods that yield local (sampled) surface facets over methods that merely provide you with positions of fiducial points.

Intuitively this makes sense because a mere point is scarcely a sample of a *surface* at all. A sample of a surface should in any case include some information on *the two-fold extended nature, that is, about the tangent plane*. You have to sample the *tangent bundle* rather than merely the surface.

It would be better, of course, to sample even higher order properties of the surface (such as curvature) *directly* instead of having to infer them from point or facet samples. This is not impossible in principle (for instance, many scattering phenomena depend critically on curvature), but present-day technology is largely preoccupied with point sampling through "ranging."

6.2.8.5   The Monge patch

♠ INTERMEZZO—BACK OF THE ENVELOPE CALCULATIONS.

Let $(\vec{e}_1, \vec{e}_2, \vec{e}_3)$ be a fixed frame field for Euclidean 3-space such that the third-frame vector is the normal at the origin. Then the map

$$\vec{x}\,(u,v) = u\,\vec{e}_1 + v\,\vec{e}_2 + w(u,v)\,\vec{e}_3$$

is called a "Monge patch," and w is the "height" as a function of u and v. Note that the inverse of the map is now merely a parallel projection of space on the $\vec{e}_1$-$\vec{e}_2$ plane obtained by ignoring the $\vec{e}_3$ variation. The Monge patch representation lends itself particularly well for visualization and for quick and dirty "back of the envelope" calculations. You should thoroughly familiarize yourself with it. In a local frame you can always use the Monge patch representation for a small neighborhood. Very often you can cover whole surfaces with just a few Monge patches.

The normal can be expressed as

$$\vec{n}(u,v) = \frac{-\frac{\partial w}{\partial u}\,\vec{e}_1 - \frac{\partial w}{\partial v}\,\vec{e}_2 + \vec{e}_3}{\sqrt{1 + (\frac{\partial w}{\partial u})^2 + (\frac{\partial w}{\partial v})^2}}$$

and the second fundamental form has the matrix

$$II(u,v) = (1 + (\frac{\partial w}{\partial u})^2 + (\frac{\partial w}{\partial v})^2)^{-\frac{1}{2}} \left(\begin{array}{cc} \frac{\partial^2 w}{\partial u^2} & \frac{\partial^2 w}{\partial u \partial v} \\ \frac{\partial^2 w}{\partial u \partial v} & \frac{\partial^2 w}{\partial v^2} \end{array} \right),$$

whereas the first fundamental form has the matrix

$$I(u,v) = \left(\begin{array}{cc} 1 + (\frac{\partial w}{\partial u})^2 & \frac{\partial w}{\partial u}\frac{\partial w}{\partial v} \\ \frac{\partial w}{\partial u}\frac{\partial w}{\partial v} & 1 + (\frac{\partial w}{\partial v})^2 \end{array} \right).$$

In most cases you will consider only the immediate neighborhood of the origin and you will make sure that you take the third frame vector in the normal direction. Then the expressions simplify quite a bit. For instance, $I(u,v)$ becomes the identity, whereas the denominator $\sqrt{1 + (\frac{\partial w}{\partial u})^2 + (\frac{\partial w}{\partial v})^2}$ can be dropped in the expression for the normal and the second fundamental form. The osculating quadric is just the second-order part of the Taylor expansion of w:

$$\frac{1}{2}(\frac{\partial^2 w}{\partial u^2}\,u^2 + 2\frac{\partial^2 w}{\partial u \partial v}\,uv + \frac{\partial^2 w}{\partial v^2}\,v^2).$$

The sign of the Gaussian curvature is the sign of the Hessian of w, which is an *exact* result and is often of great convenience in practical investigations.

It is often highly convenient to treat the surface as a series of Monge patches, each defined with respect to the frame for a given fiducial point. A principal frame is even better since then the mixed partial derivative vanishes, but you can usually not pick them *a priori* except in cases of exceptionally high symmetry.

6.2.8.6　Surface equations in principal coordinates

♠ INTERMEZZO—TO CARRY IN YOUR HEAD.

Parametrizations such that the principal directions are along the coordinate directions are especially convenient and will most often be the prime choice in applications. All equations take on their simplest guise.

Let $\vec{n}$ be the surface normal and $\vec{a}$, $\vec{b}$ unit vectors along the principal directions. If the parametrization is by (u, v), then I will denote the derivatives with respect to arclength along the parameter curves as $\vec{\partial}_a$ and $\vec{\partial}_b$. You have

$$\frac{\partial s_u}{\partial u} \vec{\partial}_a = \vec{\partial}_u$$

where s_u measures the arclength along the u-parameter curve and similarly for the v-parameter. The number $\frac{\partial s_u}{\partial u}$ measures the spacing of the v-parameter curves, and so forth. It is most convenient to introduce the normal curvatures κ_a, κ_b and the geodesic curvatures g_a, g_b of the lines of curvature too.

Then you have

The geodesic curvatures are:

$$\begin{aligned}
g_a &= -\vec{\partial}_b \left[\ln \frac{\partial s_u}{\partial u} \right] \\
g_b &= \vec{\partial}_a \left[\ln \frac{\partial s_v}{\partial v} \right]
\end{aligned}$$

These equations should be pictorially evident to you: think of a little rectangle with lines of curvature as sides. If two opposite sides have slightly different length, then it must be the case that they are *curved* because the "rectangle" is wedged. The angular spread due to the curvature must equal the wedge angle, which amounts to the length difference divided by the (average) length of the other sides. Such is the significance of these formulas.

The Gauss equations (notice that the spin of the frame about the normal is described through the geodesic curvatures, the nosedives through the normal curvatures; these equations are also pictorially evident) are:

$$\begin{aligned}
\nabla_{\vec{\partial}_a} \vec{a} &= & g_a \vec{b} & +\kappa_a \vec{n} \\
\nabla_{\vec{\partial}_a} \vec{b} &= -g_a \vec{a} & & \\
\nabla_{\vec{\partial}_b} \vec{a} &= & g_b \vec{b} & \\
\nabla_{\vec{\partial}_b} \vec{b} &= -g_b \vec{a} & & +\kappa_b \vec{n} \, .
\end{aligned}$$

Please take a good look at the nice structure of these equations. This will make it very easy for you to keep them in mind. The geodesic curvatures merely have the expected effect of a *spin* about the normal, whereas the nosedives are caused by the normal curvatures.

The Weingarten equations (in this case equal to Rodriguez's formulas, with a clear pictorial meaning) are:

$$\begin{aligned}
\nabla_{\vec{\partial}_a} \vec{n} &= -\kappa_a \vec{a} \\
\nabla_{\vec{\partial}_b} \vec{n} &= -\kappa_b \vec{b} \, .
\end{aligned}$$

These equations complete the description of the nosedives. Because of the nosedives the pair $(\vec{n}, \vec{a})$ rotates about $\vec{b}$ and the pair $(\vec{n}, \vec{b})$ about $\vec{a}$.

The symmetry equation vanishes identically.

The Mainardi-Codazzi equations are:

$$\vec{\partial}_b[\kappa_a] = g_a(\kappa_a - \kappa_b)$$
$$\vec{\partial}_a[\kappa_b] = g_b(\kappa_a - \kappa_b) .$$

These equations are harder to understand visually. This makes sense, because they express the constraints due to the embedding in three-space.

Gauss's *Theorema egregium* takes on the simple form:

$$K = \vec{\partial}_a[g_a] - g_a{}^2 - \vec{\partial}_b[g_b] - g_b{}^2 .$$

This is an intrinsic equation. The extrinsic equation is, of course, simply:

$$K = \kappa_1 \kappa_2 .$$

The first fundamental form (in this case Pythagoras's theorem) is:

$$I = ds^2 = da^2 + db^2 .$$

The second fundamental form is:

$$II = d^2\vec{x} \cdot \vec{n} = \kappa_a\, da^2 + \kappa_b\, db^2 .$$

Notice how the classical notation becomes much less objectionable when you use principal frames. The equations can be memorized rather easily because they actually capture some intuitive meaning. Even so you should be aware of obvious limitations. It is, for instance, less easy to derive properties of the asymptotic ray manifold in these frames, and this entity is very important in optical applications. For certain applications you should not hesitate to consider alternative frames.

No doubt the principal frame is the prime choice for almost any type of numerical work involving surface patches. You fit a tangent frame, turn it about the normal to obtain a principal frame, at the same time obtaining the osculating quadric and cubic. The point is that changing to a principal frame involves only calculations that you would have performed anyway.

The quadric yields the principal curvatures and the cubic the gradients of the principal curvatures. These in turn immediately yield the geodesic curvatures of the lines of principal curvature. The Gauss-Weingarten equations then provide you with the connection, the turning and twisting of the frame. In the majority of applications this will be all you need.

For applications of an optical nature you usually also need the asymptotic ray manifold. This causes no problems since the asymptotic directions can be obtained simply from the quadric.

If you want more, say the geodesic curvature of the asymptotic lines, it is best to rotate about the normal to obtain a frame of which one tangent vector is asymptotic. Then the coefficients of the cubic (in that frame) provide you with your needs. This makes it possible to find flecnodal points without much ado, for instance.[17]

6.2.8.7   The curvature of intersections with arbitrary planes

Euler's theorem allows you to calculate the normal curvature for arbitrary directions in terms of the principal curvatures and the orientation of the normal plane with respect to the principal normal planes. What about the curvature of planar intersections when you *slant* the intersecting plane with respect to the normal plane? Although this sounds as if it might well be complicated, it is actually a surprisingly simple problem. It was solved by Meusnier in 1776. Meusnier's formula is:

$$\kappa(\varphi) = \frac{\kappa_n}{\cos \varphi}.$$

Here $\kappa(\varphi)$ is the curvature of a planar section that slants by an angle φ with respect to the normal plane that intersects the tangent plane along the same line (fig. 169). The normal curvature is κ_n and can be

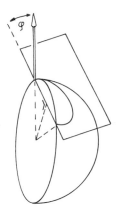
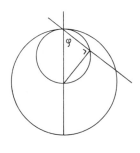

169

obtained from Euler's formula.[18] The formula is immediately evident

---

[17]These are points for which the intersection of the surface with the tangent plane is composed of two intersecting branches, one of which has an inflection at the origin. More on flecnodals later.

[18]Euler's formula expresses the normal curvature in terms of the principal curvatures, for any direction subtending an angle φ (say) with the first principal direction.

for the special case of the sphere. This is useful if you need a simple pictorial interpretation to remember Meusnier's formula.

Heuristic: *The radius of the small circle obtained as a section of a sphere of radius R with a plane that is inclined with respect to a normal plane at an angle φ is at cursory inspection seen to equal $R \cos \varphi$.*

The interesting news is that this is in fact the general result.

All osculating circles to curves with the same tangent direction thus describe a *sphere*, which may be called the "Meusnier sphere." It is a geometrical object that is at times useful in intuitive, heuristic thought. All Meusnier spheres have their centers on the normal ray on the stretch defined by the two centers of principal spherical curvature. You may guess that curves on the surface considered as space curves whose osculating spheres coincide with the Meusnier sphere do have an especially intimate contact with the surface. Instances of this will occur later on.

The geometric interpretation is as follows. Consider a normal section of the surface at a point $\mathcal{P}$ and construct the osculating circle Σ (say) to the planar curve of intersection of the surface with the normal, sectioning plane. Let $\mathcal{M}$ be the center of Σ. Let σ be the circle in the sectioning plane with diameter $\mathcal{PM}$. Then all curves that have the sectioning plane as their normal plane, thus with tangents orthogonal to the intersection, do have the centers $\mathcal{C}$ of their osculating circles on σ. Their polar axes meet the line $\mathcal{PM}$ in $\mathcal{M}$. (Thus $\mathcal{PCM}$ is a right angle.) This is—again immediately evident in the special case of the sphere.

6.2.8.8   Peano's Surface: A classical warning

♠ INTERMEZZO— SHOCK THERAPY.

You are in for some surprises if you believe that the set of normal curvatures at a point define the local shape pretty well. Peano provided a classical warning. Considering the following surface in Monge patch representation:

$$\vec{x}(u, v) = u\vec{e}_1 + v\vec{e}_2 + (2u^2 - v)(v - u^2)\vec{e}_3.$$

If the third coordinate indicates the "height" above the uv-plane, then all normal sections have a maximum at $u = v = 0$; yet the height in no way assumes a local maximum there.

For if you take a section in a plane at an angle φ with the u-direction you find that the normal curvature is minus twice the square of the sine of φ, whereas along the u-direction itself the height changes as a minus twice the fourth power of u. Thus indeed every normal section has a *maximum* at the

---

It is a trivial exercise to derive the often useful expression: $\kappa_n = \kappa_1 \cos^2 \varphi + \kappa_2 \sin^2 \varphi$.

origin. But along the curve $v = \frac{3}{2}u^2$ you have a local *minimum* at the origin because the height changes as plus one quarter of the fourth power of u!

Thus it doesn't suffice to look at the normal sections through a point $\mathcal{P}$ if you want to ascertain the presence of an extremum at $\mathcal{P}$. You have to consider the totality of curves through $\mathcal{P}$.

You will find plaster models of Peano's surface on show in the more venerable math departments as a lasting warning for generations of students to come. It looks very decorative.

6.2.9   Typical local surface forms

The study of local surface forms has a venerable tradition. Perhaps Alberti was the first to put forward something like a modern classification. This is a passage from his *Della Pittura* from the early fifteenth century:

> *We have now to treat of other qualities which rest like a skin over all the surface of the plane. These are divided into three sorts. Some planes are flat, others are hollowed out, and others are swollen outward and are spherical. To these a fourth may be added which is composed of any two of the above. The flat plane is that which a straight ruler will touch in every part if drawn over it. The surface of the water is similar to this. The spherical plane is similar to the exterior of a sphere. We say the sphere is a round body, continuous in every part; any part on the extremity of that body is equidistant from its center. The hollowed plane is within and under the outermost extremities of the spherical plane as in the interior of an egg-shell. The compound plane is in one part flat and in another hollowed or spherical like those on the interior of reeds or on the exterior of columns.*

It is remarkable how the (extremely bright and thoughtful) Alberti completely misses the hyperbolic shapes! Even more remarkable is the fact that *even in this century* writers on solid shape (*e.g.*, on the art of sculpture) follow Alberti as if Karl Friedrich Gauss had never existed![19] It would appear that one can't trust the spatial intuition of the average educated human on this issue.

In order to start to develop a solid gut feeling for the shape operator, you may consider first of all what the indicatrix typically looks like. Its shape depends on the values of the eigenvalues κ_1, κ_2. Typically both are different from zero. On certain curves on the surface one of the two

---

[19]For example Kurt Badt in his *Wesen der Plastik*, or even a scientist like James Gibson in his *Perception of the Visual World*.

may vanish. Then there could be isolated points for which the values of the eigenvalues coincide:

$\kappa_1, \kappa_2 = 0$	a "planar point"	(non-generic)
$\kappa_1 = 0$ or $\kappa_2 = 0$	a "parabolic point"	(generically on curves)
$\kappa_1 \kappa_2 < 0$	a "hyperbolic point"	(generically patchwise)
$\kappa_1 + \kappa_2 = 0$	a "minimal point"	(generically on curves)
$\kappa_1 \kappa_2 > 0$	an "elliptic point"	(generically patchwise)
$\kappa_1 = \kappa_2 \neq 0$	an "umbilic point"	(generically isolated points)

The typical cases are the hyperbolic and the elliptic points. At a hyperbolic point the indicatrix is a pair of hyperbolas. This probably inspired the name in the first place. Another more descriptive term is "anticlastic point" meaning "curved in opposite directions." (According to Webster's:

> **an.ti.clas'tic**, *a.*[Gr. *antiklān*; *anti*, back, and *klān*, to bend.] in mathematics, curved oppositely in different directions: applied to a surface having concave and convex curvatures transversely opposite, as that of a saddle: opposed to *syn-clastic*.

Who says the language of math is hard to follow; the standard dictionary is certainly worse!) Indeed, at an anticlastic point the surface is curved in one way for some directions and in the opposite sense for others. It looks like a saddle or pass, which is most clearly perceived when $\kappa_1 = -\kappa_2$ which is the condition for a "minimal point." In a way the minimal points are "as anticlastic as you can get." Figures 170 and 171 illustrate an anticlastic point and its Gaussian image. The Gaussian image has the opposite orientation of the surface, a fact that I will discuss in detail at a later point.

Note that the anticlastic surface patch *lies at both sides of its tangent plane*. The tangent plane intersects the surface in a pair of transverse curves that act as asymptotes for the lines of equal distance to the tangent plane ("height"). The shape of these height contours is similar to the shape of Dupin's indicatrix. Thus the indicatrix clearly indicates the local shape.

At an elliptic point the indicatrix is an ellipse. The ellipse can be an indicatrix for a *concavity* or a *convexity*. You can have "positive or negative height." For the outward normal both eigenvalues are positive for a *concavity*, both negative for a *convexity*. Thus, it would in fact

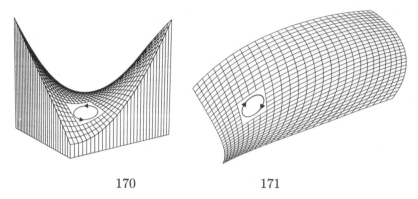

170   171

make sense to use an *oriented curve* for the indicatrix in order to skip
ambiguities right from the start. For some reason or other this is by no
means the common practice, however.

An elliptic point is also known as "synclastic" because the surface is
curved with equal sense for all directions. In this case Webster's has:

> **syn.clas'tic**, *a.*[*syn-*, and Gr. *klastos*, broken.] having cur-
> vatures all in the same direction, that is, all convex or all
> concave, at any given point: said of a surface, as of a sphere:
> opposed to *anticlastic*.

These terms describe the visual appearance quite well, and consequently I prefer[20] "anticlastic" and "synclastic" over "hyperbolic" and
"elliptic." The mathematically oriented literature is of the opposite
opinion, though.

Figures 172 and 173 illustrate a convexity with its Gauss map, whereas
figures 174 and 175 illustrate a concavity with its Gauss map. Both
Gauss maps have the same orientation as the patch itself. Clearly the
Gauss map is a nice one-to-one map of the patch, just as in the anticlastic
case. For the convexity the tangent plane lies completely outside of the
patch; for the concavity it lies inside.

If $\kappa_1 = \kappa_2$ the point is called an "umbilic" or a "navel point." The
indicatrix is singular and the eigenspace is degenerated. This is where
you meet problems when you want to define principal frame fields. Since
any unbalance of the principal curvatures makes the shape tend to the

---

[20]The more so because "hyperbolic" and "elliptic" appear in many different contexts and heighten the chances of unfortunate confusions.

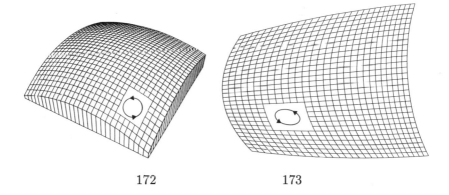

172   173

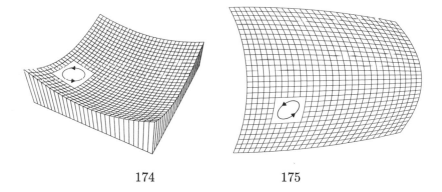

174   175

cylindrical, the umbilical points are in a way "as synclastic as you can get." There obviously cannot be umbilics on anticlastic patches; thus you never run into problems there.

A patch is said to be *locally convex* if the surface is confined to a half-space, and *strictly locally convex* if it has only a single point in common with the tangent plane. A patch is strictly locally convex if the Gaussian curvature is positive, whereas local convexity implies that the Gaussian curvature is not negative. The converse of the latter property is *not true*. That is, $K \geq 0$ does not imply local convexity. This is shown by the example[21] $z = x^3(1 + y^2)$. Of course this example is a rather contrived one. If the principal curvatures do not have different signs, you may conclude that the patch is locally convex.

An eigenvector points in a "principal direction." If you consider the strip along a principal direction, you find that it is a curvature strip because the change of normal is along the tangent to the strip. The rate of change is merely the *normal curvature*. Classically this result is due to Olinde Rodriguez. The change in the normal in a principal direction is simply $\triangle \vec{n} = -\kappa_i \triangle \vec{x}$ for the principal direction i. The sign does not depend on the convention for the normal. The reason is that if you flip the orientation of the normal you automatically also flip the sign of the curvature.

If two points on a curve of principal curvature are at a small distance d apart, then the dihedral angle between their tangent planes equals the corresponding principal curvature times d. Or taken the other way around,

Useful heuristic: *curvature is the "dihedral angle per unit distance"*.

The "edge," that is, the line of intersection of the two tangent planes, is along the other principal direction. This is the geometrical content of Rodriguez's formula.

If you take a strip that is not in a principal direction, the change of the normal has a component perpendicular to the strip's tangent, and consequently the strip must be *twisted*. If you proceed in a tangent direction $\vec{t}$, the change of the normal is made up of a component in the direction of $\vec{t}$, that is, a "nose dive" or a "climb," and a component perpendicular to $\vec{t}$, which is a "spin." A spin induces a *twist* of the geodesic strip defined by the direction $\vec{t}$.

There are two *untwisted* strips ("curvature strips," remember?) through each generic point on a surface. They are mutually perpen-

---

[21] I found it in Do Carmo's book. You should do some quick calculations in the margin. The example is simple enough to grasp in a minute or so.

dicular. The amount of twist on strips for other directions depends on
the difference of the eigenvalues and the direction with respect to the
eigenvectors. For hyperbolic patches you can even find strips that are
"completely twisted" and have no normal curvature at all. This happens when you take the strip along an "asymptotic direction," that is,
a direction for which $II(\vec{t},\vec{t}) = 0$. *The asymptotic strips are completely
twisted.* On the other hand, *at an umbilic all strips are not twisted.* This
characterizes the umbilical points.

   You can give a strip a geodesic curvature by curving it in the tangent plane. You have already seen that this does not affect the normal
curvature at all. The normal curvature depends only on the direction
of the strip's tangent. This is classically known as Meusnier's theorem.
(Meusnier, 1776) Together with Euler's theorem this is one of the few
interesting results in surface theory before Gauss. If you express the
normal curvature purely in terms of direction, which is almost trivial,
you find the classical expression known as Euler's formula.

   For strips I have defined a "conjugated direction" as the direction of
the "hinge" between subsequent faces. You can do the same for the
patch. In fact this is trivially possible if you just *think of the patch as
a sheaf of strips.* Think of strips of adhesive tape criss-crossed over a
point as if to mend a hole in the surface.

   Suppose you are at a point $\mathcal{P}$ of a patch. For any given direction
from $\mathcal{P}$ and tangent vector $\vec{t}$ (thus $\vec{t}$ has its tail at $\mathcal{P}$ and points in the
given direction), the tangent plane at the tip of $\vec{t}$ is given by $II(\vec{t})$. The
"hinge" is by definition the common line of intersection of the plane
$II(\vec{t})$ and the tangent plane at $\mathcal{P}$. Thus you obtain the tangent plane
at the tip of $\vec{t}$ from that at the tail of $\vec{t}$ through a small rotation about
the "hinge," which can be represented through its direction, which is
given through some tangent vector $\vec{h}$ (say). The direction of $\vec{h}$ is given
through $II(\vec{t})\langle\vec{h}\rangle = 0$. Thus the condition is $II(\vec{t},\vec{h}) = 0$ and you see
that it is mutual, because the second principal form is symmetrical in its
slots (fig. 168). One says that the directions of $\vec{t}$ and $\vec{h}$ are "conjugated
directions." If $\vec{h}$ is the hinge for the direction $\vec{t}$, then $\vec{t}$ is the hinge
for the direction $\vec{h}$. You also see that the principal directions are also
mutually conjugate directions and that the asymptotic directions are
self-conjugate.

Powerful heuristic: *A simple way to visualize the conjugated directions is to shine a light beam from the direction of $\vec{t}$. Then the
   edge of the attached shadow is along $\vec{h}$. Similarly, if you look
   along $\vec{t}$ the occlusion boundary is along $\vec{h}$ and vice versa.*

It is hard to overestimate the importance of the simple concept of conjugated directions. A major reason is that the notion doesn't depend on the metric and thus carries over to the projection of a surface. That's why the conjugation relations turn up at the drop of a hat in optical applications. If you deal with a problem that has some important direction in its specification (line of sight, direction of illumination . . .), your best bet is to find its conjugated direction first without much further thought: it will be an important entity for sure!

On an elliptic patch you can easily find the *characteristic directions* as those conjugated directions that subtend the smallest angle among all possible conjugated pairs. The largest angle is just $\frac{\pi}{2}$ and it occurs for the principal directions which form a conjugated pair. The smallest is zero for a hyperbolic patch because the asymptotic directions are self-conjugated, but has some finite value for an elliptic patch. In a certain vague sense the characteristic directions are thus generalizations of the asymptotic directions for an elliptic patch. The characteristic directions make equal angles with a principal direction. The angle between them depends on the ratio $\frac{\kappa_1}{\kappa_2}$.

As an exercise in conjugation you may try to make sense of an attractive theorem due to Blaschke. It is worth the effort because it finds numerous applications.

Theorem: *The meridians and latitude circles of the sphere have the following generalization:*

The curves along which osculating cones with their apices on a straight line touch a surface, together with the curves of intersection of that surface with the planes through that line, define a net of conjugated directions on the surface. (My translation. Believe me, the original German is even more opaque.)

Notice that for the special case of a sphere and a straight line through its center you obtain the usual meridians and latitude circles. If you move a point source over the line, the shadow boundary describes the latitude circles; if you move your eye along the line, the "occlusion boundary" does likewise. This is trivial for the sphere with the polar axis, but Blaschke's theorem generalizes these facts for *arbitrary* surfaces. It allows you to draw the shadow boundaries on the *Venus de Milo* for arbitrary positions of the light source. Who says differential geometry is useless in real life?

6.2.10 Special local surface forms

When one eigenvalue vanishes, or worse, when two vanish—but generically you don't have to reckon with that—the quadric is degencrated and the indicatrix becomes a bit less useful. This only happens in rare cases though because the *parabolic points* generically occur only on curves, not on patches. In such cases you may use higher order indicatrices; for instance, you truncate the local Taylor development for the normal deviation from the tangent plane at a higher order.

The good news is that the possibilities are not endless. Generically there are only five types of *local projections* on the normal. Projections on the normal arc another way to look at the local shape when you come to think of it. They are of thc following simple types (fig. 176 shows you some rough sketches of the height functions):

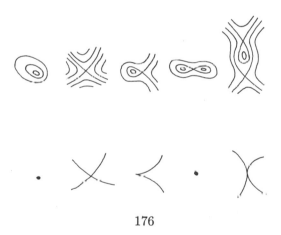

176

No.	Monge form	codim	Morse ind.	Zero level curve
1	$x^2 + y^2$	0	+1	point
2	$x^2 - y^2$	0	−1	node
3	$x^2 + y^3$	1	0	cusp (or spinode)
4	$x^2 + y^4$	2	+1	unode
5	$x^2 - y^4$	2	−1	tacnode

The "unode" appears as a point, but a small perturbation reveals it as not a single, but as a double extremum.

I have already discussed the first two cases, namely an elliptic point and a hyperbolic point. The third is that of a parabolic point, and cases four and five are "cusps of the Gauss map," or "ruffles."

Let $\vec{m}$ denote a direction that is close to the normal direction. Then you can find $c + 1$ points (c the "codimension given in the table) in the neighborhood of $x = y = 0$ with the identical normal direction $\vec{m}$. Equivalently, if you slightly tilt the shape, you obtain $c + 1$ critical points, points with a horizontal tangent plane. The "Morse index" is the number of resulting extrema minus the number of resulting saddles. Thus you have an extremum for the elliptic point and a saddle for the hyperbolic point, as should be.

For the parabolic point you obtain an extremum-saddle pair. The cuspidal zero level curve can be understood as a "fusion" of the pair. Because of the shape of the zero level curve, the parabolic points are also known as "spinodal points." A more descriptive term would be "monoclastic points," so called because the surface is locally curved in a single direction only. This term seems not to be in such general use as "synclastic" and "anticlastic" for the elliptic and hyperbolic points, as Webster's dictionary reveals (fig. 177). You will usually distinguish

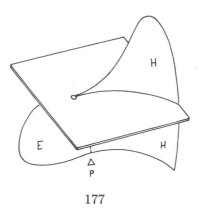

177

between rut-type and crest-type spinodal points. The former look like the inside of a gutter, the latter like the outside of a cylindrical rod. One is the "inside-out" version of the other.

Case (4) is an "elliptic cusp point." It can be considered to be the fusion of two extrema and a saddle (figs. 178 and 179). At such a point the surface looks locally like the "foot of a mountain" or—viewed from the other side—the end of a valley. Hence I often refer to such points as "pedal" or "foot" points. A more classical name would be "unode."[22]

---

[22]Webster's has:

ū.nō.de, *n.* in geometry, a conical point of a surface in which the tangent cone has become a pair of coincident planes: also called *uniplanar point.*

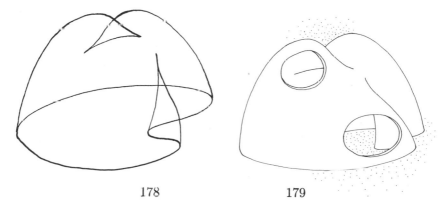

178   179

The tangent plane touches the surface at two coincident places.

The fifth case is a so called "hyperbolic cusp point." I will refer often to it as a "tacnodal point" because of the shape of the zero-level curve.[23] This type of special point can be understood as the fusion of two saddle points with an extremum (figs. 180 and 181).

The unodal and the tacnodal points, or "ruffles," are prominent shape features. Unodes occur on the boundary of the region of exposed points of a surface because you have *bitangent planes* for arbitrary small neighborhoods of both unodal and tacnodal points. For the unodes, the bitangent planes touch the surface at *elliptic points*; for tacnodes, at the *hyperbolic points*. The limiting bitangent plane of an exposed unode is a special feature of the convex hull that I have pointed out in a previous chapter. The principal direction for which the principal curvature vanishes is *tangent* to the parabolic curve at the unodal and tacnodal points. The corresponding "line of curvature," that is, the curvature strip, runs through the elliptic region for the unodes and through the

---

My usage is slightly different, but since at a unode you have a bitangent plane that touches the surface at two coincident points, the analogy is a close one.

[23] Webster's has:

tac̲'nō.de, *n.* in geometry, the point of tangency of two or more branches of the same curve.

Thus the term is descriptive of the (quartic) indicatrix.

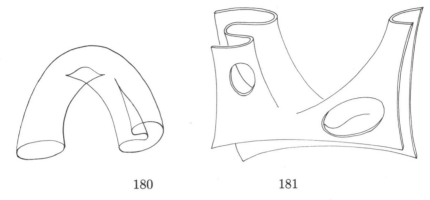

180   181

hyperbolic region for the tacnodes.

Because the unodes are the endings of the bitangent developables of the convex hull, you have a simple relation between the number of exposed unodes (U), the number of exposed tritangent support planes (T), and the topology of the region of exposed points (χ_E denotes the Euler number of this region):

$$U - T = 4 - 2\chi_E$$

You will appreciate this intuitively if you make a few drawings of possible configurations and do a little counting in the margin.

6.2.11   The Gauss map for triangulations

♠ INTERMEZZO—SPHERICAL HONEYCOMBS.

A typical triangulation will largely consist of 6-vertices and triangular faces. Each face is planar and thus maps to a *point* of the Gauss map. An edge will map to an *edge* because it represents the dihedral angle between two planes. A vertex maps to an *area* of the Gauss map because the normals at a vertex fill a finite solid angle, the "spherical excess."

As a consequence of these considerations it is intuitively evident that the vertices must map to sometimes fantastically warped *spherical hexagons*. Indeed, the typical Gauss map of a triangulation looks like a warped spherical honeycomb.

This is what you obtain if you compute the Gauss map of a triangulated surface by computing the normals of the faces and then drawing geodesic arcs between images of neighboring facets in order to obtain a graphic image.

At spinodal points and—even worse—at the ruffles, the hexagons must *fold over*. As a consequence their vertices get scrambled up. Your computer graphics will look terrible, which is one reason why most computer-oriented people restrict the use of the Gauss map to convex shapes (ovoids). However, when you want to move on to interesting applications, I advise you not to chicken out.

Even in the messed-up computer graphics you can detect something useful: it is possible, though not trivial, to write algorithms that classify the local surface singularities from the shape of the hexagons. This exercise took a student of mine half a year. You may be smarter or the problem may be difficult indeed.

The best way to get rid of the mess is to make a bold move: forget about the meshes and *concentrate on the folds themselves*. If you only draw the folds and pleats, your graphics will assume that clean, crisp look again. Moreover, you now zoom in on the features of real interest.

It is easy enough to find the folds computationally. First, find the spinodal locus through interpolation of the Gaussian curvature (which is known at the vertices) over the faces of your triangulation. Then map the locus to the unit sphere through the (likewise interpolated) normals at the spinodal curve. This is how I did the pictures for this book.

6.2.12 The Gauss map in crystallography

♠ INTERMEZZO—GAUSS MAPS IN NATURE.

The "shape of a crystal" does conventionally have two completely different meanings, the so-called "habitus"—that is more or less what the crystal looks like to the ordinary citizen—and the "structure." The structure is what the crystal looks like to the crystallographer, or rather what the crystallographer looks for in the crystal. The latter sense is the more important because it remains the same for a given substance even if crystals have a very different habitus, and it is often of decisive importance in technical applications. The "structure" is the relation between the orientations of the facets of the crystal, which is nothing else but *the Gauss map of the (growth planes of the) crystal*.

Nicolaus Steno, physician-in-ordinary of the Grandduke Ferdinand II at Florence, observed (in 1669!) that all crystals of the same mineral have identical Gaussian images (even though that entity had not yet been introduced formally) although they may have a complete dissimilar habitus. (*De Solido intra Solidum naturaliter contento Dissertationis Prodomus—Florence 1669.*) Surely an extraordinary keen observation!

An "explanation" of this observation, based on the idea that solids are built from regular "bricks" (the "molécule integrante"), was published by the Abbé Haüy in 1784. (*Essai d'une théorie sur la structure des crystaux . . .*) This was also an extremely keen observation, of course, this time of a more abstract, mathematical nature.

The crystallographer has the tools to measure the Gauss map of crystals with high precision ("goniometry") and uses special methods to handle properties of the Gauss map of polyhedra with various symmetries. The structure may also be obtained via X-ray diffraction methods. Indeed, this is the preferred method nowadays. The symmetries of the Gauss map are of interest to the modern scientist because they reveal the way the elementary building blocks of the solid state are spatially configured. This again reveals the nature of the forces between the building blocks.

The reference books on crystallography conventionally depict the Gauss map of the crystal in stereographical projection. I have followed this—highly convenient—tradition in this book.

It is somehow interesting to ponder the fact that the "growth planes" of crystals arise because crystals can be regarded—in a rather naive view of solid state physics—as "piles of sugar cubes." The X-ray diffraction methods basically determine the rules according to which the cubes may be stacked, the rules of the game, so to speak. If you experiment with piles of sugar cubes, you will no doubt soon notice the fact that only certain growth planes are possible. This is very noticeable in attempts to portray rounded objects with Lego blocks, which you may often see in toy shops.

The sphere is the solution of a problem which could be considered a paradox, were it not demonstrable by geometry that the sphere is an infinite polyhedron. Thus the most infinite degree of variety derives from the most perfect symmetry. For if we suppose the surface of the globe to be divided into points, one of these points meets the eye perpendicularly, and all the others will appear at an immense number of angles.

—ETIENNE-LOUIS BOULLEÉ, *Architecture, an essay on art (1770–84)*

6.2.13   Surfaces of constant curvature

In general the surfaces of *things growing or blown up from the inside*
tend to possess positive Gaussian curvature. Just ponder awhile over
what is common to eggs, soap bubbles, bulging muscles, ripe fruits like
melons, female breasts ... The answer is that the ovoids are the "type"
here. *The ovoid shape somehow suggests life and growth,* which is the
reason that artists tend to depict living things as agglomerations of ovoid
shapes.

The sculpture of many cultures reveals this very clearly. Very often
the negatively curved parts are reduced to narrow V-shaped grooves
between the bulging ovoid parts. An extreme example is the famous

182

"Venus of Willendorf" from Paleolithic origin (*ca.* 11 000 B.C.). Clearly
this fact that we all seem to know from introspection is not a short-
lived "cultural whim," but somehow pervades human visual perception
throughout known history and over all cultures. European art from
many stylistic periods, as well as Indian and Eastern Asiatic art provide
numerous examples. Here I show an example (fig. 182) from a didactical
book on the art of drawing. As you see, a human head has been reduced

to a cluster of ovoids. In artistic theory one often speaks of the "bunch
of grapes."

On the other hand, *things shrinking or drying out tend to have large,
negatively curved surface patches.* Think of dried fruits. Negative Gaussian curvature tends to suggest processes associated with decay and
death. In living things the negatively curved patches appear at best
as a "glue" or transition between ovoidal patches, although they sometimes appear in things unfolding (leaves bursting forth from the bud) or
convoluted (like ears).

These general properties arise from the fact that positively curved
patches are most economical with their surface area for a given volume.
They can't be pushed flat without rupture, remember?

In contradistinction, negatively curved areas have a surplus of surface
area for their volume. They tend to wrinkle when pushed flat.

Thus the negatively curved patches don't look filled out to full capacity. In their role as "glue," the negatively curved patches tend at least
to minimize area for a fixed boundary curve. This is why transitional
parts in bodies covered with an elastic skin are often almost minimal
surfaces. These are the "most anticlastic" patches you can get. Because
the boundary is often clearly seen to constrain the surface, such minimal
surfaces don't necessarily look "wrinkled"; you tend to associate them
with transitional parts of athletic bodies with taut skins.

This does not hold for organs that are designed to *maximize* surface
area, of course, such as ears which have a cooling function in large species
like elephants.[24] Nor does it hold for the case that the surface area is
"just there" and the skin merely flaps about as something superfluous.
Such cases are typically associated with decay and death.

One way to obtain a feeling for what the curvatures are about is to
consider *surfaces of constant curvature.* What do they have in common,
and in what do they differ?

Surfaces of vanishing Gaussian curvature are planar patches, pieces
of cylinders or cone mantles, or pieces of the tangent developable of a
general space curve. You can obtain all such surfaces by bending a sheet
of paper.

Surfaces of constant positive Gaussian curvature are like egg shells; the
spheres, for example. But if you take a piece of a sphere, you may bend
it into surface patches that don't look very spherical at all. I will give
examples in the chapter on shape in flux. One common characteristic is

---

[24]Of course, this is not a well-posed problem! You may make the observation more
precise yourself. The problem of the elephant's ears is not unlike the problem faced
by the designer of a central heating system.

that the geodesics radiating out from any point are certain to converge again on the "opposite pole."

Surfaces of constant negative Gaussian curvature are different in this respect. The geodesics radiating outward from a point will never meet again. Such surfaces are like pieces of a trumpet, but again you may subject them to severe bendings that destroy the rotational symmetry of the trumpet.

No blob can be completely "clothed" with anticlastic surface. Thus negatively curved surface is not fit to *bound* things. This is in sharp contradistinction with synclastic patches: even small pathes (I mean: with a limited total spread of normals) look as if they bound something, either material (for convexities) or pockets of air (for concavities).

Surfaces of vanishing mean curvature are known as "minimal surfaces." You may physically realize them by dipping arbitrarily bent copper wires into a soap solution. The resulting soap film approximates a minimal surface rather well. Clearly the plane is a trivial example. It is intuitively obvious that minimal surfaces cannot have positive Gaussian curvature because the principle curvatures must have opposite signs.

A well-known example is the "catenoid." It is illustrated fairly often because it can easily be bent into a surface that looks quite different, namely the helicoid, and thus makes for a fine classroom demonstration. Although the helicoid has the same Gaussian curvature as the catenoid— that's inherent in the notion of "bending"—it isn't obvious that it also has the same mean curvature. Yet the helicoid is a ruled surface, whereas the catenoid isn't. These surfaces look quite different from each other. This shows that even the mean and the Gaussian curvature together do not determine the local geometry of the surface completely.

For the unwary: *Two surfaces may posses equal Gaussian and average curvatures at corresponding points but still look quite different! Curvature isn't all there is to surfaces.*

Figures 183 and 184 depict the catenoid from nearby, and figures 185 and 186 the same surface from far away. From a distance, the catenoid looks like a plane with multiplicity two that hangs together at the origin. This is in fact a general property of minimal surfaces. When seen from infinity they look like sets of planes. Figure 187 depicts a single turn of the helicoid, which looks like an infinite spiral staircase.

Surfaces of constant but nonvanishing mean curvature can be realized with soap films if you employ, let's say, a straw to introduce a pressure difference. This is the art of "blowing bubbles," something you may remember from bygone times.

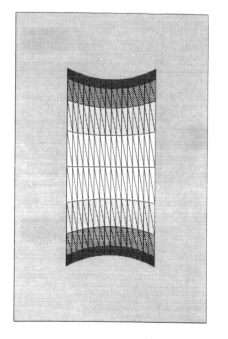 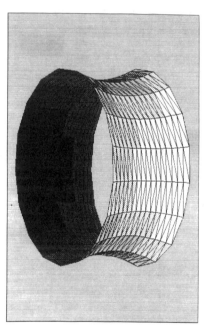

183   184

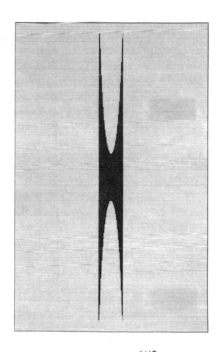
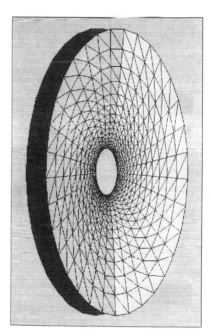

185   186

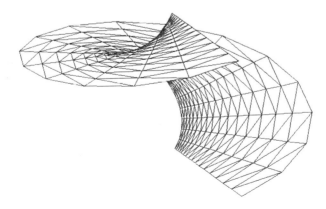

187

Such surfaces do not appear to have received much attention from geometers. The surfaces of revolution of this type were studied by Delaunay (1841) and have found some application in the morphological study of biological organisms. The Delaunay surfaces of revolution are known as the "Unduloid" and the "Nodoid." They can be generated as the surfaces of revolution of planar curves that are themselves generated as the geometrical loci of a focus of a quadric that is rolled over the axis of symmetry. The cylinder and a string of spherical beads are the extreme cases; the catenoid is also a special case.

Such surfaces can often be seen on fine columns of water falling from a jet. It helps to experiment with the faucet of your kitchen sink. The simplest shape is a cylindrical column, but very often you will notice undulations on the column that physically realize the "unduloid." Figure 188 shows a jet of water; figure 189 an unduloid. As the "necks" shrink to zero, the column breaks up into spherical drops. At the very limit the column has the shape of a beaded string. The beaded string is one of the limiting shapes of the unduloid. The cylinder is the other limit.

Of course the drops tend to separate quickly after the unduloid degenerates to the beaded form, so you won't have much time to admire this transitional shape. Such beaded strings may often be studied at ease in the fibers of a spider web, but you need a magnifying glass to get an eyeful (fig. 190).

The nodoid can only be realized in small pieces because this surface has a self-intersection, so it obviously can't bound a volume. You can see the nodoid in pieces of elastic tube under pressure. The catenoid is closely related to these shapes. You get the catenoid when you stretch a soap film between two parallel, circular wire loops. When you somehow raise the pressure on the inside, the catenoid deforms into a nodoid.

The unduloid is quite common in the shapes of simple aquatic creatures like the *Foraminifera*. One may find all the shapes described here, from the cylinder to the beaded string (fig. 191). In many respects, such creatures behave—at least shape-wise—as mere drops of water.

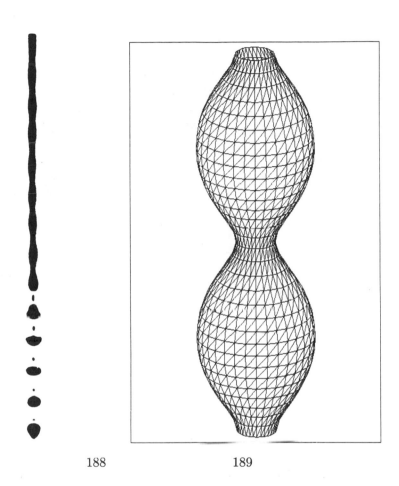

188   189

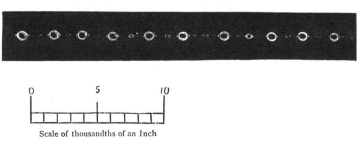

0   5   10

Scale of thousandths of an Inch

190

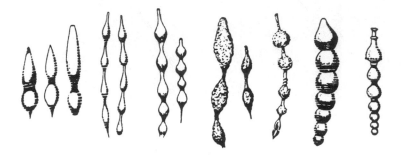

191

From a reiterated experience,
and a close comparison of the objects of Nature,
an artist becomes possessed of the idea of that central form,
if I may so express it,
from which every deviation is a deformity.
—SIR JOSHUA REYNOLDS, (1723–1792) *Third Discourse*

6.3 Intrinsic Curvature

I have introduced the Gaussian curvature as an algebraic expression, essentially as the product of the two principal curvatures. This throws some light on the Gaussian curvature as an algebraic invariant and connects it with *extrinsic* geometry. For the mathematically inclined, however, the really interesting significance of the Gaussian curvature is as an *intrinsic* geometrical invariant.

The structural equation $d\tilde{\omega}^{12} = -K\,\tilde{\sigma}^1 \wedge \tilde{\sigma}^2$ can be interpreted as a definition of K as *the common second-order derivative of all frame fields.* This identifies the Gaussian curvature as "the" curvature of the surface. You would expect the Gaussian curvature to play an important role in all problems that intuitively depend on deviation from flatness. And you would be right.

The intrinsic significance of the Gaussian curvature is revealed clearly through the *holonomy.* When you transport a vector over a closed loop in the sense of Levi-Civita, it returns after a circumnavigation with a net turn that equals the integral of the Gaussian curvature—Gauss's *"curvatura integra"* again—over the area enclosed by the loop. (Bonnet, 1848) It is easy to get an intuitive feel for this when you consider the sphere again.

When you transport a vector over a latitude circle, it is especially easy to assess the result of a Levi-Civita transport.[25] Note that a right circular cone with semi-top angle $\frac{\pi}{2} - \vartheta$ touches the sphere along a latitude circle of polar distance ϑ. The length of a generator from apex to the tangency to the sphere is $R\tan\vartheta$ (R denotes the radius of the sphere). The circumference of a latitude circle is $2\pi R \sin\vartheta$. When you spread the cone mantle in the plane, you get a sector of a circle with radius $R\tan\vartheta$ and arclength $2\pi R \sin\vartheta$. Thus the sector angle is $\frac{2\pi R \sin\vartheta}{R\tan\vartheta} = 2\pi\cos\vartheta$. It is pictorially evident that this sector angle is the sought for holonomy angle. At the equator ($\vartheta = \frac{\pi}{2}$) the holonomy angle vanishes, as it should (the cone degenerates into a cylinder), and near the pole (where the cone degenerates into a tangent plane) it amounts to almost a full turn, which is again a small amount since an integral number of turns doesn't count.

---

[25]It is *absolutely necessary* that you do some doodling in the margin! Don't skip it unless you want to miss your chance to understand something important.

If you transport a vector over a curvilinear quadrangle:

1. $\quad\quad\quad \vartheta \quad \to \quad \vartheta + \triangle\vartheta \quad$ constant azimuth
2. $\quad\quad\quad \varphi \quad \to \quad \varphi + \triangle\varphi \quad$ constant polar angle
3. $\quad \vartheta + \triangle\vartheta \quad \to \quad \vartheta \quad\quad$ constant azimuth
4. $\quad \varphi + \triangle\varphi \quad \to \quad \varphi \quad\quad$ constant polar angle

you obtain a holonomy angle of

$$0 + \triangle\varphi.\cos(\vartheta + \triangle\vartheta) + 0 - \triangle\varphi.\cos\vartheta \approx -\triangle\varphi.\sin\vartheta.\triangle\vartheta.$$

The area of the quadrangle is nearly

$$R^2 \sin\vartheta.\triangle\vartheta.\triangle\varphi,$$

thus the *curvatura integra* should equal

$$R^2 K.\sin\vartheta.\triangle\vartheta.\triangle\varphi.$$

As would be expected, things work out okay because K indeed equals R^{-2}.

You can derive many easy results from these relations when you apply them judiciously. For instance, if you construct geodesic tangents at two nearby points on a curve, you obtain an infinitesimal curvilinear triangle to which you can apply the theorem. You then obtain an intuitively attractive lemma due to Bonnet:

Bonnet's Lemma: *The geodesic curvature of the curve is the limiting value, for the case when the geodesic tangents approach each other, of the angle between the geodesic tangents divided by the arclength increment.*

This is a very simple application, but there is a catch here. The trick you need is to notice that the area of the triangle vanishes faster than its perimeter. That is why the term with the Gaussian curvature is absent.

From these same relations it also follows that an area bounded by two smooth geodesic arcs cannot exist in a hyperbolic area. That such a case is possible in elliptic areas is evident when you think of the region between two meridians on the earth's globe.

In many cases of practical interest you can apply Bonnet's theorem easily and to good advantage.

Near the pole of the geographical globe you have a system of geodesic polar coordinates. The meridians are geodesics; the latitude circles

geodesic circles in the sense that they have constant geodesic distance
to the pole. The first fundamental form is easily written down. Notice how I use the old-fashioned notation, which often recommends itself
when you do sloppy "back of the envelope" calculations. You construct
"dee-es-squared" from "infinitesimal displacements":

$$ds^2 = d\text{PolarDistance}^2 + \text{Radius}^2 d\text{Azimuth}^2 =$$
$$ds^2 = d\varrho^2 + K^{-1}\sin^2(\sqrt{K}.\varrho).d\varphi^2 = d\varrho^2 + G(\varrho).d\varphi^2,$$

where ϱ equals the Radius times the PolarDistance and $K = \text{Radius}^{-2}$.
This interesting formula is in fact valid for surfaces with arbitrary but
constant Gaussian curvature. For $K = 0$ you obtain the usual polar
coordinates of the Euclidean plane. For $K < 0$ you obtain the hyperbolic
plane. Note that $\sin\sqrt{-|K|}\varrho = \sinh\sqrt{|K|}\varrho$. Near the pole you have
approximately:

$$ds^2 = d\varrho^2 + \left(\varrho - \frac{\varrho^3}{6}K + \ldots\right)^2 d\varphi^2.$$

This expression can be used to calculate a few geometrically very significant entities:

The circumference of a geodesic circle is

$$L = 2\pi\varrho - \frac{\pi}{3}\varrho^3 K + \ldots$$

and its area is

$$A = \pi\varrho^2 - \frac{\pi}{12}\varrho^4 K + \ldots$$

From these results you can immediately regain the formulas of Diguet
(1848) relating the Gaussian curvature to the growth-rate of area as a
function of radius, and of Bertrand and Puisseux (1848) who similarly
relate it to the growth rate of perimeter. These results can be obtained
for the case of the sphere by way of elementary geometry. Just do the
sums and then develop your results in a Taylor series for ϱ. This is a
very instructive exercise.

Two geodesics that issue from a point in "almost the same direction"
separate according to the differential equation:

$$\frac{\partial^2 \Delta\vec{n}}{\partial\varrho^2} + K(\varrho)\Delta\vec{n} = 0$$

(Here $\Delta\vec{n}$ is the separation vector. That is to say, suppose that you have
a two parameter family of geodesics $\gamma(s,t)$, where t measures "which

geodesic" and s the arclength along the geodesics, and moreover such
that $\gamma(0, t)$ equals a single common point for all members of the family.
Then the separation vector measures the separation from $\gamma(s, t)$ to the
equivalent point on the nearby geodesic $\gamma(s, t + \Delta t)$.)

When K vanishes, the separation increases *linearly*, as in the Euclidean plane, but on the unit sphere you obtain a *periodic solution*.
For the globe the geodesics meet again at the opposite pole. This can
never happen if K is negative, as is already clear from the Gauss-Bonnet
theorem, which specifies the dependence of the holonomy angle on the
curvatura integra. This type of equation describes the "tidal forces,"
the forces that drive apart two free particles on nearby parallel orbits in
Einstein's theory of gravitation. Free particles traverse geodesic orbits
in this theory.

A useful parametrization is by means of "Riemann normal coordinates." They are *the nearest thing to a Cartesian net on the surface.* Of
course this applies only to a small neighborhood of a point.

To see how this works, first consider the bundle of all geodesics through
a point $\mathcal{P}$. They can be labeled with their direction at $\mathcal{P}$, say through
an angle φ. Let ϱ measure the geodesic distance from $\mathcal{P}$; then (ϱ, φ) are
"geodesic polar coordinates" at $\mathcal{P}$. This basic idea is simple enough.

According to Gauss, the first fundamental form is $ds^2 = d\varrho^2$
$+ G(\varrho, \varphi) \, d\varphi^2$. (You should refer to the case of the spherical coordinates that I discussed earlier to see how this works out for a simple
situation.) From the first fundamental form, you see that the "circles"
$\varrho = constant$ intersect the geodesic radii orthogonally.[26]

If you define new parameters (u, v) according to the scheme $u =$
$\varrho \cos \varphi$, $v = \varrho \sin \varphi$ you obtain Riemann's canonical parametrization.
The trick is clear: first you construct a geodesic polar coordinate sys-
tem, and then you use the standard relation between polar and Cartesian
coordinates from the Euclidean plane to arrive at Riemann's "normal coordinates." These coordinates are usually much nicer than the geodesic
polar coordinates because they avoid the singular nature of the origin.

If you do the sums, you will find out that $G(\varrho, \varphi)$ must have a devel-

---

[26]It is possible to define "circles" in various ways. The curves defined here may be
called "distance circles." Another definition uses the isoperimetric property of circles.
Then you obtain curves with a fixed geodesic curvature, called "geodesic circles" by
Lie and by Darboux. Only if the surface is a surface of constant curvature do the
distance circles and the geodesic circles coincide.

opment around $\mathcal{P}$ of the form[27]

$$G(\varrho, \varphi) = \varrho^2 + \alpha \varrho^4 + \varrho^5 (\beta \cos \varphi + \gamma \sin \varphi) + \ldots$$

whereas the first fundamental form in normal coordinates must be like

$$ds^2 = du^2 + dv^2 + \alpha (u\, dv - v\, du)^2 + \ldots$$

which looks very much like Pythagoras' theorem, but with a "correction."

If you now rotate the polar coordinate system about $\mathcal{P}$, then ϱ can't change, whereas φ varies in step with the rotation. The point is that α remains at a fixed value during the rotation: *it is an intrinsic invariant.*

Indeed, it is not hard to show that α equals minus one-third of the Gaussian curvature at the point $\mathcal{P}$. (Again: try it for the sphere!) From Gauss's princely theorem you obtain

$$K = -\frac{1}{\sqrt{G}} \frac{\partial^2}{\partial \varrho^2} \sqrt{G}$$

From these formulas you may once again derive the familiar relations of Diguet and of Bertrand and Puisseux.

The angles of a triangle with geodesic arcs as sides add up to

$$\alpha_1 + \alpha_2 + \alpha_3 = \pi + \int \text{ curvatura integra } dA.$$

Thus the proverbial intelligent ant can actually *measure the Gaussian curvature* of its space through simple trigonometry![28]

You get angle sums of more than π on the sphere and less than π on the pseudosphere, which is a surface of constant negative Gaussian curvature.

This simple fact has interesting consequences. For instance, you can't pave the plane with regular pentagons because the angles are 108 degrees, so a vertex of 3 pentagons adds up to 324 and of 4 to 432 degrees. On the pseudosphere you can find a size such that the angles are 90 degrees. Then you *can* fit four pentagons at a vertex. Similarly, you can't

---

[27]If the surface is a surface of *constant curvature*, the constants β and γ vanish. Thus you won't find these terms if you try the example of the sphere.

[28]Gauss himself took this observation very seriously indeed and considered the human condition as little above the mythical ant's status. He went through the considerable trouble of *actually measuring* the angles (remember he was a mathematician!) of a rather large triangle, one formed by three hilltops that were conveniently located, Hohenhagen, Brocken and Inselsberg. The angle sum came out to π within the observational accuracy.

have right-angled equilateral triangles in the plane. You can easily construct them on the sphere, however. You can tessellate the sphere with eight of them: they are merely the conventional *octants* of the sphere.

From the fact that the angle sum of a triangle depends on the total curvature calculated over the area of the triangle, you may conclude that on surfaces with constant Gaussian curvature, *similar triangles of different size cannot exist*, except for the case of vanishing curvature of course. Only in the Euclidean plane can you have similarities. On the sphere or pseudosphere, a triangle changes its shape when you let it grow in size.

For $K = 0$ you obtain the usual formulas of the Euclidean plane. For $K > 0$ you get some facts that are intuitively clear from a consideration of the sphere, namely that the area and perimeter of circles grows less rapidly with the radius than in the Euclidean plane. This is precisely why you can't spread a spherical cap out in the plane (fig. 192). There

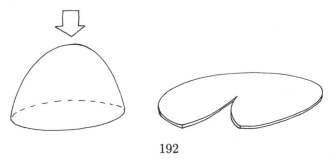

192

is a lack of material for that. On the other hand if $K < 0$, there is a surplus of material. You can't push a hyperbolic "cap" in the plane without wrinkling it because there is a surplus of material (fig. 193).

A figure taken from Fokker's book on the theory of relativity and gravitation based on drawing implements illustrates this basic fact very nicely (fig. 194).

I could go on like this for quite a while and come up with one fascinating generalization of the geometry of the Euclidean plane after another. I will not do so, however, since the main emphasis of the book is on *extrinsic geometry*.

One final remark: For the case of elliptic curvature there exist simple relations between the volume (V) and area (A) of a cap of height h and

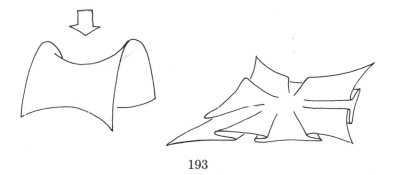

193

194

the Gaussian curvature K. Thus you have the limits

$$K = \lim_{h \to 0} \frac{\pi^2 h^4}{V^2}$$
$$\text{and}$$
$$K = \lim_{h \to 0} \frac{4\pi^2 h^2}{A^2}.$$

Note how these formulas are completely extrinsic in contradistinction with the superficially similar theorems of Diguet or Bertrand and Puisseux, which are of a purely intrinsic nature. The height and the volume have no counterparts in the intrinsic description; they depend entirely on the nature of the embedding.

Here is a simple but infallible rule of thumb that lets you spot the amateur geometer:

Useful fact: *No professional will miss the fundamentally different nature of intrinsic and extrinsic properties, whereas the tyro presents you with an indiscriminate hodge-podge.*

When you start noticing these things, you will discover that the applications-oriented literature is quite rich in papers where these elementary distinctions are completely neglected.

I call our world Flatland, not because we call it so,
but to make its nature clear to you,
my happy readers, who are privileged to live in Space.
—EDWIN A. ABBOT (1838–1926), *Flatland*

6.4 Extrinsic Curvature

I have introduced the Gauss map as a mapping that maps points of the surface on their normals or—equivalently—on points of the Gaussian sphere. There are other ways to think about the Gaussian image that are often of considerable heuristic value. You have to be familiar with all these angles in order to get a firm, intuitive hold on what goes on.

One of the more useful insights is the following. Consider the *family of parallel surfaces* for a given patch. By this I mean the surfaces you get when you move a surface along its normal over a given distance (ε, say). You get another surface which is at constant distance ε from the original one.

Parallel surfaces arise in practice when you coat an object with a layer of constant thickness ("paint"). Sometimes, parallel surfaces are required in CAD-CAM, for instance if machine tools of finite size have to be used (not uncommon!) in the computer-controlled machining of parts. The renaissance sculptor Benvenuto Cellini describes in his *Vita* how he produced clay models for statues that were a *constant amount too thin*, then coated them with wax to the correct proportions in order to speed up the process of obtaining molds for bronzes via the "lost wax" process.

Parallel surface are also common in theories of physical phenomena: the isophasal surfaces of a wave are parallel surfaces when the medium in which the wave propagates is homogeneous and isotropic. In such theories the Gauss map also figures prominently; it is then known as the "far field," or "Fraunhofer region."

Figure 195 shows the construction of parallel surfaces for a convex patch. Here the parallel surface is nice and smooth, and looks in fact very much like the original patch itself. This is usually the case when ε is small (things don't change their shape very much when you paint them). It is no longer true whenever ε is of the order of (or larger than) one or both of the principal radii of curvature (you remove pinholes of a surface when you paint it). Thus it may happen that the parallel surface intersects with itself or that it develops non-smooth parts. Don't let this worry you one bit; this is just a thought construction anyway. (It is important in CAM, though: you can't produce concavities with a curvature higher than that of your machine tool! In the wave theories, self-intersections are quite common and are not considered a problem.)

Here is a fact that is interesting about the parallel surfaces: if you construct them for larger and larger distances, they all *become spherical* regardless of what the original shape was.

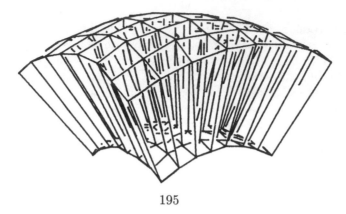

195

The parallel surfaces also become *larger* for greater distances, of course. Figures 196 to 198 show a set of parallel surfaces for the convex patch for

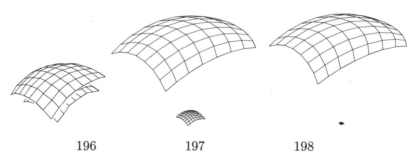

196   197   198

increasingly greater distances. Of course, the figures had to be scaled in order to fit the page. Scaling is a good idea in fact. Notice that the growth in size can be compensated for by a scaling by a factor $(1 + \varepsilon^2)^{-1/2}$. This scaling is particularly convenient for computer graphics purposes, since now all members of the family of parallel surfaces fit neatly on your screen or plotter paper.

When you do this scaling, you obtain a *continuous transformation between the surface patch itself and a piece of the unit sphere*. I contend that this map is just the Gaussian spherical image. In fact this is trivially the case because by construction all parallel surfaces have the same normals at corresponding points. Thus you arrive at the tremendously important and useful insight:

Important heuristic: *The Gaussian image can be said to represent the parallel surface at infinity.*

This is essentially the same notion that the physicist uses: the far field represents the angular spectrum of the wave. Similarly, the parallel surface at infinity represents the angular distribution of normals of the surface.

You will find it most instructive to prepare and run short computer animations that display this transition from a surface patch to its spherical image. There is no better way that I know of to obtain an intuitive grasp of the curvature of surfaces in three-space. Usually a dozen or so well-picked frames amply suffice to make a fine movie if you just see-saw back and forth through the frames.[29]

If you repeat this procedure for a *concave* patch, you find that the parallel surface first shrinks and then may assume fantastic crumpled-up shapes, but eventually unwraps again and develops into a nice spherical cap, as it should. In the process the surface was *pulled inside out twice*, the net effect being that the orientation of the spherical image equals that of the original patch, just as with the convexity. Only in this case it is a bit less obvious to the mind's eye (figs. 199 to 201). In the final figure I show a top view. This enables you to appreciate the crumpling better.

If you try this technique on an anticlastic patch, something novel happens: the patch gets turned inside out only *once*. Thus the net effect is that the spherical image has *the reverse orientation* (figs. 202 and 203).

The image is a neatly spherical cap for the convexity and concavity, and the anticlastic origin shows only in the orientation reversal.

Note that the convexity-concavity distinction cannot be decided from an inspection of the spherical image at all. Clearly there exist concave and convex patches with the same orientation in the family of parallel surfaces, and clearly they possess identical spherical images.

You have seen that in the case of polyhedra the vertices have their normals spread out over a solid angle, whereas the edges have them spread out over a spherical arc. The magnitude of the solid angle is a measure of the "curvature" at the vertex. It is completely analogous to the *Gaussian curvature*, which measures solid angle on the Gaussian sphere per surface area of the patch. This curvature of the vertices is a *curvatura integra* with vanishing support; that is, concentrated in a point.

---

[29]Use wire-frame graphics and switch off the hidden lines removal.

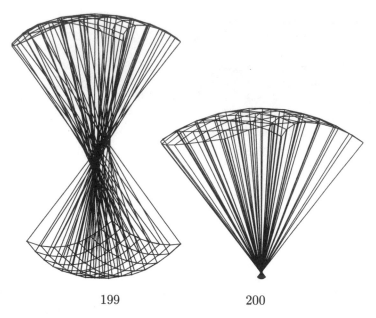

199   200

You can find a similar interpretation for the trace of the second fundamental form, the number I denoted H and which is known as the "mean curvature." A small arc on the patch will map to an arc on the Gaussian sphere. The length magnification is just the normal curvature of the patch. Thus the normal curvature is very much like the dihedral angle at a polyhedral edge, only there isn't any obvious edge around so the direction of the arc has to be arbitrary. If you *average* the magnification over all possible directions, you obtain the *mean curvature H*. This explains the term "mean" curvature and it also shows its kinship to the *dihedral angles* in polyhedra. The average of the normal curvature for any two orthogonal directions is independent of the specific choice and also equals the mean curvature.

Since the Gaussian curvature is the square of the geometrical average, just as the mean curvature is the arithmetical mean, you may well wonder whether a similar nice theorem holds for the Gaussian curvature, especially if you are fond of formal symmetries. Such is indeed the case, although the theorem is less obvious than you might expect offhand. I will return to this later.

There is another way to show the relations between Gaussian curvature and vertices and mean curvature and edges. It has to do with the surface area of the parallel surfaces in cases where you don't do the

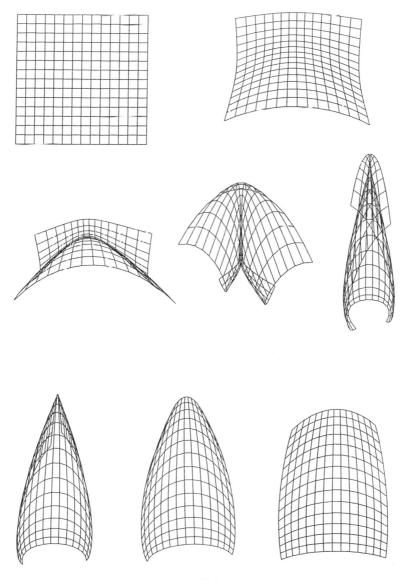

201

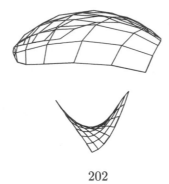

202

scaling by $(1 + \varepsilon^2)^{-1/2}$. For a polyhedron the calculation is simple. The faces are unchanged when you go to the parallel surface, so they contribute just their original area. The *edges* give rise to cylindrical pieces with an area equal to edge length times dihedral angle times ε. The vertices give rise to spherical triangles of area "spherical excess" times ε squared. Thus the area of the parallel surface consists of three terms, namely a constant term due to the faces, a linear term in ε due to the edges, and a quadratic term in ε due to the vertices (fig. 204).

When you compute the area of a parallel surface for an ovoid, you also obtain three terms. You may try this on the sphere of radius R (Gaussian curvature $K = R^{-2}$, mean curvature $H = R^{-1}$, area $A = 4\pi R^2$). The area of the parallel surface at distance ε is $4\pi(R + \varepsilon)^2$, which can be written as $A + 2AH\,\varepsilon + AK\,\varepsilon^2$. The constant term is just the area of the ovoid, the linear term depends on the mean curvature integrated over the ovoid, and the quadratic term depends on the Gaussian curvature integrated over the ovoid (the *curvatura integra*).

This shows once again that the identification of the mean curvature with edges and the Gaussian curvature with vertices makes a lot of sense.

Useful heuristic: *The Gaussian curvature is similar to the curvature of polyhedral vertices spread out over the surface, whereas the mean curvature is similar to the curvature of the dihedral edges similarly spread out over the surface.*

From the heuristic picture of the Gauss map as the parallel surface at infinity you at once obtain several interesting insights. For instance, it is pictorially evident that the Gaussian image of a curvature strip must be parallel to its original (fig. 205), whereas the Gaussian image of an asymptotic strip must be orthogonal to its own original (fig. 206).

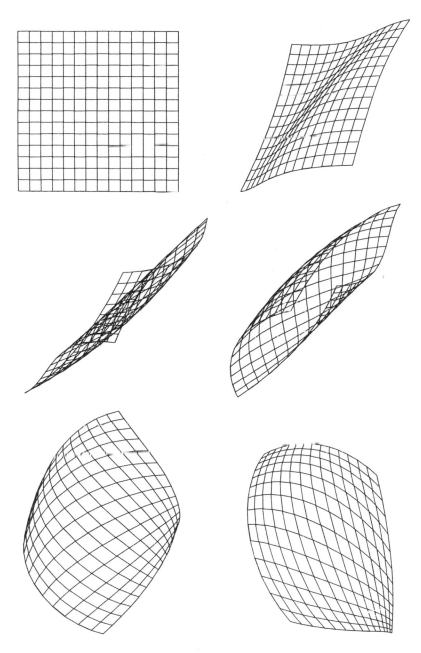

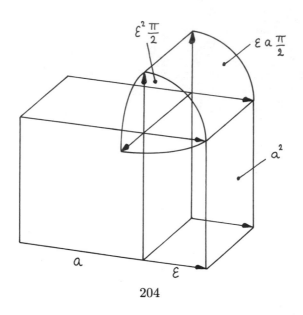

$$\varepsilon^2 \frac{\pi}{2}$$

$$\varepsilon \, a \, \frac{\pi}{2}$$

$$a^2$$

$$a$$

$$\varepsilon$$

204

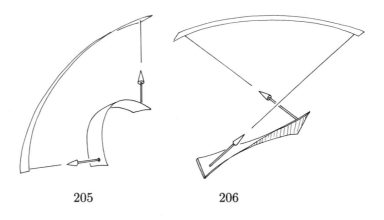

205   206

This is where the twist shows. The "lines of curvature," which are the integral curves of the principal directions, are thus exceptionally nice tools to study the Gaussian image. The line magnification along a line of curvature just equals the principal curvature, and its direction is unchanged.

People sometimes introduce the "third fundamental form" $III = d\vec{n} \cdot d\vec{n}$, which is just the "line element" or first fundamental form of the unit sphere. Since you already know all you ever wanted to know about the metric of the unit sphere, you may well wonder what all the fuss is about. The point is that III really only makes sense if you write it in a common parametrization that applies to both your patch and the unit sphere. It is the way the patch maps on the sphere that really interests you. The form III can be simply expressed in terms of the first and second fundamental forms, so it really doesn't add many novel insights. You have:

$$III = 2H\,II - K\,I.$$

For principal coordinates you obtain quite simply

$$III = \kappa_1{}^2 ds_1{}^2 + \kappa_2{}^2 ds_2{}^2,$$

as was to be expected. This shows explicitly the shape of the ellipse on the Gaussian sphere, which is the image of a small circle—the gauge figure again—on the surface patch. The latter form is in fact the most convenient if you want amuse yourself by trying to imagine what, for instance, the Gauss map of a human face would look like. This is an interesting exercise! The tip of the nose would easily fill a hemisphere, just like the whole front of the face. Of course, there is a complicated network of folds and pleats for a human face.

When a *principal curvature vanishes*, the line magnification of the corresponding line of curvature vanishes. It changes sign; thus the image of the line of curvature must flip its direction by 180°. The images of the lines of curvature *cusp* at such points, all cusps lying on a curve that is the image of the parabolic curve on the patch. On the Gaussian sphere the parabolic curve thus becomes a *fold*. You meet often with such singularities and indeed:

Fact: *The Gauss map is primarily of interest because it brings out the surface inflexions so clearly through its singularities.*

I have emphasized this remark because—for reasons incomprehensible to me—applications-oriented people appear to restrict their use of the Gauss map, which taken by itself is a rare enough occurrence, to cases

that are *free of singularities*. I do not understand the rationale behind
wanting to compute Gauss maps for ovoids in the first place, although
it seems to be a popular exercise in the field of "computer vision." The
concentration on the trivial cases may be due to the general phobia
concerning singularities.[30]

I illustrate a common nontrivial case (figs. 207 to 209).   Here you

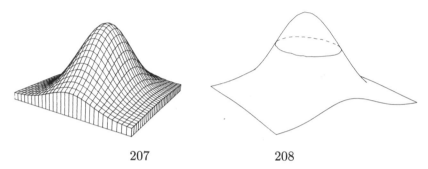

207   208

have a smooth hill on a plane. It is a Gaussian profile, to be precise,
although the precise form doesn't matter very much. It stands to reason
that the far regions of the plane must map to the north pole of the
Gaussian sphere since the slope of the terrain almost vanishes there.
But it is equally clear that the very summit of the hill must also map
to the north pole. Thus the Gaussian image must *fold over* somewhere.
This is indeed what a computation of the Gauss map reveals. You may
take this as a standard example of a fold. The pre-image of the fold is
a smooth curve on the surface. It contains the spinodal points of the
surface, which lie on a loop that bounds the convexity of the summit
from the saddle-like parts of the footplains of the hill.

Even more gruesome things happen when the line of curvature is not
transverse but tangent to the parabolic line. I use "gruesome" very much
in the sense applicable to Dracula-type movies here: the gruesomeness is
actually quite agreeable. In this case the Gauss map shows a *pleat*. This
is technically known as a—Whitney—"cusp of the Gauss map." On the
surface this is a "ruffle."[31]

---

[30]There exists a general feeling among engineers and physicists that any singularity
is intrinsically bad. This derives from the usual drilling in calculus. In real life most
of the interest and charm of any structure is in its singular "skeleton." The smooth
parts tend to be relatively boring "filling in."

[31]I have taken the term from Jim Callahan. It is used in the meaning of "a narrow

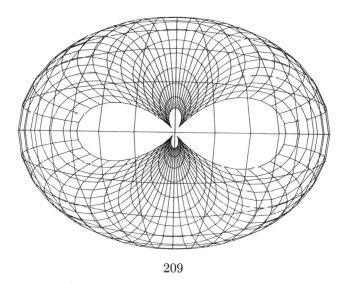

209

Thus the order of covering of the Gauss map may change suddenly from place to place. This can easily be traced to the patch itself, of course. Near a parabolic line you find *pairs of parallel normals*, near a ruffle (the pre-image of a pleat) you find *triples of parallel normals*.

Figures 210 to 212 show the situation for a ruffle. Notice that the

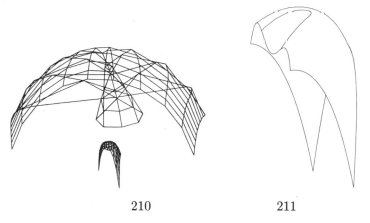

210   211

parabolic curve—the pre-image of the cusped fold in the Gauss map—is completely smooth. Figure 210 also shows a parallel surface and you may

ornamental pleat or trimming of cloth, lace, *etc.*" (One of the meanings listed in Webster's.)

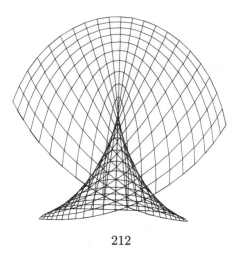

212

amuse yourself imagining how the surface manages to pleat itself when you run through the family of parallel surfaces. Such spiritual exercises are much to be recommended since they develop your intuitive grasp of the geometry and will increase by no small amount in complicated situations the odds of your "guessing right."

> ... we become aware of inclined and dipping surfaces,
> in fact we "feel" the form.
> The inclines and dips give a sensation of movement
> and one of my aims is to show that it is possible to learn
> to express movement by first feeling the movement
> made by changes of plane across a form.
> —JOHN CRONEY, *Drawing Figure Movement* (1983)

6.5   The asymptotic spherical image

At any anticlastic point you have two asymptotic directions. As in the case of the principal directions, you may divide them into two "families" such that each family admits of a smooth field of integral curves, the so-called "asymptotic curves." In order to differentiate between them, you may (arbitrarily!) assign "colors" to the different families: "red" and "blue," say.[32]

These curves are general space curves. You obtain an impression of the asymptotic curves in the neighborhood of a point if you consider the intersection of the surface with a tangent plane. This can be considered a generalization of the indicatrix of Dupin. However, you must be careful, because a theorem of Beltrami reveals that the curvature of the intersection is *not equal to*, but amounts to exactly *two-thirds* of the curvature of the asymptotic curve. At least the intersection reveals the *sign* correctly; thus the intuition—which doesn't seem to be a very quantitatively oriented faculty—is not hampered by this fact. You may want to prove Beltrami's relation to your own satisfaction.[33]

Just as I obtained the Gauss map as a spherical image of normals, I can obtain an "asymptotic spherical image" as a spherical image of asymptotic directions. Here are some facts to be aware of:

- Clearly only the anticlastic, not the synclastic parts have an asymptotic spherical image. Thus the asymptotic spherical image of an ovoid is void. Only part of the surface will appear in the image.

- There usually exist two distinct asymptotic directions at a anticlastic point; thus you obtain two distinct asymptotic spherical images of different color. They may or may not *overlap*.

- You usually want to consider *both directions* of an asymptotic line of a given color. Thus you consider each anticlastic point to be mapped on two antipodal points on the unit sphere. The image of a anticlastic patch due to one color may actually overlap its own antipodal image. You must be rather careful with your interpretation. It is generally best to treat the asymptotic rays as *not oriented*, in which case their spherical images are not single but *two* (diametrically opposite) points on the unit sphere. Thus you won't lose much if you discard one hemisphere! The remaining

---

[32]This is merely a device to keep things neatly sorted out in the mind. If you do computer graphics, you may take the colors in a literal sense.

[33]Not exactly hard, though the margin may be to narrow to contain your proof.

hemisphere can be mapped (using the stereographical projection) on a circular disc. Thus the asymptotic spherical image can be neatly displayed on your CRT. The manifold of not-oriented directions is the *projective plane* $\mathbf{P}^2$, rather than the unit sphere $\mathbf{S}^2$. In this book I often show *more than a hemisphere*. Then some directions appear *twice* in the picture. Beware!

Although a line that is tangent to a surface usually "grazes the surface" but does not penetrate it, which means that it has first-order contact with the surface, an asymptotic ray generically has second-order contact with the surface. It grazes the surface but also penetrates it (fig. 213).

213

Remember that "second order of contact" can be construed to mean that the ray pierces the surface an odd number of times (three times) and so must ultimately pass from one side of the surface to the other. Thus you can associate a well-defined direction with the asymptotic ray, namely the direction that *sticks out of the surface*. In some cases you may want to use this to consider merely one-sided asymptotic rays, in which case the asymptotic spherical image naturally simplifies a bit.[34] I will rarely do this in this text because you easily lose track of the connectivity of the asymptotic spherical image when you truncate it in this manner. This is more useful in the case of the normal ray congruence because all normal rays, without exception, are transverse to the surface.

In applications it matters a lot whether a ray roams through the air or sticks into the material, of course. You have to keep track of this in

---

[34]In this case you treat the asymptotic rays as *oriented* lines. Then the manifold of asymptotic directions is not the projective plane, but the unit sphere. Then you proceed as you would with the normal ray manifold (the Gaussian image).

real-life applications.

It is known that line congruences with only a single caustic surface (I discuss caustics in more detail later) are of such a nature that all the developables contained in the congruence envelop the caustic surface along the members of one family of asymptotic curves of the caustic. *Thus the asymptotic ray family of a surface cannot possess a caustic other than the surface itself, and must be skew.* In other words, asymptotic rays from nearby points never meet. Figure 214 shows the asymptotic spher-

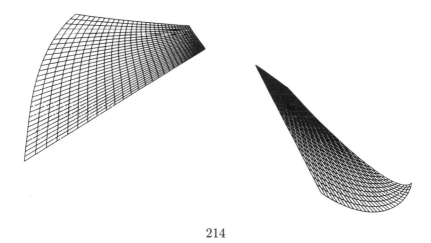

214

ical image of the asymptotes sticking out of the surface for the anticlastic patch already illustrated before (fig. 202). As you see, it is as nice as you could have wished in every respect.

It is pictorially most advantageous to draw a geometric picture of the asymptotic spherical image for a certain special kind of net on a surface, namely the net obtained by drawing both families of "asymptotic curves." Figure 215 shows an example of such a net for the surface of the kind of whirl that appears on the surface of the water surface of your bathtub when you drain it (fig. 216). An arc of such an asymptotic curve maps on an arc on the asymptotic spherical image with a linear magnification that is simply the geodesic curvature of the curve. The area magnification also involves the *twist*. I will treat this problem in the next chapter.

This suggests that the asymptotic spherical image could well have folds because the linear magnification could possibly vanish, and so it is.

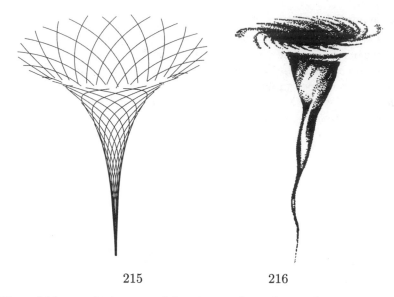

215   216

These folds are the images of the curves where the geodesic curvature of one of the lines of the net vanishes. Such curves indeed occur frequently in applications and are known as "flecnodal curves," the points on them as "flecnodal points."

Clearly the flecnodal curves also come in two colors, red or blue according the family they belong to. At a flecnode the asymptotic ray has *third-order contact* with the surface. Thus it does not penetrate the surface as the generic asymptotic rays do. It has an even number of intersections—four—remember? Figure 217 shows a surface seen from the immediate neighborhood of a flecnodal ray. You look into two asymptotic directions of the same color of points close to the flecnodal line, which is again of the same color. This was to be expected, for if the flecnodal curve maps to a fold of the asymptotic spherical image, a ray close to a flecnodal ray should be parallel to either none or to a pair of asymptotic rays.

In practice you will often fit frame fields with one surface vector along one of the asymptotic directions and the other one orthogonally to the first. The normal curvature along the latter direction is then given by twice the mean curvature, since the normal curvature along the first direction has to vanish. Remember the definition of an asymptotic strip. When the mean curvature vanishes, that is, on a curve of "minimal" points, the second direction is evidently the other asymptotic direction. In nongeneric cases the mean curvature might even vanish identically

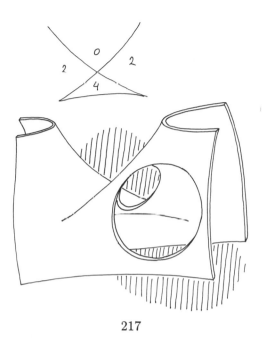

217

and you could set up a frame field such that two of the frame vectors were asymptotic directions. You will hardly ever meet this case in practice though, so most of the time you will need another frame field for calculations involving the family of the other color.

Other special curves for the asymptotic ray manifold are the *parabolic curves*. You have already seen them illustrated in the discussion of the folds of the Gauss map. At a parabolic curve the two asymptotic directions—"red" and "blue"—coalesce. The single "purple asymptotic direction" that is left may be called a "cylinder axis," since the surface is locally cylindrical, or rather, conical, with the asymptotic direction as a generator. Clearly the red and blue asymptotic spherical images hang together at the ("purple") images of the parabolic curves.

The parabolic curves and the flecnodal curves thus "organize" the asymptotic spherical image. Away from these features the mapping is regular.

It may happen, be it only at isolated points, that the flecnodal is not transverse, but tangential to an asymptotic curve of the same color. In that case the asymptotic spherical image develops a pleat. Such points are known under various names, including "biflecnodal points." They are also colored. Figure 218 shows a surface seen from a direction close

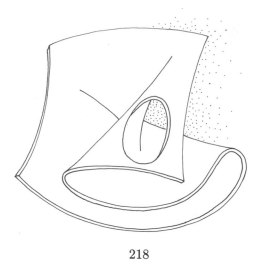

218

to a biflecnodal ray. As you see you are looking into *three* asymptotic
directions of like color, now. For directions close to that of a biflecnodal
ray you find either a single or a triple of asymptotic directions parallel
to your fiducial direction. The biflecnodes are generically isolated points
on the flecnodal curves. The biflecnodal ray has fourth order of contact
with the surface, which is the highest order that is generically possible.
The intersection of the surface with its tangent plane at such a point is
composed of a pair of curves, one of which has an *undulation*.

6.6   The osculating cubic

Instead of fitting a *quadric* to each point of the surface, which is essentially the second fundamental form, you may fit higher order approximations, such as the *osculating cubic or even the quartic or quintic*. The
zeroth order of the cubic gives position, the first the tangent plane, the
second the osculating quadric. The quadric is equivalent to a field of tangent planes. The third order specifies the deviations from the quadric.
Again, an equivalent description specifies a field of quadrics. This is
exactly why the cubic is of interest. It "patches the different quadrics
together"; it effectively gives the derivative of the second fundamental
form or shape operator.[35]

---

[35]The second fundamental form maps tangent vectors to linear maps of tangent
vectors to the real numbers. The cubic likewise maps pairs of tangent vectors to linear
maps of linear maps, *etc.* Thus the cubic is a trilinear, trisymmetric slot machine.

I will use the osculating cubic less for its metrical properties than for its *affine properties*. This concept needs a bit of explanation. The second fundamental form defines an osculating quadric, or better, an osculating paraboloid, for it is by no means the quadric with the highest order of contact with the surface. This is to say that you may find better approximating quadrics than the second fundamental form.

To give an example of this right away, the best approximating quadric for the triaxial ellipsoid is obviously *the ellipsoid itself*; indeed it is blatantly clear that the fit could hardly be better. Yet the second fundamental forms on the ellipsoid are paraboloids that deviate quite markedly from the ellipsoid if you are far from the fiducial point of contact. Please be clear about this; I often notice confusion on this point in discussions. Thus you will be motivated to study these higher order osculating quadrics. If you analytically develop such a quadric near the point of contact, the second-order terms obviously define the second fundamental form, but there will also be third-order terms in general. There will be for the ellipsoid.

Geometrically, the best-fitting quadric defines a unique vector, namely the vector with its tail at the point of contact and the tip at the center of the best-fitting quadric. For the ellipsoid these vectors all have their tips at the same point! The ellipsoid is an "affine sphere." This vector is known as the "affine normal"; it is obviously transverse to the surface and thus an "extrinsic object," although it typically doesn't coincide with the *Euclidean normal*.

There are several ways to find the affine normal direction geometrically that help to develop this geometrical object into a heuristically useful tool. They differ essentially for elliptic and hyperbolic patches. This is a phenomenon to take good notice of.

Mark well: *There exist two quite distinct types of affine differential geometry, one for the elliptic and one for the hyperbolic patches.*

The patches governed by different regimes can never be bridged, and for a good reason too. At their common border—the parabolic curve—the affine normal cannot be defined. At the parabolic points one cannot have such a thing as an "affine differential geometry."

For an elliptic patch you *slice* the object along planes parallel to the tangent plane and find the centers of gravity of the slices considered as homogeneous slabs. You thus obtain a curve, the locus of these centers of gravity (fig. 219). The tangent to this curve where it reaches the surface—it obviously also ends there—defines the affine normal direction.

For a hyperbolic patch you surround the fiducial point by a small
"parallelogram" with asymptotic directions as the sides (fig. 220). This

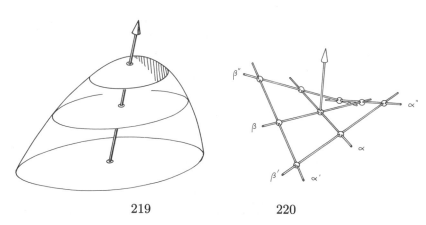

219   220

will, of course, fail to be a *planar* figure. Opposite sides of this quadri-
lateral are *skew*. Now two skew lines define a unique plane through the
fiducial point such that both lines are parallel to this plane. You obtain
two unique planes, one for each pair of opposite edges of the quadrilat-
eral. These two planes have a unique line in common, which is the affine
surface normal. Alternatively, you may consider a triple of asymptotic
rays of one family at nearby points on an asymptotic curve of the other
family. Three skew lines define a unique quadric, and in the limit for
coinciding points you obtain the *quadric of Lie*. It doesn't matter from
which family you started, you will obtain the same quadric. The affine
normal is the axis of the quadric of Lie.

Note that these constructions make no use of Euclidean but only of
affine properties. These include incidence, parallelity, and bisection of
line pieces.[36] The affine normal remains invariant under arbitrary volume preserving affinities. Thus the affine normals of the ellipsoid are an
affine picture of the radii of the unit sphere. Note that you could easily
define an affine spherical image now because you associate a unique direction with each surface element. This could be the start for an affine
differential geometry. There does indeed exist such a discipline. I will

---

[36]These are by no means exhaustive or independent properties. *E.g.*, you may
define bisection via parallel transport, and *vice versa*.

refrain from a development of this theory, however, and just use a few convenient properties.

An "affine frame" is a triad of vectors with the affine normal as the third one, the other two spanning the tangent plane. Please take good notice of the fact that although I use the term "frame" here, in this section (and only in this section!) it really refers to a "basis." In affine geometry, neither orthogonality nor normality makes sense, remember? Affine differential geometry teaches you how to pick this frame in such a way that the osculating cubic assumes a very simple "canonical form." As said before, the theory quite naturally falls apart in two quite distinct pieces, one for the elliptic and one for the hyperbolic patches (elliptic and hyperbolic are used in the Euclidean sense). *There is no way to bridge the pieces because the affine surface normal cannot be defined at the parabolic points.*

The affine frames have a simple relation to the approximating quadrics and cubics. The cubic will have curves in common with the quadric, and thus *directions* in common at the point of contact. For hyperbolic patches this is a *single direction*; for elliptic patches there are *three* of them.

For the affine frame directions I take the affine normal and the two asymptotic directions in the hyperbolic case, whereas I take the affine normal and two of the directions where the osculating cubic has contact with the osculating quadric in the elliptic case. In terms of such frames the "canonical forms" are

$$z = \frac{1}{2}(x^2 + y^2) + \frac{I}{6}(x^3 - 3xy^2) + \dots$$

at a generic elliptic point, and

$$z = xy + \frac{J}{6}(x^3 + y^3) + \dots$$

at a generic hyperbolic point. The constants are known as "Pick's invariant."

Special directions defined through the cubic indicatrix are also apparent in the Euclidean description when you consider the shapes of the normal sections at a point of the surface. Typically the osculating circles of the normal sections have a second order of contact with the surface. There exist special directions, however, for which the order of contact is higher (Transon, 1841). These circles may be called "superosculating circles." For each point on a surface you may find the directions of the normal planes for which the circles superosculate. In this way

you obtain fields of directions on the surface that may be integrated to
yield the families of "superosculating lines" on the surface. There exist
either three or just a single superosculating direction at any point. The
superosculating directions are also known as "Darboux tangents."

The Darboux tangents often show up in practical problems; for instance, at the flecnodes the asymptotic curves are tangent to a Darboux
tangent.[37] Then the order of contact is especially high.

It is possible, of course, to express the affine frame—which is a "basis,"
rather than a "frame"—in terms of the principal frames (say). This
is not a popular procedure with mathematicians who study the affine
geometry for its own beauty and consider the Euclidean case to be a
specific restricted case of it. However, my present objectives are of a
different, decidedly utilitarian nature.

The main constructions I need are the directions of the affine frame
vectors as projected on the tangent plane. I have already shown how
to do this for the vectors that span the tangent plane. These are the
asymptotic directions for the hyperbolic patches, the tangents to curves
of intersection of the osculating ellipsoid with the osculating paraboloid
for the elliptic patches.

For the affine normal you have the simple rule that its projection on
the tangent plane equals that of the conjugated direction of the curves
of constant Gaussian curvature. Thus the affine normal is one way to
think of the variations in the Gaussian curvature. This is of some interest because you can often estimate the affine normal quite well by
eye, especially in the case of elliptic patches, where it appears as a certain "skewness" or a deviation from symmetry. Thus you are apparently
somewhat visually sensitive to the gradient of the Gaussian curvature.

The third-order approximation in terms of the *principal frame* (this
time "frame" has regained its original meaning!) is simply:

$$z = \frac{1}{2}(\kappa_x x^2 + \kappa_y y^2) + \frac{1}{6}\left(\frac{\partial \kappa_x}{\partial x}x^3 + 3\frac{\partial \kappa_x}{\partial y}x^2 y + 3\frac{\partial \kappa_y}{\partial x}xy^2 + \frac{\partial \kappa_y}{\partial y}y^3\right) + R(x,y)$$

where the remainder $R(x,y)$ is composed of fourth- and higher-order
terms in x and y. Thus the coefficients of the third-order terms in
the osculating cubic have intuitively very simple meanings if you use a
representation in terms of principal frames. They are the components
of the gradients of the principal curvatures in the principal directions.

---

[37]So-called "Darboux tangents" of the same name but of a different kind also
appear in *the theory of surface strips* as those strips for which the osculating sphere
of the carrier curve is everywhere tangential to the strip. Beware!

In practice you may study the third-order structure most conveniently through the local differential structure of the field of Dupin indicatrices. This works especially well if you use computer graphics as a tool. The eye seems quite well able to interpret such a field if you display the indicatrices in a regular array.

If you use a principal frame field, the coefficients of the osculating cubic are nothing but the components of the gradients of the principal curvatures. This fact can be extremely useful in applications. It allows you to find ridges (see below) in the simplest manner, for instance.

Sculpture is quite simply the art of depression and protuberance. There is no getting away from that.
—AUGUSTE RODIN (1840–1917)

6.7   Special patches

6.7.1   Types of local features

By now, I have reviewed most of the properties of generic patches, the typical elliptic or hyperbolic patches. It remains to discuss the "special occasions" which can again be ordered in terms of genericity. Some occur on curves and are thus more general than those which occur as isolated points. The special points lie on the singular curves. Specifically you have

- typical patches:
    - convex patches
    - concave patches
    - saddle-like patches
- singular curves:
    - spinodal curves (folds of Gauss map)
    - flecnodal curves (folds of asymptotic spherical image)
    - ridges (vertices of normal curvature)
- isolated singular points:
    - umbilics (on ridges)
    - biflecnodal points (on flecnodal curves)
    - ruffles (they are simultaneously on parabolic curves, on flecnodals, and on ridges)
    - gutter points (on parabolic curves)

Some interesting points do occur on the transversal crossing of two singular curves—for instance flecnodal curves—but I won't treat them here.

6.7.2   The ridges

The strip defined by a line of curvature carries normals that are the rulings of a developable surface the edge of regression of which is a locus of centers of normal curvature. This locus may have cusps at isolated points. These refer to the *vertices of normal curvature*. If you consider a family of curvature strips, indexed via the family of orthogonal lines of curvature, you obtain a family of edges of regression that lie on a surface, the *centro-surface* or *caustic*. Notice that the terms "centro-surface," "caustic," "caustic surface," or "focal surface" are completely interchangeable. You will encounter them all in the literature.

The centro-surface is associated with a given family of lines of curvature. Each family has its own centro-surface, so there are two of them.

The cusps due to the vertices all lie on certain cuspidal edges of the centro-surfaces called the *ribs*. The pre-image on the surface of the cuspidal edge is a *ridge*. Figures 221 to 223 show a simple example. The

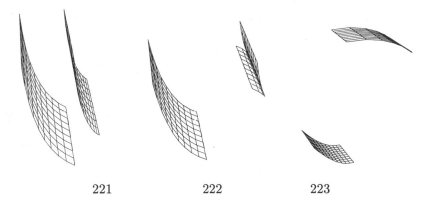

221   222   223

parallel surfaces for some intermediary distances develop a cuspidal edge. If you follow this edge for different distances, you see that it describes a surface (fig. 224), which is one of the caustic surfaces. These surfaces are also the surfaces that are the loci of intersection of normal rays. For certain patches a focal surface may itself have a cuspidal edge or "rib." The pre-image of the rib is a "ridge."

The principal directions always come in pairs, and again you may assign "colors" to keep them apart—"red" and "blue," say.[38] Then the centro-surfaces, the ribs and the ridges also assume either the red or the blue color. In computer graphics you will use the colors quite literally, of course.

A worthwhile object for contemplation is the oblate ellipsoid of revolution. Here the equator is a ridge. In fact the intersection of any surface with one of its planes of symmetry—if any—must be a ridge for pictorially rather obvious reasons.

---

[38]Of course these colors have nothing to do with the "colors" of the asymptotic direction!

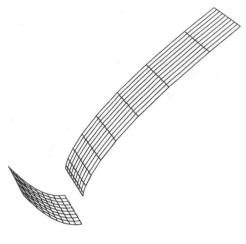

224

Please notice that *ridges are not lines of principal curvature.* In this respect the example of the ellipsoids is rather bad because of the extreme degeneration. Ridges generically intersect the lines of curvature of their own color *transversely*, except at the umbilics and at certain special, isolated points. Such points are known as "ordinary turning points." At a generic point of the ridge the principal curvature assumes an extreme value along the line of curvature. At a turning point the principal curvature has an inflection along the line of principal curvature.

At a ridge point the center of spherical curvature of a line of principal curvature considered as a space curve coincides with the center of curvature of the surface; that is, it lies on the normal ray. Another way to express this is to say that the Meusnier sphere coincides with the osculating sphere of the line of curvature.

The ridge is the surface analog of the *vertex* of the planar curve. The cusp associated with a vertex of a planar curve, for instance, is very well brought out for a parabola. The higher-dimensional case is still more complicated because the ridge is a *curve*, not a *point*, and because there are *two* centro-surfaces (fig. 225), hence two systems of ridges. A normal ray is tangent to *both* centro-surfaces, but usually only to a cuspidal edge of one of them. Figure 226 shows a caustic surface for a parabolic cylinder. This is merely the picture of the parabola drawn out in the extra dimension. Thus a section orthogonal to the axis is the familiar figure for the planar case of the parabola again. Figure 227 shows a small bundle of normal rays for a general surface element. This is just the "astigmatic bundle of light rays"—the surface is the "wavefront"—from

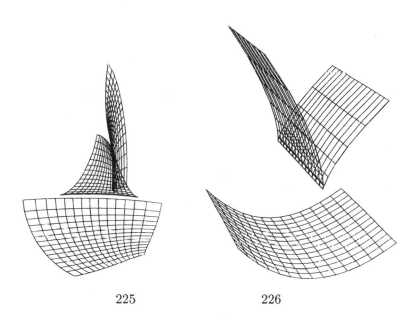

225   226

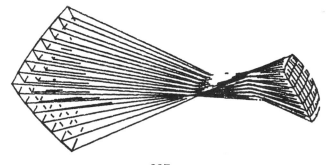

227

the elementary optics courses. Some old-fashioned classrooms still retain very attractive wire models of astigmatic beams. These are constructed from two crossed elliptical frames with equally-spaced points on the circumferences connected crosswise with taut strings. This wire bundle is then seen to contract into a line piece at two distinct places. These two "focal lines" lie on the caustic surfaces. Figure 225 shows a surface patch with its two caustic surfaces. Every bitangent of the caustics, that is, tangent to both caustic surfaces, is also a normal ray of the surface patch.

The ridges are also special if you study the spheres that have multiple tangencies with the surface. Such spheres are important, for instance, in the theory of "medial axes" of shapes. The latter are popular in pattern recognition and are discussed in a later chapter. Near a point of a ridge you can find two points such that there exists a sphere that touches the surface at these two points. This is intuitively an easily understood property that often enables you to guess at the position of the ridges if you have a well-trained eye.

6.7.3   The flecnodal curves

The flecnodal curves are the pre-images on the patch of the *folds of the asymptotic spherical image.*

Figure 228 displays the asymptotic directions for a patch with a flecnodal point in the middle, and figure 229 illustrates the asymptotic

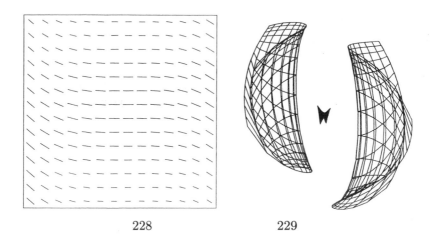

228   229

parallel surfaces for a great distance.

Clearly the asymptotic curves have an inflection, whereas the parallel surface already shows the fold that will distinguish the asymptotic spherical image. Thus the flecnodal curves are naturally associated with one family of asymptotic curves. They are curves that are generically transverse to the asymptotic curves and are loci of points at which the geodesic curvature of the asymptotic curves vanishes.

The flecnodal points are special because of the fact that the order of contact of the asymptotic ray with the surface is higher than it is at generic anticlastic points, that is, third-order instead of second-order. Remember that the typical order of contact of a ray tangent to the surface is only one. Typically the ray grazes the surface but cannot pierce it. Not so at the generic hyperbolic point; then *the ray both grazes and pierces* (fig. 230).

The result is that *you cannot look through along the typical asymptotic ray.* Instead, your sight is stopped by the surface. On the other hand you *can* see through at a flecnodal point. The visual contour has a sharp V-shaped notch there. This is often seen when you look at ridges of rounded hills (fig. 231).

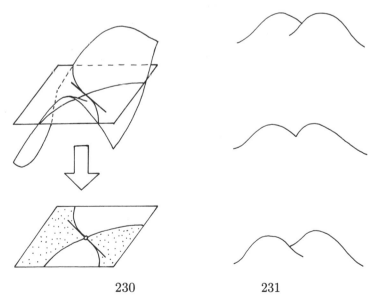

230   231

This see-through condition seems to be the main geometrical property by which flecnodal points distinguish themselves. Thus "see-through-point" would be an apt descriptive name for flecnodal points. You can even use this property to find flecnodal points on an unknown surface; they appear as "winding valleys." A local model of a typical flecnodal point is:[39]

$$z = x^2 + xy + y^4.$$

6.7.4 The biflecnodal points

If an asymptotic curve is not transverse but *tangential* to a flecnodal curve of its own color, you have a very special situation in which the asymptotic ray has *fourth-order contact* with the surface. Geometrically it is clear that there must exist two distinct types, depending on whether the asymptotic curve is on the convex or concave side of the flecnodal curve. Singularity theory lets one indeed predict that there exist two generically distinct types with local models

$$\begin{aligned} z &= x^2 + xy + xy^3 + y^5 \\ z &= xy - xy^3 + y^5. \end{aligned}$$

But singularity theory does not yield any further insight into the geometrical significance. The only geometrically significant difference between the two flavors that I can think of is based on a comparison of the senses of the curvatures of the asymptotic curves and the flecnodal curve at the biflecnodal points.

Otherwise the biflecnodes do not appear as very salient geometrical features on a surface. This may just be my shortsightedness. However, everybody else seems just about as myopic. On the asymptotic spherical image the biflecnodes appear as pleats, as you can easily check by programming the local models.

I have yet to *find* a biflecnode in a practical application, which is as well because there is still a lot that is uncertain about them. For instance, can there exist closed flecnodal curves that can be shrunk to a point within the hyperbolic area with two biflecnodes on them? There certainly exist *closed* flecnodal curves—for instance for the torus where the inner equator must be such a curve by symmetry. But the inner

---

[39]I give simple instances of local patches for you to try on your computer. You will usually have to do some scaling (apply affinities) to make things come out as visually pleasing. The fastest way to get results is to program these expressions with lots of extraneous parameters so you can interactively seek good instances. For instance, given the expression for the flecnodal point I would put scaling factors on x, y and z as well as on two of the three terms. Sometimes the addition of higher-order terms is needed to achieve more "generality." Of course, you can easily provide your program with all the partial derivatives it needs; this speeds up the calculations.

equator of the torus can't be shrunk to a point. It is not hard to formulate other down-to-earth questions about the biflecnodes that nobody can answer for you.[40]

6.7.5   The parabolic curves (loci of spinodal points)

A parabolic curve is a curve on which the Gaussian curvature vanishes, or—more specifically—where one of the principal curvatures vanishes while the other one is of constant sign. Thus you may assign *colors* to the parabolic curves, namely the color of the lines of principle curvature for which the curvature happens to vanish. Parabolic curves are always of a uniform color.

The parabolic curves are the higher dimensional analogs of the *inflections* of planar curves. It is indeed quite to the point to refer to the parabolic curves as the "curves of inflection of the surface."

There is nothing special about the strips along the curves of principal curvature of the other color; that is, in general the corresponding curvature doesn't vanish along them. The lines of the principal curvature that changes sign carry ribbons that are special, though. At the parabolic point the centro-surface has an asymptote; thus the parabolic curve carries normal rays that are the generators of an asymptotic surface for one of the caustics.

These asymptotic surfaces approximate the caustic surfaces very well in the "far field," that is, at distances from the object that are large compared to its (largest) diameter. They can often *replace* the caustics in applications, which is very convenient.

This asymptotic surface divides the centro-surface into two parts, just as the asymptotic line of a hyperbola divides the hyperbola into two branches. For any point near a parabolic curve you can find another point at the other side of the parabolic curve that has a normal parallel to the normal at the first point. In other words, the parabolic curve can be regarded as a locus of merged pairs of points whose normals are parallel. This, of course, is also evident from the Gauss map where the patch along a parabolic curve is folded over.

Since the patch must be anticlastic on one side of the parabolic curve, the parabolic curve shows up as a boundary of the asymptotic spherical image of the anticlastic patch. The two images—one for each family of asymptotic curves—hang together via the asymptotic spherical image of the parabolic curve.

The cubical indicatrix at a parabolic point is a cubical parabola, that

---

[40]I'd appreciate reprints if you happen to do original work on these issues.

is, a cusped curve. Which part of it lies above the tangent plane depends on whether the neighboring synclastic area is convex or concave. The axis of the cubical parabola, that is, the direction of the cusp, is known as the "cylinder axis." Indeed, the osculating quadric $(\frac{1}{2}II(\vec{t},\vec{t}))$ is a cylinder that touches the surface along a generator. Thus Dupin's indicatrix is highly degenerated, and consists of just two parallel lines. This means that *any direction on the surface has the cylinder axis as its conjugated direction*, a property that has extremely far reaching consequences in optical applications.

Important heuristic: *Pictorially the surface strip along a parabolic curve acts very much like any other developable. Remember that for the cylinder the body shadow is always along a generator and the contour is always the projection of a generator. You have essentially the same phenomenon at the parabolic curves. Here the cylinder axes act as the generators.*

If you consider the totality of cylinder axes along a parabolic curve, you find that they are the generators of a developable surface. It is developable because the cylinder axes are everywhere the conjugates of the tangent to the curve. Its edge of regression is of obvious geometrical importance. It contains the *apices of superosculating cones*. These are the right circular cones with apex at this edge of regression and the same curvature as the osculating cylinder. Figure 239 shows a particularly nice example.

The apex of the superosculating cones is either at the anticlastic or at the synclastic side of the surface. Thus there exist *two distinct types* of parabolic arc. This distinction also shows up in the normal spherical image. One type has a convex, the other a concave fold. These facts have great practical importance, for they govern much of the structure of the optical contour and of the shadow boundary. Typical examples of both kinds are:

$$z = x^2 \pm x^2 y + y^3.$$

Figure 232 shows one type of parabolic line. Notice that the contour of the surface shows an inflection, which is a sure sign that you are looking at a parabolic point. A convex patch will show up with a convex contour whereas a concave point can never be on the contour at all. An anticlastic point can be a point of the contour, depending on the vantage point, and it will always be on a concave part. I discuss this in greater detail later on.

It is very hard to see what kind of parabolic arc you are confronted with. Even after considerable practice I can't be sure when the surface is viewed from *this* particular angle. However, one glimpse of the Gauss map removes all doubt (fig. 233). The fold is clearly *convex*. That means

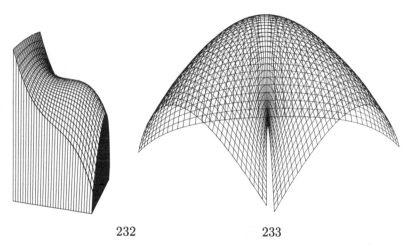

232   233

that the cylinder axes must point to an apex on the synclastic side of the parabolic curve. An explicit computation of the asymptotic directions shows this in detail (fig. 234).

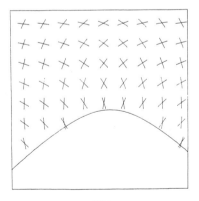

234

As you see, the asymptotic directions approximate each other as you get closer to the parabolic line because they must *coincide* there. At the parabolic line they assume a single, common asymptotic direction, the cylinder axis, and these clearly converge towards the synclastic side. You can verify this when you draw the cylinder axis, prolonged to both sides (fig. 235). Their edge of regression is indeed on the synclastic side.

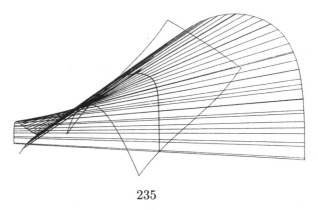

235

Figure 236 shows the other kind of parabolic arc. Notice that the surface looks superficially quite similar to the previous type. Again the inflection in the contour is the most conspicuous feature. However, the Gauss map (fig. 237) now has a *concave* fold. For this patch, I have also drawn a parallel surface (fig. 238), which shows especially nicely how the fold develops. You may conclude that the apices of the developable surface of cylinder axes (fig. 239) must now be on the anticlastic side of the parabolic curve, and so it is.

It should be clear from these examples that you have to deal with *two quite distinct types of parabolic arcs*. They appear as completely different patches in most practical applications, especially all applications of an optical kind. Thus it is most remarkable that the two kinds of inflexion are not at all distinguished in the traditional textbooks and that they have received no distinct names.

Indeed, you will encounter several rather special spinodal points in computational differential geometry that don't seem to figure in the classical literature. It is perhaps easiest to classify them on the basis of the behavior of the cylinder axes developable. For the general spinodal points, the edge of this surface is a general space curve, which can be at the synclastic or the anticlastic side of the spinodal locus. At the so-called "gutter points" (to be discussed in detail) the edge of regression

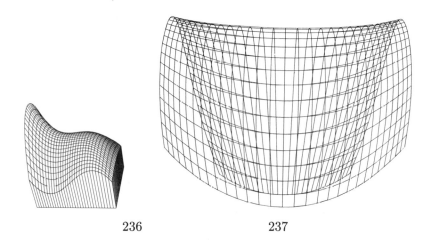

236   237

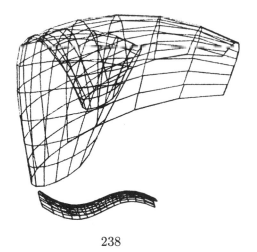

238

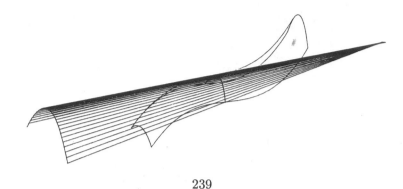

239

has an asymptote, and crosses over from one side of the spinodal locus
to the other. At a "ruffle" (that is, a cusp of the Gauss map), the edge
of regression *osculates* the spinodal locus. Finally, there exist isolated
points where the edge of regression *cusps*. (Then the developable of
cylinder axes has a swallowtail singularity.) At such points the cylinder
axes very closely converge to a single point: the developable of cylinder
axes is almost conical, with the singular point as apex. I call such
spinodal points "conical points," but I'm not aware of any classical term.
The spinodal points depicted in figure 235 are fairly regular (all cylinder
axes are tangent to a general space curve), but the depiction in figure 239
is special because the spinodal arc contains a conical point. For a conical
point the "apex" can be at either side of the spinodal curve. Thus they
come in two flavors.

Both types of generic spinodal point look like "shoe surfaces" in the
first rough approximation. The tip of a shoe is clearly an synclastic
patch, whereas the region near the instep is clearly anticlastic. Thus
shoes typically have a parabolic line on the leather somewhere in the
middle part. This is very easily visible on smooth polished shoes and
boots where the specularities clearly reveal the local normal direction.

Just remember that a parabolic curve is an *inflection* of the surface; thus you find pairs of points with parallel normals straddling the
parabolic curve. These must produce pairs of specularities if the sun
shines on them, and they certainly do. The difference shows up most
clearly when you view them in the direction of a cylinder axis. I illustrate
this later on. Perhaps it is best to distinguish them as an "elliptic inflex-

ion" when the Gauss map is a convex fold and a "hyperbolic inflexion" when the Gauss map is a concave fold.

The easiest way to distinguish these surfaces on sight is to view them from directions that are close to a cylinder axis. Then the elliptic type may develop a split-off contour (fig. 240). On the other hand, the hyperbolic type will either show a double fold or—on just a small excursion of the vantage point—a pair of cusped contours facing each other (fig. 241).

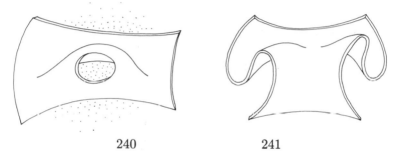

240   241

These events of the visual contour will be discussed in somewhat greater detail in a later chapter. They are often known by the technical names of "lips" and "beaks," which are literal translations from the French "*singularité lèvre*" and "*singularité boo à boo*" proposed by René Thom.

6.7.6   The gutterpoints

I have shown that there exist two decidedly different flavors of parabolic arc. Remember that for one type the apices of the osculating cones lie on the hyperbolic; for the other, on the elliptic side of the patch. There exist isolated points on the parabolic curves that are "transition points" for these two regimes. At these points the angle between the cylinder axes and the parabolic arc is stationary; thus locally the osculating cones degenerate into a true cylinder. You can't find anything more like a cylinder on a generic patch.

These very cylindrical points are termed "*pointes gouttières*" in the French literature. I'm not aware of any classical term, although there may well be one that I have failed to "translate" into modern terminology. The French term literally means "gutterpoints" and so I have baptized them, since the term seems very descriptive indeed. The only problem is that the "gutter" might as well be "inside out," in which case the surface looks locally like the outside of a cylindrical rod instead of like the inside of a reed (a "gutter").

The image of a parabolic arc in the Gaussian image must show an *inflection* at the image of the gutterpoint. Less obvious is the fact that the asymptotic spherical image of the parabolic curves has a *cusp* there. The Gaussian and asymptotic spherical images of parabolic curves are "duals" in many respects. In any case their cusps correspond to inflections, and *vice versa*.

A typical example of a gutterpoint is:

$$z = x^2 + y^3 + x^3y.$$

The gutterpoint tends to look like any other parabolic point at first sight (fig. 242). However, from the side the surface looks a bit funny (fig. 243). There is a very long "almost contour" where your view almost

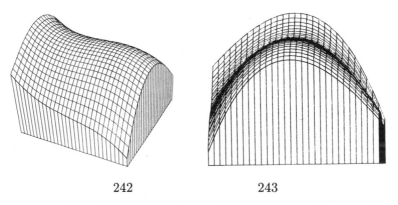

242   243

grazes the surface. The precise shape of the contour will be considered in a later part of the book; it is rather complicated. If you want to distinguish the different types of parabolic arc, your best bet is to view them from this direction, that is, as close as possible to the cylinder axes. Then the differences show up in the clearest way. The Gauss map (fig. 244) makes the difference immediately explicit. It depicts an inflected fold.

Much as you would expect, the apices of the cylinder axes change over from one side of the parabolic line to the other at the gutterpoint (fig. 245). Of course the apices *don't move in toward the parabolic line* to cross over. The apices move to infinity and reappear in the antipodal

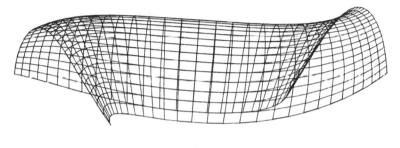

244

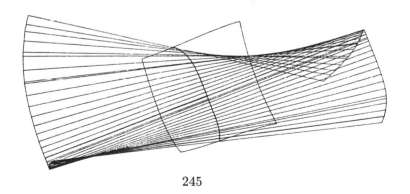

245

direction because the cylinder axes must be locally parallel at the gutterpoint. The cylinder axis at the gutterpoint is an asymptote of the axes
at both sides of the edge of regression of the cylinder axes' developable
surface.

For this example, I have also computed the asymptotic spherical image
for one family of asymptotic directions at the hyperbolic side of the
parabolic line. You can see that the image of the parabolic curve *cusps*
there (fig. 246). The gutterpoint is a transitional case between the two
types of generic spinodal points (fig. 247).

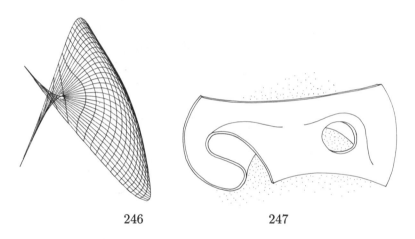

246   247

6.7.7   Ruffles

When a line of principal curvature touches the parabolic curve for which
that principal curvature vanishes, you encounter a special situation. The
derivative of the principal curvature along the line of principal curvature
vanishes. Note that this defines the condition for a ridge. This special
situation occurs when a ridge and a parabolic curve belonging to the
same principal curvature cross transversely. A tangential meeting is not
generic.

There are two distinct flavors. The figures depict an example of a
unode (fig. 248), and an example of a tacnodal point (fig. 249). Both
are examples of the conditions sketched above.

The French call such a point "godron" which can be translated as
"ruffle." (Jim Callahan taught me the English word.) Ruffle is indeed
a nice descriptive term. The only problem I have with it is that there

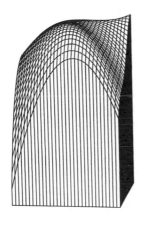
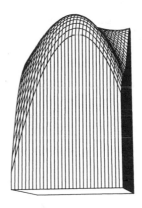

248

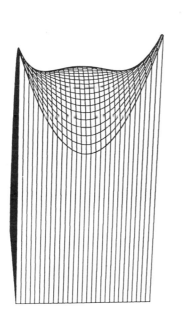
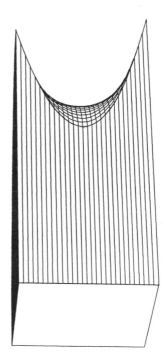

249

is no obvious way to distinguish between tacnodes and unodes, whereas this distinction is often crucial in applications.[41]

The spherical images of the lines of principal curvature must map to double cusped curves for curves on one side of the critical one and to regular curves for those on the other side. The cusps lie on curves that are the images of the two branches of parabolic curve at each side of the critical point. Because conjugated directions map to orthogonal curves on the Gaussian sphere, it must be the case that the image of the parabolic curve also cusps, with the axis of the cusp transverse to the cusps on the images of the lines of curvature.

The two distinct types of ruffle differ geometrically in many interesting and characteristic ways. One way to distinguish them is to see whether the curvature strip for the principal direction with the vanishing normal curvature runs in the hyperbolic or the elliptic part of the patch. One type may be understood as an elliptic intrusion in a hyperbolic patch, the other as the other way around. The two types look decidedly different from almost all viewpoints. Typical representatives are:

$$z = \pm x^2 + x^2 y + x y^2 + y^4.$$

The asymptotic spherical image of the parabolic curve near a ruffle displays an inflection (fig. 250). At the inflection a fold starts off in

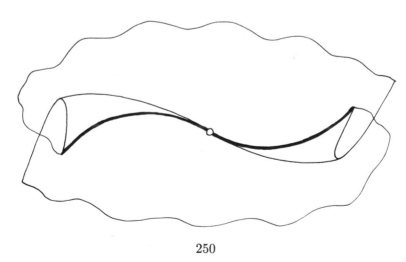

250

either direction, each fold belonging to a distinct family of asymptotic

---

[41] Are there different kinds of ruffle that could be used?

directions. These folds are of course the asymptotic images of the flecnodal curves. You have already seen that the flecnodal curves osculate
the spinodal curves at the ruffles. The "cylinder axis" at the ruffle obviously runs tangential to the parabolic curve (fig. 251 is a unode, fig. 252

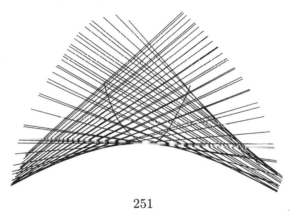

251

is a tacnode). This is clearly evident in the quartic indicatrix of the

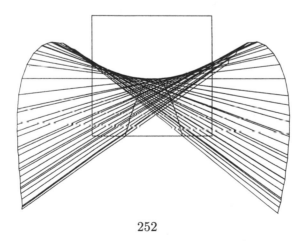

252

tacnodal point, which consists of two osculating curves.

The pattern of asymptotic curves in the neighborhood of a ruffle is
highly characteristic. There exist three distinct types of patterns. I will
discuss them in the next chapter.

Figure 248 shows one type of ruffle, the *unodal* type. I have prepared a map of asymptotic directions (fig. 253). As you see, they are tangent to the parabolic curve at the unode, whereas they are transverse to the curve at the typical parabolic points. The Gaussian image of the parabolic line is *concave* near the unode; thus the parabolic points are of the hyperbolic type. When you prolong the cylinder axes, you obtain an impression of the edge of regression of the cylinder axes developable (fig. 251) . It is tangent to the parabolic curve at the unode. When you draw the normal rays on the parabolic curve, you see the smooth parabolic curve gradually transforming into the sharp cusp in the Gaussian image (fig. 254).

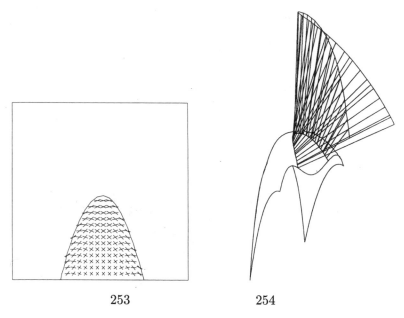

253   254

I also illustrate the other type of ruffle (fig. 255), the tacnode. The tacnode can be understood as an elliptic intrusion in a globally hyperbolic area, as the figure shows. For the unode you have a "hyperbolic finger" pointing into the elliptic area, for the tacnodal point an "elliptic finger" pointing into the hyperbolic region. At first sight, the Gaussian image and thus the parallel surfaces look very much like those for the unode, unless you look carefully for the orientation (fig. 256). I have again prepared a chart showing the asymptotic directions (fig. 257). They are tangent to the parabolic curve at the tacnode. The edge of regression

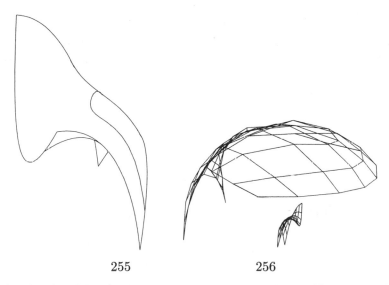

255   256

of the developable of cylinder axes is again similar to the picture for
the unode (fig. 252), and so is the developable of parabolic normal rays
(fig. 258).

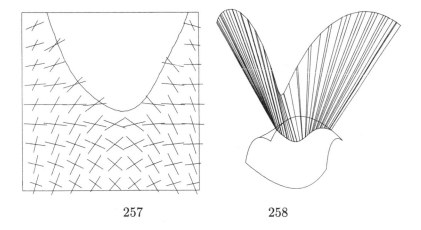

257   258

6.7.7.1   Bitangent rays near a ruffle

"Bitangent rays" graze the surface at two distinct points. You have
seen before that the limiting bitangents are the generators of "bitangent
developables." The edge of regression of these surfaces contains the
apices of osculating bitangent cones. At a ruffle you have the remarkable
phenomenon that the bitangent developable surface *ends* in a singular

bitangent ray for which the points of contact finally *merge* into a single double contact. The apex of the "final osculating bitangent cone" defines a singular point in space that is part of the geometrical structure of the ruffle. It has remarkable properties for the visual projection. To my knowledge this was first pointed out quite recently (and in a pictorially rather opaque manner) by Arnold.

6.7.8   Umbilics

The umbilics correspond to higher-order singularities of the normal ray manifold. (A variant of "umbilic" is "umbilicus," Webster's has:

> **um.bil'ic**, *n*. **1**. the navel; the center. [Obs.]
> **2**. in geometry, an umbilicus.

> **um.bil'i.cus**, *n.;pl.* **um.bil'i.cī**, [L]. **1**. in anatomy, the navel; the cicatrix which marks the site of the entry of the umbilical cord.
> . . .
> **5**. in geometry, a focus; also, a point at which the radii of curvature are equal.[obs.]
> . . .

> **um.bil'i.căl**, *a.*[L. *umbilicus*, the navel]
> **1**. of or like an umbilicus, or navel.
> **2**. . . . *umbilical points*; in mathematics, same as *foci*.
> . . .

Thus the main emphasis appears to lie on a certain "focal" property.) The typical lowest-order singularity is just the centro-surface. The next higher order is the cuspidal edge of the centro-surface. A still higher order singularity is a cusp of the cuspidal edge. At such points the two centro-surfaces hang together and their cuspidal edges connect. There exist two generically different types. For the *elliptic umbilic* three cuspidal edges from both centro-surfaces meet (fig. 259). For the *hyperbolic umbilic* one cuspidal edge from one surface meets one from the other (fig.260).

These facts clearly show up in the connectivity pattern of the ridges. For the elliptic umbilic, three ridges of each type meet; for the hyperbolic umbilic, one ridge of one type meets one of the other. There exist four hyperbolic umbilics on the triaxial ellipsoid, which have often been reproduced from Hilbert and Cohn-Vossen's remarkable book. These occur as the "circular points" of the ellipsoid. These are so called because all intersections of the ellipsoid with planes parallel to the tangent planes

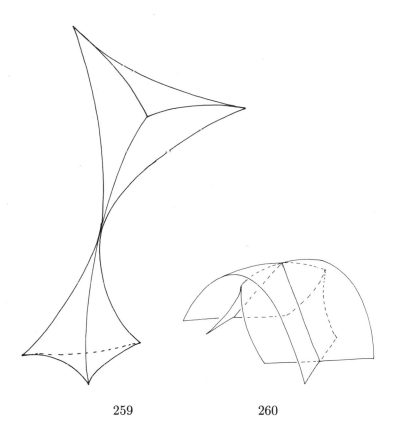

259   260

at the circular points are circles. There exist two such families of circular sections for the triaxial ellipsoid and intuitively these appear as the "reason" for the four umbilical points. An example of the elliptic umbilic is the equally famous "monkey-saddle."[42]

When you consider the pattern of lines of curvature near an umbilic, you find that there exist really three generically distinct types, although two of them are quite similar in many topological respects (fig. 261). The patterns of lines of curvature near an umbilic cannot be field lines

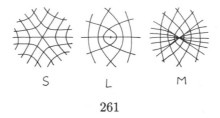

261

for an oriented vector field. They defy the attempts to define global frame fields on a surface that contains umbilics. Any surface but the torus must—I guess—contain some of these bothersome points.

It is possible to understand the "lemon-type" pattern as a *Cartesian grid that lacks a half-plane* (fig. 262), whereas it is possible to understand

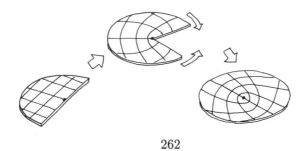

262

the "star-type" pattern as a *Cartesian grid with a superfluous half-plane* (fig. 263). Of course some cutting, sewing, and stretching or shrinking has to be performed to actually make this happen. This very vividly illustrates the inaptness of the umbilics to admit a neighborhood where

---

[42]There is an impossible drawing of the indicatrix in Hilbert and Cohn-Vossen's book. This original mistake can be traced forward in time to several more recent books. The monkey saddle is treated in some detail later in this chapter.

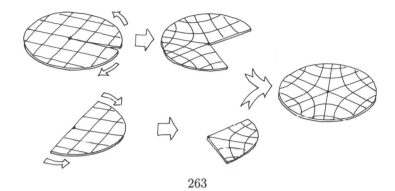

263

the principal directions define a neat Cartesian mesh.

When you *compute* the principal directions, you don't know *a priori* how to make out which one is the "first" and which one the "second" one. Consequently you only get a *pair of orientations* and it is not easy to integrate them to neat families of lines of curvature. Moreover, your

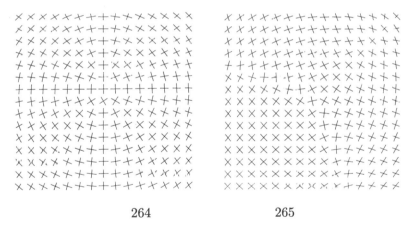

264   265

program yields mere *line segments* without any preferred sense to them, so you don't even know how you should "line them up." Figures 264 and 265 give an impression of the kind of result to expect. These figures were obtained by changing the values of the coefficients of the third-order terms of the osculating cubic at an umbilical point. Such fields cannot be ordered such that you have two parameter line like families. They are the worst nuisance in numerical work.

When you consider the parallel surfaces for the umbilics, you meet

with some incredibly complicated cases. Because the two caustic surfaces hang together on the focal points of the umbilics, the crumpling is
especially thorough there. With some effort you can distinguish "monkey saddle"- and "handkerchief surface"-like cases. These singularities
will be considered in more detail at the end of this chapter (figs. 266 and
267).

When I paint an apple my eye is inside the apple.
—PAUL CÉZANNE (1839–1906)

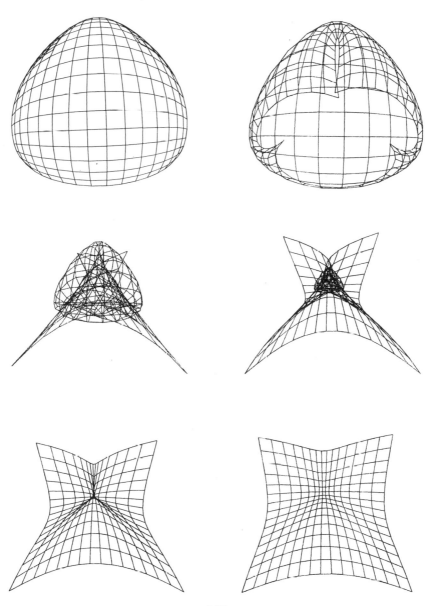

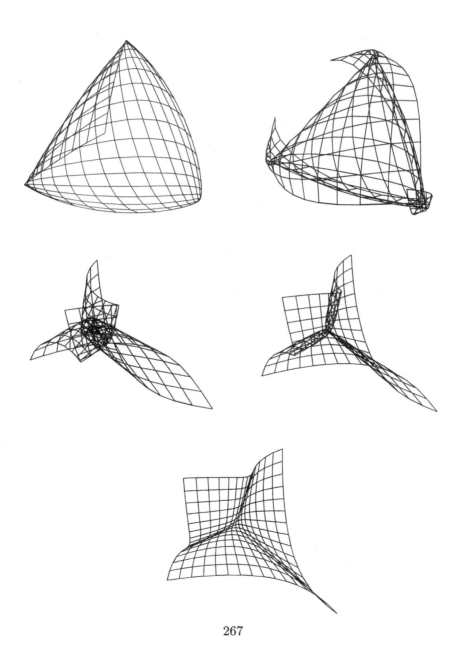

267

6.8   The local shape index

How unimportant the actual depth measure of the figure is for the
spatial understanding of the visual act is for instance illustrated when I
remove a relief from its background and put it at a distance; it becomes
difficult then to discern whether it is a relief or a figure in the round.
—ADOLF VON HILDEBRAND, *The Problem of Form in Visual Art (1893)*

It is intuitively evident that the shape of a patch does not depend on
its orientation and position in space. This may be taken as a *definition*
of shape. Shape is the geometrical structure that does not depend on
isometries. This means that *local shape* depends only on the values of
the principal curvatures.

But people very often mean by "shape" something that is also invariant against homotheties, that is, uniform scalings. For instance, a
copy of a statue on a smaller scale still has the "same shape" as the
original.[43]. If this were not the case, then the very idea of a "copy" on
a scale different from true size would lose much of its sense.

There is little doubt that the man in the street will agree with the
dictum that "all spheres have the same shape." But this notion is not
at all captured by any of the shape measures I taught you up till now!
Somehow there ought to be a way to ascribe a "shape" (a quality) and
a "size" (a quantity) to a sphere.

There doesn't seem to exist any general formalism that captures these
notions and that people seem to agree on, although there are no essential
difficulties involved here. I will just force my own favorite method on
you. You can define two parameters R and S.[44] For the moment I will
refer to the parameter R as the "curvedness" (I will change its precise
definition slightly in a moment). I refer to the parameter S as the
"shape index." These parameters are defined in terms of the principal

---

[43]You can stretch the definition of "shape" even further. For instance, consider
the question whether a rendering as sculpture in the round has "the same shape" as
a rendering of that same object in relief (*rilievo alto, basso* or *stiaccato* as the case
may be). If you admit such to be the case, as most sculptors would (from a little
distance you can't discriminate the renderings), you declare "shape" to be invariant
under a class of projectivities.

[44]Alternative definitions might be considered. For instance, you could define a
"curvedness" through the root-mean-square normal curvature calculated over all directions. This leads to a slightly different characterization. I prefer the method explained in this section, but I grant you that other methods may be just as convenient.

curvatures in the following way:[45]

$$
\begin{aligned}
R &= \sqrt{(\kappa_{min}^2 + \kappa_{max}^2)/2} \\
S &= -\frac{2}{\pi} \arctan \frac{\kappa_{max} + \kappa_{min}}{\kappa_{max} - \kappa_{min}}.
\end{aligned}
$$

The curvedness is a measure of the *size*, the shape index of the *shape* of a local patch.

Every distinct shape except for the planar points corresponds to a unique value of the shape index. A planar point has vanishing curvedness and an indeterminate shape index. The new parameters (R, S) are merely polar coordinates in the (κ_1, κ_2)-plane, centered on the case of the planar point.

Note that all shapes, except for the plane, can be mapped to the unit circle in this plane. The unit circle contains the shapes with unit curvedness. Rays through the origin contain identical shapes that merely differ in their curvedness.

Diametrically opposite points on the unit circle denote shapes that are each other's "negatives," *i.e.*, they stand in the relation of a shape and its mold. The shape $S = 0$, which is a minimal point, or a symmetrical saddle, is very special indeed, because *it equals its own mold.* The other shapes clearly differ from their molds: the in- and outside of an egg-shell (pits and peaks), the saddle ridge and saddle rut, and so forth (fig. 268).

Not all shapes on the unit circle are to be distinguished, however. When you permute the principal curvatures, you merely rotate the shapes over ninety degrees. Such a permutation is a reflection about the line $\kappa_1 = \kappa_2$, which is the ray representing the umbilics. Clearly the umbilics themselves are not affected by the permutation.

This latter observation means that *all shapes can be mapped on the interval $S \in [-1, +1]$.* I have implicitly introduced this convention already in the formal definition of S, because you are supposed to use the $(-\frac{\pi}{2}, \frac{\pi}{2})$ branch of the arctangent function.

The endpoints of the interval $S \in [-1, +1]$ are the concave and convex umbilics. These are as different as shapes can be, at least when you consider the boundaries of blobs.[46]

---

[45]There is no magic in the coefficient $-2/\pi$ in the expression for the shape index. It merely serves to map shapes neatly on the interval minus unity to plus unity, with the convex umbilics mapping to the value $+1$.

Likewise, there is no magic in the division by two in the expression for the curvedness. This merely serves to normalize the scale such that the surface of the unit sphere has unit curvedness.

[46]The mathematician doesn't make the distinction!

268

All shapes with positive index are "convex," those with negative index "concave." Notice that this generalizes the convex-concave distinction to the anticlastic points. This actually makes good sense if you think of anticlastic points that are close to being cylindrical.

The symmetrical saddle $S = 0$ has indeterminate sign, and it is indeed neither convex nor concave because it equals its own mold. This generalized notion of convexity is often useful.

The convex synclastic and the concave synclastic points are represented by two subintervals that are kept apart by the single interval of anticlastic points. On the boundary are the (distinct) chimeric monoclastic shapes, namely the inside and the outside of the cylinder mantle. Notice how the S scale has a topology that captures the introspective, pictorial notion of "local shape" very well.

An even better representation is in terms of the shape index S and the logarithm of the curvedness $C = \frac{2}{\pi} \ln R$. The Cartesian plane with the parameters (S, C) as coordinates is merely a conformal image of the $\kappa_1 >= \kappa_2$ part of the (κ_1, κ_2)-plane (fig. 269). This representation is so nice that I will from now on forget about R, and when I refer to the "curvedness," I will refer to the new parameter C.

The new representation has all the advantages of a neat Cartesian mesh, but also introduces a not only visually more pleasing, but actually physically more useful curvedness scale: equal increments now have a *scale independent* effect. You no longer have to worry about your yardstick.

In the new coordinates all shapes are mapped on a strip of infinite length in the C-direction. However, in real life this range is restricted by the fact that you perceive with limited resolution and that you can only interact with objects of limited extent. If your smallest discriminable

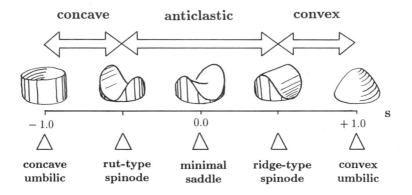

concave   anticlastic   convex

−1.0   0.0   +1.0   s

concave   rut-type   minimal   ridge-type   convex
umbilic   spinode   saddle   spinode   umbilic

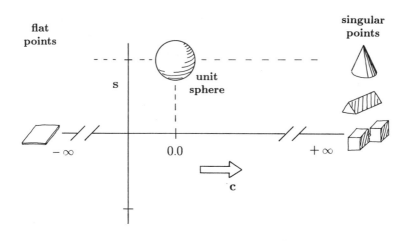

flat   singular
points   points

s

unit
sphere

−∞   0.0   +∞

c

distance is ε, and the size of your laboratory E, then the C range is within the (approximate) limits $\frac{2}{\pi} \ln \varepsilon^{-1}$ and $\frac{2}{\pi} \ln \frac{8\varepsilon}{E^2}$. The planar points are no longer represented (you can only assert that the curvedness has to be less than some value, never that it is zero), and infinitely sharp knife edges or needle points likewise don't occur.

This representation of shape is an extremely *natural* one in the sense that you can easily train yourself to gauge shapes by eye. The shape index is a convenient measure of "which" shape, and the curvedness of "how much" shape. They are related like hue and brightness, in that the one is categorical and on an interval scale, the other merely intensional and on a ratio scale.

Indeed, the analogy between the dichromatic "red-green" space and the local shape space is extremely close. Red and green are the opposite endpoints of the hue scale and correspond to Convex and Concave umbilics. (Convexity and concavity in their purest form.) The center of the hue scale is *yellow*, which is neither red nor green. Similarly the symmetric saddle is neither convex nor concave (it is its own mold). The brightness dimension corresponds to the curvedness. Total darkness is hueless, and all colored lights, when sufficiently attenuated, approach this state. For the shapes, the flatpoint assumes this role. When you decrease the curvedness of an arbitrary shape, it approaches this form.

If you like the analogy, you may think of the points on a surface as "colored" by their shape index, and "shaded" by their curvedness. If you practice computer graphics, you may even take the analogy in a literal sense, if you like. If you study human visual perception, you may come to think of the shape continuum as a parameter space like color space, in which structure can be investigated through psychophysical experiments aimed at the measurement of detection and discrimination thresholds. Here lies a job that could keep a generation of psychophysicists occupied!

6.8.1 Curvature measures

♠ INTERMEZZO.

By now I have introduced many different measures for the curvature of surface patches; namely,

$\kappa_{1,2}$	the principal curvatures
H	the mean curvature
K	the Gaussian curvature
C	the curvedness
S	the shape index

and various other measures related to various ways into which you may cut up the surface. All these entities have their obvious uses. K is, of course, the only measure of interest if you want to study the intrinsic curvature.

If you want to study extrinsic curvature too, the two principal curvatures are usually most apt. In the majority of applications dealing in one way or another with the perception of form, the shape index is the most valuable measure and the curvedness comes next. In a way the shape index gives you all the qualitative information you want, whereas the curvedness carries the quantitative "size-like" information.

Notice that planar points are fully specified through their infinitely negative curvedness. This is often an intuitively agreeable and practically useful property.

When you work your way through the literature, you will find no sign of the "shape index" and the "curvedness." That's because I made them up. In practical morphology these entities are very useful, even if the mathematician manages to do without them.

... to make a bust does not consist in executing the different surfaces and their details one after another, successively making the forehead, the cheeks, the chin, and then the eyes, nose, and mouth. On the contrary, from the first sitting the whole mass must be conceived and constructed in its various circumferences; that is to say, in each of its profiles ...

—AUGUSTE RODIN (1840–1917)

6.9 Assorted singular points

6.9.1 Singular features

Given time you can easily construct infinitely many singular cases that don't fit the discussion of generic patches at all but have to be attacked via special methods. It makes me feel very good that I can safely skip them because they are unstable against infinitesimal perturbations, saving me an infinite amount of trouble . . .

A few cases are nonetheless instructive. They are connected with such childish questions as, "*Why can't parabolic curves cross?*" or "*Why don't you have planar points on the generic surface?*". Although the general arguments should really silence all this, it is still of considerable didactical value to construct would-be examples and then "explode them" into generic features.

I will treat three arbitrary but useful examples. Some nongeneric cases appear more often than others in practice; perhaps you need a notion of "generic nongeneric cases". . . These cases also throw some light on the kinds of creasing that go on in the families of parallel surfaces of the umbilics.

6.9.2 The monkey saddle

A simple planar point is the surface (in Monge representation)

$$z = y^3 - 3yx^2,$$

which is a homogeneous polynomial of the third order that happens to be interesting because of the structure of its Gauss map. Notice that the polynomial has the identical algebraic structure as the third-order terms in the canonical form of the shape of an elliptic surface patch in affine differential geometry, which we encountered earlier. Figure 270 depicts the general shape of this surface. This may serve to clarify the funny name of this monster. Consider where the tail should go . . .

The Gaussian curvature is approximately $z_{xx}z_{yy} - z_{xy}^2 = -36(x^2+y^2)$ for small values of $x^2 + y^2$. Thus the patch is hyperbolic everywhere, except at the origin where you have a planar point. It is planar because the principal curvatures are seen to be zero: all second-order partial derivatives of z vanish at the origin. At the origin the normal is in the z-direction; thus it maps to the north pole of the Gaussian sphere.

Close to the north pole the Gauss map (which I will fit out with the standard spherical coordinate system (ϑ, φ), the colatitude and the longitude) is easily expressed in terms of the usual polar coordinates

$r = \sqrt{x^2 + y^2}$ and $\psi = \arctan(\frac{y}{x})$ in the (x, y) parameter plane. You have, in the lowest approximation:

$$\vartheta = 3r^2$$
$$\varphi = 2\psi$$

from which you may conclude two things:

1. The Gaussmap collapses at the pole because of the second power in r, and

2. The image of the (x, y)-plane is *wrapped twice around the pole.* Such a point is generally known as a "ramification point."

Figure 271 depicts the Gauss map which you will now be able to

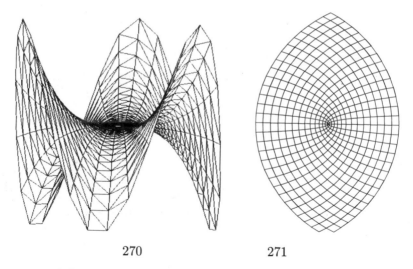

270   271

interpret. When you take the trouble to compute the family of parallel surfaces (fig. 272), you get an impression of how the Gauss map manages to wrap the plane around the origin *twice* in a continuous manner.

Next consider what happens when you perturb the monkey saddle. It suffices to add almost any second-order perturbation whatsoever. Typically the Gaussian image explodes into a triple-pointed star, that is, into three ruffles connected by folds. When you compute the Gaussian

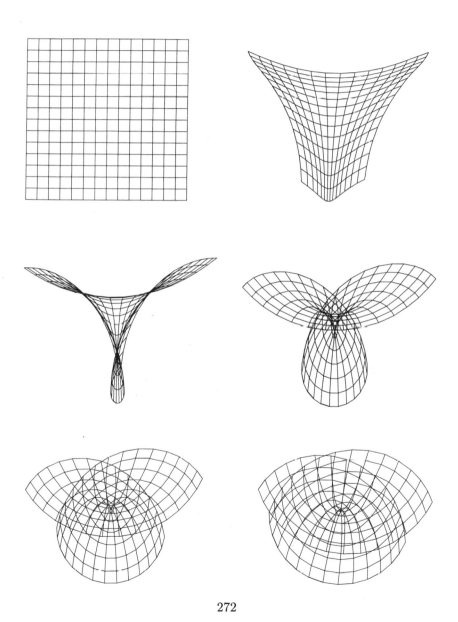

272

curvature, you see that you have obtained a synclastic island within an anticlastic sea.   Figure 273 shows the general appearance of the perturbed surface with the parabolic line drawn in it.   Figure 274 shows

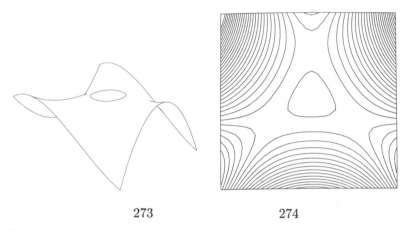

273   274

lines of equal height for the surface considered as a landscape.   In the center you spot oval loops.   They reveal the indicatrix of a synclastic patch at that place.   Thus the ruffles must be of the tacnodal type.

The perturbed Gauss map gives a very vivid impression of how you can wrap a plane about a point twice (fig. 275).

The trick involves a triple of cusps (fig. 276).   Why they have to be thrown in can be understood as follows.   If you consider a large ribbon cut more or less along a circle that encircles but avoids the funny cusped structure, you find—on a precise examination, and maybe you need to do some tracing with a pencil—that this is a *single ribbon that encircles the origin twice* (fig. 277).   It is equivalent to a doubly covered plane (fig. 278).   Thus it captures a ramification point and cannot comfortably be extended over the interior of the loop.   This is why the thing is called singular in the first place.   Now if you cut a much smaller ribbon encircling the origin, also avoiding the cusps but this time because it runs completely *inside* the triangular fold structure, you find—perhaps to your surprise—that this "ribbon" is actually composed of a *pair of ribbons* (fig. 279).   Both members of the pair happen to *encircle the origin once*.   Thus you can fill in their interiors ("span a membrane") without any trouble.   Somehow you have moved all singular structure to

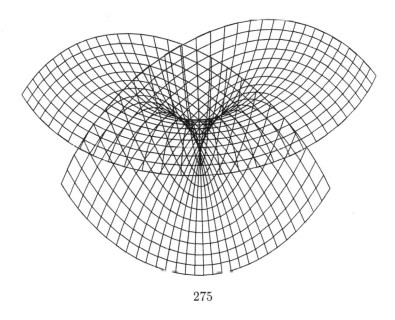

275

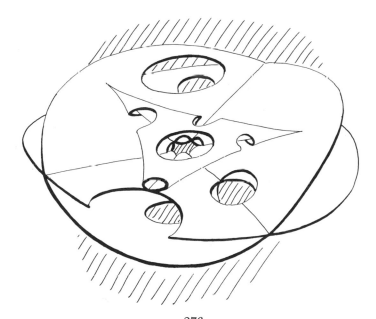

276

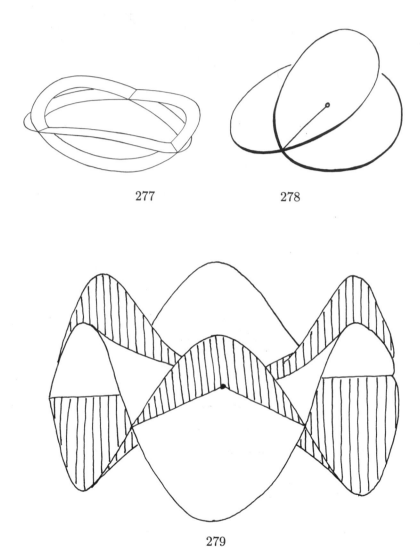

277

278

279

the thrice-cusped structure. Because this structure contains only regular folds and cusps, it is structurally stable. You have succeeded in "taming" the ramification point.

A simple scheme to assemble the whole thing from simple components starts from three identical parts (fig. 280). Each part contains a 120°

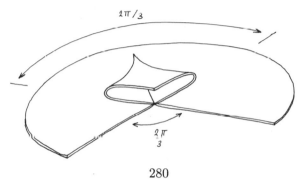

280

sector with a piece of cusp. You can easily sew the three parts together such that the cusped structure becomes an integral whole. Then you are left with three flaps in the shape of 240° sectors. After some self-intersecting exercises they can be sewn together to form a plane that wraps twice about the origin.

6.9.3   The handkerchief surface

The surface

$$z = \frac{x^3 + y^3}{6}$$

is known as the "handkerchief surface" (christened "*mouchoir plié en quatre*" by René Thom) for reasons that will become clear when you calculate the Gauss map. Notice that the polynomial has the identical algebraic structure as the third-order terms in the canonical form for the hyperbolic surface patch from affine differential geometry. The Gaussian curvature is (for small $x^2 + y^2$) approximately $K = xy$; thus this patch is a good candidate for a *transverse crossing of two parabolic curves*. These parabolic curves would be the coordinate axes themselves.

The patch is synclastic when x and y have like sign, and anticlastic otherwise. Notice that the quadrant $x > 0$, $y > 0$ contains concave, whereas the quadrant $x < 0$, $y < 0$ contains convex points. This is also immediately apparent from the general appearance of the patch (fig. 281). Again, the origin of the x-y-plane maps to the north pole of he Gauss map.

Let (u, v) denote Cartesian coordinates in the tangent plane to the north pole. Then the Gauss map is approximately:

$$u = -\tfrac{1}{2}x^2$$
$$v = -\tfrac{1}{2}y^2.$$

This is a very intriguing result because obviously both u and v are confined to a single quadrant. All quadruples of points

$$x = \pm a$$
$$y = \pm b$$

map onto a *single point of the Gaussian sphere* (fig. 282). The Gauss

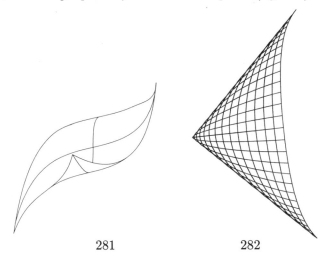

281   282

map is like a handkerchief that has been folded twice, once about the x-axis, then about the y-axis or *vice versa*. In fact, if you take the trouble to compute the family of parallel surfaces, you will actually see it happen (fig. 283). This makes for a spectacular computer movie!

When you perturb the surface ever so little—it doesn't matter very much exactly how—the neat folding degenerates into a smooth fold and a pleat (fig. 284). This is exactly what you get when you pull a bit on a neatly folded handkerchief (fig. 285). You may construct another but equivalent interpretation (fig. 286). Take your pick.

The perturbation works both ways; when you change the sign of the perturbation the pleat transfers from one branch to the other. Notice

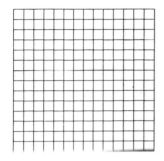

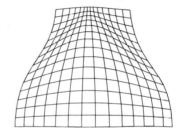

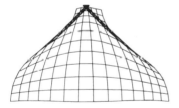

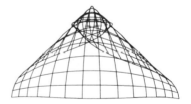

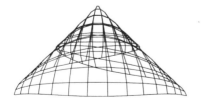

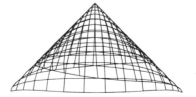

283

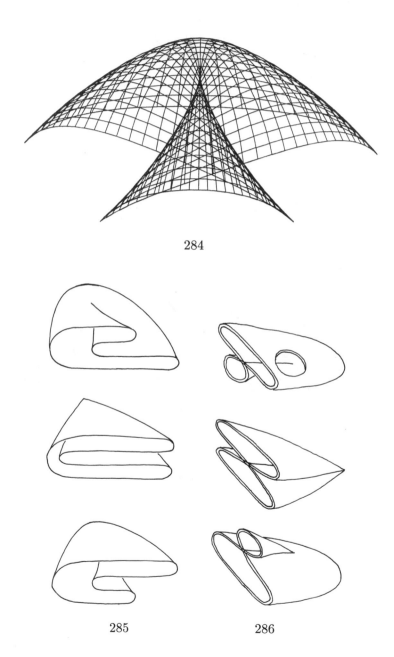

284

285   286

that the types of the parabolic arcs change then. Look for the polarity of the curvatures in the Gauss map.

If you compute the parabolic curves, you see that the perturbations always induce a *hyperbolic bridge that separates the elliptic parts* (fig. 287). This makes perfect sense because the elliptic parts are of opposite types—

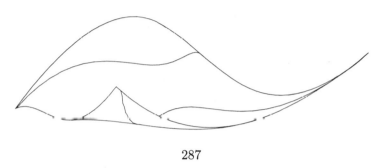

287

convex and concave—and so they can't fuse in any case. Consequently the ruffle is always of the tacnodal type.

6.9.4   The planar parabolic curve

In general the *parabolic arcs are space curves*. Yet everybody tends to think of the most singular example first if he thinks of a parabolic curve: the parabolic curves of the torus. These are *very special*, in fact, because they are actually *planar* curves; their torsion vanishes identically along the curve. In fact it makes sense to consider these curves as being composed completely of unodes. These curves map to *points* of the Gauss map, not to arcs at all (fig. 288).

Planar parabolic curves are a typical feature of the family of surfaces of revolution. The reason is very simple: when you rotate a template curve about an axis, you generate a surface that sports two quite distinct types of parabolic curves.

- The curves that are generated by the points of inflection of the (planar!) template curve. These are nicely behaved parabolic curves.

- The curves that are generated by the points on the template curve whose tangents are orthogonal to the axis of rotation. It is pictorially evident that all points on this curve will have *a common tangent plane.* This is a real monster, because of the singular nature of surfaces of revolution. The parabolic curves of the torus are of this type. So is one of the parabolic curves of the "dimple of revolution," a case treated in depth in the next chapter.

It is pictorially evident that the Gauss map collapses in the most spectacular fashion (at least if you are sensitive to such abstract trivia!) for points on the second type of curve.

If you compute the asymptotic directions, they prove to be asymptotically *tangent* to the parabolic curve instead of being *transverse*, as a well-behaved asymptotic direction should (fig. 289). Remember that

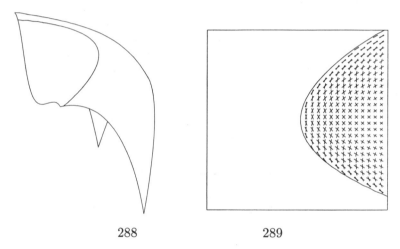

288   289

this is the condition for a *ruffle*. Indeed, the Gaussian image of the spinodal curve is squashed into a mere point (fig. 290).

It stands to reason that this situation is not at all stable. In fact there exists an infinite family of perturbations with distinct effects. Think of how you might impose an azimuthal perturbation on the torus with *arbitrary wavelength* except for the condition of periodicity. Then you obtain an arbitrary number of ruffles in the unfolding.[47]

Although this case is highly degenerate, it is actually not uncommon to meet with it in practice because the—nongeneric—objects of revolution are so common when you consider human artifacts.

---

[47] At least as long as you construe "arbitrary" to mean "even and larger than four."

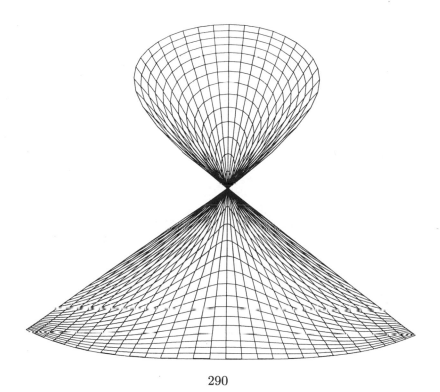

290

My whole originality, therefore,
consists in having made improbable beings live humanly
according to the laws of the probable,
by as far as possible putting the logic of the visible
at the service of the invisible.
—ODILON REDON, *(1898)*

6.10   The Fundamental Theorem

For curves I have discussed the simple and intuitively agreeable result
that curvature and torsion suffice to determine the curve up to Euclidean
isometries. One would very much like to prove a similar result for surfaces. For instance, given the Gaussian and the mean curvature, is the
surface determined up to movements? *The answer is no*, you have to
make sure that these functions are *compatible with any surface at all*.
That means that Cartan's equations of compatibility have to be satisfied, and even then the Gaussian and the mean curvature don't specify
a unique surface, as the example of the helicoid and the catenoid given
earlier shows.

Bonnet showed (1867) that the specification of the first and second
fundamental forms determines a unique surface if the Codazzi-Mainardi
equations of compatibility are satisfied, and that two surfaces that have
identical first and second fundamental forms must be congruent. You
may regard this result as a formal analogue of the fundamental theorem
of the theory of curves.

People have tried to prove many different flavors of the "Fundamental
Theorem of Surfaces." Some of these are of interest. For instance, Cartan has proved that under certain mild conditions an analytic curve and
a second fundamental form define a unique surface. Similarly, Thomas
has shown that *locally a surface patch is determined, at least up to arbitrary isometries, through its first and second fundamental forms*.

Surfaces are much more interesting objects than curves. Although
any curve is intrinsically isometric to any other, this does not apply
to surfaces. There may exist intrinsically isometric surfaces that are
not extrinsically congruent. Sometimes such surfaces can be bent into
each other, sometimes not. And again, there do exist (compact and
complete[48]) surfaces that are completely determined through their intrinsic geometry.

Many surface patches can be bent. Bending a piece of paper is the
prototypical example of this. The plane and the cylinder are isometric if
distances are measured along the surface, but are obviously not congruent. A bending changes the mean curvature but conserves the Gaussian
curvature. This can be studied by taking a flexible polyhedral vertex
and changing its dihedral angles. You may think of a construction with
hinged edges between the facets. This changes the shape, but not the

---

[48]You will find an explanation of these terms in a later chapter. Just read on if
you miss their meaning at this place.

spherical excess. (This is the paradigmatic case that led Gauss to his great invention in the first place.)

Don't jump to the conclusion that two surfaces with the same Gaussian curvature at corresponding places are necessarily isometric. The first fundamental form must also agree. I present an example of two nonisometric surfaces with the same Gaussian curvature at corresponding points here (fig. 291). At the vertices of the coordinate quadrangles,

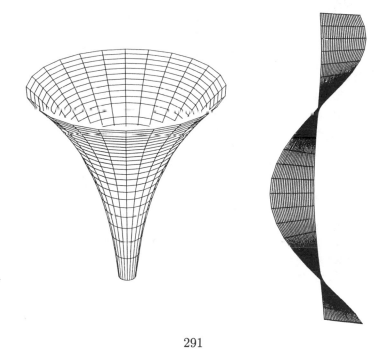

291

the Gaussian curvatures correspond. The first fundamental forms differ.

People say that the "natural order of differentiation" for curves is three because any Euclidean invariant can be expressed in terms of the curvature and torsion, that is, in terms of derivatives up to the third order. For *affine* properties the natural order is five; obviously it depends on the geometry you consider. For a *surface* this notion is much more involved. Third-order derivatives do appear in the integrability conditions, but these are only needed in integrated form as far as the "fundamental theorem" is concerned. Thus order two seems to suffice. Affine properties need an order of five. Some of the generic singularities for the case of the visual projection (the "contour") contain even higher order terms. Thus I find it hard to say what the "natural order of differentiation" is supposed to mean for the case of surfaces in three-space.

If you specify a surface locally up to an isometry, you pose the problem of the realization of a surface "in the small." You have to specify the first fundamental form, that is, the intrinsic metric, at a point. You also have to worry about how many times you want to be able to smoothly differentiate your patch, and so forth. Then you ask for a surface that realizes this metric. In general you must expect to find large families of solutions. The next question then is whether all these solutions are somehow connected; that is, can you find a continuous series of solutions between any pair (a "bending")? In general you cannot. This is intuitively obvious if you think of small elliptical caps, for although convex and concave versions may have *identical metrics* you cannot expect to be able to bend the one into the other because you can't push the cap flat. But this is indeed the *only* problem that prevents the family of solutions from being connected. For each of these families of solutions you may bend any solution into any other. This type of problem is extremely intricate and probably of minor—or no—practical relevance, as questions of differentiability play a decisive role.

The problems associated with bendings, or one-parameter families of isometries, and congruence, that is, the existence of surfaces, are rather intricate. I don't treat them here but will return to these problems several times later.

The boundaries of bodies are the boundaries of their planes,
and the boundaries of the planes are lines.
Which lines do not form part of the size of the planes,
nor of the atmosphere which surrounds these planes;
therefore that which is not part of anything is invisible
as is proved in geometry.
—LEONARDO DA VINCI (1452–1519)

IV STATIC SHAPE

7 Global Patches

Is it—the Venus de' Medici—not marvelous?
Confess that you did not expect to discover so much detail.
Just look at the numberless undulations of the hollow
which unites the body and the thigh ...
Notice all the voluptuous curvings of the hip ...
And now, here, the adorable dimples along the loins ...
It is truly flesh ...
You would think it moulded by caresses!
—AUGUSTE RODIN (1840–1917)

7.1 Local & Global

A short explanation of the terms "global," "local," and so forth may be helpful. I use the following system more or less consistently. A property is

global if it applies to the manifold as a whole,

local if it applies to some neighborhood of any point,

infinitesimal if it is defined in terms of a differential equation, that is to say, if it is defined with respect to a connection, and

punctal if it applies merely to the tangent space of every point.

I will often proceed in a somewhat cavalier manner and not care to distinguish sharply between local, infinitesimal, and punctal, although there is little excuse for such sloppiness.

A manifold is called "complete" if you can extend any geodesic arbitrarily far in any direction. Then geodesics run on forever just like the lines of the Euclidean plane. Notice that they also do this on the unit sphere. Thus a plane is complete, and so is a sphere. Intuitively, "completeness" means something like "without border."

A surface is "compact" if you can use a finite atlas for it. Thus the sphere is compact and complete, for you can simply cover it with two charts, but the plane is not compact because of the fact that you need infinitely many tiles to cover it. Intuitively compactness means "finite size," and for our purposes, which always imply a limited resolution, this interpretation is reasonable.

The ovoids are both complete and compact and so are all the surfaces that bound your blobs of finite size looked at with a finite resolution. In short: *all surfaces of practical interest are both complete and compact.*

O God! I could be bounded in a nutshell,
and count myself king of infinite space,
were it not that I have bad dreams.
—SHAKESPEARE, *Hamlet*

7.2   Curve congruences

> *Observe the motion of the surface of the water,*
> *how it resembles that of hair,*
> *which has two movements—one depends on the weight of the hair,*
> *the other on the direction of the curls;*
> *thus the water forms whirling eddies,*
> *one part following the impetus of the chief current,*
> *and the other following the incidental motion and return flow.*
> —LEONARDO DA VINCI (1452–1519), *with a drawing*
> *showing water taking the form of hair*

7.2.1   Curves on surfaces

In many practical cases you have to deal with curves or families of curves on a surface. They occur as boundaries of special areas, for instance, the parabolic curves, as integral curves of tangent vector fields, as boundaries of the elliptic areas, as parameter curves, or as the geometric loci of some extraneous condition such as shadow boundaries.

The fact that a curve is constrained to some surface is most important. For instance, there exist properties of curves on a surface that depend merely on their *tangent direction*. This is a most remarkable fact. Such a possibility is unheard of in the case of a general space curve. For general space curves the properties depend only on the curvature and torsion, which can be prescribed in the freest manner.

Consider a well-known example: Laguerre has shown that the derivative of the normal curvature with respect to arclength minus twice the product of the geodesic curvature and the geodesic torsion must be the same for all curves on the surface with the same tangent.

You may well wonder how anybody could ever hit on such a weird relation except through the very rarest of coincidences. For a long time I wondered too, until I got wise to the fact that *there are* in fact ways to make such a theorem intuitively acceptable. I won't discuss it any further here. You might consult Spivak.

There exist examples that are more easily penetrated. For instance, it is intuitively clear that spherical curves must have curvatures in excess of the inverse of the radius of the sphere, and so on.

Curves on surfaces are in many respects similar to planar curves. For a unit speed curve $\vec{c}(s)$ the tangent is $\vec{T} = d\vec{c}/ds$. You can define the "normal" of the curve $\vec{N}$ by requiring that the triple of vectors $\vec{T}$, $\vec{N}$

and the outer surface normal form a unit crate in three-space. Torsion doesn't make sense, of course, but a curvature can easily be defined: $\vec{T}' = \kappa_g \vec{N}$ defines a curvature κ_g which is nothing but the geodesic curvature you have met before. Notice that the geodesic curvature has a well-defined *sign*. If ψ denotes the angle between the first surface frame vector $\vec{f}_1$ and $\vec{T}$, then you have the equation

$$\kappa_g = \frac{d\psi}{ds} + \tilde{\omega}^{12}\langle \vec{T} \rangle$$

for the geodesic curvature, an equation quite similar to what you have in the Euclidean plane. Very intuitive and nice! For arbitrary curves $\vec{p}(t)$ the first derivative is the speed (v, say) times $\vec{T}$, whereas the acceleration is dv/dt times $\vec{T}$ plus a component that deflects the orbiting particle from a straight course. This latter component is velocity squared times κ_g, again, exactly what you would expect on the basis of your experience with the Euclidean plane.

7.2.2   Types of curve

I have already introduced several remarkable curves on surfaces, to wit: geodesics, lines of curvature, asymptotic and parabolic curves, flecnodal curves, and ridge curves.

On any patch you can construct *geodesics* through every point running in every direction. The geodesics are special because their osculating planes contain the surface normal, so that their geodesic curvature vanishes. Consequently they are the straightest paths on the surface. A particle traversing a geodesic orbit suffers an acceleration that is purely normal to the surface.

The geodesics are most simply characterized by the geometrically significant equation $\nabla_{\vec{x}}\vec{x} = 0$. This equation expresses the fact that the tangents are parallel transported along the curve. The geodesics are "autoparallels." This constrains their curvature to equal the normal curvature

$$\kappa_n = \kappa_1 \cos^2\vartheta + \kappa_2 \sin^2\vartheta = II(\vec{x}, \vec{x})$$

and their torsion τ_g to

$$\tau_g = (\kappa_1 - \kappa_2)\frac{\sin 2\vartheta}{2} = II(\vec{x}, \underline{\vec{x}}),$$

where ϑ measures the angle of the tangent with the first principal direction and $\vec{x}$ denotes the tangent to the curve, $\underline{\vec{x}}$ the orthogonal tangential

direction. It is easy to show that the torsions of orthogonal geodesics
are equal except for the sign.

A "geodesic" obtains its name from the property of the great circles
on the sphere to cut the sphere exactly into two equal parts. They are
intuitively the curves that do not swerve either way; thus there is no
reason why they should cut the sphere in unequal halves. They are the
most "uncommitted" of curves.

The curvature of an arbitrary curve can be decomposed into a normal and a geodesic contribution. The curvature of the space curve is
composed in the Pythagorean way: $\sqrt{\kappa_n^2 + \kappa_g^2}$. Elsewhere I have explained the geodesic curvature κ_g in terms of the Levi-Civita parallel
displacement. It is the rate, in terms of arclength, at which the tangents at the curve turn relative to the tangential geodesic. If you use
an orthogonal parameter net whose parameter curves have the geodesic
curvatures κ_{g_1} and κ_{g_2}, you can compute the geodesic curvature from
Liouville's formula

$$\kappa_g = \frac{\partial \mu}{\partial s} + \kappa_{g_1} \cos \mu + \kappa_{g_2} \sin \mu,$$

where μ is the angle between the curve's tangent and the first parameter line. This is a simple generalization of a similar relation in planar
Euclidean geometry. The geodesic torsion equals that of the geodesic
augmented with the term $\frac{\partial \varphi}{\partial s}$, which is the derivative with respect to
arclength of the angle φ between the principal normal of the curve and
the surface normal.

Asymptotic curves can only be found in the anticlastic regions. Exactly two of them pass through every point. For an asymptotic curve,
the osculating planes of these curves coincide with the tangent plane.
This is true by definition, if you like. Thus their curvature is purely
geodesic, since the normal curvature vanishes. A particle traversing an
asymptotic orbit has no tendency whatsoever to leave the surface; the
acceleration only deflects the orbit within the tangent plane. You have
already seen that the curvature is a fixed constant times the curvature
of the intersection of the surface with its tangent plane. The curvature
of the asymptotic curve is

$$\frac{\|\nabla_{\vec{x}} II(\vec{x}, \vec{x})\|}{2\sqrt{-K}},$$

where $\vec{x}$ denotes the asymptotic direction. It depends on the covariant
derivative of the second fundamental form. A famous theorem of Beltrami and Enneper that dates from 1870 says that the magnitude of the

torsion of an asymptotic curve at any point equals the square root of
the absolute value of the Gaussian curvature.

Lines of curvature can be found all over the surface. Through any
point you have an orthogonal pair of them. The geodesic curvature
of a line of curvature equals the normal curvature times the geodesic
curvature of their Gaussian image except for the sign. Their geodesic
torsion vanishes by definition.

7.2.3   Congruences

A one-parameter family of curves is called a "congruence" or "curve congruence." The parameter lines, the lines of curvature, and the asymptotic curves are all examples of pairs of curve congruences. A congruence
is partly characterized by the properties of its members. The relations
between the member curves are also of considerable interest, however.
Of special interest are the *envelopes of the congruence*, if they exist.
These are a kind of caustics for the congruence. Consider, for instance,
the meridians of a sphere; here the poles are degenerated caustics.

You may expect special geometrical relations for the loci of normal
or geodesic inflexion of the curves or their orthogonals. A curve of
geodesic inflexion of the orthogonals is known as a "curve of striction."
Curves of geodesic inflexion are especially important for the asymptotic
curves. You have already met them as the flecnodal curves. In the case
of the curves of principal curvature the striction curve happens to be
an important locus if you are interested in the inflexions of the visual
contour of blobs.

7.2.4   Spherical images

An excellent way to study a congruence is to consider its *spherical image*. Just map the point $\vec{x}(u, v)$ of the surface patch on the direction
$\vec{t}(u, v)$ of the member of the congruence at that point. The tangents
obviously roam over the unit sphere; hence the term spherical image. I
have already introduced the asymptotic spherical image, but you may
equally well study spherical images for any congruence whatsoever. In
all cases you can find continuous deformations of the same surface patch
into a spherical image through the construction of generalized "parallel
surfaces"[1]:

---

[1]By a "generalized parallel surface" I mean the following: Let $\vec{x}(u, v)$ be a surface
and $\vec{v}(u, v)$ any unit-vector field, not necessarily tangential. Then the surface $\vec{x}(u, v)+$
$\varepsilon\vec{v}(u, v)$ is a generalized parallel surface (for the given vector field) at distance ε. *The
parallel surface is the case for which the normal specifies the vector field.* For a
tangential field the parallel surface is like the wavefront of a wave that "sprays off

Important heuristic: *A spherical image is the generalized parallel sur-
    face at infinity.*

The "magnification" of the spherical image provides a convenient way
to study the angular spread of the tangents to the congruence over a
small surface element. Consider how such an angular spread over a solid
angle may be generated intuitively, that is, pictorially. There are two
possibilities (fig. 292). The figures show the situation for a planar patch

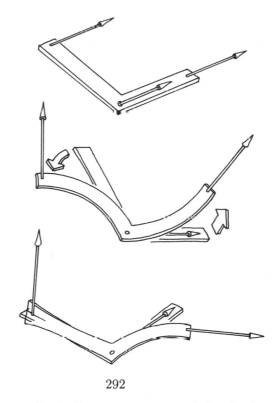

292

and a Cartesian coordinate lines congruence. Obviously the spherical
image for each of the coordinate line congruences degenerates into a
mere point. All the tangents are parallel for every point of the surface.
Thus you can encounter the situations that (the underlined quantities
belong to the orthogonals):

---

the surface." Such wavefronts do indeed occur in nature for geodesic congruences.
Otherwise these surfaces are convenient thought constructions. They are of value in
computer graphics studies of curve congruences.

- In the tangent direction the tangent turns over an angle κ_n times ds_1 toward the normal for a progression ds_1, whereas for a progression ds_2 along the orthogonal the tangent turns over κ_g times ds_2 toward the orthogonal. You obtain a solid angle $\kappa_n \times \overline{\kappa_g}$ times the area $ds_1 ds_2$ (fig. 292).

- In the tangent direction you turn over an angle $\kappa_g ds_1$ toward the orthogonal whereas in the orthogonal direction you turn over an angle $\tau_g ds_2$ toward the normal (fig. 292).

Usually these twists and turns occur in combination.

Of course, the nice way to do the calculation is by way of the connection equations. They capture exactly the geometric content of the previous discussion. It is a routine exercise to obtain:

$$d\vec{\Omega} = \det \begin{vmatrix} \tilde{\omega}^{12}\langle \vec{f_1} \rangle & \tilde{\omega}^{12}\langle \vec{f_2} \rangle \\ \tilde{\omega}^{13}\langle \vec{f_1} \rangle & \tilde{\omega}^{13}\langle \vec{f_2} \rangle \end{vmatrix} d\vec{A},$$

where $d\vec{A}$ denotes the area bivector and $d\vec{\Omega}$ denotes the solid angle bivector. An interpretation of the connection forms in terms of the curvatures and torsions of the members of the congruence and their orthogonals yields the magnification M:

$$M = \kappa_g \underline{\tau_g} + \kappa_n \underline{\kappa_g}$$

as expected.

Consider the congruence defined by one family of lines of principal curvature. Then the orthogonals are also lines of principal curvature; hence their geodesic torsion vanishes. Consequently the magnification reduces to the product of the normal curvature of a curve of the congruence and the geodesic curvature of its orthogonal. Thus you will appreciate that the spherical image will have a fold in any of the two following cases:

- The lines of curvature cross a parabolic curve at which the corresponding normal curvature vanishes. Thus the folds of the principal spherical image are also folds of the Gauss map in this case.

- The orthogonals have a geodesic inflexion. Then the pre-image of the fold is a curve of striction of the congruence. Such curves of striction can also be spotted on the Gauss map because the spherical images of the orthogonals inflect on the Gauss map of the curve of striction.

Next consider a congruence defined through one family of asymptotic lines. Their normal curvature vanishes. Consequently the magnification reduces to the product of the geodesic curvature with the geodesic torsion of the orthogonals. Since the geodesic torsions of orthogonal curves are merely each other's negatives, and moreover the magnitude of the torsion of an asymptotic curve is the square root of the magnitude of the Gaussian curvature, the magnitude of the magnification for an asymptotic congruence equals the curvature of the curves times $\sqrt{-K}$. Thus the magnification vanishes for the parabolic points, although you cannot strictly speak of a "fold" there because there are no asymptotic directions on the elliptic side of a parabolic curve. There is a true fold on the curve of geodesic inflexions of the family: this is just a flecnodal curve.

For a congruence of geodesics the magnification is the normal curvature times the geodesic curvature of the orthogonals. Thus there must be folds where the geodesics cross the parabolic curves and where they cross their curves of striction.

The geodesics are special because *there are so many of them*. Through each point of the surface you may construct infinitely many geodesics, remember? One way to put some order into this mess is to consider *subsets*, say "pencils," of geodesics. This can be done in an advantageous and elegant way if you consider the geodesics as the characteristics of a certain differential equation, the so-called "eikonal equation." This equation can easily be obtained when you consider the directional derivatives of some scalar function on the surface. The maximum of the square of the directional derivatives is known as "Beltrami's first differentiator" of the scalar function.[2] If you set this derivative equal to unity, you have obtained the eikonal equation: $\nabla(\varphi, \varphi) = \max|\frac{\partial \varphi}{\partial s}|^2 = 1$. Let a solution be $\varphi(u, v, c)$; then the curve $\frac{\partial \varphi}{\partial c} = constant$ is a geodesic.

When you think about it, this method simply defines the geodesics as (at least locally) the shortest arcs.

Useful heuristic *Locally a geodesic is the shortest arc for any pair of its points.*

---

[2]In the classical literature one merely defines $\nabla \psi = \nabla(\psi, \psi) = \frac{E\psi_v^2 - 2F\psi_u\psi_v + G\psi_u^2}{EG - F^2}$ and proves invariance with respect to parameter changes. The expression already occurs in Gauss's work. This dirty hat-trick makes Beltrami's differentiator look very mysterious indeed. In fact the result is merely $d\psi\langle \sharp d\psi \rangle$; thus the modulus of the gradient of the scalar field ψ. This makes the geometrical content immediately crystal clear. This is a good example of the elegance and utility of the tools at your disposal. You will come to value it when you try a piece of the classical literature, for a change. Use Strubecker as an easy entrance into the esoteric field of "absolute parameter invariants."

The eikonal equation also appears in the theory of geometrical optics, the geodesics are like "rays of light" constrained to the surface. Their orthogonals are the wavefronts of a surface wave. The analogy may be used to construct interesting geodesic ray congruences, such as the pencil of rays issued forth by a point source or the normals to a "wave" started off from some arbitrary curve. In any case you may conclude that the "surface waves" spray off in such a way that their caustics are due to the parabolic curves and to the lines of striction. The lines of striction are the inflexions of the wavefront. Thus you obtain a simple *physicist's insight* into these relations: the folds in the far field due to inflections of wavefronts are better known as *rainbows*.

Important heuristic: *Geodesic pencils describe the rays of a surface wave; the orthogonals are the wavefronts.*

The term "first differentiator of Beltrami" probably makes you curious about other differentiators. There does in fact also exist a "Beltrami's second differentiator." In orthogonal coordinates this differentiator is (Cesàro):

$$\triangle\varphi = \frac{\partial^2 \varphi}{\partial u^2} + \frac{\partial^2 \varphi}{\partial v^2} + \kappa_2 \frac{\partial \varphi}{\partial u} + \kappa_1 \frac{\partial \varphi}{\partial v}$$

where $\kappa_{1,2}$ denote the geodesic curvature of the u, v "axes." This "differentiator" reverts to the "Laplacean" in the Euclidean case ($\kappa_{1,2} = 0$).[3] You may want to try the formula for a case that you know well (*e.g.*, if you are a physicist you will know the expression for the Laplacean in spherical coordinates by heart). Beltrami's second differentiator appears prominently in the theory of "minimal surfaces." Whereas the first differentiator can be used to spot curves of extremal length, the geodesics, the second can be used to find patches of extremal area for a given boundary.[4]

---

[3] You can derive the Laplacean in a way that brings out its geometrical invariance by using the $*d*d$ operator. This does away with the mystique that surrounds the classical definition:

$$\triangle\psi = \frac{1}{W} \left[\frac{\partial}{\partial u} \left(\frac{G\psi_u - F\psi_v}{W} \right) + \frac{\partial}{\partial v} \left(\frac{E\psi_v - F\psi_u}{W} \right) \right],$$

with $W = \sqrt{EG - F^2}$.

[4] Strubecker is a convenient reference.

7.3 Patches

...I saw as masses with surfaces which were convex, concave, angular,
planimetrical, etc.
Next I realised that the different contours resulting from
the surfaces of these bodies, determined their appearance
and emphasized their shapes.
I noticed further that the number and complication of the irregular
appearances of the surfaces, resulted in (I must not say "variety")
confusion.
—ÉTIENNE LOUIS BOUILLÉE, *Note on architecture, (around 1770)*

7.3.1 Synclastic areas

Synclastic areas occur in two flavors, convex areas and concave areas. The difference is of a purely extrinsic character, so it is usually totally disregarded in the textbooks. Yet the difference could hardly be greater from a practical point of view. In this section I follow the custom, however.

First consider a patch that doesn't contain umbilics or ridges. Such patches are about the simplest pieces of surface you ever have to deal with. There certainly exists a nice principal-lines-of-curvature parameter mesh. In a region without umbilics and ridges the principal curvatures take their extreme values on the boundary of the patch. Thus you could also take the principal curvatures themselves as parameters in this case.

The caustic surfaces both lie on one and the same side of the surface. They lie in the air for a concave patch, beneath the material of the surface for the convex patch. In the latter case they usually are of little practical interest except for the case where the surface is used as a mirror.[5]

You can easily find the caustic surfaces in applications by plotting points at a distance equal to the reciprocal of a principal curvature along the normal. That is how I made the figures. The caustics are neat, smooth surfaces too, except when the surface is degenerated. The normal rays map the lines of curvature on the corresponding sheet of the caustic of "the same color."

These "raised lines of curvature" can be shown to be geodesics of the caustic surface. They have everywhere nonzero curvature. That they are geodesics is indeed evident to the physical intuition. The original

---

[5]At least when you are concerned with "ranging data." The next chapter goes into detail.

surface is just one wavefront out of many of the surface-wave over the caustic that "sprays off" the normal rays. Then Fermat's principle from geometrical optics ("a ray is an extremal path") yields the result that the "rays on the surface" must be geodesics.

In all cases of practical interest you will have to reckon with the presence of umbilics and ridges. As Caratheodory has shown, *every ovoid has at least two umbilics.* I guess next to nothing is known about the general object. However, it is a reasonable assumption that you will hardly ever meet an object without several umbilics and a network of ridges connecting them. Notice that they are not impossible: the torus has no umbilics. It appears to depend on the topological structure of the surface, probably on the Euler number, *whether you have to have an umbilic or not.* Indeed, the sum of indices of all umbilics for the surface of some blob must equal the Euler number. For an object without holes the indices have to add up to two. A simple example is the triaxial ellipsoid, which features *four* umbilical points of index one-half. In this case you have a convenient geometrical insight into the "origin" of the umbilics, because they represent the *circular points* of the ellipsoid.

Where a line of curvature transversely crosses a ridge "of the same color," the corresponding principle curvature assumes an extreme value along the curve. If the line of curvature happens to be tangent to the ridge, the principle curvature has an "inflexion." These points may be called "turning points" of the ridge with respect to the lines of curvature.

The ridges on the surface correspond to edges of regression of the caustic. These are the "ribs" corresponding to the "ridges." If you construct spheres tangent to the surface with centers on the caustic, then it is clear that such spheres have a high order of contact with the surface. They intersect the surface at a cusped curve. If you take the center on an edge of regression, the contact is even tighter. Then *the intersection looks like the indicatrix of a ruffle.*[6]

In fact the points I have christened ruffles in this book arise similarly for the case of osculating spheres with centers at infinity.

For a given stretch of ridge that contains no higher-order singularities you obtain either all tacnodes or all unodes.[7] Thus ridges come in two flavors. These have been named "fertile" (the tacnodal case) and "sterile" (the unodal case) by Montaldi, a student of Portuous, and for

---

[6]That is to say, if you study the intersections with spheres of slightly lesser or larger radii, these look like the intersection with planes close to and parallel to the tangent plane at a ruffle.

[7]All references in this section to tacnodes, unodes, *etc.* are of the "generalized type" discussed here, that is, relative to the osculating spheres rather than the tangent planes. Watch out!

a good reason too. In a one-parameter deformation of a surface, pairs of ridges can be created or annihilated. This occurs only on the fertile ridges; it is impossible on the sterile ridges.

Ridges may well *intersect* if they are of different color. Porteous calls this a "flyover," which, I understand, is a term used by the British to denote traffic crossing at unequal heights (an overpass). Crossings of ridges of the same color do not occur for the generic surface.

A ridge changes color as it passes from one sheet of the focal surface to the other. An example is offered by the ridges of the triaxial ellipsoid. There are two ridges that each completely encircle the ellipsoid and contain no umbilic—a red and a blue one say. Then there is another ridge that encircles the ellipsoid and that contains the four umbilics. This ridge changes color as it passes an umbilic. You have to color it such that the transverse crossings imply only red-blue pairs. These properties are obvious because the ellipsoid has three planes of symmetry that must necessarily intersect the ellipsoid along the ridges; the condition at the flyover points then constrains the coloring completely.

The umbilics are definitely a curse in computational differential geometry: they frustrate your attempts to establish a regular coordinate mesh based on principal directions. Instead of a mesh you get a mess. There are only two ways out. Either you cut up your patch, for instance along the ridges, or you use a coordinate system that is not based on the directions of principal curvature.[8] The latter escape is the easiest. It isn't really so bad to use an arbitrary coordinate mesh, although it complicates the expressions quite a bit.

In any case you will not be able to tell one caustic surface from another in a systematic way. This is because you can't label principal directions consistently. This tends to be the cause of the ugly spikes that are bound to disfigure your graphics: your algorithm will suddenly jump from one caustic to the other because the principal directions get mixed up. It is a real nuisance, especially when your graphics look so good otherwise!

The pattern of lines of curvature in the vicinity of an umbilic has already been illustrated in the previous chapter. There are three topologically distinct types. For two of these types the foliation by the lines of curvature has index $+\frac{1}{2}$. These are known as the "lemon" and the "(le-)monstar." The third type is known as the "star," and has index

---

[8]But in general you will not be able to cover your shape with a single mesh. You must use an "atlas" with several overlapping meshes. In the overlap regions you have a choice of charts. If you have constructed a faithful atlas the results will never depend on that choice, though. The construction of atlases is discussed in most books on the structure of manifolds; in fact, manifolds are usually *defined* in terms of atlases.

$-\frac{1}{2}$. The funny names have been picked in such a way that you will find it easy to remember the patterns of lines of curvature.

The umbilics and ridges completely determine the qualitative structure of the caustics. Hence their enormous importance. Any problem that involves caustics has a need for the calculation of umbilics and ridges. Examples include ranging problems, specular reflections, and many more. Fortunately, it is not very hard to compute them. It is merely a matter of comparing principal curvatures and differentiating them. Or—equivalently—looking for sign changes of the coefficients of the osculating cubic for a principal frame field representation. In practice you interpolate the values of the third order coefficients in principal coordinates on the faces of your triangulation.

7.3.2 Ovoids

Technically "complete surfaces" are surfaces for which the geodesics cannot be extended any further. In practice the skin of a blob is a complete surface. An ovoid, that is, a convex blob, is bounded by a complete elliptic patch. This fact constrains the geometry enormously, and the number of theorems that concern these surfaces is really gigantic.

You would intuitively expect that the size of an ovoid would somehow be connected with its curvature. The larger the curvature is the smaller you would expect the object to be. For instance, spheres of diameter d have Gaussian curvature $\frac{4}{d^2}$; thus the diameter of a sphere with Gaussian curvature K is $\frac{2}{\sqrt{K}}$. This is also true for *intrinsic size*: Bonnet has proved that if the Gaussian curvature exceeds a number $\delta > 0$ the greatest geodesic distance between any of its two points is less than $\frac{\pi}{\sqrt{\delta}}$. For the sphere you have $\delta = R^{-2}$ and the semi-great circles have a length of exactly $\frac{\pi}{\sqrt{\delta}} = \pi R$

It is also possible to talk sense about projections in this case. For instance, if the Gaussian curvature is within the limits A^{-2} and B^{-2}, then the areas of the projections on the coordinate planes are within the limits πA^2 and πB^2. Notice that this yields the exact value in the case of spheres.

An ovoid that is well known and shows most of the generic features is the triaxial ellipsoid. The pattern of umbilics—there are four of them—and of the ridges is equally well known. Hilbert and Cohn-Vossen's book has a beautiful figure that has been copied by many authors since.[9] The

---

[9] Portuous told me that Monge is reported to have designed a room with a hemi-ellipsoidal dome, tiled in the pattern of the principal directions, with chandeliers suspended from the umbilics! How delightfully irrational rationality can get!

lines of curvature are families of confocal geodesic ellipses (fig. 293). It is fairly easy to cut up the ellipsoid in patches where the principal

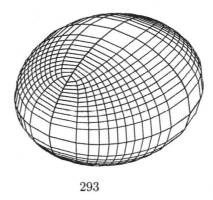

293

directions can be ordered. You just use octants. This case can very easily be programmed in order to study it interactively at your ease. As noted before, this case is highly degenerate though, so take care! The ridges coincide with lines of principal curvature, which is most remarkable and not at all generic.

The sphere is essentially different from the ellipsoid: it has umbilics all over its surface. Slight perturbations immediately cure this singular behavior. The simplest, that is, the lowest-order perturbations or "bumpy spheres," are the surfaces

$$x^2 + y^2 + z^2 + \varepsilon C(x, y, z) = 1,$$

where $C(x, y, z)$ denotes a homogeneous polynomial of the third degree. Such shapes have been investigated by Montaldi. Interesting paradigms are the "bumpy cube" ($C = xyz$), the "bumpy orange" ($C = x^3 - 3xy^2$), the "bumpy tennisball" ($C = xy^2$), and the "bumpy sphere of revolution" ($C = x^3$). These exhaust the possibilities in a way because any small deformation of the sphere leads to a linear combination of these prototypes. If you draw the pattern of ridges, you will understand that the names are quite descriptive. These shapes may easily be embedded in one-parameter families. Thus they can easily be used to program interesting computer graphics animations. These, again, can be used to obtain an insight in the possible changes of the curvature landscape.

On *any* smooth compact and complete surface, not just on ovoids, the sum of the indices of all umbilics must add up to the Euler characteristic of the surface. This means among other things that

Important fact: *any perturbation of the shape can only produce or remove umbilics in pairs.*

Such a twin must add nothing to the index sum and thus must consist of an umbilic with positive index and one with a negative index. Such events are indeed possible on the fertile ridges.

7.3.3   Caustics

In practice you will only be interested in the caustics of *concave* elliptic patches, as they are buried beneath the material of the object for the convexities.

On a typical normal ray you have *two focal points* at distances from the surface that are equal to the reciprocal of the principal curvatures. Their geometrical significance is that the focal points are the loci where nearby normal rays of curvature strips meet each other.

Another important geometrical fact is that if you are on parts of the normal ray that are far from the object, then the distance function assumes a local maximum. In that case *both focal points are between you and the surface.* You are looking into a *concavity,* remember? When your eye is so close to the surface that *both focal points are behind you,* the distance function assumes a local minimum, *even though the patch is a "hollow"!*

Many people I have met considered this fact to be "counter-intuitive" when they first came to think about it. When you put your eye *in between the focal points,* the distance function has a local saddle. I will discuss such fundamental relations more thoroughly in a later chapter. You should certainly ponder these relations until you find them "self-evident truths." Believe me, it will happen.

For a generic patch the focal points lie on smooth focal surfaces, also known as "caustics" or "centro-surfaces." Singularities occur at ridges and umbilics.

For special surfaces the caustics may be degenerate, of course. For instance, the sphere is composed of merely umbilical points: both caustics degenerate into a single common point. Well-known degenerations occur for the surfaces of revolution, where one caustic degenerates into the axis of symmetry, and for "canal surfaces," which are the envelopes of one-parameter families of spheres, where one caustic degenerates into a general space curve. In this case each sphere touches a surface along a circular line of curvature; hence the degeneration.

Such surfaces conventionally receive a lot of attention in differential geometry classes because they easily yield to the type of analysis that one expects in the classroom. Nowadays they have become popular in the field of computer vision. Sad thought that such surfaces are singularly ill suited to bring the student into contact with real-life shapes, for which such highly degenerated surfaces are of relatively minor importance.

The caustics are worth your special attention in many respects. The reasons—among others—are the following:

- The parallel surfaces have their cuspidal edges on the caustics.

- The number of normal rays through a fiducial point outside the blob changes when the fiducial point crosses a caustic.

- The normal rays are tangent to both caustics; in fact this property determines the complete normal ray manifold if you have the caustics. Thus you also have all parallel surfaces, including the Gaussian image and the surface itself.

The final observation carries a lot of intuitive content: you may consider the parallel surfaces as the "wavefronts" of the bundle of normal rays. The surface itself is one wavefront and the Gauss map is the "wavefront at infinity," or the "far field," in the usual parlance of optical theory. In a way the caustics determine the normal ray manifold, and the original surface appears as a mere "incident." It is merely one wave surface among an infinite host of the same.

It is an easy matter to derive lots of special theorems on the shape of the caustics and the nature of special curves on them. The classical books on differential geometry make a big show of this. I won't follow their example here because you will seldom be interested in such matters. It usually suffices to be able to calculate the caustics themselves, an ability you have already acquired. It is of some importance to have a grasp of the generic singularities of the caustics though.

As said before, caustic surfaces may display *cuspidal edges*, the ribs, that occur for the ridges on the surface. The distance function has a higher order degeneracy for a point on the cuspidal edge, or—what amounts to the same thing—the contact of spheres with their centers on the edge is especially tight. The rib points in a way generalize the unodal and tacnodal points, just as the generic points of the caustic generalize the spinodal points. Indeed, the spheres with centers at these focal points intersect the surface in figures that are like the intersections of the tangent planes with the surface at the special surface points. This is intuitively reasonable because the spheres in fact *equal* the tangent planes at parabolic points.

The caustic surfaces hang together at the foci of the umbilics. There the ribs show a singular behavior. That the caustic surfaces meet is clear because the focal points on an umbilic normal ray coincide.

There are two topologically different types of umbilics: the "hyperbolic" and the "elliptic" umbilic. These have been illustrated in the previous chapter. The triaxial ellipsoid illustrates the hyperbolic umbilic case.

Local models are:

$$z(x, y) = \frac{x^2 + y^2}{2R} + \frac{1}{6}(\alpha x^3 + 3\beta x^2 y + 3\gamma x y^2 + \delta y^3),$$

where the sign of

$$4(\alpha\gamma - \beta^2)(\beta\delta - \gamma^2) - (\alpha\delta - \beta\gamma)^2$$

determines the type: *elliptic* if positive, *hyperbolic* if negative.

Of course, you may also expect *transversal crossings* (generic mutual intersections) of caustic surfaces. Such effects are very important in practice, yet they are never treated in the mathematical literature because they are so trivial. Trivial as they may be, they can be very important in applications.

The configurations of the ridges for the two types of umbilic have been discussed in the previous chapter. The congruence of principal directions is singular near an umbilic. The elliptic umbilics always show a characteristic star pattern. However, the hyperbolic umbilics may show one of three quite different types, namely—apart from the star— the "lemon" and the "(le-)monstar." The star pattern has topological index $-\frac{1}{2}$, the other types topological index $+\frac{1}{2}$, signifying that *the principal directions rotate counterclockwise for a clockwise traversal of the umbilic in the star case and clockwise for the other cases.*[10]

7.3.4   Anticlastic areas

At an anticlastic point the surface is locally saddle-shaped; in a way it is convex and concave at the same time. One caustic surface is *inside the material,* the other one is "in the air" *outside.* Hyperbolic patches are numerically extremely nice because the principal curvatures are always unequal—they are of different sign. There are no umbilics. When you have served your time in computational differential geometry you will know when it is time to rejoice.

---

[10]I'm sorry that the figures in this book are not colored. You will have to figure out for yourself how the different colors of the ridges are arranged around the umbilics.

The asymptotic curves—the integral curves of the asymptotic directions—are neatly transversal on a hyperbolic patch. They can be used as coordinate curves if you wish.[11] The angle between the asymptotic directions is a measure of "how saddle-shaped" the surface really is; they are orthogonal when the mean curvature vanishes. In the latter case you have the "minimal points."

Figure 294 shows a well-known *all-minimal* example, namely "Scherk's surface." The parameter lines shown in the figure are not asymptotic curves though. The same surface triangulated on the basis of an asymptotic net is shown in figure 295.

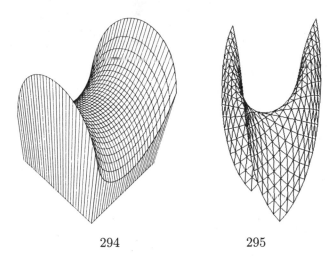

294   295

The angle between the asymptotic directions is simply the arctangent of $\frac{\sqrt{-K}}{H}$ and becomes increasingly acute as you approach a parabolic curve.

By the way, the "minimal surfaces" minimize—or rather extremize—the *area* of a patch if you keep the boundary fixed. This is known as "Plateau's problem" (Plateau, 1866). Such surfaces can be realized as soap films stretched—but not inflated—over space curves. Generic surfaces are never minimal of course, but there exist *curves* on generic hyperbolic patches where the surface is *locally* minimal. In the computer vision community such curves would likely be called "zero crossings." Obviously, it is not possible for such curves to exist on elliptic patches

---

[11]But of course the coordinate curves can hardly be expected to turn out to be orthogonal.

because the average curvature can't vanish there.

Figure 296 shows an asymptotic net on a "whirl surface," the kind

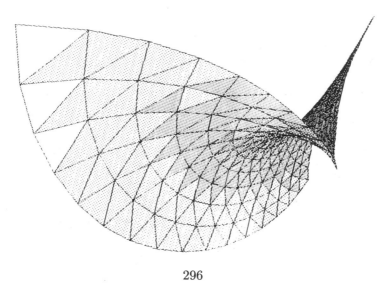

296

of surface you might observe while draining your bathtub. This patch
is a parameterline parallelogram, even if it may not look that way at
a cursory glance.[12] In the Monge patch representation the height is a
logarithmic function of the distance to the axis, whereas the asymptotic
curves, when projected on the x-y plane, are logarithmic spirals. They
look much as you would expect the stream lines in your tub to look.

Notice that the asymptotic curves are special in that their osculating
plane coincides with the tangent plane. Thus an "asymptotic net" must
have *planar vertices* in the sense that the edges belonging to the parameter curves are coplanar. A polyhedral model based on the asymptotic
nets has similarly "planar" vertices.[13]

From an intrinsic point of view the intuitively simplest hyperbolic
patches are those of constant negative curvature, the so-called "pseudo-
spheres." The minimal surfaces are about the simplest from an extrinsic

---

[12]*I.e.*, for a parametrization by (u, v), a region $\{(u, v) \mid u_1 < u < u_2, v_1 < v < v_2\}$.

[13]But please notice that the edges belonging to the "diagonals" of the coordinate
mesh are not coplanar with the other edges. Otherwise you could not have a curved
surface at all.

point of view. The latter admit of asymptotic nets whose normal spherical images are "Chebyshev nets": the meshes are parallelograms with geodesic edges. Thus all dihedral angles are equal. A quadrangle formed by asymptotic lines on a pseudosphere of Gaussian curvature minus unity has an *area* that equals the excess of the sum of the interior angles of the parallelogram over 2π (Hazzidakis).

The most salient feature of the hyperbolic patches from the point of view of applications is their asymptotic ray manifold, because this largely determines the possible contact of the patch with straight lines. This is often important in applications (*e.g.*, the line of sight in an optical application). Since the asymptotic ray manifold is skew you should not go out to hunt for "asymptotic caustics" in the air because this would keep you busy for the rest of your lifetime. If you want to put it that way, then *the surface itself* can be considered to be the two—merged—caustic surfaces.

Thus most of the structure of interest is already contained in the *asymptotic spherical image*. It is easy enough to compute. The second fundamental form immediately gives you access to the asymptotic rays. You need the osculating *cubic* to decide which side sticks into the surface and which side sticks into the air though. You decide this on the basis of the curvature of the indicatrix, as has been illustrated in the previous chapter.

When you are on a flecnodal point, you can't arrive at a decision because the indicatrix inflects. Then *the asymptotic rays stick out in both directions*. This defines a very special "see-through" condition. In practice, you find the flecnodal curve by calculating the curvature of the indicatrix for all points of the patch and drawing the zero-level curve by interpolation. The only numerical problems occur near the ruffles, where the surface is locally exceptionally flat. But at such places the flecnodals nearly coincide with the parabolic curve anyway and are of minor practical interest. At such locations the parabolic curve yields all the structure you are likely to need.

Again:

Good news: *Computationally the hyperbolic patches are by far the easiest objects around.*

7.3.5 The pattern of inflexion

You distinguish convex or concave, that is, synclastic, and saddle-like or anticlastic patches on the surface of a blob. In the simplest case the blob is an ovoid and thus an all-convex patch. There will always be a

convex patch in fact. This is intuitively obvious because any blob must
have exposed points and the exposed points are necessarily convex. If
there are concavities, then there have also to be some saddle-like patches,
because convexities and concavities cannot be contiguous but must be
separated by hyperbolic regions. This is because the boundaries of the
patches are parabolic curves at which one of the principal curvatures
vanishes. If *both* principal curvatures vanish you have a planar point,
which is a nongeneric entity: the slightest perturbation removes it. Thus
both the convex and the concave patches must be surrounded by saddle-
like points.

The Gauss map of the surface of a blob covers the unit sphere completely. The image of the surface of the blob can be imagined as being
"wrapped around the sphere" in a continuous fashion, introducing folds
and pleats if so required. For any shape that is more complicated than an
ovoid you will certainly need folds because the saddle-like patches map
to an "inside out" cover of the sphere. This is a rather tight topological
constraint that you can use to good advantage in heuristic thought. For
instance, will the introduction of a disc-like island of saddle-like points
on an ovoid introduce pleats? Obviously yes, because the simplest way
to do it is to "pinch" the Gaussian sphere and fold it over, thus introducing two pleats at the same time (figs. 297 and 298). It is intuitively

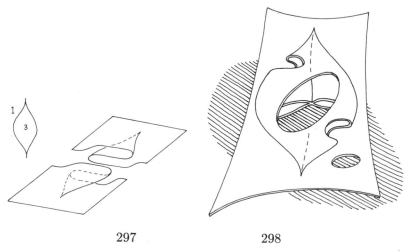

297   298

clear that there is no way to "iron them out" without destroying the hyperbolic area in the process. You may, of course, introduce complications by introducing "spurious" pleats on a fold (figs. 299 and 300). The latter pair of pleats can easily be "ironed out" without affecting the

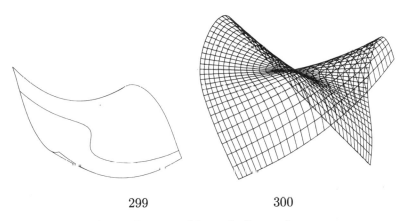

299 300

general layout of the elliptic and hyperbolic patches.

The parabolic curves are general space curves. If their curvature doesn't vanish, which is the generic case, then the torsion vanishes at the ruffles which are the pleats of the Gauss map. This is often an easy cue to spot these special points on the surface. The ruffles must satisfy certain topological constraints. Thus you have:

Useful Fact: *The number of unodes minus the number of tacnodes equals the Euler characteristic of the hyperbolic region.*

This shows you that a simply connected hyperbolic island in a global ovoidal shape must at least possess a pair of unodes. Similarly,

Useful Fact: *The number of exposed unodes minus the number of tritangent support planes equals four minus twice the Euler characteristic of the region of exposed points.*

Such rules can often be put to good use in applications. However, you must be a bit careful with your interpretation, as will be shown later.

Because the pattern of folds and pleats is so important, it is intuitively useful to think of the following complex as the framework or skeleton that roughly captures the global shape of the surface:

- the parabolic curves
- the flecnodal curves
- the ruffles
- the ridges
- the gutterpoints
- the conical points
- the umbilics
- the biflecnodes

This complex roughly determines the qualitative pattern of principal directions and convexities-concavities. For a quantitative representation you merely have to sew the flesh on the bones because the qualitative framework has been established. The umbilics only occur on the elliptic parts, of course. The ridges also traverse the hyperbolic areas. The ruffles mark the points where a ridge and a parabolic curve belonging to the principal curvature of like color cross transversely. Given the complex, you can qualitatively sketch the Gauss map. This is a first step toward the description of global shape. A useful refinement is obtained by indicating the position of the *gutterpoints*: they decide which parts of the parabolic curves go to convex and which to concave folds on the Gauss map.

If you also want an indication of the structure of the asymptotic ray manifold, you need an indication of the *flecnodal curves*. They always issue forth from the ruffles and run through the hyperbolic areas. The pattern of parabolic curves, gutterpoints, flecnodal curves, and perhaps biflecnodal points on the latter, qualitatively determine the asymptotic spherical image. They also qualitatively determine the pattern of the asymptotic curves.

The pattern of asymptotic curves within the hyperbolic areas is always trivial because *there are no singular points.* Near the parabolic curves the curvature of the asymptotic curve approaches zero as they meet the parabolic curve transversely. Both families approach the parabolic curve in the same direction; thus you get a characteristic cusped pattern.

In figures 301 and 302 this has been drawn for the "Gaussian hill" ($z = \exp(-(x^2 + y^2)/2)$).

In the neighborhood of a ruffle the asymptotic directions tend to be tangent to the parabolic curve. In certain degenerate cases the parabolic curve may turn out to be "all ruffle" and consequently the asymptotic curves are nowhere transverse to the parabolic curve, as should

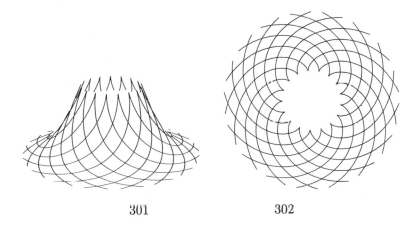

301   302

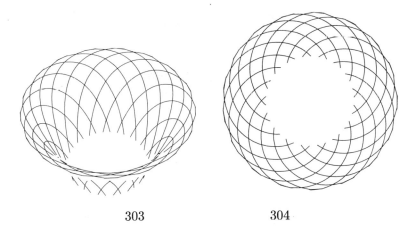

303   304

be (figs. 303 and 304). This is the case for the torus, for instance. It is a highly unstable situation, as you can imagine. It is true that even a small warping of the torus restores the nice generic pattern. But of course the asymptotic directions will remain *almost* parallel to the parabolic curve; thus you will meet with some numerical problems in computational differential geometry.

There exist three topologically distinct patterns of the asymptotic curves near a ruffle (figs. 305 to 307). At a unode you get to see one of

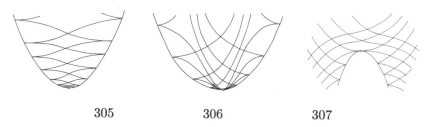

305   306   307

the patterns of figures 305 and 306, whereas the pattern of figure 307 is typical for the tacnode.

If you wish to have a fairly complete picture of the normal ray congruence, which is important, for instance, in ranging applications, you will also want a representation of the singular features of the caustics. Note that the skeleton described above already specifies the important singularities:

- The umbilics specify the points where the caustics meet.

- The ridges specify the cuspidal edge of the caustics.

- The parabolic curves specify the asymptotic cones of the caustics.

And so forth!

It is often convenient to regard the Gauss map of the parabolic curves as an image of the "caustics at infinity." In applications it is often useful to construct the ruled surfaces described by the parabolic normal rays. They are easily computed in practice because you only need the osculating quadric.

Useful construction: *The surfaces described by the parabolic normal rays are asymptotic cones of the caustic surfaces and can be used as convenient approximations of the latter in the far field.*

Similarly, if you are interested in the asymptotic ray manifold, which might well be the case if you are involved in optical applications, you will want the ruled surfaces described by the cylinder axes at the parabolic curves and the "see-through rays" at the flecnodal curves. Again, these are easily computed. You need the third-order description to find the see-through rays though. These entities can be used to approximate the structure of the asymptotic ray manifold in the far field. In many applications the asymptotic—or far field—structure is essentially all that you will ever need.

These entities are of the utmost importance for practical applications. However, they are rarely described in the usual textbooks. Again, they are only appreciated in a clear fashion for *generic blobs*. In the usual examples they tend to be degenerated and often merge. For instance, consider the torus (a real freak case!):

- The surfaces of normal parabolic rays are right circular cylinders; thus the Gauss map degenerates into a pair of points.

- The surface of cylinder axes degenerates into two doubly covered planes with circular discs removed.

- The surfaces of see-through rays are hyperboloids of one sheet: they coincide for the two families of asymptotic rays.

- The parabolic curves are "all ruffle."

- The lines of curvature have ridge points everywhere.

If you ever so slightly warp the torus, the degeneracies vanish and the coincident features explode into something generic that may well look horribly complicated to you at the first sight but is in fact *a lot nicer* than the degenerated junk because it is at least *stable* against, for instance, the perturbations caused by the numerical tolerances of your algorithms. Although it might seem that, because the generic structures are on such a fine scale when you are close to a degenerated case, you might as well use the degenerated case as an approximation, this would mean that you give up generality. You would have to treat each instance as a special case. This is much too costly, of course—unless you happen to live in a very dull universe indeed.

Mark well: *Generality implies genericity.*

It is obviously impossible to describe the full complexity of all the wonderful variety that might occur in practice. On the other hand you do have a complete overview of the generically possible features. Later[14]

---

[14]The "Examples" section.

I describe several specific surfaces that reveal "families" of features that
you will meet over and over again in applications. They may be thought
of as a kind of "canonical examples." They are not properly "canonical" in the sense of forming an exhaustive set of distinct possibilities.
However, you will find them extremely practical and common, and a
close acquaintance with these examples will prepare you for almost all
shapes. They are much more useful than the typical textbook collection
of objects, which merely constitute a cabinet of freak cases.

7.3.6   The bitangent ray congruence

The tangent plane at some convex point P will in general intersect the
surface of the object in a closed curve not containing P. On this curve
there will be points Q, Q', Q'', ... such that the rays $PQ, PQ', \dots PQ'^{\cdots \prime}$
will be tangent to the loop and thus to the surface. There must at least
be *two* of those if P is an elliptic point and the intersection is not void.
Such special rays are tangent to the blob at two points and are known
as "bitangent rays." There pass a finite number of bitangents through
every point of the surface. The number might well be zero, of course.

When you change the position of the point P, it may happen that
two bitangent rays PQ', PQ'' become *coincident* for a given position.
This may happen because the loop of intersection shrinks to a point or
because the point $Q'(=Q'')$ becomes an inflexion of the loop.

At such limiting positions the limiting plane $PQ'Q''$ will be a *bitangent
plane* of the surface. The normal rays at P and Q' $(=Q'')$ are parallel
in such a case. The normals themselves may be parallel or anti-parallel:
you have "inner" and "outer" bitangent planes. If the bitangent plane
is also a support plane, they will be parallel, of course.

The bitangent planes envelop a ruled surface, the "limiting bitangent
developable." *This surface appears also as a boundary for the bitangent
ray manifold.*

An example may clarify the situation. Consider an "object" composed
of two disjunct ovoids. Figures 308 and 309 illustrate a simple example.
If you object that this "object" is really "two objects," you may put
your mind at rest by soldering a thin wire between the two. Obviously
this will in no way affect the argument. If the ovoids are spheres, then
clearly for a point on one sphere there are either zero, a single, or two
bitangents. There exist two distinct types of bitangent planes, one with
parallel and one with anti-parallel normals. The bitangent developables
are cones in this simple case. The bitangent ray manifold fills the space
between the two conical surfaces.

You are familiar with this example from the phenomena you experi-

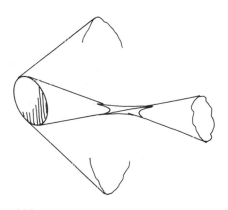

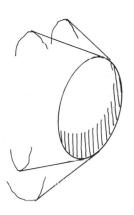

308

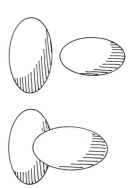

309

ence when you put your eye (or better: when your eye is being put) in different locations relative to those heavenly bodies our sun and moon. The cases of juxtaposition and annular and total eclipses corresponds to different locations relative to the bitangent ray manifold.

The apices of the cones in the example are special, of course; they are like foci for the bitangent ray congruence. In this overly symmetrical case they are degenerated. In the general case they "explode" and you have to reckon with the *edges of regression* ("cuspidal edges") of the bitangent developable and with isolated swallowtail-like cusps on these edges. The structure is identical with the "astigmatic pencil of rays" often illustrated in elementary courses in geometrical optics in the chapter on aberrations of imaging systems.

At a cuspidal edge point of the bitangent developable you have a similar situation *locally*, as in the apices of the cones in the example. Their importance in computer graphics and computer vision is great because they govern the genesis of "T-junctions" in the outlines. Consider the example of the spheres. Again, if you interpret the large sphere as the sun and the small one as our moon, then the position of the earth with respect to the apex of the cone of outer bitangent rays determines whether you will experience a "total" or "annular" solar eclipse.

I have already discussed the appearance of the bitangent developables in the composition of the *convex hull* of blobs. There I also discussed the fact that the developables might just *end* at a unode as the points of contact with the object merge there. The limiting bitangent plane at a unode necessarily contains the cylinder axis there. Thus the bitangent developable also meshes with the developable of cylinder axes, or the bitangent congruence with the asymptotic ray congruence.

The close connection between the bitangent ray congruence and the asymptotic ray congruence is also evident when you consider the see-through condition near a flecnodal point. This has been illustrated in the previous chapter. Near a see-through ray you must have a single T-junction—that means a single bitangent ray. The flecnodal scroll acts as a boundary for this congruence, and again the flecnodal scroll contains the limiting cylinder axis at the ruffles.

The structure of the bitangent ray manifold and its intermeshing with the asymptotic ray manifold has not been studied in great detail up till now, despite their great *practical importance*. The reason is that the bitangents are *global*, or at least "bilocal," rather than local entities, and are scarcely amenable to the usual differential geometric techniques. It is a real pity that they are also expensive to study *numerically*: it takes a lot of computation to find them because you have to try N^2 cases for a patch described through N points.

The best way seems to imply the Gauss map: for any point $\mathcal{P}$ find its Gaussian image $\mathcal{P}^*$. For this image you can then find the pre-images $\mathcal{P}'$, $\mathcal{P}''$, ... and antipodal pre-images $\underline{\mathcal{P}}'$, $\underline{\mathcal{P}}''$, ... Points $\mathcal{P}$, $\mathcal{P}'$, ..., $\underline{\mathcal{P}}'^{\cdots'}$ have at least parallel tangent planes. The signed distance of the tangent planes at $\mathcal{P}$ and $\mathcal{P}'$ (say) is a function of $\mathcal{P}$, and you want to find the locus of its zeros. Although this leads to a reasonable algorithm, it still takes me ages to compute the loci in detail; my initial attempts are not especially encouraging. It certainly worked though. Moreover, the algorithm is suitable for parallel processing. Maybe I should just lean back and wait for technology to catch up!

The air is full of infinite straight and radiating lines
intersected and interwoven with one another,
without one occupying the place of another.
They represent to whatever object the true form of their cause.
—LEONARDO DA VINCI (1452–1519)

7.4   Examples

> *Schließlich mache ich noch auf die im Dyckschen Kataloge als*
> *"bohnenförmige Versuchskörper" bezeichneten Modelle aufmerksam,*
> *auf denen man die einzelnen Punkte hyperbolischer, elliptischer oder*
> *parabolischer Krümmung markieren soll. Es zeigt sich, daß unser*
> *Augenmaß da sehr unsicher ist, so daß die Definitionen der*
> *Elementaren Krümmungstheorie bereits einen sehr abstrakten*
> *Charakter zu besitzen scheinen. Man empfindet dies besonders lebhaft,*
> *wenn man die betreffende Aufgabe an einer so verwickelten, empirisch*
> *vorgelegte Fläche, wie sie etwa eine Porträtbüste vorstellt,*
> *durchzuführen sucht. Ich empfehle, dies zu studieren.*
> —FELIX KLEIN, *Von der Versinnlichung idealer Gebilde (1928)*

I will skip the example of the ovoid here. The triaxial ellipsoid has
already been illustrated in some detail. The interesting cases concern
undulations, not necessarily in the sense of an alternation of convex and
concave parts but in the sense that not all sections of the blob ought to
be completely convex. Specifically I will describe (note that agricultural
terms seem to agree especially well with these shapes)

the **Furrow:** A hyperbolic patch or "dent" in an overall ovoidal shape.[15]
This may be called a "kidney bean" or "banana" surface. Although
this blob is not all convex *it contains no concavities.*

the **Dimple:** A concavity in a globally ovoidal shape,[16] which could
be called a "pot hole" or an "apple" surface. The concavity is
surrounded by an annular hyperbolic patch.

the **Bell:** The "bell shape": a strongly curved convex "wart" on a globally ovoid shape.[17] It may be called a "pear" surface. The "bell"
is surrounded by an annular hyperbolic patch.

---

[15] "a narrow groove in the earth made by a plow; anything resembling this ....
[ME, *forowe, furwe*; AS, *furh*, a furrow; O.H.G., *furuh*; Dan. *fure*; Sw. *fara*; Ice.
for, a drain]." The root doesn't quite cover the nonconcave nature, but is fairly close.

[16] "a slight depression or dent occurring in some soft part of the body, as on the
cheek or chin, ... [Late ME. *dimpul*, from base of Eng. dial. *dump*, deep pit filled
with water, and -*le*, dim. suffix.]." The root clearly covers the present meaning.

[17] "..., anything in the form of a bell, as the cup or calyx of a flower, ... [ME. *bell,
belle*; AS. *belle*, a bell]." The shape of a cup or calyx of a flower covers the meaning
intended here well.

the Hump: A convex "island" within a hyperbolic "sea."[18] The hyperbolic sea may be understood as part of the surface of some much larger blob.

Together these examples exhaust much of the complexity you will meet in practice. A study of the examples will at least prepare you for an analysis of the kind of junk you have to expect from computer outputs—mainly of the graphical kind—in your attempts at computational differential geometry. If you don't have any idea what to look for, you are apt to be puzzled most of the time. You can cut down on the time spent in utter bewilderment if you practice a bit on the examples.

The examples are in the nature of a picture story or comic book: you are expected to spend your time largely with the figures. Use the text to figure out what is being illustrated if you can't guess it. Perhaps the text will direct your attention to features you might otherwise miss. But the main thing is to look at the figures until you fully understand their mutual interrelation and until you can interprete them almost as easily as a run-of-the-mill perspective rendering of the surface.

7.4.1 The furrow

The "kidney-bean surface" is a classic in differential geometry; it appeared in catalogs of mathematical models of more than a century ago.[19]

The surface depicted in figure 310 is basically *globally convex* except that it has received a kind of "dent." Clearly the dent, or "furrow," is not convex but also *not concave*: you can't keep a liquid there because it will flow off in whatever position you hold the object! I have often noticed that people have considerable difficulty calling up such an object before their mind's eye. For the majority of people *nonconvexity* seems to imply *concavity*. The point to grasp here is that there exists a third possibility for local shape: in addition to the inside and outside of egg shells there are the saddle shapes. Most people think intuitively of surface curvature as something essentially structured through a dichotomy (you have either a protrusion or a hollow) and completely miss

---

[18]"a rounded, protruding lump, as the fleshy mass on the back of a camel: in man, a hump is formed by a deformity of the spine; a hummock, mound, ... [17th c.; probably from international nautical usage; cf. L.G. *hump*, a heap, hill.]." The root doesn't cover the saddle-shaped surrounding, but I was at a loss to find anything covering this.

[19]Felix Klein refers to a catalog of the German educational fair, Chicago, 1893 (W. Dyck, Spezialkatalog der Math. Ausstellung (Deutche Unterrichtsaustellung in Chikago 1893), Berlin 1893, S. 52), for a "bean-shaped experimental object" for the empirical study of surface curvatures.

the trichotomy offered to them. (Is this perhaps because of the two-dimensional nature of the visual field? Or do we think in sections? This is a problem of a psychological nature to which I know of no answer.)

If you do have this difficulty, try to adjust your mental optics, for it is important to grasp fully what is going on here. For the case of the furrow you have a local anticlastic island in a much larger synclastic sea.

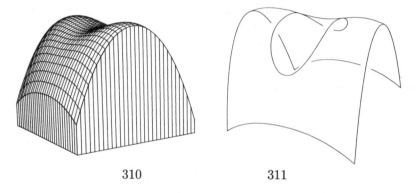

310   311

The problem was first discussed in relation to the curvature theory of surfaces by Felix Klein. (Of course, sculptors had been aware of the facts for a long time, but in their writings—which are rare enough—the lack of mathematical background detracts from the clarity of the discussion.) Klein notes that our "eye-measure" cannot really be trusted in the case of surface curvature, and that consequently curvature theory must be on a high level of abstraction from perceptual reality.

Figure 311 shows the parabolic curve, which is apparently a closed, twisted space curve. The Gauss map of the parabolic curve is shown in figure 312. I have superimposed a coordinate grid. Figure 313 displays the Gauss map of the patch. The fold of this map is, of course, the Gaussian image of the parabolic curve. As you see, the image of the patch on the Gaussian sphere contains *two cusps*. They are pleats of the Gauss map, as is evident from the deformation of the coordinate grid on the Gaussian sphere. The pre-images of these pleats occur on *torsion*

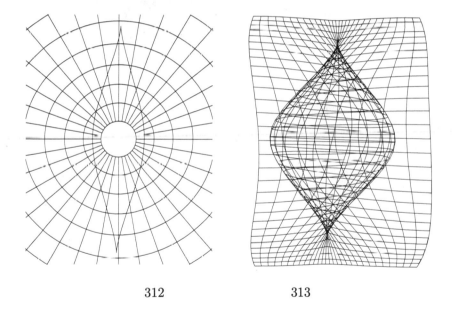

312 313

zeros of the spinodal curve. How this comes about can be followed in
detail when you consider the family of parallel surfaces.

At first the furrow merely articulates, but then it develops a veritable
"pinch" (fig. 314). The surface then manages to intersect itself and

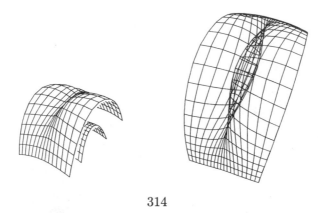

314

forms the fold and pleat structure. If you follow the parabolic curve
over the family of parallel surfaces (figs. 315 to 317), you see how the

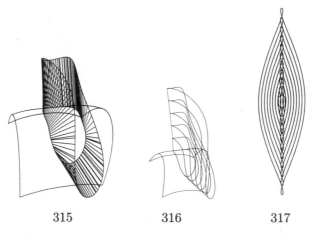

315   316   317

space curve becomes a spherical curve and how it manages to pull itself
inside out. The two loops that are formed in the process finally form the
cusps. The family of parallel surfaces is a wonderful tool in the study

of solid shape. It gives you a solid grasp of the singular structure of the Gauss map and the relation to the original surface undulations. The method is especially powerful if you use animations. Then you can "see" the surface deform to its own Gauss map, and *vice versa*. There is no tool remotely as powerful as this to let you gain a true gut feeling for the significance of the Gaussian image. Everyone should try this a few times. It is more than worth your time!

The cusps of the Gauss map correspond to "footpoints" (in this case, unodes) on the surface. This becomes clear when you compute the flecnodal curves in the anticlastic area, for instance. The flecnodal curves touch the parabolic curve at two points which are the ruffles (fig. 318).

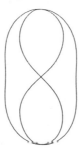

318

You can spot the footpoints visually if you look for the curvature of the contour. If this flips from convex to concave, or *vice versa*, you have crossed the tangent plane of a footpoint. At the moment of this event the contour has a point of zero curvature which must be the projection of a footpoint. Figure 319 illustrates this for a "banana surface," which is much like the kidney bean.

The phenomenon illustrated here, in which a concave arc of the contour develops a concavity, is a useful sign for the presence of a unode. Although the method is not very sensitive, you can use it to find unodes on statues, for instance. You should try it: it is a most instructive exercise.

Figure 298 attempts to illustrate the structure of the Gauss map. I have tried especially to make the multiplicity and connectivity of the covering pictorially clear. In order to do this, I have made a liberal use of cut-out "windows," and you may need some time to adjust to that device. Windows "put into series" allow you to determine the multiplicity of the covering by mere counting. For instance, you count three lamina

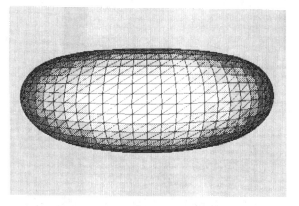

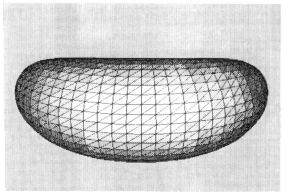

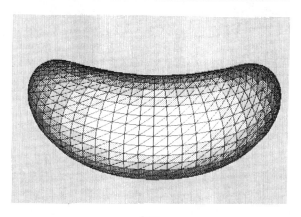

319

in the middle of the figure before you can see the hatched background. From this you may conclude that for any point of the anticlastic area you should be able to find two points in the synclastic area that possess matching normal directions. This is, of course, pictorially almost self evident.

If you use computer graphics with wireframe representation without hidden line removal, you *have* to become thoroughly familiar with the multiple covering of the Gauss map, because the graphics will overwrite themselves in multiply covered regions. This is also a very good method of developing a solid feel for what goes on here.

The developable of cylinder axes has a rather complicated edge of regression: one branch touches the ruffles, whereas the other branch cusps somewhere in the air (figs. 320 and 321). The cusp is due to

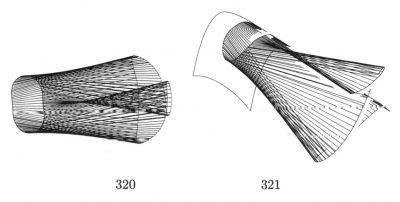

320   321

the existence of a "conical point." Clearly there must be chimeric "in between" points where the cylinder axes are not diverging either way but are parallel, and these are the gutterpoints. You see that there are four gutterpoints in total. In retrospect you should have gotten this from the Gauss map, because the gutterpoints correspond to inflexions of the Gaussian image of the parabolic curve. Evidently there are two inflexions on each fold connecting the two pleats.

When you follow the developable of cylinder axes in space, you see a curious hourglass shaped structure emerging (fig. 322). This will prove to be a very prominent feature of the asymptotic spherical image. The swallowtail point in the developable is evidently a very special type of point. It has to do with a vertex-like point of the field of cylinder axes at the spinodal curve.

When you circumnavigate a parabolic curve, you might pay special

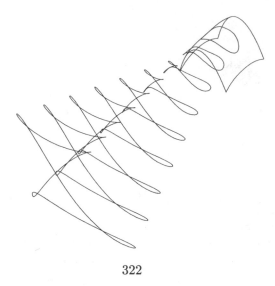

322

attention to the direction of the cylinder axes. At certain points the distance at which nearby cylinder axes intersect may prove to be stationary: then you have arrived at such a vertex-like point. Such points are clearly very special geometrical features, although I know of hardly a mention of them in the literature—only one cursory remark by Arnold, as far as I am aware. They have never received a special name. You could call them "conical points" or "funnel points," because the developable of cylinder axes is nowhere more like a true cone than at these points.

Similarly, you can calculate the flecnodal scroll (fig. 323). It doesn't

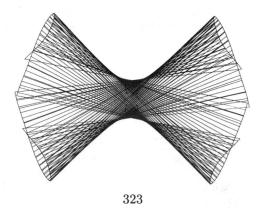

323

display any obvious special features. The spherical image of the flecnodal curves appears as a very prominent feature in the asymptotic spherical image, though.

You get an impression of the asymptotic spherical image if you compute the asymptotic parallel surface for a large distance (fig. 324). You

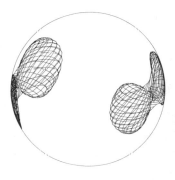

324

may detect the hourglass nucleus due to the cylinderaxis developable with enormous butterfly shaped puffs at both sides bounded by the flecnodal rays. These boundaries are apparently *folds* of the asymptotic spherical image. You also see that the asymptotic spherical image covers only part of the unit sphere. If you plot only those asymptotic rays that *stick out of the surface*, the picture simplifies a lot (fig. 325). This figure is composed of the image by the *two* families of asymptotic directions.

For practical purposes you want to plot the structure of the asymptotic spherical image on the "viewing sphere" (fig. 326).[20] Then you can easily determine what will happen to the image of the shape when you change the vantage point.

There does in fact exist a somewhat simpler type of furrow, one that contains only a single pair of gutterpoints (fig. 327). Of course, you can easily construct much more complicated examples, too.

I have illustrated the asymptotic spherical image in some detail. It is rather important to grasp the structure fully because this is one of the simplest cases you will ever encounter in real life.

First try to obtain an insight in the covering due to a family of asymptotic directions of a single color. Part of the sphere is covered twice, part only once, and part thrice. Of course, some directions do not occur at all. The structure for the family of the other color is very similar: it is

---

[20]This entity will be discussed fully in the next chapter. You may regard it as the "sphere at infinity" centered on the object, for the sake of the present discussion.

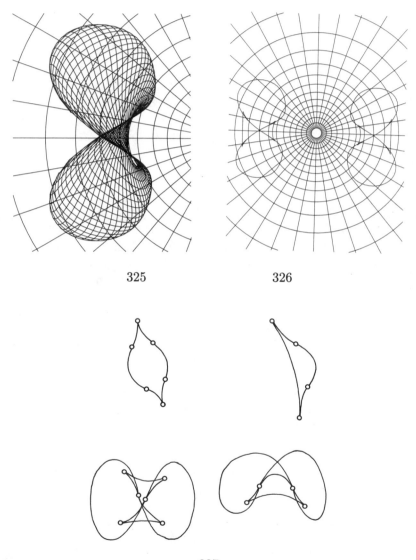

325   326

327

a kind of mirror image and covers predominantly the other flank of the lips-shaped figure. Part of the sphere is now doubly covered, once by each color. For many practical purposes it is rather important to distinguish between a double covering of one color and a double covering of two colors.

Notice that the fancy "occlusions" in the sketch are merely a pictorial device to indicate the nature of the connectivity: many other choices could have been made that would have been equally valid. Try to extract the essence and to forget about the mere pictorial embellishments. The best way to do this is to try to make some alternative sketches on your own.

Once you understand the structure fully, you will find that a more austere diagram showing only the spinodal and flecnodal curves with some numbers indicating the multiplicity will serve you better (figs. 328 and 329).

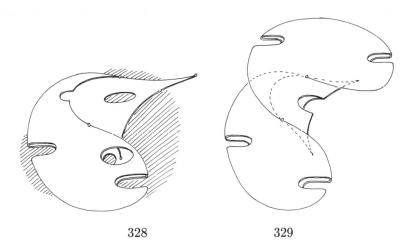

328   329

7.4.2   The dimple

Doth the Eagle know
What is in the pit,
Or wilt thou go ask the mole?
—WILLIAM BLAKE (1757–1827)

When you first roll an ovoid out of a blob of clay and then produce a concavity by pushing in your thumb somewhere, you produce a "dimple," or pothole (fig. 330). Unlike the case of the furrow you *can* keep water

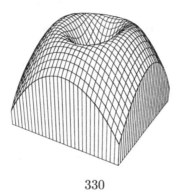

330

in this hole. This is what most people understand as a "concavity in a convexity." You have a concave synclastic patch contained in a much larger convex synclastic patch (namely the overall ovoid shape), kept apart from each other by an annular anticlastic region.

Notice that this shape does have a certain similarity with the torus. In the case of the dimple you also find a ring-shaped area with a parabolic curve on top. One difference is that the hole in the torus is a through hole, whereas the hole of the dimple has a bottom. Most of the geometrically interesting (because almost singular!) structure of the dimple derives from its similarity to the torus. If you want to study the dimple geometry in other differential geometry books, your best bet is to look up the torus in the index.

Because a concave patch cannot touch a convex patch there must exist an annular hyperbolic patch to keep the two apart. Thus, you have to reckon with two concentric parabolic loops. This is indeed the case, as figures 331 and 332 show. Both parabolic loops are general space curves. It is of crucial importance to understand the fact that these parabolic

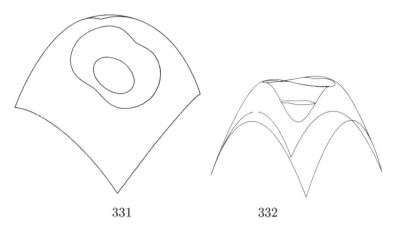

331   332

loops are of a *completely different nature.*

If you want to develop an appreciation for this fundamental difference between the two parabolic loops, you may compare the inner one with the parabolic loop of the Gaussian hill and the outer one with the parabolic loop of the torus. The inner one is thus completely "normal," whereas the outer one is of an almost singular type. Remember that the parabolic loop of the torus maps into a single point of the Gaussian image. This clearly illustrates the singular nature of this parabolic curve. As you will remember, this entails that the asymptotic directions be almost parallel to the parabolic curve instead of being decidedly transverse.

The state of affairs is shown in dramatic detail if you consider an overly symmetric example, such as $z(x, y) = -(x^2 + y^2)^2 + (x^2 + y^2)$ in the usual Cartesian coordinates or $z(\varrho, \varphi) = -\varrho^4 + \varrho^2$ in cylindrical coordinates.

The inner parabolic loop is located at $\varrho = 0.408\ldots$, whereas the outer one is located at $\varrho = 0.707\ldots$. For the outer loop the normal is vertical for all points;[21] thus *the Gauss map degenerates into a single point*, exactly as in the case of the torus. The inner loop maps onto a small circle of radius $28.56\ldots$ degrees and behaves very much as the inner loop of the bell. It is also a simple matter to derive the cylinder axes analytically for this case. For the inner loop the asymptotic curves neatly cusp and their directions are radial with an inclination of $61.439\ldots$ degrees with respect to the vertical. For the outer loop *the asymptotic curves are*

---

[21] This one of the nongeneric monsters was treated at the end of the previous chapter.

tangent to the loop and lie in a horizontal plane. Thus the cylinder axis developable for the inner loop is a cone with its apex inside the material when the normal points in the positive z- direction. For the outer loop you obtain a doubly covered horizontal plane without a disc of radius 0.707.... Note that there are no flecnodal points in this example; the asymptotic curves inflect nowhere.

This is a very revealing example that you can easily check on the back of an envelope. It makes a lot of sense to start doing this right now. It will provide you with a head start over lazier readers as far as an understanding of what follows is concerned.

Consider how the features of this simple and overly symmetric model appear in a generic case. First of all notice that I have illustrated only the simplest generic version. You may make the example generic, or "unfold it," by applying azimuthal perturbations of arbitrarily high frequency. I have picked the lowest frequency possible. However, you will have no difficulty imagining more complicated perturbations because they are all very similar, once you catch the pattern.

First of all you may consider the family of parallel surfaces (fig. 333). Observe how the inner part of the patch contracts, pinches into a singular point, then crosses itself and blows out into a large bubble. The crossover point looks like a four-cusped asteroid shape if you scrutinize it carefully. This is more clearly perceived in the Gaussian image of the parabolic curves (fig. 334). The outer loop in the Gauss map is the image of the inner parabolic loop. This was to be expected because the concave patch is highly curved; thus it maps onto a large part of the Gaussian sphere. This outer loop is just a neat regular fold of the Gauss map, absolutely nothing special!

The asteroid is the image of the outer parabolic loop. Its size depends very critically on the magnitude of the perturbation, in sharp contradistinction with the other loop for which the magnitude of the (small) perturbation is not at all critical. The reason is clear enough: the parabolic normal rays on the outer loop are almost the generators of a cylinder. They are *exactly* the generators of a *cylinder* in the symmetric case. Thus the slightest perturbation throws them way off (fig. 335). The type of perturbation is also critical, and it is only too easy to produce much more complicated star shapes.

Inside this asteroid the Gauss map is quintuply covered. This is evident if you draw equal height curves for the surface: you obtain two hills, one valley, and two passes (fig. 336).

It is not very hard to figure out the connectivity of the multiple covering of the Gauss map, although the exercise is largely of an academic

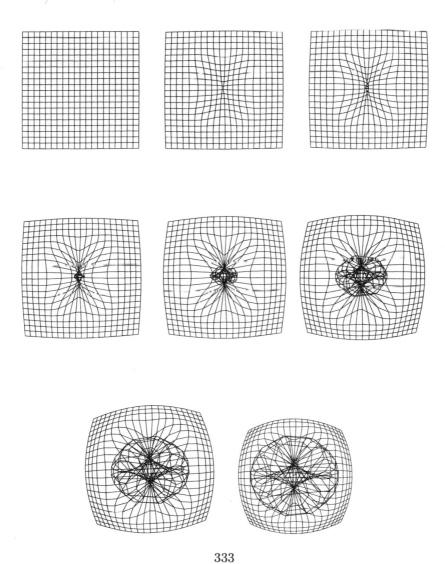

333

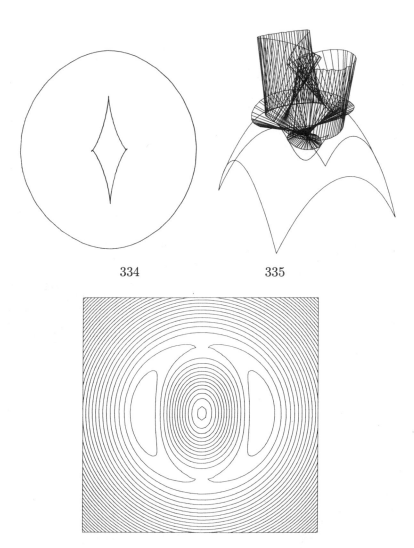

334   335

336

nature. In practice, it often suffices to treat the asteroid as a point and to neglect its inner structure. In any case, it is useful to keep the point representation in mind as a convenient overall model of the asteroid.

Figures 337 to 339 are an attempt to clarify the structure of the

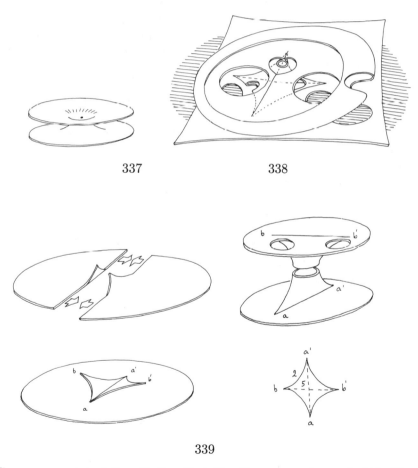

337   338

339

Gauss map pictorially. Notice that the Gauss map has a bubble-like outgrowth that is attached to the main covering in a remarkable manner: two sheets of the covering hang together (almost) *at a point*. However, this coarse view—although heuristically useful—is not generic. When you look closely, the "point" reveals a highly complex structure of folds and pleats. In the figures I use the simplest type of unfolding in which the point has been exploded into a quadruply cusped asteroid figure. You may use the window cut-outs to determine the multiplicity of the covering at different places in the sketch.

It is also very instructive to try to figure out how diverse routes over the surface would map on the Gaussian sphere. The routes are mapped on sometimes rather convoluted orbits because you double back on yourself when you meet a fold. For instance, try to figure out in how many different ways you can obtain split-off loops for straight-line cuts through the Gauss map. Such an exercise has a rather direct bearing on the study of possible illuminance patterns of the shape for various positions of the light source. I will discuss this application in more detail in a later chapter.

The decisive fact that makes the outer parabolic loop so singular is the circumstance that the principal direction for the zero principal curvature, that is, the direction that "causes" the parabolic loop, is *almost tangent to the parabolic curve*. For the inner loop the crossing is nearly *orthogonal*. The condition of nontransversality of the cylinder axis (the principal direction that "causes" the parabolic curve) and the parabolic curve is typical for a ruffle; thus the parabolic points on the outer loop are all very close to being ruffles. Figure 340 shows the principal direc-

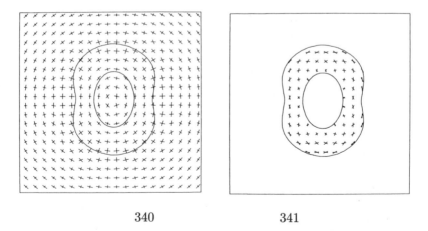

340   341

tions and figure 341 the asymptotic directions for the dimple. Again, the asymptotic directions are almost tangent to the outer loop, almost orthogonal to the inner one.

When you calculate the developable of cylinder axes, you find that the inner loop generates almost a cone. Notice that the apex is more complicated than a point if you look at it with high resolution though. It is composed of edges of regression and swallowtail points. On the other hand the outer loop generates two intermeshed, almost coincident surfaces that "share a common hole," that is to say, are sewn together in such a way as to approximate a double lamina with a common closed loop as an inner boundary. The latter doubly sheeted surface is the generic version of the doubly covered plane with a circular disc punched out of it in the symmetric example (fig. 342).

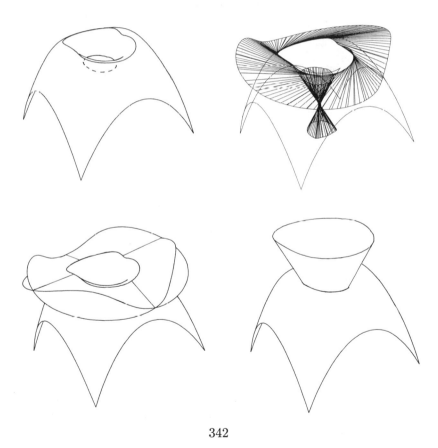

342

The structure of the asymptotic spherical image is somewhat complicated, and you may need a while to figure it out. Figure 343 shows the asymptotic parallel surface from a great distance and gives perhaps the clearest impression. Don't try to find the flecnodals in these figures; al-

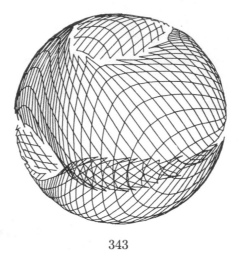

343

though present, they are hardly visible at all. In this case, the flecnodals *almost* (but not quite!) coincide with the parabolic curves. This makes them very hard to detect. Figures 344 to 346 show the image of the

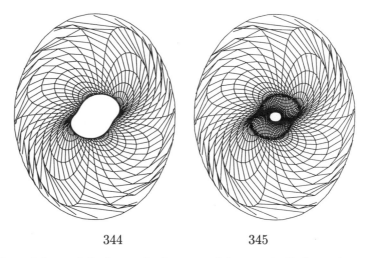

344   345

patch and figure 347 shows the images of the parabolic loops in stereographic projection. Each loop *appears twice* because I have also plotted the antipodal images. Each family of asymptotic directions generates an annular spherical image that *overlaps with its antipodal image*. This feature threw me for a while. It is essential for the understanding of the structure though. The images of the two families hang together at the images of the parabolic loops. Thus the sphere is largely covered with

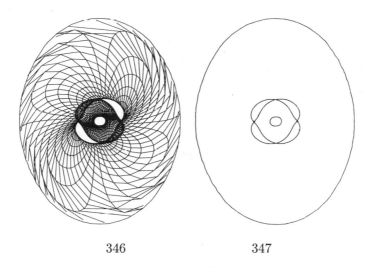

346   347

various degrees of multiplicity; only at the two poles are there uncovered
patches. They have the image of the inner parabolic loop as boundary.
The image of the outer parabolic loop winds around the equator, crossing it several times and thus also crossing its own antipodal image. This
generates a multiple covering of the sphere.

> Soft dimpled hands, white neck, and creamy breast,
> Are things on which the dazzled senses rest
> Till the fond, fixed eyes forget they stare.
> —JOHN KEATS, *Woman! when I behold thee*
> *flippant, vain (1817)*

7.4.3   The bell

The simple bell surface is another classic example in differential geometry. It was used by Hilbert and Cohn-Vossen ("Glocke") to illustrate a
simple fold of the Gauss map.

It is instructive to consider a slightly simplified form of the bell first,
namely the Gaussian hill (fig 348). There is only a single parabolic loop.

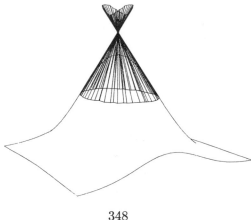

348

The summit of the hill is a convexity, whereas the rest of the surface is
saddle-like. The normals along the parabolic curve form a cone with the
apex buried inside the blob. The summit must map on an appreciable
area of the Gauss map because of its high curvature, whereas most of
the remainder of the surface is hardly curved at all and must map on a
relatively small area. This is evident from a look at the family of parallel
surfaces: the center indeed blows up considerably, and you get an oval
fold (fig. 349).

The cylinder axes are almost orthogonal to the parabolic curve, and
they generate an almost conical surface. This cone is clearly visible in
the asymptotic spherical image, where it is the boundary of the "gap"
(uncovered area). Figure 350 shows the asymptotic parallel surface at a
large distance, and figure 351 a stereographical projection of the asymptotic spherical image. Each family of asymptotic directions covers the
sphere completely except for this gap. In fact it is a hemisphere and its
antipodal image: the points at infinite distance from the summit map
to the equator.

This simple situation is only slightly more complicated when you con-

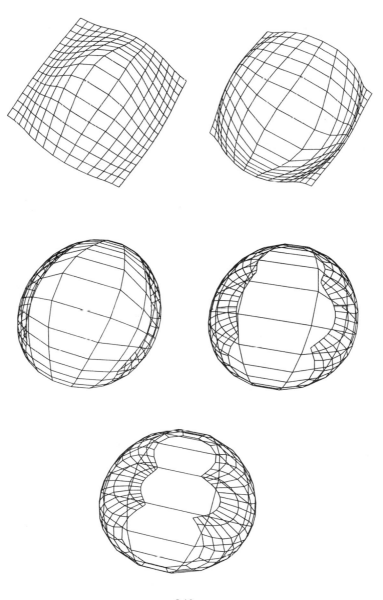

349

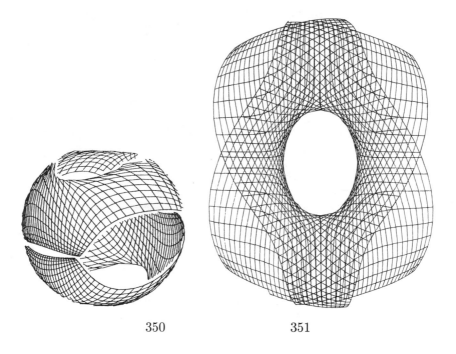

350   351

sider the "bell," which is a highly curved "wart" on an ovoid. The wart is surrounded by an anticlastic ring (figs. 352 and 353). The parallel sur-

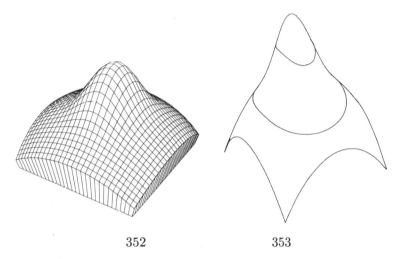

352   353

faces and the Gaussian image are quite similar to the Gaussian hill, with the exception that the overall convexity forces a second fold (figs. 354 to 356). Here you have an example of a complicated, *multiply covered Gaussian image without pleats,* for the Gauss maps of both parabolic curves are as smooth as can be. Figure 357 shows a fancy interpretation of the nature of the Gauss map.

This situation is much different from that of the dimple because for the bell *both* parabolic loops are of the "nice" type. This is clearly brought out by the pattern of principal and asymptotic directions. Figure 358 shows the principal directions, figure 359 displays the asymptotic directions.

The principal curvature vanishes on both parabolic loops for the principal direction that is almost orthogonal to them. This is possible for a convexity on a convexity but not for a concavity on a convexity, because in the latter case *both* principal curvatures must change sign. Thus you appreciate intuitively that the dimple *has* to have a "bad" parabolic loop, whereas it is *natural* for the bell to be "nice."

You may already have spotted the flecnodal curves in figure 359. An explicit calculation shows them encircling the summit. Of course, they can never reach the parabolic curves because there are no ruffles (fig. 360).

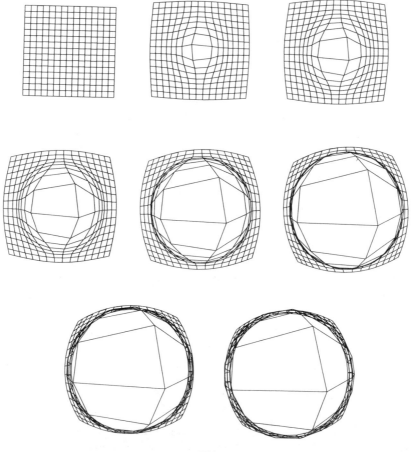

354

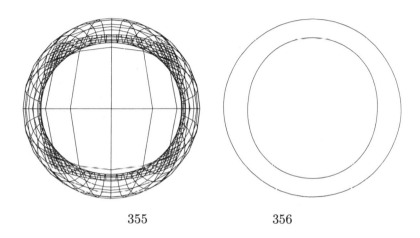

355   356

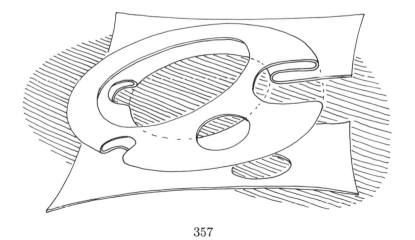

357

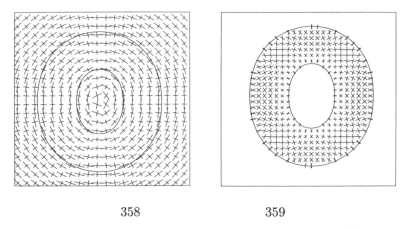

358   359

The developable surfaces generated by the cylinder axes of the parabolic points are indicated summarily in figure 361). These surfaces look

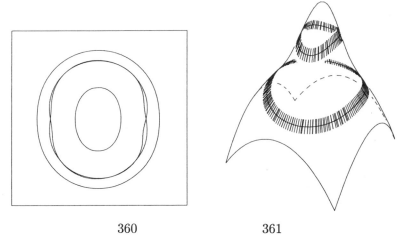

360   361

like "perturbed cones," I mean, like cones with their apices exploded
into an edge of regression. Indeed, cones as such are nongeneric entities.
The generic developable surface is the envelope of osculating planes of a
general space curve (its edge of regression).

When you compute the asymptotic spherical images of the parabolic
curves and flecnodal curves, including their antipodals, you obtain the
complicated pattern of figures 362 to 364.   The asymptotic parallel

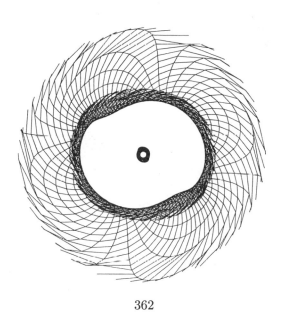

362

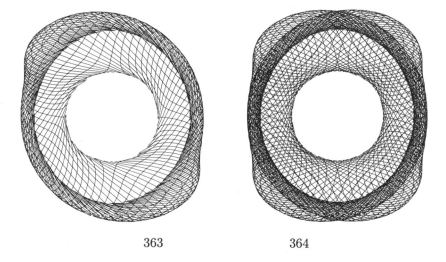

363 364

surface at a great distance for a single family may clarify what goes on
(figs. 365 and 366). At one side the image is bounded by the image of the

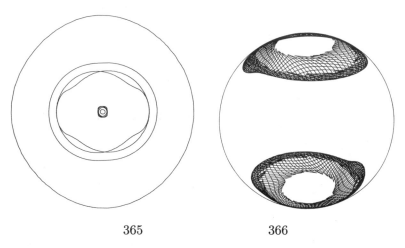

365   366

inner parabolic loop, which is the "gap" near the poles. At the other side
you have a *fold*, which is the image of a flecnodal curve and which bounds
the image against an annular equatorial gap. The image of the outer
parabolic loop lies within the covered part. When you put the images of
the two asymptotic families together, you obtain a complicated, multiply
covered image. Although it looks horrible it carries a lot of intuitive
content when you interpret it in terms of the visual projections of the
surface as seen from a variety of vantage points. I will discuss it at
length in a later chapter.

> *... what an oak blossom is like; only I know its bracts get together*
> *and make a cup of themselves afterwards, which the Italians call,*
> *as they do the dome of St. Peter's 'cupola' ...*
> —JOHN RUSKIN, *Proserpina (1874)*

7.4.4 The hump

The furrow is a hyperbolic island in an elliptic sea; its converse is the "hump": a convexity in the middle of a saddle-like area (figs. 367 and 368). Of course, this cannot occur unless the saddle-like area is itself

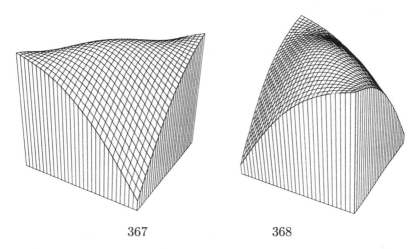

367   368

embedded (as a furrow say) in a larger context. Of course, it would be possible to consider furrow and hump as essentially *equivalent* because they are both made up from (topological) synclastic and anticlastic discs sewn together at the circumferences. However, I will distinguish them because I want to be able to consider the limiting cases in which you have either very small synclastic or very small anticlastic intrusions. You will understand the significance of this idea when you have read the chapter on morphogenetic sequences.

In contradistinction to the bell, dimple, and bean, the hump doesn't seem to belong to the waxworks of classical surfaces from differential geometry—at least I can't recall an example like it.

The Gauss map of the hump is very similar to that of the furrow, but of course, all orientations are reversed (figs. 369 and 370). Indeed, the hump is in many respects merely an "inside out" furrow. Again, you have two smooth folds ending in two pleats. However, this time the ruffles are not unodes, as in the case of the furrow, but tacnodes. *The hyperbolic part is outside the parabolic loop, not inside it.*

The pattern of principal directions for the hump is almost trivial;

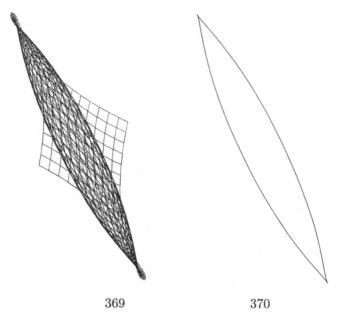

369   370

you can easily spot the tacnodal points where the principal direction of
zero curvature touches the parabolic curve (fig. 371). The asymptotic
directions also display the expected pattern (fig. 372). It is somewhat
difficult to spot the flecnodals in the previous picture, but an easy matter
to compute them (fig. 373). As you see, the hump is indeed in very many
respects just an "inside out" furrow.

The asymptotic spherical image of the hump is also very similar to
that of the furrow. Figure 374 shows the asymptotic parallel image at
a great distance. Figures 375 and 376 show several views of the stereographical projection of the asymptotical spherical image: figure 375 the
singular curves and figure 376 the coordinate patch with antipodes missing. Again you see the characteristic hourglass figure. This was to be
expected because the asymptotic spherical image of the parabolic curve
is a dual of the Gaussian image; thus inflexions correspond to cusps and
vice versa. The flecnodal scroll is different, however. It can't close, as
is the case with the furrow, because the hyperbolic area is not enclosed
within the parabolic loop but instead, extends to unknown distances
outside it.

Of course, you may dream up quite different types of "hump," or elliptic islands in hyperbolic seas. An example would be the perturbed

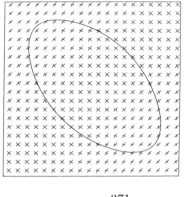

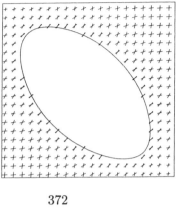

371   372

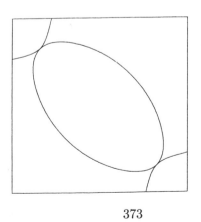

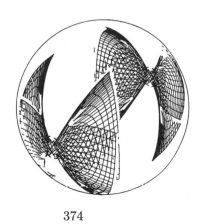

373   374

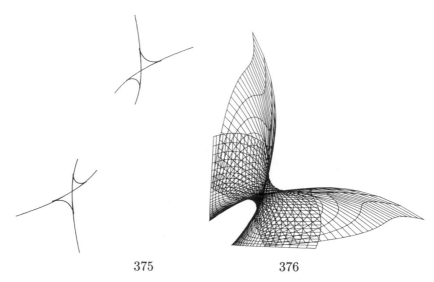

375   376

monkey saddle[22] with a triple-cusped asteroid as fold on the Gaussian
sphere. However, the present example is more interesting in the sense
that *you may blur it away*, which indicates that this hump can be regarded as the *simplest* local perturbation of a hyperbolic sea that gives
rise to an elliptic island. You can easily confirm that this doesn't work
for the perturbed monkey saddle.

The real rationale behind these remarks will only become clearer when
I discuss the fate of surface undulations under a blurring of blobs. The
furrow and the hump then appear as simple local articulations. If you
introduce the resolution of your density measurement as a parameter,
the notion of "simple undulation" indeed acquires an exact meaning:
a "simple undulation" is a feature that is lost if the resolution is below some threshold, and that suddenly appears when you increase the
resolution by an arbitrarily small amount.

Within this context the dimple proves to be of a more complicated
nature than the furrow in the following sense: if you start with a "primordial egg" or ovoid blob and "deblur" it, you have to pass through
a furrow stage before you can arrive at anything like the dimple. In a
later stage a hump arises within the anticlastic area of the furrow. Then
further changes occur that lead to the dimple as discussed earlier. This

---

[22]This example has been explained in detail at the close of the previous chapter.

involves a fairly complicated "script" involving local singularities of the "handkerchief surface" type.

This illustrates the intimate relations between the "furrow," the "hump," and the "dimple." In a later chapter I will illustrate an example in which *a single shape* appears as ovoid, ovoid with furrow, ovoid with furrow and hump, or ovoid with dimple, according to the *resolution* of your density measurement.

Nachdem ich diese Behauptungen aufgestellt,
bleibt für jeden einzelnen von Ihnen die Forderung bestehen,
sie an den Modellen selber zu prüfen
und dadurch seine Anschauung zu beleben.
—FELIX KLEIN, *Von der Versinnlichung idealer Gebilde durch Zeichnungen und Modelle (1928)*

7.5   Global Gauss-Bonnet

I really do not dare to pass up the opportunity to mention the summit of the differential geometry of surfaces, that is, the GLOBAL GAUSS-BONNET THEOREM. Most textbooks on differential geometry really work their way up to this glorious crescendo.

You have already been exposed to the fact that the integrated Gaussian curvature equals the holonomy angle for a traversal of the boundary of the patch. Consider what happens when you take all of the surface for your patch. Obviously the holonomy angle must be a multiple of 2π then, but *what multiple*? That the answer is not simple can be gleaned from the fact that the totally integrated Gaussian curvature must equal the algebraic surface of the covering of the Gauss map. At least so much is evident from the interpretation of the Gaussian curvature as the magnification of the Gauss map. Thus you understand right away that the ovoids have an integrated Gaussian curvature of 4π. Moreover the torus covers the Gaussian sphere twice, but with opposite signs: thus the algebraic surface area of the covering vanishes.

From topological arguments you may arrive at the conclusion that the integrated Gaussian curvature must equal 2π times the Euler number of the surface. This can be found, for instance, by considering simple triangulations of the surface.

This elegant "Gauss-Bonnet theorem" is extremely important in the development of the intrinsic geometry of surfaces involving global properties. It is only of minor importance for the purposes of this book, however, since the emphasis is almost completely on extrinsic, fairly local geometrical properties. I will make no further use of the theorem. If you are a geometer interested in geometry for its own sake and not a hard-nosed engineer interested in 3D extrinsic geometry for profit, you must realize that I have left out the best parts. Don't feel cheated—you know very well that you should be reading other books than this one.

8 Application to Ecological Optics

> *Painting consists of Outline drawing, Composition, and Reception of Light.*
> —LEON BATTISTA ALBERTI, *Della Pittura (1435)*

8.1 Ranging data

In many practical applications a shape is given through "ranging data," that is, the field of distances of the surface of the object with respect to some "vantage point." The mutual positions of object and vantage point are often *variable*, which complicates the problem because you now obtain *sets of ranging data* (a three-parameter family of scalar fields) and the problem arises of how to reconcile them.

I will consider both very distant and rather near vantage points. For the near vantage points the result will depend on the *position*, and consequently will depend on *three parameters*. I will refer to this case as the "near zone." For the very distant vantage points the distance itself doesn't really matter very much and the result depends essentially on *two parameters*, namely the visual direction, which can be neatly parametrized as a point on the "viewing sphere," that is, the manifold of all visual directions. In such cases the projection is almost a parallel projection.

The "visual directions" should be understood *not with respect to any particular vantage point*, of course. The notion often puzzles people, so I will spell it out somewhat further.

A *direction* in Euclidean space is best represented with a *line congruence*, namely a family of all lines parallel to a given one. Usually one gives the lines a sense of direction (all the same, of course). Such a congruence is indeed a pure direction without reference to any specific vantage point. In many applications the family of all planes orthogonal to the congruence ("orthotomics") are also very useful. The planes are the duals of the lines.

If you consider the unit sphere centered on an arbitrary point, then a direction can be mapped on a unique point of that sphere, namely the point where the member of the family of lines through the center meets the sphere. You may also arrive at this idea through the following intuitive construction:

Surround the object with a sphere (the center doesn't matter as long as the object is conveniently contained in it), then blow up the radius of the sphere a zillion times. Now scale the object and the sphere together such that the sphere becomes a unit sphere. As a consequence the object is reduced to a mere point (in fact as small as you want), at the center of the sphere. You have constructed "the viewing sphere of the object." You see that the viewing sphere is much like a sphere at infinity centered on the object. In physics one would call the viewing sphere the "far field," for a planar wave decomposition of which the orthotomic planes are the wavefronts and the directed lines the rays.

Sorry to have bothered you with all this, but I have noticed that many people have wrong ideas about the notion of the "viewing sphere."[1]

If the object has a largest diameter D, then you obtain essentially a parallel projection in the limit $\frac{D}{d} \ll 1$. Here d denotes the distance. Notice that *it does not suffice to have a small field of view in order to be permitted to invoke the parallel projection paradigm.* For example, the apparent size of the moon by far exceeds that of the planet Jupiter as you can sometimes see during conjunctions of these heavenly bodies. Yet we know very well that Jupiter is a huge body when compared with the earth's moon. Here parallel projection—the main virtue of which is that it preserves the size orthogonal to the line of sight—obviously doesn't apply at all, even though a field of view of only half a degree suffices to obtain full projections of these bodies. In the present formalism D would be the distance from the moon to Jupiter; thus the ratio $\frac{D}{d}$ is of the order of unity and certainly not small. I refer to the case $\frac{D}{d} \ll 1$ as the "far zone." Thus the problem with the moon and Jupiter is that *taken as a pair they are in the near zone,* although each *taken alone is in the far zone.* Trivial as all this may seem, people usually manage to screw things up, as you are bound to notice when you peruse the literature.[2]

For the near zone you can *parcellate* the ambient space of the object into cells such that you have *equivalent views* for all points within a cell. I will define the equivalence classes more precisely later on, but the general idea should be intuitively clear.[3] For the far zone the distance drops out as a relevant parameter, and only the viewing direction matters. Then you can parcellate the "viewing sphere" in the same manner.

---

[1] In the literature on computer vision, the viewing sphere is often confused with the Gaussian image. Why? I don't know.

[2] People usually assume that you can use the approximation of parallel projection if you just restrict the field of view sufficiently. This is—of course—an erroneous notion. For *arbitrarily* small fields of view you may obtain arbitrarily large effects of apparent size because of the unrestricted distance range.

[3] For instance, you may think of the "frontal," "side," and "rear" views of a building.

On the viewing sphere you will have polygonal cells of equivalent views, which I will later call "stable views."[4] These views are *stable* in the sense that you stay within the same equivalence class of views for a small movement. The cells are bounded with arcs that I will call "generic events" because a certain change of view occurs—you jump from one equivalence class to the next when you cross the arc—*no matter how you do it*. Thus the arc also represents an equivalence class of orbits that take you from one cell to the next.

The vertices of the polygonal cells are unimportant in the sense that it is infinitely unlikely to encounter them for a random orbit. They are very important from a structural point of view, however. That is because they "organize" the structure of the polygonal parcellation, and I will refer to them as *organizers*. In *space*, that is for the near zone, you have polyhedral cells corresponding to stable views, polyhedral faces that correspond to generic events, and polyhedral edges and vertices as organizers.

It has been pointed out [that] the artist, with his problem of making a unitary picture out of his complicated ideas of the three-dimensional, is compelled to separate clearly the two-dimensional appearance of the object from the general subjective idea of depth. Thus he arrives at a simple idea of volumes as a plane continuing in the distance. To make this manner of presentation quite clear, think of two planes of glass standing parallel, and between them a figure whose position is such that its outer points touch them. The figure then occupies a space of uniform depth measurement and its members are all arranged within this depth. When the figure, now, is seen from the front through the glass, it becomes unified into a unitary pictorial surface, and, furthermore, the perception of its volume, of itself quite a complicated perception, is now made uncommonly easy through the conception of so simple a volume as the total space here presented. The figure lives, we may say, in one layer of uniform depth ...

... The total volume of a picture will then consist, according to the objects represented, of a greater or lesser number of such imaginary layers arranged one behind the other, yet all together uniting into one appearance having one uniform depth measurement. ...
—ADOLF VON HILDEBRAND (1847-1921), *The Problem of Form*

---

[4]Of course, the edges need not be geodesics of the sphere; in fact they are usually curved and may even have singularities such as cusps.

8.1.1   The distance function

Let $\mathcal{P}(u, v)$ be a parametrization of the object and $\mathcal{V} = (x, y, z)$ the "vantage point." Then $d^2(u, v; x, y, z) = \|\mathcal{P} - \mathcal{V}\|^2$ is the "distance squared function," properly a map from $\mathbf{R}^2 \times \mathbf{R}^3$ to the positive reals ($\mathbf{R}^+$):

$$d^2 : \mathbf{R}^2 \times \mathbf{R}^3 \to \mathbf{R}^+$$

I will call it the "ranging map," for future reference.

Ranging data usually provide you with a set of sampled datapoints from this map, where (u, v) often will denote the "direction of sight." This dataset is usually very incomplete; just remember that you usually see only "the front" and not "the back" of an object. Moreover, you can only sample from a rather limited number of vantage points. Examples include radar, laser scanning, Moiré topography, and many more.

From differential topology you have the encouraging result that *for almost all vantage points the distance squared map is "Morse"*. This technical term means merely that the critical points of the ranging map will be isolated and nondegenerate and its critical values distinct. "Almost all" means that *if the function is not Morse, then an infinitesimal displacement suffices to bring this desirable situation about*.

The "bad" points lie on *surfaces* that meet along *curves*, which again are connected through points. Thus the "bifurcation set" parcellates space into cells such that you have a single topologically distinct view from a cell, whereas a "catastrophic" bifurcation occurs if you cross from one cell to the next. When the vantage point describes some orbit with respect to the object, then bifurcations will almost certainly occur.

However, *it will almost always be the case that a bifurcation has to do with the crossing of a boundary surface*. For it is infinitely unlikely that you will ever meet a singular *curve*, that is, an edge between two faces of the cells, or even less likely that you will ever find yourself at a singular *point*, that is, a vertex of a cell. The smallest deformation of the orbit would certainly suffice to prevent that.

Thus the generic events occur when you traverse a face of a cell, and you need consider no other singular cases.

8.1.1.1   How to take a view of the distance function

♠ Intermezzo—How to sample depth.

A simple but very effective way to actually *view the distance function in real time for arbitrary objects*, such as the faces of your friends, is to use "Moiré topography."

The principle is very simple. You place a regular grid of opaque strips with a dutycyle of 50 % and a wavelength of a few millimeters between your eye and the object. People have used fish line, wound over threaded rods and sprayed a dull black, with much satisfaction. I use grating patterns silkscreened on perspex sheets. My method has the advantage that I can mass produce screens if necessary and the disadvantage that it takes an initial investment. You may have more restricted aims.

The illumination is by a point source that is placed on your side of the fence. Then the shadow of the grid on the object consists of a complicated family of planar curves. Since you have to view these shadows through the grid, you get to see the well-known *Moiré beats*, which you may already be familiar with if you have some experience with garden fences. It is a simple matter of high-school geometry to show that these Moiré fringes happen to be *curves of equal depth*.

Such a machine is very easy and cheap to assemble and set up, but the result is little less than spectacular. I have spent hours trying to identify the generic surface undulations on real objects. It is really satisfying to be able to *see* the geometry without any fancy computation whatsoever. Just let the machine perform the stupid "number crunching" in the most elegant analog fashion—instant results—and lean back to enjoy the scene.

There are other ways to obtain a pictorial impression of the distance function: for instance, "structured light" devices (*German: "Schnittbildwerfer"*). You can also experiment with such devices at little cost. Just place a slide, opaque except for a narrow slit, into your slide projector and project it on your object at right angles from your line of sight. You then see an equal depth contour on the illuminated side of the object. This does work well in a way, but it is much less spectacular than the Moiré set up. Instead of a slit you may as well use a grating pattern, of course; then the results are much more spectacular. Some "official" versions have a *pair* of projectors beaming at the object from the left as well as from the right.

A classical but rather messy method also works rather well and is particularly easy to implement. You dip the object in a bath and somehow regulate the degree of partial immersion by such artifices as draining the bath, slowly lifting the object, and so forth. You obtain an equal height contour at the edge of the meniscus where the object dips into the fluid. Make sure that your objects are not the kind that dissolve. White objects dipped into a dark liquid are especially successful.

Sometimes you can see this method in the large, when you view submerged or flooded terrain from an aeroplane.

In the sixties, photographer Sam Haskins shook the world with his picture of a nude lady (white object) reclining in a bath of black coffee (dark liquid) with rather interesting results from a scientific point of view, although you may consider it funny, distasteful or artistic according to your mental makeup.[5] (Look for his album "Cowboy Jane.") Michelangelo is reputed to have invented this method, and much later the German sculptor Hildebrand based a once-famous artistic theory of solid shape on the principle.

8.1.2   The stable views

I call it outline for the sake of immediate intelligibility—strictly speaking, it is merely the edge of the shade; no pupil in my class being ever allowed to draw an outline in the ordinary sense. It is pointed out to him, from the first, that Nature relieves one mass, or one tint, against another; but outlines none.
—JOHN RUSKIN, *The Elements of Drawing (1857)*

A "stable view" is a ranging map from a generic vantage point. It looks pretty simple. For almost all viewing directions the *linear approximation* to the ranging data yields an excellent local approximation. It is usually described via values for the *tilt* and the *slant* of the local surface element.

Tilt and slant are the natural parameters to specify the tangent plane with respect to the vantage point. If the ranging map graphically displays curves of equal distance to the vantage point, then the tilt specifies the orientation of these curves, whereas the slant specifies their spacing. This is just another method to specify a *one-form*, of course, since slant and tilt just define the depth gradient.

There exist basically two types of singular elements for the stable views: the critical points of the distance function and the *envelope of the curves of equal distance*—or equivalently, the locus of slant equal to $\frac{\pi}{2}$. The latter singularity is the contour where the tangent planes are viewed "edge on." *The tangent planes project onto lines*, which is very degenerated compared to the generic case where they project onto *planes*. The former type of singularities are "specular points." Look perpendicularly to the tangent plane and you would see a reflection of your eye, if the surface were mirror-like.

The specular points come in three flavors: the extrema of the distance function, called "near" and "far" points, and the saddle points for which the surface curves toward the vantage point for some directions and away from it for others.

---

[5] Haskins gives some technical details: "The model is lying in 8 inches of black coffee. This was the only substance available at the time of the shooting with which we could darken the water—which incidentally was held in a plastic sheet draped over a wooden frame. The coffee had no harmful effects on the model's skin."

At a "near point" the surface curves away from the vantage point and the surface is locally convex, saddle-like or concave. It is likely to be *convex* if you are far away. At a "far point" the surface curves apparently toward the vantage point and the surface is locally concave. If the curvature equaled the inverse of the distance, the point would appear to be "flat," in the sense of "equidistant."

There is a simple rule to find out whether a surface patch will appear as a far, a near, or a saddle point. This rule is based on a count of the number of focal points on the line segment, that connects the vantage point with the object. A focal point is a point where the segment meets a caustic surface. If both centers of principal curvature are on the segment, the point appears as a far point. Of course this situation can only occur if the patch is a concavity. If no centers are on the segment, the point appears as a near point. This is always the case for a convexity, but notice that it might equally well occur for a concavity or a saddle-shaped patch! If only one center appears on the segment, the point appears as a saddle of the distance. This may happen for a saddle-shaped patch, but equally well for a concavity.

Thus, convexities appear as near points in all cases, hyperbolic points may appear either as saddles or as near points, and concavities may appear as far, as near, or as saddle points.

Figure 377 depicts lines of equal distance on a concavity for different

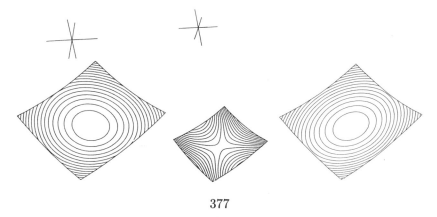

377

distances of the vantage point. From nearby you have a "near point," from an intermediate distance a saddle, and for a large distance a "far point." Figure 378 depicts the case for an anticlastic point. From nearby

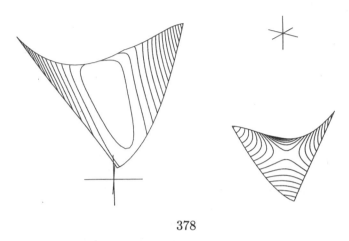

378

you get a near point; from afar, a saddle, in this case.

The distribution of the caustic surfaces in space obviously decides the issue. The cells of stable view are just the parcellation due to the caustic surfaces. This fact explains the *operational significance of the caustic surfaces*. For the far zone the caustic surfaces become asymptotic cones that are completely equivalent to the folds of the Gauss map. Thus the parcellation of the viewing sphere is simply the pattern of folds of the Gauss map.

This has been illustrated in the previous chapter for the "furrow." If the vantage point is located within the folded over part of the Gaussian sphere, you get one saddle and two near points (fig. 379). When the vantage point is outside this region (fig. 380), you get a single near point.

You need a bit of terminology to be prepared for a discussion of the structure of the *contour*. There exists no agreement on these terms, and I unashamedly employ my own inventions here.

These are the facts: if you look at an opaque object, there will be pieces of its surface that are *visible* and pieces that are *not visible* on account of the fact that pieces of the object are interposed between that piece of surface and your eye.

This is *the most basic fact of life as far as vision is concerned*, and you would expect it to be mentioned on the very first page of every book on vision. In fact it is typically left out altogether—probably because

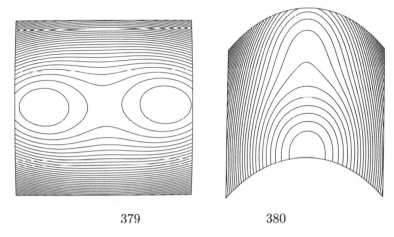

379   380

it's so obvious. The curve on the surface that divides these two regimes of visibility is sometimes called the "occlusion boundary,"[6] sometimes the "terminator,"[7] but I will use the term *rim*.[8]

In the natural projection the image of the rim appears as a curve called the *contour*.[9] Again, this is my terminology, and you are certain to encounter other uses of the same terms. Several variant expressions are in use.

The part of the contour which bounds that part of the visual field occupied by the projection of the object, which is commonly called the

---

[6]Obviously compounded from "occlusion" and "boundary." Webster's has: "oc.clù'sion (-zhun), *n.* (1) an occluding or being occluded." "**bound'à.ry,** *n.*; *pl.* **bound'à.ries** (-riz), [from *bound*, a limit; LL. *bunnarium, bonnarium,* a field with limits.] a limit; a bound; anything marking a limit. Sensation and reflection are the boundaries of our thoughts—Locke. **Syn.**—limit, border, bound, confine, extent, termination, margin, edge, wedge."

[7]Webster's has: "**tẽr'mi.nā.tŏr,** *n.* (1) one who or that which terminates. (2) in astronomy, the line dividing the illuminated and dark parts of the disc of the moon or a planet."

[8]Webster's has: "**rim,** *n.* [ME. *rime*; AS. *rima,* an edge, border] (1) the edge, border or margin, especially of something circular; often, a raised or projecting edge or border. **Syn.**—brim, brink, verge, edge, margin, circumference, periphery, ring."

[9]Webster's has: "**con.töur,** *n.* [Fr. *contour,* a circuit, circumference, from LL. *contornare,* to go around; from *com–*, intens., and *tornare* to turn; *tornus,* a lathe; Gr. *torsios,* a tool to make a circle with.] (1) the outline of a figure, a mass, land, etc. (2) the representation of such an outline. (3) in fortification, the horizontal outline of works of defense."

silhouette,[10] I call the *outline*.[11]

If you are an addicted reader of *footnotes* you will have noticed that the terminology is a real mess, and you will probably forgive me the coining of idiosyncratic terms. If you are not you may read on (probably a bit irritated) without missing a thing.

If you pretend that the object is made out of "tinted air," so you can *see through* it, you would see the fold of the natural projection of the surface of the object. This you can study in X-ray photographs. Bones make nice objects for studying the folds, especially their knobby parts near the joints.

Clearly the *outline* is a part of the *contour*, whereas the *contour* is part of the *fold*. Part of the *rim* belongs to the pre-image of the fold on the surface.

This pre-image is by far the simplest geometrical locus considered here. For a smooth object it is a smooth space curve; moreover, it is *closed*, although it may be composed of several disconnected loops.

In contradistinction with this nice entity, the fold may have cusps and self-intersections and thus is not necessarily smooth, although it too is closed. The contour is not even a closed curve, as it may "just end" at places. The rim is more complicated because it may involve obscuration by non-contiguous parts of the object. This is a "cast shadow"-like effect. This always happens when the fold self-intersects.

The structure of the contour depends in a complicated way on the position of the vantage point. This problem is treated in another section. Here I consider just two other types of singular points that have to do with the contour, namely its *near and far points*.

The locus of points on the object for which the tangent planes are seen edge-on, because they define the contour, is a smooth curve whose tangent is the conjugated direction of the line of sight. This is intuitively obvious if you remember the interpretation of conjugated directions in terms of surface "facets." Evidently the intersection of tangent planes that touch the surface at points along the direction of sight is the conjugated direction of the line of sight but is also the tangent to the locus of edge points. As you may recall, the conjugated directions are typically transverse but not orthogonal.

---

[10]Webster's has: "**sil.hŏu.ette'** (-ŏ-et'), *n.* [from Étienne de *Silhouette*, French minister of finance in 1759] (1) an outline drawing, especially a profile portrait, filled in with solid color: silhouettes are usually cut from black paper, and fixed on a light background. (2) any dark shape as outline seen against a light background."

[11]Webster's has: "**out'līne**, *n.* (1) a profile line; line bounding the limits of an object. (2) a sketch showing only the contours of an object without use of shading. **Syn.**—delineation, sketch, contour, draft, skeleton."

Thus *the locus typically runs into depth* and is not orthogonal to the line of sight, as it would be for a sphere. This is one of those facts of life that many people hate to accept. The true state of affairs is misrepresented in a great many texts and research papers on computer vision. I keep meeting people who'd rather disbelieve me than face the facts straight on. Be sure to adjust your inner vision if you sense a problem. It should suffice to study a single example.[12] *Typically the locus is not a planar curve, but a general space curve.*

Consider the far and near points on the locus. *At these points the locus must be orthogonal to the line of sight,* which means that the conjugated directions are *principal* directions. The conclusion is that you obtain a far or near point of the contour if the line of sight coincides with a principal ray, that is, a line that grazes the surface along a principal direction. The locus then touches the other principal direction. This indicates that you should study the "principal ray manifold" and the "principal spherical image." If you are in a portion of space where one or more principal rays go through every point, one will stably obtain that number of near and far points.

It is pictorially evident that you will at least obtain one near and one far point, but in fact the number may be larger than this. It may be infinite in the degenerate case of the sphere, but generically it will be some finite number. Thus you meet with yet another parcellation of space, one that is induced by the boundaries of the principal ray manifold. For very large viewing distances the principal spherical image suffices and the cells are defined through the folds of the principal spherical image. These folds are the images of the points at which the curves of principal curvature on the object cross their parabolic curves and points where the other principal direction has a geodesic inflexion. This is the curve of striction of the congruence.

The principal ray manifold seems not to have been treated in much detail in the literature. It appears to be hard to make any general observations about these manifolds without an extensive analysis. This need not bother you in the case of any applications, however. It is easy enough to compute the principal ray manifold in any special case. I have forged all the tools you need in the previous chapters.

It is an easy matter to obtain an insight in the local pattern of equidis-

---

[12]It should be obvious that the locus runs into depth for a *cube*. If you think this is typical for a polyhedron, you might consider a *cylinder*. If you believe the facts to be due to the singular nature of the cylinder, try an *ellipsoid*. If you are the stubborn type, you will grant that the locus runs into depth but tell me that it certainly has to be a planar curve. In that case you really have to do some homework. For instance try the *torus*.

tance curves near a contour for both the generic arc and for the near and
far points (fig. 381). The pattern of projections of lines of curvature is

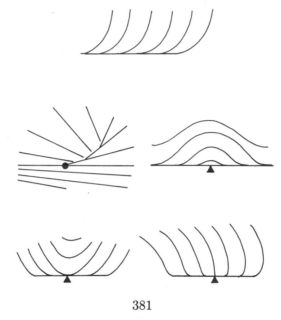

381

also characteristic. Notice that at the near and far points of the contour
the projection must show a cusp because you view the line of curvature
from a tangent direction.

There is one additional singularity of the contour that merits attention. This is the fact that at certain places the contour itself may cusp
because you view it in the tangent direction. Of course, its pre-image
is smooth and in no way cusps. Figures 382 and 383 show it in realistic
detail. *This will be the case when you look into an asymptotic direction
because the asymptotic directions are self-conjugate.* Of course, you will
only be able to see one branch of the cusp because the other branch
must be hidden, occluded by the object itself. Thus *you look at an
ending contour.*

The ending contours will be created when you cross a fold of the
asymptotic spherical image.

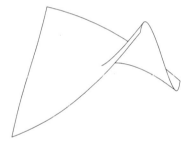

382

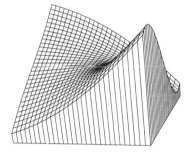

383

8.1.2.1   How to view the outlines of shapes

♠ INTERMEZZO—SHADOW PLAY.

A good way to study the changes in the outline of a shape is to place it on (let's say a record-) turntable in front of a translucent screen illuminated from behind. Alternatively you may view the shadow on a screen thrown by the shape when you place it in the beam of a slide projector. Since you can't make out surface detail in such circumstances, you must judge the shape purely on the basis of the outline. The genesis of pairs of inflexions is especially clear in this setup. The shadow method is very nice since you can also study the pre-image of the outline on the object itself. It is simply the edge of the attached body shadow. This is a simple method to find many important special points and curves on the object.

A drawback of both setups is that *you can't see contours within the outline.* This is actually possible if you don't use opaque bodies but surfaces bent out of wire mesh, such as copper gauze with relatively wide mazes. I have performed some successful demonstrations with common gauze curtain material. It is a rather spectacular sight to see the cusps develop in such a setup. In radiography you often see nice examples in X-ray pictures of bones, especially at the joints where the bones develop interesting shapes. This technique works much better than looking at transparent—say glass—objects in visible light (fig. 384). This is the case because the refractive indices for the X-rays are essentially unity, whereas the index for most transparent objects (such as the bottoms of broken beer bottles) is much higher than that of the surrounding air. The refraction spoils much of the fun because it warps the visual projection of contours that are behind curved surfaces.

8.1.3   The generic events

You can find the generic events via "catastrophe theory." You have the case of a *potential*, the distance squared function, with two variables (u, v) and a single control parameter, the arclength of the orbit. I don't treat catastrophe theory in this book, but merely provide a short primer. For the distance field within the projection, sufficiently far away from the contour, a generic event is the creation or destruction of an extremum-saddle pair. The extremum could either be a near or a far point.

What happens in the case of a creation—for a destruction the script simply runs backward, of course—is that an equidistance curve develops a vertex of ever-increasing curvature. When the curvature reaches an

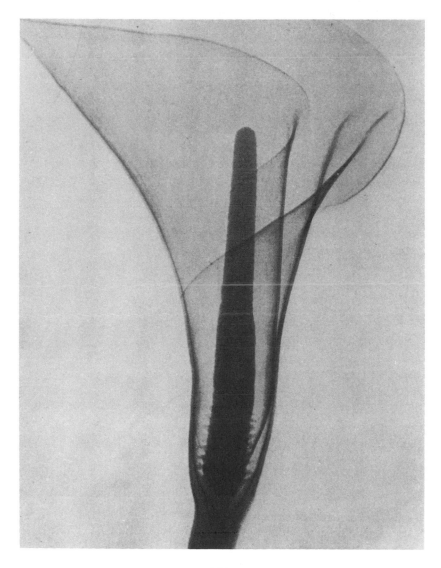

384

infinite value, the vertex changes momentarily into a cusp which then immediately splits into a saddle and an extremum.[13]

This kind of event is dramatically demonstrated via a Moiré contouring set up where you can observe the equidistance curves in real time. It can also be demonstrated via computer graphics, of course, although only in real time if you have a very powerful machine. Figures 385 to 387 illustrate the process for the Gaussian hill. The bifurcation set for the

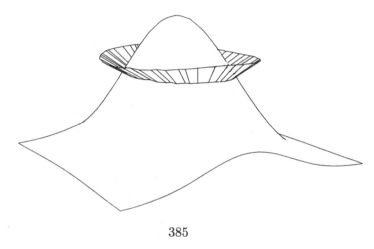

385

large distances is just the cone of parabolic normal rays. When you cross it, you create an extremum-saddle pair. The figure also illustrates the chimeric "in between" situation, namely a cusped equidistance contour.

You seldom have the opportunity to catch the chimerical "in between" case in practice, although I managed to find an example in a paper on Moiré contouring techniques in medical engineering (fig. 388). In this photograph of a mannequin you easily find near and far points, saddles, the contour as envelope with near and far points of the contour and a clearly cusped equidistance contour on the *sternum*. This example merits careful study. Can you point out synclastic and anticlastic points?

For the far distance you obtain more complicated patterns for the ruffles. In the near zone these same patterns occur on the edges of regression

---

[13]You can often observe a similar phenomenon during slide shows when the slides are of the old-fashioned glass framed type. The heat of the projector makes the film bulge, with the result that the air space between film and glass becomes a hilly landscape that changes with time. Interference fringes conveniently throw curves of equal thickness on the screen. (At this point someone in the audience usually warns in a loud voice that the slide is melting.) You observe the event mentioned here when new loops split off or when existing loops merge.

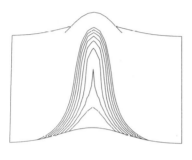

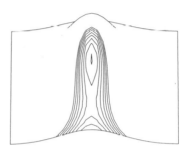

386 387

388

of the caustic surfaces. They are the familiar Dupin's indicatrices of the ruffles. In the near zone you also have special *points*, namely the cusps on the edges of regression of the caustics—the ribs—that are the foci of the umbilical points. These patterns are similar to the indicatrices of the handkerchief surface and the monkey saddle, but I will not elaborate this any further.

The events having to do with near and far points of the contour are of a very different kind. The contour appears as the envelope of equidistance curves. At a far or near point of the contour the equidistance curves are approaching from different directions at both sides of the point. A versal event means the creation or destruction of a pair consisting of a near and a far point.

For the far zone this obviously happens when the direction of view crosses a fold of the principal spherical image. Here you have a boundary where you have a pair of principal directions on one side and no principal directions on the other. The events at the contour are more complicated and do not yield to the methods of simple catastrophe theory. The main problems involving the topological structure of the contour have only been solved in recent years by—mainly—Gaffney and Arnold.

8.1.4   Bulges and hollows

The topological structure of the field of equidistance contours is governed by just a few singular elements. These are:

- the far, the near and the saddle points

- the contour

- the near and far points of the contour

- the points of ending contour

- the tangencies of contours and equidistance contours on remote patches (fig. 389)

- the equidistance curves through these singular points.

The curves divide the visible surface into cells, which can be divided into *bulges and hollows*. "Bulge" and "hollow" should not be confused with the terms "convex" and "concave." The latter terms are reserved for the "absolute" shape description used in the previous chapters; the former are *relative to the vantage point*. Thus a concavity may be a

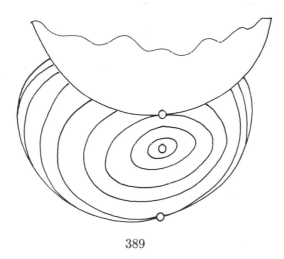

389

"bulge" if you are nearby. When you change the vantage point, the pattern of bulges and hollows changes at each event.[14]

The bulges and hollows are connected with each other via the saddle points. There are four distinct types of combination. These will be found nested to sometimes appreciable depth and juxtaposed in typical applications (fig. 390).

Simple topological considerations yield a mild but useful constraint on the number of critical points.

Useful fact: *The number of extrema minus the number of saddles equals the Euler characteristic of the surface.*

Thus you must have equal numbers of extrema and saddles on the torus, whereas you can have a situation with just two extrema (no saddles at all) on the sphere. Such relations are intuitively obvious for simple shapes, but sometimes useful for more complicated ones.

Because the rule only applies to *the surface as a whole,* you will rarely be able to apply it to real ranging data: you typically see only the frontal side.

---

[14]There don't appear to exist unambiguous terms that take the difference into account. All terms relating to shape are of the "absolute" type. "Bulge" is defined by Webster's as "[ME. *bulge,* a swelling, lump; Sw. *bulgja,* to swell; AS. *belgan,* to swell.] the protuberant or most convex portion of a thing; a part that swells out ..." and "hollow" as "[AS. *holge, holh,* a hole] a depression or excavation below the general level or in the substance of anything ...." I guess that, strictly speaking, these terms don't apply very well. No language known to me seems to recognize the distinction.

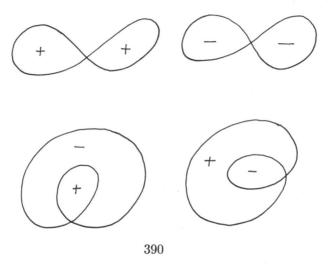

390

. . . painting does not, as a matter of fact, extend beyond the surface;
and it is by the surface that the body of any visible thing is
represented.
—LEONARDO DA VINCI (1452–1519)

8.2 The contour

8.2.1 The apparent curvature

Suppose you view a point $\mathcal{P}$ on the surface that happens to lie on the contour. At the contour the tangent planes have a slant of ninety degrees and thus must have a degenerate projection. They get squashed into a line. Figure 391 shows a schematic figure of this situation.

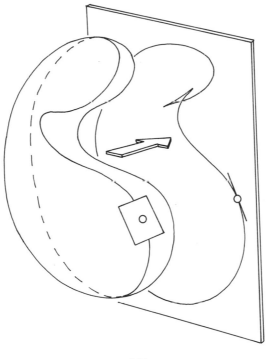

391

If you are at a great distance, the visual rays that *graze the surface* near $\mathcal{P}$ will be the generators of a cylindrical surface (fig. 392). A little thinking will reveal the (pictorially rather obvious) fact that the curvature of the section of this cylinder of grazing visual rays with a plane that is orthogonal to the rays equals *the curvature of the contour in parallel projection.* What is its value?

This problem is easily solved with the methods presented in the previ-

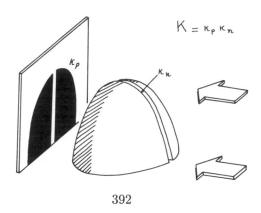

$$K = \kappa_p \, \kappa_n$$

392

ous chapters. In fact it was solved by Blaschke more than half a century ago with the result (κ_c denotes the cylindrical curvature):

$$\kappa_c^{-1}(\varphi) = \kappa_1^{-1}\sin^2\varphi + \kappa_2^{-1}\cos^2\varphi,$$

where φ denotes the angle of the visual ray with respect to the first principal direction. The theorem appears as a formal "dual" of the theorem of Euler. Remember that Euler's formula gives the normal curvature for an arbitrary normal section of the blob. You may attempt to prove it yourself. It is a straightforward enough "classroom-variety" problem.

You may well be curious whether it would be possible to derive something similar for the near zone. It is indeed possible to find a convenient expression. The problem becomes manageable if you use a lemma, which Blaschke generously ascribes to Mannheim, that is, a formal "dual" of the theorem of Meusnier. Remember that Meusnier's theorem gives the curvature for planar sections with arbitrary inclinations with respect to the normal plane. You have:

Mannheim's Sphere: *Let α be a visual ray grazing the surface at $\mathcal{P}$. Consider the osculating cones of visual rays that graze the surface for different points $\mathcal{Q}$ on α. Then these cones envelope a sphere that osculates the surface in P (the so-called "Mannheim sphere").*

The radius of the Mannheim sphere is $\kappa_c(\varphi)^{-1}$ because the tangent cylinder is one of the osculating cones (namely for the infinitely far point on α), and the sphere must have the same radius as the cylinder.

The osculating cones can equally well be thought of as *small circles* on the sphere of visual directions. Just imagine a sphere centered on the vantage point and look for the intersection with the osculating cone. The geodesic curvature of the circle on the sphere corresponding to a cone with semi-top angle ϑ is $\cot\vartheta$. For a distance d from the vantage point Q to P the semi-top angle is $\arctan\frac{R}{d}$, where R is the radius of the Mannheim sphere.

Combining these expressions, you obtain the apparent curvature of the contour as:

$$\kappa_a(d,\varphi) = \frac{dK}{H - \frac{\kappa_2 - \kappa_1}{2}\cos 2\varphi},$$

an expression that neatly expresses the curvature of the projection in terms of the principal curvatures of the surface and the position of the vantage point relative to the surface. The position dependence is expressed through the dependence on the parameters φ and d.

The practical importance of this expression in the science of natural perspective, hence also for robot vision and human vision, can hardly be overestimated. Yet the relation is not very well known and I have yet to encounter it in the literature. It comes as a surprise that Blaschke did not hit upon this theorem, especially since there is an especially pleasing and elegant interpretation of the result (see below) of exactly the type that Blaschke seems to have enjoyed.

Notice that Euler's formula allows you to express the curvature of the normal section of the object *in the direction of the line of sight* in terms of the angle φ. You begin with:

$$\kappa_n(\varphi) = \kappa_1\cos^2\varphi + \kappa_2\sin^2\varphi = H - \frac{\kappa_2 - \kappa_1}{2}\cos 2\varphi$$

You may eliminate φ from the expression for the apparent curvature. The result is

$$\kappa_a = \frac{dK}{\kappa_n},$$

or, if you want the appropriate result for parallel projection:

$$K = \kappa_c\kappa_n,$$

surely a very elegant result. Here the Gaussian curvature appears as an "average curvature," not an average in the arithmetic but in the geometrical sense, and not of orthogonal normal sections but of a normal section and a projected outline.

This extremely simple expression is very convenient in practice. The key point to notice is that

Important triviality: *κ_n always has the same sign because the visual ray runs through the air and not through the material of the blob.*

Thus

Important fact: *the sign of the apparent curvature is the sign of the Gaussian curvature.*

Anticlastic points look concave (figs. 393 to 396), convex points look

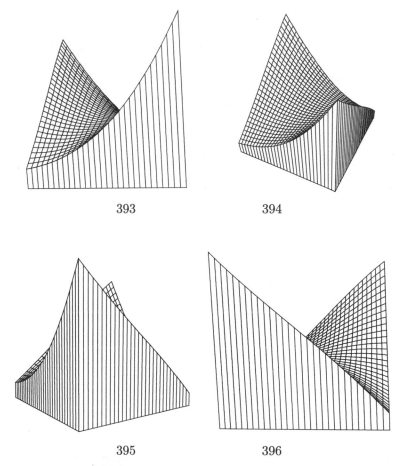

393   394

395   396

convex (figs. 397 to 400), and parabolic points lead to inflexions of the contour.

It is a trivial consequence of these relations that *a concave point never appears on the contour at all* (figs. 401 to 404). The fact is nevertheless

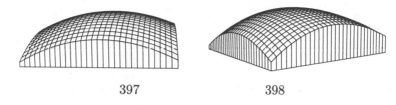

397 398

399 400

401 402

of the greatest *practical* importance.

403   404

The expression for the apparent curvature carries a lot of intuitive content and it is important to grasp it fully. Several of the dependencies are almost trivial, such as the linear dependence on the distance.

Just think of a sphere of radius r at distance d. The apparent radius of the disc is approximately rd^{-1} and thus the curvature $\frac{d}{r}$. The interesting news is that the linear relation holds *exactly* for arbitrary distances.

The proportionality with $\frac{K}{\kappa_n}$ is trivial if you look in a principal direction, because then this expression is equal to the other radius of principal curvature. Again, the interesting news is that this relation holds *exactly* for arbitrary directions.

Notice that the present discussion suggests an intuitively and formally attractive parallel to the well-known result that the mean curvature equals the mean of the normal curvature of any pair of mutually orthogonal normal cuts. As far as I know, no text attempts to formulate anything similar to this for the Gaussian curvature. Here you have arrived at the conclusion that the Gaussian curvature is the square of the *geometrical mean* of the curvature of any normal section and the curvature of the projection on an orthogonal plane. For any but the principal directions this is an elegant and nontrivial result. It is possible to give a completely elementary proof of this result (next subsection).

Several straightforward consequences of these results are extremely important in a great many applications:

Important Facts: *The curvature of the contour reflects the curvature of the surface in the following ways*:

- *Synclastic patches yield convex contours for convexities, whereas there is no contour for concavities.*

- *Anticlastic patches yield concave contours for those lines of sight that give rise to a contour at all.*

- *The inflexions of the contour occur on the projection of the parabolic curves; thus "inflexions project to inflexions."*

- *In the asymptotic directions the normal curvature vanishes; thus the apparent curvature becomes infinite (you have already seen that the contour cusps at such points).*

Thus you can really tell quite a lot about the nature of the local surface patch from the nature of the visual contour.

8.2.1.1   An elementary proof of the theorem on projected curvature

♠ Intermezzo—How elementary can you get?

Take a coordinate system with x, y in the tangent plane, z along the normal. Then the Hessian of the height function

$$z(x,y) = \frac{1}{2}(z_{xx}x^2 + 2z_{xy}xy + z_{yy}y^2) + \ldots$$

determines the surface locally.

When you set $x = 0$ you obtain the curve $z = \frac{1}{2}z_{yy}y^2$ in the y-z-plane. Thus you may conclude that the curvature of the normal cut with the y-z-plane equals z_{yy}. Similarly the curvature of the normal cut with the x-z-plane is z_{xx}. The sum of these curvatures is the trace of the Hessian.

The parallel projection on the y-z-plane is obtained when you set $z_x = 0$; thus $z_{xx}x + z_{xy}y = 0$. This expression can be used to eliminate the coordinate x from the height function, giving you $z = (z_{xx}z_{yy} - z_{xy}{}^2)y^2/2z_{xx}$. This is the desired projection. You appreciate that the product of the curvature of the projection (which is seen to equal the determinant of the Hessian divided by z_{xx}) with the curvature of the normal cut by the x-z-plane (which equals z_{xx}) is just the determinant of the Hessian.

The trace and the determinant of the Hessian are invariant against rotations in the tangent plane. Thus you have reached the conclusions:

Fact 1: *The trace equals the sum of the curvatures of any pair of mutually orthogonal normal sections.*

Fact 2: *The determinant equals the product of the curvature of any normal section with the curvature of the projection of the surface on an orthogonal plane.*

The first observation is nothing but the well-known fact that the mean curvature can be found from the sum of the normal curvatures of any pair of orthogonal normal cuts. The second observation is never mentioned, as far as I know, but appears to be equally noteworthy:

Theorem: *the Gaussian curvature can be found from the product of the normal curvature of an arbitrary plane with the curvature of the projection on an orthogonal plane.*

8.2.2   The stable views

Each profile is actually the outer evidence of the interior mass; each is
the perceptible surface of a deep section, like the slices of a melon, so
that if one is faithful to the accuracy of these profiles, the reality of the
model, instead of being a superficial reproduction, seems to emanate
from within. The solidity of the whole, the accuracy of the plan, and
the veritable life of a work of art, proceed therefrom . . .
—AUGUSTE RODIN (1840–1917)

The shape of the contour can lead to surprises at first sight. It is
possible to obtain some general insight when you first study the *local
stable features.*

From the previous section you can guesstimate the stable views of a
piece of the contour. The official way makes use of "catastrophe theory"-
like methods again. The following possibilities exist for a local surface
patch (fig. 405):

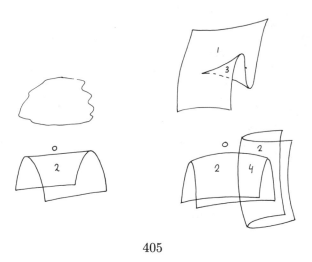

405

- The patch isn't on the contour at all. Then the visual image is
  just a deformed map of the surface patch without singularities.

- The simple fold, that is, a smooth piece of contour. If you are
  interested in the curvature you may make a subdivision into:

    − a convex arc

- a concave arc

- an inflexion.

- The pleat, that is a cusp of the contour. Because you look into an asymptotic direction, the patch must be anticlastic; hence the ending contour is necessarily concave.

- The T-junction. This is a bilocal rather than a local feature. If you are so disposed, you may distinguish different flavors of T-junctions according to the curvature of the branches.

The final possibility—the T-junction—is merely a transversal crossing of two folds. This is *not a local* but at best a *bilocal* feature. I will discuss it at greater length in the next section.

Thus the structure of the contour is very simple indeed. If you disregard occlusion ("objects of tinted air"), the contour consists of a number of loops which may display inflexions and cusps. There exist more constraints, though. For instance, although self-intersections are not forbidden, not just any old self-intersection is allowed (no figure-eight-shaped contours); and although cusps are common, you can't have a loop with a single cusp. This is not the place to elaborate such constraints. They are of a topological type.

Remember that I discuss only *generic cases*. When you experiment with man-made objects, you will often fail to verify the rules given here because all kinds of degenerations due to symmetries compound the singularities.

A good example is the torus. Here you have some extremely degenerated views because the two parabolic curves are planar and completely made up of unodes. When you perturb the torus a bit, you obtain shapes that satisfy the general observations in full detail, of course. I illustrate such a warped torus here (figs. 406 to 409). You will be able to detect many of the singularities mentioned in the text in these figures. It is an interesting exercise to try to relate the generic views of the warped torus to the degenerated views of the true one. This will give you some inkling of the complications you are likely to encounter when you play with overly symmetrical objects.

8.2.2.1 A quick primer on "Catastrophe Theory"

♠ Intermezzo—For those who missed Thom.

First of all you shouldn't miss Thom: his book should really be part of your general cultural background. If you *have* read him you should skip this

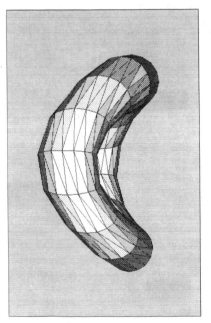 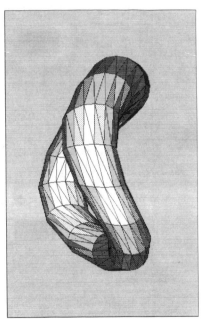

406   407

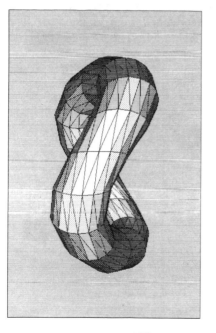 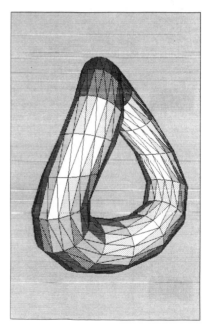

408 409

section. If you haven't, you can expect to obtain at least an inkling of what catastrophe theory is about.

Since the subject commonly known as "catastrophe theory" (well-known for its catchy name) is of rather minor importance in the context of this book—although I make use of its results several times—I will not spend a great deal of space on it. I will merely indicate some of the superficial flavor. The discussion will be slanted toward applications rather than deep understanding. The subject is of an algebraic rather than of a true geometric nature, which is why it fits in rather badly in the present text.

A "natural" setting from the standpoint of the physicist is that of the caustics in geometrical optics. I will adopt the language of this discipline here, rather than use abstract algebraic concepts.

The "rays" of geometrical optics can be defined in many different ways. One particularly advantageous method is to use Fermat's principle of extremal length. Fermat's principle constrains possible rays to those curves that extremize the "optical pathlength." You may recall, or perhaps you want to look it up in an optics textbook, that Fermat's principle allows you to derive the reflection and refraction laws in a particularly elegant and simple manner.

Let Φ denote the optical pathlength. It depends on essentially two completely different types of parameters, the so-called *state variables* and the *control parameters*. What is meant by that can be explained as follows.

The state variables label the possible rays so far as they are compatible with the given problem. For example, the rays transmitted from a point source could be labeled by their directions. The control parameters are of a completely different nature. They essentially specify possible perturbations of the problem itself. For instance, they might specify the position of the point source. I will write $\Phi(s; c)$, where s denotes the state variables $\{s_1, \ldots\}$ and c the control variables $\{c_1, \ldots\}$. The value of Φ is merely the pathlength for the ray labeled by s that satisfies the condition c.

Fermat's principle specifies that the only rays that occur in geometrical optics are those for which the pathlength is extremal, that is, $\Phi(s + \triangle s; c)$ should vanish to the first order in $\triangle s$. You could also write $\delta\Phi = 0$, "the first variation of Φ vanishes." In general there may well exist multiple solutions, which I will label s^ξ for $\xi = \{0, 1, \ldots\}$. In heuristic terms the solutions are merely the peaks, pits, and passes of the "landscape" Φ considered as a function of the state variables.

When you then proceed to turn the knobs on the control variables, you really *change the topography of the landscape*. That means that you may actually introduce extra critical points and thus change the multiplicity of the solution.

This is indeed a well-known phenomenon in geometrical optics. The multiplicity of rays through a point in space often jumps at certain singular surfaces known as the caustics of the ray congruence. At a caustic, *rays merge*; thus the local ray density must be very high. In a very real sense *the caustics are*

the only features of ray manifolds that you can actually observe. Just blow a
little smoke into the light beam and they immediately light up. It is of obvious
importance to be able to compute the caustics.

Intuitively the caustics occur when peaks or pits of the landscape collide
with a pass when you change the controls. This happens when the critical
point is not Morse, that is, whenever the determinant of the Hessian vanishes
at a critical point. Thus the conditions for a caustic are:

$$\frac{\partial \Phi}{\partial s_i} = 0 \quad \text{for all } i$$
$$\det \left\| \frac{\partial^2 \Phi}{\partial s_i \, \partial s_j} \right\| = 0 \quad ,$$

for then Fermat's principle is satisfied to an even higher degree than merely
the first order.

This condition is not at all generic, of course. For almost all points in control
space it will not be satisfied. Because there is one condition "too much,"
you may guess that the special conditions will be satisfied on manifolds of a
dimensionality that is one less than the dimensionality of control space. Thus
"the caustics are of codimension one." They will be surfaces in three-space,
or curves in the plane, and so forth.

Catastrophe theory permits you to obtain a complete overview of the zoo
of a class of singular structures—in this example the "caustics." The classification is in terms of equivalence classes that comprise shapes that are diffeo-
morphic. That means that equivalent forms are the same up to an arbitrary
smooth coordinate transformation in control space. Locally this looks—to the
first order—like an affine transformation. Such an equivalence class is known
as a "catastrophe."

In simple, that is, low-dimensional cases such as you encounter in this book,
these equivalence classes are structurally stable, that is, stable against infinitesimal perturbations of the function Φ. This means that the theory disregards "degenerated cases" completely. An example would be the caustic of
a spherical wavefront. This is a mere point, which escapes the classification
of catastrophe theory. However, such cases are in some sense "infinitely unlikely," which is why people are prepared to spend a lot of money on camera
lenses that are supposed to be able to generate spherical wavefronts, whereas
any junk piece of glass such as the bottom of a broken beer bottle will give
you a nice generic caustic for free.

The standard classification is in terms of the "codimension." What is meant
is the dimension of the control space decreased by the dimensionality of the
singularity. This amounts simply to the number of essentially available control
parameters. In books on the subject you will find tables that specify simple
representatives of the equivalence classes, typically nonlinear polynomials in
the state variables augmented with linear terms in the control variables. For
the applications in this book the control variables will either be a position in
three-space, where you will have three control parameters—say the Cartesian
coordinates (x, y, z)—or else a direction of view which can be parametrized

with two variables, say azimuth and elevation. These cases are covered by Thom's famous "theorem of the seven." But you don't need them all for the present purpose. I introduce only a five-tuple of "The Seven." The so called "normal forms" are:

The Fold $\hspace{8cm} \frac{s^3}{3} + cs$

The Cusp $\hspace{6cm} \frac{s^4}{4} + c_2\frac{s^2}{2} + c_1 s$

The Swallowtail $\hspace{4cm} \frac{s^5}{5} + c_3\frac{s^3}{3} + c_2\frac{s^2}{2} + c_1 s$

The Elliptic Umbilic $\hspace{2cm} s_1{}^3 - 3s_1 s_2{}^2 - c_3(s_1{}^2 + s_2{}^2) - c_2 s_2 - c_1 s_1$

The Hyperbolic Umbilic $\hspace{2cm} s_1{}^3 + s_2{}^3 - c_3 s_1 s_2 - c_2 s_2 - c_1 s_1$

The fold has codimension 1, the cusp codimension 2, whereas the swallowtail, and the two umbilics—don't confuse these normal forms with the umbilics defined in the text—are of codimension 3.

Let's try a simple example. For planar curves you may consider the distance of some arbitrary point (u, v) from the curve $(x(t), y(t))$. This distance is $\Phi(t; u, v) = (x(t) - u)^2 + (y(t) - v)^2$. I have taken the distance squared function, rather than the distance itself, simply because it is more convenient to work with. The "rays" in this example are obviously the straight lines that meet the curve orthogonally, or in other words the normal ray congruence of the curve. Since you have a two-dimensional control space, you expect folds and cusps, the folds being one-dimensional singularities and the cusps mere points. Just count the codimension. Let's consider the fold by way of an example. The conditions for the caustic are:

$$s^2 + c = 0 \quad \text{and} \quad 2s = 0,$$

thus $s = c = 0$; hence the singularity sits at the origin. The rays are $s = \pm\sqrt{-c}$; thus you will have no rays at all if $c > 0$, whereas you have two rays if $c < 0$.

Similarly, for the cusp the conditions are

$$s^3 + c_2 s + c_1 = 0 \quad \text{and} \quad 3s^2 + c_2 = 0,$$

thus $c_2 = -3s^2$ and $c_1 = -2s^3$; again the singularity sits at the origin. That's built into the normal forms. By elimination of s you arrive at the relation $4c_2{}^3 + 27c_1{}^2 = 0$ for the shape of the singular set in control space. This curve in control space has a cusped shape, hence the name for this particular singularity. The ray equation is of the third order and you obtain either a single or a triple solution.

You may explicitly consider a simple case—for instance, the parabola $(t, t^2/2)$, for which the squared distance function is:

$$\Phi(t; u, v) = (t - u)^2 + (\frac{t^2}{2} - v)^2 = \frac{t^4}{4} + (1 - v)t^2 - 2ut + u^2 + v^2,$$

which indeed can be transformed at the origin to the normal form of the cusp through a translation and a nonhomogeneous scaling.

The strength of the approach via catastrophe theory is, of course, that you need no longer attack special problems at all if you are only interested in the things that could conceivably happen.

8.2.3 The T-junctions

A transversal crossing of two folds of the projection is usually known as a "T-junction." The name derives from the fact that only half of one of the folds can be visible: the other half is necessarily occluded by the part of the object to which the other fold belongs. Thus you obtain a "T-shaped" configuration of the contour.

The T-junctions are extremely important in daily vision because they give you a static cue to radial order in depth. Notice that they cannot reveal a depth *scale*, but only an order. It is interesting from a psychological viewpoint that the visual system automatically assumes something for which it has no explicit evidence in the retinal image, namely that the cut-off contour *exists* even if invisible behind the occluder.

The pieces of the fold locus on the object that correspond to the pieces of contour that make up the T-junction are *not adjacent* on the surface; they only meet in the projection. Thus T-junctions cannot be understood from a local approximation to the surface. They are at least of a bilocal nature.

At a T-junction, you happen to look along a general *bitangent ray*. That the T-junction is stable is clear enough, since as you know, the bitangents form ray congruences. That is to say they form families of straight lines such that a finite number of rays pass through an arbitrary vantage point. If you move your eye, the T-junction remains stubbornly present, although the two points at which it grazes the surface do change all the time, of course.

The example of the two spheres that I introduced previously illustrates the stability very well. For the typical vantage point the perimeters of the apparent discs are either completely disjunct or intersect in a pair of T-junctions. Clearly both situations are stable against small excursions of the vantage point. Qualitative changes only occur near the vantage points from which *the apparent discs are tangential*, that is, on the limiting bitangent developable surfaces.

8.2.4   The generic events

It is fairly easy to guess at the possible generic *events* because you now have a feeling for the geometrical reasons behind the nature of the stable views. The official manner is to invoke singularity-theory-like methods. This problem was solved only a few years ago by Gaffney and Arnold. A problem is that it is rather hard to interpret the—algebraic—results in terms of geometrical content. I will completely skip the formal derivations here and just describe the results. This makes sense because there is hardly any need for such theory in ordinary applications. You do it once and for all for the canonical case. On the other hand it is of great use to be able to generate the geometrical insights that make the results look natural or, after a certain period of mental adjustment, even obvious.

You have to understand basically three processes, namely the genesis of inflexions of the contour, the genesis of cusps, and the genesis of T-junctions. The genesis of extra loops of contour proves to be a special case of the genesis of cusps. I will discuss these processes in sequence.

Inflexions of the contour always occur in pairs, such as in the case when a convex arc develops a concave dent and you obtain a pair of inflexions. The concave arc must run in anticlastic territory, whereas the overall convex arc points at a synclastic region. When you gain the concavity, the contour must have been momentarily *flat*, in other words, must have possessed a tangent with fourth-order contact. This tangent in the projection together with the vantage point defines a *tangent plane* with the order of contact that is typical for a ruffle.

This is indeed how pairs of inflexions are generated: when you cross the tangent plane of a ruffle. If the point is a unode, you develop a local dent in a globally convex contour; if it is a tacnodal point, you develop a hump on a globally concave contour. In the first case this means that you get a glimpse of an anticlastic "finger," in the second case, of a synclastic "finger" (figs. 410 to 412).

The remaining events deal with the local differential topological structure of the contour. There exist only a few distinct types of event (fig. 413).

Cusps are also *generated in pairs*. Because cusps occur when you look into an asymptotic direction, it is clear that the generation of a pair of cusps has to do with the crossing of the vantage point of one of the boundaries of the asymptotic ray manifold. These are of two basic types, namely the flecnodal scrolls and the developables of cylinder axes. These two types give rise to completely different events.

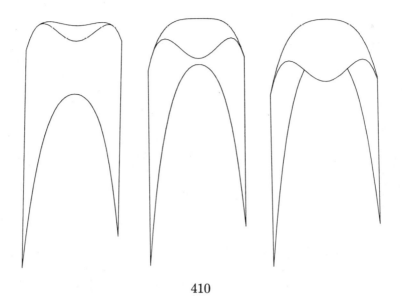

410

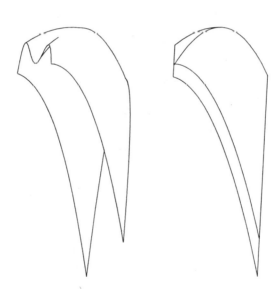

411

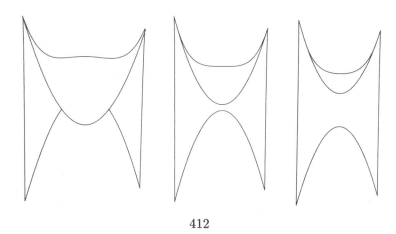

412

If you cross a flecnodal scroll, you gain—or lose—two asymptotic directions, that is, a pair of cusps. The two asymptotic directions are necessarily members of one and the same family. The contour then suddenly develops a swallowtailed structure with two cusps and a T-junction. Only one of the cusps can be visible (fig. 414).

You can often observe this kind of process in nature, notably when you drive along ranges of nicely rounded and preferably bald hills. The southern Californian coast road (Highway 1) is ideally suited, if you care to share the experience.

The other type of event happens when you cross the developable of cylinder axes. You again gain or lose a pair of asymptotic directions, but this time each member of the pair belongs to a distinct family. What happens depends on which side of the edge of regression you are, or rather whether the edge of regression is between you and the surface. You have met a similar condition in the depth map where the number of foci on a normal ray was decisive. In order to keep things fairly simple, I will restrict the discussion here to the far zone. Then the decisive factor is on what side of the parabolic curve the edge of regression is.

A simple way to remember the geometry is to throw up the Gauss map before your mind's eye. The curve on the Gauss map that corresponds to the contour is a *great circle*, for you have to consider all points with normals orthogonal to the visual direction. Thus the locus on the object that is on the contour is always the pre-image of a great circle of the Gauss map. Consider how the topology of this pre-image could change. It will certainly change if the circle sweeps over a fold, because the multiplicity of the pre-image suddenly changes at a fold.

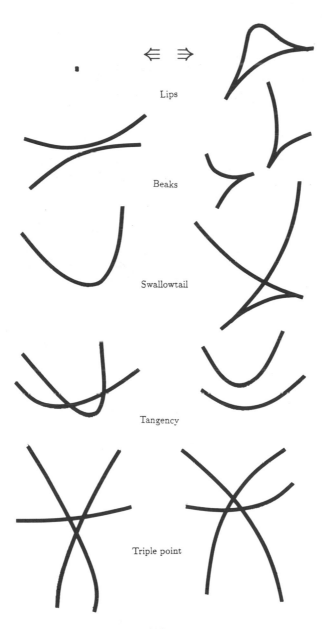

Lips

Beaks

Swallowtail

Tangency

Triple point

413

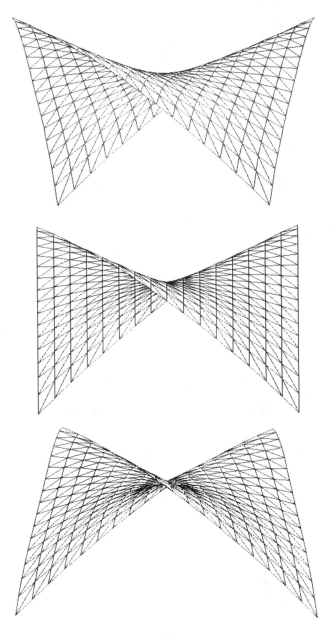

Some pictorial consideration reveals that you will *gain a loop for a convex fold*, whereas you will have a *change of connectivity for a pair of contours for a concave fold*. The first process is in fact the unique way in which the contour can gain or lose loops. Figure 415 illustrates these

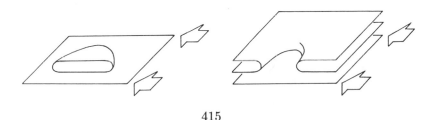

415

processes. Because the Gaussian images of the asymptotic curves are tangential to the images of the parabolic curves, you will certainly gain a pair of cusps in both cases.

The two cases show characteristic differences, and it is good to be well acquainted with them. Figures 416 to 418   show in detail what happens when you move the vantage point so as to move the great circle over a convex or a concave fold. Both a few selected views and selected pictures of the pre-image of the fold of the projection, in its relation to the parabolic curve, are shown here. Due to the shape of the contours these cases are known in the literature as the "lips" and the "beaks." (Thom christened them *singularité lèvre* and *bec-à-bec*.) These sequences show the difference between the two types of parabolic arc to the best advantage, whereas seen from a direction about $\frac{\pi}{2}$ further on, both shapes tend to look deceptively similar. Both then display an inflected contour. The figures also illustrate the loci on the surfaces that are on the visual contour, which is the pre-image of a great circle, with the parabolic curves drawn in. It is clear that the small loops that have appeared are *centered on the parabolic curves*, as should indeed be the case.

These events are very basic; they are the main way in which the topological structure of the contour changes as you move about. You should thoroughly familiarize yourself with them. You can make a start by carefully studying simple objects such as apples and pears, viewed from as many sides as you like. Such small objects are especially convenient, as you can easily rotate them in your hand to detect the singular views and transitions. When you feel at home with the possible events, you

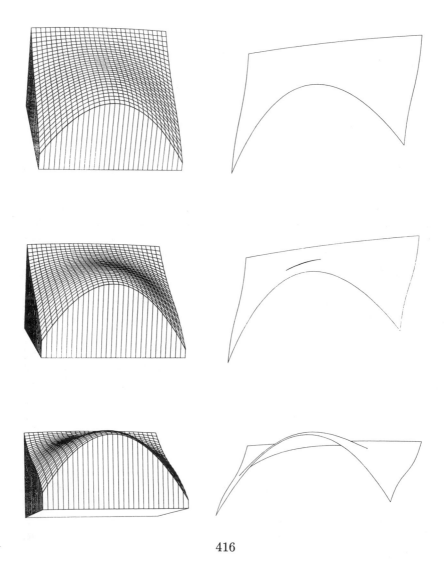

416

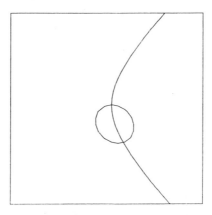

417

can graduate to a plaster-cast gallery and study much more complicated objects, such as (generalized) human bodies. Once you know what to look for, you will be able to cope with the complexity.

The T-junctions are generated when the vantage point crosses the developables of limiting bitangents. The example of the two spheres offers an excellent example of this. When the vantage point is on one of the two cones, you can have an inner or outer tangency between the apparent discs. Special cases include the tritangent ray (fig. 419) and the tangent ray that happens to be asymptotic at another point.

The T-junctions are visually very conspicuous, and you will experience few surprises if you study them in natural objects. This does not detract from their importance though.

The *organizers* are rather complicated geometrical features, and I will not discuss them in detail or even completely enumerate them. There are a dozen distinct types for parallel projection and disregarding curvature. It is of some interest to consider a few of them, though. But remember that it is infinitely unlikely ever to be at such a point or on such a curve for a random orbit.

The organizers are all due to singular features of the special surfaces I have described earlier, the cylinder axes developable, the flecnodal scroll, and the developable of limiting bitangents. The developables have edges of regression and swallowtail points, and that's where the organizers are. If the edges of regression have asymptotes, you will also meet the organizers in the far zone. An example is the edge of regression of the cylinder axes developable. In the far zone this corresponds to an inflexion of a fold of the Gauss map. This singularity is fondly known

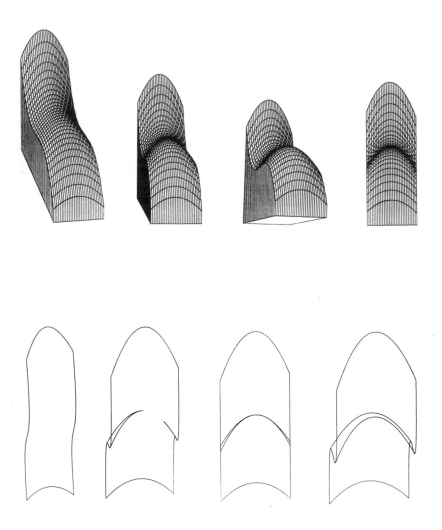

418

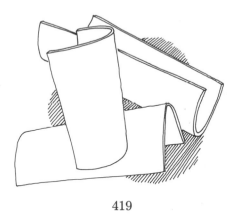

419

as the "goose" (fig. 420).

I add as a handy reference a short review of "normal forms" of the singularities that have to do with the structure of the contour. In all cases the interesting singular direction is the Y-axis. Thus you should study the views for viewing directions

$$\vec{v} = \xi\vec{e}_x + \vec{e}_y + \eta\vec{e}_z,$$

where ξ and η denote small perturbations ($\xi, \eta << 1$). The table is only complete for parallel projection and takes no account of T-junctions.

You could use these forms as a point of departure when you want to try some graphics. You will soon discover that some of the higher order singularities "don't like to be photographed." You will have to do some judicious scaling and even some "sculpting," that is, trying to devise the kinds of perturbations that make the picture come out nicely. This needs skill, which again is bred only through practice.[15] In short, don't quit too soon!

It should be possible to obtain reasonably nice pictures for most of the cases after some trials. I find that the most stubborn cases are the biflecnodes ("butterfly" catastrophes). It is not all that difficult to produce pictures that convince you visually that things are indeed as they should be, but it is hard to obtain anything visually pleasing.

---

[15] Your best bet is to program generalized versions of the normal forms that contain plenty of parameters. These parameters are so many "knobs" you can twiddle. A little thought is needed if you want the "knobs" to control the configuration in a way that you intuitively understand. The actual programming is easy, even with very many knobs, because the normal forms are so simple. You will spend most of your time looking at the graphics output, trying to decide which knobs to twiddle next and by what amount.

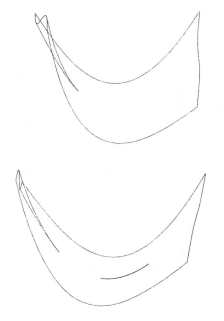

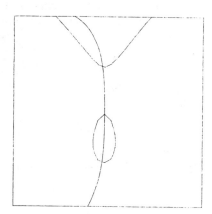

420

The possibilities are:

Contour Curvature: I have divided this item into the stable views and the typical events. You have:

> **The stable cases:** There are only three possibilities. You can have
>
> - An Elliptic Fold, which always signifies a synclastic point. A local model is:
> $$z = x^2 + y^2.$$
>
> - A Hyperbolic Fold, which always signifies an anticlastic point. A local model is:
> $$z = -x^2 + y^2.$$
>
> - A Parabolic Fold, that is, an inflected contour, which signifies a spinode. A local model is
> $$z = y^2 + x^3 + xy^2.$$
>
> **The generation of pairs of inflections:** It may happen that the contour suddenly develops a pair of inflections, that is, an undulation. You can expect to encounter:
>
> - An Elliptic Undulation, a concavity developing in a globally convex contour. This signifies a unode. A local model is
> $$z = y^2 + x^2y + xy^2 + x^4.$$
>
> - A Hyperbolic Undulation, a convexity developing in a globally concave contour. This signifies a tacnode. A local model is
> $$z = -y^2 + x^2y + xy^2 + x^4.$$

Cusps of the Contour: It may be the case that the contour is cusped, or starts to develop cusps. Of course, then you will see T-junctions and ending contours. Again, I distinguish the generic views and the typical events.

> **The stable case:** There is only one, namely:
>
> - A Cusp, an ending contour, which signifies an anticlastic point. A local model is
> $$z = x^2 + xy + y^3.$$

The generation of cusps: There exist many interesting possibilities, namely:

- A Swallowtail, the case of a concave contour that develops a T-junction with an ending contour. This signifies
  a flecnode. A local model is

$$z = x^2 + xy + y^4.$$

- A Butterfly, a concave contour that develops a complicated structure composed of two T-junctions and two
  ending contours. This case signifies a biflecnode. A local
  model is
$$z = x^2 + xy + xy^3 + y^5.$$

- A Butterfly (2nd type), very similar to the previous case.
  A local model is

$$z = xy - xy^3 + y^5.$$

- The Lips, the generation of an extra loop of the fold,
  which appears as a split-off piece of contour with two
  endpoints. It signifies a spinode with convex fold of the
  Gauss map. A local model is

$$z = x^2 + x^2 y + y^3.$$

- The Beaks, a complicated event in which two pieces of
  the fold meet and move out again but with a different
  connectivity. This event signifies a spinode with concave
  fold of the Gauss map. A local model is

$$z = x^2 - x^2 y + y^3.$$

- The Goose, a very complicated situation pending between the lips and the beaks. It signifies a gutterpoint.
  A local model is

$$z = x^2 + y^3 + x^3 y.$$

Bifurcating Contours: In some singular cases the contour *appears
to branch.* An example is the torus of revolution seen "edge
on." Then the contour is composed of two circles that are somehow "joined" to two straight-line pieces. The "gulls" unfold such
branchings. You have:

- The Elliptic Gull, the type of gull you have in the case of the "furrow" described before. It signifies a unode. A local model is

$$z = x^2 + x^2y + xy^2 + y^4.$$

- The Hyperbolic Gull, the type of gull you already encountered in the case of the "hump." It signifies a tacnode. A local model is

$$z = -x^2 + x^2y + xy^2 + y^4.$$

Contour crossings: There exist essentially two different types of event that generate transversal crossings of the contour: local and multilocal ones. You have:

- For the Swallowtail and the Butterfly, you obtain crossings in a purely local fashion. The same is true for the ruffles if you study finite viewing distances.

- The multilocal types can be classified according to the structure of the bitangent developable. This doesn't fit in quite well in the present list, so I'll skip this issue here.

It should be a relief that that's all there is! People used to entertain the romantic notion that three-dimensional shapes could be enjoyed in *infinite variety*. Such is not the case. The visually distinct possibilities for the local structure are rich but *limited*. The complexity is of a combinatorial type, thus, in a way, geometrically trivial. (You may put as many furrows and dimples in a blob as you like, thus raising its combinatorial complexity. But you cannot add anything unexpected, that is, *qualitatively novel*, no matter how much of a genius you are as a sculptor!)

One and the same attitude is shown in an infinite number of variations,
because it can be viewed from an infinite number of places
and these places are of a continuous quantity,
and a continuous quantity is divisible into an infinite number of parts.
Consequently every human action shows itself
in an infinite variety of situations.
—LEONARDO DA VINCI (1452–1519)

8.3   Furrow, dimple & bell revisited

The examples that I introduced earlier suffice to illustrate most of the interesting features in a way that easily sticks in the memory. I will consider them separately and will treat only the far zone. Then a glance at the Gaussian and the asymptotic spherical images suffices to grasp what goes on. (This section—again—has the character of a picture story. The pictures are actually more important than the words, so you should spend most of your time on them.)

Furrow: I have already used this example to illustrate the use of the Gauss map to understand ranging data. If the visual direction is in the thrice-covered part of the Gaussian sphere, you have two near points and a saddle, otherwise merely a near point. I just forget about the invisible far point on the back, here.

The asymptotic spherical image is most suited to discuss the contour (fig. 421). The parabolic arc maps on the curious hourglass-

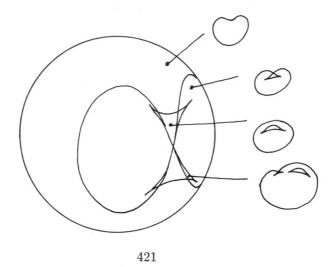

421

like structure. Its cusps correspond to the inflections of the folds of the Gauss map. Thus you have two arcs where you can expect lips and two where you can expect beaks, separated by the cusps. The beak-type arcs are inflected; the inflections correspond to the ruffles. Thus the flecnodal folds run from the inflection on the one beak type arc to the inflection on the other.

Figure 421 doesn't contain *all* relevant structure. For instance,
I have not indicated either the tangentplanes of the ruffles or the
bitangent developable. (These entities can be represented as curves
in the asymptotic spherical image.) At the tangent planes of the
ruffles, you have the creation or annihilation of a pair of inflections
of the contour (a dent). Thus, figure 421 does not even differentiate
between fully convex contours and one with an indentation (as
shown in the figure). You can try to complete the figure yourself.
This is an instructive exercise, although the figure becomes rather
complicated.

When you cross the flecnodal fold, you get a swallowtail type singularity in the contour. All this is easily illustrated in the numerical
study (fig. 422). When you first compute the asymptotic spherical
image, it is a simple matter to predict from which vantage points
you will obtain specific shapes of the contour.

Thus the asymptotic spherical image is really a very convenient
tool in computer graphics, although few people seem to be aware
of the fact. I have yet to see it used in an application except for the
graphics on my own home computer. You will come to value this a
lot after you have struggled for a time with some computer-defined
object in order to get characteristic views or even transitional views
on your screen using trial and error. You may *never* find some of
the rarer views that subtend small areas on the viewing sphere,
unless you are really determined and are prepared to spend ages.
If on the other hand you use the asymptotic spherical image you
will find that you zoom in at a jiffy! I am at a loss to understand
why other people refuse to be as lazy as I am.

A few characteristic views (fig. 423) have been illustrated in somewhat more elaborate detail, sporting a liberal sprinkle of window
cut-outs, both juxtaposed and in series to a considerable depth.
You may need a few moments to really appreciate a structure, at
times. What you gain is a good insight into the multiplicity of the
covering of the projection—the different depth layers or the radial
order, so to speak. Thus the figures allow you to develop a vivid
visualization of the "deep structure" of the images of the shapes.

Please notice that these schematic drawings are exactly what they
look like, that is *schematic*. A lot of detail has been suppressed.
Everything having to do with changes in curvature or self-occlusion
has been left out, for instance. You should be able to sketch in most
of the omitted detail, in a qualitative fashion, making use of the

422

interrelations between the geometrical entities I have noted earlier. Remember that changes of curvature have to do with the unodal tangent planes, the self-occlusions with the bitangent developable, and so on. Trying to complete the schematic sketches as far as you can is really a very worthwhile exercise. You will notice how the number of qualitatively different views is really rather high, even for such very simple surface modulations.

Figures 424 and 425 depict some views of the *banana surface*. The

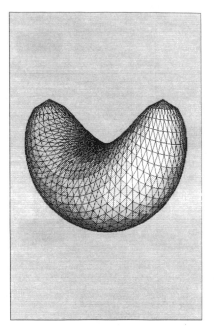 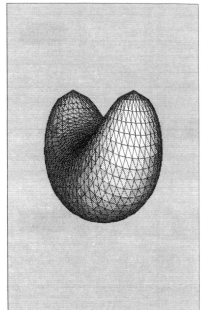

424

event leading from a concave contour to an ending contour with a T-junction is illustrated. I have also drawn the triangulation without hidden line removal. Although it looks like a mess at first sight, the swallowtail structure stands out quite well. Figure 426 shows the emergence of a lips structure. You can study such transitions quite easily in real objects, of course.

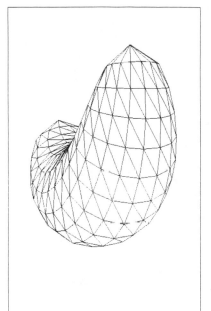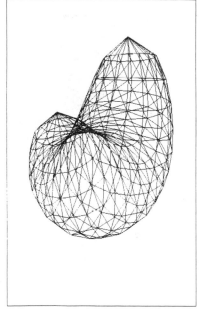

425

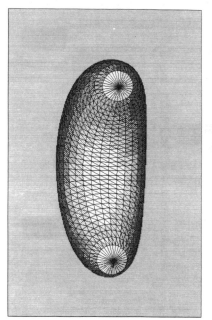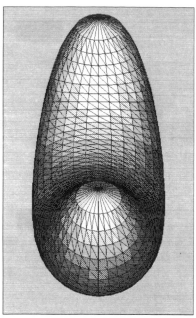

426

Once you know what to look for, you will notice the generic features all over the place.

It is worth the effort to try to throw up a vivid image of the furrow before your mind's eye and to relate the different views to both the shape and the asymptotic spherical image.

Such exercises will enable you to guess at the structure of the spherical images of new shapes or to dream up the shape of some object for which you know the spherical images.

Dimple: The dimple and the bell are of heuristic interest, especially when you contrast them as a pair. Both are essentially ovoids with local patches of high elliptic curvature superimposed. Only in one case, the perturbation is of *like* (convex); in the other, of *unlike* (concave) curvature. The dimple possesses in many ways the more intricate and confusing structure of the two.

Figure 427 shows some of the typical views of a sphere with a dimple with hidden lines removed. You see a lips event very clearly, but when the visible contour of the lips gets near to the contour of the overall shape, things start to look messy.

The dimple is not an easy case to illustrate. As you will readily appreciate while perusing these figures, a problem of a practical—computer graphics—nature is that it is almost impossible to get a good view of what goes on at the edge of the pit.

This is equally true for many differential geometrical objects of major interest. One example that especially bugged me when I was making illustrations for this book concerns the flecnodal scroll. The flecnodal fold is almost coincident with the outer parabolic loop. However, because you know the canonical behavior of the flecnodals, it is an easy matter to *imagine* how they run. They start at the inflections of the parabolic curve and end at the next one. I have schematically indicated their structure in figure 428.

Imagine what happens when you look into the dimple from above. You just get the contour of the overall ovoid shape. Nothing special. When you lower the altitude of the direction of view you reach a point where you cross the developable of cylinder axes for the inner loop (fig. 429). Notice that this loop is a convex fold on the Gauss map; thus you will get a lips.

When you lower the altitude still more, you first have to cross a flecnodal, and thus will gain two cusps. This is usually a scarcely

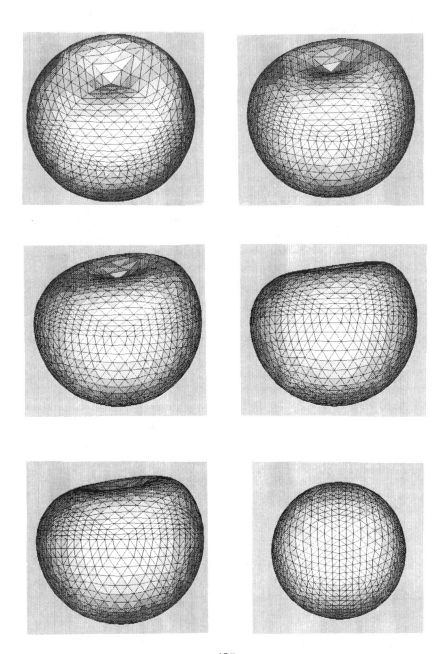

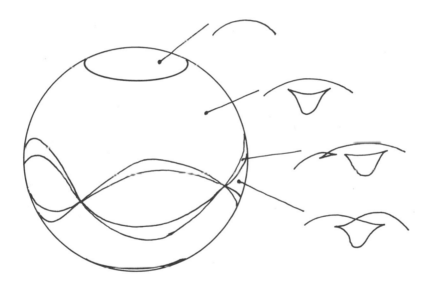

428

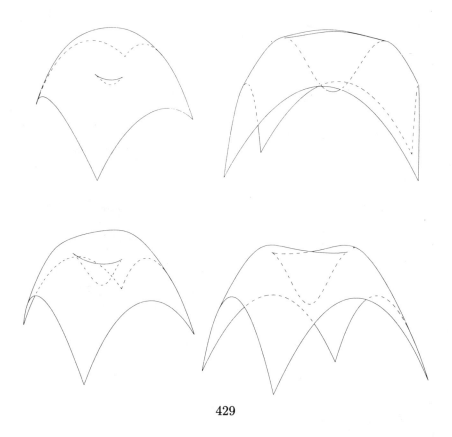

429

noticeable event, because for a little lower altitude still, you will
cross the second developable of cylinder axis and this time contract
a beaks. What happens is that one cusp from the bell-shaped loop
will meet one of the cusps from the swallowtail-like inflection such
that the loop will merge with the contour of the overall ovoid.

I illustrate this case again with a few rather freely rendered interpretations (fig. 430). In the case of the dimple they serve an

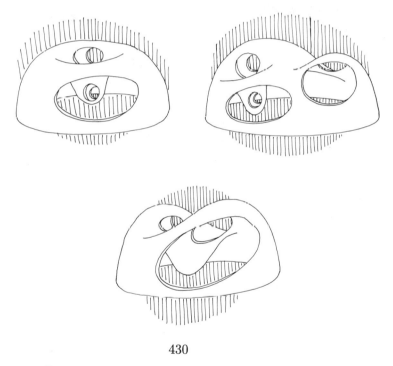

430

especially good purpose because the many windows allow you to
see what goes on. But yes, you may have to look for a while before
you get things into focus. Compare these figures to the "official"
figure 427.

Bell: A few typical views of a sphere with a "wart" are depicted in
figure 431. All events of interest can be seen quite clearly, except perhaps the occurrence of the swallowtail event when the lips

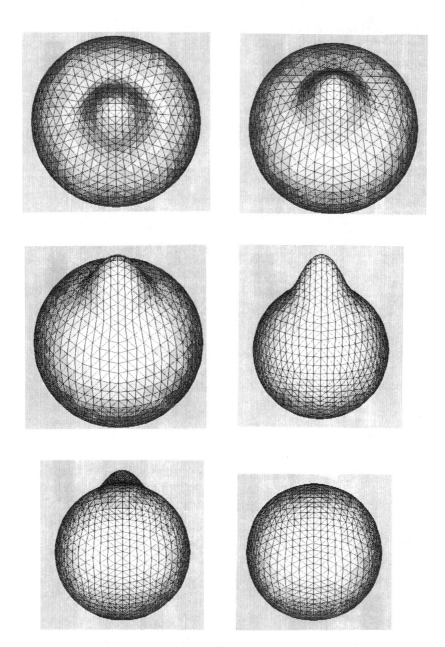

contour manages to attach itself to the overall outer contour.

The bell can be analyzed in a similar way as the dimple. Figure 432 gives you the asymptotic spherical image, figure 433 a few key

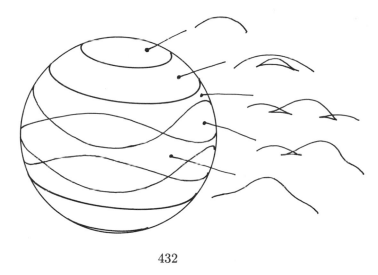

432

projections.

Start with a view from above. Then the contour doesn't depend on the wart at all; it is just that of the overall ovoid. When you lower the direction of view, you must cross the developable of cylinder axes for the inner parabolic loop. Since it is a convex fold on the Gauss map, you get a lips again. Only this time it is upside down, as compared with the dimple. (But perhaps it would make more sense to call the dimple upside down, because in the case of the bell the convexity of the new loop is of the same sense as that of the overall ovoid shape.)

When you lower the viewing direction, you have to cross the other cylinder axes developable and you will contract a beaks event. As a result you lose the extra loop again, as it gets converted in two swallowtail-like inflections of the overall ovoid contour.

When you lower the direction of view still further, you will cross the two flecnodals in succession, losing the two swallowtailed inflections in the overall contour one after the other. From a very low viewing angle you get a smooth, pear-shaped contour. This is

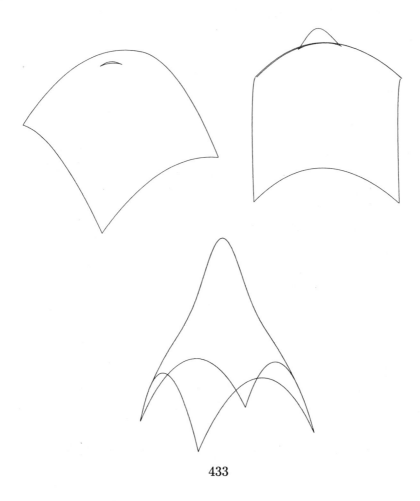

433

the "canonical view" that most people will intuitively pick when asked to "draw a pear."

Once again I have added some assorted fancy interpretations (fig. 434). In this case you may find that the "official" views are just as easy to read. Yet you may notice that these schematic sketches let you judge the multiplicity of the covering of the visual field by the projection especially well. You will probably have to think hard and count explicitly to arrive at a recognition of the *quintuple covering* at the middle part of this shape.

... the artist finds himself compelled to do away with that gracefulness that he had achieved in the first view in order to harmonize it with all the others. This difficulty is so great that no figure has ever been known to look right from every direction.
—BENVENUTO CELLINI (1500–1571)

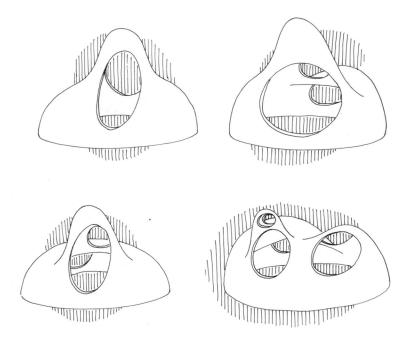

434

8.4 The illuminance

The incidence of light consists in knowing the shadow which a body, placed on a certain plane, and exposed to a given light, ought to make upon that plane; a knowledge easily attained from the books of perspective. By the incidence of lights we therefore understand the lights and shades proper to particular objects. And by the word claro-obscuro is meant the art of advantageously distributing the lights and shades which ought to appear in a picture, as well for the repose and satisfaction of the eye, as for the effect of the whole together.
—ROGER DE PILES (1635-1709)

An interesting problem of some practical interest is to find the pattern of illuminance due to, for example, a point source of light, as it depends on the shape. The problem is very similar to that of the ranging problem.

However, the function you will consider is of a slightly different nature. Although this is not at all necessary, in order to keep the exposition within rather restricted bounds, I will consider here only the case of parallel beam illumination. This has the advantage that only *directions* are relevant, so you can do all necessary geometry via spherical images. In this case you don't use a "viewing sphere" but the manifold of all directions of illumination.

You may think of a diffuse light field where the "direction" is the direction of the net flux vector. But the photometry proper isn't too important here, so I will skip a discussion of photometric problems. The only fact you need to appreciate in the remainder of this chapter is that the *illumination* is in most cases approximately a function of the angle between the surface normal and some "direction of illumination."

In the typical outdoors situation in my country this direction is from above: the sky tends to be uniformly grey, so you have the simple photometric case of a hemispherical uniform source. This type of illumination has many advantages from an artistic viewpoint: there are virtually no cast shadows and hardly any attached shadows, but the surface relief is beautifully revealed through soft gradations. This is the type of illumination that brings out surface modulations (in, for example, marble statuary) to the best advantage. Portrait photographers value this type of light field for the same reason. This is the type of situation implied in this chapter.

8.4.1   The slant function

Consider the function $S(u, v; p, q) : \mathbf{R}^2 \times \mathbf{S}^2 \to \mathbf{R}$, called the *slant function*. The parameters (u, v) denote the coordinates on the patch, whereas (p, q) denote the direction of the light source. The value of S is the interior product of the surface normal at the point $\vec{x}(u, v)$ of the surface and the direction of the source. This value is proportional with the illumination if the value is positive and there are no cast shadows, whereas the patch is in shadow if it is negative. The slant function is Morse for most directions of illumination. These nice directions define cells on the sphere of all directions of illumination. The boundaries of these cells are the bifurcation set.

8.4.1.1   Families of curves in the projection

It is often of considerable practical interest to understand how families of curves on a surface will appear in the projection. For instance, the curves of equal irradiance of a Lambertian surface will appear as curves of equal radiance in the visual field.[16] Dufour has classified the generic possibilities. I will merely describe them here.

There are six distinct possibilities:

The regular case A regular foliation of the surface appears as a regular foliation in the projection. This is, of course, the most frequent case that will apply to most of the image. Not very exciting.

Morse singularities (extrema and saddles) appear as such in the projection. Again, so what?

A fold This is more interesting: it is your typical "occluding boundary." The contour appears as an envelope of the projections of the members of the family of curves.

A Morse singularity on the fold This is an extremum of the irradiance along the contour (not on the surface but on the contour). Then a curve of the projected family has an undulation on the contour.

---

[16]The "Lambertian surface" is a mythical entity that appears in elementary optics classes and computer vision research papers. It is the "ideal diffuse reflector" that is supposed to remit all radiation impinging on it equally in all directions, such that the remitted radiance doesn't depend on the viewing angle. The Lambertian surface is probably unphysical, but if you aren't too picky, many matte surfaces may be acceptable representatives. For most of the discussion of this chapter, it is largely immaterial whether the surface is truly Lambertian or not.

A generic singularity of the fold ("Whitney umbrella") Another interesting case to take note of.

A cusp You have met this singularity before.

Figure 435 illustrates these basic possibilities.

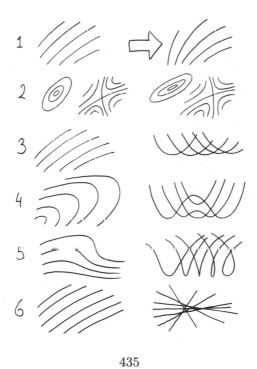

435

Polished wooden sculpture displaying the wood grain very clearly allows you to study these effects to best advantage. The paper by Dufour will fill you in on many details.

8.4.1.2 How to view the illuminance pattern

♠ INTERMEZZO—MAKE YOUR WAY INTO THE WHITE WORLD.

The main problems in judging illuminances are the effects of reflexes, which arise because of multiple scattering on different surface facets or surfaces in the surrounding, and variations of pigmentation of the surface itself, otherwise known as "stains."

This is why the academic artist of the long-forgotten days, when all art was supposed to be in the likeness of something, had to spend several years of his life in the "white world" of plaster casts before he was permitted to work from the rosy flesh.

You can get rid of the stains if you carefully spray the object with dull white or gray paint and subsequently handle it very carefully. Only pick it up with gloves or a clean tissue. Don't forget that any smudge on such a pristine white thing will appear as a surface depression.

People studying shape have successfully sprayed such diverse objects as bottles, cauliflowers, and even nudes. Different techniques apply to different classes of objects. The optical principles involved apply to all cases, however.

Reflexes from the environment can be minimized when you place the object in an open box that has been painted a dull black on the inside. You obtain what photographers call a "lunar effect."

Vignetting of the source is a problem that cannot be circumvented but only minimized using objects with only very shallow relief. Vignetting is very noticeable if your object contains relatively deep pot holes. The holes tend to look dark irrespective of the exact surface tilt and slant of the patches that are deeply recessed. This is usually evident in portraits of caucasian people in which the eye sockets stand out as dark patches in the face. (Of course, the skull is the prototypical example here.) It is also particularly evident at deep crevices where two parts of the body are pressed together, like an upper arm against the torso, where you see an almost black line at the junction.

Reflexes from part of the object itself, which only occur when the object is not an ovoid, can only be minimized by taking a medium gray rather than a white object, but you will never be able to get rid of them completely. By the time you have sprayed your object black in order to get rid of all traces of reflexes, you have also lost your chiaroscuro!

An illumination by a point source is not at all necessary to see the effects described in the text. In fact you should avoid such sources because they obliterate half of your object through the attached body shadow. A transilluminated gauze screen or piece of opal glass in fact gives the best results because it minimizes the area of the object filled by the attached body shadow. You have to be alert for too-strong effects of vignetting, though. Vignetting means an obscuration of parts of the source by distant parts of the object itself.

It may well take you some initial training period before you are able to appreciate the smooth illuminance gradients and notice the changes when you turn the object. Remember that the old-fashioned academic artist needed several years to tune in. Some people would never learn and were expelled from the academies. Don't give up too soon.

In case you never learn, you may take to photography and use special techniques ("solarization") to bring out the equiluminance contours on the film. Special materials and developers are available that make this task a relatively simple one if you have any darkroom experience. Of course, computer image processing is nowadays a simple and a less messy substitute, but you will need a frame grabber on your home computer.

8.4.2 The generic events

The versal events are the same as in the case of the ranging problem, that is, you may expect the destruction or creation of a saddle-extremum pair.

In this case it is extremely easy to get an intuitive picture of what happens. For a family of parallel surfaces the illumination is equal on corresponding points for all members of the family. The Gaussian sphere in particular is illuminated in exactly the same way as the object itself. But the illumination pattern of the sphere is trivial, since the isoilluminance contours are just the "latitude circles" that have the direction of illumination and its diametrical opposite point as the poles. You will appreciate that:

Useful Insight: *The family of curves of equal illuminance of the object are the pre-images of a family of latitude circles on the Gaussian sphere.*

The poles have the points on the object as pre-images where the tangent planes are perpendicular to the direction of illumination. These extrema—a maximum and a minimum—are most strongly tied to the direction of the source. If you change the direction of the source, then the pre-images move over the surface and *they can essentially be anywhere*.

There exists a more interesting family of singular points, however. They occur where the latitude circles on the Gaussian sphere touch the folds of the Gauss map. The pre-images are either extrema or saddles, depending on whether the fold is convex or concave. The interesting fact is that these singularities always cling to the pre-images of the folds, that is, to the parabolic curves.

Thus this class of singularities is tied every bit as closely to the object structure as to the direction of the source. *It is these light and dark spots that truly reveal the surface undulations.*

The versal events are completely dependent on the structure of the folds, that is, on the direction of the pleats (ruffles) and the inflections (gutter points). They are the points where things happen when you change the direction of the source. Yet these points are tied only to the surface and not to the source at all. Changing the source merely serves to reveal them. They are pure shape properties and have nothing to do with any incidental setup.

One way to think of these phenomena is to say that you actually see the multiplicity of the Gauss map reflected in the chiaroscuro. This is not *quite* true to the extent that the illuminance corresponds to a *curve*, not to a *point* on the Gaussian sphere. This degeneracy could be lifted through the use of colored lights. You might, for instance, illuminate with a red and a green beam at 90° angular separation. Then a color does neatly correspond to a certain normal direction. Thus the colored illumination pattern can be inverted and you can calculate the Gauss map from it. The same color at different places immediately signifies a multiple covering of the Gauss map.

Although this is not quite true for simple white light illumination, the chiaroscuro does a remarkable job of revealing the surface undulations. Chiaroscuro was one of the main tools used by the old-fashioned academic artist to reveal shape. It is striking how convincingly you may render three dimensional shape on paper through a judicious use of charcoal smudges. What you really get from this is a sampling of their folds of the Gauss map.

A few examples may clarify these observations. Figure 436 illustrates the illumination of the Gaussian hill. The altitude of the source is such that it exceeds the elevation of the normal parabolic rays. There are two light spots, one on the summit and one in the "footplains," connected with a saddle that is on the parabolic curve. There is also a dark spot on the other side of the hill, centered on the parabolic curve. When you move the source, the parabolic curve remains the structure that organizes the whole light-dark distribution.

Figure 437 shows the example of the furrow. You see a saddle and an extremum of the illuminance on the parabolic curve. Again, they will cling to the parabolic curve when you move the source. It is easy to imagine the qualitative situation on the Gaussian sphere and to use this image to be able to predict what will happen for specific movements of the source.

To many people it appears "intuitively absurd" that a certain class of critical points of the illuminance should be confined to the parabolic curves instead of "breaking loose" when you move the source. Even some of my mathematical friends expressed disbelief. This goes to show that the *ratio* is not to be despised, even though we like to intuit things. The best antidote is to have the conditions expressed with the Gauss map in mind. But perhaps it might also help to consider a lower dimensional example.

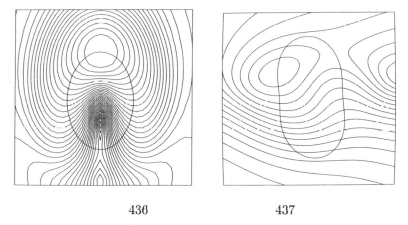

436   437

Try the curve $y = \frac{x^3}{6} + x$, which has a "parabolic line," an "inflection" in this case, at $x = 0$. Let the direction toward the source be $\cos \varphi \vec{e}_x + \sin \varphi \vec{e}_y$. The direction of the normal to the "surface" is in the direction $\cos \psi \vec{e}_x + \sin \psi \vec{e}_y$ with $\tan \psi = -(\frac{\partial y}{\partial x})^{-1} = -(1 + \frac{x^2}{2})^{-1}$. The slant depends on the difference of the angles φ and ψ. This difference clearly has an extremum at $x = 0$ because the tangent function is monotonic. The precise value of φ doesn't even matter! Thus the position of the source is again immaterial, and there will be a fixed critical point of the illuminance at the inflection. You will understand this geometrically if you make a sketch of this example. The higher-dimensional case is not different in principle. I guess these facts of life just take getting used to. In due time they will appear to you as self-evident truths. Take heart!

There are other interesting invariances having to do with the parabolic curves. This has to do with the fact that any direction is conjugated to the direction of the cylinder axis. This means that if you change the direction of the source then the equi-illuminance curves change all over the place, except that their direction on the surface is invariant at the parabolic curves.

You have discovered the interesting fact that the illuminance distribution over curved bodies is completely determined by the structure of parabolic curves, ruffles, and gutter points. They are the crucial geometrical entities, in this case.

A true drawing is nothing but the shadow of a relief.
Thus relief turns out to be the father of all drawing ...
—BENVENUTO CELLINI (1500–1571)

8.4.3   Specularities

A "specularity" is an image due to reflection of the light source. Specularities are only of interest for sources of small apparent size. "Small" is a somewhat ill-defined term here. The precise definition would have to depend on the curvature of the surface too, for the higher the curvature the larger the source may be. For a tiny droplet of mercury such as you sometimes find in the physics laboratory, you obtain a nice specularity from the sky. However, I will not enter into this kind of problem area here. In this section I will treat infinitely distant point sources of finite size only ("stars"). In practice the sun is often an excellent approximation.

For a source in the direction $\vec{s}$, defined such that the arrow of $\vec{s}$ points toward the source, you will see a specularity in the direction $\underline{\vec{s}}$, defined such that the arrow of $\underline{\vec{s}}$ points from the eye toward the specularity. Geometrical optics allows you to write down the relation $\underline{\vec{s}} = \vec{s} - 2(\vec{n} \cdot \vec{s})\vec{n}$ for a surface patch with either inward or outward normal $\vec{n}$. What happens here is that *the normal component of the light ray reverses*.

Notice that the orientation of the normal is curiously immaterial. The vector $\vec{n}$ occurs twice in the same term; thus its sign cancels out.

If the viewing direction is $\vec{v}$—tail of $\vec{v}$ at the eye—then $\vec{v} = \underline{\vec{s}}$ is an equation for $\vec{n}$, that is, for a point on the Gaussian sphere. The specular points on the object will be the pre-images of this point on the Gaussian sphere. This should be clear enough because their normals are identical.

From this simple discussion you at once draw several interesting conclusions:

Useful Facts: 1. *The number of specular points equals the multiplicity of the Gauss map.*

2. *When you move either the eye or the source you will gain or lose a pair of specular points when the solution of $\vec{v} = \underline{\vec{s}}$ crosses a fold of the Gauss map.*

The latter observation can be extended a bit. When you gain a pair of specular points, they are generated on a parabolic curve. One of the pair will move into the anticlastic, the other into the synclastic area. The pair moves transversely to the parabolic curve with an initially infinite velocity if you move the vantage point or the source with finite velocity. The latter conclusion directly follows from the fact that the principal curvatures determine the principal magnifications of the Gaussian image. These conclusions can easily be verified with the solar reflection in a

polished spoon. In many cases this provides a simple and very sensitive
method to find the positions of parabolic arcs on a (shiny) surface.

These conclusions are equally true when the object itself *deforms* while
the vantage point and the sources remain stationary. Then you can
imagine a changing Gaussian image with folds and pleats being formed
and straightened out repeatedly.

A simple example is the rippled surface of a pond. If the pond is
even and unrippled, the Gaussian image is a mere point. If it is rippling
through the action of the wind and surface mechanics, you obtain a
Gaussian image of extreme complexity, and the multiplicity may run
into the thousands. You can be sure, however, that the "twinkles" on
the pond will come and go in pairs, usually one on the convex ridge
of a wave, the other on the saddle-like flank of the wave. Although I
know of no practical use for this fact, it is somewhat of an intellectual
satisfaction to be aware of it.

Of course, there is a continuous transition between the diffuse reflection and the specular case. You can obtain such transitions when you
raise the slant function to higher and higher powers.[17] Figures 438 and
439 illustrate such "almost specularities" for the furrow. In figure 438

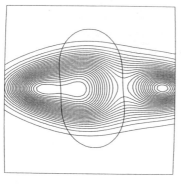
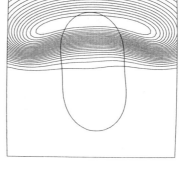

438   439

there are two saddles on the parabolic curve. Notice how one of the
saddles almost merges with the two associated extrema to a thin line
that represents the "glint" of the local cylinder axis. Figure 439 shows a
similar situation near one of the unodes. The cylinder axis is even more
prominent and is clearly seen as being tangent to the parabolic curve.

---

[17]This simulates the simple case in which the viewing direction coincides with the
direction of the incident light.

8.4.3.1   How to view specularities

♠ INTERMEZZO—USE THE SILVERWORK.

Specularities are easiest to interpret if the source is at the position of the eye itself. Although this might sound like impossible advice, you can easily bring this about by using a half-silvered mirror or a beam splitting cube. Alternatively you can take your distance and simply place your head close to the source.

You have to use polished objects such as spoons, of course. Polished metallic sculpture is even better, but is quite rare since sculptors are well aware that mirror-like surfaces tend to "dematerialize" an object. Most sculptors don't like the effect because they enjoy ponderable matter.

It is worth the inconvenience to build such a setup in a neat way, because it allows you to spot the spinodal points very easily and with considerable precision. When you turn your spoon, you will easily find orientations where a single specular point suddenly splits up into a pair of the same. This happens exactly at the spinodal points. Similarly you can look for the ruffles where a triple of specular points come together.

Water surfaces rippling in the breeze also yield most interesting material for study. In this case the sheer number of specularities may be enormous. It depends critically on eye height, though, so in many situations you can manipulate this number within very wide limits. Most often a statistical approach is indicated. The paper by Longuett-Higgins is a classic on this subject. The book by Minnaert will put you on the track of interesting observations, such as the columns of sparkling light on the sea surface when the sun sets.

> *The highlight or lustre on an object*
> *is not necessarily situated in the middle of the illuminated part,*
> *but moves as the eye moves in looking at it.*
> —LEONARDO DA VINCI (1452–1519)

8.5   Felix Klein's Conjecture

*Die parabolische Kurven sind von F. Klein zu einer eigenartigen
Untersuchung herangezogen worden. Er nahm an, dass die
künstlerische Schönheit eines Gesichts ihren Grund in gewissen
mathematischen Beziehungen hätte, und liess derhalb auf der Apollo
von Belvedere, dessen Gesichtszüge uns ein besonders hohen Grad von
klassischen Schönheit wiedergeben, sämtlichen parabolischen Kurven
einzeichnen. Diese Kurven besassen aber weder einen besonderes
einfache Gestalt, noch liess sich ein allgemeines Gesetz ausfindig
machen, dem sie gehorchten.*
—*Footnote in* HILBERT & COHN-VOSSEN'S *Anschauliche Geometrie.*

During the time that Felix Klein was professor at Göttingen University
he must have pursued the research to which Hilbert and Cohn-Vossen
devoted this note essentially as a sideline, probably as a kind of hobby.
Except for a short side remark that probably alludes to it, Klein's complete works contain no hint of this endeavor. At least I have been unable
to find it.

According to the note Klein "had the parabolic curves drawn on the
Apollo of Belvedere." The Apollo of Belvedere is a marble copy of a
Hellenistic bronze that has been at the Vatican since the early Renaissance. It became famous in Germany through Winckelmann's lyrical
description and was in fact generally acclaimed as the very summit of
classical beauty, a view that Hilbert and Cohn-Vossen also share. The
fame of the Apollo in fact derives rather more from the literary capabil-
ities of Winckelmann than from a true visual appreciation of the source.
The rather optimistic estimate of Winckelmann as to the antiquity of
the piece must also have fired the romantic imagination. I must say the
Apollo Belvedere fails to impress me as an outstanding achievement.

However this may be, when Felix Klein looked for a paradigmatic case
to experiment with notions concerning the aesthetics, this choice must
indeed have been a very natural one. We may guess that Klein ordered
a copy from the cast factory at Berlin (it still exists), which turned out
such plaster casts in considerable numbers. Klein used a scaled-down
copy of the bust of the Apollo (which is itself a life-size full figure),
something a professor could have on his desk.

It is not clear how Klein actually managed to get the parabolic lines
drawn on the cast (although Hilbert and Cohn-Vossen's text says that
he just "had them drawn," but it is unlikely that Klein had an assistant
who could take such an order), nor whether the drawn curves *are at all*

close to the real thing. Maybe Klein thought of some method (he was a very practical geometer, who had experience with the construction of mathematical models) and gave the task to a smart student.

Since the bust has survived the war (it is in the collection of the department of mathematics of Göttingen University) (fig. 440), it is in

440

principle possible to check the curves with modern methods (say laser ranging or Moiré topography). For the moment let's just assume that the curves are close to the true curves of inflection of the surface.

We do not know what brought Klein to formulate the hypothesis that the parabolic curves were the key to the beauty of a face, nor do we know how he expected the parabolic curves to turn out. (Perhaps showing such nice symmetrical properties as, for instance, the hyperbolic arcs of the outlines of certain Greek pottery?) Hilbert and Cohn-Vossen speak of "mathematical relations concerning artistic beauty," but I wonder whether they had any clear idea what kind of structure such a theory could possibly assume. There exists very little literature of what could be called "mathematical esthetics." A measure that is most often used is the amount of information needed to generate the shape relative to its configurational complexity. Beauty then becomes a measure for the total amount of symmetry present, or—equivalently—the economy of the possible descriptions. However, we can't be sure that Felix Klein had anything specific in mind.

I don't know whether Klein was at all familiar with the (considerable) literature on visual esthetics. One (remote) possibility is that he knew the book *Analysis of Beauty* by the painter William Hogarth. In this book Hogarth based beauty on *inflections of planar curves*. This idea goes back to Lomazzo's *figura serpentinata*, which again derives from the *contraposto* stance, which dates back to classical antiquity. It is not unlikely that he was aware of Lomazzo's theories, which were quite generally known. Thus Hogarth writes:

> *The eye hath this sort of enjoyment in winding walks, the serpentine rivers, and all sorts of objects, whose forms, as we shall see hereafter, are composed principally of what, I call, the waving and serpentine lines.*

Hogarth refers to the inflected arc as "the line of beauty." Since the parabolic curves are the natural higher-dimensional generalization of the inflections of planar curves, it is just possible that Klein attempted to generalize Hogarth's concept to higher dimensions.

In any case, Klein's hypothesis is by no means as singular as Hilbert and Cohn-Vossen suggest; its roots can be traced back in the history of the theory of visual esthetics.

As Hilbert and Cohn-Vossen relate, the result disappointed Felix Klein sufficiently that he gave up his research in this field. Was he betting on the wrong horse? I think not: apart from the fact that we don't expect to be able to formulate "laws of beauty" any more (the notion itself is repulsive to the modern mind), it is nevertheless clear that the parabolic curves play a decisive role in the structure of the optical input in our optical interaction with solid shapes. Thus *any* conceivable theory of vision that applies to solid shape can *a priori* be expected to be based on the properties of parabolic curves in some way or other. (Of course, the author of such a theory need not explicitly state this fact, nor even notice it himself!)

It will be clear by now that the parabolic curves are very special entities, and are worth your attention for many different reasons:

- The parabolic curves determine the inflections of the visual contour of a shape.

- The parabolic curves determine the possible *changes* of the topology of the contour when you move the vantage point or the body.

- The parabolic curves determine the qualitative structure of the illuminance distribution or *chiaroscuro*, that is, the placement and nesting of lights and shadows.

- The parabolic curves determine where new shadow patches will be formed when you move the light source or the object.

- The parabolic curves determine where pairs of highlights will appear or disappear when source, object, and vantage point move.

- The parabolic curves are the boundaries of the "thing-like" parts and of the "holes" (pockets of air) that make up the object.

You can probably add several more equally interesting properties yourself.

This much is certain: Felix Klein's hunch of the importance of the parabolic curves for our visual appreciation of the world was absolutely to the point.

> For though beauty is seen and confessed by all, yet,
> from the many fruitless attempts to account for the cause of it being so,
> enquiries on the head have almost been given up;
> and the subject is generally thought to be a matter of
> too high and too delicate a nature
> to admit any true or intelligible discussion.
> —WILLIAM HOGARTH, The Analysis of Beauty (1753)

V DYNAMIC SHAPE

9 Morphogenesis

*In a very large part of morphology, our essential task lies in the
comparison of related forms rather than in the precise definition of
each;
and the deformation of a complicated figure may be a phenomenon
easy of comprehension, though the figure itself
have to be left unanalysed and undefined.*
—D'ARCY THOMPSON, *On Growth and Form* (1917)

9.1   Evolutionary processes

When you come to think of it, there exist a great many notions in daily
use that play an important and often decisive role in intuitive thought
and visualization and that are very relevant to the description of shapes
but appear to have no counterpart in the mathematical description at
all. This is brought out most dramatically when you analyze the ways
artists, by which I mean draftsmen and sculptors in this context, talk
about "shape." It is almost as if there were no relation with differential
geometry whatsoever. Clearly this is an intolerable state of affairs. It
may be partly due to the difference in language, but this is certainly
not the full story. After all, there are also many notions of artistic
relevance that *do* have clear-cut mathematical counterparts. Just think
of painter's perspective in relation to projective geometry, to offer the
most obvious example.

What is actually lacking here is a bit hard to pin down. It may be
best to consider some examples. You may have been struck at times
by the fact that both artistically and perceptually a dumbbell is not
very different from two juxtaposed but disjunct spheres. Clear enough,
from certain vantage points these two shapes—notice how I count the
pair of spheres as a single shape—look *identical*, but the perceptual
similarity is not at all restricted to such vantage points (fig. 441). You
may have noticed quick artist's sketches in which the human torso, which
is roughly a dumbbell shape if you disregard the extremities, has actually
been represented by two *disjunct ovoids*, the ribcage somehow hovering
in the air over the pelvic girdle. Such representations are very effective
and are intuitively understood by persons of any wit. Now this is a very
strange situation, from the obvious geometrical standpoint. Since the
two objects even have a *different connectivity*, they are automatically in
entirely different ballparks, and there is no need to consider more refined
shape measures at all. *They can't be more dissimilar.*

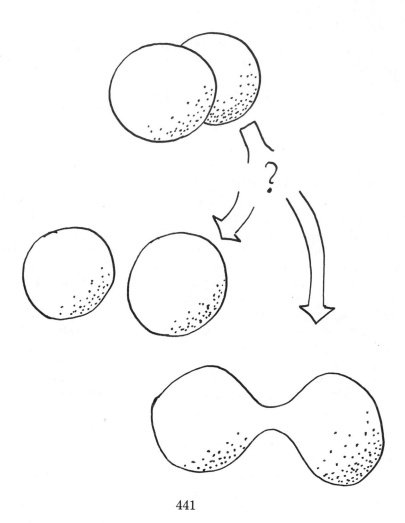

441

Yet, when you consider the situation intuitively or—what appears to be the same thing—pictorially, you may notice certain striking similarities. For instance, the developable of cylinder axes and the flecnodal scroll of the dumbbell and the inner limiting bitangent cone of the pair of spheres play in many respects similar roles. They help you decide how the objects look from certain portions of space, and some of these looks are similar or even identical. But how could you ever establish an equivalence relation between such very different geometrical objects? There is no answer to be expected from the classical literature.

One way to go about this is to imagine a *morphogenetic sequence* that leads from the pair of spheres to the dumbbell and vice versa. A very simple model would be to consider the "ovals of Cassini" with the polar description $r^4 + 1 - 2r^2 \cos 2\varphi = a^4$, rotated about the x-axis. For $a^2 < 1$ you obtain *two ovoids*, for $a^2 > 1$ *dumbbells*.[1] The shapes in this sequence can easily be studied by way of the methods developed earlier. Then you actually get a *cinematographic impression* of the limiting bitangent developable changing into the complicated structures associated with the hyperbolic "collar" of the dumbbell.

Here is the

Key Observation: *Relations that do not even exist for a single shape can be defined in such a morphogenetic sequence.*

This seems to be a natural way of describing shape from a perceptual standpoint *even if you are confronted with a single shape*. The "sequence" is completely imaginary. In artistic practice the sequence is sometimes explicit in the sense that you can trace it in the sequence of the technical progress of the work. *Any shape* may start as an ovoid in the sketch.

This is a general phenomenon. The intuition likes cinematographical sequences very much because they yield novel relations. It functions very much like reasoning by analogy. These relations then enrich properties that can also be defined in terms of the individual frames. For instance, your understanding of the Gauss map is expanded greatly when you see the Gaussian image as a frame in the cinematographical sequence defined through the parallel surfaces of a given surface.

In most cases the perceptually relevant morphogenetic sequences are less than arbitrary. For instance, they always tend to progress from the simple to the complicated. The members of the sequence become

---

[1] For $a = 1$ the curve is a lemniscate. Then the shape has a singular point that looks like the apex of a (double) right circular cone.

more and more articulate if you follow the sequence in one direction. I call such morphogenetic sequences *causal* and I will offer a technical definition of this concept later.

It proves to be the case that the concept of the morphogenetic sequence has very important consequences for the study of shape, the main reason being that it allows you to compare apparently different properties of the differential geometry. Consider the hyperbolic collar of the dumbbell and the inner limiting bitangent cone of the pair of spheres. It also allows you to put a *hierarchical order* on the geometrical features of a given shape.

For instance, feature $\mathcal{A}$ may appear before feature $\mathcal{B}$ when you develop the shape from its primordial ovoid nucleus. These hierarchies are the logical bases for the syntax of "shape languages." Moreover, it allows you to group certain features in "feature clusters" and treat them essentially as the manifestations of a single event. For example, when you push a dimple in an ovoid you have to generate two parabolic loops. These belong together as it were. There is no way in which you could produce the dimple without generating *both* loops. Further on, you will see how clusters of features will often be generated in one go when a singularity "explodes."

The main objection to the evolutionary sequence idea from the mathematician's point of view is that it is a vacuous exercise if there isn't a *unique* way to embed a given shape into such a sequence. If this weren't the case, everybody's old sequence would have equal rights to cosmic significance and you couldn't decide different claims as to what would constitute a feature cluster—clearly an unacceptable state of affairs. The whole thing would be utterly subjective.[2]

Somehow the sequence has to be constructed from the vantage point of the Eye of Eternity. There is actually a reasonable way to do something like this. There exists only a single sensible way to embed a shape in an evolutionary sequence if you agree on a few general and seemingly "obvious" constraints. You have to take this for granted until I explain it.

The evolutionary sequence is actually dormantly present in the concept of shapes defined in physical terms. In physics the value of a physical intrinsic parameter (a "density") is not defined unless you specify the resolution of the method of measurement. Thus any *real*, that is, operationally defined density is already a one-parameter family or mor-

---

[2]Most artists loudly would welcome such an observation, I guess. However, when you analyze their way of grasping shape it is very clear that their sequences are anything but arbitrary and that there are definite patterns to be observed.

phogenetic sequence with the resolution as the parameter.

This is the final key toward the solution of the problem. In retrospect it is clear that the "parameter" of the perceptual families is the *resolution*.

To any draftsman, a generic oak tree is a hemisphere resting on a cylinder; the boughs and leaves appear only later in the sequence. Here one turns from blurred to clear vision. Artists will often tell you to "screw up your eyes." Similarly, the human is a dumbbell-like torso first. The bulges due to the musculature appear only later.

Again, resolution is the key.

9.1.1   Shape diffusion

The concept of "shape diffusion" is not really novel, although it is never discussed in books on differential geometry. It has been used in image processing and pattern recognition for years. For instance, a typical method for curves uses a low-pass filtering technique on the (usually polar) coordinates of the curve. People typically conserve the total arclength of the curve in the process.

It is of some interest to consider this example, as it illustrates some of the more obvious pitfalls.

Suppose the curve is a circle of unit radius. Let the resolution be c. That means that all shapes within a distance ε of the given shape are treated as equivalent.

The notion of "distance" between shapes has been introduced in the first chapter. Then the perimeter is a patch of length 2π and width ε. It has a *finite area* $2\pi\varepsilon$; thus there is sufficient room to cram a wrinkled curve of *arbitrary length* into this patch! This means that there exist curves with arbitrarily long perimeters within a distance ε of the given curve. You shouldn't be surprised if this method of "blurring" leads you to arbitrary dilated circles. Just imagine: you blur a somewhat serrated circle of an inch diameter and it blows up on you to a somewhat less-serrated circle with a diameter of a mile! Of what use is such a method?

The lesson is that for curves you shouldn't conserve the total arclength at all. Nor should you conserve the total surface area for 3D shapes. The only global entity that it would not be unreasonable to conserve in n-dimensional space is the n-dimensional volume. But I can think of no compelling reason why you should, except when you are handling a blob of clay or something like that.

But there are other, more serious problems. Suppose the curve were a "figure eight" shape with a *self-intersection* in the middle. What would the blurred result be like? This kind of algorithm always tends to *decrease the local curvature.* In fact this is the main point of departure in most cases. Intuitively any closed curve should eventually blur into a circle. But you can't blur the figure eight into a circle without *increasing* the curvature at some points, because you have to straighten the extraneous loop out somehow.

What is the sermon this time? It can only be that these methods are somehow *basically wrong.* You shouldn't have been facing the dilemma of being asked to blur an entity with self-intersections in the first place.

Consider yet another case, a "curve" consisting of a pair of juxtaposed circles. They will never be blurred into the desired end result—which again would have to be a *single circle*—either. There is just no way to change the connectivity with this type of algorithm. The lesson is that it isn't at all necessary or even desirable to try to conserve the topological structure of the shape in every case.

It is possible to do away with all such problems in one sweep. Simply abstain from blurring geometrical entities of nonzero codimension (curves, surfaces, . . .) completely. If you consider a surface to be a boundary of a level set of the density of some physical intrinsic quantity, then *you should blur the density itself.* Once you do that, there is no reason whatsoever why the connectivity of a level curve shouldn't change. This happens all the time when a region is flooded and islands are created, or *vice versa.* From this viewpoint it is also clear that it doesn't make any physical sense to try to conserve areas or volumes.

What should be conserved is the total amount of "stuff," that is the volume integral of the density. Only this makes solid operational sense.[3]

9.2   Scale space

When you regard some intrinsic quantity as a function of both the space (or space-time, but I will disregard time in this book) and the resolution parameter, you describe it in "scale space," a term that people seem to agree on nowadays. In this section I will describe the rationale of the scale space idea and some of its more useful mathematical properties.

---

[3]This is of course the standpoint of the physicist. If you are a mathematician, you will not be impressed. Some people appear to believe that I advocate the blurring of "characteristic functions." This is not the case. Characteristic functions have no meaning in the physical sense. If your shapes are not physical densities but purely mathematical entities, don't ask me what to do. Basically anything goes; it depends on your mood. "Right" and "wrong" are a binary measure of efficaciousness and apply only to your interaction with the natural environment. In mathematics they are mere whimsicalities.

I will skip derivations and proofs, which are available in the literature, but concentrate on the concepts involved and the heuristics of the idea.

First of all I will consider the meaning of the concepts of "scale" and "resolution" and provide a simple example of scale space that is familiar to everybody—the geographical atlas.

9.2.1 Scale and resolution

"Scale" is a term used in widely different senses. I will introduce the technical meanings with the help of an example.

Consider photographs of a scene of the natural world. The photographic material limits the "resolution" of the result.[4] Thus it is of no avail to scrutinize the photograph with a microscope because this gives you the structure of the photographic material, not of the world. This limit is the "pixel size" or, as I will call it, the *inner scale* of the measurement. A photograph can be considered to represent a *measurement* (or "observation," if you like). To be precise, for the sake of convenience I will use "inner scale" for the pixel size converted to scene dimensions. If the photographic graininess just obliterates the leaves of an image of a tree, the inner scale must be a few inches.

There is another limit to the amount of data in the measurement. It is the *size* of the photograph, again in terms of the scene dimensions. What isn't in the photograph has not been measured. I call this the "outer scale" of the measurement. The inner and outer scale together determine the "logon content" or "total number of degrees of freedom" of the measurement. In image-processing terms this logon content is but the total number of pixels or voxels.

The observational errors in the data for any degree of freedom and the dynamic range of the process determine the "metron content" per pixel. In image-processing terms, the number of significant bits per pixel or voxel. In this discussion I assume the metron content to be ample; thus the bottleneck is in the inner scale.[5]

You can easily change the inner and outer scale by means of well-known processes:[6]

---

[4]I assume the lenses are never the bottleneck. In practice they may be, but it doesn't matter to the present argument.

[5]Yet I assume the metron content to be *limited*. Infinite metrical resolution leads to unphysical phenomena ("superresolution"). This subject is technically quite complicated. Although it is important, I leave out a discussion because the material is not strictly on "solid shape."

[6]There exist less obvious methods to change the depiction of 3D scenes like "travel shots," and so forth, but they are not relevant to the present argument.

"Trim" the picture (decrease outerscale). Producing a "blow-up" on the same format has the identical effect.

"Blur" the picture (increase the inner scale).

"Zoom" the picture, that is, decrease the inner scale and decrease the outer scale in proportion. This is done when you change lenses, that is, from wide-angle to tele lenses.

"Pan" the picture, which is done by pointing the camera away.

Here I am primarily interested in the effects of inner scale. That is, I will assume the outer scale to be ample in order to avoid "boundary effects." Then the key question is the following:

Question: *How to establish a relation between pictures of the same scene at different inner scales (resolution)?*

This is by no means a trivial or an easy problem. In many cases it may be entirely hopeless. In some cases it may be in fact manageable though. When you see a *long shot* and a *close up* of some scene, you can usually point out some common features in both and so establish a relation between light and dark spots or patches in the two photographs. In other cases it may be impossible.

An example would be the task of pointing out the spot corresponding to a leaf on a close-up of a tree in a long shot that contains the same tree. The problem is that the "corresponding" configuration of light and dark spots isn't there at all; when you change to the long shot, all kinds of tiny light-dark articulations *merge and disappear*.

The nature of this problem can be clarified by considering a well-known example of the same type, namely the *geographical atlas*. Everybody is familiar with its basic properties. When I need to find my home town in the atlas, I don't turn to the first page, which depicts the globe as a whole. I know I won't find it, and for a good reason, too. In a map of my country the town is probably represented by way of some conventional, that is arbitrary, sign.[7] It is a *mere point* in the sense that it is devoid of structure. It doesn't help to look at the map through a magnifying glass. When I turn to more detailed maps of the countryside near my home town, I get to see some structure, such as the rough outlines, perhaps the fact that it is divided by a river. I won't be able to spot my house, however. In order to do that, I need a very detailed town plan, which the usual atlas doesn't contain.

---

[7]In cartography this is known as "generalization."

The point is that

Key Observation: *an atlas has a tree structure.*

The first page, which presents the global view, splits into more and more maps showing continents, countries ... When I pick out one possible series of maps graded by "resolution," all containing my home town, I have an *evolutionary sequence* with very interesting properties.

For instance, you will appreciate that some details are completely absent on some maps because they are below the inner scale. Small fish swim right through the net designed for large fish. On the other hand, some details are absent on some maps because they don't fit the outer scale. You can't catch whales in a net designed for herring.

A mere *point* on a coarse map will "explode" into structure when I move to more detailed maps. Remember the representation of my home town. This "explosion" is just the tree structure of the atlas that exists at all scales.

This is the typical structure of scale space. Scale space has a tree structure with a clearly defined direction toward which the paths split off. For certain features you will be able to point out singular points where a point explodes into a spatial pattern.

In fact, the main constraint that makes scale space unique is the existence of a *causal structure*, that is, a tree-like structure in the sense of computer data structures.

There are two properties that you use when you try to point out the feature on a coarse map corresponding to some feature on a finer map. You only attempt to do this if the inner scales are not very different, though; otherwise the problem is hopeless from the very start.

These properties are:

Spatial proximity: It doesn't make sense to look for the feature very far away from where you expect it to be on the basis of its position on the finer map.

Metrical identity: The two features should have identical, or at least very similar properties.

These properties can easily be used in the case of the physical densities. Just look for the same value of the density as near to the point where you are as possible.

This leads to a very simple structure. You may conceive of scale space as space augmented with an extra dimension, the inner scale. The density is a scalar field in this augmented space, and you may consider its level surfaces. Then you have to look on the same level surface in order to fulfill the second requirement (metrical identity). In order to fulfill the first requirement, too, you must look along the direction of steepest increase of the inner scale. This completely determines the correspondence between the "maps" at different resolution.

The problem is easily stated as a least squares problem, and the solution is a trivial task. The geometrical characterization as paths of steepest increase of the inner scale on the surfaces of equal density is of heuristic value, and in fact suffices to explain most of the structure of scale space in a pictorial, intuitive fashion. The analytical expression has its uses though. The paths are the integral curves of the vector field: (Φ denotes the density, s the innerscale, x... the spatial coordinates)

$$\vec{p} = -\Phi_s \Phi_x \vec{e}_x + \ldots + (\Phi_x{}^2 + \ldots)\vec{e}_s$$

I will call the integral curves of the vector field $\vec{p}$ the curves of "canonical projection."

A simple example may help to drive these points home. Consider a density $\Phi(x)$ over a 1D space. Then scale space must be a function of two variables, namely the spatial coordinate x and a parameter s (say), which denotes the inner scale. Thus I write $\Phi(x; s)$. The canonical projections are the integral curves of $\vec{p} = -\Phi_x \Phi_s \vec{e}_x + \Phi_x{}^2 \vec{e}_s$. Take the case $\Phi = \frac{x^2}{2} + s$. The vector field is $\vec{p} = -x \vec{e}_x + x^2 \vec{e}_s$. The integral curves are simply $s + \frac{x^2}{2} = constant$; thus they are a family of parabolas with different shifts along the s-axis. Consequently the structure of the projection is very simple: the curves of projection all end on the singular line $x = 0$, which is seen to consist of merely branching points. The branches split off toward the direction of decreasing inner scale, which is just the condition of causality. Thus, this example is a possible "atlas." If you consider the example $\Psi(x; s) = \frac{x^2}{2} - s$, which is just Φ "upside down," you have an instance of a *noncausal structure*. Such a case should be strictly forbidden, as it represents an atlas where you get to see more fine detail if you turn from a city plan to the world map. Clearly this cannot be tolerated.

You should contemplate these trivial examples until you fully grasp what's going on here. If you miss the point about causality, I'm afraid it doesn't make much sense to read on.

In order to be able to construct scale space for any given density, you need an algorithm that *guarantees* you will get a nice atlas structure. It is not very hard to come up with such an algorithm.

First you may take notice of the fact that a branching can only occur

at the critical points of the density, that is, those points where the
gradient, which comprises all first-order partial derivatives with respect
to the spatial coordinates, vanishes. Only at such points, the canonical
projection vectors do not exist. If Φ_x vanishes in the 1D example you
can easily calculate the curvature of integral curves. It is $-\frac{\Phi_{xx}}{\Phi_s}$. For
a causal structure *this curvature has to be negative*. Only then is the
branching toward the correct direction. Thus you obtain the *necessary
condition*: $\{\Phi_x = 0 \to \Phi_{xx}\Phi_s > 0\}$.

If you are interested in the higher-order differential structure too,
the same condition must hold for *arbitrary partial derivatives of Φ with
respect to the spatial coordinates*. This is certainly guaranteed if the one-
parameter family $\Phi(x; s)$ is a solution of the *diffusion equation* (that is,
$\Phi_{xx} = \Phi_s$) with boundary condition $\Phi(x; 0) = \Phi(x)$. Thus solutions of
the diffusion equation are necessarily causal atlases. That they are the
only possibility can also be shown, but the proof is not very enlightening
from an intuitive point of view.

For arbitrary dimension (n say) the diffusion equation is:

$$\triangle \Phi = \Phi_\sigma$$

where σ is again a measure of the inner scale. The kernel or Green's function for this partial differential equation is the Gaussian. For dimension
three ($n = 3$; "just space") you have:[8]

$$G_{000}(x, y, z; \sigma) = \frac{e^{-\frac{x^2+y^2+z^2}{4\sigma}}}{(4\pi\sigma)^{\frac{3}{2}}}$$

The "width" of this bloblike function is about $s = 2.8 \ldots \sqrt{\sigma}$, where s
denotes the "inner scale." Instead of running the diffusion equation, you
may convolve with the "window" G_{000}, or—what amounts to the same—
replace the density with its average value over the window of diameter
s.

If you introduce the vector $\vec{C} = -\text{grad}\,\Phi$ as a "current," the diffusion
equation becomes $\text{div}\,\vec{C} + \Phi_\sigma = 0$, which can be interpreted as an *equation of continuity*.[9] The current $\vec{C}$ "transports" the density in such a
way as to conserve the "source material" Φ very much in the spirit of
what happens when you fool around with a blob of clay.

The total influx of current through a closed surface equals the increase
of material, which is represented by the volume integral of the density, for

---

[8] Relax! I will explain the notation with the funny lower indices soon enough.

[9] I intentionally use "physics-notation" here; you may want to convert the formalism to the much nicer differential form notation.

any change of the inner scale. The current "redistributes" the material in such a way that *the density becomes smoother when you increase the inner scale.*

The smoothing process can be followed easily in the 1D case. Consider a local solution of the type $\Phi(\triangle x; \triangle \sigma) = \frac{\triangle x^2}{2} + \triangle \sigma$. For $\triangle \sigma < 0$ you have two zeroes of Φ, for positive $\triangle \sigma$ none. Thus pairs of zeroes vanish when you increase the inner scale. The same process goes on for partial derivatives of arbitrary order.

9.2.2 Singularities

> *Mountains rising from the midst of the sea in the*
> *far distance, though there may be ample space between*
> *them for the free passage of a fleet,*
> *look as if linked together in a single island.*
> —LUCRETIUS (C. 100–C. 55 B.C.), *On the Nature of the Universe*

The singularities of scale space are of a simple type and can be classified via catastrophe theory. Again the 1D case offers a simple example. The singularities are all of the type $\Phi(\triangle x; \triangle \sigma) = \frac{1}{6}\triangle x^3 + \triangle x \triangle \sigma$. For $\triangle \sigma$ *increasing* from zero there are no extrema, whereas for $\triangle \sigma$ *decreasing* from zero you have a maximum and a minimum. Thus the singularity consists of a "collision" of a minimum with a maximum. Under blurring the pair annihilates; under deblurring it is created. When you deblur the point $\triangle x = 0$, $\triangle \sigma = 0$ suddenly explodes into structure. You obtain a pair of critical points.

For higher dimensions the situation can be more complicated and interesting. I will return to such problems later on.

9.2.3 Pyramids

In practical applications, which usually means computer implementation, you have to *sample* scale space in order to arrive at a finite, combinatorial data structure.

It is not hard to do this for any *given* inner scale. You just use the conventional method and compute the "Nyquist sample frequency" for a given tolerance.

It is not immediately apparent how to go about the sampling in "the resolution domain" though. One lead can be used though. Since there is *no preferred scale*, the sampling density should be *scale invariant.* This fixes the functional dependence of the sample rate right away to a uniform sampling on a logarithmic scale. What this means is that the inner scale should be stepped up by fixed percentages of the present value.

Since the blurred functions are smoother than the unblurred ones, you have lower Nyquist sample frequencies for more blurred functions. You may predeform scale space so as to make the sampling intervals isotropic and homogeneous. Then a given region leads to an exponentially tapered "pyramid" in the predeformed scale space. Such structures were in fact the first to be described in the literature and are generally referred to as "pyramids" (fig. 442).[10] Rosenfeld's book gives a good introduction.

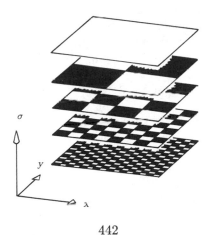

442

9.3   Theory of measurement

Up to this point I have treated scale space more or less as a *mathematical fiction*. But instead of such a treatment I could have introduced it via a *physical operational definition* of densities. In order to make the point more tangible, I will use the paradigm of an *atmospheric cloud*.

What do people mean by the concept "a cloud"? The more you know of the actual constitution of clouds, the more mysterious the problem appears. Perhaps the most useful definition is: a somewhat localized region with an exceptionally high concentration of condensed water in

---

[10]The "pyramid" structures as they are commonly used in image processing *seriously undersample* scale space. Thus their properties reflect the idiosyncratic sampling as well as the properties of scale space itself. This makes these structures hard to deal with conceptually.

the earth's atmosphere. Consider a typical continental cumulus cloud. You can expect a few hundred water droplets per cubical centimeter with droplet diameters in the range of 3-30 micrometers. A typical density of condensed water is quoted as 0.4 grams per cubical meter.

What is actually meant by "density" here? This is yet another term that appears simple enough at first glance but as rather ill-defined and mysterious when you give it some thought. It very clearly depends on the inner scale. For an inner scale of a micrometer the density is either that of liquid water or that of air, depending critically on the position within the cloud. For an inner scale of ten miles the density is low because the sample in the "window" is heavily "diluted." Most of the window is outside the cloud. Both results are essentially *useless*. For a reasonable estimate of the density the right inner scale is about a meter, with maybe an order of magnitude "play" on both sides.

The *physical density* is a ratio between the sampled flux, which is the total amount of condensed water in the sampling window, and the volume of the sampling window. This is similar to the *mathematical definition* except for the fact that the physicist cannot and *should not* take the limit for vanishing inner scale. The physical density depends essentially on its operationalization; in other words, on the inner scale. "The" physical density is really a one-parameter family of densities.

In most cases of practical interest it doesn't matter very much what the actual shape of the sampling window is. However, it becomes important when you are interested in the spatial structure of the density at the highest levels of resolution, the level of the inner scale. Then you encounter the phenomenon of "spurious resolution" or "false detail," due to a less than fortunate choice of the shape of the sampling window. The only shape that avoids spurious resolution altogether is the Gaussian weighted sample window. But in that case *the physical density is merely an operational realization of the abstract scale space* introduced previously.

> In visual art we are aware of forms as charged with a tension
> to be thus manifest.
> They are the simple showing products of complication;
> they are faces: they disclose, they spread:
> they are unfolded like the open face of the rose:
> a folded cycle is unfurled as a shape.
> —ADRIAN STOKES, *Colour and Form (1937)*

9.4   Densities and Level Sets

You may define a "cloud" as a blob of atmospheric space where the density of condensed water measured at an inner scale of a meter exceeds about 0.2 grams per cubical meter. Thus you pick a *fiducial density* $\Phi^*$and define the *object* as the set

$$\{\vec{x} \mid \Phi(\vec{x};\sigma) \geq \Phi^*\}.$$

The *level set* $\Phi(\vec{x};\sigma) = \Phi^*$ is the "surface" of the object. Thus the "cloud" has a *smooth surface* despite the fact that it consists of a dispersion of disjunct spheres of liquid water.

The level sets depend on the parameter σ; thus you deal with a one-parameter family of surfaces rather than with a single one.

It proves to be advantageous to introduce a *normalized density* as follows: $\varphi(\vec{x};\sigma) = \frac{\Phi(\vec{x};\sigma)}{\Phi^*}$. The level sets are just $\varphi = 1$. The advantage derives from the fact that φ is *dimensionless*, whereas Φ isn't.

9.4.1   Set theory

The normalized densities can be used in set theoretical operations. Consider a simple example. You may treat *treetops* in the same way as I did the cloud. Instead of the amount of condensed water in a sampling window you just weigh the total biomass. A "treetop" presupposes an inner scale of about a foot. Then oaktrees are more or less hemispherical, whereas the typical cypress is conical.

Using the normalized density, you may compute the *union* or *intersection* of an apple and an orange tree as follows (note that the *normalization* allows you to mix apples—the set $\mathcal{A}$—and oranges—the set $\mathcal{O}$!). Intersection and union are defined as:

$$\mathcal{A} \cap \mathcal{O} = \{\vec{x} \mid \varphi_{\mathcal{A}} \cdot \varphi_{\mathcal{O}} \geq 1\}$$
$$\mathcal{A} \cup \mathcal{O} = \{\vec{x} \mid \varphi_{\mathcal{A}} + \varphi_{\mathcal{O}} \geq 1\}.$$

The union makes immediate physical sense. For the union of two apple trees you find a result that treats the pair as a single tree.

The intersection is more enigmatic. You may appreciate that this definition is very much like a cross-correlation. Notice that a "true" cross-correlation of two dispersed systems usually yields a void result. This is certainly the case for the trees in the example. Because the leaves have to occupy their own portions of space, they can in no sense "overlap." It actually makes more *sense* to correlate the blurred versions than to blur the correlation. In these terms the present definition

is an operationally reasonable prescription to find the cross-correlation
(figs. 443 to 446).

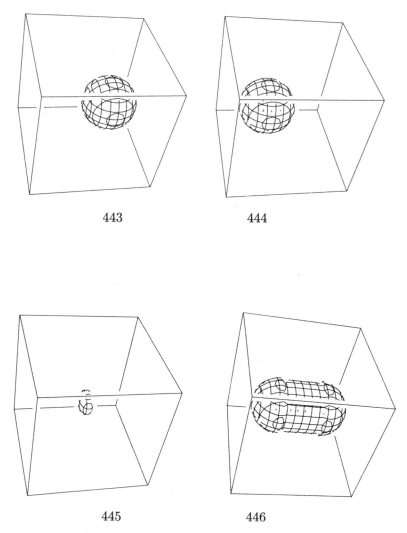

443   444

445   446

This leads to a "set theory" that differs a bit from the usual version:
the present definition lacks the notion of complementation because there

doesn't exist a notion of the "universal set". Most theorems in this set theory are somewhat weaker versions of the corresponding theorems in the "official" set theory. Some theorems are actually identical.

A distant tree is not a flat and even piece of colour,
but a more or less globular mass of a downy or bloomy texture,
partly passing into a misty vagueness. I find, practically,
this lovely softness of far-away trees
the most difficult of all characters to reach ...
—JOHN RUSKIN, *The Elements of Drawing (1857)*

9.4.2   Differential Geometry

*Now, in the first place, this term "the figure of the Earth," which
seems to have a certain definite & determinate meaning, is really very
vague & indefinite. The surface which bounds the seas, the lakes, the
rivers, the mountains, the plains & the valleys, is really something
quite irregular, at least to us; & moreover it is also unstable; for it
changes with the slightest motion of the waves & the soil. But those
who investigate "the figure of the Earth," do not deal with this figure
of the Earth; they substitute for it another figure which, although to
some extent regular, yet approximates closely to the former true figure;
that is to say, it has mountains & the hills leveled off, whilst the valleys
are filled up. ...*
    *Also, there can be an infinite number of surfaces, & these too quite
different from one another, which satisfy the problem; & all of them, of
such a kind that they have manifest humps, as far as they can be
detected; & this term even contains no true definiteness.*
—ROGERIO JOSEPHO BOSCOVICH, S.J. (1711–1787), *Expeditio
Litteraria per Pontificam ditionem*

Given the normalized density $\varphi(\vec{x}; \sigma)$, you want an entrance to the
differential geometrical treatment of the object. I will keep the inner
scale fixed in this section, and I will then leave out references to σ.

It is an easy matter to find the *surface* of the object. It is just the
level curve $\varphi(\vec{x}) = 1$. It is equally easy to define a field of—inward—unit
normals on the surface because the gradient of the density is obviously
orthogonal to the level surface. Thus you have

$$\vec{n}(\vec{x}) = \frac{\vec{\nabla}\varphi}{\|\vec{\nabla}\varphi\|}.$$

Notice that the normal is defined over most of the space, not just at
the surface. The only points where it is undefined are the critical points
of the normalized density. Thus you obtain a rather extended tubular
neighborhood.

You may establish local coordinates (x, y, z) with z increasing in the
normal direction. Then it is not hard to show that for such a Monge
patch the eigenvectors of the quadratic form $\varphi_{xx}x^2 + 2\varphi_{xy}xy + \varphi_{yy}y^2$
are the principal directions of the level surfaces. Again, they are defined
almost everywhere. You obtain a frame field in a rather voluminous
tubular neighborhood of the level set.

The upshot of all this is that you obtain the frame field through the partial derivatives of the normalized density and that these partial derivatives do not depend critically on the exact localization of the level set. For instance, you can compute the normal and the principal directions without first finding the level set at all.

9.4.3 Partial derivatives

The partial derivatives of the normalized density with respect to the spatial coordinates open the way to the differential geometry of the surface, which is merely the unit level set of the density. It is of considerable interest to study how they depend on the inner scale.

You may construct kernels that yield the *partial derivatives* for arbitrary inner scales. Consider the following simple result, which is a trivial consequence of the fact that the diffusion equation is linear:

$$\frac{\partial}{\partial x}(\varphi \otimes G_{000}) = \frac{\partial \varphi}{\partial x} \otimes G_{000} = \varphi \otimes G_{100}.$$

with

$$G_{100} = \frac{\partial G_{000}}{\partial x}$$

or in words:

Useful Fact: *the partial derivative of the blurred density equals the blurred partial derivative of the density and also equals the convolution of the density with a kernel that is the same partial derivative of the window function.*

Thus the general kernel for arbitrary partial derivatives is

$$G_{klm} = \frac{\partial^{k+l+m} G_{000}}{\partial x^k y^l z^m}.$$

It is a simple though rather tedious exercise to express these derivatives in terms of "special functions," in this case the Hermite polynomials and the Gaussian. These kernels are numerically very robust operators because they combine a differentiating with an integrating behavior. They are analytically as convenient as can be because they satisfy all the rules of differential calculus in the obvious manner.

I will use the term "fuzzy differentiators" for these kernels, a term that aptly describes their main properties. They are very important because all features familiar from local differential geometry can be expressed as algebraic combinations of partial derivatives. You may directly substitute fuzzy derivatives and thus arrive at the evolution of the features with nary an effort.

You obtain finite operators, namely spatial weighing functions or "neighborhood operators," that represent various geometrical objects in their operational garb *exactly*. For instance, the weighing function $G_{100}(x, y, z; \sigma)$ represents the unit vector in the x-direction. The integral of any scalar field multiplied with this weighting function indeed equals the partial derivative with respect to the x-coordinate of the blurred (parameter σ) version of that scalar field and thus is identical to the operation of $\vec{e}_x$ on the blurred field.

Important Observation *This completely eliminates the need for an "infinitesimal domain" and allows you to handle geometrical objects such as vectors in an exact sense on numerically specified scalar fields.*

9.4.4   Shape calculations

♠ Intermezzo—In case you want to program it.

The surface is a level set $\varphi(x, y, z) = 1$ of the normalized density. Thus you have to solve a nasty nonlinear equation in order to calculate points of the surface. In computational differential geometry you probably have the density sampled on some spatial grid, and you find the surface through search and interpolation. If you use a "pile of sugarcubes" representation, you are all set from the very start, since you merely have to compare your voxel values with the fiducial density.

You can find the *normal direction* in terms of the first-order spatial derivatives, that is, in terms of the gradient. Notice that it is not necessary to find the surface first. The accuracy by which you determine the surface points need have no influence on the accuracy by which you determine the normal. The normal direction is defined all over space, except at the critical points of the density.

The gradient

$$\vec{G} = \vec{\nabla}\varphi = \varphi_x \vec{e}_x + \varphi_y \vec{e}_y + \varphi_z \vec{e}_z$$

is a vector in the normal direction. Thus the normal is $\vec{n} = \frac{\vec{G}}{\|\vec{G}\|}$. For other inner scales you simply use the expression

$$\vec{G} = G_{100} \otimes \varphi \vec{e}_x + G_{010} \otimes \varphi \vec{e}_y + G_{001} \otimes \varphi \vec{e}_z,$$

where the derivations have been replaced with convolutions with first-order fuzzy derivatives. This is a very practical and robust method in computational differential geometry.

In practice you may just find the *direction* for which the first-order directional fuzzy derivatives assume a maximum. That is the normal direction.

After finding the normal direction, you rotate the coordinate system such that $\vec{e}_x$ and $\vec{e}_y$ span the tangent plane of the level set. Next you look for a direction $\vec{e}_r$ (say) in the tangent plane for which the second derivative $\frac{\partial^2}{\partial r^2}$ assumes a maximum. In practice you will substitute a fuzzy derivative, of course. In general there will be two orthogonal directions for which this is the case. These are the principal directions. Once you have found the principal directions, you rotate the frame such that the principal directions coincide with $\vec{e}_x$, $\vec{e}_y$. You have constructed a principal frame.

The *principal curvatures* are

$$\kappa_x = \frac{G_{200}\otimes\varphi}{|G_{001}\otimes\varphi|} \quad \kappa_y = \frac{G_{020}\otimes\varphi}{|G_{001}\otimes\varphi|}$$

and you have a fairly complete basis from which to start your differential geometrical investigations.

Alternatively you may compute the matrices of the first and second derivatives of the density (φ_i and φ_{ij}). In computational differential geometry you use fuzzy derivatives of course. You bring the matrix of second derivatives (the Hessian) to diagonal form through a suitable rotation.

Then you find the Gaussian curvature from

$$K = \frac{\varphi_1{}^2\varphi_{22}\varphi_{33} + \varphi_2{}^2\varphi_{11}\varphi_{33} + \varphi_3{}^2\varphi_{11}\varphi_{22}}{(\varphi_1{}^2 + \varphi_2{}^2 + \varphi_3{}^2)^2},$$

and the mean curvature from

$$H = \frac{\varphi_1{}^2(\varphi_{22} + \varphi_{33}) + \varphi_2{}^2(\varphi_{11} + \varphi_{33}) + \varphi_3{}^2(\varphi_{11} + \varphi_{22})}{2(\varphi_1{}^2 + \varphi_2{}^2 + \varphi_3{}^2)^{\frac{3}{2}}}.$$

You can find the asymptotic directions from the simultaneous conditions ($\vec{a}$ denotes the asymptotic direction):

$$\vec{a}.\{\varphi_{ij}\}\vec{a} = 0$$
$$\vec{a}.\vec{n} = 0.$$

The second condition is merely the requirement that the asymptotic direction lie in the tangent plane.

Similarly, you can find the principal directions from the conditions ($\vec{d}$ denotes a principal direction):

$$\vec{n} \wedge \vec{d} \wedge \{\varphi_{ij}\}\vec{d} = 0$$
$$\vec{d}.\vec{n} = 0.$$

(The first condition merely expresses the coplanarity of the gradient, the principal direction, and the *change of the normal* along the principal direction.)

The importance of all these relations is that you can derive all the differential geometry of the *surface* via differential operations on the *scalar field* of the density in *space*. These you can conveniently calculate by way of the fuzzy differentiators. Thus, you gain access to the differential geometry of the surfaces of your objects at any level of resolution in a way that is eminently suited to computer implementation.

The method is robust, and can be applied to empirically determined densities (*e.g.*, three-dimensional images from nuclear medicine, such as scintigrams). Tolerances can be adjusted to suit the observational errors. Moreover, all relevant measures arise as volume integral subject to certain localized weighing functions. It is a neat and convenient way to use all the data and avoids many of the problems that beset operations with *surfaces*, as contrasted with *volumes*.

9.4.4.1   Density Ridges

♠ INTERMEZZO—JUST A CURIOSITY.

The density is a scalar function in three-space. The *density ridges* are the surfaces generated by the singular integral curves of the gradient, that is, those integral curves that separate the families of curves going to distinct extrema. This is much like the way the main watershed acts as the medial axis of an island. These surfaces have many features in common with the medial axis, although this similarity is not at all self-evident from a formal point of view.

If you find yourself at a minimum and follow the integral curves of the fastest increase of the density ("walk uphill"), you are bound to end up at one or another maximum. *Which exact maximum it will be* depends on the precise direction in which you started your journey.

If you start to walk blindly uphill from inside a valley, it all depends on your initial direction which summit you will reach. Some paths lead to one maximum and some to another.

The families of paths that run into a single extremum are separated by singular surfaces that are the three-dimensional analogues of the "watersheds" and "watercourses" of a geographical landscape. As the latter divide the landscape into natural districts ("hills" or "dales"), so the former divide space into space cells labeled by density extrema.

One difference with the medial axes is that the ridges don't end in midair the way the medial axes do, but run right through the level surfaces. Thus they also generate special curves, namely those of their intersection, on the level surface.

These latter curves are a kind of "ridges," distinct from the ridges defined by the normal ray manifold of the level surface. They are, if anything, of even greater practical utility. In order to distinguish these entities from the ridges you already know, I will refer to them as "crests." Depending on whether they are convex or concave, they can be used to define "crests" and "natural part boundaries."

There exists a good deal of classical literature on this kind of description, including polemics over the "correct" definition of the "Thalweg" and so forth, starting with the seminal publications of Cayley and of Maxwell on the description of geographical terrain in terms of "hills" and "dales." The third volume of the *Enzyklopaedie der mathematischen Wissenschaften* will put you on the track.

> ... you must therefore try to discover some mode of execution
> which will more or less imitate, by its own variety and mystery,
> the variety and mystery of Nature,
> without absolute delineation of detail.
> —JOHN RUSKIN, *The Elements of Drawing (1857)*

9.5   Singularities

When you consider the evolutionary sequence of a level set, you will
immediately notice two types of singularities: changes of the connectivity
such as merges and splittings of blobs, and changes in the curvature
landscape such as the emergence of furrows, and so forth. Such events
always take place in a stereotyped manner and it is not very hard to
come up with a complete taxonomy. I will consider both types of events
here.

These two types do not at all exhaust the changes that might well
interest you, of course. For instance, it is also quite interesting to find
the events that change the medial axes.

9.5.1   The Connectivity

A generic piece of the level set cannot split or merge when you vary the
inner scale somewhat. This is immediately clear when you consider the
local Taylor expansion of the density for a point on the unit level set:

$$\varphi(x, y, z; \sigma) = 1 + a_x x + a_y y + a_z z + b\sigma + \dots$$

The coefficient b depends on the second-order terms in the spatial coordinates, of course, because φ must satisfy the diffusion equation. Thus
you must have $b = a_{xx} + a_{yy} + a_{zz}$ in the present notation. The unit
level set is the locus $\varphi = 1$; thus the level surface is approximately given
by the "plane" $a_x x + a_y y + a_z z + b\sigma = 0$, that is, a moving plane in
space. "Moving" when you turn the knob on σ, that is. Thus the level
surface *moves about* when you change the resolution but doesn't change
into something else.

You obtain a completely different behavior if the point is a *critical
point* of the density. For a given inner scale you cannot expect to find
critical points of the density on the level set. However, for the evolutionary *family* you will encounter singular members for which this actually
happens. It is a "versal" event. Near such a point the Hessian of the
density can be used to describe the density locally. I replace the coefficient b with the Laplacean, using the diffusion equation explicitly. The
result is

$$\varphi(x, y, z; \sigma) = \quad 1$$
$$+ \tfrac{1}{2}(a_{xx}x^2 + 2a_{xy}xy + 2a_{xz}xz + a_{yy}y^2 + 2a_{yz}yz + a_{zz}z^2)$$
$$+ \dots + (a_{xx} + a_{yy} + a_{zz})\sigma + \dots$$

This time you obtain a *one-parameter family of general quadrics* in
space. The parameter is σ.

With a suitable rotation of the coordinate axes you can bring about
the following simple canonical form:

$$\frac{1}{2}(ax^2 + by^2 + cz^2) + (a+b+c)\sigma = 0$$

where you may (re-)label the axes such that $a \geq b \geq c$. This simplifies
the discussion quite a lot because by now you have freed yourself from
most of the rococo embellishments. You can obtain the taxonomy of
singular events by just considering the signs of a, b, c, and $d = a+b+c$.
The resulting events can be classified in certain equivalence classes as
follows (fig. 447; of course, I made up the fancy names for the occasion;
there is no established convention here):

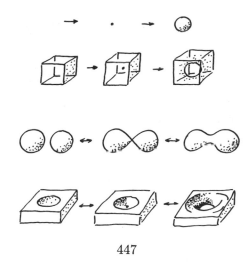

447

Emergence processes The parameters a, b, and c are all of the same
sign. Then the parameter d obviously must posses the same sign.
Thus you have two possibilities, depending on the sign:

   a blob when the sign is negative

   a bubble when the sign is positive

Accretion processes The parameter a is positive, the parameters b
and c, negative. There exist two distinct cases depending on the
sign of the parameter d:

   a merge when d is negative

a split when d is positive

Versification processes The parameters a and b are both positive, the parameter c, negative. Again, there exist two distinct cases according to the sign of the parameter d:

a hole-collapse when d is negative

a punch-through when d is positive.

The geometrical significance of these processes is the following:

- The "emergence processes" describe purely local events, the creation or annihilation of a volume. This may be a "bubble," that is, an ovoid hole, or a "blob," which represents a chunk of material. These processes run only one way. You easily check that the bubbles or blobs are created on deblurring and annihilated on blurring.

- The "accretion processes" describe the sudden union or separation of existing structures. For the "merge," a neck or bridge forms on blurring. This neck connects two chunks of material. The "split" is the converse of the merge; on blurring, a chunk of material splits into two pieces.

- The "versification processes" do not change the number of components but do change the connectivity (the Euler number). This is equally true for the "bubble" creation. The versification processes are special because they can run *both ways*, though. The "hole-collapse" fills a through-hole on blurring. Thus a hole-collapse will blur a torus into an ovoid with two dimples. The "punch-through" has the reverse effect; thus it can *create* a through-hole and produce a torus out of a double-dimpled ovoid.

Many people seem to experience the split and the punch-through intuitively as "noncausal" events because they complicate the topology on blurring instead of simplifying it. Yet these processes are intuitively very "natural" when considered from the right point of view. Consider two spheres with a very thin wire soldered between them. When you blur this scene, it stands to reason that you will lose sight of the wire. This is a "split."

You can often observe this effect in nature in the following way. You easily change the resolution—relative to the linear dimensions of your object—by changing the viewing distance. If you look at a leaved branch

against the sky—overcast sky is best for this exercise—then from a sufficient distance you lose sight of the stems of the leaves. Now the leaves,
which are still clearly perceived, apparently have detached themselves
from the branch and seemingly just hover in the air. This effect, to the
best of my knowledge, was first described in detail by John Ruskin in his
influential and rather delightful book, the "The Elements of Drawing,"
which first appeared in 1857 (fig. 448).

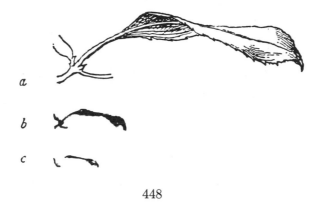

448

You now appreciate the possible connection between the dumbbell
and the pair of spheres. They are almost similar, indeed, being divided
by a mere "merge" event. Figure 449 shows the pair of spheres at the
very moment of the merge, and also after some additional blurring.

9.5.2 The Curvature

It is very hard to classify the events that change the curvature on the basis of the structure of the density function. This is because the principal
curvatures depend in a complicated way on the partial derivatives of the
density with respect to the spatial coordinates. It is possible to take a
kind of "short cut," however, and deal with the curvature directly. This
method has the greater heuristic value, which is the reason I introduce
it at this place.

Suppose the local radius of curvature of the level surface is large with
respect to the inner scale. Then the surface can be considered as *almost
flat* as far as the blurring process is concerned. This is an approximation,
of course. It only applies to these situations where the inverses of the
principal curvatures, the radii of curvature, are large with respect to the
resolution, that is, the square root of σ. In the cases of most interest this
always applies, however. For whenever curvatures change in interesting

449

ways, they become zero in the process.[11]

In such cases it is possible to show that the local surface relief $z(x, y)$ (where x and y denote coordinates in the tangent plane, whereas z points along the normal direction) is also *blurred via the diffusion equation*; thus you have $z_{xx} + z_{yy} = z_\sigma$. Of course, the same relation holds for arbitrary partial derivatives of the relief. This approach has the disadvantage of being less elegant, because you use an unnecessary approximation, but the considerable advantage that it provides a rather direct, intuitive insight into the evolution of the curvature landscape.

That you don't need the approximation is clear because of the following reasoning. It is sufficient to solve for the relief as a function of the inner scale and find $z(x, y, \sigma)$. The Gauss map is just the map from the tangent plane (x, y) to the "gradient space" $(u = -z_x, v = -z_y)$. An elementary application of catastrophe theory, basically just a table lookup in Thom's table, then suffices to find the generic singularities.[12]

In order to get a feeling for what happens, you may consider a lower order example first. Think, for instance, of a one-dimensional relief $z(x)$, that is, the shape of the boundary of a planar blob. A simple solution of the diffusion equation is $z(x) = \frac{x^4}{24} + \sigma\frac{x^2}{2} + \frac{\sigma^2}{2}$. The inflections are located at $z_{xx} = 0 = \frac{x^2}{2} + \sigma$. Thus you observe a pair of inflections at

---

[11] If you feel uneasy about this approximation, you may rest assured that the results can also be obtained directly without using the approximation at all. However, the approximation makes things more easily graspable by the inner vision.

[12] There is a problem here that I glibly skip but will return to.

the points $\pm\sqrt{-2\sigma}$ for deblurring and no inflections at all on blurring. The pair separates at a rate $\frac{1}{\sqrt{-2\sigma}}$; thus they move with infinite velocity at the moment of creation. You observe a veritable "explosion" of the singularity at $\sigma = 0$. This is how the boundary of a planar blob articulates when you deblur the blob. Pairs of inflections appear at singular points and very rapidly separate. On blurring the reverse process takes place and inflections are pairwise removed until the shape is ovoid.

For the 3D case the situation is somewhat more complicated. You don't have to consider *points* of inflection but the *parabolic curves*, which are "curves of inflection of the surface." When an ovoid articulates in an evolutionary sequence, it must somehow develop parabolic loops. When a number of loops exist, you may also expect interactions between the loops.

In the parlance of catastrophe theory you have a "potential" depending on two "state variables" (x and y) and three "control variables," namely the coordinates u, v on the Gaussian sphere, and the inner scale σ. Then a standard result of catastrophe theory is that you will have the *lips*, the *beaks*, the *swallowtail*, and the elliptic and hyperbolic *umbilic* as the singularities that govern the evolutionary sequences of the surface relief.

Figure 450 illustrates the possible events that change the Gauss map.

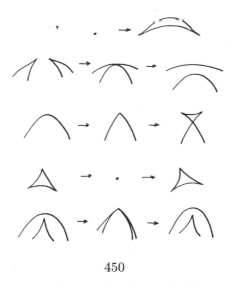

450

This is the easiest way to visualize the changes in the curvature landscape of surfaces. These terms are technical and somewhat misleading. What I mean is that you should not associate them with the surface undulations that I introduced earlier under similar names, at least not in a simple-minded manner.

This application of catastrophe theory is not altogether trivial because of the constraint imposed by the diffusion equation; thus the "unfolding" due to the control variable σ is not quite free. Problems can be expected when the linear term in σ vanishes, that is to say, when the surface is locally minimal. I skip these complications here. They do not yield much that is of interest for the present purpose, anyway.

Of these singularities *only the lips can generate novel parabolic loops*. What happens is that an elliptic patch develops a flat point and this singularity immediately explodes into a parabolic loop. The resulting structure is similar to the *furrow* I described earlier in some detail; thus you get a hyperbolic island. Once you have hyperbolic patches, you may also expect lips events that generate elliptic islands in them. Such undulations are similar to the *hump*, described in detail in chapter seven. By now you will appreciate the more than just exemplary importance of these basic surface undulations. Any shape evolves from an—all-convex—ovoid, and the undulations originate by stages from initially simple structures like the furrow and the hump. Note that *you will only gain parabolic loops on deblurring* but will never lose them, insofar as the shape diffusion is causal.

The other singularities merely articulate the undulations through processes that either complicate the structure of a parabolic loop or involve interactions between disjunct parabolic loops.

The *swallowtail* generates a pair of ruffles on a parabolic arc. This only happens on deblurring the shape. I have illustrated this event already in an earlier chapter. The parabolic curve is smooth and remains smooth, although it tends to have an obvious wriggle. The fold of the Gauss map changes between a smooth curve and a curve with two cusps and a self-intersection ("swallowtail shape"). Thus the event creates a pair of ruffles, a unode, and a tacnode. You should look up the figure in the chapter on global patches.

The *elliptic umbilic* is similar to the perturbed monkey saddle. What happens is that an elliptic island bounded with a parabolic loop possessing three ruffles changes from convex to concave or vice versa, passing through a flat point at the event itself.

The *beaks* and the *hyperbolic umbilic* are the main mechanisms through which the existing pattern of parabolic loops may change its topological structure.

The *beaks* event changes the connectivity of the hyperbolic area in the following manner. In the Gaussian image two pleats approach each other and merge. After the blending you are left with two smooth folds that are made up of parts that once belonged to the folds connected to two different pleats. In the reverse direction two folds approach and when they have become tangent split into two pleats. The pleats may belong to two different parabolic loops or to a single one, that is, a *global* rather than a *local* matter. Thus it is possible for the two pleats in the fold of a furrow to approach each other and go through a beaks event. The result is two concentric parabolic loops.

This is typically how you obtain the "bell" type of undulation. You can't obtain a bell in one go when you deblur some ovoid shape; it isn't generic. You can get a "feel" for this if you imagine yourself just sitting there with an ovoid of clay in your hands wanting to raise a local mound on it. You will find that *whatever move you make will cause an indentation first*. What you get is the initial creation of a furrow. The furrow grows and bends around, then "bites its own tail." This is the beaks event that lets you lose the pleats. You are left with a bell. In this sense the two parabolic loops of the bell belong intimately together; they were once of one piece.

The *hyperbolic umbilic* involves the interaction between a pleat and a fold. It is similar to the perturbed handkerchief surface. A pleat is transferred from one fold to another. At the singularity you have two intersecting parabolic arcs. The hyperbolic umbilic is involved in the evolution of the typical "dimple." The evolution can be described as follows: you start with an ovoid and first contract a furrow. The furrow grows and the hyperbolic area develops a hump. You have now two concentric parabolic arcs. Each has two pleats in the Gaussian image. Then two successive events of the hyperbolic umbilic type serve to transfer all pleats to the outer parabolic loop. The result is the dimple as described in chapter seven. Thus the parabolic loops of the dimple are a *true pair*, they were never one but were created at different times.

9.6 Canonical projection

The canonical projection of scale space also induces a canonical projection between the level sets at different inner scales. The projection is neatly one-to-one except at the critical points of the density, that is, at the singularities of the connectivity. At such places the projection bifurcates. For instance, at a "merge" the singular point of momentary contact projects to a curve encircling the freshly formed "neck." Such a curve can be regarded as "the seam" that necessarily has to be created in order to join the two blobs.

Similarly, at a "split" each of the resulting chunks carries a "scar" that is due to the section (fig. 451).

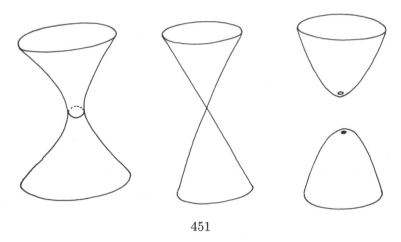

451

Similar observations apply to the other topological events. The scars and seams are of great interest because they can be used as a means to induce a division of a shape into *natural subparts,* an ability that is fundamental for any "shape grammar."

9.6.1   The primordial egg

When you increase the inner scale far enough, you can annihilate *any* blob completely. Clear enough, when the sampling window becomes huge, the samples are so much "diluted" through inclusion of the "background" that you will lose sight of the object.

At the moment of annihilation the shape of the blob must be a triaxial ellipsoid because it is just the "blob" type of emergence process described above. Thus any shape can be blurred into an ovoid with four umbilical points. Conversely, the evolutionary sequence leading up to any shape has to start with such an ovoid. In many cases an evolutionary sequence will "assemble" a blob from several or even many of such ovoids that are created at different times. The hyperbolic areas of a surface are either inherited from the assemblage and are "blown out" seams or are articulated furrows starting with lips events.

In this sense the ovoid is really the simplest shape around, and it appears as the "primordial egg" from which any shape may develop.

> When we see the square towers
> of a city in the distance,
> they often appear round.
> —LUCRETIUS (c. 100–c. 55 B.C.), On the Nature of the Universe

9.7   Morphological scripts

I will conclude this chapter with the description of some typical evolutionary sequences. It is, of course, impossible to do anything toward a complete enumeration of shapes. The examples are just that: *examples*. They are of interest as paradigms because you will not find this kind of illustration in the usual textbooks.

I have found that most of my fellow scientists tend to be puzzled by the kind of complexity you routinely meet with in even simple shapes. When I show computer movies of really rather simple examples, even many mathematical friends look surprised at what they see. The reason is probably that the usual textbook material only prepares you for examinations, not for real life applications. The examples may serve to prepare you for the kinds of things you will inevitably find when you (computer-)process realistic shapes.

Of course, I can only cushion the shock somewhat since it is out of the question to be complete. Nobody knows what "complete" could actually mean. It isn't so bad after all, for since you have a complete catalog of local events, the surprises are only in the global, combinatorial phenomena.

9.7.1   Furrow

The creation of a *furrow* is by far the simplest nontrivial example of a morphogenetic evolution of the curvature landscape. I use it as a start to let you develop a feeling for shape evolutions.

You should start with a look at the first parts of the figure sequences (figs. 452 to 459, the surface with parabolic curves; figs. 460 to 466, the patch as seen from the normal direction at the center, with parabolic and flecnodal curves; figs. 467 to 473, the folds of the normal spherical images; and figs. 474 to 479, the structure of the asymptotic spherical images).

These figures illustrate different aspects of the same evolutionary sequence. You start with the primordial ovoid—in this case just a *patch* of an eggshell—and then go through the *lips event*, which is in fact the only possible change from the eggshell.

As you will remember, the Gaussian image of the parabolic loop that was created is such that the fold has two pleats. It is clear from a topological standpoint that you can't have a single—this is essential—closed fold with just a *single* pleat. What happened was the simplest possibility. Even so the lips can lead to *two qualitatively different kinds*

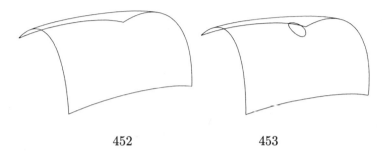

452   453

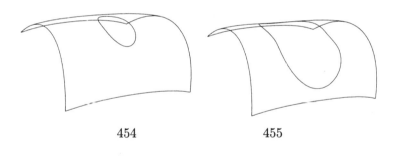

454   455

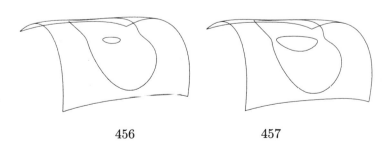

456   457

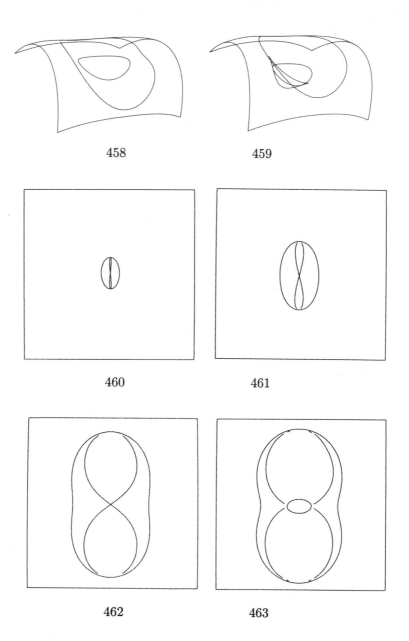

458   459

460   461

462   463

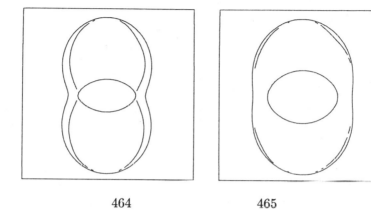

464 465

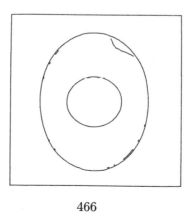

466

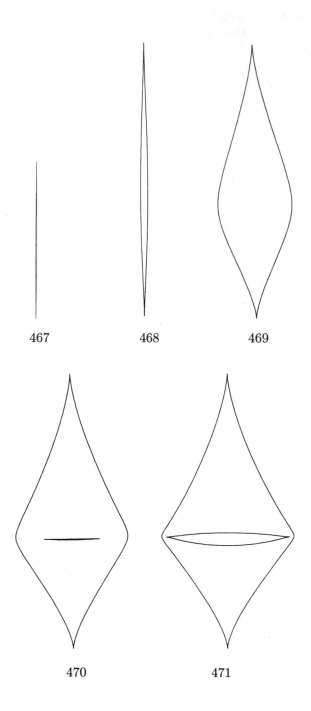

467   468   469

470   471

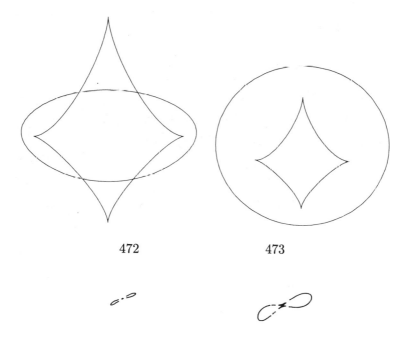

472

473

474

475

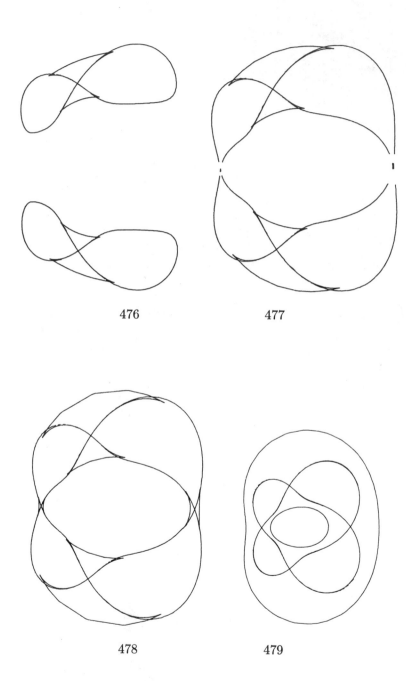

476

477

478

479

of furrow. One possibility is the furrow discussed in chapter seven. It has two inflections on each of the folds that connect the pleats. These map to the cusps of the parabolic curves in the asymptotic spherical image, remember? The other possibility is *that only one of these folds has a pair of inflections,* whereas the other is all concave.

The figures actually illustrate a complicated sequence that only *initiates* with the genesis of a furrow. This is typical of *all* sequences because an ovoid can only start on any evolution by first going through the furrow stage.

In figures 452 to 455 you have illustrations of the patch with the parabolic curve drawn in. In figure 452 the patch is still all elliptic; in figure 453 a small furrow has been created that manages to enlarge its territory in figures 454 and 455. Figures 460 to 462 show a top view with the flecnodal curves drawn in. As you see, the furrow springs to life "fully armed," flecnodals and all, like Athena from the brow of Zeus.

The pattern *grows* in figures 461 and 469 but doesn't change qualitatively.

Figures 467 to 469 show the evolution of the Gauss map. The pattern starts as a very narrow double fold with a pleat at both ends and simply blows up.

Similar remarks apply to the asymptotic spherical image. Right after the genesis of the furrow, all the structure is already there (fig. 174). The full structure explodes out of a point in one go. As the structure blows up, you get a clearer picture (figs. 475 and 476) but there are no qualitative changes.

9.7.2 Hump

The hump is a synclastic island within an anticlastic sea. Thus you can't develop a hump on an ovoid. You have to develop a hyperbolic area first, and this has to be through a lips event.

Once you have a hyperbolic area, you can get a hump through a simple additional lips event. The whole thing is quite similar to the previous case.

You may witness the creation of a hump in figures 455 and 456. In figures 463 and 464 you see how the flecnodals of the hump that just went "out there" in the local picture of the hump neatly mesh in with the flecnodals of the furrow that happens to contain this hump.

In the Gauss map (figs. 470 and 471) the hump just introduces the folds and pleats of its own, but the asymptotic spherical image (figures 477 and 478) again clearly shows how the hump meshes with the external structure.

The furrow and hump fit snugly together as bolt and nut. Figure 480 shows this for the asymptotic spherical image.

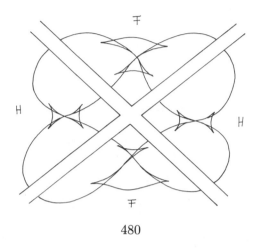

480

9.7.3   Bell

The bell is a somewhat more complicated undulation than the simple furrow. Take a look at the figure sequences (figs. 481 to 486, the surface with parabolic curves; figs. 487 to 491, the surface as seen from the normal direction at the center, with parabolic and flecnodal curves; figs. 492 to 495, the asymptotic spherical images; and figs. 496 to 499) to get a feel for the complexity.

There are several possible evolutionary sequences that all lead to a bell at some stage; thus you might say that there exist *qualitatively different versions of the bell* in the sense that their evolutions differ.

The hyperbolic annulus of the bell has to originate somehow. This has to occur after a preliminary stage in which you have one or more furrows. In the simplest case you have a single furrow of the type that has only one pair of inflections. This furrow curves around and loses its pleats through a beaks event. The result is a "bell."

This is clearly illustrated in figures 481 to 486. In figure 481 you have the pristine, all-elliptic patch. Then a furrow is created (fig. 482), this time of the simple type, different from the furrow treated above, as is evident from the Gauss map (figs. 492 to 494) and especially the asymptotic spherical image (figs. 496 to 499).

The Gauss map again consists of two folds and two pleats, but the

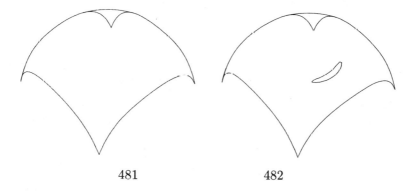

481 482

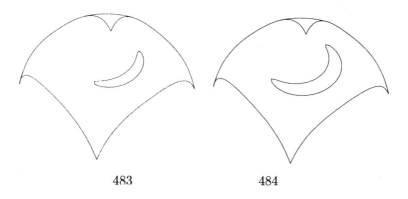

483 484

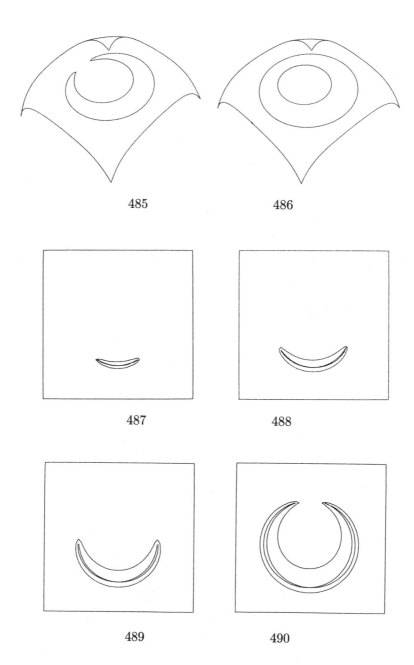

485

486

487

488

489

490

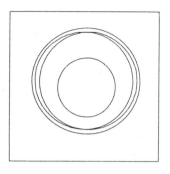

491

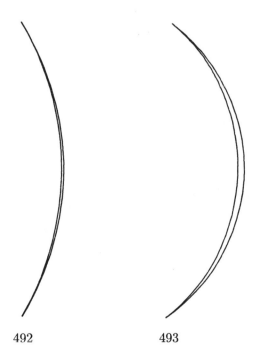

492 493

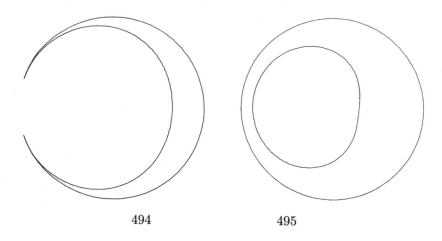

494   495

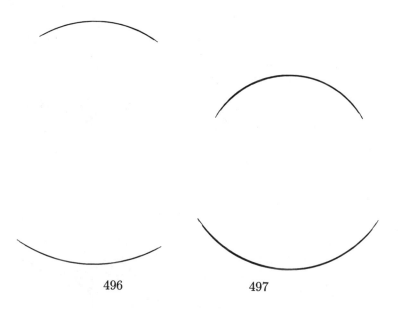

496   497

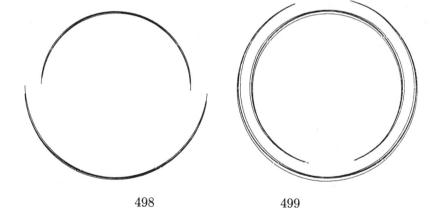

498 499

difference with the previous furrow is that the present one has one all-concave fold. Thus the present furrow has only *two* gutterpoints.

The pattern of flecnodals is in every respect like that of the previous furrow (figs. 487 to 490). The bell is created when the two pleats of the Gauss map meet and merge by way of a beaks event (figs. 494 and 495; figs. 485 and 486; and figs. 490 and 491). Notice what happens to the flecnodals (fig. 491) after the merge. You go from the furrow pattern to the bell pattern, which means that the flecnodals have to break free from the parabolic curve. They exchange the pleats for an intersection. In this case the asymptotic spherical image is too squashed together to be very enlightening.

But, nice as this is, still other scenarios are possible. For instance, you can also have a case in which several furrows merge sequentially so as to form a hyperbolic annulus in the end (figs. 500 to 502, the patch with parabolic curves; figs. 503 to 508, the patch as seen from the normal direction for the center, with parabolic and flecnodal curves; figs. 509 to 511, the folds of the Gauss map; and figs. 512 to 515, the structure of the asymptotic spherical images).The example illustrates a simple case with just two furrows. Notice that the example is a bit too symmetrical to be truly generic. However, the general idea should be illustrated well enough.

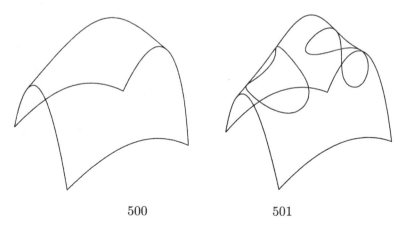

500   501

Figures 500 to 502 illustrate the general layout. The ovoid shell is illustrated in figure 500. Then in figure 501 the two furrows have sprung into existence. Figures 503 to 508 show the pattern of flecnodals, figures 509 to 511 the Gauss map, and figures 512 to 515 the asymptotic spherical image. From the Gauss map you see that both furrows are of

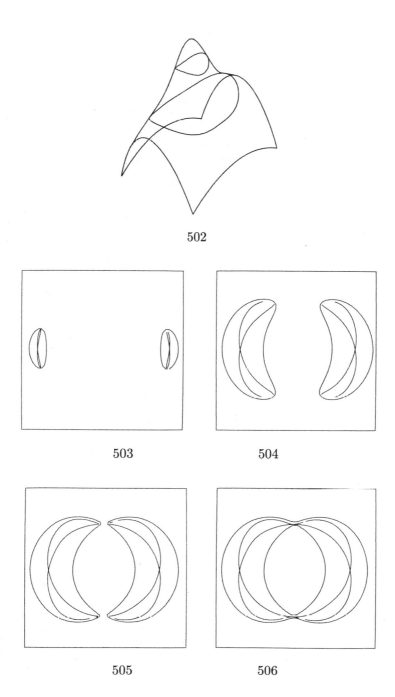

502

503 504

505 506

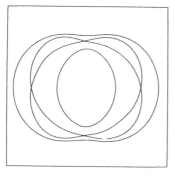

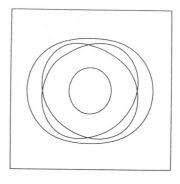

507 508

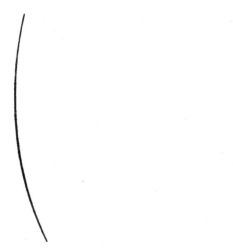

509

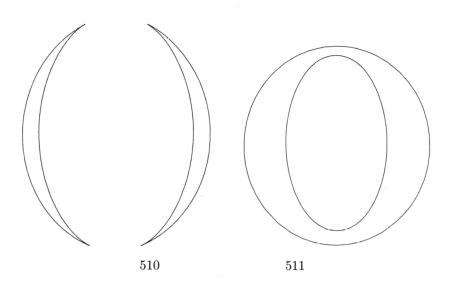

510   511

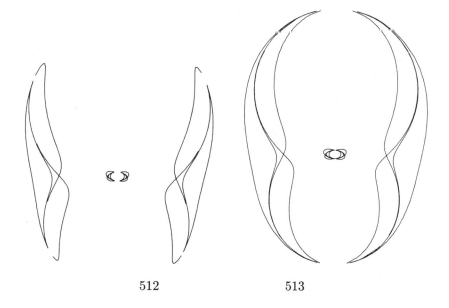

512   513

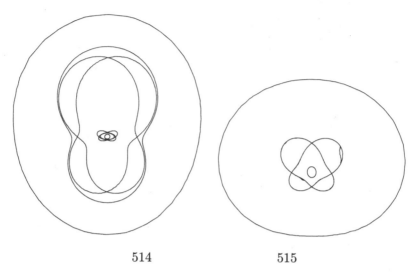

514   515

the two-gutterpoint type. This is especially clear from the asymptotic spherical images.

The merge of the furrows can be brought about through two successive beaks events. In figures 502 and 511 these have just occurred. The change of connectivity in the flecnodal pattern can be especially nicely followed in figures 505 to 507.

9.7.4   Dimple

Like the bell, the dimple is also necessarily a later stage of evolution. You can obtain it from a furrow with a hump in it that is of the opposite type of synclastic shape as the far surroundings—for instance, from an— almost—ovoid with a furrow on it that has a *concave* hump.

In a way such a structure already has some rights to the title of "dimple," since it is indeed a concavity in a convexity. However, it is certainly very much different from the slightly perturbed dimple of revolution because it doesn't have a smooth, closed fold.

The furrow-hump example shown before actually evolves into a dimple (figs. 452 to 479). Two "hyperbolic umbilic" events suffice to transfer the pleats of one parabolic curve to the other and thus to produce a dimple of the type I described earlier (figs. 458 and 459).

After the transfer of the pleats of the Gauss map from one fold to the other, the flecnodals cling closely to the almost singular outer parabolic curve, and my algorithm runs into numerical problems and doesn't quite succeed in computing them very well any more (figs. 465 and 466). The actual transfer of the pleats occurs between figures 471 and 472 in the Gauss map.

After the transfer the four-cusped fold just shrinks in the Gauss map (fig. 473). Remember that it is a mere point in the rotationally symmetric dimple. It is most interesting to see how the "hourglass" figures of the humps and furrows are transformed in the asymptotic spherical image. Their self-intersections are neatly preserved as the most conspicuous features of the dimple pattern (fig. 479).

Notice how the "hourglass figures" in the asymptotic spherical image due to the furrow and the hump neatly mesh so as to prepare for the changeover to the final dimple configuration. Notice also how the flecnodals are transferred and how they become squashed onto the parabolic curves so as to become almost unnoticeable.

In the process you go through an intermediary stage where *only one pleat has been transferred.* Then you have a very interesting configuration of pleats and folds of the Gauss map. For instance, you have a closed parabolic curve that maps to *a fold with a single pleat.* This is *impossible for a single parabolic loop,* but it is nevertheless possible here because the *two* loops form a kind of single entity as the boundary of a simply connected hyperbolic patch. It remains true that the Gauss map of the boundary of a simply connected hyperbolic area is a fold with an even number of pleats. It is an interesting and worthwhile exercise to figure out the way the Gauss map wrinkles the surface on the unit sphere and to follow this process from the ovoid stage to the fully developed dimple.

In figures 516 to 519 this same phenomenon is illustrated for a slightly different—but quite similar—case.   In figure 516 you see a projection of this ugly patch, figure 517 shows the pattern of parabolic curves, and figures 518 and 519 show the Gauss map.

Whereas figure 519 clearly indicates the multiplicity and folding, figure 518 clearly reveals the strange fact that makes this case interesting in the first place. You have—apparently—a closed fold with a single cusp. A simple model (figs. 520 and 521) shows the folds of the Gauss map and may help to anchor this phenomenon in your mind.

Figure 520 shows that this animal has two closed folds—each with a single cusp. Figure 521 shows that you can actually come up with a quite respectable interpretation.

As you see, you need a self-intersection, or figure-eight-shaped cross sections, to construct such pairs of closed loops with a single cusp. This signifies that you cannot have this type of phenomenon in the contour

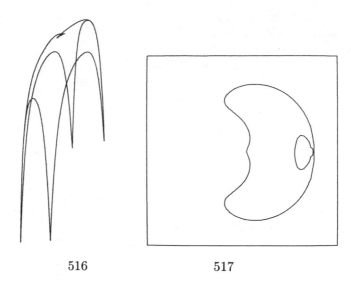

516   517

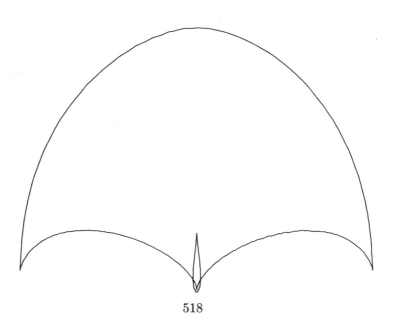

518

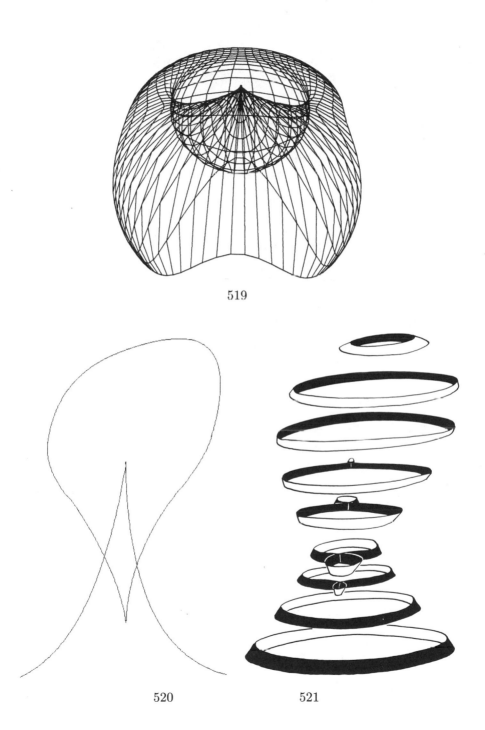

519

520 521

of the projection of bodies. But on the Gauss map it is allowed.

The dimple and the bell look superficially similar. You have a concavity on an egg or a convexity on an egg, both surrounded by an annular anticlastic annulus. But, of course, they are vastly different structures. This is brought out very clearly by their evolutions.

This is illustrated in figure 522; in both cases I have drawn very simple evolutions. Of course, various complications could make these scenarios more involved.

522

My purpose is to tell of bodies which have been transformed into shapes of a different kind. You heavenly powers, since you were responsible for those changes, as for all else, look favorably on my attempts, ...
—PUBLIUS OVIDIUS NASO (43 B.C.–A.D. 17), *Metamorphoses*

9.7.5 Dumbbell

This is the simplest example of an "aggregated" shape. In a way this is mere word play, because the bell can also be regarded as a kind of dumbbell and its evolution is indeed exemplary for certain families of dumbbells. I focus on a different flavor of dumbbell in this section, however.

The "true dumbbell" is the aggregate of two ovoids (fig. 523). You

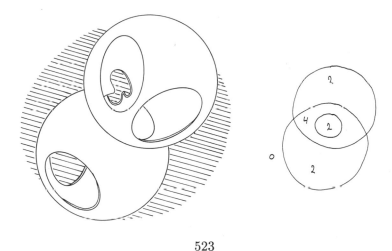

523

may define it as the kind of structure that can lead to a projection like that shown in the figure. A closed loop has been split off that runs completely through the hyperbolic annulus. This clearly distinguishes what you would like to call a "dumbbell" from the "bell" that has the same pattern of elliptic and hyperbolic areas. The evolutionary sequence first passes through the stages of a single and then two juxtaposed ovoids. Then a merge forms a bridge between the components. You have a shape with a narrow neck encircled by a seam and an annular hyperbolic area that need not contain points that map to pleats on the Gauss map.

In this case you don't have an event of the kind that potentially changes only the curvature landscape but something much more complicated. At the merge the surface is locally a double cone; thus it is intrinsically rather flat. This is necessary because the dumbbell has a hyperbolic waist, whereas the spheres are elliptic all over.

9.7.6 Torus

The torus is also a very instructive example because there exist essentially *two varieties*. One family is of the "pinched sphere" type (fig. 524), the other of the "strangled torus" type (fig. 525).

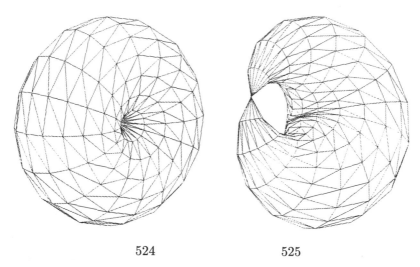

524   525

The "pinched sphere" is obtained if you start with a spherical balloon and push at two points from the outside in order to move the "north and the south poles" toward each other. When they meet, you have the pinched sphere.

The "strangled torus" is obtained if you throw a wire loop round the torus—you have to stick the wire through the hole first—and then pull it tight ("strangle") such as to reduce the diameter to nothing at all.

The pinched sphere variety of torus evolves in the following manner. First you develop two dimples on roughly antipodal positions on an ovoid. Then the dimples grow inward and meet, going through the "punch-through" event. You obtain a torus with a seam encircling the hole. This kind of torus is usually produced through a drilling process, as in the manufacture of beads.

The strangled torus variety evolves through *accretion*. You start with one or more, perhaps very many ovoids and go through a series of merges that take you to the torus. In the simplest case you have just a single ovoid that grows to a crooked sausage shape and merges with itself. This variety of torus has seams that do not encircle the hole. People usually produce this type via an assemblage process, mostly through "gluing" or a similar process to that used in the production of elastic bands for the office, via pressing of many small parts or via casting.

Notice that the "torus by accretion" might just as well assemble from a ring of "dust." Here you have an example of an *infinite family of qualitatively different tori.*

9.8   "Shape Language"

The method of describing a shape by way of an imaginary but uniquely defined evolution that also makes physical sense is eminently suited for the development of *shape languages.*

The usual methods of differential geometry do yield the *symbols* for a shape language—features such as umbilical points, footpoints, parabolic curves, and what have you. They do not yield a *syntax,* however.

The evolutionary sequences do yield a natural *syntax* in the sense that they reveal partial orders between the features. Moreover, they extend the vocabulary of symbols in important ways. For instance, the structure of seams divides the object in natural parts that are in themselves conglomerates of elementary symbols. Seams play no part in differential geometry except when you are prepared to consider evolutionary sequences. In the literature of visual perception attempts have been made to define seams as loci of minimum concave principal curvature.

> *He alone can conceive and compose,*
> *who sees the whole at once before him.*
> —HENRI FUSELI (1741–1825), *Aphorisms on art, item 72*

10 Shape in Flux

When as in silks my Julia goes,
Then, (me thinks) how sweetly flowes
That liquefaction of her clothes.
Next, when I cast mine eyes and see
That brave Vibrations each way free;
O how that glittering taketh me.
—HERRICK, *Upon Julia's Clothes*

There are many kinds of transformation of shape that are worth a closer look. I consider only a few simple types in this book.

In the previous chapter I discussed special cases of very general transformations of objects as volumes where the topology of the surface is not conserved. Not so in the present section. Here I consider only transformations that do conserve the topology, and I treat the "skins" *as such*, not their enclosed volumes.

Many such transformations are of recurring interest. A few are especially common, but so trivial that I may omit them altogether: I mean the Euclidean movements, their reflections, similarities, and combinations. Some transformations are of primarily academic interest and I will not treat them either. Examples include such things as conformal mappings in which the metric is scaled by some scalar function, affinities or projective transformations, mappings that carry geodesics to—perhaps reparametrized—geodesics, and so forth.

Of obvious practical interest are arbitrary smooth deformations. Such transformations are always locally equal to an affinity and this is the way they are usually treated. This affinity is the "Cauchy-Green tensor" of the kinematical theory of deformable media. There exists a host of literature on this and many readers will be quite familiar with it. Because of the easy availability of digestible material on this important subject I omit it in this book.

An important special case is that of the volume-preserving transformations. This is what you get when you knead a lump of clay if you don't "join" or break off pieces. I'm not aware of any *general* theory of volume preserving transformations and I won't treat the subject here.[1]

Special cases of interesting transformations include the infinitesimal ones. Note that infinitesimal maps can be represented by vector fields,

---

[1] An important class of transformations of this type can be handled via the theory of incompressible fluid flow.

which describe *displacement fields*, and conversely vector fields define infinitesimal transformations. The infinitesimal *isometries* are important in differential geometry and are known as "Killing vector fields."

In this chapter I concentrate on isometries or at least infinitesimal isometries. In the former case distances measured along the surface are preserved, whereas in the latter case distances along the surface don't change to the first order.

Such an isometry usually involves an—extrinsic—change of shape. If not, you have a *movement*, or *congruence*, which doesn't concern me here. If the surface admits a continuous family of isometries that are not Euclidean movements people say that the surface is *bendable*. Such families are called *bendings*. If the surface only admits of infinitesimal isometries that are not movements, it is called *flabby*. If a surface does not admit bendings or infinitesimal isometries that are not movements, it is called *rigid*.

If there exists an isometry between two surfaces but not a continuous transition from the one to the other, you can still imagine a *catastrophic change* from one form to the other. People then often say that the surface has received a *dent*. This is the kind of thing that routinely happens to the fender of your car when you hit something. Figure 526 shows a hemisphere that has received a simple dent such that one polar cap became a concavity, and figure 527 shows how a series of such events may lead to an interesting isometric deformation of a hemisphere into a circular disc of arbitrarily small thickness ε in cross section.   The

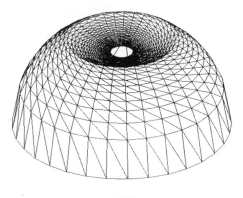

526

transformation is merely a finite number of dents. In practice there must be a limit to such an endeavor because the spherical shell will have

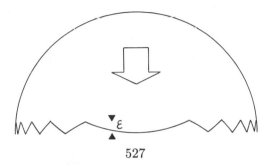

527

some thickness to it. You can go rather far though as the harm inflicted to car bodies in junk yards convincingly shows.

There exist noncomplete surface patches that do not admit a bending; an example is a semi-torus, cut via the symmetry plane perpendicular to the axis of rotational symmetry (fig. 528). Hence the common use

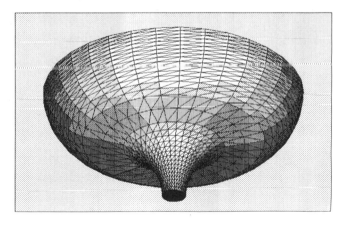

528

of a similarly shaped *rim at the top of pails*. It makes the pail much more rigid than would otherwise be the case. That is why the tinsmith produces a rolled fringe at the edges of cups and buckets. The reason is primarily mechanical rather than decorative or protective.

For the semi-torus you can easily specify a warping, that is an isometry that is not a bending, nor a movement. You cut the semi-torus along the parabolic curve and substitute the mirror image for one of the pieces. You can map points on the original and on the shape you tinkered with by relating points with the same azimuth and with the same distance from the axis of rotational symmetry. This is trivially an isometry because you did not change the surface at all—intrinsically, that is. Yet it is neither a bending nor a movement. Sometimes you meet with rubber rings of similar shape and you will find that you can flip them between two stable configurations.

That many complete surfaces are practically rigid is clear from the example of, for instance, the common ping-pong ball.

These problems are mathematically of a very subtle nature. The only thing I can do here is to offer examples of the different kinds of transformations and to point out the kinds of properties that are typical for certain families of surfaces.

If you preserve the smoothness but allow any number of sharp jumps in the curvature, that is, the nonexistence of the second derivative, then surfaces as a whole can be almost arbitrarily deformed. You can crumple a sphere into a smooth, much smaller ball having very shallow creases. This process can be observed in junk yards where it is applied to car bodies with rather spectacular results. Elastic movements will resist such a process, as the example of the ping-pong ball convincingly shows. (You may also have noticed that once you manage to produce a dent, it is even harder to get it out again. Here the problem is of a physical, rather than a mathematical nature, however.)

The practical implication of the mathematical analysis in these cases is often of a doubtful nature. In practice much depends on the physical nature of the problem. For instance, consider the well-known fact that *an ovoid is rigid*. That is to say, you can easily hit an ovoid shell and produce a dent, but there exists no bending of an ovoid into another shape. This is well borne out for a metal spherical shell, a bit less for a rubber tennis ball because a little "play" introduced through noninfinite values of elastic constants suffices to deform the sphere. If you consider a clay shell, the situation is different again. Here the surface is not conserved at all, but under the typical transformations exercised by the potter only volume is conserved. Finally, consider a sphere woven as a cloth such as a hollow silk sphere. Clearly this can be crumpled without any problem at all—you can crumple it into a very small sphere if so desired. As you know a spherical paper lantern can be pushed flat in order to transport it (fig. 527).

In the mathematical problem—for whatever it is worth—it is the *local* metric that is conserved and together with it intrinsic invariants such as the Gaussian curvature and the geodesics.

10.1 Applicability

Under flexion the metric on the surface is invariant. Thus the first fundamental form that embodies the metric, the Gaussian curvature, and the geodesics are conserved.

The so-called "first problem of applicability" or "Minding's problem" (1839) is that of deciding whether two surfaces can be shown to be "applicable."

Technically speaking, "applicable" means that you may find a mapping from the one surface to the other that leaves the first fundamental form invariant.

The problem was solved by Minding. Roughly speaking, Minding has shown that if you are given two first fundamental forms in parameters (u, v) and (u', v'), the surfaces are applicable if and only if there exist functions $\Phi(u, v) = \Phi'(u', v')$ and $\Psi(u, v) = \Psi'(u', v')$ that transform the first fundamental forms into each other and that satisfy the conditions that the moduli of their gradients are equal, and similarly the scalar products of their gradients agree. If $K(u, v)$ and $K'(u', v')$ are the Gaussian curvatures, then it suffices to take $\Phi = K$ and $\Psi = \|\vec{\nabla} K\|^2$, and check the conditions.

A so-called "bending," that is to say, a single-parameter family of applications (figs. 529 to 534) is possible if $\|\vec{\nabla} K\|^2 = f(K)$, $\|\vec{\nabla}' K'\|^2 = f(K')$ and $\triangle K = F(K)$, $\triangle' K' = F(K')$ apart from the obvious requirement $K = K'$.

In that case both surfaces are applicable to the same surface of revolution. Each surface can be deformed in itself such that the curves $K = constant$ slide over each other. These curves are simply the *latitude circles* of the corresponding surface of revolution. This gives you an intuitive insight into what goes on here: if you take a surface of revolution and cut it open along a meridian, you can bend it inward and outward, or give it a torsion. Then you produce surfaces that are all applicable onto each other and can slide over the prior latitude circles.

Further on I show examples for the case of the sphere (for the moment regarded as a surface of revolution).

If K is constant, the surface is deformable in itself and two such surfaces admit a *three-parameter family of applications.* That is the utmost freedom, equal to the freedom yielded by the translation-rotation group of the Euclidean plane.

Indeed, the surfaces of constant curvature have an intrinsic geometry that make them in many respects similar to the Euclidean plane. One

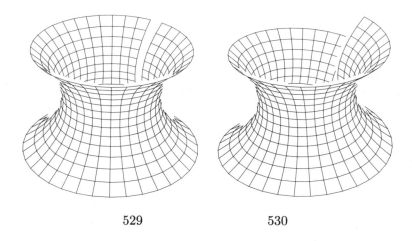

529   530

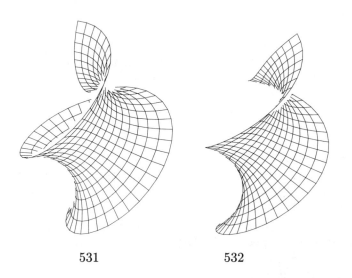

531   532

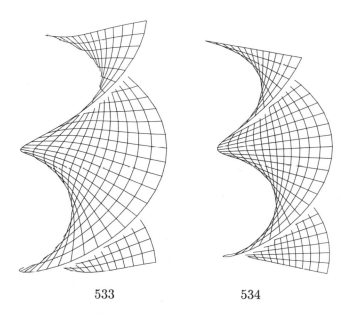

533   534

major difference with the Euclidean plane is that you can have no similar figures of different size if the Gaussian curvature differs from zero. You saw way back that triangles have angle sums that depend on their area and exceed π for positive Gaussian curvature, are less than π for negative Gaussian curvature. Surfaces of constant Gaussian curvature serve as realizations of elliptic or hyperbolic nonEuclidean geometry.

The so-called "second problem of applicability" is *to find all surfaces applicable to a given one.* No general complete solution is known, but many special cases have been solved.

Some results on surface patches have a general interest:

- Every *small piece* of surface is bendable *except* when the Gaussian curvature vanishes somewhere. If the Gaussian curvature vanishes *everywhere*, the story is completely different. If K vanishes at isolated points, the patch may actually be rigid. (Efimov, 1940 gives an—extremely contrived—example.)

- Given a curve C on a surface patch S, I can deform it into a given curve C' on a surface patch S' if the curvature of C' everywhere exceeds the geodesic curvature of C. The necessity of this condition is indeed intuitively obvious if you think of a plane paper strip with the geodesic curvature of C. You would have to tear it in order to sin against the theorem, because the curvature can never be less than the geodesic curvature, no matter how you flex your strip.

- Suppose that $C = C'$, that is, you try to deform the surface S into S' under the constraint that the curve C remains fixed. This has interesting consequences.

  The surface strip of S' along C has either the same tangent plane as S or a symmetrically positioned tangent plane relative to the osculating plane of C. This is the case because both the geodesic as well as the absolute curvature of C have to remain invariant. This is true *except* when the tangent plane of S' coincides with the osculating plane of C, that is, when C is an asymptotic curve of S': in that case the two possibilities coincide.

  This proves that a bending along C is only possible if C is an asymptotic curve. Clearly the asymptotic curves play a very special role for the bendings.

- If $C \neq C'$ and the aforementioned condition has been satisfied, then there are generally two possible bendings. This is intuitively reasonable because the tangent plane of S' may assume two symmetric positions with respect to the osculating plane of C'.

  An exception occurs when the curve is asymptotic to begin with, in which case there is an infinity of possible bendings.

- You may deform a surface patch so as to keep a given asymptotic curve rigid while it remains an asymptotic curve, a result that does not hold for any other curve.[2]

  As a simple example you may consider ruled surfaces, where the asymptotic curves of at least one family are degenerated into straight lines.

  The hyperboloid of revolution of one sheet given through the constraint $x^2 + y^2 - z^2 = 1$ can be deformed into the skew screw surface given by $z = \sqrt{x^2 + y^2} + \operatorname{arctg}\frac{y}{x}$ leaving the generators rigid (figs. 535 and 536). This property is at least intuitively reasonable if you consider the properties of asymptotic strips. Changing the twist cannot imply the application of any stretch.

- It is possible to deform a surface patch in an infinity of ways such that any given curve on it becomes a line of curvature. This needs

---

[2]The asymptotic curves play indeed a key role in the theory of surfaces. If you specify a surface through an initial strip and its second fundamental form, then the asymptotic curves bound the region where the resulting problem has a unique solution. I don't discuss such problems here because the methods needed are based on the theory of differential equations and have no immediate geometrical content.

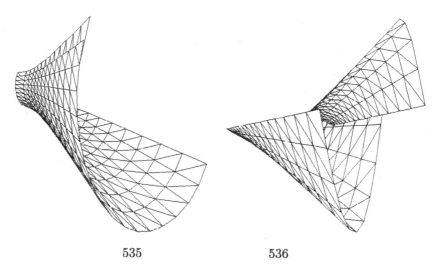

535   536

thinking over; it isn't in any way *obvious*. It doesn't hurt the intuition, but it doesn't seem to touch it, either.

- Surfaces of *constant curvature* behave in a singular way with respect to bendings. Such surfaces essentially allow the free movement of figures like the Euclidean plane. Thus any two surface patches of *constant* but not vanishing curvature are in two ways applicable such that a given point and a geodesic through it on one surface correspond to a given point and a geodesic through it on the other.

The development of the sphere and other bodies whose surface has a double flexure would be impossible, unless we considered them as consisting of a great number of plane faces or of simple curvatures, as the cylinder and the cone.
—JOSEPH GWILT, F.S.A., F.R.A.S. *The Encyclopedia of Architecture*
(1867)

10.2   Special results

10.2.1   Ovoids & convex caps

Many interesting special results concern the ovoids, or certain parts of ovoids, most often the parts known as "caps." A cap is a topological disc cut out of an ovoid in such a way that its boundary curve is planar and there exists a parallel projection of the cap on the plane of its boundary that is neatly one-to-one. Thus any small circle divides the sphere into a cap and a sphere without a cap. This latter piece is itself not a cap, of course.

If you specify an arbitrary but positive definite "first fundamental form" and an everywhere positive but otherwise arbitrary "Gaussian curvature" on a sphere, then Weyl has shown in 1915 that there always exists an ovoid with that metric.

Aleksandrov has given a very geometrically appealing interpretation of this. He considers abstract triangulations with the Euler number of the ovoids and such that the sum of all sector angles at a vertex is less than 2π for all vertices. Such triangulations have positive Gaussian curvature and intuitively should represent convex polyhedra, which are the nearest piecewise flat combinatorial objects similar to ovoids. Aleksandrov manages to show by elementary means that there always exists a convex polyhedron that realizes the metric implied by the triangulation. Moreover, this polyhedron is unique except for movements and symmetries.

But there is a catch to be aware of: Aleksandrov allows for possible folding of the faces; that is, the faces of the polyhedron need not be the faces of the triangulation.

Figure 537 shows a triangulation with a convex metric. (You may want to verify this.) Indeed, it is not hard to find a convex polyhedron for it. This must be unique.[3]

Amazingly at first sight, Blaschke showed how to paste up a *nonconvex* polyhedron from this *same* triangulation. Thus, there do exist convex and nonconvex polyhedra with the same intrinsic metric. In retrospect this is not so unreasonable, because after all the sphere and the dented sphere are isometric too. If you allow edges almost anything goes.

To continue with the ovoids: Cohn-Vossen showed that in the class of three-times smoothly differentiable surfaces every ovoid is uniquely determined (again: up to movements and symmetries).

---

[3]The catch mentioned above doesn't hurt because Cauchy has shown that closed convex polyhedra are uniquely determined by their facets.

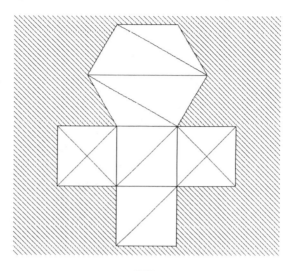

537

Famous Fact: *The Ovoids are Rigid.*

You may well wonder whether caps are rigid too. In a very limited way they are. Liebmann showed in 1920 that caps will not allow bendings that leave their boundary curve planar. This is known as a "Gleitver-biegung" or—literally—"shift-bending."

Pogorelow showed that isometric caps are congruent and that every intrinsically convex geodesic region is realizable in the form of a cap. If you allow deformation of the boundary curve into a space curve, caps become flabby. Pogorelow shows that you may specify an *arbitrarily shaped* convex region on the Gaussian sphere, and as long as its area equals the *curvatura integra* of the cap, there will exist some bending that takes the spherical image of your cap to that specified shape. I find it intuitively almost shocking that the caps are *that* bendable.

Ovoids with holes cut into them, but not necessarily caps, are also bendable. All isometric punched ovoids can be bent into each other if the hole is a geodesically convex disc, at least if the ovoid is three times smoothly differentiable. Thus you won't have to use brute force to move from one isometric form to any other.

10.2.2   Bour's result

A result that does hold some general interest is that a surface that can be continuously deformed on itself is either a helicoid, a cylinder or a surface of revolution. *Any screw surface can be bent into a surface of revolution* (Bour, 1862).

Almost the only example the typical texts give of a continuous bending, is indeed the famous example of the helicoid being bent into a catenoid of revolution. This is simple because one can use special methods—imported from complex analysis—to deal with minimal surfaces.

Figures 535 and 536 show the simple example of a hyperboloid of one sheet, which is a surface of revolution, bent into a skew helicoid. The "waist" of the hyperboloid becomes the axis of the screw. The—straight—generators remain straight during the bending. In the example above, you see that a full turn of the screw surface only suffices to cover part of the hyperboloid.

Other simple examples are the bendings of simple surfaces of revolution such as, for instance, *spheres*. You can cut a sector between two meridians and then bend the surface so as to close up the gap. Figures 538 and 539 show how to bend a hemisphere into a spindle-shaped body in this manner. Similarly, a sphere with two polar caps deleted

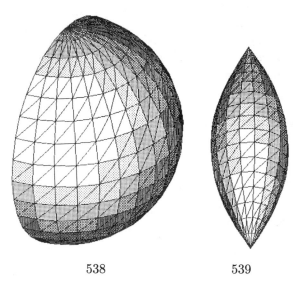

538   539

can be sliced open along a meridian and then bent open until the edges at the highest latitude develop a common tangent plane perpendicular to the polar axis. You then obtain a surface that looks a bit like a car fender.

Figures 540 and 541 illustrate this process. Of course, you can then

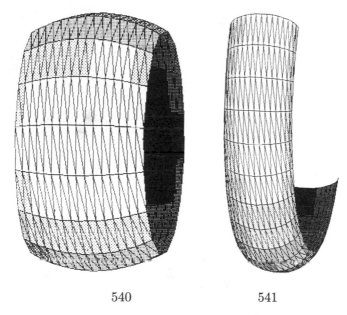

540   541

twist the thing, as you can any surface of revolution, and thus produce a helicoidal surface that is isometric with the sphere (figs. 542 to 544). If you use more turns of the helicoidal surface, you obtain part of the surface of a spiraling column that can be wrapped several times around the sphere by a bending (figs. 545 and 546).

This latter example can be very nicely illustrated with mechanical models sometimes found at the math departments of the older universities. They have a plaster sphere and a plaster column that are isometric. A piece of brass plate has been forced to the correct Gaussian curvature. It can be applied equally well to the sphere and to the column in many different ways. This is really a most interesting and impressive toy.

Similarly, you may bend the *plane*—which for the occasion can be considered as a surface of revolution—into right circular cones of revolution, namely $z = \frac{\sqrt{1-m^2}}{m}\sqrt{x^2 + y^2}$. For $m = 1$ you obtain the plane

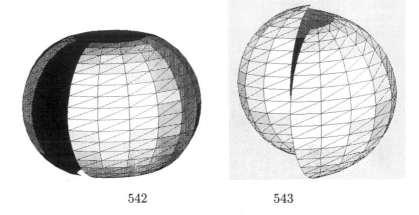

542   543

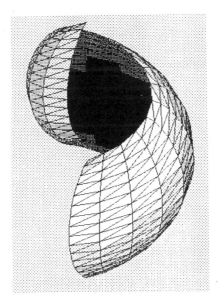

544

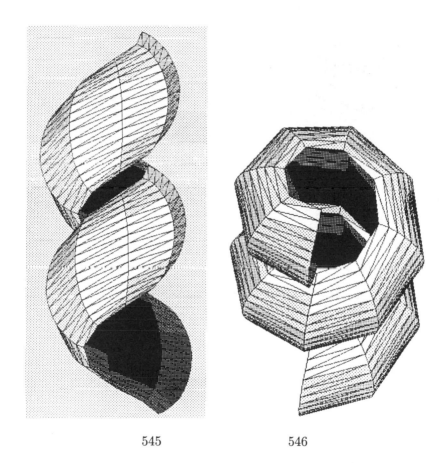

545   546

itself, but when you decrease m you obtain cones with semi-top angles equal to $\arccos m$. Figure 547 shows how to bend a half-plane into a right circular cone. For $m = 0$ you have wrapped the plane infinitely

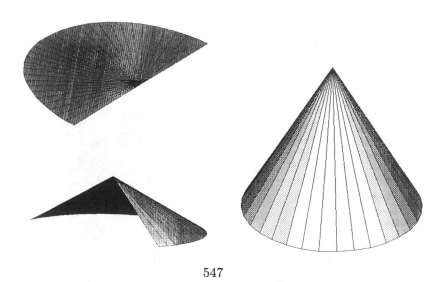

547

many times around the positive z-axis.

Such cases make nice subject matter for spectacular computer movies and are actually very easy to program.

10.2.3   The Sphere

♠ INTERMEZZO—A HISTORICAL CURIOSITY.

Hilbert and Cohn-Vossen have a delicious section on the possibility of *bending* a sphere in which you have punched a hole. Since it is impossible to outstrip these authors in clarity of exposition, I translate the section for you:

The authors first relate the classical result that *the sphere is rigid*, that is to say, there exist no isometries except Euclidean movements. This is a classical result, guessed by Minding (1838) and proved by Liebmann (1900), for arbitrary ovoids by Herglotz (1943). They continue:

Because it is intuitively clear that there exist spherical pieces that can be bent the question arises how large a hole you have to cut in a sphere in order to make it bendable. It is at least conceivable that such a hole should possess a certain minimum size, e.g., a hemisphere. However, it is possible to prove that such is not the case; the sphere becomes already bendable when you cut an arbitrarily small hole in it, it suffices even to slice the sphere open along an arbitrarily short stretch of a great circle. It has not been decided, however, whether the sphere becomes bendable already when one or more isolated points are left out.

That a sphere becomes bendable when I cut out an arbitrarily small piece can be brought in a curious relation with the properties of soap films. Namely, it is easily possible to show analytically: When I start from a patch $\mathcal{F}$ of constant mean curvature c and when I push the surface $\mathcal{F}$ forward in the normal direction by a stretch $1/2c$ toward a certain direction, then the new patch $\mathcal{G}$ that is described by the end points of these normal stretches doesn't have a constant mean curvature, but it does have a constant Gaussian curvature of magnitude $4c^2$. One says that $\mathcal{G}$ is the parallel surface of $\mathcal{F}$ at the distance $1/2c$. If you do this to a spherical patch, then $\mathcal{G}$ is a piece of a sphere that is concentric with the sphere of $\mathcal{F}$ and conversely, $\mathcal{G}$ is only spherical if $\mathcal{F}$ is, too. This must be true because one may show that the normals of $\mathcal{F}$ are orthogonal to $\mathcal{G}$ in the corresponding points. —The side of $\mathcal{F}$ toward which I have to erect the normal stretches is not arbitrary; you can easily refine the prescription when you think of $\mathcal{F}$ as like a soap bubble on a closed rim of a pipe; you have to pass into the interior of the enclosed volume of air.

I now conceive of a small closed curve $\mathcal{R}$ drawn on a sphere of radius $1/c$, that is, with mean curvature c, and of a continuous deformation of this curve such that the deformed curves no longer lie on a spherical surface. It is plausible that I can construct soap films with constant average curvature c through all these curves if the deformation is not too extreme. For if I construct a soap film through the original curve $\mathcal{R}$, I can always arrive at a mean curvature c if I blow it up to the desired degree; for the sphere that contains $\mathcal{R}$ is such a surface, and when I blow from the correct side I must at some stage obtain the larger of the spherical patches bounded by $\mathcal{R}$. From a continuity argument it is evident that when I regulate the supply of air judiciously through the deformation of $\mathcal{R}$, I can make sure that the soap film that started as the piece of a sphere deforms in such a way that the value of the mean curvature remains invariant; but then the deformed soap films cannot be spherical any more because—by construction—the deformed curves do not lie on spheres. Now we construct to all these soap films the inner parallel surfaces at distance $1/2c$. Then we obtain a continuous sequence of surfaces that have a constant Gaussian curvature $4c^2$ according to the theorem explained earlier. The first of these surfaces is a sphere of radius $1/2c$, with a little hole in it that is bounded by a curve similar to $\mathcal{R}$ and in a similar position as $\mathcal{R}$. All other surfaces are continuously bendable into the original one; but they can't be spherical because otherwise all the soap films would have to be spherical. Thus a sphere with an arbitrarily small hole in it is apparently bendable.

The possibility of bending bordered and not bordered surfaces has been investigated for much more general cases. Rigid are all closed convex surfaces such as ellipsoids. Also rigid are all convex surfaces with boundaries, if the surface along these boundaries possesses but a single tangent plane; an example of such a surface (with boundaries) is the convex part of the surface of the torus.

If you cut an arbitrarily small hole in a closed convex surface it becomes bendable. It isn't clear yet whether it is sufficient just to slice the surface open or even to punch out isolated points.

There would appear to be a catch in the argument: the authors silently assume that it is sufficient to show that the members of the family are applicable if their Gaussian curvatures agree. An additional argument is needed in order to make it intuitively clear that the local metrics agree too. This is an example of the kind of partial proof that easily sticks in one's memory and is worth remembering because it is so intuitively appealing, although it is not a complete proof.

The surface that you obtain when you slit a sphere along an arc of a great circle, get hold of the endpoints of the arc, and pull the arc into a straight line segment, is known. It is the so-called "Rembs's surface," a famous classical example of a nontrivial bending. Since the analytical expression is not very enlightening, I don't give it here.

It is possible to find the explicit transformation of the sphere into Rembs's surface, but since this is numerically quite elaborate, I have not illustrated it. Figures 548 and 549 show Rembs's surface for the case where a meridian has been sliced open for one quarter and pulled straight.

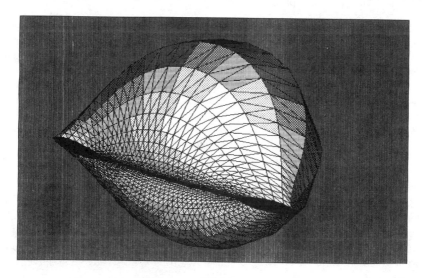

548

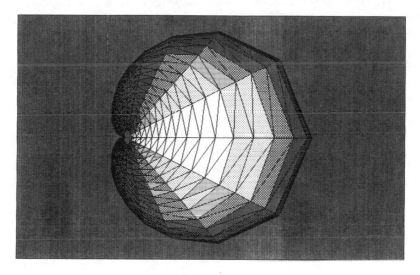

549

The surface can be admired in many plaster cast galleries to be found in the more venerable mathematics departments.

Similar bendings are known for the prolate and oblate ellipsoids of revolution. You will find them in Efimov's book.

10.2.4   Paper surfaces

Sometimes he made clay models, draping the figures with rags dipped in plaster, and then drawing them painstakingly on fine Rheims cloth or prepared linen. These drawings were done in black and white with the point of the brush . . .
—GIORGIO VASARI, *Life of Leonardo da Vinci (1550)*

A flat piece of paper can be bent and folded (creased) into many different shapes. Any developable surface is applicable to itself and to any other developable in a triple infinity of ways. It serves as a physical implementation of a surface of zero Gaussian curvature. If the surface has assumed a certain shape, then it will be either planar or approximately cylindrical in the neighborhood of each of its points. In the latter case there will be a unique "generator," that is, a straight line that goes through the point and lies completely within the surface.

If you imagine the generators to be drawn on the surface, you may flatten the paper again and study their pattern. The generators may nowhere cross each other unless there is some kind of discontinuity or crease, a case I will cover later. Thus the generators must end at the edge of the paper.

If you take a rectangular piece of paper, the generators typically cross the boundary transversely or coincide with it. The flat pieces are bounded by the boundary of the paper and-or the generators. If they are completely bounded by generators within the surface, they are of triangular shape with the vertices on the boundary of the paper.

If the paper is not rectangular but has pieces of concave boundary, the generators may also be tangent to the boundary and the surface is the tangent surface of a space curve. Even if the paper is rectangular you may prolong the generators in your imagination and notice that they are tangents to a space curve outside the paper.

Degenerate cases are the cylinder and the cone.

If you *crease* the paper, more interesting effects occur. You may, for instance, consider the "dented cone" (fig. 550). Here the crease is

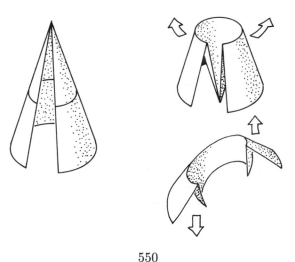

550

a planar curve, a circle. If you flex the paper, you can change the curvature of it, changing the dihedral angle at the crease at the same time. The sine of the semi-dihedral-angle is the ratio $\frac{\kappa_0}{\kappa}$, where κ_0 is the curvature of the—planar—crease when the paper is pushed flat, and κ the curvature after the creasing.

If you put a *twist* on the crease and make it into a space curve, the generators move through the paper, the angle at which they meet the crease being determined by the torsion.

A special case of a crease is an apex. You obtain a general cone with convex and concave pieces on the cone mantle (fig. 551). The typical "node" or "eye" of a fold in drapery can be modeled quite well with an apex and a crease (fig. 552). Such "models" can often be admired in

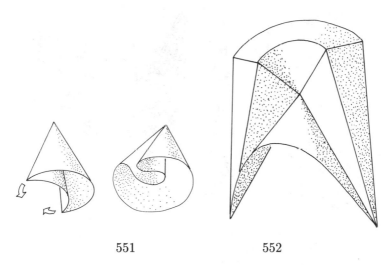

551   552

medieval and renaissance paintings (figs. 553 and 554).

If several creases meet at a vertex, you obtain a generalized polyhedral vertex—"generalized" because the faces need not be planar but may be pieces of cone mantles.

It is an interesting exercise to follow the bendings and creases of a paper surface on the Gaussian sphere. Because the surface is always isometric to a plane, the Gauss map is degenerated and consists of arcs and points. Near an apex or vertex you obtain closed arcs that bound a zero algebraic area because there can be no spherical excess.

10.3 Deformation of a curve

Suppose you apply an arbitrary field of deformation to a curve, that is, a vector field $\vec{d}(s)$ of displacements as a function of arclength s. The point $\mathcal{P}(s)$ of the curve is supposed to be moved over $\vec{d}(s)$ to $\mathcal{P}(s) + \vec{d}(s)$. What happens to the shape?

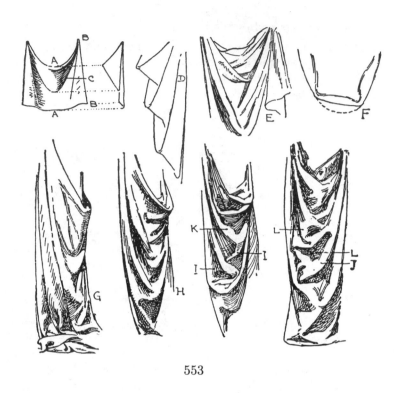

553

554

You can obtain some insight by looking at a rod model for a plane curve first. If you consider the three universal joints between successive rods, which themselves can no longer be considered rigid for an arbitrary deformation, it makes sense to develop the vector field into the following components:

- A rigid movement with six degrees of freedom compounded of

    - a rigid translation
    - a rigid rotation.

- A flexion at the joint yielding one degree of freedom. This component does not affect the intrinsic geometry, of course. You lose no generality if the flexion is only in the osculating plane.

- Changes of the intrinsic geometry describe the remaining two degrees of freedom. This type of change is a dilation or contraction of the rods. As components you may take

    - a uniform dilation (same factor for both rods)
    - a deformation (one rod extends, the other shrinks by the same factor).

Together these transformations explain nine degrees of freedom, which is exactly what you imposed through three arbitrary deformation vectors.

Essentially the same thing happens in the general case of a smooth, twisted space curve. (You may want to take a look at the chapter on curves to refresh your memory here.) There is a modulus of extension $\varepsilon = \vec{t} \cdot \vec{d}'$ which represents the increase of length per unit length of the curve. The flexion appears in the change of curvature. It consists of two terms, namely an amount $-2\varepsilon\kappa$ due to the dilation (if you shrink a circle the curvature obviously increases) and a contribution $\vec{n} \cdot \vec{d}''$ due to the flexion proper.

Similarly the torsion change can be described by way of three terms, namely a term $-\varepsilon\tau$ due to the dilation, a term $\kappa\,\vec{b} \cdot \vec{d}'$ due to the deformation and finally a term $(\kappa^{-1}\,\vec{b} \cdot \vec{d}'')'$ due to the flexion.

You can understand these relations pictorially once you obtain a feeling for the turning and twisting of the frame field due to the perturbation.

The Frenet frame suffers small rotation due to the deformation. The frame turns by an amount $\frac{1}{\kappa}\,\vec{b} \cdot \vec{d}''$ about the tangent, an amount $-\vec{b} \cdot \vec{d}'$ about the normal, and an amount $\vec{n} \cdot \vec{d}'$ about the binormal.

The turns about the normal and binormal are indeed pictorially evident. For the turn about the tangent you may have to prepare a little sketch. In order to understand this spin pictorially, it is best to think of the change of orientation of the osculating plane. Thus your little drawing should include three points of the curve, that is, two successive rods of the rod model.[4]

Usually you will describe the deformation field in terms of the Frenet frame itself: $\vec{d} = \alpha\,\vec{t} + \beta\,\vec{n} + \gamma\,\vec{b}$. For the case of a bent wire (inextensional deformation) you have $\alpha' = \kappa\beta$ as the condition for which the modulus of extension ε vanishes identically.

Weatherburn's book has a useful section on these problems.

10.4   Deformation of a surface

To obtain a quick insight, I first consider a triangulated surface with a vector field of deformation $\vec{d}$ defined on the vertices.

It is an easy matter to obtain an insight in the change of the intrinsic geometry. Consider the first fundamental form, that is the metric, first. Clearly it suffices if you consider a face and the three components of the deformation vectors in the plane of the face. Even this is a redundant description because you can still subtract a planar movement, a translation, and rotation; thus you disregard three degrees of freedom. The planar deformation has only three degrees of freedom left, then.

The most convenient description is the following: first find a direction of greatest dilation, which accounts for one degree of freedom, and two scalars, which describe the dilation in that and in an orthogonal direction. Alternatively these scalars can be expressed in terms of a homogeneous dilation or area magnification and a true deformation or shear that is an expansion in one and a contraction in the orthogonal direction with a conservation of area. This is useful because the area magnification is truly rotationally invariant. It is a simple matter to compute these quantities from only the relative positions of the vertices with respect to each other. This is the best method for computational purposes. For a *bending* the shear and dilation must vanish identically, of course.

The change in the intrinsic geometry determines the change of the Gaussian curvature. Consider a vertex. The change in the metric deter-

---

[4]Notice that you can understand the turns by considering what happens to a single rod—but of course you use the Frenet frame; thus implicitly you also consider three successive points.

mines the sector angles and thus the spherical excess. Thus there is no need for further calculation.

The modulus of extension (ϵ) for a direction $\vec{t}$ on the surface is a number $\mathbf{E}(\vec{t})\langle\vec{t}\rangle$, where $\mathbf{E}$ denotes an operator that maps tangent vectors on 1-forms, very much like the shape operator does. The operator $\mathbf{E}$ can be expressed in terms of the derivatives of $\vec{d}$ with respect to the frame vectors $\vec{e}_i$. The directions for which $\mathbf{E}(\vec{t})\langle\vec{t}\rangle$ is extremal are the principal axes of strain and are the equivalents of the axes of the pure shear considered in the discrete case.

The changes of the shape, or extrinsic geometry, are reflected in the change of the dihedral angles between the faces. You can attach a unique frame to an edge by finding its midpoint and using the direction of the edge and the bisectrix of the normals to the faces as axes. The third axis is determined through the orthonormality condition. If you do this before and after the deformation, the change of frame determines a unique translation and rotation. This accounts for six degrees of freedom. The change of shape of the faces takes up another five degrees of freedom, namely the length change of the edge and the shift of the outer vertices in the plane of the faces. The deformation has four times three is twelve degrees of freedom in all because there are four deformation vectors and the single degree of freedom left must clearly be the change of dihedral angle. As you have seen before, this is equivalent to a change in the mean curvature.

Weatherburn's book has useful formulas if you are interested in numerical applications of this type of material.

The case dear to the heart of differential geometricians is the special case of the isometric deformation. In that case there isn't any shear.

In terms of your polyhedral the only allowable perturbations are changes of the dihedral angles. Thus the edges can be used as hinges between the rigid faces of the model. It is intuitively clear (at least to people with some mechanical insight) that such constructions are not likely to be bendable although they may be "wobbly." It is indeed the case that polyhedral models of bendable surfaces are often rigid! (Although wobbly.)

Thus these alleged "models" are not true models in this area: you have stretched the domain of applicability of the model too far. These problems are very complicated indeed. In general, it can be said that "polyhedral models" are more of a hindrance than a help in investigations of bendings of smooth surfaces. They can be of value in mechanical investigations where you include the effects of the elastic constants though. Take care!

"Isometric" is used as an intrinsic term here, of course. This is a hard problem and the finite element models usually lead to misleading results. It is not necessarily a useful problem either, for in many practical cases the deformation is either not isometric at all, or it is merely "almost" isometric. Just a little "play" in the hinges or elasticity in the faces make the models pliable.

For example: a planar vertex can easily be deformed into a pyramid because this change affects the metric only to the second order. (Easy to prove if you remember Pythagoras's Theorem.) This has led to a theory of "infinitesimal deformations" keeping the metric constant to the first order. (See below.)

10.4.1 Curves of bending

If you have a correspondence between two isometric surfaces, you may look for corresponding nets that are conjugated nets *on both surfaces simultaneously*. Remember that two directions $\vec{a}$, $\vec{b}$ are called conjugated if $II(\vec{a}, \vec{b}) = 0$, where II denotes the second fundamental form. The two conditions generically lead to a unique solution. Peterson (1868) first defined such simultaneously conjugated nets and called their parameter curves "curves of bending."

Important heuristic: *The parameter parallelograms for doubly conjugated nets are planar and their size and shape must remain fixed. Thus the "hinges" must be along the parameter curves. These nets are by far the best way to visualize a given bending.*

Consider a simple application: if you cut two polar caps from a sphere and slice it open along a meridian, you may bend what is left into the shape of a car fender. The conjugated nets are simply the meridians and latitude circles in this case. Along the latitude circles the surface facets bend inward, having the effect of increasing the curvature, whereas along the meridians they bend outward, having the effect of decreasing the curvature.

After some mental exercises you may obtain almost a "muscular" feeling for the bending.

10.5 Infinitesimal bending

For an infinitesimal bending you require that the first fundamental form does not change to the first order in the perturbation. Suppose you have a surface $\vec{x}(u,v)$ and you deform it into the surface $\underline{\vec{x}}(u,v;\varepsilon) =$

$\vec{x}(u,v) + \varepsilon\,\vec{y}(u,v)$. Then you must require that

$$\|\underline{\vec{x}}(u + \triangle u, v + \triangle v) - \underline{\vec{x}}(u,v)\|^2$$

does not depend on ε to the first order. This implies that corresponding tangent vectors of the surfaces $\vec{x}$ and $\vec{y}$ are orthogonal for all values of (u,v), as you may easily verify. From this fact you may deduce that there must exist a field of infinitesimal rotations on the surface such that a tangent vector of $\vec{y}$ is obtained from the corresponding tangent vector of $\vec{x}$ through such a rotation.

You may similarly define a field of translations and so obtain the fields of translation and rotation for infinitesimal surface elements of the surface for that infinitesimal bending.

The relations are especially simple in the case of the Monge patch representation $z = f(x,y)$. You may find the formulas in Efimov's book, for instance. A simple example is the case of the paraboloid of revolution $z = (x^2 + y^2)/2$. One possible deformation is:

$$(x - \varepsilon\,(x^2 y + \frac{1}{3}y^3))\,\vec{e}_x + (y - \varepsilon\,(xy^2 + \frac{1}{3}x^3))\,\vec{e}_y + (\frac{x^2 + y^2}{2} + 2\varepsilon\,xy)\,\vec{e}_z.$$

This deformation is depicted in figure 555 for values of ε of 0 and ±0.2.

This deformation merely adds $2\varepsilon\,xy$ to the height, and warps the indicatrix into oblong shapes. The rotation field is $2\varepsilon\,(x\,\vec{e}_x - y\,\vec{e}_y - \frac{1}{2}(x - y)^2\vec{e}_z)$.

For this example you easily check explicitly that both the first fundamental form and the Gaussian curvature do not depend on ε to the first order. The curves of bending are along the relative rotation vectors and are families of hyperbolic curves in this case, much as you could have guessed.

Sometimes you get surprising results. For instance, *the plane $z = 0$ is bendable into an arbitrary shape $z = \varepsilon\,f(x,y)$* because the first fundamental form is only changed to the second order in the process and so is—consequently—the Gaussian curvature. This flabbiness of planar surfaces is, of course, a well-known fact in practical life. It explains why a steel plate has to be embossed or rolled into a periodic wave pattern to make it withstand bendings and be useful as a cheap construction material. In fact a slight cylindrical curvature is sufficient to sustain a load in the direction of the generators. You can try checking the idea with some pieces of paper and a weight, such as a brick. A few pieces of writing paper will carry a brick if you first introduce a zig-zag folding.

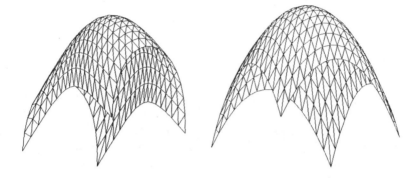

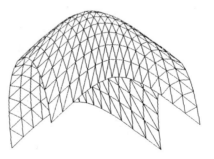

555

10.5.1   Monge patch representation

♠ INTERMEZZO—TO TRY ON YOUR COMPUTER.

Suppose you have a surface patch parametrized as

$$\vec{r}\,(x,y) = x\,\vec{e}_x + y\,\vec{e}_y + z(x,y)\,\vec{e}_z,$$

that is, a Monge patch representation. Let the perturbed surface be

$$\vec{r}' = \vec{r} + \varepsilon\,\vec{s},$$

with

$$\vec{s}\,(x,y) = \xi\,\vec{e}_x + \eta\,\vec{e}_y + \zeta\,\vec{e}_z.$$

Then the condition that the perturbation be a bending is

$$\triangle x\,\triangle\xi + \triangle y\,\triangle\eta + \triangle z\,\triangle\zeta = 0,$$

thus you obtain the simultaneous equations

$$
\begin{array}{rcl}
\xi_x + z_x\zeta_x & = & 0 \\
\eta_y + z_y\zeta_y & = & 0 \\
\xi_y + \eta_x + z_x\zeta_y + z_y\zeta_x & = & 0.
\end{array}
$$

From this you obtain a second-order differential equation for ζ:

$$z_{xx}\,\zeta_{yy} - 2z_{xy}\,\zeta_{xy} + z_{yy}\,\zeta_{xx} = 0.$$

Now you are all set: from every solution to this equation you immediately get a perturbation that is isometric to the first order in ε. You can obtain the field of infinitesimal rotations from the perturbation ($\vec{R}$ the rotation vector):

$$\vec{R} = \zeta_y\,\vec{e}_x - \zeta_x\,\vec{e}_y + (\eta_x + z_x\,\zeta_y)\,\vec{e}_z.$$

In the case of the paraboloid of rotation, with the Monge parametrization $z(x,y) = (x^2+y^2)/2$, the differential equation for ζ is just the *Laplace equation*, namely $\zeta_{xx} + \zeta_{yy} = 0$. That is very convenient, because as a consequence any solution to Laplace's equation immediately yields an isometry.

In the example of the cap I gave in the previous section, I just took what amounts to about the simplest nontrivial solution of Laplace's equation, namely $\zeta = xy$. It may amuse you to do some graphics with more complicated solutions.

We have to be grateful to Liebmann (1919) for these very convenient equations.

10.6   Final Remark

As I have said before, I don't think the mathematical theory of isometries or even infinitesimal isometries is of much use in practice, except in a few obvious applications of a rather qualitative nature. In practice, it will virtually always be necessary to model the *material properties* of the object, be it only very roughly. The elastic properties are really *decisive* in almost any case. It makes little sense to model shape changes without their explicit consideration, except as an academic exercise. In practice, you will probably always do best to consider a finite element approach on the actual mechanics right away.

> *. . . It was his opinion that there were sixty-four basic varieties of grimaces.*
> *When I visited him, he had completed sixty different heads, some in marble, others in a mixture of lead and pewter, most of them the size of life.*
> *He had spent no fewer than eleven years in this unfortunate labor, working with astonishing patience. All the heads were self-portraits.*
> *I saw him work on the sixty-first head.*
> *He would look into the mirror every half minute and assume precisely the grimace he wanted. Considered as works of art,*
> *the heads are admirable masterpieces, especially the more natural ones.*
> *But the majority represent strangely contorted faces, . . .*
> —C. FRIEDRICH NICOLAI, *Reisebeschreibung durch Deutschland und die Schweiz im Jahre 1781;* on a visit to Franz Xaver Messerschmidt

VI EPILOGUE

11 Shape models

...the cherry-tree is of the character of the fir-tree as regards its ramifications which is placed in steps round its stem; and its branches spring in fours, fives and sixes opposite one another; and the tips of the topmost shoots form a pyramid from the centre upward; and the walnut and the oak from the center upward form a half-sphere.
—LEONARDO DA VINCI (1452–1519)

...treat Nature by the sphere, the cylinder and the cone ...
—PAUL CÉZANNE (1839–1906)

In this overly short and rather sketchy chapter I review some common models for shapes and indicate their typical use. Of course, I can't be exhaustive because new models are being invented every day. If you long for more, you will find the recent literature on "CAD," "computer graphics," and "computer vision" a veritable cornucopia.

11.1 Axes

Many shapes lend themselves very well to a description in terms of "axes." For instance, an interesting model of a man is the stick figure so often drawn by children and already known from Stone-Age cave paintings. Figure 556 shows a sixteenth-century example attributed to the Renaissance artist Erhardt Schön. Although the similarity to the

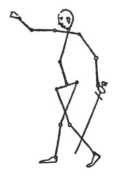

556

shape of a real man may be slight, the stick man is often remarkably useful, especially when describing human movements. The reason is clear enough. Because human postural movements—not facial expressions and phenomena like that—depend mainly on the constraints due to the mechanical linkages—skeletal joints—and are thus piece-wise rigid, the "phase space" for human movement is identical to the phase space for the stick man. This is the reason why the stick figures immediately convey the mood of a certain posture or the style of a certain movement such as walking, running, dancing, ...

Systems of piece-wise rigid, joined parts can easily be converted to this type of representation, the axes being defined mainly by the linkages. The engineer setting up the phase-space for a system is essentially doing just that.

There are other forms of description via axes that must not be confused with the stick-man principles. They make use of the so-called "medial axis" which is the locus of centers of "maximal spheres." A maximal sphere is a sphere that snugly fits into the object—conceptually of course—and has one degree of freedom left. It touches the surface at two points. The medial axis brings out some of the symmetries of a shape. It is sometimes known as the "symmetry set" of the shape. Its main drawback is that it is extremely sensitive to small perturbations of the surface. This makes the medial axis mainly useful for mathematically defined very smooth shapes or in the context of low resolution descriptions of an object. Seen with a slightly blurred view, the wrinkles on the surface disappear; then the problems for the medial axis approach become less severe. The "medial axis" is not a true arborized axis system, but contains pieces of surface.

You obtain the medial axes when you construct the *family of parallel surfaces* and find the loci of *self-intersection* of them. For a given distance the self-intersection of a parallel surface must generically be a *curve*. When you vary the distance, these curves sweep out a *surface*, which is the medial "axis."[1] This surface is not a "complete surface" but will in general have a boundary curve. The boundary curve is the locus of points where the parallel surfaces develop a swallowtail; that is how the self-intersection starts.

This whole process is much simpler in a lower dimensional case, say the medial axis for a planar *curve* (fig. 557). It is particularly easy to construct it explicitly for the parabola, for instance. You appreciate then that the boundary of the medial axis is nothing but the cusp (2D) or cuspidal edge (3D) of the *caustic surfaces*.

---

[1] The terminology is not very fortunate: the medial axis is a curve for a planar shape, whereas this is really a surface for a solid blob.

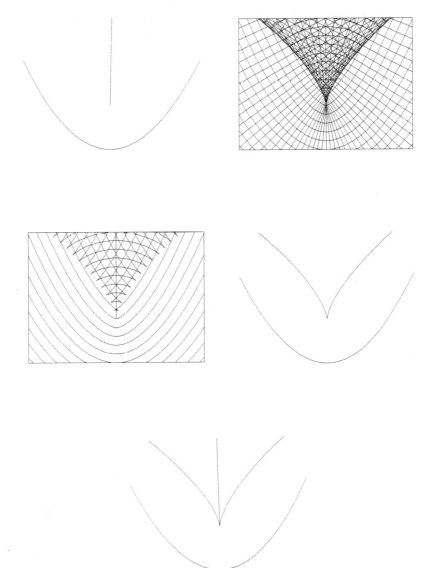

557

This is not very amazing in retrospect, for at the singular points of the caustic you have the centers of spheres that have an exceptionally high order of contact with the surface, that is, a multiple point of contact. The points of the medial axis are the centers of spheres with at least two points of tangency with the surface. For the boundary points the points of tangency coincide, which is just the condition for a singularity of the caustic. It is not hard to derive the generic singularities of the medial axis itself.

In many cases of practical interest the medial axes are not necessarily of much relevance. Consider a rocky island, for instance (fig. 558). Its

558

shape is given by the curve of its coast line, the zero level line, at a given resolution. The medial axis is some imaginary curve that need not have the slightest relation with the remainder of the surface topography at all. In such a case a much more important "medial axis" is the *crest line* of the mountain range that makes up the island. It is the crest that constrains the traffic for the islanders and that decides whether you will be able to see the east coast or the west coast or both.

Similarly, if the surface is some level surface for a fiducial value of the density of some physical parameter, it is much more natural to relate the "medial axis" to *the density function as an entity* than to any single level surface alone.

There is a decisive mathematical difference between the medial axis in the sense of a "symmetry set" and in the sense of a "crest." The symmetry set is an entity that depends merely on a single level curve, whereas the crest depends on the density as a scalar field. The crests originate at *maxima* of the density and are made up from special integral curves of the gradient of the density, namely those that end at saddle points. This fact immediately shows the way toward a complete classification of the generic singularities of the crests.

Despite the enormous mathematical differences between the symmetry set and the crests, they are often qualitatively very similar and can usually be considered as essentially equivalent from a practical point of view.

In 3D the families of integral curves of the gradient that run from a given maximum to a given minimum are separated from each other by singular surfaces, which again meet each other in singular curves. The surfaces meet the boundary of a level set in curves, which may be taken as the crests and ruts of that surface. The situation is quite like that in 2D, with obvious changes in the relevant dimensions.

Some surfaces can be represented in a most natural way by reference to an axis system. For instance, all objects of revolution are naturally referred to their axis of symmetry. Tube surfaces are defined as the envelopes of spheres with their centers on an arbitrary space curve, the radius of the sphere being constant (fig. 559). If you make the radius

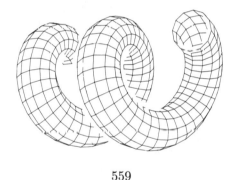

559

a function of arclength, you may meet the problem that the envelope contains no contributions from certain parts of the curve. Basically the rate of increase of the radius should be less than the increase in arclength along the axis.

The torus is an example of both a surface of revolution and a tube surface. The axis defined in the latter way appears as a natural "body axis," the axis of rotation lying completely outside the body.

11.1.1   Singularities of the medial axis

♠ INTERMEZZO—TECHNICALITIES.

People have defined the medial axis in apparently different, but usually equivalent ways (for instance, via "grass fires," maximum discs, symmetry, and so forth). An abstract way to formulate a problem that has the medial axis as a solution would be:

Let t be a parameter that specifies a point on a (closed) curve. Let (u, v)

specify a point within the loop $(x(t), y(t))$. Then the function

$$\Phi(t; u, v) = (x(t) - u)^2 + (y(t) - v)^2$$

is *the distance squared function for the loop*. You can define a function of the position (u, v) and the loop as a whole as follows:

$$\Psi(u, v) = \min_t \Phi(t; u, v).$$

The function Ψ cannot be assumed to be a smooth function of position, *even if the loop is as smooth as you could wish*. This comes about because the function Ψ considered as a function of t will in general have a number of minima, and if you vary the "control parameters" u, v you must expect that the global minimum will *jump from one local minimum to the other* at certain singular points and curves in control space. (The effect is analogous to the case of the landscape composed of smooth hills in which the *horizon* is only piece-wise smooth because of the presence of "T-junctions," one hill apparently being in front of another.) These singular sets are exactly the loci that make up the medial axis.

This abstract structure immediately suggests a relation with catastrophe theory. The normal form for the cusp has the expression

$$\Phi(t; u, v) = \frac{t^4}{4} + \frac{ut^2}{2} + vt.$$

The extrema are located at the points $t^3 + ut + v = 0$. For $v = 0$ they are $t = 0$ and $t = +/ - \sqrt{-u}$. The latter specify a pair of minima that both lead to a value of Φ equal to $-u^2/4$. This is exactly the singular condition for the function Ψ; thus you find that the negative u-axis is a medial axis. The upshot of this all is that one normal form for the singular sets of Φ is an ending curve. The endpoint of the medial axis is exactly a cusp point of the distance squared function.

Arnold has classified the possible singularities of the function Ψ. In 2D there exist three possible normal forms up to addition of a smooth function of the parameters and a parameter transformation:

$$\begin{aligned}
\Psi(u, v) &= & \|u\| \\
\Psi(u, v) &= & \max(u, v, u + v) \\
\Psi(u, v) &= & \max_x(-x^4 + ux^2 + vx).
\end{aligned}$$

The first is merely a crest, that is, a normal piece of medial axis. The second is more interesting; it represents a branch point of the medial axis: three semi-lines meet at a point subtending finite angles with each other. The third case looks complicated at first sight, but is really nothing but the ending medial axis that I discussed above.

For the 3D case there are five more possibilities.

11.1.2   Tubular surfaces

♠ INTERMEZZO—SOME SPECIAL SURFACES.

The tubular surfaces are rather degenerated objects. They have attracted a lot of attention in graphics and computer vision, however. Tubular surfaces are sometimes defined as envelopes of one-parameter (parameter s, say) families of spheres with radius function $R(s)$ and centers on a space curve $\vec{x}(s)$. It is assumed that each sphere touches the envelope along a circle, which will automatically be a line of principal curvature. (The condition is $|\partial R/\partial s| < 1$.) There exist several other less precisely defined and often very complicated notions of what are often called "generalized cylinders." In some cases the definitions are so broad that it is hard to see what surfaces do not belong to the intended class. In such cases the notion becomes obviously less natural, and usually other methods will serve the goal better.

A simple case that is much in the spirit of the "generalized cylinder" approach is that of the surfaces of the "garden hose" variety, namely

$$\vec{x}(s) = \vec{y}(s) + R\,(\vec{n}(s)\,\cos\varphi + \vec{b}(s)\,\sin\varphi),$$

where $\vec{y}(s)$ is a general space curve parametrized with respect to arclength and normal $\vec{n}(s)$, binormal $\vec{b}(s)$. Thus you have a circle of radius R that is moved orthogonal to a space curve and thus sweeps out a volume that looks like a garden hose. It is assumed that certain obvious limits are observed; you obviously shouldn't use bends that are much sharper than the diameter of the hose, for instance.

You obtain the normal to the tube surface through straightforward differentiation. It is

$$\vec{N} = \vec{n}\,\cos\varphi + \vec{b}\,\sin\varphi$$

and the Gaussian curvature is

$$K(s,\varphi) = \frac{-\kappa(s)\cos\varphi}{R(1 - R\kappa(s)\cos\varphi)}.$$

Thus the parabolic curves are $\varphi = \frac{\pi}{2}$ and $\varphi = \frac{3\pi}{2}$, a very simple result. (κ is the curvature of the space curve.) The extreme values of the Gaussian curvature are $-\kappa/R(1 - \kappa R)$ and $\kappa/R(1 + \kappa R)$. If the radius of the tube is much smaller than the radius of curvature of the space curve, you just get plus or minus κ/R, as you could have guessed beforehand. If the product κR equals unity, you are in trouble; thus a garden hose with radius R will tolerate curvatures of the axis up to $1/R$. If you try to curve it even more, it will develop a kink.

For the ordinary torus you have $\kappa = 1/A$, where A is the radius of the center circle. Thus

$$K = \frac{-\cos\varphi}{AR(1 - \frac{R}{A}\cos\varphi)}.$$

It is somewhat more interesting and indeed a rewarding exercise to investigate the perturbed torus. You find, and this is in fact a general property, that the Gauss map develops pleats exactly where the axis of the tubular surface has a torsion zero. The situation is more complicated in the degenerated case that the rate of change of the torsion vanishes at the torsion zero.

The axial directions are the dominant force "felt" between the outside contour. Our feeling for movement is thus energised by the dominant force and as we put down our marks to feel the form sooner or later we want to draw its outside or contour.
—JOHN CRONEY, Drawing figure movement (1983)

11.2 Cratings & polyhedral approximations

Beautiful forms are straight planes rounded.
—JEAN AUGUSTE DOMINIQUE INGRES (1780–1867)

A "crating" is often called a "box" in computer graphics. It is not a true approximation of a shape—at least it is not meant to be. Instead, it defines a region—usually as tightly as possible—that is constrained to have a simple shape such as a crate with sides parallel to three specified orthogonal directions and that contains the object. Many geometrical problems can be decided at least approximately on the basis of crates rather than the objects themselves. Using the crates then yields great increases in the efficiency of the algorithms. Many objects are generated via a sequence of operations that takes them through a crate stage, an activity that is known by sculptors as "blocking out."

If you elaborate the blocking-out process, you go toward a true *approximation* of the shape. This is commonly done by draftsmen when they have to copy an intricate shape by eye. It is a simple and very effective process that can be carried to arbitrary precision.

A polyhedral approximation should be distinguished from a crating, although the distinction is one of aim, rather than of structure *per se.* The aim of a polyhedral approximation is to approximate the shape in some specified way, that is to say, to define another object that shares a set of decisive shape measures with a given object. The polyhedral approximation is then substituted for the object itself. Thus different shapes may have identical cratings, but they must have different polyhedral approximations in order to be counted as different.

There are many ways to arrive at a polyhedral approximation. Here are two of them:

1. You pick a triangulation of the surface and replace the surface by the polyhedron formed by the faces defined by the chords of the triangulation.

2. You pick a set of points on the surface and construct their tangent planes. The polyhedron is defined by the facets that appear when you intersect the tangent planes with one another. For objects that are not ovoids this necessitates certain nontrivial decisions.

Note that—for ease of reference I speak of the ovoid case—for the first method the polyhedron lies *inside the surface*, whereas for the second

method it lies *outside*. If for some reason you want the polyhedron to
have the same volume as the object, you need still another method.
The quality of the approximation can be measured by many and very
different means and all yield different results. The overall impressions
will be similar, of course. One example of a quality measure is the total
volume of the shape defined by the "skin" between the approximation
and the object. Another quality measure is the "ε-distance" (which
you may recall from many chapters back) between the shape and its
approximation.

Polyhedral approximations are often nice because it is so easy and
natural to control the "resolution" of the approximation. This is often
used in artistic practice. First one gets the "major planes" right, and
then articulates by subdivision based on the shapes of the minor masses.
Figure 560 shows an example from a book of the "how to draw" variety.

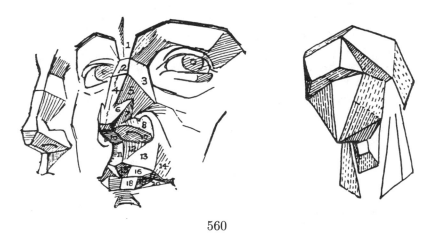

560

Schwarz (1890) has discussed a very simple example that clearly illustrates some of the problems to be aware of. He considers a cylinder
of unit height erected over the unit circle. Divide the height into equal
parts 0, $1/k$, $2/k$, ..., $(k-1)/k$, $k/k = 1$, and the circumference into
n equal parts. Then you obtain a triangulation of $2kn$ equal triangles
(fig. 561), and it is an easy though somewhat tedious exercise to compute
the surface area of this "lantern surface." Its value is

$$A(k,n) = 2n \sin \frac{\pi}{n} \sqrt{1 + 4k^2 \sin^4 \frac{\pi}{2n}}.$$

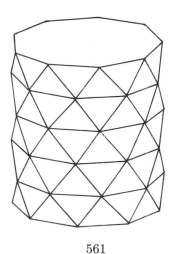

561

Now you may consider the limit for infinitely fine triangulations.

It is straightforward to show that *the limit depends on the way in which you refine the triangulation*: suppose you take $k = n^s$ and let n approach infinity. (Of course, you can take infinitely many different routes toward the smooth cylinder! I have made an essentially arbitrary choice here, mainly inspired by the desire to obtain a tractable problem.) Then you may verify that

- For $s = 1$ you obtain 2π;

- For $s = 2$ you get $2\pi\sqrt{1 + \frac{\pi^4}{4}}$;

- For $s = 3$ you see that the limit doesn't exist.

Clearly this is not such a good model if you are interested in surface area. The observation that $A(k, n) \geq 2n \sin \frac{\pi}{n}$, whereas the limit for n to infinity of the latter estimate is 2π, shows that the surface of the cylinder is the *limes inferior* of the total area of the triangulation. It is intuitively reasonable to expect that this could be a general property of triangulations.

The upshot is that

Mark well: *you should be suspicious of any method that proposes to make use of surface area of a polyhedral model.*

As I remarked many times earlier, only volumometric measures make much operational sense in the real world. The model of the cylinder clearly illustrates some of the problems involved. It should also serve as a warning against the heedless use of combinatorial models for smooth geometrical entities: if surface area doesn't converge to the real thing when you refine the triangulation, then what about other properties of interest to you? Clearly you have to be very careful.

The primary part of painting, therefore, are the planes.
That grace in bodies which we call beauty is born from
the composition of the planes.
A face which has its planes here large and there small—similar to
the faces of old women—would be most ugly in appearance.
Those faces which have the planes joined in such a way
that they take shades and light agreeable and pleasantly,
and have no harshness of the relief angles,
these we should certainly say are beautiful and delicate faces.
—LEON BATTISTA ALBERTI, Della Pittura (1435)

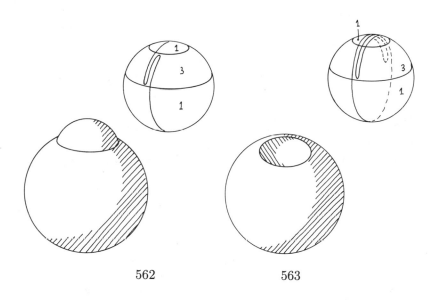

562

563

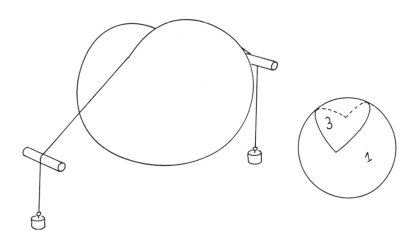

564

11.3   Ovoid assemblies

> *Fancy not to compose an ideal form by mixing up a mass of*
> *promiscuous beauties; for, unless you consulted what was homogeneous*
> *and what was possible in Nature, you have hatched only a monster:*
> *this, we suppose was understood by Zeuxis when he collected the*
> *beauties of Agrigentum to compose the perfect female.*
> —HENRI FUSELI (1741-1825), *Aphorisms on Art, item 103*

Ovoids are in many respects the simplest shapes around: for instance,
many of the intricate problems related to inflexions of the surface and
high order of contact of tangent lines or planes with the object do not
occur for them.

This suggests a method of shape approximation in which you combine
ovoids into clusters. In order to arrive at anything reasonable, you have
to tolerate overlaps of the ovoids. Thus you arrive at the approximations
based on *set theoretical combinations of ovoids.* Such "ovoid assemblies"
are patch-wise simple, or even trivial, and the problematic areas become
concentrated in the boundary curves, the crests and V-shaped furrows,
and the general spatial layout (figs. 562 and 563).

You can generalize this notion somewhat by including all-synclastic
surfaces that are permitted to possess singular curves of the V-groove
type. Such surfaces can be generated physically by "strangling" balloons
with taut wires (fig. 564).   The addition of such surfaces to the basic
repertoire is useful because they permit simple models of the furrow
type depressions—something that cannot be done elegantly with the set
theoretical combination of ovoids.

The use of all-synclastic surfaces as parts in the assemblage of general
surfaces is a method that has been extensively used in the art of drawing
from the Renaissance to the baroque eras. Modern applications abound
in graphical methods in organic chemistry, where large molecules are
often modeled as ovoid assemblies. The example is interesting because
in this discipline, as in the art of drawing, people often employ the axis
and the ovoid assembly models in combination, with apparently good
results.

Many of the complex inflexional structures on surfaces can easily be
modeled in terms of ovoid assemblies, just as they can be modeled by
polyhedral patches. This is an interesting field of inquiry that yet has to
be developed. In such models the smooth patches of the surface are all
synclastic in nature, and the "anticlastic parts" are *completely concen-*
trated in singular curves and points. On the Gauss map the synclastical

parts map to bounded patches of the same orientation *whose boundaries do not mesh.* You find ample illustrations in the previous chapters. The singular curves also map on patches, and these connect the synclastic parts.

In this way it is natural to think of the anticlastic parts of a surface as a kind of "glue" that is needed to patch the convexities and concavities together. Figures 562 to 564 illustrate this for a "furrow," a "dimple," and a "bell."

Instead of the ovoid assembly, people often use an "ovoid cladding" on some simplified object such as a tubular surface, a large ovoid, a plane ... This has been a repeatedly used tool in the art of drawing, where some artists model humans as basically inflated stick men with an ovoid cladding to represent the musculature. This simplifies many later operations such as shading. Each of the ovoids is shaded for its own sake, which is a relatively simple process. Then a general shading suggesting the inflated stick-man surface is superimposed over the shaded ovoids to blend it all together. In most cases the latter overall shading is simplified again by using a polyhedral model for the shape ("the general planes," fig. 565).

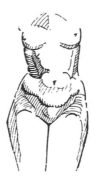

565

The "medial axis transform" expresses a shape as a union of infinitely many "maximal spheres." If you merely *sample* or discretize the integrand, you obtain a sum over finitely many spheres as an approximation of the shape. This is an easy and well-defined manner to build ovoid assemblies. The problem is that you tend to use an overdose of ovoids in this way. This will certainly dawn on you when you consider the case of an ellipsoid which is after all nothing but a rather simple ovoid. It appears only slightly less than ludicrous to approximate the ellipsoid with an infinity of spheres.

What you really want is a series of increasingly precise approximations to a shape such that any truncated part of the series makes sense by itself. In most cases reasonable approximations should use less than, say, three or four well-picked ovoids.

Surface patches such as the anticlastic patch of the torus do not yield very gracefully to the ovoid treatment. They only look reasonable in the limit of very many ovoids.

11.3.1   Ridges and grooves

When you consider set theoretical combinations of blobs, you will have to deal with "crests" and "grooves," which are singular lines on the surface where the tangent planes are not defined. Rather, you can define a "left" and a "right" tangent plane at each point of the singular line.

A first rough taxonomy of such singular curves is obtained when you consider the position of their osculating planes with respect to the right and left tangent planes. If the right and left outward normals point to *one side* of the osculating plane, you obtain a typical groove or crest of the "collar type" (figs. 566 and 567). Whether it is one or the other

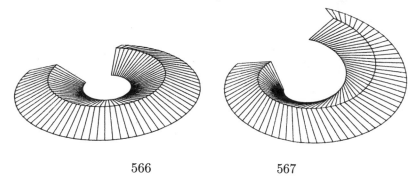

566   567

depends on the order of the normals and the binormals of the curve.

If the normals are at *both sides* of the osculating plane, the crest or groove is like the edge of a discus, or like a "waist" (figs. 568 and 569). Of course the singular curve will have a torsion in the general case.

The parameters describing these singular lines are:

- the parameters of the singular curve as a space curve

- the *average normal* (of left and right surface strips) along the curve

- the dihedral angle along the curve.

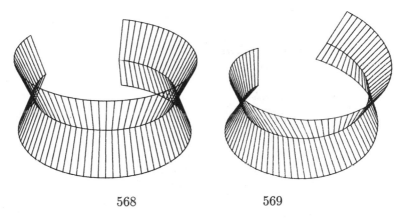

568   569

They may all be arbitrary functions of arclength, except for the constraints:

- the curvature is *strictly positive*

- the dihedral angle varies between 0 and 2π (π would be a smooth join).

The general case can look awfully complicated (fig. 570).

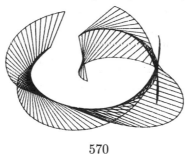

570

You can easily generate crests and grooves if you have made a program
that generates space curves and have subsequently converted (or augmented) it to produce ribbons. The same program will produce crests
if you code for the dihedral angle.

In special cases you may be able to exploit the resulting simplifica-
tions; for instance, for the set theoretical combination of spheres the
singular curves must obviously be planar and the dihedral angle must
be constant along the curve.

In the earlier literature you can find a lot of material that could be
useful in practice, such as formulas relating normal curvatures of the
surfaces to the left and the right of a crest with the curvature of the
crest as a space curve, and so on.

11.3.2   Triple orthogonal surfaces

♠ INTERMEZZO—FROM THE MUSEUM.

Intersecting surfaces have been very important in applications where curvilinear coordinates were required. In 1813 Dupin proved that the surfaces of a threefold orthogonal system of surfaces meet pair-wise along lines of curvature. Darboux showed that, at least in some tubular neighborhood of a surface, you can embed any given surface into such a three-fold orthogonal system.

Thus any sole family belonging to a triple orthogonal system cuts the surfaces of the other families into shreds that are perfect curvature ribbons. This is how people have arrived at the nice pictures of the principal directions of the triaxial ellipsoid in fact.

A somewhat more general result is that of Terquem-Joachimsthal: if two surfaces intersect at a constant angle, the curve of intersection is principal on both surfaces, and *vice versa*.

The triply orthogonal surfaces once were a major tool in the hand of theoretical physicists. Many of the "classical solutions" from the physics textbooks were constructed via a shrewd use of the known triply orthogonal systems.

From a threefold orthogonal system you can easily derive interesting shapes with well-defined crests with a $\frac{\pi}{2}$ crest angle. Because of the simple relation to the principal directions such surfaces are relatively easy to manufacture. The simplest example is, of course, the rectangular crate that can be obtained from the triple orthogonal set of surfaces $x = constant$, $y = constant$ and $z = constant$. In fact, many useful shapes can very simply be "mapped" on such cratings if you take the crates from some triple orthogonal system. The only condition is that your crating should not cover a singularity, like the poles for the geographical coordinates, of the curvilinear coordinate system.

A density $\Phi(x, y, z)$ can be converted to a triple orthogonal system very easily. One family is composed of the level surfaces $\Phi = constant$. You then use the principal directions on the level surfaces and the normal directions to generate the other two families. Conversely, each triple orthogonal system can be put into relation with densities in many possible ways such that one family represents a set of equal density contours.

> To arrive at la belle forme *one must model in the round and without interior details.*
> —JEAN AUGUSTE DOMINIQUE INGRES (1780–1867)

> *Les antiques prenaient par les milieux, au lieu que la Renaissance prenait par la ligne.*
> —EUGÈNE DELACROIX (1798–1863)

11.4   Nets

Like the chain models or linked-rod models for curves, people use "net models" for surfaces. In order for these to be useful, you should put some restrictions on the net; for instance, all of its edges are often constrained to be of the same length (fig. 571).

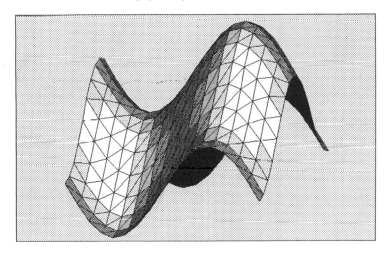

571

Please note that the "diagonals" of the parameter net don't belong to the Chebyshev net! Their lengths may vary a lot.

Such nets have been pioneered by Chebyshev and are usually called "Chebyshev nets" after him. Chebyshev wrote a famous mathematical paper entitled "On the cut of our clothes" in which he introduced the concept, the idea being that these nets approximate the structure of the cloth used to make your suit. As we all know you can't in general make a piece of clothing fit without cutting and sewing, and Chebyshev required a tight, smooth, sexy fit. Chebyshev may have simplified the problem a bit too much to be useful in real life. Stoker has an interesting discussion.

In any Chebyshev system the tangent to either family undergoes a parallel displacement along each curve of the other family (and *vice versa*).

The main parameter that describes such a net locally is the angle between the coordinate curves, (ω, say). The first fundamental form has $u^2 + 2\cos\omega\, uv + v^2 = 1$ as its gauge figure and is simply related to the Gaussian curvature via the equation

$$K = -\frac{1}{\sin\omega}\,\frac{\partial^2\omega}{\partial u\partial v}.$$

Geometrically the nets are special in that the edges in one family are carried over into each other via parallel displacement, in Levi-Civita's sense, along the curves of the other family. The converse also holds.

The parallel displacement property is the reason why Chebyshev nets are quite common in engineering practice. They are automatically generated by the coordinate curves of all *surfaces of translation* (German: *"Schiebfläche"*, French: *"Surfaces moulures"*), which are those families of—very special—surfaces for which $\vec{X}(u,v) = \vec{U}(u) + \vec{V}(v)$. Such surfaces are especially easy to assemble because you can prefabricate a series of planar ribs of the shape $\vec{U}(u)$ and stack them in parallel layers with the possible introduction of a one parameter—vertical—shift. If you also have "prefab" planar ribs of the shape $\vec{V}(v)$, you only have to connect the ribs at premarked points (fig. 572). (This is, of course, the origin of

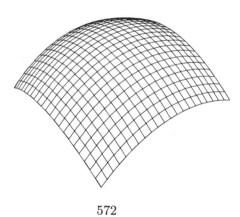

572

the French term for these surfaces.) Again, the "diagonals" don't belong to the net! The parameter curves of such nets are mutually conjugated, and thus the meshes are planar.

There exist many other well-known nets with interesting properties. The classical literature has a lot of material on nets, much of it of quite some interest from the point of view of applications in CAD-CAM.

11.5 Functions with "knobs"

An often-used method to approximate given surfaces is to use functions with a sufficient number of "knobs," the "control variables" that can be twiddled to make something that approximates the shape. The many kinds of "splines" that dominate computer graphics and CAD-CAM are the obvious examples.

A simple example is the "bilinear Monge patch"

$$z(x, y) = a + b\,x + c\,y + d\,xy,$$

which describes a hyberboloid surface. People like it because it can be used to fill out the rectangles on a surface that has been obtained through the sampling on a Cartesian grid. You have simply:

$$
\begin{aligned}
a &= z(x, y) \\
b &= \frac{z(x+\triangle x, y) - z(x,y)}{\triangle x} \\
c &= \frac{z(x, y+\triangle y) - z(x,y)}{\triangle y} \\
d &= \frac{z(x+\triangle x, y+\triangle y) + z(x,y) - z(x+\triangle x, y) - z(x, y+\triangle y)}{\triangle x \triangle y}
\end{aligned}
$$

for the rectangle defined by the points (x, y), $(x+\triangle x, y)$, $(x+\triangle x, y+\triangle y)$ and $(x, y+\triangle y)$ in the parameter plane. People tend to prefer this over a triangulation (in which you can interpolate linearly within the triangular areas defined by the sample points) because the simple "wire-frame"-graphics look better for the bilinear mesh than for the triangulation.

Most often, however, people forget about this background and act as if the little squares in their wire-frame graphics represent *little planar parallelograms*. This is just an approximation, of course. One actually has a surface pieced together from hyperboloid patches, with singular edges and vertices as in the polyhedral case.

If you don't like dihedral edges or vertices on your surface, you have to use higher-order interpolations. This is perfectly possible, of course, and a large literature exists to assist you. The "splines" are the most convenient tools here because they have such nice "controls."

The differential geometry for such functions is easy to work out because they are algebraic surfaces, although many of the really interesting results, such as the detection of the flecnodals, are not readily available from the standard references. The classical literature on the differential geometry of algebraic surfaces is directly applicable here, although it is no fun because of the old-fashioned insistence on the use of coordinate language.

If you are interested in higher-order phenomena, such as the structure of the asymptotic ray manifold, you must "blend" the patches extremely smoothly, which means that you must go to much higher orders than is the usual practice. If you don't take care, the singularities will be on the "edges" of the patches, and you are in a similar situation as with the polyhedral approximation if you study the Gauss map. In the case of the Gauss map for polyhedra all the curvature is in the vertices and edges, remember? The important generic singularities of surfaces are of a higher order than the typical order of the template functions as they are being used in practice.

You will only confuse your representation of the muscles
and their location, derivation, and purpose
if you first do not show the network of the small muscles ...
—LEONARDO DA VINCI (1452–1519)

11.6 Piles of sugar cubes

A very simple and algorithmically nice method is related to "crating." You segment space into a regular tessellation of cubes, which can be indexed (i, j, k) where i, j, k are integer values. A given shape is then replaced with a pile consisting of those cubes that "hit" the shape (fig. 573). If you are interested in the shape only, you then delete all

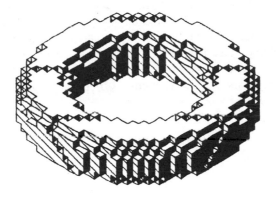

573

faces that belong to two cubes sharing the common face. The resulting "surface" can easily be represented as a linked datastructure.

This method is nowadays popular in medical image processing, where more and more 3D data are forthcoming.

The "surface" of this pile of cubes is obviously less smooth than could be desired. It is visually evident, for example, that it is not easy to define reasonable tangent planes. Thus the Gauss map of the pile looks rather messy.

However, these models are well suited for purposes of volumometric integral geometry, which I do not treat in this text, and for display purposes.

They are almost worthless for the study of the shape through its *surface*. If you are interested in the latter, you will be much better off to treat the voxel values as samples of some smooth 3D density function and to attack this via the methods presented earlier. This will mean that you will lose some resolution. However, this is more or less what you ask for if you want to get rid of the cubical texture.

In many cases, such as the generation of graphics from sugar cubes type data bases, it may not at all be necessary to go through the motions to figure out a smooth surface that fits the sugar cubes representation.

It often suffices to use a form of "ray casting" and use the densities represented by the cubes to simulate an "optical medium" for the rays to interact with. Then you can compute pictures that the eye interprets easily enough as an "illuminated surface in space." Here the eye does most of the job.

This general type of technique is of interest because it completely disregards surface-type representations. If these techniques come into general use, I will have to change the emphasis of this book not a little.

These models are in a class of their own when it comes to integral geometry. As a simple example you may consider the computation of the volume of a shape. This is no big deal in the sugar cube representation but extremely hard in almost any other. Clearly, it may be of value to entertain multiple models for the same object, each one tailored for a certain family of problems.

Philosophy is written in this great book—by which I mean
the universe—which stands always open to our views,
but it cannot be understood unless one first learns to comprehend
the language and interpret the symbols in which it is written,
and its symbols are triangles, circles and other geometric figures,
without which it is not humanly possible to comprehend
even one word of it;
without these one wanders in a dark labyrinth.
—GALILEI GALILEO (1564–1642)

12 How to draw and use diagrams

..., even if your problem is not a problem of geometry, you may try to draw a figure. To find a lucid geometric representation for your nongeometrical problem could be an important step toward the solution.
—G. POLYA, *How to solve it (1945).*

Trivial as the task may seem at first sight, it does make some sense to review the *basics* concerning the preparation of diagrams, be it only summarily. Of course, much depends on whether you are just making a quick thumbnail sketch to explain a point to a fellow scientist or to help to bring your own thoughts to some focus, or whether you are actually preparing a diagram for publication. In the latter case you will be prepared to spend some time on the job; in the former case the sketch has to progress at the same pace as your verbal explanation or your wandering thoughts.

In both cases it is of value to be aware of certain conventional attitudes that most people—including ourselves—seem to assume when confronted with geometrical diagrams. When you exploit these, you will be able to imprint a pattern of thought on your audience, whereas a neglect of these matters is certain to get you in trouble. From such a neglect many surprises arise in audience and speaker alike, and it is often the case that a lecturer spends more time on the explanation of irrelevant details of his sketch than on the subject matter he wanted to raise. Worse still, the result is often irritation and misunderstanding.

Consider sketching an important enterprise. If done for yourself, it can either pin you down in some *cul de sac* or let you roam freely through imaginary spaces; if done for an audience, it can either put you in a position to imprint *your* pattern of thought on *their* minds or lead to utter confusion.

You must be explicitly aware of your goal. The goal is to manipulate other people's minds with your sketch. Remember that vision is the main gateway to the brain in terms of sheer numbers of input connections. Thus, if you are really serious about wanting to influence people, you had better exploit it in the most effective manner, for you will not be granted a better opportunity. It really pays to assume a thoroughly Machiavellian attitude in this respect.

With *any* sketch you must depend on a certain *visual maturity* of the reader. For example, you are not going to explain that certain scribbles—arrows—are meant to "point" to other scribbles, and so forth, although such tacit knowledge is actually far from trivial. It is at least *conceivable* that there could be cultures that draw their arrows "the wrong way." Certain features of the sketch—such as the arrows—must by necessity be indicated with *conventional signs*. Others are meant to establish *patterns of reading* and specify eye movements. For example, a bolder type will attract the attention more easily than a light type.

Still other features are silently understood to be irrelevant to the matter at hand. An example would be the indication of a "point" through a "little sphere," that is a circle in the sketch, perhaps with some stylized shadowing. Such irrelevant details are not mere baroque embellishment. The little sphere convention to indicate points allows you to indicate which of two points is nearer to the viewer. You use overlap if the points are close in the sketch and a size cue when they are far apart.

If details happen to be *really* irrelevant, you should remove these rococo frills: manipulating other people is difficult enough without such distractions, and you should consciously exclude any unnecessary sources of possible confusion.

If some details included in the sketch are irrelevant, it is equally true that most sketches include relevant detail that has not been drawn. You should be aware of such visible invisibles. An example would be the line-segment between two points that are drawn but remain unconnected in the sketch. The line-segment may not have been drawn, but it is nevertheless present because the reader will notice the moment you introduce a third point on the segment. Even more remarkable, the third point will assume a depth value that interpolates the depths of the original pair of points. If the third point happens to be at a different depth, you have to take some countermeasures.

Readers who are not conversant with such conventions as arrows, points of finite size, and so forth will typically come up with interpretations of your sketch that are completely off the mark. This will lead to unnecessary misunderstanding, and it pays to be aware of the possibility that such impossible people exist. In many cases you can avoid some of the trouble by explicitly mentioning the irrelevancy of certain details. Of course, you will almost automatically mention those facts that are relevant. You must make a conscious effort at the converse though.

When you talk while sketching or when you write a caption for a sketch, you are using two different types of instruction. One type is aimed at focusing and shifting the focus of attention of the audience. You want to enforce a pattern of eye movements as part of your brainwashing attempt. The other type is aimed at the association of certain details of the sketch with certain meanings that cannot be drawn. An example of the latter kind would be such a remark as "the vector $\vec{E}$ represents the electric field."

You refer to details in the sketch by content ("the triangle") or by relative position to other details that are referred to by content ("the vector that represents the displacement $\mathcal{A}$ to $\mathcal{A}'$," "the point $\mathcal{B}$ immediately to the right of $\mathcal{A}$").

I assume you are aware of such elementary matters as the fact that a lecturer should never say things like "this vector"—while pointing at a detail in his sketch. If you say "the vector $\vec{\mathcal{A}\mathcal{A}'}$," you will even be understood by the member of the audience who happened to be examining his fingernails instead of your sketch.

Remarks of the second kind include instructions about (ir-)relevancy. For instance the remark "the points $\mathcal{A}$, $\mathcal{B}$, $\mathcal{C}$ are in general position" communicates that the actual shape of the triangle $\mathcal{ABC}$ in the sketch is immaterial.

Both types of remark can be crucial, so it makes sense to consider them with an eye on their most effective exploitation. The first type tends to be the most difficult but is extremely important because you need to establish a pattern of eye movements in order to manipulate your audience.

An introductory textbook on the arts of layout and graphic design is most helpful to obtain a grasp of the basics. I assume you already possess some rudimentary knowledge, as most scientists do who are used to lecturing. Due to sheer exposure most people have some tacit understanding, but you need an explicit one. I will skip this subject here, but it is worth pondering that most art directors selling soap are much more effective and professional in these areas than is considered professional standard for the scientist. Soap is sold through the subtle use of crude methods, and much the same principles apply to the problem of producing and using scientific illustrations.

It is surprisingly difficult to scribble lines on a surface in such a way that the result has a "flat" quality. Usually there will be some *illusory depth*. Thus it would seem to be mere child's play to evoke solid-looking 3D artwork on flat paper. Such is not the case, however. In order to be effective you need to do some careful engineering. The kinds of tricks you play are essentially those of the comic book artist of the "Marvel" type.

Consider the simple example of drawing a vector based on a point $\mathcal{P}$. The typical textbook drawing looks like the sketch in figure 574.

Although this certainly has a professional, "clean" look, you miss quite a few opportunities to imprint a pattern on your audience using this technique. For instance, is the vector pointing toward you or away from you? There is no way to find out. The drawing is inherently ambiguous in this respect. Most people will probably understand the vector as existing in a frontoparallel plane of undefined depth.

If you throw in a little "irrelevant" detail, you can do much better. Consider putting a little solid arrowhead on the shaft. Your audience may believe that you do this merely to have the arrow look cute, but in fact this enables you to have the vector point toward or away from you in an obvious manner (fig. 575).

This effect depends on several "depth cues." The strongest one is that of "occlusion." Either the shaft occludes the arrowhead or vice versa. The effect is lost if you color the vector all black. The same trick works perfectly well on the base of the vector (fig. 576).

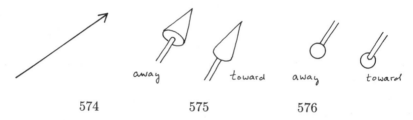

574   575   576

You can use these techniques in combination, of course. Be careful not to have them disagree. It is even possible to evoke the effect by way of the shaft alone, if you *taper* it (fig. 577). This also works for black vectors, but the effect is weaker and hard to use in printed material. It also takes a lot of time, so I seldom use the tapering trick except in quick sketches. It is only when you make the final figures that the time factor comes in and the method becomes burdensome. In a quick sketch almost anything goes, timewise. All these methods may be combined (fig. 578).

If you have to sketch a *frame*, you are in an even better position. Because the frame vectors are understood to be orthogonal, the sketch is especially easily interpreted in 3D if you have the frame in "general position" with respect to the projection. The remaining ambiguity can be lifted through the use of exaggerated and not necessarily "true"— it is seldom necessary to actually go to perspective constructions— perspective.

The only ambiguity that can not be lifted is the identification of the individual frame vectors. Here you need symbolic labels, such as numbers. Conventions that distinguish the frame vectors through multiple arrowheads and so forth are burdensome and tend to clutter up the sketch. They had better be avoided altogether (fig. 579).

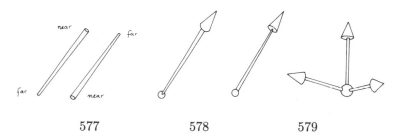

577   578   579

A circle for a point that is nowhere occluded tends to look quite flat. A little conventional shadow turns it into a little sphere (fig. 580).

If you use this method, you should shadow all other points as well, albeit in a cursory fashion. It looks a lot better if you respect a common "direction of the illuminating beam" (fig. 581).

580   581

The thickened shafts of vectors are extremely helpful when you have to indicate *depth order* where the shafts intersect in your sketch (fig. 582). The impression is so powerful that many sketches gain clarity when you throw in a few of such intersections. If you overdo it you will lose all your gains.

Draw a shaft in one go even when it is partially occluded. This is the only way to avoid "crooked" or even "broken" shafts; such defects really destroy your drawing (fig. 583).

Occlusion is by far the most powerful depth cue that you can draw on. If you can't use it, you must rely on other cues though. An example is the case of isolated points. You may indicate their depth order through apparent size or "atmospheric perspective" (fig. 584). The latter cue is better avoided for art work that has to be printed, of course. It works very well and can be drawn with real speed if you draw with a soft pencil.

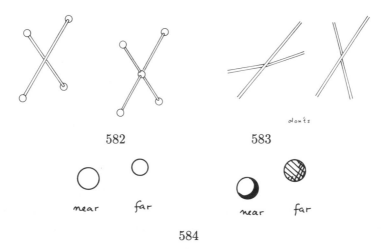

582   583

near   far   near   far

584

Often you need some dynamics in the picture, to indicate a direction of movement or flow, for instance.

The main thing to remember is to avoid arrows that look like vectors. The difference should be as immediately obvious as can be. A good substitute is the "flat cutout." Direction in depth is easily indicated if you give them some thickness. A double outline and a bolder outline will both do the job for you. Self-occlusion and exaggerated perspective are also quite effective (figs. 585 to 587).

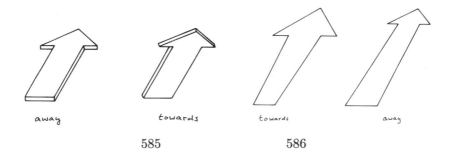

away   towards   towards   away

585   586

The same method applies to the indication of planes, such as tangent planes, bivectors, one-forms, etc. The one- and two-forms are especially easy because they will nearly always allow you to use as many overlaps as you like (fig. 588).

587

588

General smooth surfaces are perhaps the hardest subjects. The more "general surfaces," that is, those with convoluted shapes with many bulges and hollows, are actually the easiest to portray. This is because they at least give you something to draw, except from an eventual patch boundary, and you will often have the opportunity to introduce powerful depth cues such as self-occlusions.

Almost flat surfaces are the most problematic of all. Without special care they look like flat paper cut-outs. The tools at your disposal to counteract this regrettable effect are basically the *edge of the patch*, the contour, and—whenever you are able to introduce them—*ending contours* and *T-junctions*. The sign of the curvature of the contour reveals the sign of the Gaussian curvature of the surface. This is a very useful property, one you should exploit. You must try to find a viewpoint such that you obtain a nice distribution of self-occlusions and ending contours while at the same time leaving uncluttered those parts of the surface that have to be given a special treatment.

In many cases you will be quite free to determine the shape of the edge, and you can put this to good advantage. The easiest to "read" are edges that suggest a bent rectangular patch and those where the edge results from the intersection of the surface with a rectangular box or a sphere. The treatment of the edge can be decisive. Here is yet another example of essential "irrelevant detail" (fig. 589).

It is usually not necessary to introduce shading such as hatching, stip-

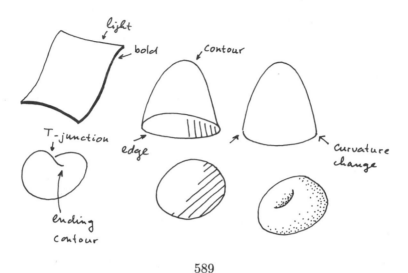

589

pling, tone wash, and so forth, although this looks great and is thrown in
almost for free in the thumbnail sketch. Use rough hatching in a single
direction with the pen, or rubbed tone with a soft pencil. I used some
rudimentary shading for several sketches in this book. For reproduction
purposes I kept it as open as possible and never used cross-hatching.[1]

"Shadowing" may be of the "naturalistic" type and take account of
the direction of some imaginary illumination. Other methods are often
more effective though. For instance, you may use the medieval trick of
shading in rough proportion to the slant; that is, you darken what curves
away from you. This produces very nice and easily readable designs and
leads to an attractive "edge crispening." This method of using tone is
often encountered in the working drawings of sculptors because it tends
to clarify solid shape and avoids the introduction of an irrelevant light
source. The light source is a mere "incident" and should be disregarded
if you view the shape with the eye of eternity. Other uses of tone are to
accentuate "undercuts" (fig. 590).

Multi-sheeted coverings are best treated in the same way as surfaces.
For instance, the austere diagram from the typical textbook indicating a
pleat with triple cover inside, single cover outside the cusp looks a whole
lot clearer when you draw it with an "irrelevant" edge (fig. 591). This
kind of trick often determines whether you lose part of your audience
or not. Sometimes it is desirable to add some irrelevant 3D by "lifting"

---

[1] A good way to judge your artwork is to reduce it several times with a xerox
copier or to view it through a negative lens.

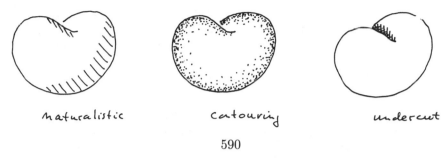

naturalistic   catouring   undercut

590

the covers from each other (fig. 592). This is a bit dangerous because it

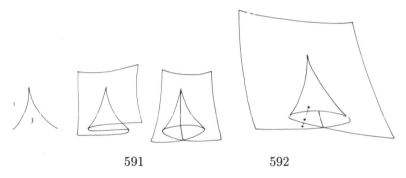

591   592

asks for a certain understanding on the part of the reader. You count on the silent agreement to consider only the "horizontal" directions as relevant, whereas the "vertical" dimension should be discounted. The reader has to squash the surfaces flat in his mind's eye. Because the sheets have been "lifted," you can now actually show a single point as multiple—identical—copies, one on each sheet. This is sometimes called the "stack of discs theorem." It is often convenient and tends to be easily understood, especially if you remove the ambiguity through a stippled, "ghostlike" vertical line "identifying" the copies as a single point.

A problem with surfaces and multiple sheets alike is that you have to decide on their degree of "transparency." Opaque surfaces obviously look more "solid" and their depth relations are less ambiguous. The drawback is that you cannot see the back of the head if you look at the face.

A trick that works is to cut some "window" in the frontal surface that allows a glimpse of the far surface to be seen. You use windows in places where they happen to reveal important things going on at the back. Windows easily lead to cluttered design. Another problem is that you have to establish them as windows as distinct from surface markings. This is best done through such depth cues as occlusion or—fancy—atmospheric perspective. If you use windows in a clumsy way, they destroy your work.

It will often be possible to avoid such crutches if you carefully lay out your design. Windows can be "put in parallel," that is, juxtaposed, or "in series." In the latter case one window yields a view of another one, and so forth. Due care must be taken to establish mutual depth order and to specify windows very clearly as such and not as—potentially relevant—geometrical structure. Multiple windows are better avoided altogether, but in topologically involved situations there may be no other way out.

I have used some rather complicated multiple window views in some chapters. These perhaps cross the borderline of what can be considered reasonable (fig. 593). You may be able to do better.

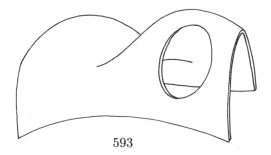

593

It will rarely be necessary to draw *several objects* distributed over space. If this is necessary, you must establish their mutual depth relations in some way or other, preferably without running into unclarities from unnecessary occlusions. In short, careful design is required.

The best method is the "tomographic" one. This means that you divide your subject into a few well-defined "depth planes." This is the ancient method used by painters to suggest space in landscapes. It can be very effective indeed. But don't think it is easy. Painters need a long apprenticeship before they can cope with the problems in an effective manner. If you are not an accomplished painter or draftsman, then foreground, middleground, and background are about the complexity you can expect to be able to handle.

Distribute your objects within these depth layers and the layers with respect to each other such that occlusions will clearly indicate the depth planes but not obliterate important detail. Apparent size or atmospheric perspective are most effective to clearly assign individual objects to their respective depth plane.

Once again: to do this kind of job at all well is really something for the professional. You would be wise to avoid it.

After reiterated endeavours to apprehend the general idea of a triangle, I have found it altogether incomprehensible. And surely if anyone were able to introduce that idea into my mind, it must be the author of the Essay concerning Human Understanding; *he who has so far distinguished himself from the generality of writers by the clearness and significancy of what he says. Let us therefore see how this celebrated author describes the general or abstract idea of a triangle.*

"It must be (says he) neither oblique nor rectangular, neither equilateral, nor scalenum; but all and none of these at once. In effect, it is somewhat imperfect that cannot exist; an idea, wherein some parts of several different and inconsistent ideas are put together."

It is therefore plain that visible figures are of the same use in geometry that words are: and the one may as well be accounted the object of that science as the other, neither of them being otherwise concerned therein than as they represent or suggest to the mind the particular tangible figures connected with them.

—BISHOP BERKELEY, *An Essay towards a New Theory of Vision (1709)*

12.1   What to avoid

There are so many things to avoid that it hardly seems possible to arrive at an effective sketch from scratch in every case. Practice will increase your number of "hits," though. It is good to have some explicit notions of the most common pitfalls; this will help you to increase your effectiveness in the beginning. With practice you will automatically avoid common blunders without thinking twice.

It is obviously bad practice to come up with a cluttered design. If your sketch looks complicated, as most first tries do, you should try to make clear to yourself what the essentials are and put them in focus at the expense of irrelevant details. It may be advantageous to split the sketch into a number of sketches or to split off parts as an "inset," perhaps showing a "microscopic view" in enlarged form. The more complicated the drawing the less its impact will be and the greater the possibilities for incorrect interpretations.

But some impossible people will invariably find their way to read any sketch incorrectly. And in retrospect it is no less than miraculous that so many people catch on right away. Consider a sketch successful if about three quarters of a professional audience gets the meaning right away. This doesn't happen to me very often. You may be more effective that way.

Cluttering may be concentrated; I mean a rather simple drawing may be rendered ineffective through the fact that the point it makes is made in only 5 % of the area of the sketch. The rule is to try to disperse the important features evenly over the extent of your artwork.

The things to avoid like the plague are "accidents." An example of such an accident is the case of three points that are collinear in the drawing but not collinear in space. The cure is obvious. Another case is that of an important feature that is hidden. Again the cure is obvious. Or consider a point that is not on a surface but appears to lie in it. A possible cure is to "lift" the point, preferably by not having it coincide with the projection of the surface. If this can't be helped, a little "shadow" will also lift the point but is a potential source of confusion. If you have to do this, you should clearly establish the shadow as such and avoid the possibility of its being read as a point. Blurring the edges of the shadow does the trick, but don't count on this for work that has to be reproduced.

The problem with "accidents" is that you may fail to notice them yourself and only detect their presence when something seems to go awry with your audience's readings. Try to develop an awareness of possible

misreadings and consciously scan your sketches for possible mishaps of
different kinds. Try to assume the attitude that something is wrong
with any sketch and that the only problem is to find out where the
trouble is located (figs. 594 and 595).   Remember the immutable law

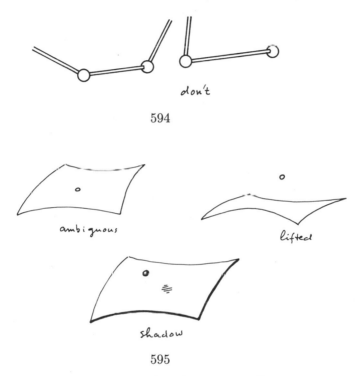

that collinearity in the drawing should indicate collinearity in space;
otherwise the result will almost certainly be an incorrect reading. This
applies equally to "almost collinearity." You should make the differences
appreciable. Exaggeration is the key to drawings that appear clear at
the first glance.

Tangencies of contours and curves should only occur if they indicate
an actual tangency of the spatial configuration. This holds equally true
for T-junctions. You must substitute—almost—orthogonality for mere
transversality because otherwise it is quite likely that your intention will
not clearly register (fig. 596). The obvious general law is that all inci-
dents and coincidences should be absent—and clearly so—except when
you explicitly want to exploit their effect. Avoid features that are overly
simplistic or symmetric. Try to draw the "general case"; since you don't

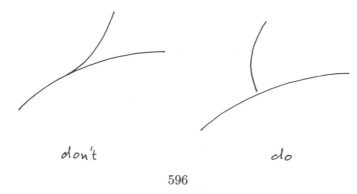

don't   do

596

have to write a computer program for it, there is no need to make your
surface look like another "generalized cylinder."

The reason is that the reader will unconsciously associate any obvious symmetry present in your drawing with the geometrical facts you
attempt to illustrate. This will often hinder his understanding in the
sense that it usually prevents him from any application to more general,
usually less symmetrical, cases. Again, if you want to portray something as not possessing a certain symmetry, you had better make sure
that your drawing is *obviously* not symmetrical. You have to be crude!

Irrelevant symmetry is a type of irrelevant detail that must be elim-
inated. Many textbook figures suffer from this flaw; it appears to be
the obvious mistake to make. You better watch out. The authors of
textbooks may actually use this on *purpose* in order to use the "simplest" setting possible. It is really a disservice to the reader though.
Irrelevant symmetries are often the reason why freehand sketches are so
much more satisfactory than the finished artwork for a publication. For
finished line work you usually use drawing instruments that encourage
you to introduce irrelevant symmetries. Be aware of this and avoid it.

Expect to spend, say, ten seconds on a simple and maybe one minute
on a more complicated sketch. Taking too much time over a sketch will
lead to wooden and overworked designs. It is much better to produce
fifty quick sketches from which you select one in an hour than spending
the hour on a single design if you are trying to find a good way to represent some geometrical fact. Usually five to ten trials for a complicated
situation will help you converge on something reasonable, though. It is
only when you deal with complicated topologies that you must reckon
with much time to zoom in on some nice layout. For final publication
you have to spend somewhat more time on careful finishing. I used
about five minutes on the average to produce each of the sketches for
this book.

The point is to avoid the use of drawing instruments and elaborate construction work. The drawings should have a slightly "sloppy" look, which they will acquire for free if you abstain from the use of drawing implements such as rulers, compasses, or french curves in order to encourage the reader to take them merely as suggestions and not as the real thing. Their meaning is purely metaphoric, and they shouldn't look like photographically precise renderings of something that really exists.

If you produce artwork by computer, the basic rules do not change at all, only you tend to have less control. The thing to do is to produce many drawings, changing parameters continually until you obtain something at least slightly to your taste.

You can always draw as well as you know how to.
I flatter myself that I feel more than I express on canvas;
but I know that is not so.
—WILLIAM MORRIS HUNT (1824–1879)

A Your way into the literature

...I know of an uncouth region whose librarians repudiate the vain and superstitious custom of finding a meaning in books and equate it with that of finding a meaning in dreams or in the chaotic lines of one's palm...
They admit that the inventors of this writing imitated the twenty-five natural symbols, but maintain that this application is incidental and that the books signify nothing in themselves.
This dictum, as we shall see, is not entirely fallacious.
—JORGE LUIS BORGES, *The Library of Babel (1964)*

I will assume that the reader is not a mathematician and is familiar with mathematical subject matter largely through books directed at the engineer or physicist. He or she is supposed to wish to gain some mode of access to the available mathematical knowledge without spending too much time on it. Thus I will not attempt to flood you with large lists of useful references here. I have also consciously used the utmost restraint with regard to references in the previous chapters of this book. I take it that the reader is not at all interested in a flood of references to specialistic literature *per se*. References to general texts and selective references enabling relatively painless entrance in some specific fields put together at the end of the book seemed optimal. If you are so disposed, you can always follow up the references given here and the usual chain reaction will soon provide you with more than your needs.

I will try to achieve two goals in this short chapter. First, to indicate a few modern textbooks that should prove particularly helpful to obtain a quick grounding in several of the fields touched on in this book, and second, to give a few hints as to how to start mining the wealth of knowledge buried in the older literature. Clearly trying to aim at any level of "completeness" would not only be very hard but also certainly counterproductive. I am certain to offend many people who will miss their pet books. Indeed, in a different mood my own choices might have been different! But if you have any strong feelings about this, you should not have started reading this chapter—or probably even this book!—in the first place; so no apologies are offered.

A.1   Some helpful literature

There exist a great many books treating "Differential Geometry" with some stress on lower dimensional (2- and 3D) examples or applications.

Although they differ greatly in the level of mathematical sophistication, there appears to be some kind of consensus concerning the general subject matter. If you have studied one or two rather well, you should be able to go through many others rather quickly.

Skimming through an armful is not altogether a waste of time because you become acquainted with various notations and alternative methods that will greatly help you to judge whether it is worth your while to read or skip some paper in the future.

Moreover, different authors tend to use their own pet examples, and if you are applications-oriented, the more examples you see the better. Some may be of direct use to you, now or in the future.

I will list a few books you may find helpful, sorted according to level and taste. I don't aim at anything like completeness.

Books stressing intuitive understanding:

Hilbert and Cohn-Vossen The classical masterpiece. This is a "must" and a joy to read. It contains a wealth of material, getting by with an incredible minimum of tools. Everybody should read it as part of a general cultural background.

Aleksandrov (1) Easy to read, more limited in scope but almost as nice as Hilbert and Cohn-Vossen. Appeals especially to the physicist. It has been reprinted as part of a series of volumes on different subjects in mathematics, and all volumes are worth reading.

Felix Klein A very nice little treatise by a real master. It is remarkable how Klein stresses the operational—in the physicist's sense—meaning of geometrical entities, and how he really cares about tolerances and things like that. According to Klein, geometry is about spatial relations and objects (the models are the essence, the theory is merely *about them*), rather than about formalism, a standpoint that sets him well apart from most of his fellow mathematicians.[1]

Griffiths A by now classic on the combinatorial topology of surfaces, including such subjects as Morse theory. A pleasure to read. Invites you to pick up paper and scissors and glue together your own surfaces. Fairly easy going.

---

[1] Does it show that Felix Klein is one of my heroes?

Aleksandrov (2)   A nice little book on topology, explaining in few pages and almost without formalism what the Betti groups are about. This is easily the cheapest entry in the field.

Berger   Delightful book on all forms of geometry. This will give you a lot of novel insights and help you develop your intuition. Not hard to read, but not kid's stuff, either. Lots of very good illustrations; looking at the pictures alone is worth your time. Very worthwhile references.

Ewald   Nice and easy going. If you are vague about problems of smoothness, differentiability, and all that, this is an easy update with lots of pictures and lucid examples. Painless but effective.

Francis   This is a book that stresses the pictorial side of differential topology. It makes you think about the way pictures convey geometrical insights. Francis also teaches you how to produce effective figures yourself. The pictures alone make the book worth your attention.

The topics are sometimes close, but more often rather far from the material covered in this book. You will learn about knotty problems.

Müller and Wölpert   "Anschauliche Topologie": does the title ring a bell? A nice little book on many topics of point set topology, combinatorial topology, knot theory, graphs, ... Lucid, well-illustrated, elementary, a good starting point.

Books especially aimed at the physicist:

Burke   Not exactly easy going, but sensible and nice with many concrete examples that should appeal to the physicist. You will learn about fiberbundles, Lie groups, and so forth in a manner quite different from what the mathematical texts offer you. Burke teaches you very effective tools and how to handle them.

I like the book, especially because it throws a new light on problems in fields of physics that I know reasonably well in the "old-fashioned" way.

Misner, Thorne, and Wheeler   You can't pass up such a gigantic paperback at such a reasonable price! This is a great text on a subject that is drenched in differential geometry. As a physicist I have read this book purely for pleasure.

It has a lot to offer if you want an entry in the field of differential geometry, too. One mathematical friend confessed to me that he understood covectors for the first time when he looked at the figures. This is remarkable because the geometrical interpretation advocated by these authors was well-known in the nineteenth century! It clearly reveals the lacunae in modern teaching methods.

This book may be your best source for an understanding of the Riemann curvature tensor and its inherent symmetries.

Flanders This nice little book served as the introduction to "differential forms" for many physicists.

Abraham I don't particularly like the text but have found that it motivated many of my students who are all majoring in physics. There has to be something here.

Abraham and Shaw Nice because of the illustrations. Easy, on an intuitive level. A very successful attempt to make complicated scientific concepts pellucid. Such effective illustrations are very rare. A study of the graphic design is indeed as rewarding as the study of the scientific meat. Don't miss it.

Boys This well-known book on soap bubbles is something you should enjoy. The messy background (you will get your clothes wet if you repeat the experiments) on minimal surfaces is here.

d'Arcy Thompson A classic. If you have always been curious whether your eggs have left the hen point first or the other way around, then this is your book. The author explains how Albertus Magnus got the answer right for the wrong reasons. This is a veritable mine of ideas.

The author covers an incredibly broad spectrum of problems.

General texts on an intermediate level in "nice" notation:

O'Neill This is a book that I personally enjoyed reading. Much recommended. The author uses essentially the same type of notation I used in this text, but, of course, he really justifies every step whereas I glibly skipped over all proofs. This book gives you the flavor of modern differential geometry and some facility in pulling the strings yourself without unnecessary ballast and in the most lucid manner. Everything is geometrically motivated so you actually see what is going on. What a pity the author didn't carry on the good work much further!

Spivak "The Great American Differential Geometry Book." You're not going to read this book in one go! It is worth the effort though and has become a bible for many, physicist and mathematician alike. The book is remarkable in that the author shows you most (or all?) of the different routes that lead to certain goals and really takes you *explicitly* through all the motions! If you want to understand a subject, then Spivak may be your best bet. People complain that I have borrowed the copy (of five volumes!) in my department's library for my lifetime. I owe a lot to Spivak. The bibliography at the close of the fifth volume is definitely not the thing to skip.

If you want to learn differential geometry from scratch (background in linear algebra and calculus understood!), then probably the easiest road is to start with O'Neill and then move to Spivak. After that you can spread your wings and fly.

Guggenheimer In a somewhat "in between" notation. Useful, you can learn about Lie groups and affine differential geometry in an accessible way. Lots of interesting examples. Readable. Lots of interesting problems.

Lehmann and Sacré One of those books I like a lot. Modern in spirit, good choice of examples, extremely clear.

General texts for the hopeless coordinate addict:

Eisenhart A real classic in its field. You should understand that I personally hate this book; I never use it. The number of references to the book speaks for its popularity, though. I'll never understand people.

Do Carmo Although I don't care much for the notation, I still consider this a worthwhile book. It is useful because the author seems to understand where naive people invariably go wrong and sprinkles warnings throughout the text in the form of enlightening examples. Another nice point is the sheer number of interesting special cases to be found here. Well illustrated too. You should definitely take a look at it.

Struik Vanilla variety. Some nice passages on bendings and on mappings of surfaces on surfaces, though. Struik is not the only author who copied the—wrong!—indicatrix of Dupin for the monkey saddle from Hilbert and Cohn-Vossen's book.

Stoker   Different from most. I don't particularly like it and I know
that some mathematical friends of mine positively hate it. Yet
the book has some passages that will appeal to the engineer and
physicist and cannot easily be found elsewhere. Example: remarks
concerning Chebyshev nets.

Laugwitz   A pity about the old-fashioned notation, because this is
a *nice* book, very readable and with many passages on subjects
difficult to find elsewhere. If you like the fancy tensor notation,
this is the book for you.

General texts with a "cookbook" flavor:

Lipschutz   Friends of mine consider the cookbook variety texts a poi-
son for their students. Yet I often see the book on shelves (people
apologize in different ways), and I have been known to refer to it
for some expression I didn't seem to have correctly in my head.
Well organized and to the point. Notice that much of the meat is
in the problems sections.

A.2   Pedestrian's guide to the past

You will need a strong stomach to digest the older literature if you like
the elegant modern way of expressing simple things simply, but if you
are a hard-nosed coordinate addict you will rejoice.

Even if you abhor the old-fashioned notations, you will probably appreciate the way the nineteenth-century authors succeed in motivating
their researches. Instead of throwing some elegant blurb at you in the
expectation that the meaning will eventually dawn on you, they actually
appear to speak about something. It is rarely necessary to spend much
time wondering about how anybody could have thought of something in
the first place, as is all too common nowadays.

A prerequisite is that you become somewhat familiar with notations
of previous generations. The easiest way to make progress here is to
read some books by authors who make this task enjoyable. Don't start
reading Darboux, even though he seems to be the author who did everything first. I'm afraid that you are doomed to find out only *after* having
understood the problem by yourself first. Some more recent texts that
are written in the archaic style may also be helpful here. I suggest:

Weatherburn   I like it and have consulted it a lot. A very useful book
that could be of value in many applications. The notation includes

many old-fashioned geometrical objects such as "dyadics" and so forth. The chapters on curve congruences are particularly useful and contain results that I wouldn't know where to find elsewhere.

Someone should "translate" what is here in modern notation. Many readers would be most grateful.

Blaschke I consider myself lucky to have found a copy of Blaschke's *Differential Geometrie* in a secondhand bookstore early in my life. Fun to read because of the truly geometrical motivation behind the formalism. Many interesting classical special cases. Useful references. The volume on affine differential geometry makes that subject appear interesting and useful. I like the earlier editions much better than the later one, which uses differential forms and tensors in a rather opaque manner. The earlier texts have a true geometrical flavor.

Blaschke wrote many books on many aspects of geometry. All of them are worth reading.

Strubecker An example of a modern text that may help you to get a feeling for what the ancients did. (Of course, the ancients are nineteenth- and early-twentieth-century ones in this context!) Lots of excellent illustrations. Very useful examples, some of them hard to find elsewhere. You will appreciate this after you have noticed that authors tend to use the same examples over and over again, really *ad nauseum.*

Fischer A somewhat different category. This book presents a picture gallery of classical (plaster, wire, paper, . . .) models with interesting historical remarks. You shouldn't miss it if you have not been raised among cabinets of mysterious dusty plaster casts with illegible tags . . .

After this you are on your own. If you want to delve into a subject, your best bet is to try to trace the references to be found in recent texts written by authors with some historical sense. They are actually quite rare.

Other possibilities are to go to the standard texts from so many decades ago. They are easy to find because modern textbooks refer to them as a matter of course and start following references from there.

An excellent source of key references that you should not pass up in any case is the Enzyklopaedie der mathematischen Wissenschaften. This is a very rich mine that is comparatively easy to explore. The volume you want is the third one.

If you are really determined and can stand a lot, it may be worth your while to consult Darboux's monumental treatise.

A.3   Special subjects

There are a great many "special subjects" as measured against the contents of this book, which might be of interest to you in some context. I will mention a few possible entries into fields that osculate the subject matter treated here:

General topology:

O'Neil   A very lucid and readable introduction. Much recommended.

Combinatorial topology:

Aleksandrov (3)   Not easy but nice and appealing to the intuition. The methods used in this book are of the type that seem most fit for computer implementation. About time computer-oriented people discover this text.

Moise   This is a good book to get started. Lucid, nice examples and pictures. Introductory level.

Differential topology:

Guillemin and Pollack   Generally acclaimed as an excellent and easy introduction. Appeals to the intuition and motivates the really very minimal formalism through excellent examples. I profited a lot from this text. Like it a lot.

Milnor   A generally acclaimed didactical monument. On Morse theory, but you will get a lot more out of this nice book, which really appeals to the geometrical intuition. Not especially *easy*, though.

Bruce and Giblin   With a sprinkling of catastrophe theory. This is a didactically extremely well-written book and is a joy to read. Lots of motivating examples, good pictures. Modern-style math. Very much worth your time.

Eells   I find this book useful, although it doesn't turn me on. You will have to bring some geometrical insights with you in order to "translate" some of the results into digestible terms.

Lehmann and Sacré Nice, clean and modern. With differential geometry proper. Clear examples.

Arnold, Gusein-Zade, and Varchenko Arnold is the person who usually turns out to have done things first. Not easy! More of an algebraic than a truly geometrical flavor, I'm afraid.

Callahan Two very lucid papers on mappings from the plane into the plane with excellent illustrations. You really shouldn't miss this. Jim Callahan is great as an illustrator.

Bröcker and Jänich Nice and modern. Good pictures. Everything nicely motivated through very geometrical examples. You will learn about "sprays," an alternative way to arrive at a connection. Nice!

Linear algebra:

Brieskorn Modern and extremely nice. Makes the subject appear novel and exciting. Lots of intriguing examples. Wish I had been taught the subject this way! It's too late now.

Catastrophe theory:

Poston and Stewart Every beginner should start here. Good examples, every move motivated through geometrical examples. Useful and nice. After reading this you can decide whether it would be worth your while to delve deeper into this field.

Most of the technical texts are algebraic rather than geometric in nature—be warned!

Thom The master's voice. Read Poston and Stewart first or you will be lost. You will either hate or love this book because of its flagrant mysticism.

Arnold An easy introduction by one of the masters.

Special curves:

Fladt A book on algebraic curves, a subject that tends to bore me stiff. In this book I actually found some sections that I read with interest.

Brieskorn and Knörrer This is an admirable book. Lots of tricks and facts that are useful or interesting, all very nicely motivated through an appeal to the geometrical intuition and an attempt to show the "roots." A book to read over several rainy weekends.

Special surfaces:

Fladt and Baur   The first part of this book gives an introduction
to general computational methods in differential geometry (lots of
coordinate expressions) that some people find useful as reference
for their work in computer implementation. I find it rather dull.

The second part is the nice part: scores of special surfaces with
lots of detail of academic interest and extremely effective pictures.

Once I started noticing, I see Fladt's pictures all over the place;
everybody seems to borrow them.

Descriptive differential geometry:

Sauer   This is a rare bird among differential geometry texts. About
the only example I know that treats differential geometry as the
limiting case of "difference geometry." Especially useful sections
on bendings and infinitesimal bendings. Watch out for printing
errors in the formulas.

Kruppa   This book has an awful lot to offer. A must if you are
interested in graphics. The book goes much farther than most
introductory level differential geometry books in some respects.
For instance, the section on the cubical indicatrix is very useful.
Many results that are hard to find anywhere, for instance, the
curvature of the central projection of a general space curve. Not
easy reading.

Distance geometry:

I have included this subject because it has become important in many
settings of computational science, such as chemistry.

Blumenthal   Not for the timid.

Projective differential geometry:

Bol   This book is somewhat readable for the courageous. The subject
has many applications in machine vision but is largely neglected
because there are no introductory texts.

I'm sure that Bol's book contains many useful results on the geometry of the asymptotic ray manifold that I have as yet failed to
extract. I'm afraid this will have to wait until after my retirement.
Maybe you have more time to spare.

Ruffles (cusps of the Gauss map):

Banchoff, Gaffney, and McCrory   They tell you about all you are ever likely to need to know about cusps of the Gauss map. They write in a very lucid and didactical style. In this one little reference you will find a great number of facts that may well prove to be very useful to you in applications.

Thomas Banchoff is a master of didactics. He must have been one of the first mathematicians to discover the power of computer graphics as a tool in geometrical reasoning and exploration.

Symmetry sets:

Blum   This is the inventor of the "medial axis" as defined through "grass fires." He proposes to develop a novel geometry that is more fit for biology than the conventional geometries. I'm not certain that he actually succeeded in this, but the effort was worth it, anyway. His basic entity is the bloblike region, which he describes by way of its symmetry axes. Nice and readable. Very biological flavor.

Bruce, Giblin, and Brassett; Bruce, Giblin, and Gibson   These papers are a must for you if you ever want to do anything in this area. They really bring you on the level.

Don't forget the book by Bruce and Giblin.

Integral geometry:

Féjès Tòth   A delightful book. You will learn how to pack ovals and ovoids in a tight space.

"Varifolds":

Almgren   I'm not sure whether anybody but Almgren himself uses "varifolds" very much, but this is an exciting and conceptually novel way to define surfaces as equivalence classes of operators on two-forms. It may well be important for parts of theoretical physics. For years I have had a guilty feeling about not really using his stuff. Perhaps you will. A nice book with interesting applications to the theory of minimal surfaces.

The normal ray manifold: Caustics, umbilics, etc.:

Montaldi and Porteous   Extremely lucid and geometrically well-motivated papers. You will have to read them, as this material is not yet available in any textbook that I know off.

> Mit der Mathematik ist es wie mit der bildenden Kunst.
> Es ist nicht nur nützlich, sondern durchaus notwendig,
> daß man von seinen Vorgängern lernt.
> Wenn man sich aber ausschließlich auf das Studium des
> Überkommenen beschränkt, also nur auf dem weiterbaut, was man in
> den Büchern liest, so entsteht das,
> was ich als scholastisches System bezeichne.
> Hiergegen ergeht dann die Mahnung:
> Zurück zur eigenen lebendigen Auffassung, zurück zur Natur,
> welche die erste Lehrmeisterin bleibt!
> —FELIX KLEIN, *Von der Versinnlichung idealer Gebilde durch*
> *Zeichnungen und Modelle (1928)*

B Glossary

A glossary seemed a good thing to do for this book because I use many terms in the text that you will not encounter in the standard literature. Moreover, the book is directed at scientists who are not primarily mathematicians, as well as mathematicians who don't mind dirtying their hands by reading a text that skips proofs. Even worse, I use terms in an idiosyncratic manner—sometimes the meaning even changes with the context. If you are really at a loss, try the glossary. You should try to find a general term that more or less coincides with your problem and look for it. If you can't find it, try something close. Of course, you can use the index and the glossary together in various ways to home in.

A

Accretion A process that changes the connectivity of a shape by a fusion of originally disjunct parts. Example: a string of beads (without the string; *i.e.*, a circle of disjunct spheres) becomes a "torus by accretion" to the blurred vision. I use the term in a technical sense in the chapter on shape evolution.

Affine geometry is basically the geometry of a linear vector space without an origin. You are allowed to carry out constructions with a ruler, and you are allowed to displace the ruler parallel to itself. Yardsticks, dividers, and protractors are strictly out. Many objects and operations of great practical utility are of an affine nature. The ability to discriminate between Euclidean and affine properties is something you should strive to acquire. The text mentions the key points, but it is easy to skip over it. Watch out!

Agglomeration I always use this term in a sloppy way. It is then synonymous with "accretion" if you strip that term of its technical meaning: basically building a shape through the fusion of parts.

Anholonomic bases are bases that are not based on coordinates.

Anticlastic point At an anticlastic point the tangent plane intersects the surface in two transversely intersecting smooth curves. Thus the shape lies at *both sides* of the tangent plane. Synonyms are "hyperbolic point" and "saddle-like point."

Apparent curvature The curvature of the visual projection of a curve
or the visual outline of a surface is called the "apparent curvature."
It is the geodesic curvature of the projection on a unit sphere
centered on the vantage point. Thus the apparent curvature of
the horizon is zero; that of the disc of the full moon ($0° 30'$ of arc
diameter) is 229.18.

Applicability Two surfaces are said to be "applicable" if you can find
a correspondence between them that respects the surface metric.

Approximation An approximation of something is another entity that
can be substituted for it in specified situations with a guaranteed
tolerance. A cube might be a perfect approximation to a sphere
if you are interested in *volume*; an icosidodecahedron a bearable
approximation if you are interested in *diameters* (passing through
sieves, *etc.*). Approximations should not be confused with models.

Art is a human endeavor that is supposed to be the orthogonal complement of science. Skip references to it if you are of this opinion. Your loss will be some useful heuristics that can help you
understand shape. In the text I mention a few of the methods
traditionally used by artists to suggest solid shape. References are
scattered throughout the text.

Asymptotic spherical image The spherical image of all rays (parametrized through their points of contact with the surface) that
graze the surface but also pierce it is of decisive importance in all
interactions of an optical nature. For instance, cusps of the visual
contour occur when the visual direction coincides with such a ray.

Attitude transformation You could think of a *frame field* as of an
isometry $I(\mathcal{P})$ that moves the standard Euclidean frame from the
origin $\mathcal{O}$ to the fiducial point $\mathcal{P}$. It is composed of a *translational
part* $T = \mathcal{P} - \mathcal{O}$ and a rotational part A. Only the latter part is
important; it changes the *attitude* of the frame and may well be
called the "attitude transformation."

Autoparallel Fix the steering wheel of your car in the straight ahead
position and hit the accelerator: you will realize an orbit that
is an "autoparallel" of the landscape. Autoparallels are geodesics
without the unit speed parametrization. Sometimes they are called
"pregeodesics."

Azimuth One of the components of the polar spherical coordinate system. On the globe "azimuth" corresponds to "latitude."

B

Beaks A technical term for a singularity of the visual contour for a change of vantage point. The term is descriptive of the shape of the contour: two smooth folds approach, osculate and split. After the split you have two cusped contours facing each other. Of course, this scenario could run backward. The French "bec-à-bec" is even more descriptive.

Bell My term for a wart-like protrusion on a convex patch. A local region of high convex curvature within a larger convexity, isolated from it through an annular anticlastic region. The protrusion looks like a church bell or the calyx of a flower, if you like.

Bendings A highly technical term for a certain class of deformations of surfaces. A bending leaves the *local metric* invariant; *i.e.*, the inhabitants of the surface would never notice a bending.

Bicycle chain A bicycle chain is a useful mechanical model for a general planar curve. It has a single degree of freedom at the joints and is constrained to remain in a plane. Since all the rods are of equal length, the angles at the joints divided by rod length are a convenient measure of the curvature.

Biflecnode from Latin *flectere*, to bend, and *nodus*, a node. Often used for the *undulations* of planar curves, which are points with vanishing curvature as well as rate of curvature. I use the term for the special anticlastic points of a *surface* where one of the asymptotic curves has an undulation. (One of the branches of the intersection with the tangent plane has an undulation, too.) Such points occur generically as isolated points. The biflecnodes lie on the *flecnodal curves*.

Bilocal entity A geometrical object that is defined with respect to an ordered pair of disjunct points. Vectors of Euclidean space are the prototypical bilocal objects: ordered pairs of points $(\mathcal{P}, \mathcal{Q})$ can be regarded as a vector $\mathcal{PQ}$ at point of application $\mathcal{P}$. For curved submanifolds you have to be cautious, but *heuristically* and *pictorially* vectors will always remain bilocal entities.

Bitangent One of the components of the Frenet-frame of a point on a general space curve. The bitangent is normal to the osculating plane of the curve.

Bivectors are oriented area elements.

Blob I use "blob" very often in this text, and I use it in several different senses. The general feeling is that of a material object with a smooth, somewhat ill defined (because of observational inaccuracies) skin of no particular symmetry. I think of a potato, a human torso, a cloud, or a treetop as typical blobs. In some contexts I use blob as a volume that appears as the "window," or "aperture" for the physical measurement of some density. For instance, a cloud may measure so many droplets per cubic foot. It doesn't matter much what the shape of the cubic foot is; think of it as a potato-like blob.

Blocking out is a technical term used in the craft of sculpting. You remove large chunks of material from your stone until you have "blocked out" the rough form of your bust or torso. Usually done by the underpaid apprentice. After blocking out the master takes over as the chips become smaller and smaller.

Blurring is a technique that reveals macrostructure at the cost of the ability to discriminate microstructure. If you can't see the wood for the trees you know it is time to start blurring your vision. Artists practice blurred vision to detect the main features of shapes. The best procedure is to use adjustable blurring, so you can see *both* the leaves *and* the shape of the treetop. In mathematics blurring paves the road for the use of *differential analysis* in the study of nonlocal features. The technical development leads to "scale-space."

Body shadow One usually discriminates between "body shadow" (or attached shadow) and "cast shadow." In the real world you need dark, approximately convex bodies and point sources to get well-defined body shadows. In geometry you simply define the body shadow as that part of a surface where the source is on the inside of the tangent plane. The boundary of this geometrical body shadow has remarkable properties that are most important for the study of shape. Use the index to find many places where the body shadow is mentioned in the text.

Bubble I use "bubble" in the same sense as "blob," except that for the bubble the material is *outside*. Thus a bubble is a "pocket of air," or a cyst.

Bulge A bulge is something protruding outward. I use the term in a technical sense, though. A bulge sticks out *toward the vantage point*. Thus a *plane* is technically a "bulge," because the distance between points on the plain and the eye has a single minimum. If you compute the "hills and dales" of the distance as a function of visual direction, you can divide the visual field—and thus the scene—in bulges. (Or, if you want, in "hollows.")

C

CAD is an acronym for Computer-Aided-Design.

CAM is an acronym for Computer-Aided-Manufacture.

Canonical form In the text I give "canonical forms" for most of the features that are being discussed. "Canonical" usually implies "standard" or even "simplest" in many context. It has the connotation of bringing an entity *in vitro*, stripped from all unnecessary frills. In this book, however, I don't aspire to such heights. The "canonical forms" are to be understood as examples, simple specimen that you can easily program and play with. Remember that—in the majority of cases—you can subject these examples to arbitrary affinities and freely add higher-order terms, to make them look better or remove accidental degeneracies.

Canonical projection I use this term in a precise technical sense to denote the relation between instances of the same density function at different levels of resolution. The canonical projection gives scale-space the structure of a continuous tree ("tree" in the sense of a computer data structure).

Cap A cap is a convex patch with a planar boundary, such that there exists a parallel projection of the patch on the interior of the boundary curve. If you take a chip off any ovoid with a planar knife, then it will always be a cap, if it is small enough. A convex Monge patch over a plane ovaloid area is a cap.

Carrier curve A curve on a surface considered as the carrier of a surface strip. You can think of the envelope of tangent planes along the curve, or of an infinitesimal surface strip cut along the curve.

Cartan matrix The transformation that describes the rotation of the frame for a shift of the point of application.

Catastrophe theory classifies the structure of the singularities of potentials (real functions) as depending on the dimensions of the spaces of state and control variables. It has numerous applications to the study of shape. It is not, however, powerful enough to derive, for example, the singularities of the visual contour. Because of its simplicity I present the general flavor in the text. The more powerful tools of differential geometry are skipped here as too technical to present in an intuitive fashion in a book of this size.

Cauchy-Green tensor In the theory of deformable media the Cauchy-Green tensor describes the local linear approximation of the movement of the medium.

Causality is not used in the sense usually associated with the word. I use it to describe the one-way character of the blurring operation: you never pick up structure by blurring, you only get rid of it. A blurring method is causal if it consistently destroys structure.

Caustics of a congruence (usually a line or curve congruence) are the envelopes of the congruence.

Central projection is the mapping that assigns to every point $\mathcal{P}$ (say) a unique *direction* relative to a given vantage point $\mathcal{V}$. (Restriction: $\mathcal{P} \neq \mathcal{V}$.)

One generally takes one step further and assigns to $\mathcal{P}$ the point $\mathcal{Q}$ with the same direction (if it exists) that lies on a given "*picture plane.*" Then one also speaks of "perspective projection." I don't take the latter step in this book. Although this is usual in the applied literature, I feel it is rarely necessary and usually complicates the problem in an unnecessary way.

Centro-surface The focal surfaces of a surface are often denoted "centro-surfaces." "Surfaces of centers," "caustics," or "caustic surfaces" are other synonyms that you will frequently encounter.

Chiaroscuro, literally clear-dark (from Italian), is (according to Webster's):

- a style of painting, drawing, *etc.* using only light and shade in order to achieve the effect of a third dimension;

- the effect achieved by such a style;

- the way that an artist uses light and shade;

- a painting, *etc.*, in which chiaroscuro is used.

Codimension of a submanifold is the dimension of the normal spaces. It thus depends on the dimension of the space the submanifold lives in. The difference between planar and space curves is due to their different codimensions.

Computational differential geometry, as I use the term, is not yet an established discipline, but it soon will be. At this moment there is a discipline sometimes called such, but it only deals with *intrinsic* geometry and its uses are mainly restricted to cosmology and theoretical high-energy physics.

Concentrated curvature exists in the edges of polyhedra, the corners of cubes, and the apices of cones. If you slightly blur such features, you appreciate that they are small regions with a large spread of the surface normals.

Conjugated directions on a surface can be found empirically by illumination with a candle: the edge of the body shadow is conjugated to the direction of the light ray. Conjugated directions often appear in optical applications, since the notion is of a projective, rather than a Euclidean nature.

Connection equations describe the structure of framefields. They reflect the basic constraints due to the embedding space.

Contact in the technical sense measures the degree of "fit" of two geometrical entities that meet at some point. Intuitively, the degree of fit determines the structure of the intersection if you slightly perturb the relative positions or the shapes. Technically the order of contact is measured by the order of the initial part of a Taylor series in a common parametrization.

Contour The "visual contour" is a curve in the visual field (or—equivalently—a cone of visual directions) that is the projection of the *rim*, the locus on the object that divides visible from not visible regions.

Contraction is a very basic operation that actualizes the potential meaning of vectors and covectors. The contraction of a vector on a covector yields a *number*, that is, a nongeometrical entity.

Control variables appear in catastrophe theory. They are like "knobs" or "controls" on a machine: by twiddling the knobs you actually *specify a new machine.*

Convexity A patch on the surface of a blob is a convexity if all the surface normals *diverge* consistently. A point is on a convexity if it is on a cap. Notice that convexity only makes sense for a material blob, otherwise the concave-convex distinction becomes arbitrary.

Corkscrews are the memory elements for the *orientation of space.*

Covectors are (formally!) linear maps of vectors to the reals. Physically they are gradients, geometrically they are stacks of oriented planes.

Crate Crating is related to the "blocking out" process. A crating of an object encloses the object in a polyhedron with faces parallel to the Euclidean coordinate planes. Often a crating is just a "box," that is, the smallest parallelepiped that contains the blob. Boxes are often used in computer graphics. Draftsmen use progressively refined cratings to get their proportions right.

Crease A crease is an edge of a curvilinear polyhedron. Creases are the singular features of set theoretical combinations of smooth blobs. They are common as "V-grooves" in styles of sculpture based on ovoid assemblies.

Crest The crest of a mountain range is its watershed. It can also be defined for densities in three-space. It then occurs as a kind of "skeleton" of a blob. The "medial axis" of a planar curve is the crest of the function that assigns the shortest distance to the curve for any point in its interior. Thus there is a connection between crests and symmetry sets.

Cross correlation between densities is a problematic concept. Suppose that two clouds of flyspecks of different colors "overlap," but that no pair of specks coincides. Are the clouds correlated? They are if you consider the cross-correlation at a suitable level of resolution. They are not on the microscopic level. This problem makes the definition of Leibnitz's rule for "fuzzy derivatives" a nontrivial problem.

Crumpling is an operation that destroys the smoothness of a surface through the introduction of discontinuities of the normal ray congruence.

Curvatura Integra is the "total curvature," that is, the total spread of the normals.

Curvedness is a measure coined by me to quantify the amount of external curvature. It is proportional to the logarithm of the sum of squares of the principal directions.

Curves of bending are integral curves of the instantaneous "hinges" for a surface that is being subjected to a bending. The curves of bending form a conjugated net on the surface and the meshes of the net suffer an instantaneous first-order Euclidean isometry, whereas the dihedral angles at the edges change.

Cusp The term "cusp" is used in at least three different senses:

- it describes the shape of the cubic parabola $x^2 = y^3$;
- it is used for a singularity of a map of the plane into the plane of the type $u = x^3 - xy$, $v = y$;
- it is used to indicate a surface point where the Gauss map has the singularity mentioned in the previous item.

The second type is often called a "Whitney cusp," but I call it a "pleat." The third type is called a "ruffle" in this book. I reserve the term "cusp" for the first type.

D

Data structure I use data structure in the same sense as the computer scientist: A set of items with a system of cross-references between them. The simplest example is an ordered triple of reals with a pointer to a frame as the coordinate representation of a vector.

Deblurring is the reverse of "blurring." Thus when you deblur you
increase the resolution. Whereas blurring is a computationally
robust process, deblurring is computationally highly unstable.
That's not what I intend you to do. When I urge you to deblur, you should look at a *blurring process*, but "run the movie
backward."

Dee-es-square is the quasi-phonetic spelling of "ds^2," that is, the
squared "infinitesimal displacement" of your fiducial surface point
$\mathcal{P}$. Implied is the Pythagorean Theorem $ds^2 = du^2 + dv^2$ for an
as yet unspecified displacement (du, dv) on the surface. It is the
classical way to refer to the metric, or first fundamental form of
the surface at $\mathcal{P}$.

Deformation I use the term to denote arbitrary smooth transformations that conserve the connectivity. "Diffeomorphism" is the official term.

Degeneration is an ill defined term to denote situations with an overdose of order; order of the type that is destroyed by small perturbations. A four legged table that doesn't wobble is a degenerated
case. "Degeneration" is usually precisely defined and depends on
the exact context. In this book I'm rather sloppy, but you will
usually be able to fill in the details.

Density is used by me as a generic term for some physical intensive
parameter, "this much $\mathcal{X}$ per cubic foot," where $\mathcal{X}$ may stand for
mass, flyspecks, electrons, droplets, or what have you. In this book
it *makes a difference* whether the density is in cubic microns, feet,
or miles!

Depth is distance relative to the current vantage point. This usage
is different from the common notion that depth is the shortest
distance to the picture plane. Take care!

Derivative is a generic term for a measure that indicates how an entity
defined over space varies in the neighborhood of a point. Taking
the derivative of something that changes is something you can
always do, and it usually makes sense to do so. To define a sensible
derivative of something by something is typically an important
conceptual advance. In this text many different types of derivatives
are used; don't confuse them.

Developable of cylinder axes If the surface isn't curved in a certain direction, that direction defines a "cylinder axis." Generically this only applies to points on certain curves; thus you have one-parameter families of cylinder axes to reckon with. It can be shown that the axes are generators of a developable surface. This surface plays an important role in many applications.

Diffusion is a physical phenomenon that redistributes material in such a way that the distribution becomes smoother with time. The only causal blurring procedure is formally identical with such a physical process. Thus the "diffusion equation" governs the structure of scale-space.

Dihedral angle Dihedral angles are defined for polyhedra. In this text I use the term in a more general way: the dihedral angle is a function that assigns the angular separation of the tangent planes to any two distinct points of a surface.

Dimple is a term I use for a surface feature that represents a local concavity contained in a larger convexity. It is a kind of "inverted bell." The Gauss map of a dimple is like a blister attached to the main covering at a single point (generically a small, highly singular area).

Discrete models are very useful heuristic aids. The bicycle chain model for planar curves is a paradigmatic case. Discrete models of surfaces are not trivial constructs though; in this book I underplay the difficulties involved. The discipline of "difference geometry" is rather underdeveloped and could benefit from your genius!

Distance squared function The distance function assigns the distance from a given vantage point to any point on a given submanifold. Technical reasons make it preferable to use the squared distance instead. No doubt you couldn't care less.

Doodling kills time and can be fun. In this book I use the word to suggest the generation of *sloppy* drawings that fire the imagination and suggest possible relations. Doodling is a way of "brainstorming" that seems to be indispensable to the true geometer. According to Webster's, doodling is an archaic term for playing the bagpipe (German: *Dudeln*).

Drapery is a technical artistic term for the handling of folds in clothing, *etc.* It often suffices to look at the drapery to date a painting or even guess at its author, if you are at all sensitive to such things. In this book "drapery" applies to surfaces that are intrinsically flat but extrinsically curved or even creased.

Dupin's Indicatrix is the figure you obtain when you take a very thin slice off an object, parallel to the tangent plane. The edge of the wound is the indicatrix. This important figure sums up the curvature of the surface at the location of the wound.

Dynamics applies strictly to mechanics and hence to physics. However, in geometry one often introduces a "dynamics" based on parametrization. Think of curves as orbits; then the velocity and acceleration are defined with respect to the parametrization (although the parameter is a formal one, rather than physical time). "Unit speed curves" are referred to arclength.

E

Elastic constants are physical entities and have nothing to do with geometry. They are often of decisive importance in your dealings with the shapes of real things, though. Their appearance in this book reveals that I'm not a mathematician.

Emergence processes occur when you "deblur" a density. The paradigmatic case is the geographical atlas: as you flip pages to smaller and smaller regions (globe, continent, country, provence, city, block ...), you witness a progressive *emergence* of features.

Enantiotropy Enantiotropic objects are mirror-reversed copies. This is usually done to gloves, corkscrews or sugar molecules, for obvious reasons. You turn a space curve into its enantiotropic mate when you flip the sign of the torsion. The glove case was made famous by Kant, although he didn't exactly distinguish himself by it.

Ending contour It may happen that the visual contour of a blob "just ends." In such a case you look into an asymptotic direction.

Equidistance contours are curves of equal distance to a submanifold in the visual field. (Or—equivalently—cones of rays through the vantage point that meet the manifold at a fixed distance.) They are the projection of the intersections of the manifold with spheres concentric with the vantage point.

Equivalence classes are an important tool to induce relevant structure. It may be the most common method in mathematics to arrive at novel entities. Physical entities are always equivalence classes of cases that can't be discriminated due to operational tolerances. All entities that admit of a physical interpretation (are "real") thus have to be defined as equivalence classes.

Exposure A point on a surface is "exposed" if it can be seen from at least a half-space.

Evolution in the sense of Darwin doesn't figure in this book. I use "evolution" to describe the unfolding of structures under deblurring.

The Eye of Eternity is completely unprejudiced and never admits descriptions that put like members in unlike positions. (To the Eye of Eternity there can't be an "origin" in Euclidean space. Cartesian coordinates make no sense.) I use the term to indicate the attitude that never admits *ad hoc* or accidental constructs. Elegance in geometry is judged by the Eye of Eternity. Practical people express disbelief in its existence. I use it as a guiding principle.

F

Facets are defined for polyhedra, but I use the term just as well for the tangent planes of the points on a smooth surface.

Far field In physical optics the far field is the disturbance at infinity, usually brought within reach at the focal plane of a lens. In mathematics one does the same through *scaling*. Thus all lines can be represented as points on an infinite sphere, which is then scaled back to the unit sphere. (All parallel lines then map on the same "vanishing point.") *Spherical images* are such representations of the far field of different entities.

Far points are those points on a submanifold whose distances to some fiducial vantage point assume a local maximum.

Feature cluster If you put a dent in a circle you create two inflections and a bitangent at the same time: you can't introduce these objects one after another. Such a collection of objects I call a "feature cluster." It is not uncommon to find fallacious reasonings in (amateur) geometrical arguments that arise from a neglect of such clusters.

Field lines are the physicist's way of representing a two-form in three-space. The operational meaning is that the number of field lines through an oriented area is a measurable quantity: the *flux* through the area. Thus, field lines are used in the same way as a two-form that can be contracted on area elements (bivectors). The "tube," or "spaghetti" picture used in this book is quite close to the physicist's notion.

Flabby is a technical term for a surface (patch) that admits of non-trivial isometries or bendings. A plane is flabby because it can be bent into a cylinder; the sphere isn't flabby but rigid.

Flat as a noun denotes a maximally extended linear subspace. (Plane, line, point.) A surface patch is called flat if the local intrinsic geometry is everywhere identical to that of the Euclidean plane. (Thus a cone is flat.) A flat-point of a surface is a point for which the curvature of arbitrary normal sections vanishes.

Flecnode A flecnode is often used as a synonym for a point of inflection of a planar curve. In this book I use "flecnode" to denote an anticlastic point at which one asymptotic curve has a geodesic inflection. (The intersection with the tangent plane then also has an inflected branch.) Flecnodes generically occur on curves (flecnodal curves). The biflecnodes are isolated points on these curves.

Flux is used in the sense of something captured by an aperture. In physics a flux is a quantity actually measured. Thus, a density is not a measurable quantity, but the flux sampled in some sampling volume is. Fluxes are used to give operational definitions of intensive parameters like densities. Similarly a two-form is not measurable (field strength), but the contraction on a bivector (flux through a wire loop) is.

Folding model An instructive model of a general space curve is the folding model. You build it from sectors bounded by tangents at finite distances along a planar curve. If you hinge the sectors, you can flex the model into a space structure, changing the torsion but not the curvature.

Foot point The "foot" of a mountain can be defined as a point in which immediate neighborhood triples of points with parallel normals can be found. The footpoints appear as pleats in the Gaussian image. I usually call these points "unodes," a kind of "ruffle."

Frame field See Attitude transformation.

Freaks are often encountered in the classroom but rarely in the real world. Freaks can be recognized easily, because they are destroyed through even mild perturbations. Don't be afraid of freaks—just perturb them.

Furrow I use "furrow" for the simplest type of nonconvex local perturbation you can inflict on an ovoid. It is a small saddle-like island within a global convexity.

Fuzzy derivative Derivatives make no physical sense because you can't take any limit in which a size goes to zero: the density of anything behaves wildly at the molecular level and spacetime may not even exist at yet deeper levels. Only derivatives of suitably blurred densities make any sense. Such derivatives can be arrived at by finite operations. I call these "fuzzy derivatives."

G

Gauge figure The gauge figure is a geometrical object that allows you to measure lengths and angles. In Euclidean space the unit sphere fulfills this role. In the text I show how to measure by mere construction and counting based on the gauge figure. Closely related are the notions of "metric," "metrical tensor," "sharp operator," and "first fundamental form."

General Custer's hat is a valuable pictorial aid to help you remember the meaning of the notion of the inward surface normal.

Geodesy is an ancient art used to decide on the ownership of fields. I is the physical operationalization of the metric of space.

Glue is what holds parts together. In many cultures the anticlastic points are treated (or rather: ignored) as the "glue" that is between the parts (convexities and concavities).

Gutterpoint or (French) *pointe gouttière* is a special parabolic point of a surface singled out by the property that the rate of turn of the cylinder axis along the parabolic curve vanishes. The gutterpoints separate the two operationally quite distinct types of parabolic arc.

H

Handkerchief surface Thom's "mouchoir plié en quatre" is a surface patch near a special planar point at which two parabolic curves intersect transversely. The Gauss map is like a handkerchief folded in the conventional manner.

Heuristics or the *Ars Inveniendi* is not taught in the regular courses but picked up through apprenticeship or developed from scratch. It differs from intuition by the fact that it uses *methods*. Because it is an art rather than a science it is generally in bad repute. Yet science would be in a sorry state if scientists didn't use heuristic methods! In this book I compromise myself by concentrating my attention on heuristics rather than hard proofs. Some people will refuse to speak to me again.

Hidden elements are usually suppressed in computer graphics: if you show a frontal view of a face you don't want the back of the head to shine through. In geometrical diagrams hidden elements are usually not suppressed. This book takes an uneasy middle road.

Hills and Dales were the subject of one of Clerk Maxwell's papers on what now has become Morse theory. Basically, the watercourses divide a landscape into hills and the watersheds divide it into dales. Hills and dales are thus dual systems of "natural districts."

Hinge I use mechanical models like the folding model of space curves that rely on planar faces attached to each other via hinged joints. Such models can be flexed at the joints. I often think of the edges of polyhedral models as hinged: sometimes these polyhedral patches can then be "flexed." On smooth surfaces "hinges" can be defined relative to a fiducial direction: take two points on a curve through that direction. Then the intersection of the tangent planes at those points defines the direction of the "hinge."

Hole The term "hole" is somewhat ambiguous. I use it in two different senses. A torus has a through-hole. (I then speak of through-holes, rather than holes.) A dimple, or "pothole" is a local concavity in a larger convexity: it can be used to keep water in. (I try to reserve the term "dimple" for such features.)

Please notice that a furrow is not a hole.

Hollow A hollow is a region of maximum distance relative to some vantage point. Hollows and bulges are the hills and dales (or natural districts) of the distance function. Notice that the inside of an eggshell need not be a "hollow": whether it is or not depends on the distance. (In the typical kitchen environment it usually is.)

Holonomy is a term that relates to the total curvature of a surface patch. If you transport a compass body around the circumference, you will find it rotated over the "holonomy angle" after the trip. A "holonomic basis" is just a coordinate basis.

Hump I use the term "hump" for a local synclastic island in a much larger anticlastic area, especially for those cases that are generated on deblurring through a single event.

I

Illuminance is a concept from photometry. The total radiant energy received by a surface from all directions per unit surface area is the *irradiance* of that surface. The illuminance is like the irradiance, but weighted to account for the "average" (by committee) sensitivity of the human eye. The eye doesn't collect the irradiance of a surface, but rather the radiant energy scattered by the surface toward the eye. (This involves the bidirectional reflectance function.) In this book I take several shortcuts and in fact construe "illuminance" to mean little more than "slant function with respect to a point (the 'source')."

Indicatrix See Dupin's Indicatrix.

Infinitesimals are used in mad abandon by physicists and engineers. In fact they make little sense in the real world. One way to make sense of them is by way of the scale-space approach.

Information is a key concept in modern physics. Information theory is the discipline to use in the analysis of physics's operational methods. It is closely connected with concepts such as sampling density, tolerance, scale of resolution, etc. that figure heavily in this book. I decided to skip an exposition of information theory, but you are missing important concepts here.

Inner scale is a term coined by me to indicate the ultimate "grain" of the measurement process. In image processing the inner scale is set by the "pixels." If you approximate a surface with a triangulation, the length of the edges sets the inner scale. It never makes sense to look for features smaller than the inner scale: then you study the method of measurement, rather than the object.

Intelligent ant Intelligent ants appear in La Fontaine (especially as opposed to the stupid cricket), but also in geometry books as inhabitants of submanifolds that can't look outside of the manifold and thus deal only with intrinsic geometry. Most of them are practising geodesy, measure angle sums of triangles, check holonomy angles, *etc.*

Intuition cannot be understood but is something that happens to people. In retrospect you can often detect a pattern, however. Generally, it seems to be the case that intuitions have many of the traits of conclusions arrived at through reasoning by analogy and metaphor. Thus, it must be good for you to make mental notes of analogies between unlikes, of remarkable configurations that pop up in different contexts, *etc.* This may help you "develop your intuition."

Invariants are all we can perceive in the Heraclitean flux. All geometrical objects are defined as invariants. The group of transformations for which they are invariant characterizes the geometry itself. For instance, a vector is a geometrical object that is invariant against arbitrary smooth deformations of the space: the temperature difference between tip and tail of the vector is clearly a conserved quantity. Vectors consequently belong to differential geometry.

J

Join The join of a collection of objects is the convex hull of their union. For instance, the join of a point pair is a line segment.

K

Kinematics is a subdiscipline of mechanics that abstracts from "causes" such as forces. It is thus also a branch of mathematics. The "models" I present in the book are kinematical models: you should abstract from the physics.

L

Lambertian surface The only reflecting surfaces (apart from mirrors) treated in introductory physics texts are Lambertian surfaces. Advanced texts hardly mention them because they are an embarrassment: there are no such surfaces in the real world. The Lambertian surface is a convenient mathematical fiction. It is convenient because it looks equally bright from all angles, no matter how you irradiate it. That's why I use the notion in this book: it lets me skip the real physics!

Lemon Not a fruit, but a certain type of umbilical point named after the pattern of the integral curves of the principal directions in its vicinity. There are four lemon-type umbilics on the triaxial ellipsoid.

Level of resolution You can't speak of any object unless you indicate the level of resolution at which you intend to consider it. This is a truism in physics, but resolution is not a common notion in geometry. The surface of the sea is different every minute, yet we call it plane or (if we are astronauts) spherical. A geometry in which resolution is naturally incorporated doesn't exist at this moment. I merely indicate some of the problems and possibilities in the text.

Level set Surfaces don't exist in any physical (that is, operational) sense. In three-space you have only volumes. The concept of a level set of a physical density (that is, for a specified resolution) makes solid operational sense, though: this is the way to define a "surface." Many of the problems that plague the usual constructions of surfaces then disappear automatically.

Linked rod model A very useful difference model of a space curve is constructed from rigid rods of like lengths connected with universal joints. The model can be flexed with the utmost freedom, and all properties of general space curves are easily visualized.

Lips A technical term for a singularity of the visual contour as you change the vantage point. The contour becomes suddenly enriched with an extra component (two ending contours) that spring to life from nowhere (or *vice versa*). At the moment of creation (or annihilation) you look along the cylinder axis of a certain type of parabolic point.

Local I'm being very sloppy in this book. "Local" means different things in different contexts. Usually I mean a *finite* size patch, of a size that is sufficiently small to prevent phenomena that are irrelevant to the discussion from intruding.

M

Machine concept A useful notion that is closely connected to the classical notion of "tensors" but avoids coordinate language is that of the slot machine. A "machine" is an object that pops out a *number* (that is, a real) when you feed it other objects, if all its slots are filled. I consider only linear machines; thus slot machines are multilinear maps that take multivectors and multi-covectors as arguments. If not all slots are filled, the machine becomes another machine with fewer slots. The paradigmatic case is the Riemann curvature tensor. The curvature tensor has slots for an oriented area element (bivector) and for a vector. The curvature tensor also has a slot that takes a covector. If you only feed it a vector and a bivector, the curvature tensor has an empty slot and behaves like a vector: this vector is the change of the vector you dropped in the slot after circumnavigating the area of the bivector you dropped into the other slot. This completely describes the holonomy. The machine concept is perfectly adapted for computational differential geometry: machines are algorithms, and *vice versa*.

Major planes The "major planes" of a figure or a head are the subject of teaching in old-fashioned art classes. They are canonical polyhedral approximations of various levels of resolution. Despite the modern scorn for such methods they are crucial if you want to catch a likeness.

Mathematical proof is something you won't find in this book.

Maximal spheres are spheres that fit into a volume in such a way that their freedom is limited by the surface. Different interpretations are in actual use. A sphere that touches two points can only roll in one way (a single degree of freedom), whereas a sphere that touches three points is kinematically determined (no freedom). The centers of maximal spheres describe the "medial axis."

Mechanical models are useful heuristic aids for geometrical reasoning. I even invert this and hold that geometry is *about* mechanical implementations; they are the essence, geometry the model. This shows that I'm a physicist. But Felix Klein was of the same opinion, so I find myself in good company.

Microscopes reveal novel structure in the real world, but in the mathematics of smooth entities microscopes trivialize anything to the study of flats. This is most useful. Even "infinitesimals" have been made respectable through the suitable construction of microscopic domains (the hyperreal number system).

The mind's eye is actually more often used than the physical eye in geometrical reasoning, probably because both depend on the same hardware. Real vision is continually recalibrated and makes you fit for interaction with the real world; it *has* to yield empirically true results. The mind's eye doesn't have such constraints and may lead you astray. The way to counteract such problems is to try to visualize theorems known to be true by logical reasoning in as vivid a way as possible. This calibrates the mind's eye for future use.

Models are your only way to make sense of the world. Because the intuition appears to like analogy and often transplants models to new domains, you should consciously enrich your store of models as well as your potential to use them in manifold ways. Models can, of course, be in many different domains (formal, sensory, sensorimotor). Your world can be as complex as your models allow. In a pessimistic mood you may grant that it is *limited* by them.

Moiré contouring is a simple optical technique to visualize or measure the distance function.

Monstar A technical term for a specific type of umbilical point. The pattern of principal directions in its vicinity is between that of the (le-)mon and that of the star. (But more like the lemon in many respects.)

Morpho-... I distinguish morphology, morphonomy, morphometry in the text. They all have to do with the study of shape, but the range is like that between astro-*etc.*

Morphogenetic sequence Any blob looks like a speck (or even nothing at all) if the resolution is low. When blobs become distinguishable, they are all ovoid. When you run the sequence backward and *deblur*, you have the blob developing from a "primordial egg." I call this a "morphogenetic sequence." Just as embryology throws light on human anatomy, morphogenetic sequence reveals a lot about shape.

Myopia is a necessary condition for the geometer. All differential geometry is an exploitation of the locally trivial structure of things. Smooth objects become flats, linear maps, *etc.* It's the pillar upon which differential geometry is founded.

N

Nabla is an Assyrian harp. In the context of this book it denotes the covariant derivative operator.

Natural perspective is a map that assigns a direction (relative to some vantage point V) to every point of space (except V). Euclid's Optics is the first systematic treatise on natural perspective, although it is usually considered a (flawed) treatise on linear perspective.

Near point A point on a submanifold is a near point of that submanifold relative to a vantage point if the distance funtion assumes a local minimum for that point.

Near zone When the diameter of an object is of the order, or larger than, the distance of the object to some vantage point, the object is said to be in the "near zone." Parallel projection is a bad approximation to natural perspective, in that case.

Neighborhood operator A "neighborhood operator" is a weighted average with a weighing function that is negligible except for a small local region centered about the point of application of that operator. A neighborhood operator maps a density to another density.

Net Two curve congruences whose members intersect transversely. A net is like a curvilinear parameter mesh.

Nose dive A "nose dive" of a frame for a step into a certain direction is a rotation of the frame about any direction but the direction of progression.

O

Obscuration The term is used in the sense of "interposition": object $\mathcal{A}$ obscures object $\mathcal{B}$ (relative to a given vantage point $\mathcal{V}$), if $\mathcal{B}$ can't be seen from $\mathcal{V}$ because $\mathcal{A}$ gets in the way. I also speak of "occlusion."

Operational definitions are the rule in the natural sciences. You don't define a physical entity and then proceed to measure it: the method of measurement is the definition of the entity! "First define your terms" is a maxim that applies to mathematical exposition, but not to real life. This book is about shape, but I don't define the term.

Optics is a chapter of physics, so it doesn't belong in a book on geometry. One way to define shape is through interactions of an optical nature; thus optics is necessary in many studies of shape.

Organizers is used by me for singular elements that specify the global structure of an entity at least qualitatively. For instance, the poles and zeros are the organizers of a complex function. I use the term most often for certain elements that determine the parcellation of the viewing sphere for the topological structure of the visual contour.

Orthotomics are the "orthogonals" of a congruence. For instance, the spheres about the origin are the orthotomics of the rays through the origin, and *vice versa*. An "orthotomic system" is a congruence with its orthotomics: in physics, the system of rays and wavefronts, for instance.

Osculation is a Victorian synonym for "kissing." ("Do you propose osculation, Mr. Longbottom?") In geometry the term is generally used for first-order contact, or the "touching" (rather than intersection) of submanifolds. A ball resting upon the tabletop "kisses" that surface.

Outer normals are normal to the surface of a blob and point from the "material" into the "air."

Outer scale The outer scale of a sampled entity is its "scope": for instance for a photograph, the size of the picture. (In the latter case the grain of the photographic material would set the "inner scale.")

Outline I use the term "outline" for the part of the contour that bounds the region of the visual field occupied by the projection of an object.

Ovoids are strictly convex blobs; *i.e.*, every two points of the blob can be joined with a straight line segment that runs entirely within the material of the blob.

Ovoid cladding is an artistic technique in which a globally smooth shape is articulated with ovoid patches. Look for the Renaissance and mannerist knotty muscular figures as exaggerated examples. The technique is very characteristic for many cultures and periods, though.

P

Painting algorithms "paint" a region in a recursive manner: you pick an element ("seed") and paint it. Then you paint the neighbors of every painted element until there isn't anything more to be painted. If the "paint" is a compass-direction, the process may never end!

Paper is a material widely available in the university environment that closely simulates nonstretchable parabolic surface patches. Thus, it is perfectly suited for empirical studies of such surfaces.

Parabolic curves are the loci of inflection of generic surfaces.

Patch A "patch" is a piece of surface of finite extent. It is picked in such a way that the boundary of the patch isn't bothersome and that the surface character is relatively constant. Thus, patches are the ideal entities to bring local shape features *in vitro*.

Peel A synonym for "strip," except that it suggests a reference to a larger surface from which it was a part. (A "strip" is often defined only in the immediate neighborhood of some carrier curve, without reference to any surface from which it would be part.)

Perturbations are "small changes" of some entity. In general you embed the entity in a smooth N-parameter family of entities and study what happens in the family in the neighborhood of the fiducial member.

Physics and mathematics are in different universes. This book is about "mathematical physics," rather than mathematics. The tools needed for the construction of formal descriptions of real world operations are easily confused with mathematics though. Don't let this fool you.

Pictures are important vehicles for the heuristic investigation of a problem. Drawing a picture is *identical* to putting forward a hypothesis (thus it is never a proof); only the syntax is different. A drawing is in the same class as a verbalization: imprecise, suggestive, basically ideolectic. It doesn't stand for something formally determined but has the power to trigger ideas in you and certain others (native speakers of the language, people who are used to your doodling). Like speech, drawing can be formalized and made precise, but at a cost.

Piercing is used for the transverse intersection of a curve or line with a surface in three-space.

Pixels A short term (or slang) for "picture element."

Pleat I often use "pleat" for what is technically known as a (Whitney) cusp.

Plumbing is the art of building complicated surfaces from pieces of cylinders, spherical caps, and "T-pieces," or "cute pants," which are topological spheres with three disjunct discs removed.

Points are "that which has no extension." Thus points don't exist in real life. In the scale-space paradigm a point is a (finite size) neighborhood operator. The points take a bite from scalar fields; the result is a sample of the density at a certain level of resolution. Such points are operationally defined in a physical sense.

Polyhedral models are extremely common in applications, *e.g.*, in computer graphics, machine vision, ... The curvature is concentrated in the edges and vertices.

Porcupine A harmless animal that serves as a convenient model for the outward surface normal.

Pragmatic truth applies only to that what really exists and is operationally defined. It is the physicist's truth (or it should be), not the mathematician's truth.

Primordial egg An ovoid is the simplest shape in the sense that it appears as an ovoid on every level of resolution. *Any* blob becomes ovoid if you blur it enough. If you then *deblur*, the shape develops from a "primordial egg." I use the term because it is catchy, not because it means anything.

Projections are important but rather trivial transformations. If you just make sure to use an adapted frame, the projection entails that you *ignore* a certain number of coordinates.

Punch-through I use the term "punch-through" for a certain topological singularity that occurs in shape evolution. If a simply connected blob changes into a topological torus, a punch-through has occurred.

R

Raised lines of curvature are the traces on the caustic surface of the normal rays on lines of principal curvature. I owe the term to Portuous.

Ranging data are obtained from SONAR, RADAR, laser scanning, stereo-algorithms, *etc.* It is the physical operationalization of the distance function.

Rays are (usually) oriented straight lines. However, in some parts of the text I use "rays" in the geometrical optical sense, as the curves satisfying Fermat's principle of extremal path length. Take care!

Reflex is the term artists use for what is an "interreflection" in photometry: one part of an illuminated object may scatter light onto other parts. Reflexes are one of several reasons why many "shape from illumination" algorithms are virtually worthless.

Resolution is a very important parameter that turns up in every physical operationalization. It means that the infinitesimal domain is forbidden territory for real-life probing. A value of a physical parameter is completely noninformative unless the resolution is being specified. Few mathematicians care about such real-life problems: a geometry in which resolution appears doesn't exist.

Ribbons A synonym for peels or strips.

Ribs are the edges of regression of the focal surfaces.

Ridges are the loci on the surface on which a principal curvature assumes an extremum along the corresponding line of principal curvature. The ribs are raised ridges; *i.e.*, the normal rays on a ridge meet the focal surface at the rib.

Rigidity doesn't occur in nature, although certain materials come close, for practical purposes. "Rigid movement" is synonymous with "isometry." Systems that propose to develop geometry on the basis of measurement are usually based on transactions involving rigid bodies such as "yardsticks." (Helmholtz, Killing.)

Rim The rim is the locus on a surface of an object that divides visible from not visible parts.

Rounded edge A mathematical cube has "sharp edges," but at a certain level of resolution the sharp edges become rounded off. Real cubes have such rounded edges. This is evident from the chiaroscuro: you can often see how the edges of a real cube have a brightness that doesn't interpolate the brightness of the two faces at each side. The reason is that the tangent planes on the rounded edge may face the source whereas the faces don't. You may often watch this on buildings.

Ruffle is Jim Callahan's translation of René Thom's *godron*; a point on a surface giving rise to a cusp of the Gauss map.

S

Sampling is what you do with continua such as densities. Clearly you couldn't fill a telephone book with an infinity of values; you have to make a choice. Since the resolution is finite anyway, it doesn't make sense to sample denser than the resolution parameter. Formal theories of the sampling problem exist, but I don't use them in this book.

Sculpture is an art and a craft that has no relation whatsoever with the study of three-dimensional shape—at least judging from the frequency with which the term appears in the index of treatises on differential geometry. Sculptors don't refer to differential geometrical work, either.

See-through-rays are very special rays that touch the surface with third-order contact. When you look along such a ray, the contour has a sharp V-shaped dip: you look through a "winding valley." See-through-rays exist only for points of certain curves in anticlastic regions.

Shadow boundaries are everywhere conjugated to the direction of the light rays. Thus the rays are the hinges for the strip along the shadow boundary.

Shape is an ill-defined term that somehow has to do with the configurations of matter in space. I use it as a generic term for the information you can gather about a blob relative to a specific type of physical interaction. Thus things may have an optical shape, a haptic shape ...

Shape diffusion is a term that describes the cinematic sequence you obtain when you progressively blur a configuration. Formally it is described by the action of the "diffusion equation."

Shape generation denotes a process that generates a blob—for instance the rotation of a planar curve to generate a surface of revolution (action of a milling machine).

Shape index The shape index and the curvedness are concepts used by me to characterize extrinsic curvature. The shape index measures the direction from the origin in the parameter plane of the two principal curvatures.

Shape languages are used by artists and people interested in object recognition (*e.g.*, for robotics purposes). The "words" of the language are usually entities like ovoid blobs, major planes, *etc.*, that is, "natural subparts." The syntax describes the configurational aspects of aggregation, such as hierarchical nesting, axes, *etc.* This field remains in a rather underdeveloped state.

Silhouettes are the blobs in the visual field occupied by the projections of objects.

Simple cases are favorites for classroom purposes and are necessary crutches to commit things to memory. The main problem is that "simplicity" is a matter of judgment and taste. Seeing "generalized cylinders" all over the place is a professional deformation rather than a help.

Simultaneous presence is one of the categories of experience. Is is the foundation upon which we build geometry and space.

Slant describes the spatial orientation of a surface element relative to some direction, *e.g.*, a visual direction or a light ray. For a given vantage point or point source of light you obtain a scalar field on the surfaces of blobs, the "slant field." In the photometric case of distant sources the slant field determines the irradiation

Slot machines are tensors without coordinates, that is, multilinear maps that map ordered sets of tangent vectors and covectors to the reals. The "slots" are like the formal parameters of an algorithm: you fill the slots, the machine grinds awhile and pops out a number. The metric is a simple machine: it has two slots. If you fill both with the same vector, the machine spews out its squared length. Very often you don't fill all of the slots. For instance, if you don't fill a slot that accepts a covector, the partly filled slot machine behaves like a vector.

Smoothness ought to be precisely defined in mathematical contexts. According to my mathematical friends all physicists are sloppy in this department, and I certainly am. If you are a physicist like me, you won't see the problem. If you are a mathematician, you will have a lot of fun inserting the right assumptions at the right places.

Soap films are fun and can be used as models for surfaces of constant average curvature, for instance, the minimal surfaces. Basically the pressure difference over the membrane governs the average curvature.

Space is a generic term for various structures put on simultaneous presences. According to Riemann's famous paper the only spaces we know from experience are the space we move in and the space of colors. This book is about the space we move in.

Specular points are (at least in this book) the critical points of the distance function. Not to be confused with "specularities," that is, highlights due to specular reflection.

Spin When the frame rotates about the direction of progression, I speak of a "spin" of the frame. In a completely different sense I call "spin" the rotation about the normal when you move over a surface for a frame field adapted to that surface. It will be clear from the context what is being meant.

Spinodes are also known as "parabolic points" and are the points of zero Gaussian curvature on a surface. The cubic indicatrix is then a cusped curve or "spine," hence "spinode."

Split The split is a singularity you meet in evolutionary sequences. For instance, if you deblur a raincloud it fragments into water droplets due to myriads of "split" events.

Spread of normals The spread of normals per volume of some object measures its deviation from flatness, hence its curvature. The spread of normals per unit arclength is the curvature of a curve; the spread of normals per unit area is the Gaussian curvature of a surface.

Spurious resolution is a term used in the optics of imaging instruments for the phenomenon that defocused images may show structure that is apparently not in the object. I use it in the more general sense for noncausal blurring.

Squashed coordinate systems are very bad. This is what happens at the north pole (in what direction should you point to indicate the south pole? How do you point eastward?). Yet you wouldn't know you were at the north pole if someone didn't tell you. The north pole is nothing special: it's not the manifold that is bad, just the coordinate system. Squashed coordinate systems are nuisances that you evade by having spare coordinate systems ready to draw on when necessary.

Stable features don't go away that easily when you perturb a configuration. You can even be sure to find them if your method of measurement is not infinitely precise. That suggests that all real features (the ones you can see) are stable features. It makes sense to concentrate on such features with your theories.

Star The "star" is an umbilical with a configuration of principal directions that reminds you of a star pattern.

State variables describe the state of a physical system. They are contrasted with the "control variables," which parametrize the system intrinsically. For instance, if the system is a cart driving on a hilly landscape, then the state variables describe the position and momentum of that cart. The control variables describe the landscape. (As a physicist you will understand right away that the landscape symbolizes any potential.)

Sterile ridges are ridges that never give birth to new umbilicals when you deform the surface.

Stereographical projection is used for the pictures of spherical images in this book. It has the advantage of being conformal and of accommodating a sphere except for a single point.

Structured light is a generic term in robotics for devices that measure three-dimensional shape in images via a special kind of illumination.

Sugar cubes are great for building piles. Such piles are interesting models for blobs. The cubes are often called "voxels."

Support planes are planes that have at least a point in common with your blob and are such that the blob is situated on *one side* of the support plane. A tabletop is the support plane for all objects put upon it.

Surfaces are geometric entities of a rather bothersome kind. In physics there are no such things as surfaces. Many different definitions for surfaces are in use. In this book surfaces are level sets of densities at a given level of resolution.

Swallowtail is a technical term in catastrophe theory. The term was inspired by the appearance of the bifurcation set. In this book the swallowtail often appears in the description of developable surfaces: their singular features are the edge of regression and swallowtail points (at which the edge of regression cusps).

Symmetry is invariance with respect to some transformation.

Synclastic points are points where the surface is concave or convex, "curves in the same sense in all directions." These points are also known as elliptic points.

T

Tacnodes are points where a surface has a special type of high-order contact with its tangent plane. The quartic indicatrix is a pair of osculating parabolas; hence the name.

Taut strings are useful implements for the geodesic exploration of surfaces. In differential geometry one uses a special brand of string that never lifts off the surface. These are not to be found in the physics laboratory.

Tinted air Blobs of tinted air are perfect for the study of the visual contour: there are no problems with obscuration. You have an excellent physical approximation in X-ray pictures of objects.

Tolerances are not things that keep mathematicians awake. For the physicist a measurement is completely uninformative unless he knows the tolerance. (Physicists are touchy about the subject, mistrust tolerances specified by colleagues, *etc.* People have lost their jobs because of tolerance problems.) Real things are equivalence classes of physical entities relative to some tolerance.

Torso "The" torso is the Belvedere Torso made famous by Michelangelo and Winckelmann. "A" torso is a piece of sculpture that is inspired by the human body and includes at least the thorax, but certainly not the head and extremities. When I say "typical blob," you may substitute the Belvedere Torso without harm.

Transition layers are the physicist's answer to the "surfaces" of the mathematician. The thickness of a transition layer depends not just on the object but also on the tolerances of the measurement, that is, on the resolution.

Tubes are used in two different contexts in this book:

- As thought models of the geometrical meaning of the differential two-form. One thinks of infinite space-filling bunches of spaghetti.

- As the simple surfaces that appear as envelopes of one-parameter families of spheres. The garden hose variety is treated in the text.

Turn I use "turn" for a rotation of a frame about an axis that is orthogonal to the direction of movement. The component of the rotation about the direction of movement would be a "spin" of the frame. I often use "nose-dive" as synonym for "turn."

Twist I use "twist" for a spin of an adapted frame on a surface strip when you move along the carrier of the strip.

Type converters are algorithms that are used to convert the representation of an entity; for example, a type converter may take an unsigned integer (say, 2) and change it to a real (+2.0E00). I use it in a somewhat generalized sense. Thus, the metric is a machine that can be used as a "type converter" that converts vectors into covectors.

U

Umbilics or "navel points" are points on a surface where the principal curvatures coincide. All normal sections have the same curvature. Dupin's indicatrix is a circle. Generically the umbilics are isolated points. Even in isolation they are enough of a nuisance to the computational differential geometrician.

Unfolding An "unfolding" of a degenerated configuration is a perturbation that breaks the symmetry and is stable in the sense that additional perturbation don't bring about any qualitative changes.

Universal joints can be used to connect rigid rods in such a manner that their relative movement has two degrees of freedom. This contrasts with the single degree of freedom offered by the hinges of a bicycle chain.

Unodes are points on a surface where the tangent plane and the surface have an unusually high order of contact. The intersection is a single point (hence the name), but in the immediate vicinity of a unode you can find *triples* of points with parallel normals. Contrast this with a generic synclastic point (also a point as intersection with the tangent plane) where *no* point has a mate with a parallel normal.

V

Vantage point A vantage point is a point that you single out as the point from which to view a blob. In the physical operationalization the vantage point would be the center of the entrance pupil of the objective of your camera.

Vectors are your prototypical "geometrical objects." Formally a vector is a directional derivative. Physically it is a rate. Pictorially a vector is an ordered pair of points or an equivalence class of curves.

Versification is a singularity of an evolutionary sequence that changes the connectivity of your blob and may occur either on blurring or on deblurring.

V-grooves are conspicuous features of the sculpture of many cultures and periods. They typically occur on the interface of two ovoid patches. In European Renaissance sculpture you often see rather overdeveloped muscle groups in depictions of the male nude, with sharp V-grooves in between (*e.g.*, the pectoral, deltoid, biceps and triceps of the upper arm region). The grooves take the place of the anticlastic patches.

Viewing sphere The "viewing sphere" is the space of visual directions for parallel projection (the "far field").

Vignetting is a term used in photometry for the obscuration of the source by parts of the object. (Or the dioptric apparatus, but that is of no importance in the context of this book). Vignetting and interreflection are the two main mechanisms that challenge the basic assumption that irradiance depends on slant alone.

Vision is what happens when you open your eyes. Nowadays "vision" is also used as an abbreviation for machine vision, which is an odd mixture of image processing, pattern recognition, and robotics.

Visualization is what happens in your visual field when you close your eyes. Vision is for a large part visualization, and visualization is a faculty that exists because humans have vision.

Voxels are a slang expression for "volume elements."

W

Watersheds are the boundaries of "dales." I also call them "crests." The crests of densities are useful as skeletons or axes systems of blobs.

Waves are physical phenomena, but the concept is useful in any context in which "Fermat's principle" occurs. One example is in the geodesic congruences on surfaces. Geodesic pencils are solutions of the Eikonal equation that satisfy Fermat's principle automatically. The orthotomics of a geodesic pencil are the "wavefronts" of a surface wave. The idea helps physicists to understand geodesic congruences intuitively. Forget about it if you are a mathematician.

Bibliography

[1] Abraham, R: *Foundations of mechanics*, W. A. Benjamin, Inc., New York, 1967.

[2] Abraham, R. H., and R. Shaw: *Dynamics—The geometry of behavior*, 4 Vols., Aerial Press, Inc., Santa Cruz, Ca, 1985.

[3] Aleksandrov, A. D.: *Kurven und Flächen*, VEB Deutscher Verlag der Wissenschaften, Berlin, 1959.

[4] Aleksandrov, P. S.: *Combinatorial topology*, Graylock Press, Albany, N.Y., 1960.

[5] Almgren, F. J., Jr.: *Plateau's problem*, W. A. Benjamin, Inc., New York, 1966.

[6] d'Arcy Thompson, W.: *Growth and Form*, Cambridge University Press, Cambridge, (abridged edition), 1961.

[7] Arnold, V. I., S. M. Gusein-Zade, and A.N. Varchenko: *Singularities of differentiable maps*, Vol. 1, Birkhäuser, Boston, 1985.

[8] Arnold, V. I.: *Catastrophe theory*, Springer, Berlin, 1984.

[9] Banchoff, T., T. Gaffney, and C. McCrory: *Cusps of Gauss mappings*, Pitman, Boston, 1982.

[10] Berger, M.: *Geometrie*, 5 Vols., 2nd ed., Cedic/Fernand Natlan, Paris, 1979.

[11] Blaschke, W.: *Differential Geometrie*, ? Vols., Chelsea, New York, 1967.

[12] —: Volume 3, Springer, Berlin, 1929.

[13] Blum, H.: *Biological shape and visual science*, J.theor.Biol. **38**, pp. 205–287, 1973.

[14] Blumenthal, L. M.: *Theory and applications of distance geometry*, 2nd ed., Chelsea, New York, 1970.

[15] Bol, G.: *Projektive Differentialgeometrie*, 3 Vols., Vandenhoeck & Ruprecht, Göttingen, 1950.

[16] Boys, C. V.: *Soap bubbles, their colors and the forces that mold them*, 3rd ed., Dover, New York, 1959.

[17] Brieskorn, E.: *Lineare Algebra und analytische Geometrie*, 2 Vols., Friedr. Vieweg & Sohn, Braunschweig, 1983.

[18] Brieskorn, E., and H. Knörrer: *Ebene algebraische Kurven*, Birkhäuser, Basel, 1981.

[19] Bröcker, T., and K. Jänich: *Einführung in die Differentialtopologie*, Springer, Berlin, 1973.

[20] Bruce, J. W., and P. J. Giblin: *Curves and singularities*, Cambridge University Press, Cambridge, 1984.

[21] Bruce, J. W., P. J. Giblin, and C. G. Gibson: *Symmetry sets*, Proc.Royal Soc. Edinburgh, **101A**, pp. 163–186, 1985.

[22] Bruce, J. W., and P. J. Giblin: *Growth, motion and 1-parameter families of symmetry sets*, Proc.Royal Soc. Edinburgh, **104A**, pp. 179–204, 1986.

[23] Burke, W. L.: *Applied differential geometry*, Cambridge University Press, Cambridge, 1985.

[24] Callahan, J.: *Singularities and plane maps*, Am.Math.Monthly **81**, pp. 211–240, 1974.

[25] —:Am.Math.Monthly **84**, pp. 765–803, 1977.

[26] Carmo, M.P. do: *Differential geometry of curves and surfaces*, Prentice-Hall, Inc., Englewood Cliffs, N.J., 1976.

[27] Darboux, G.: *Leçons sur la théorie génerale des surfaces*, 4 Vols., 3rd ed., Chelsea, New York, 1972.

[28] Dufour, J.-P.: *Familles de courbes planes differentiables*, Topology **22**, pp. 449–474, 1983.

[29] Eells, J., Jr.: *Singularities of smooth maps*, Gordon and Breach, New York, 1967.

[30] Efimov, N. W.: *Flächenverbiegung im Grossen*, Akademie Verlag, Berlin, 1957.

[31] Eisenhart, L. P.: *A treatise on the differential geometry of curves and surfaces*, Dover, New York, 1960.

[32] Enzyklopædie der mathematischen Wissenschaften mit Einschluss ihrer Anwendungen, III. Band: *Geometrie*, in 3 Teilen (29 Hefte), Eds. W. Fr. Meyer and H. Mohrmann, Leipzich, 1902–1929.

[33] Ewald, G.: *Probleme der geometrischen Analysis*, Bibliographisches Institut Mannheim/Wien/Zürich, B.I.-Wissenschaftsverlag, 1982.

[34] Fabricius-Bjerre, Fr.: *On the double tangents of plane closed curves*, Math.Scand. **11**, pp. 113–116, 1962.

[35] Féjès Tòth, L.: *Lagerungen in der Ebene auf der Kugel und im Raum*, Springer, Berlin, 1953.

[36] Fischer, G.(Ed.): *Mathematical Models*, Friedrich Vieweg & Sohn, Braunschweig/Wiesbaden, 1986.

[37] Fladt, K.: *Analytische Geometrie spezieller ebenen Kurven*, Akademische Verlagsgesellschaft, Frankfurt a/M, 1962.

[38] Fladt, K., and A. Baur: *Analytische Geometrie spezieller Flächen und Raumkurven*, Friedr. Vieweg & Sohn, Braunschweig, 1975.

[39] Flanders, H.: *Differential forms*, Academic Press, New York, 1963.

[40] Fokker, A. D.: *Tijd en ruimte, traagheid en zwaarte*, De Haan, Zeist, 1960.

[41] Francis, G. K.: *A topological picture book*, Springer, New York, 1987.

[42] Gaffney, T.: *A note on the order of determinacy of a finitely determined germ*, Invent.Math. **52**, pp. 127–130, 1979.

[43] Giblin, P. J., and S. A. Brassett: *Local symmetry of plane curves*, Am.Math.Monthly **92**, pp. 689–707, 1985.

[44] Griffiths, H. B.: *Surfaces*, Cambridge University Press, Cambridge, 1976.

[45] Guggenheimer, H. W.: *Differential geometry*, McGraw-Hill, New York, 1963.

[46] Guillemin, V., and A. Pollack: *Differential topology*, Prentice Hall, Englewood Cliffs, N.J., 1974.

[47] Helmholtz, H. von: *Über die Thatsachen, die der Geometrie zugrunde liegen*, Nachrichten von der kön. Gesellschaft der Wiss. zu Göttingen, **9**, June 3, pp. 193–221, 1868.

[48] Hestenes, D.: *Vectors, spinors, and complex numbers in classical and quantum physics*, Am.J.Physics **39**, pp. 1013–1037, 1971.

[49] Hilbert, D., and S. Cohn-Vossen: *Anschauliche Geometrie*, Dover, New York, 1944.

[50] Huntington, E. V.: *A set of postulates for abstract geometry expressed in terms of the single relation of inclusion*, Math.Ann. **73**, pp. 522–559, 1913.

[51] Klein, F.: *Elementarmathematik vom höheren Standpunkte aus*, 3rd ed., Springer, Berlin, 1928; Dritter Teil: *Von der Versinnlichung idealer Gebilde durch Zeichnungen und Modelle*

[52] Klein, F.: *Vergleichende Betrachtungen über neuere geometrische Forschungen ("Erlanger Programm")*, Math.Ann. **43**, pp. 63–100, 1893.

[53] Kruppa, E.: *Analytische und konstruktive Differentialgeometrie*, Springer, Wien, 1957.

[54] Laugwitz, D.: *Differentialgeometrie*, B.G.Teubner, Stuttgart, 1960.

[55] Lehmann, D., and C. Sacré: *Géometrie et topologie des surfaces*, Presses universitaires de France, Paris, 1982.

[56] Lipschutz, M. M.: *Differential geometry*, Schaum's Outline Series, McGraw-Hill, New York, 1969.

[57] Longuet-Higgins, M. S.: *Reflection and refraction at a random moving surface. I. Pattern and paths of specular points*, J.Opt.Soc.Amer. **50**, pp. 838–844, 1960.

[58] Milnor, J. W.: *Morse theory*, Princeton University Press, Princeton, N.J., 1963.

[59] Minkowski, H.: *Über die Begriffe Länge, Oberfläche und Volumen*, Jahresber.D.Math.Ver. **9**, pp. 115–121, 1900.

[60] Minnaert, M.: *De natuurkunde van het vrije veld*, Vol. I: *Licht en kleur in het landschap*, W.J.Thieme & cie, Zutphen, 1937, 5th ed. 1968.

[61] Misner, C. W., K. S. Thorne, and J. A. Wheeler: *Gravitation*, Freeman, San Francisco, 1973.

[62] Moise, E. E.: *Geometric topology in dimensions 2 and 3*, Springer, New York, 1977.

[63] Montaldi, J. A.: *Surfaces in 3-space and their contact with circles*, J.Diff.Geom. **23**, pp. 109–126, 1986.

[64] Müller, K. P., and H. Wölpert: *Anschauliche Topologie*, B.G.Teubner, Stuttgart, 1976.

[65] O'Neil, P. V.: *Fundamental concepts of topology*, Gordon and Breach, New York, 1972.

[66] O'Neill, B.: *Elementary differential geometry*, Academic Press, New York, 1966.

[67] Polya, G.: *How to solve it*, Princeton University Press, Princeton, N.J., 1945.

[68] Porteous,   I.R.:   *The normal singularities of surfaces in* $\mathbf{R}^3$, Proc.Symp.Pure Math. **40**, part 2, pp. 379–393, 1983.

[69] —: *The normal singularities of a submanifold*, J.Diff.Geom. **5**, pp. 543–564, 1971.

[70] Poston, T., and I. Stewart: *Catastrophe theory and its applications*, Pitman, London, 1978.

[71] Riemann, B.: *Über die Hypothesen, welche der Geometrie zugrunde liegen*, Werke, 2nd ed., p.272, 1892.

[72] Rosenfeld, A. (Ed.): *Multiresolution image processing and analysis*, Springer, Berlin, 1984.

[73] Ruskin, J.: *The Elements of Drawing*, 1st ed., 1857; many later editions, I used George Allen, Sunny Side, Orpington, 1900.

[74] Sauer, R.: *Differenzengeometrie*, Springer, Berlin, 1970.

[75] Schouten, J. A.: *Ricci calculus*, 2nd ed., Springer, Berlin, 1954.

[76] Spivak, M.: *Differential Geometry*, 5 Vols., Publish or perish, Inc., Berkeley, Ca., 1970, 1970, 1975, 1975, 1975.

[77] Stoker, J. J.: *Differential geometry*, Wiley-Interscience, New York, 1969.

[78] Strubecker, K.: *Differentialgeometrie*, 3 Vols., Walter de Gruyter & Co., Berlin, 1964, 1969, 1969.

[79] Struik, D. J.: *Lectures on classical differential geometry*, Addison-Wesley, Reading, Mass., 1961.

[80] Thom, R.: *Stabilité structurelle et morphogénèse*, Benjamin, New York, 1972.

[81] Weatherburn, C. E.: *Differential geometry of three dimensions*, Cambridge University Press, Cambridge, 1927.

[82] Whitney, H.: *On singularities of mappings of Euclidean spaces. I: Mappings of the plane into the plane*, Ann. of Math. **62**, pp. 374–410, 1955.

Index

The MIT Press, with Peter Denning as general consulting editor, publishes computer science books in the following series:

ACM Doctoral Dissertation Award and Distinguished Dissertation Series

Artificial Intelligence
Patrick Winston, founding editor
Michael Brady, Daniel Bobrow, and Randall Davis, editors

Charles Babbage Institute Reprint Series for the History of Computing
Martin Campbell-Kelly, editor

Computer Systems
Herb Schwetman, editor

Exploring with Logo
E. Paul Goldenberg, editor

Foundations of Computing
Michael Garey and Albert Meyer, editors

Information Systems
Michael Lesk, editor

Logic Programming
Ehud Shapiro, Editor; Fernando Pereira, Koichi Furukawa, Jean-Louis Lassez, and David H. D. Warren, associate editors

The MIT Press Electrical Engineering and Computer Science Series

Research Monographs in Parallel and Distributed Processing
Christopher Jesshope and David Klappholz, editors

Scientific and Engineering Computation
Janusz Kowalik, editor

Technical Communication
Ed Barrett, editor